中国城市发展报告

（2014）

主　办

中　国　市　长　协　会

承　办

国际欧亚科学院中国科学中心

《中国城市发展报告》编委会　编

中国城市出版社

·北京·

图书在版编目（CIP）数据

中国城市发展报告.2014/《中国城市发展报告》编委会编.—北京：中国城市出版社，2015.8

ISBN 978-7-5074-3034-9

Ⅰ.①中… Ⅱ.①中… Ⅲ.①城市经济—经济发展—研究报告—中国—2014 Ⅳ.①F299.21

中国版本图书馆 CIP 数据核字（2015）第 142723 号

责任编辑	孙湛波　陈夕涛　宋　凯
装帧设计	美信书籍设计工作室
责任技术编辑	张建军
出版发行	中国城市出版社
地　　址	北京市海淀区三里河路 9 号（邮编　100835）
网　　址	www.citypress.cn
发行部电话	(010) 63454857　63289949
发行部传真	(010) 63421417
总编室电话	(010) 58933140
总编室信箱	citypress@sina.com
经　　销	新华书店
印　　刷	北京圣夫亚美印刷有限公司
字　　数	628 千字　　印张　28.5
开　　本	889×1194（毫米）　1/16
版　　次	2015 年 8 月第 1 版
印　　次	2015 年 8 月第 1 次印刷
定　　价	398.00 元

《中国城市发展报告(2014)》
机构组成名单

《中国城市发展报告(2014)》总顾问

路甬祥　全国人民代表大会常务委员会原副委员长

成思危　全国人民代表大会常务委员会原副委员长

周光召　全国人民代表大会常务委员会原副委员长

徐匡迪　中国人民政治协商会议全国委员会原副主席

罗豪才　中国人民政治协商会议全国委员会原副主席

《中国城市发展报告(2014)》顾问

汪光焘　全国人大环境与资源保护委员会原主任委员，
　　　　国际欧亚科学院秘书长，中国科学中心常务副主席

王梦奎　国务院发展研究中心原主任

曲格平　全国人大环境与资源保护委员会原主任

刘燕华　国家科技部原副部长

刘　江　国家发展和改革委员会原副主任

赵宝江　原国家建设部副部长

李振东　原国家建设部副部长

陶斯亮　中国市长协会顾问

《中国城市发展报告(2014)》理事会

理 事 长：蒋正华　全国人民代表大会常务委员会原副委员长
　　　　　　　　　　国际欧亚科学院执行院长，中国科学中心主席

副理事长：齐　骥　中国市长协会副会长，原住房和城乡建设部副部长

理　　事：(以下按姓氏拼音顺序排列)
　　　　崔衡德　戴　逢　李津逵　马俊如

《中国城市发展报告(2014)》学术委员会

《中国城市发展报告(2014)》编委会

《中国城市发展报告(2014)》研编机构

广州市都市发展研究会
清华大学建筑学院
北京大学数字中国研究院
中山大学城市与区域研究中心
北京师范大学资源学院
中国科学院地理科学与资源研究所
国家遥感应用工程技术研究中心

《中国城市发展报告（2014）》工作委员会

主任委员：王长远

委　　员：林家宁　方兆瑞　马海鹰　赵旺华

序　一

蒋正华

（第九届、第十届全国人大常委会副委员长、国际欧亚科学院
执行院长、国际欧亚科学院中国科学中心主席）

2014年，在中国城镇化和城市发展进程中，是具有里程碑意义的一年。3月16日，国务院出台了《国家新型城镇化规划（2014－2020年）》，这是根据党的十八大报告、《中共中央关于深化全面改革若干重大问题的决定》、中央城镇化工作会议精神、国家“十二五”经济社会发展规划和《全国主体功能区规划》而编制的，是今后一段时期指导全国城镇化健康发展的宏观性、战略性、基础性规划。

新型城镇化的“新”在于：强调以人的城镇化为核心，从开放户籍限制和公共服务均等化两个方面入手，有序推进农村转移人口市民化；以城市群为主体形态，推动大中小城市和小城镇协调发展；以综合承载力为支撑，提升城市可持续发展水平；以体制机制为保障，通过改革释放城镇化发展潜力；走出一条以人为本、四化同步、优化布局、生态文明、文化传承的中国特色新型城镇化道路。

按照《国家新型城镇化规划（2014－2020年）》要求，2020年我国按常住人口比例计算的城镇化率将达到60%左右，按户籍人口计算的城镇化率将达到45%左右。中央提出将解决“三个1亿人”问题置于优先地位，即：促进约1亿农业转移人口落户城镇，改造约1亿人居住的城镇棚户区和城中村，引导约1亿人在中西部地区就近城镇化。这既是一个令人鼓舞的规划，同时也是充满巨大压力和挑战的规划，要在有限的时空内完成如此人口规模的城镇化，在世界城镇化的历史上是前所未有的伟大创举。

围绕有序推进人口城镇化，《国家新型城镇化规划（2014－2020年）》提出了实施差别化落户政策，即：以合法稳定就业和合法稳定住所（含租赁）等为前提，全面放开建制镇和小城市落户限制，有序放开城区人口50万~100万人的中等城市落户限制，合理放开城区人口100万~300万人的大城市落户限制，合理确定城区人口300万~500万人的大城市落户条件，严格控制城区人口500万人以上特大城市人口规模。大中城市可设置参加城镇社会保险年限的要求（最高不得超过5年）；特大城市可采取积分制等方式设置阶梯式落户通

道，调控落户规模和节奏。同时，又进一步制定了农业人口进城镇落户具有可操作性的政策，强调要重点解决进城时间长、就业能力强、可以适应城镇产业转型升级和市场竞争环境的人员落户问题。并强调要切实保障农业转移人口和其他常住人口的合法权益，包括随迁子女平等享有受教育权利，并将其纳入社区卫生和城镇社会保障体系，使其和城市人口一样享有均等化的基本公共服务和社会保障服务。

为进一步落实和实施《国家新型城镇化规划（2014－2020年）》，经过半年多的调查酝酿，2015年2月4日，国家发展改革委等11个部门下发《关于开展国家新型城镇化综合试点工作的通知》及《国家新型城镇化综合试点方案》，确定将江苏、安徽两省以及62个城市（镇）作为国家新型城镇化综合试点地区和城市，其中包括宁波、大连、青岛3个计划单列市，石家庄、长春、哈尔滨、武汉、长沙、广州6个省会城市及重庆主城区，以及25个地级市（区）、25个县级市（区）和2个建制镇。试点内容主要有以下五个方面：建立农业转移人口市民化的成本分担机制，建立多元化可持续的城镇化投融资机制，改革完善农村宅基地制度，探索建立行政管理创新和行政成本降低的新型管理模式，以及综合推进体制机制改革创新。要求各试点单位于2014年年底前开始试点，将在2017年取得阶段性成果，形成可复制、可推广的经验，2018－2020年逐步在全国范围内推广试点地区和城市的成功经验。

随着城镇化的快速推进与城镇规模的不断扩张，城市公共安全问题日益凸显。2014年中国各类城市发生了30多起重大公共安全事件，包括基础设施老化引起的泄漏及坍塌事件、生产安全事件、交通安全事件、社会安全事件及食品安全事件等。其中，社会负面影响较大的有：1月，云南大理巍山古城发生重大火灾，古城楼被烧毁，此事件距香格里拉古城火灾不到1年；4月，兰州自来水苯污染事件，波及兰州主城区城关、七里河、安宁、西固四个区；8月，江苏昆山中荣金属制品公司发生特大铝粉尘爆炸事故，造成97人死亡、163人受伤，直接经济损失3.51亿元；12月，“12·31”上海外滩发生严重踩踏事件，造成36人死亡、47人受伤。上述重大公共安全事件的发生，一方面是由于城市规划与建设急功近利，公共安全理念缺失，长期重经济轻市政建设，导致城市基础设施总体供给不足，城市基础设施系统整体脆弱，长期处于高负荷运行状态；另一方面，由于城市公共安全管理体制机制不健全，缺乏相应的法律法规体系和灾害应急管理机构。同时，也与公众的防灾安全意识教育缺失、安全设施严重不足密切相关。今后，应将提高城市公共安全管理水平和体系建设作为城市精细化管理的重要组成部分，尽快制定《城市公共安全管理条例》，并将其纳入法制化的治理轨道。

《中国城市发展报告（2014）》围绕国家新型城镇化和城市公共安全两大主题，聚焦上述核心问题，内容包括城市经济、城市规划、城市建设、城市管理、城市地理、城市生态环境和城市文化等，仍按综论篇、论坛篇、观察篇、专题篇、案例篇、附录篇六部分编写，力图从不同的视角和方面较全面地反映中央城镇化工作会议以来在新型城镇化方面所取得的进展与成绩，以及存在的问题，为城市发展的决策者、管理者、研究工作者提供参考。欢迎读者提出意见、建议。

序 二

陈政高

（住房和城乡建设部部长、中国市长协会执行会长）

城市的出现是人类发展史上最伟大的创造和构建，是人类群居生活的高级形式，也是人类走向成熟和文明的重要标志。城市改变了人类的生存环境和生存条件，改变了世界的形态和走向，使之成为地球上最热闹、最复杂、最精彩的活动舞台。

城市在我国城镇化建设和发展过程中的地位尤为显著。我国目前正处于快速推进城镇化的进程中，同时工业化也处于快速发展阶段，这更需要发挥城市和城市经济的作用。城市发展决定了我国城镇化的水平、质量和速度，因为城市是市场的集聚地、消费的集中地、投资的吸引地。建设和发展好城市，才能稳定经济、促进消费、解决就业、带动农村，促进城乡、区域、大中小城市全面、协调发展。所以，我们必须建设和发展好城市，提升城市的水平和质量，为大家创造更好的生活、工作和居住环境。建设和发展好城市需要政府重视、社会和市民共同参与；需要城市的建设者、管理者付出更多的心血和努力。我们要按照国家新型城镇化的要求规划，把城市规划好、建设好、管理好，为我国的经济和社会发展做出贡献。

城市规划是为实现一定时期内城市的经济和社会发展目标服务的，要根据经济发展目标和城市的发展方向进行科学布局，合理利用城市土地。城市规划是建设和管理好城市、保证城市空间资源有效配置和土地合理利用的前提和基础，是实现城市经济和社会发展目标的重要手段之一。城市规划在城市建设和发展中的龙头作用是不可替代的。

改革开放以来，我国的城市建设和发展日新月异，但城市规划职能的作用还远远没有发挥出来，“千城一面”、浪费土地资源、重复建设等现象还比较普遍。要尽快改变这种现象，就要发挥城市规划的作用。各城市不仅要重视城市总体规划，还要制定空间规划和各专项规划；不仅要制定城市规划，还要严格实施城市规划。让城市规划促进、提升城市的建设和管理水平。对城市风格、建筑色彩、主干道绿化和灯光等都要制定专项规划，使我们的城市更美丽、更有魅力。

城市建设体现的是城市水平。城市建设好了、水平提升了，可以扩大城市的影响力，吸引来更多企业和资金。要把城市作为新型发展资源来认识，要把城市建设作为培育发展资源基础来对待。所以，城市建设不能粗犷，要精雕细琢，要使每个建筑、每个工程、每个项目都达到要求的水平和效果，要爱护节约资源、爱护环境、保护古建筑，让我们的城市历史文脉传承下去，创造出更多可留传于世的建筑和城市文化。

城市管理是当前工作中的最薄弱环节，不管是广义的城市管理，还是狭义的城市管理，都是比较复杂的系统工程。越是复杂和困难，我们越要勇往直前。现在主要的问题是对这项工作认识不足、重视不够。就拿城市市容、市貌、市政设施管理来说，看起来是一般性的工作，其意义却又非常深远。城市市容脏、市貌乱、市政设施陈旧而不完善，这些都是制约新型城镇化发展的因素。显然，这样的城市谁也不喜欢，不仅本地居民不满意，外来的客人也不喜欢，这样，如何能吸引资金和人才？又如何能更快发展？因此，我们必须从更高角度、更宽阔视野认识城市管理工作的重要性，加大资金投入，进行科学规划，实施严格管理，把更多的城市建设成宜居、绿色和美丽的城市。

《中国城市发展报告（2014）》有理论、有实践、有案例，内容比较丰富，是一个很有价值的报告。

目 录

综论篇

2014 年中国城市发展综述 …… (3)
一、城镇化进展概况 …… (3)
二、新型城镇化规划的发布与试点 …… (6)
三、加快户籍制度的改革进程 …… (7)
四、保障性住房建设和棚户区改造 …… (8)
五、城乡规划体制的改革试点与实践 …… (9)
六、城镇化理论与实践的国际交流 …… (13)
七、结语 …… (15)

An Introduction of Urban Development in China：2014 …… (16)
Ⅰ. Overview of Urbanization Progress …… (16)
Ⅱ. Release and Pilot of the New Urbanization Plan …… (21)
Ⅲ. Accelerate Reforms to the Household Registration System …… (23)
Ⅳ. Construction of Public Housing and Redevelopment of Rundown Urban Areas …… (25)
Ⅴ. Reform Pilot and Practices of Urban-Rural Planning System …… (27)
Ⅵ. International Experiencing on Theory and Practice of Urbanization …… (33)
Ⅶ. Conclusion …… (37)

2014 年中国城市发展十大事件 …… (38)
一、《国家新型城镇化规划（2014－2020 年）》出台 …… (39)
二、国家启动京津冀协同发展及城镇体系规划 …… (41)

三、国家推行户籍改革，取消城乡“二元户口” …… (43)
四、国务院调整城市规模划分，增设超大城市 …… (46)
五、上海外滩陈毅广场发生“12·31”踩踏事件 …… (47)
六、国务院设立广东、福建和天津自由贸易园区 …… (49)
七、国务院发布实施《不动产登记暂行条例》 …… (50)
八、国务院推进改革城乡居民基本养老保险制度 …… (51)
九、北京成功举办亚太经合组织领导人会议 …… (53)
十、十八届四中全会部署全面推进依法治国 …… (56)

2014 年中国城市交通发展进程 …… (59)
一、新型城镇化发展下的城市交通一体化 …… (59)
二、绿色交通主导下的交通发展与实践 …… (61)
三、行政与法治视野下的交通改革与治理 …… (64)
四、移动互联网发展下的特色交通服务与探索 …… (65)
五、智慧城市引领下的智能交通发展 …… (66)
六、交通文明下的文化建设 …… (67)
七、结语 …… (68)

2014 年中国城市信息化进展 …… (69)
一、城市信息化政策措施取得新进展 …… (69)
二、移动通信与物联网促进城市信息化落地 …… (72)
三、大数据与云计算创新城市信息化模式 …… (74)
四、地理信息技术及产业支撑城市信息化建设 …… (76)
五、城市信息化建设应用呈现新的趋势 …… (77)
六、结语 …… (79)

论坛篇

气候变化对我国沿海城市安全的影响分析 …… (83)
一、引言 …… (83)
二、气候变化对海岸带的影响及其机理 …… (83)
三、气候变化对沿海城市的影响预估 …… (84)
四、应对气候变化的策略建议 …… (86)
五、结论 …… (88)

广州南沙区域规划 …………………………………………………………………………… (91)
一、南沙规划建设的动因 ………………………………………………………………… (92)
二、南沙地区规划的核心是南沙港 ……………………………………………………… (94)
三、“大南沙”和“小南沙”、小南沙规划 …………………………………………… (100)
四、南沙地区规划 ………………………………………………………………………… (103)

关于“京津冀城市群协调发展规划”课题的几个核心问题 …………………………… (115)
一、强化背景研究 ………………………………………………………………………… (115)
二、合理界定城市群范围 ………………………………………………………………… (116)
三、创建协同机制 ………………………………………………………………………… (116)
四、制定健康发展评价标准 ……………………………………………………………… (117)
五、强化对城市群发展机制的研究 ……………………………………………………… (118)
六、开展城市群“弹性”机制的研究 …………………………………………………… (118)

我国城市噪声环境的现状及挑战 ……………………………………………………… (121)
一、引言 …………………………………………………………………………………… (121)
二、我国城市的环境噪声现状 …………………………………………………………… (122)
三、噪声图技术与应用 …………………………………………………………………… (124)
四、声景设计及运用 ……………………………………………………………………… (127)
五、结论 …………………………………………………………………………………… (129)

城市公共安全综合风险评估与评价指标体系 ………………………………………… (132)
一、前言 …………………………………………………………………………………… (132)
二、公共安全三角形理论模型 …………………………………………………………… (133)
三、城市公共安全综合风险评估 ………………………………………………………… (134)
四、安全保障型城市评价指标体系 ……………………………………………………… (136)
五、结语 …………………………………………………………………………………… (139)

关于协调区域与城乡发展的政策建议 ………………………………………………… (141)
一、我国经济社会发展到现阶段，应在逐步缩小区域间、城乡间的相对贫富差距方面加大力度 ………………………………………………………………………… (141)
二、区域政策应由协调东部与中、西部地区及东北地区的发展，进一步向协调发达或较发达的核心地区与其外围欠发达或贫困地区之间的发展深化 ……… (142)
三、发展城市群只能作为人口密集的发达地区城镇化的主体形态，不宜作为全国城镇化的主体形态 ……………………………………………………………… (142)
四、因地制宜，着力发展广大农村地区的县域经济，推进以产业化为基础的部分

农村人口在县域内就近城镇化 …………………………………………………… (143)
五、新农村建设只有与县域内部分农村人口就近城镇化密切结合，才能最终实现缩小城乡差别的城乡一体化 ……………………………………………………… (144)
六、改革现行行政区划的设市体制，允许在众多县域内设立一个或多个副县级市 ……………………………………………………………………… (145)
七、加大国家和省级财政向贫困县和欠发达县的转移支付力度，在加强县级领导班子的基础上向县放权 ……………………………………………………… (146)
八、鼓励发达地区的城市群和都市圈的资金、人才、技术、信息等要素向欠发达的农村地区流动，倡导先富市县帮带贫困县脱贫致富 ……………………… (146)

观察篇

2014年全国“两会”城乡规划建设与管理热点问题综述 ………………………… (151)
一、新型城镇化建设 ………………………………………………………………… (152)
二、保障性住房建设与房地产市场调控 …………………………………………… (154)
三、城乡生态环境建设 ……………………………………………………………… (155)
四、保障和改善民生，关注城乡软环境建设 ……………………………………… (157)
五、农业现代化建设 ………………………………………………………………… (158)
六、区域协调与发展 ………………………………………………………………… (159)

处在十字路口的中国土地城镇化
——土地有偿使用制度建立以来的历程回顾及转型展望 ………………………… (161)
一、有偿使用制度建立以来我国土地政策和土地市场的变迁 …………………… (161)
二、土地城镇化进程回顾及其双刃剑效应 ………………………………………… (163)
三、土地城镇化进程中的利益分配和运行机制 …………………………………… (168)
四、处在十字路口的土地城镇化：何去何从 ……………………………………… (170)

我国新城新区的理性建设与科学发展 ……………………………………………… (173)
一、新城新区建设取得的巨大成就 ………………………………………………… (173)
二、新城新区建设过多过大的问题十分突出 ……………………………………… (174)
三、新城新区建设失控的原因分析 ………………………………………………… (182)
四、新城新区适度理性建设的科学路径 …………………………………………… (184)

食品质量安全的问题与对策 ………………………………………………………… (188)
一、我国食品质量安全的现状、问题与面临的形势 ……………………………… (188)

二、国外发达国家食品安全问题的应对 …………………………………… (189)
三、国外发达国家食品安全问题应对给我们的启示 ……………………… (192)

2014 年中国市长协会舆情观察 …………………………………………… (196)
一、舆情综述 ……………………………………………………………… (196)
二、话题分析 ……………………………………………………………… (197)
三、教育类舆情分析 ……………………………………………………… (199)
四、交通类舆情分析 ……………………………………………………… (200)
五、和谐城市类舆情分析 ………………………………………………… (201)
六、社会保障类舆情分析 ………………………………………………… (203)
七、住房类舆情分析 ……………………………………………………… (204)
八、食品安全类舆情分析 ………………………………………………… (205)
九、物价类舆情分析 ……………………………………………………… (207)
十、市长市府类舆情分析 ………………………………………………… (208)
十一、医疗类舆情分析 …………………………………………………… (210)
十二、敏感舆情类舆情分析 ……………………………………………… (211)
十三、环境保护类舆情分析 ……………………………………………… (213)
十四、旅游和文化类舆情分析 …………………………………………… (214)

专题篇

从美国的三次债务危机看我国地方政府债务的新常态 ………………… (219)
一、引言 …………………………………………………………………… (219)
二、美国历史上的三次地方政府债务危机与四种新常态化解法 ……… (219)
三、区域经济不平衡发展的规律与地方政府的五色债务生态 ………… (222)
四、中国地方政府债务的三分结构与地方融资平台四大基本特征 …… (225)
五、中国经济的五重再造与五种政府债务风险的全方位化解 ………… (228)

我国省级公共安全综合评价指标体系研究 ……………………………… (237)
一、导论：问题的提出和研究的重要意义 ……………………………… (237)
二、公共安全的基本概念、相关理论及研究方法 ……………………… (238)
三、国内外公共安全指标体系设计文献 ………………………………… (240)
四、我国省级公共安全评价指标体系的现状和问题 …………………… (241)
五、如何构建我国省级公共安全指标框架体系 ………………………… (242)

比较视角下的中国公立医院管理效率研究 …………………………………… (262)
一、引言 …………………………………………………………………… (262)
二、国内外医院管理研究综述 ……………………………………………… (263)
三、《全球医院管理研究——中国部分》 …………………………………… (264)
四、结语 …………………………………………………………………… (271)

基于大数据开展规划决策支持的技术方法探讨 ……………………………… (273)
一、引言 …………………………………………………………………… (273)
二、基于大数据开展规划决策支持的技术路线 ……………………………… (274)
三、结论与讨论 ……………………………………………………………… (280)

绿色建筑的发展路径研究 …………………………………………………… (283)
一、我国绿色建筑的发展历程和绿色建筑的本质 …………………………… (283)
二、我国绿色建筑发展的问题 ……………………………………………… (284)
三、我国绿色建筑发展的政策建议 ………………………………………… (286)
四、绿色建筑的发展路径和技术对策 ……………………………………… (287)
五、结论与展望 ……………………………………………………………… (291)

案例篇

实施型村庄规划编制探索
——以广州市白山村美丽乡村规划为例 ……………………………………… (295)
一、广州历次村庄规划编制特点及问题 …………………………………… (295)
二、面向实施的白山村村庄规划编制探索 ………………………………… (297)
三、结语 …………………………………………………………………… (306)

加强中外社团间合作，促进新型城镇化建设
——美国保尔森基金会与中国有关团体合作介绍 ………………………… (307)
一、愿为可持续城镇化有所为 ……………………………………………… (307)
二、可持续城镇化主要项目：城市评估工具 ……………………………… (308)
三、可持续城镇化的其他项目 ……………………………………………… (311)
四、加强高端智库建设，促进新型城镇化 ………………………………… (314)

海口：国际旅游岛助推城市快速发展 ……………………………………… (316)
一、城市资源环境与城市发展条件 ………………………………………… (316)

二、海口发展定位 …………………………………………………………………… (319)
三、海口旅游发展思路与策略 ………………………………………………………… (320)
四、海口城市发展 …………………………………………………………………… (322)
五、结语 ……………………………………………………………………………… (323)

苏州申报“李光耀世界城市奖”对中国城市的启示 ………………………………… (324)
一、什么是“李光耀世界城市奖” …………………………………………………… (324)
二、苏州为什么能获奖 ……………………………………………………………… (325)
三、对中国城市有什么启示 …………………………………………………………… (334)

以新型城镇化推进广东区域协调发展的调研报告 ……………………………… (336)
一、坚持分类指导，加快打造升级核心城市圈层 ………………………………… (336)
二、强化城市群区域发展协调机制 …………………………………………………… (339)
三、完善区域协调发展的保障机制 …………………………………………………… (340)

附录篇

附录 1　2014 年中国城市发展大事记 ………………………………………………… (345)
附录 2　2014 年度中国城市相关政策法规索引 ……………………………………… (368)
附录 3　中国城市基本数据（2012 年） ……………………………………………… (373)
附录 4　2013 年中国人居环境奖获奖名单 …………………………………………… (405)
附录 5　2013 年国家园林城市、县城和城镇命名名单 ……………………………… (407)
附录 6　全国“美丽乡村”首批创建试点名单 ……………………………………… (409)
附录 7　中国城市幸福感调查推选活动资料（2007－2014） ………………………… (421)

编后语 ……………………………………………………………………………… (437)

综论篇

2014 年中国城市发展综述

2014 年是全面深化改革元年，是全国人民追逐梦想、积极适应经济发展新常态的一年。面对复杂多变的国际环境和艰巨繁重的国内发展改革稳定任务，各族人民团结一心、克难攻坚，按照中央部署，坚持稳中求进的工作总基调，全面深化改革，扎实有效地改善民生，实施创新驱动发展战略，同步推进新型工业化、信息化、城镇化和农业现代化。十八届四中全会对全面推进依法治国做出顶层设计和总体部署，党风廉政建设和反腐败工作持续深入推进，社会主义经济建设、政治建设、文化建设、社会建设和生态文明建设取得重大进展，为全面建成小康社会迈出坚实步伐。

一、城镇化进展概况

（一）城乡经济社会持续发展

2014 年，我国经济社会发展总体平稳，经济运行处于合理区间，经济结构有了新的变化，发展质量有新的提升，对外开放有新的突破，人民生活有了新的改善，南水北调中线一期工程正式通水，“一带一路”、京津冀、长江经济带三大区域发展战略稳步推进。

初步核算，全年国内生产总值636 463亿元，人均46 531元，扣除价格因素，实际增长 7.4%；第一、第二、第三产业比重为 9.2:42.6:48.2。根据城乡一体化住户调查，全年全国居民人均可支配收入20 167元，实际增长 8.0%。按常住地分，城镇居民全年人均可支配收入28 844元，实际增长 6.8%；农村居民全年人均可支配收入 10 489 元，实际增长 9.2%。2014 年全国居民收入基尼系数为 0.469。全年农民工总量 27 395 万人，比上年增加 501 万人，其中外出农民工 16 821 万人。农民工月均收入水平 2 864 元，比上年增长 9.8%。

从城乡结构看，年末全国内地总人口为 136 782 万人，比上年末增加 710 万人，自然增长率为 5.21‰。其中，城镇常住人口 74 916 万人，比上年末增加 1 805 万人，乡村常住人口 61 866万人，比上年末减少 1 095 万人，城镇人口占总人口比重为 54.77%。全国居住地和户口登记地不在同一个乡镇街道且离开户口登记地半年以上的人口（即人户分离人口）2.98 亿人，比上年末增加 944 万人，其中流动人口为 2.53 亿人，比上年末增加 800 万人。年末全国就业人员 77 253 万人，比上年末增加 276 万人，其中城镇就业人员39 310万人，比上年末增加1 070万人。年末城镇登记失业率为4.09%。

到2014年年底，全国铁路运营里程11.2万公里，其中高速铁路运营里程1.6万公里；公路通车里程446万公里，其中高速公路通车里程11.2万公里；沿海港口2 116个，通航的民用运输机场202个。宽带用户超过7.8亿户。全国有21个城市开通城市轨道交通线路，运营总里程超过2 800公里。

（二）市级行政区划的调整

2014年年末，全国有设市城市653个，其中直辖市4个，副省级市15个，地级市273个，县级市361个，县城合计近1 600个，建制镇20 401个。年内全国设市城市建制的调整变动如下：

国务院6月26日批复西藏自治区人民政府，同意撤销日喀则地区和县级日喀则市，设立地级日喀则市。日喀则市设立桑珠孜区，以原县级日喀则市的行政区域为日喀则市桑珠孜区的行政区域。

国务院10月20日批复西藏自治区人民政府，同意撤销昌都地区和昌都县，设立地级昌都市。昌都市设立卡若区，以原昌都县的行政区域为昌都市卡若区的行政区域。

根据国务院批复，撤销县级从化市，设立广州市从化区；撤销县级文登市，设立威海市文登区；撤销县级双城市，设立哈尔滨市双城区；撤销县级建阳市，设立南平市建阳区；撤销县级藁城市，设立石家庄市藁城区；撤销县级鹿泉市，设立石家庄市鹿泉区；撤销县级九台市，设立长春市九台区；撤销县级富阳市，设立杭州市富阳区。经国务院批准，新疆维吾尔自治区设立县级双河市和县级霍尔果斯市；云南省撤销香格里拉县，设立县级香格里拉市。

根据国务院批复，设立陕西西咸新区，区域范围涉及西安、咸阳两市所辖7县（区）23个乡镇和街道办事处，规划控制面积882平方公里；设立贵州贵安新区，区域范围涉及贵阳、安顺两市所辖4县（市、区）20个乡镇，规划控制面积1 795平方公里；设立青岛西海岸新区，包括青岛市黄岛区全部行政区域，其中陆域面积约2 096平方公里，海域面积约5 000平方公里；设立大连金普新区，范围包括大连市金州区全部行政区域和普兰店市部分地区，总面积约2 299平方公里；设立四川天府新区，区域范围涉及成都、眉山、资阳三市所辖7县（市、区），规划面积1 578平方公里。

据最新统计，全国现有国家级历史文化名城125处，其中2014年新增两处，分别是浙江湖州市和黑龙江齐齐哈尔市；国家级历史文化名镇252处，历史文化名村276处；有2 555个村落列入中国传统村落名录。“大运河”、“丝绸之路：长安—天山廊道的路网”被成功列入联合国教科文组织《世界遗产名录》，我国的世界遗产地增至47处，包括文化遗产29处，自然遗产10处，文化与自然双遗产4处，以及文化景观4处。

（三）城市（城区）建设

根据住房和城乡建设部统计，2013年年末，全国设市城市658个，城市城区户籍人口37 697万人，暂住人口5 621万人，建成区面积47 855平方公里。

2013年，城市市政公用设施固定资产完成投资16 349.8亿元，主要新增生产能力（或效益）是：供水日综合生产能力748万立方米，天然气储气能力2 361万立方米，集中供热蒸汽能力0.16万吨/小时，热水能力2.31万兆瓦，道路长度1.12万公里，排水管道长度1.95万公里，城市污水处理厂日处理能力1 834万立方米，城市生活垃圾无害化日处理能力4.8万吨。全国有35个城市在建轨道交通，在建线路总长度2 760公里。

2013年，全国城市用水人口4.23亿人，用水普及率97.56%，人均日生活用水量173.51升；用气人口4.08亿人，燃气普及率94.25%；集中供热面积57.2亿平方米；城市道路长度33.6万公里，人均城市道路面积14.87平方米；城市共有污水处理厂1 736座，污水处理厂集中处理率84.53%；城市共有生活垃圾无害化处理场（厂）765座，城市生活垃圾无害化处理率89.30%；城市道路清扫保洁（覆盖）面积64.6亿平方米，其中机械清扫率44.4%；全年清运生活垃圾、粪便1.89亿吨，每万人拥有公共厕所2.83座；城市建成区绿地率35.78%，人均公园绿地面积12.64平方米。2013年年末，全国共有225处国家级风景名胜区，据其中224处统计，风景名胜区面积9.7万平方公里，可游览面积4.2万平方公里，全年接待游人7.3亿人次。

据交通运输部统计，2013年年末全国有18个城市开通了轨道交通，拥有轨道交通车站1 549个，其中换乘站134个。年末城市及县城拥有公共汽电车50.96万辆、57.30万标台，拥有城市轨道交通运营车辆14 366辆、34 415标台。出租汽车运营车辆134.00万辆。城市客运轮渡422艘。拥有公共汽电车运营线路41 738条，运营线路总长度74.89万公里；轨道交通运营线路81条，运营线路总长度2 408公里。城市客运轮渡运营航线143条，运营航线总长度575公里。全年城市客运系统运送旅客1 283.35亿人，其中公共汽电车完成771.17亿人，轨道交通完成109.19亿人，出租汽车完成401.94亿人；客运轮渡完成1.06亿人，下降19.4%。城市客运系统完成的客运量构成为：公共汽电车61.1%、轨道交通8.5%、出租汽车31.3%和客运轮渡0.1%。

（四）县城建设

2013年年末，全国有县城1 613个，据其中1 582个县和15个县级特殊区域及148个新疆生产建设兵团师团部驻地统计汇总，县城户籍人口13 701万人，暂住人口1 566万人，建成区面积19 503平方公里。

2013年，全国县城市政公用设施固定资产完成投资3 833.7亿元，主要新增生产能力（或效益）是：供水日综合生产能力186万立方米，天然气储气能力681万立方米，集中供热蒸汽能力335吨/小时，热水能力7 544兆瓦，道路长度6 817公里，排水管道长度1.2万公里，污水处理厂日处理能力161万立方米，生活垃圾无害化日处理能力1万吨。

2013年，全国县城用水人口1.35亿人，用水普及率88.14%，人均日生活用水量119.06升；燃气用气人口1.08亿人，燃气普及率70.91%；集中供热面积10.3亿平方米；县城道路长度12.5万公里，人均城市道路面积14.86平方米，道路清扫保洁面积19.8亿平方米，其中机械清扫率31.7%；全年清运生活垃圾、粪便0.71亿吨，共有生活垃圾无害化处理场（厂）992 座，生活垃圾无害化处理率 66.07%；共有污水处理厂 1 504 座，污水处理厂集中处理率 76.25%。县城建成区绿地率 24.76%，人均公园绿地面积 9.47 平方米。

（五）村镇建设

2013 年年末，全国共有建制镇 20 117 个，乡 12 812 个。据 17 449 个建制镇、12 281 个乡、673 个镇乡级特殊区域和 265 万个自然村（其中村民委员会所在地 53.72 万个）统计汇总，村镇户籍总人口 9.48 亿人。其中，建制镇建成区人口 1.52 亿人，乡建成区 0.31 亿人，镇乡级特殊区域建成区 0.03 亿人，村庄 7.62 亿人。全国建制镇建成区面积 369 万公顷，乡建成区 73.7 万公顷，镇乡级特殊区域建成区 10.7 万公顷，村庄现状用地面积 1 394.3 万公顷。全国已编制村镇总体规划的情况为：建制镇 15 810 个，乡 9 055 个，镇乡级特殊区域 477 个，行政村 32.0 万个，自然村 73.8 万个。

2013 年，全国村镇建设总投资 16 235 亿元，其中房屋建设占总投资的 77.5%、市政公用设施建设占总投资的 22.5%。年末村镇实有房屋建筑面积 373.69 亿平方米，村镇人均住宅建筑面积 33.02 平方米。

2013 年，全国建制镇建成区用水普及率 81.73%，人均日生活用水量 98.58 升，燃气普及率 46.4%，人均道路面积 12.3 平方米，排水管道暗渠密度 6.75 公里/平方公里，人均公园绿地面积 2.37 平方米。乡建成区用水普及率 68.24%，人均日生活用水量 82.81 升，燃气普及率 19.5%，人均道路面积 12.1 平方米，排水管道暗渠密度 3.57 公里/平方公里，人均公园绿地面积 1.08 平方米。全国村庄内道路长度 228 万公里，其中硬化路 71 万公里；道路面积 641 亿平方米，其中硬化路 197 亿平方米；村庄内排水管道沟渠长度 50.7 万公里。年末全国 61.3% 的行政村有集中供水，9.1% 的行政村对生活污水进行了处理，54.8% 的行政村有生活垃圾收集点，36.3% 的行政村对生活垃圾进行了处理。

二、新型城镇化规划的发布与试点

2014 年 3 月 12 日，中共中央、国务院发出“关于印发《国家新型城镇化规划（2014－2020 年）》（以下简称《规划》）的通知”。通知指出，《规划》是今后一个时期指导全国城镇化健康发展的宏观性、战略性、基础性规划，是解决农业农村农民问题的重要途径，是推动区域协调发展的有力支撑，是扩大内需和促进产业升级的重要抓手。制定实施《规划》，努力走出一条以人为本、四化同步、优化布局、生态文明、文化传承的中国特色新型城镇化道路，对全面建成小康社会、加快推进社会主义现代化具有重大现实意义和深远历史意义。

《规划》提出的 2020 年发展目标是：

城镇化水平和质量稳步提升。城镇化健康有序发展，常住人口城镇化率达到 60% 左右，户籍人口城镇化率达到 45% 左右，户籍人口城镇化率与常住人口城镇化率差距缩小 2 个百分点左右，努力实现 1 亿左右农业转移人口和其他常住人口在城镇落户。

城镇化格局更加优化。“两横三纵”为主体的城镇化战略格局基本形成，城市群集聚经济、人口能力明显增强，东部地区城市群一体化水平和国际竞争力明显提高，中西部地区城市群成为推动区域协调发展的新的重要增长极。城市规模结构更加完善，中心城市辐射带动作用更加突出，中小城市数量增加，小城镇服务功能增强。

城市发展模式科学合理。密度较高、功能混用和公交导向的集约紧凑型开发模式成为主导，人均城市建设用地严格控制在 100 平方米以内，建成区人口密度逐步提高。绿色生产、绿色消费成为城市经济生活的主流，节能节水产品、再生利用产品和绿色建筑比例大幅提高。城市地下管网覆盖率明显提高。

城市生活和谐宜人。稳步推进义务教育、就业服务、基本养老、基本医疗卫生、保障性住房等城镇基本公共服务覆盖全部常住人口，基础设施和公共服务设施更加完善，消费环境更加便利，生态环境明显改善，空气质量逐步好转，饮用水安全得到保障。自然景观和文化特色得到有效保护，城市发展个性化，城市管理人性化、智能化。

城镇化体制机制不断完善。户籍管理、土地管理、社会保障、财税金融、行政管理、生态环境等制度改革取得重大进展，阻碍城镇化健康发展的体制机制障碍基本消除。

12 月 29 日，《国家新型城镇化综合试点总体实施方案》发布。试点地区确定在江苏、安徽两省，宁波等 60 个设市城市，以及浙江省苍南县龙港镇和吉林省安图县二道白河镇。试点时间自 2014 年年底前开始，并根据情况不断完善方案，预计到 2017 年各试点任务取得阶段性成果，形成可复制、可推广的经验；力争在 2018－2020 年，逐步在全国范围内推广试点地区的成功经验。试点的主要任务是：建立农业转移人口市民化成本分担机制，建立多元化可持续的城镇化投融资机制，改革完善农村宅基地制度，探索建立行政管理创新和行政成本降低的新型管理模式，以及综合推进体制机制改革创新。鼓励试点地区从推进新型城镇化实际出发，在城乡发展一体化体制机制、城乡规划编制和管理体制机制、农业现代化体制机制、城市“多规融合”制度、城市生态文明制度、城市社会治理体系，以及新型城镇化标准体系建设和创新城市、智慧城市、低碳城市、人文城市建设等方面开展形式多样、富有特色的改革探索。

三、加快户籍制度的改革进程

推进城镇化的首要任务，是促进有能力在城镇稳定就业和生活的常住人口有序实现市民化。6 月 30 日的中共中央政治局会议指出，加快户籍制度改革是涉及亿万农业转移人口的一项重大措施。要坚持以人为本，着力促进有能力在城镇稳定就业和生活的常住人口有序实现市民化，稳步推进城镇基本公共服务常住人口全覆盖。要坚持积极稳妥、规范有序的方针，既要鼓励各地大胆实践、积极探索，又要指导地方尊重客观规律，尊重群众意愿，不搞指标分配，不搞层层加码。要优先解决好进城时间长、就业能力强、可以适应城镇和市场竞争环境的人的问题，使他们及其家庭在城镇扎根落户，有序引导人口流向。要积极推进城镇基本公共服务由主要对本地户籍人口提供向对常住人口提供转变，逐步解决在城镇就业居住但未落户的农业转移人口享有城镇基本公共服务问题。要完善农村产权制度，维护好农民的土地承包经营权、宅基地使用权、集体收益分配权。要区别情况、分类指导，因地制宜地实行差别化落户政策。

7月24日，国务院发布《关于进一步推进户籍制度改革的意见》（以下简称《意见》）。《意见》要求进一步调整户口迁移政策，包括全面放开建制镇和小城市落户限制，有序放开中等城市落户限制，合理确定大城市落户条件，严格控制特大城市人口规模，有效解决户口迁移中的重点问题。认真落实优先解决存量的要求，重点解决进城时间长、就业能力强、可以适应城镇产业转型升级和市场竞争环境的人员落户问题。不断提高高校毕业生、技术工人、职业院校毕业生、留学回国人员等常住人口的城镇落户率。创新人口管理的具体措施包括：建立城乡统一的户口登记制度，取消农业户口与非农业户口性质区分和由此衍生的蓝印户口等户口类型，统一登记为居民户口，体现户籍制度的人口登记管理功能；建立居住证制度，公民离开常住户口所在地到其他设区的市级以上城市居住半年以上的，在居住地申领居住证。符合条件的居住证持有人，可以在居住地申请登记常住户口。以居住证为载体，建立健全与居住年限等条件相挂钩的基本公共服务提供机制；健全人口信息管理制度，建立健全实际居住人口登记制度，加强和完善人口统计调查，全面、准确掌握人口规模、人员结构、地区分布等情况。

为更好地实施人口和城市分类管理，国务院发布《关于调整城市规模划分标准的通知》。以城区常住人口为统计口径，将城市划分为五类七档。城区常住人口50万人以下的城市为小城市，其中20万人以上50万人以下的城市为Ⅰ型小城市，20万人以下的城市为Ⅱ型小城市；城区常住人口50万人以上100万人以下的城市为中等城市；城区常住人口100万人以上500万人以下的城市为大城市，其中300万人以上500万人以下的城市为Ⅰ型大城市，100万人以上300万人以下的城市为Ⅱ型大城市；城区常住人口500万人以上1 000万人以下的城市为特大城市；城区常住人口1 000万人以上的城市为超大城市。

四、保障性住房建设和棚户区改造

2014年国务院的政府工作报告提出，以全体人民住有所居为目标，坚持分类指导、分步实施、分级负责，加大保障性安居工程建设力度，加强配套设施建设。提高大城市保障房比例。推进公租房和廉租房并轨运行。创新政策性住房投融资机制和工具。

4月2日，国务院常务会议部署进一步发挥开发性金融对棚户区改造的支持作用。会议强调，加快棚户区改造，让亿万居民早日“出棚进楼”，是改善民生的硬任务，也可以有力拉动投资、促进消费，是以人为核心的新型城镇化的重要内容。今年要更大规模推进棚改，必须抓住资金保障这个“牛鼻子”，把政策支持和市场机制有效结合，尤其要发挥好依托国家信用、服务国家战略、资金运用保本微利的开发性金融的“供血”作用，为棚改提速提供依法合规、操作便捷、成本适当、来源稳定的融资渠道，保证棚改任务的资金需要，并努力降低资金成本。会议确定，由国家开发银行成立专门机构，实行单独核算，采取市场化方式发行住宅金融专项债券，向邮储等金融机构和其他投资者筹资，鼓励商业银行、社保基金、保险机构等积极参与，重点用于支持棚改及城市基础设施等相关工程建设。

7 月 21 日，国务院办公厅印发《关于进一步加强棚户区改造工作的通知》，要求进一步完善棚户区改造规划，摸清待改造棚户区的底数、面积、类型等情况；优化规划布局，完善安置住房选点布局，改进配套设施规划布局；加快项目前期工作，做好征收补偿工作，建立行政审批快速通道；加强质量安全管理，强化在建工程质量安全监管，开展已入住安置住房质量安全检查；加快配套设施建设，完善社区公共服务；落实好各项支持政策，确保建设用地供应，落实财税支持政策，加大金融支持力度；加强组织领导，力争超额完成 2014 年目标任务，并提前谋划 2015－2017 年棚户区改造工作。

据不完全统计，2014 年全国城镇保障性安居工程新开工 740 万套，基本建成 511 万套。棚户区改造工作自 2004 年启动至今已累计完成 2080 万户，农村危房改造工作从 2008 年起已累计完成1 600万户。

国家审计署对 2013 年全国城镇保障性安居工程（包括廉租住房、公共租赁住房、经济适用住房、限价商品住房和各类棚户区改造等）的投资、建设、分配、后续管理及相关政策执行情况进行了审计，发现的主要问题有：挪用工程财政补助、银行贷款、企业债券等专项资金；通过虚报资料、重复申报等方式，套取骗取棚户区改造资金；不符合条件家庭违规享受保障性住房实物配租和住房货币补贴；保障性住房被代建企业等单位违规销售或其他用途；未办理转用审批手续占用农用地、违规获取或处置安居工程用地等。

五、城乡规划体制的改革试点与实践

（一）开展全国性规划改革试点工作

为探索完善县（市）规划体系，推动城乡发展一体化，推进规划体制改革，住房和城乡建设部于 2014 年 1 月 24 日下发《关于开展县（市）城乡总体规划暨“三规合一”试点工作的通知》（以下简称《通知》）。《通知》指出，目前县（市）规划过多，相互矛盾，覆盖广度、深度不够，带来城乡分割、重城轻乡、用地粗放等问题，不利于规划实施的监管。特别是一些经济较为发达、人口密度高的地区，人地关系紧张，亟须加强规划统筹和管理。近年来，一些地区开始探索开展县（市）域城乡统筹规划的编制工作，取得了一定成效，为开展县（市）城乡总体规划工作试点提供了良好的基础。试点工作的主要内容是：按照城乡一体、全域管控、部门协作的要求，编制县（市）城乡总体规划，实现经济社会发展、城乡、土地利用规划的“三规合一”或“多规合一”，逐步形成统一衔接、功能互补的规划体系。

针对近年来各地村镇规划存在照搬城市规划模式、脱离村镇实际、指导性和实施性较差等问题，住房和城乡建设部于 3 月 28 日下发《关于做好 2014 年村庄规划、镇规划和县域村镇体系规划试点工作的通知》。试点的目的是探索符合新型城镇化和新农村建设要求、符合村镇实际、具有较强指导性和实施性的村庄规划、镇规划理念和编制方法，以及“多规合一”的县域村镇体系规划编制方法，形成一批有示范意义的规划范例并加以总结推广。在各地推荐申报的基础上，遴选辽宁盘锦市大洼县等5个县开展县域村镇体系规划试点，天津武清区河西务镇等17个镇开展镇规划试点，江西赣州市瑞金市黄柏镇向阳村等10个行政村开展村庄规划试点。

国家发展改革委、国土资源部、环境保护部、住房城乡建设部于8月26日下发《关于开展市县“多规合一”试点工作的通知》（以下简称《通知》），将在辽宁省大连市旅顺口区等28个市、县、区联合开展“多规合一”的试点工作。《通知》指出，开展市县“多规合一”试点，是解决市县规划自成体系、内容冲突、缺乏衔接协调等突出问题，保障市县规划有效实施的迫切要求；是强化政府空间管控能力，实现国土空间集约、高效、可持续利用的重要举措；是改革政府规划体制，建立统一衔接、功能互补、相互协调的空间规划体系的重要基础，对于加快转变经济发展方式和优化空间开发模式，坚定不移实施主体功能区制度，促进经济社会与生态环境协调发展都具有重要意义。试点的任务包括探索经济社会发展规划、城乡规划、土地利用规划、生态环境保护等规划“多规合一”的具体思路，合理确定规划期限、规划目标和规划任务，研究提出可复制可推广的“多规合一”试点方案。

（二）加强“海绵城市”建设

近几年来，“逢雨必涝”成为国内不少城市面临的重要问题。对此，习近平总书记提出，城市规划建设的每个细节都要考虑对自然的影响，更不要打破自然系统。在提升城市排水系统时要优先考虑把有限的雨水留下来，优先考虑更多利用自然力量排水，建设自然积存、自然渗透、自然净化的“海绵城市”。

为保护和改善城市生态环境，促进生态文明建设，住房和城乡建设部印发《海绵城市建设技术指南（试行)》(以下简称《指南》)。《指南》明确了城市规划、工程设计、建设、维护及管理过程中低影响开发雨水系统构建的内容、要求和方法，并提供了我国部分实践案例。

“海绵城市”，是指城市能够像海绵一样，在适应环境变化和应对自然灾害等方面具有良好的“弹性”，下雨时吸水、蓄水、渗水、净水，需要时将蓄存的水“释放”并加以利用。在“海绵城市”建设过程中，应统筹自然降水、地表水和地下水的系统性，协调给水、排水等水循环利用各环节，并考虑其复杂性和长期性。“海绵城市”的建设途径包括：对城市原有生态系统的保护，最大限度地保护原有的河流、湖泊、湿地、坑塘、沟渠等水生态敏感区；生态恢复和修复已经受到破坏的水体和其他自然环境；按照对城市生态环境影响最低的开发建设理念，合理控制开发强度。“海绵城市”建设应统筹低影响开发雨水系统、城市雨水管渠系统及超标雨水径流排放系统，三者相互补充、相互依存。

财政部、住房城乡建设部、水利部于12月31日下发《关于开展中央财政支持海绵城市建设试点工作的通知》。中央财政决定对“海绵城市”建设试点给予专项资金补助，一定三年，具体补助数额按城市规模分档确定，直辖市每年6亿元，省会城市每年5亿元，其他城市每年4亿元。对采用PPP模式达到一定比例的，将按上述补助基数奖励10%。试点城市应将城市建设成具有吸水、蓄水、净水和释水功能的海绵体，提高城市防洪排涝减灾能力。财政部、住房城乡建设部、水利部将对试点工作定期组织绩效评价，并根据绩效评价结果进行奖罚。

（三）上海启动新一轮城市总体规划编制

2014 年 2 月 13 日，上海市人民政府印发《关于编制上海新一轮城市总体规划的指导意见》。未来上海发展的目标定位是：在 2020 年基本建成国际经济、金融、贸易、航运四个中心和社会主义现代化国际大都市的基础上，努力建设成为具有全球资源配置能力、较强国际竞争力和影响力的全球城市，为打造中国经济升级版，实现中华民族伟大复兴的中国梦做出应有的贡献。建设生态良好、社会和谐、智慧低碳、安全便捷的宜居城市，建设适合各类人才成长创业的宜业城市，建设充满魅力、令人向往的国际文化大都市，打造世界级城市群的核心城市。新一轮城市总体规划的期限确定为 2040 年。

上海城市发展中存在的主要问题有：《上海市城市总体规划（1999－2020）》要求至 2020 年全市实际居住人口为1 600万人左右，但至 2013 年年末，全市常住人口总数已达 2415 万人，其中外来常住人口 990.01 万人；中心城人口疏解压力大，新城人口集聚能力不足，建设用地结构不尽合理，中心城向外连片蔓延的趋势没有得到有效遏制；中心城住宅用地整体开发强度过高，全市生态空间接近底线，城市风貌特色尚未充分展现；市政基础设施的整体供给能力、安全保障水平、基础设施配置标准和能级有待提高；总体规划实施缺乏稳定的评估机制和程序设计，缺乏连续统一的可评估的规划目标和指标，缺乏可靠的基础数据平台，缺乏与具体部门之间的实施政策制定的衔接，缺乏目标和政策修正的载体，难以与动态维护和管理有效衔接。

编制上海新一轮城市总体规划，将以提升国际竞争力、可持续发展能力和城市魅力为重点，把改善民生作为城市发展的出发点和落脚点，以建设全球城市为导向，以调整产业结构为抓手，以资源环境承载能力为底线，以公共服务和基础设施保障水平为支撑，通过优化产业结构、完善公共政策、加强社会管理，综合调控城市发展规模。严格控制人口规模和用地规模，实现人口规模适度可控，人口布局和结构不断优化；严守建设用地总量的“天花板”，实施最严格的耕地保护制度和节约集约用地制度，依靠存量优化、流量增效和质量提高满足城市发展的用地需求，实现全市规划建设用地总量“零增长”。坚持有机疏散基本理念，强化城乡空间统筹和海洋陆域资源统筹，形成以基本生态空间为底线，以市域“多心、开敞”空间结构为导向，以全覆盖空间政策体系为保障的集约型、紧凑型、网络化的城市空间格局。把提升城市品质和文化内涵的理念贯穿于城市规划、建设和管理的全过程，推进城市文化的传承与创新，努力建设具有世界影响的“海派”文化魅力和城市品质的国际文化大都市。

5 月 6 日，上海市召开第六次规划土地工作会议，正式启动和全面部署新一轮城市总体规划编制工作。会议强调了新一轮总体规划必须坚持的“四个转变”：从规模扩张型的规划向资源环境紧约束条件下有边界的规划转变，从单纯以经济发展为中心的规划向以促进人的全面发展为中心的规划转变，由注重目标制定的技术性文件向注重规划实施的综合性公共政策转变，由编制完成就一成不变的静态式规划向基于过程控制的可维护的动态式规划转变。“六个突出”：突出以人为本的发展内涵，突出区域一体化的发展格局，突出生态优先的发展底线，突出功能提升的发展方向，突出睿智增长的发展路径，突出开放包容的发展精神。“五量调控”：总量锁定、增量递减、存量优化、流量增效、质量提高。

上海市委书记韩正指出：“规划工作是百年大计，编制规划既要积极，更要稳妥，既要有为，也要无为，重视留白。该守住不能变的，就要确保不突破底线；该与时俱进、面向未来的，就要为我们的子孙留足空间。”

（四）北京城市总体规划开始修改

按照目前执行的《北京市城市总体规划（2004－2020年）》，2020年北京市实际居住人口应控制在1 800万人左右。但到2013年年末，全市常住人口已达2 114.8万人，其中常住外来人口802.7万人。随着人口过快增长，环境污染、交通拥堵、资源紧张等各种“城市病”日益突出。2014年1月16日，王安顺市长在北京市人大十四届二次会议上提出，2014年将修改城市总体规划，推进经济发展规划、城乡建设规划、土地利用规划“三规合一”，划定城市开发边界，优化城乡功能和空间布局，坚决扭转城市发展“摊大饼”，提升城镇化质量。同时，积极配合编制首都经济圈发展规划，抓紧编制空间布局、基础设施、产业发展和生态保护专项规划，建立健全区域合作发展协调机制，主动融入京津冀城市群发展。

2月25日至26日，习近平总书记在北京考察调研并主持召开座谈会，就推进北京发展和管理工作提出五点要求：一是要明确城市战略定位，坚持和强化首都全国政治中心、文化中心、国际交往中心、科技创新中心的核心功能，深入实施人文北京、科技北京、绿色北京战略，努力把北京建设成为国际一流的和谐宜居之都；二是要调整疏解非首都核心功能，优化三次产业结构，优化产业特别是工业项目选择，突出高端化、服务化、集聚化、融合化、低碳化，有效控制人口规模，增强区域人口均衡分布，促进区域均衡发展；三是要提升城市建设特别是基础设施建设质量，形成适度超前、相互衔接、满足未来需求的功能体系，遏制城市“摊大饼”式发展，以创造历史、追求艺术的高度负责精神，打造首都建设的精品力作；四是要健全城市管理体制，提高城市管理水平，尤其要加强市政设施运行管理、交通管理、环境管理、应急管理，推进城市管理目标、方法、模式现代化；五是要加大大气污染治理力度，应对雾霾污染、改善空气质量的首要任务是控制PM2.5，要从压减燃煤、严格控车、调整产业、强化管理、联防联控、依法治理等方面采取重大举措，聚焦重点领域，严格指标考核，加强环境执法监管，认真进行责任追究。

6月5日，北京市政府向国务院报送了关于修改北京市城市总体规划的请示。此次修改后的规划期限与《北京市城市总体规划》保持一致，仍为2020年。部分专题根据研究需要，可适当进行远景展望。总体规划修改的主要思路是，以人口资源环境承载能力为底线，特别是强调“以水定城、以水定地、以水定人、以水定产”，坚决做“减法”，明确和统筹规划好功能疏解、人口控制、用地减量、空间优化、生态安全、质量提升等目标任务，为深化和统筹治理“城市病”做好基础性工作，为推动国际一流的和谐宜居之都建设和京津冀协同发展发挥好规划引领作用。

8月3日，首都规划建设委员会召开第33次全体会议，研究《北京市城市总体规划》

的修改工作。北京市委书记郭金龙对《北京市城市总体规划》修改提出五点要求：一是突出“瘦身健体”，一方面下决心调整疏解非首都核心功能，另一方面在构建“高精尖”经济结构上积极作为；二是突出国际一流，努力打造城市建设精品力作，特别是把城市开发强度降下来，把“摊大饼”式的发展遏制住，把绿色空间长上去；三是要突出文化传承，处理好古都风貌保护和现代化建设的关系，延续城市历史文脉，造福人民群众；四是突出破解难题，把生态文明建设和城市环境治理作为重要内容，进一步优化城市空间布局；五是突出改革创新，使修改后的规划更好地反映首都特点、北京特色和时代特征。

六、城镇化理论与实践的国际交流

（一）第七届世界城市论坛

由联合国人居署主办的“第七届世界城市论坛”于4月5日至11日在哥伦比亚的麦德林市举行。论坛组织了约500场合作伙伴活动，设置了110个展会展台，包括中国代表团在内共有140多个国家的22 000人参会。

论坛的主题为“在发展中实现城市公平：生活型城市”。在开幕式上，联合国秘书长潘基文提出：“为消除极端贫困，我们需要实现包容性发展。”麦德林市长加维里亚呼吁：“我们要创建一个更加公平的城市，我们可以通过创新达到这个目标。”联合国人居署执行主任霍安·克洛斯指出：“我们必须考虑城市化，我们必须为此制订计划。目前世界193个国家中，只有20个国家制定了国家城市发展规划，这是不够的。”

论坛共组织了六场主题对话：城市发展的法律平等，社会融合的城市规划与设计，创新地方政府的金融工具，为城市地方产业提供公平的基本服务，提高弹性城市的标准，一个安全的城市也是一个公正平等的城市。

论坛通过了题为“公正是可持续城市发展的基础”的《麦德林宣言》。宣言说：作为第七届世界城市论坛的参会方，各国政府、私营部门、国际组织、学术界、专业人士和公民社会重申，致力于把城市公正纳入发展议程，利用现有的所有方式和资源，保障将城市转变成为人人享有的包容、安全、繁荣、和谐的空间。鉴于事态紧急，我们必须采取个人和集体的行动，使可持续城市发展造福于所有人。

宣言强调，需要促进制定新的城市议程，克服缺乏充足的法律框架和规划带来的挑战。新议程应该要求新的技术、可靠的城市数据、综合性参与式规划的举措和基于“城市，让生活更美好”的城市化模型，以便应对当前的挑战及未来城市的新兴需求。针对国家和城市多样化的文化、制度和社会状况，新城市议程应该鼓励各国政府制定和使用各种方法，如国家城市计划和政策，把当前的城市发展与未来的需求联系起来，牢固地植根于公平正义和人权的基本原则；推动更强的社会凝聚力，打破社会壁垒，通过赋权社会的所有阶层，尤其是妇女、青年和原住民，促进公正；促进参与式、包容性的地方治理，赋权所有居民；承认各级政府的重要贡献，包括地区级、次区级和市级；加强正式协作机制；确认连带责任；向各级政府提供必要的资源和刺激手段，便于其有效地发挥各自的作用；基于促进青年参与、性别平等、均衡的区域发展的城市规划，促进可持续城市发展；加强城市韧性，应对气候变化和自然灾害；改造贫民窟并防止贫民窟滋生；提供住房、基本服务和保障土地使用权；提供安全、负担得起、便利、可持续的交通；向所有人提供安全的公共空间和服务。

（二）首届世界城市日庆典

经中国政府倡议，第68届联合国大会决议，将每年的10月31日设为“世界城市日”。这是中国首次在联合国推动设立的国际日，是中国对促进全球城市可持续发展的重要贡献。经过国务院批准、联合国人居署同意，上海成为首个“世界城市日”系列纪念活动的主场城市。10月31日，由联合国人居署、中国住房和城乡建设部和上海市政府联合举办的首届“世界城市日”全球启动仪式在上海世博中心举行。

李克强总理代表中国政府和人民，对首届“世界城市日”系列活动在上海开幕表示祝贺。李克强说，城市是人类文明进步和各国经济社会发展的重要平台。“世界城市日”以“城市，让生活更美好”为总主题、以“城市转型与发展”为本年度主题，反映了城市的功能和本质，体现了人们对新时期城市发展的思考和行动。中国作为拥有13亿人口的发展中大国，正在推进新型城镇化，核心是以人为本、写好“人”的大字，实现城镇和谐、包容发展，新型城镇化和农业现代化相辅相成。国际社会应当加强绿色城市、智慧城市和城市治理、城市文化等交流与合作，让城市在历史继承中更好地创造未来。

联合国秘书长潘基文在“世界城市日”致辞说，联合国大会决定设立“世界城市日”后，我们现在就有了一个每年庆祝人类最伟大、最复杂的发明创造的日子。这个新的日子可以追溯到2010年的上海世博会，当时国际社会探讨了世界各地在城市建设方面的最佳做法和理念。因此，由上海主办这个新的联合国纪念日的首次主要活动，可谓恰如其分。把“引领城市变革”作为首个“世界城市日”的主题，突出了城市的开拓能力。全世界已有半数以上的人口生活在城市地区，因此，人类的未来在很大程度上就是城市的未来。我们必须把城市化搞好，这意味着要减少温室气体排放，增强复原能力，确保供水和环境卫生等基本服务，设计安全的公共街道和场所供大家分享。宜居城市的重要性既关系到城市居民，又关系到为可持续发展的一些关键环节提出解决办法。国际社会将在2016年共同举办第三次联合国住房和城市可持续发展会议（人居Ⅲ）。在我们展望城市的未来之际，让我们抓住城市提供的所有机会，提出一个崭新的、具有变革意义的城市议程。

上海市长杨雄致辞说，当今世界已经迈入城市时代。城市给人类既带来了繁荣和便利，也带来了交通拥堵、环境污染、资源紧缺、城市贫困、文化冲突等诸多挑战。应对这些挑战，需要各国的城市携手合作、互相借鉴，探索科学合理的城市可持续发展之路。上海作为“世界城市日”倡议的发起地，将与各国城市一道，共创更美的城市、更好的生活。

（三）北京亚太经合组织领导人会议

2014年11月5日至11日，亚太经合组织（APEC）领导人会议在北京举行。会议通过了《北京纲领：构建融合、创新、互联的亚太——亚太经合组织领导人宣言》和《共建面向未来的亚太伙伴关系——亚太经合组织成立 25 周年声明》这两份成果文件，批准了《亚太经合组织推动实现亚太自由贸易区路线图》、《亚太经合组织互联互通蓝图》和全球价值链、供应链、能力建设等领域的重要合作倡议，通过了《亚太经合组织经济创新发展、改革与增长共识》。

会议认识到亚太经合组织经济体面临的城镇化挑战和机遇，城镇化的持续健康发展有助于促进创新增长，实现亚太强劲、包容和可持续发展；会议高度评价亚太经合组织 2014 年在推动亚太城镇化合作方面开展的建设性工作，批准《亚太经合组织城镇化伙伴关系合作倡议》；会议承诺建立亚太经合组织可持续城市合作网络，共同组织生态城市和智能城市合作项目，推广低碳示范城镇项目，深入探讨建设绿色、高效能源、低碳、以人为本的新型城镇化和可持续城市发展路径；会议鼓励各成员充分利用现有资源，推进城镇化研究和能力建设，支持城镇化合作及城镇化相关项目，包括由成员自愿捐资成立亚太经合组织城镇化子基金。

为全力保障 APEC 会议期间北京地区的空气质量，北京、天津、河北、山西、内蒙古、山东、河南等会议空气质量保障的重点控制区，将停工停产、同步限行、降尘减排等保障措施落到实处，京津冀及周边地区的 PM2.5 平均浓度同比下降 29% 左右。北京市环境监测中心数据显示，从 11 月 1 日至 12 日，北京市空气中 PM2.5、PM10、SO_2、NO_2 浓度比去年同期分别下降了 55%、44%、57% 和 31%。“人努力、天帮忙”，整个会期内北京空气质量 4 天为优、7 天为良，各项污染物浓度均达到近 5 年同期最低水平。环境保护部统计，各省区市累计出动 43.4 万人（次），检查工业企业 6.1 万家、其他各类污染源 12.3 万处；在 APEC 会议期间实际停产企业9 298家，限产企业3 900家，停工工地 4 万余处，分别是环境保护部《APEC 会议空气质量保障方案》规定的 3.6 倍、2.1 倍、7.6 倍。

七、结语

时光更替，岁月前行。2015 年是全面深化改革关键之年、全面推进依法治国开局之年，也是全面完成“十二五”规划收官之年。必须清醒认识的是，我国仍处于并将长期处于社会主义初级阶段，形势依然严峻复杂，化解各种矛盾和风险，跨越“中等收入陷阱”，实现现代化，根本要靠发展。而这种发展，必须是遵循经济规律的科学发展，必须是遵循自然规律的可持续发展，必须是遵循社会规律的包容性发展。

习近平总书记在全国政协新年茶话会上的讲话中指出：“问题是时代的声音，人心是最大的政治。推进党和国家各项工作，必须坚持问题导向，倾听人民呼声。”“我们的事业是全新的事业，在前进的道路上，我们既不能因循守旧、墨守成规，也不能罔顾国情、东施效颦。我们要坚定不移走好走稳自己的路。”

（作者：毛其智，清华大学教授，国际欧亚科学院院士）

An Introduction of Urban Development in China: 2014

The year 2014 has been the first year of comprehensively deepening the reform and a year for Chinese people to pursue their dream and actively adapt themselves to new normal of economic development. In face of the complex and volatile international environment and the arduous mission to stabilize the domestic development reforms, the people of all nationalities united to tackle difficulties, insist on making progress while ensuring stability according to the deployment of the CPC Central Committee, comprehensively deepen the reform, make practical and effective improvements in the people's livelihood, carry out the innovation-driven development strategy, move ahead to carry out new types of industrialization, applications of information technologies, urbanization and agricultural modernization. The Fourth Plenary Session of the 18th CPC Central Committee made a top design and overall arrangement for thoroughly advancing the law-based governance. As the conduct and ethical governance construction and anti-corruption work are advancing continuously and thoroughly, China has made great progress in the construction of socialist economy, politics, cultures, society and eco-civilization, and make a new steady step forward to building a well-off society in an all-round way.

Ⅰ. Overview of Urbanization Progress

(Ⅰ) Urban-rural economy continuing development

China's national economy generally kept smooth and steady in 2014 and operated within an appropriate range. China achieved new changes in economic structure and development quality, new breakthroughs in opening-up and new improvements in living standard. The first phase of the middle route of the South-to-North Water Diversion Project was officially put into operation. The development strategy for three regions, the Silk Road Economic Belt and the 21st Century Maritime Silk Road, the Beijing-Tianjin-Hebei region and the Yangtze Economic Belt, has been promoted steadily.

The gross domestic product (GDP) of the year 2014 was RMB 63.6463 trillion yuan, or RMB 46 531 per capita, actually up by 7.4 % over the previous year after deducting the price factor; the proportion of three industries (primary industry, secondary industry and tertiary industry) was 9.2 : 42.6 : 48.2. The survey of urbanization residents showed that per capita disposable income of all the residents was RMB 20 167, up 8.0% actually. By the place of usual residence, per capita disposable income in urban areas was RMB 28 844, up 6.8% actually; per capita in rural areas was RMB 10 489, up 9.2% actually. The Gini's coefficient of resident income in the country was 0.469. The total number of *nongmingong* (Migrant worker) numbered 273.95 million across the country, adding 5.01 million over the previous year, and including 168.21 million who left hometown and worked in other places. Average monthly income of *nongmingong* reached RMB 2 864, up 9.8% over the previous year.

Seen from the urban-rural structure, by the end of 2014, the total number of Chinese population at the mainland reached 1 367.82 million, an increase of 7.10 million over that at the end of 2013, with a natural growth rate of 5.21‰. Among them, urban permanent residents numbered 749.16 million, adding 18.05 million over the end of previous year; rural permanent residents numbered 618.66 million, a decrease of 10.95 million; the percentage of urban population accounted for 54.77% of the total. The number of population who live in places other than their household registration reached 298 million, adding 9.44 million over the end of previous year. Among them, floating population reached 253 million, a rise of 8 million over the end of previous year. The employed persons in the country hit 772.53 million at the end of that year, adding 2.76 million, of which the employed persons in cities were 393.10 million, increasing 10.70 million. The urban registered unemployment rate was 4.09%.

By the end of 2014, the operating mileage of national railways was 112 000 kilometers, of which high-speed railways amounted to 16 000 kilometers; the length of highways in operation reached 4.46 million kilometers, including 112 000 kilometers of expressways opened to traffic; there were 2 116 coastal harbors and 202 civil airports in service. Cabled broadband users exceeded 780 million. Across the country, there have been 21 cities opening the urban rail traffic lines and the total mileage in operation exceeded 2 800 kilometers.

(Ⅱ) Adjustment on municipal administrative divisions

By the end of 2014, there have been 653 cities with municipal governments, including 4 municipalities, 15 sub-provincial-level cities, 273 prefecture-level cities and 361 county-level cities, 1 600 counties and 20 401 towns in the country. The changes on the organizational system of cities with municipal governments within this year are as follows.

The State Council approved the People's Government of Tibet Autonomous Region to cancel Xigaze Prefecture and Xigaze County-level City to set up Xigaze Prefecture-level City on June

26. The Xigaze City sets up Samzhubze District, following the original administrative regions of County-level Xigaze City.

The State Council approved the People's Government of Tibet Autonomous Region to cancel Qamdo Prefecture and Qamdo County to set up Qamdo Prefecture-level City on October 20. The Qamdo City sets up Karuo District, following the original administrative regions of Qamdo County.

The State Council also agreed to cancel Conghua County-level City and set up Conghua District of Guangzhou City; cancel Wendeng County-level City and set up Wendeng District of Weihai City; cancel Shuangcheng County-level City and set up Shuangcheng District of Harbin City; cancel Jianyang County-level City and set up Jianyang District of Nanping City; cancel Gaocheng County-level City and set up Gaocheng District of Shijiazhuang City; cancel Luquan County-level City and set up Luquan District of Shijiazhuang City; cancel Jiutai County-level City and set up Jiutai District of Changchun City; cancel Fuyang County-level City and set up Fuyang District of Hangzhou City. Upon the approval of the State Council, Xinjiang Uygur Autonomous Region set up Shuanghe County-level City and Horgos County-level City; Yunnan Province cancelled Shangri-La County to set up Shangri-La County-level City.

The State Council also approved Shaanxi Province to set up Xixian New Area which covers 23 villages and towns and street offices of 7 counties (districts) in Xi'an and Xianyang, and the planned area is 882 square kilometers; approved Guizhou Province to set up Guian New Area which covers 20 villages and towns of 4 counties (districts) in Guiyang and City, and the planned area is 1 795 square kilometers; approved Qingdao City to set up West Coast New Area covering all administrative regions in Huangdao District, of which the land area is approximately 2 096 square kilometers and sea area is approximately 5 000 square kilometers; approved Dalian City to set up Jinpu New District including all administrative regions of Jinzhou District and partial regions of Pulandian, at an area of 2 299 square kilometers; approved Sichuan Province to set up Tianfu New Area including 7 counties (cities and districts) of Chengdu, Meishan and Ziyang, at an area of 1 578 square kilometers.

According to the latest statistics, there have been 125 national-level historical and cultural cities, including two new ones added in 2014, Huzhou City of Zhejiang Province and Qiqihar City of Heilongjiang Province respectively; 252 national-level historical and cultural towns; 276 historical and cultural villages; 2 555 villages listed by traditional Chinese villages. "Grand Canal" and "Silk Road: Road Network of ChangAn-Tianshan Corridor" were included into the UNESCO *World Heritage List*, lifting the country's world heritage sites to 47, including 29 cultural heritage sites, 10 natural heritage sites, 4 cultural and natural heritage sites and 4 cultural landscapes.

(Ⅲ) Construction of cities (districts)

According to statistics of the Ministry of Housing and Urban-Rural Development, by the end of 2013, there have been 658 cities with municipal governments nationwide, urban population numbered 376.97 million, temporary residents numbered 56.21 million and total built-up areas amounted to 47 855 square kilometers.

In 2013, fixed-assets investment in municipal public utilities was RMB 1.63498 trillion. Major newly-added production capacity included daily water production capacity of 7.48 million cubic meters, natural gas storage capacity of 23.61 million cubic meters, centralized heating capacity of 1 600 tons per hour, hot water supply capacity of 23 100 megawatts, roads of 11 200 kilometers, drain pipes of 19 500 kilometers, daily treatment of municipal sewage of 18.34 million cubic meters and daily harmless treatment of urban domestic garbage of 48 000 tons. There have been 35 urban rail transits under construction, with total length of 2 760 kilometers.

In 2013, water-using population numbered 423 million, the popularization rate of water hit 97.56% and per capita daily water consumption for residential use was 173.51 liters; natural gas-using population numbered 408 million and the popularization rate of gas was 94.25%; centralized heating floor area was 5.72 billion square meters; urban roads was 336 000 kilometers and per capita road area was 14.87 square meters; there were 1 736 urban sewage treatment plants and the centralized treatment rate of sewage was 84.53%; there were 765 harmless treatment sites (plants) of urban domestic garbage and harmless treatment rate of domestic garbage averaged 89.30%; the sweeping and cleaning (coverage) area of urban roads reached 6.46 billion square meters, with the mechanical sweeping rate accounting for 44.4%; garbage and feces cleaned and removed was 189 million tons and every 10 000 people had 2.83 latrines; the green space rate of urban built-up areas was 35.78% and per capita park space was 12.64 square meters. As of the end of 2013, there have been 225 national-level scenic spots. Among them, 224 scenic spots covered a total area of 97 000 square kilometers, including 42 000 square kilometers available for sightseeing, and accepted tourists for 730 million person times in the year.

According to statistics of the Ministry of Transport, by the end of 2013, there have been 18 cities in the country opening up rail transit and owning 1 549 rail transit stations, including 134 transfer stations. End of the year, there have been 509 600 public auto and electric buses, and 14 366 rail transit vehicles in service. There have been 1.34 million taxies in service and 422 urban passenger ferries. There have been 41 738 lines in operation for public auto and electric buses, with a total length of 748 900 kilometers; 81 rail transit lines in operation, with a total length of 2 408 kilometers; 143 routes in operation for urban passenger ferries, with a total length of 575 kilometers. The urban passenger transport systems carried passengers of 128.335 billion total, including 77. 117 billion passengers by public auto and electric buses, 10. 919 billion passengers by rail transport and 40. 194 billion passengers by taxies; 106 million passengers were carried by passenger ferries, down 19. 4%. Among total passengers carried by the urban passenger transport systems, public auto and electric buses, rail transport, taxies and passenger ferries accounted for 61. 1%, 8. 5%, 31. 3% and 0. 1%, respectively.

(Ⅳ) Construction of county seats

By the end of 2013, there have been 1 613 county seats in the country. Based on statistics of 1 582 counties, 15 special areas and 148 Xinjiang Production and Construction Corps-stationed areas, total household register population numbered 137. 01 million, temporary residents were 15. 66 million, and the build-up area was 19 503 square kilometers.

In 2013, fixed-assets investments in the county seats municipal public utilities reached RMB 383. 37 billion. Major newly-added production capacity included daily water production capacity of 1. 86 million cubic meters, natural gas storage capacity of 6. 81 million cubic meters, centralized heating capacity of 335 tons per hour and hot water supply capacity of 7 544 megawatts, roads of 6 817 kilometers, drain pipes of 12 000 kilometers, daily sewage treatment capacity of 1. 61 million cubic meters and daily harmless treatment capacity of domestic garbage of 10 000 tons.

In 2013, in total county seats, water-using population numbered 135 million, the popularization rate of water was 88. 14% and per capita daily water consumption for residential use hit 119. 06 liters; natural gas-using population numbered 108 million and the popularization rate of gas was 70. 91%; centralized heating floor area was 1. 03 billion square meters; roads of county seats were 125 000 kilometers, per capita road area was 14. 86 square meters, sweeping and cleaning area of roads was 1. 98 billion square meters and the mechanical sweeping rate of roads reached 31. 7%; garbage and feces cleaned and removed was 71 million tons; there were 992 harmless domestic garbage treatment sites (plants) and harmless treatment rate of domestic garbage reached 66. 07%; there were 1 504 sewage treatment plants and the centralized sewage treatment rate was 76. 25%. The green space coverage rate of built-up area was 24. 76% and per capita public green space was 9. 47 square meters.

(Ⅴ) Construction of villages and small towns

By the end of 2013, there have been 20 117 towns and 12 812 townships. Based on data collected from 17 449 towns and 12 281 townships, 673 town-level special areas and 2. 65 million natural villages (including 537 200 ones where village committees are located), total permanent residence-registered population numbered 948 million, including 152 million in built-up areas of towns, 31 million in built-up areas of townships, 3 million in build-up areas in town-level special areas and, 762 million in villages. Built-up area in towns was 3. 69 million hectares, in townships was 737 000 hectares and in town-level special areas was 107 000 hectares. Current land area of villages covered 13. 943 million hectares. There were 15 810 towns, 9 055 townships, 477 town-level special areas, 320 000 administrative villages and 738 000 natural villages having master plans in the country.

In 2013, total investments in the construction of villages and towns were RMB 1. 6235 trillion, of which investments in housing construction accounted for 77. 5% of total and in municipal public utilities accounted for 22. 5%. As of the end of 2013, the total floor space of building stock in the villages and towns covered 37. 369 billion square meters with 33. 02 square meters of per capita housing floor space.

In 2013, in the built areas of towns, the water coverage rate was 81. 73%, daily per capita domestic water consumption was 98. 58 liters, gas coverage rate was 46. 4%, per capita area of paved roads was 12. 3 square meters, drainage pipeline and ducts density was 6. 75 kilometers per square kilometers, and per capita area of public green space was 2. 73 square meters. In the built areas of townships, the water coverage rate was 68. 24%, daily per capita domestic water consumption was 82. 81 liters, gas coverage rate was 19. 5%, per capita area of paved roads was 12. 1 square meters, drainage pipeline and ducts density was 3. 57 kilometers per square kilometers, and per capita area of public green space was 1. 08 square meters. Total roads in villages were 2. 28 million kilometers long, including hardening roads of 708 000 kilometers; roads in villages covered an area of 64. 1 billion square meters, including hardening roads of 19. 7 billion square meters; ditches of drainage channel within villages were 507 000 kilometers long. By the end of 2013, in the administrative villages nationwide, there were 61. 3% had access to central water supply, domestic wastewater had been treated in 9. 1% of the villages, domestic garbage collection facilities had been set up in 54. 8% of the villages, and 36. 6% of domestic garbage had been treated.

Ⅱ. Release and Pilot of the New Urbanization Plan

On March 12, 2014, the Central Committee of the CPC and the State Council released the "Notice on Releasing the *National New Urbanization Plan* (2014 – 2020)". According to the *Plan*, it is a macroscopic, strategic and fundamental plan, which serves as an important approach to solve the problems related to agriculture, rural areas and farmers, a strong support to promote the regional coordinated development and also a key link to expand domestic demand and promote industrial upgrade. Upon the formation and implementation of the *Plan*, China's new type urbanization should be people-oriented. Areas of modernization should develop in step with each other. The arrangement should be optimized and it should be ecologically friendly and carry forward cultural traditions. The urbanization should have great realistic meaning and profound historic significance in building a well-off society in an all-round way and accelerating the socialist modernization.

The *Plan* proposed China's objectives by 2020:

Level and quality of urbanization will be promoted steadily. With the healthy and ordered development, the urbanization rate of resident population and registered population will reach around 60% and 45% respectively, and the gap between these two figures will be narrowed by about two percentage point. We will strive to complete the registration to 100 million rural migrants and other resident population with urban permanent residence.

Urbanization pattern will be more optimized. The spatial pattern of "two-horizontal axes and three-vertical axes" urbanization strategy will be basically formed. Agglomeration economy of city clusters and population capacity will be enhanced remarkably. Integration level and international competitiveness of city clusters in the Eastern region will be promoted considerably. City clusters in the central and western regions will become a new important growth pole for the regional coordinated development in China. The scale structure of cities will be more improved, with more focus on the leading role of central cities. The number of small and medium-sized cities will be increased and the service functions of small towns will be intensified.

Urban development model will be scientific and reasonable. The intensive and compact development pattern will eventually dominate, with a highlight on higher density, mixed functions and bus orientation. Per capita urban built-up land area will be strictly controlled below 100 square meters, and the population density will be enhanced gradually. Green production and consumption will become the norm in the urban economy, which will remarkably raise the percentages of water and energy saving and recycling products as well as green buildings. The coverage rate of urban underground pipe network will be improved significantly.

Urban life will be harmonious and pleasant. Basic public services including compulsory education, employment service, basic endowment, basic medical heath and low-cost housing system will be steadily promoted and eventually accessible to all permanent urbanites. Infrastructures and public service facilities will be more perfect, consumption environment will be more convenient, eco-environment will be improved remarkably, air quality will be better gradually and the drinking water safety will be secured. Natural landscapes and cultural features will be protected effectively. The urban development will be individualized and urban management will be oriented to humanization and intellectualization.

Urbanization system and mechanism will be improved continuously. Great progress will be made in the system reforms, such as, household registration management, land management, social security, taxation and finance, administration and eco-environment. The system and mechanism barriers that impede the healthy development of urbanization will be eliminated basically.

The *Programme for Overall Implementation of Comprehensive Pilot of National New Urbanization* was released on December 29. The pilot areas were determined to locate at 60 cities, two provinces of Jiangsu and Anhui, as well as Longgang Town of Cangnan County in Zhejiang Province and Erdaobaihe Town of Antu County in Jilin Province. The pilot work was commenced from late 2014. The *Programme* will be improved continuously according to actuality. By 2017, all pilot areas will make the staged achievements in their respective task and form the experience that can be copied and extended; in 2018 – 2020, the successful experience of pilot areas will be demonstrated across the country step by step. For those pilot areas, the primary mission is to share costs associated with granting urban residency to rural people who have moved to cities, diversify the sustainable investment and financing mechanism for urban development, reform and improve the rural residential land system, explore to establish the new management model of administrative management innovation and administrative cost reduction, and comprehensively promote reforms and innovations in systems and mechanisms. Pilot areas are encouraged to start with the promotion of new urbanization and conduct the diversified and featured reforms and exploration in terms of the systems and mechanisms for urban-rural development integration, for formation and management of urban-rural planning, for agricultural modernization, for coordination of the multiple planning systems, the urban eco-civilization and social governance system, the construction of standard system for new urbanization and the construction of innovative cities, smart cities, low-carbon cities and cultural cities.

Ⅲ. Accelerate Reforms to the Household Registration System

The primary task of pressing ahead with urbanization is to promote the realization of orderly citizenization of permanent residents who are capable to take stable jobs and life in the urban areas. On June 30, the Political Bureau of the CPC pointed out that the reform of household registration system is a key measure that concerns migrant rural population of hundreds of millions. To this goal, we shall embark on the people-oriented reforms, strive to promote the realization of orderly citizenization of permanent residents who are capable to take stable jobs and life in the urban areas and steadily extend basic public services to be accessible to all permanent urbanites. We shall adhere to acting active and prudent actions and moving forward step by step. We not only encourage all places to be bold in practices and active in exploration, but also guide the local areas to respect objective laws and people's will, avoiding allocation of objectives and quotas raised at each level. Priorities shall be placed on solving the population who live in the city for a long time and have a strong employability to adapt themselves to the competition environment in the city and the market, and facilitate such population and their accompanying families to settle in the city, so as to guide the population flows in an orderly manner. We shall actively promote the transformation of providing urban basic public services from local registered population to resident population, and gradually solve the problem that the urban basic public services are accessible to migrant rural population who work and live in cities but not register their household there. The system of rural property right shall be improved. The right of operation of land contracted by peasants, the use right of house site and the distribution right of collective incomes shall be maintained properly. The household registration policy with different eligibility requirements shall be implemented in a targeted way and under classified instructions in light of different local conditions.

On July 24, the State Council released the *Opinion on Further Promoting the Reform of Household Registration System*. The *Opinion* asks to further adjust the household registration transfer policy. Specifically, we shall completely lift restrictions on new residence registration in administrative townships and small cities, relax restrictions on new residence registration in medium-sized cities in an orderly manner, lay down appropriate conditions for new residence registration in big cities, and strictly control the population size of megacities, with an aim to effectively solve the key issues of residence transfer. We shall earnestly carry out and preemptively resolve the current requirements, with a focus on the issues of residence registration of population who live in cities for a long time and have a strong employability to adapt themselves to the urban industrial upgrades and transformation and market competition environment. Continuous improvements shall be made in the registration rate of urban residence of residential population including university graduates, technical workers, graduates of vocational institutions and overseas returnees. The specific measures for innovative population management include: establish the unified household registration system in both urban and rural areas, cancel the difference in the agricultural and the non-agricultural registered permanent residence and the derived types of household registration (i. e. blue-stamped residence permit) to unify as resident household and embody the population registration management function of household registration system; establish the system of residence permit which can be applied and obtained locally by a citizen who leaves the registered permanent residence and lives in other city with districts at the city level or above for over half a year. The eligible holder of residence permit may apply for registration of local permanent residence. With the residence permit as the carrier, we shall establish and improve the accessibility mechanism of basic public services that are linked to the conditions for period of resident; the population information management system shall be improved; the registration system of actual resident population shall be enhanced; efforts shall be made to strengthen and improve the demographic research, so that we can come to a comprehensive and accurate understanding to the size, structure and regional distribution of population.

To further and effectively implement the categorized administration of population and cities, the State Council released the *Notice on Adjusting the Standards for Categorizing City Sizes*. Cities are categorized into five categories and seven grades based on the statistics of resident population in urban areas. Cities with a permanent population below 500 000 in urban areas are categorized to small cities, of which those with a permanent population between 200 000 ~ 500 000 are Grade-Ⅰ small cities and those with a permanent population below 200 000 are Grade-Ⅱ small city. Cities with a permanent population between 0. 5 ~ 1 million are categorized to medium-sized cities. Cities with a permanent population between 1 ~ 5 million are categorized to big cities, of which those with a population between 3 ~ 5 million are Grade-Ⅰ big cities and those with a population between 1 ~ 3 million are Grade-Ⅱ big cities. Cities with a permanent population between 5 ~ 10 million are categorized to megacities. And cities with a permanent population of 10 million and more are super-cities.

Ⅳ. Construction of Public Housing and Redevelopment of Rundown Urban Areas

According to the government work report of the State Council in 2014, to achieve the goal of public housing for all, we shall build more government-subsidized housing in accordance with the principle of giving targeted guidance, carrying out step-by-step implementation and having governments at different levels assume their respective responsibilities. The construction of security-oriented housing projects and related supporting infrastructure shall be strengthened. The proportion of government-subsidized housing in large cities shall be increased. The construction of public rentals and low-rent public housing shall be merged gradually. The mechanisms and instruments for securing investment and financing for policy-related housing shall be improved innovatively.

On April 2, the State Council deployed to further exert the role of development-oriented finance on supporting the rundown urban areas redevelopment. The meeting stressed it is a heavy task to speed up the shantytown reconstruction and enable hundreds of thousands of residents to live in new homes as early as possible. It not only helps stimulate investment and promote consumption but also constitutes an important content that characterize the people-oriented new urbanization. This year, the rundown urban areas redevelopment shall be advanced in large scale. To this end, we must grasp the key of fund guarantee to effectively integrate policy support with market mechanism. In particular, we shall give into play the development-oriented finance that relies on the state credit, places the emphasis on service the state strategy and utilization of capitals oriented to cost recovery and meager profit, so as to quickly provide the shantytown reconstruction with the legal and convenient financing channels that is featured with appropriate costs and stable source, and ensure the capital demands and cost reduction for the shantytown reconstruction. The meeting decided that National Development Bank shall establish a special organization to carry out the independent accounting and issue the housing finance bonds by way of marketization to attain financing from financial institutions and other investors like China Postal Savings Bank. Commercial banks, social insurance funds and insurance agencies shall be encouraged to mainly finance for the rundown urban areas redevelopment and related engineering construction of urban infrastructures.

On July 21, the General Office of the State Council released the *Notice on Further Strengthening the Work of Rundown Urban Areas Redevelopment*. As specified in the *Notice*, we shall further improve the shantytown rebuild plan and make the statistics of base number, area and type of shantytowns to be rebuilt; optimize the planning layout, perfect the site layouts of resettlement housing and improve the planning layout of supporting facilities; accelerate the work of early stage, well fulfill the acquisition and compensation and quicken the channels of administrative approvals; strengthen the quality safety control, intensify the safety supervision on the quality of construction in progress and conduct the safety inspection against the quality of resettlement housing; speed up the construction of supporting facilities and improve the community public services; implement various support policies, guarantee the supply of construction land, carry out the tax and fiscal support policies and boost the financial support; strengthen the organization and leadership to strive for over fulfilling the task in 2014 and making an advance planning for the rundown urban areas redevelopment during 2015－2017.

According to the partial statistical data, 7.4 million units of government-subsidized urban housing were built additionally in 2014, of which 5.11 million units were basically finished. Since the commencement of shantytown reconstruction in 2004, a cumulative number of 20.80 million urban housing units have been reconstructed. And 16 million dilapidated rural houses have been renovated cumulatively from its commenced in 2008.

The National Audit Office made an audit on investment, construction, distribution, subsequent management and relevant policy execution of government-subsidized housing projects in 2013 (including low-rent housing, public leasing houses, economically affordable houses, price-restricted commercial housing and various shantytown reconstruction projects). The auditing results revealed major questions as below: the special funds of engineering fiscal subsidy, bank loans and enterprise bonds were misappropriated; the capitals for rundown urban areas redevelopment were obtained illegally by way of false application information and repeated application; disqualified households were discovered to illegal enjoy the affordable rent of security-oriented houses and housing monetary subsidy; security-oriented houses were unlawfully sold or used by the construction enterprises and units for other purposes; the agricultural land was occupied without any approval of land transfer, and the land of resettlement projects was acquisitioned or disposed illegal.

V. Reform Pilot and Practices of Urban-Rural Planning System

(I) Carrying out the nationwide pilot for planning system reforms

To explore and improve the county-level (municipal) planning system, promote the urban-rural development integration and advance the reform of planning system, the Ministry of Housing and Urban-Rural Development issued the *Notice on Carrying out the Pilot Work of County-level (Municipal) Urban-rural Overall Planning and "Integrating Three Plans in One"*. The *Notice* pointed out that currently county-level (municipal) plans are too many and conflicting one another, without insufficient coverage and depth. These plans result in urban-rural separation, giving priority to cities and extensive use of urban land, whereby the implementation of plans counts against the supervision. Especially in some areas with developed economy and dense population, man-land relationship became strained and needed the intensified overall plan and management. In recent years, some areas started to explore the compilation of county-level (municipal) urban-rural master plan and have made specific achievements, providing a favorable basis for the work to launch the pilot of county-level (municipal) urban-rural overall planning. The major contents of pilot work are to county-level (municipal) urban-rural overall planning, realize the integration of plans for economic and social development, urban-rural development and land use, or merger of multiple plans into one, and gradually form the planning system with uniform engagement and complementary functions, according to the requirements of urban-rural integration, overall control and interdepartmental coordination.

In recent years, many villages and townships plans were just the "cookie-cutters" of city planning, leading to the issues that plans were separated from actuality and inferior in guidance and implementation. In this view, the Ministry of Housing and Urban-rural Development issued the *Notice on Fulfilling the Pilot Work of Village Plan, Township Plan and Urban-village System Plan in* 2014, on March 28. The aim of pilots is to explore the concepts and compilation methods of village and township plans which keep in line with the requirements for new urbanization and building a new socialist countryside, and have relatively strong guidance and implementation. Besides, it is to explore the compilation method of urban-village system planning by "Multi-Plans in One", and form a batch of model-setting plans to sum up and promote experience. Based on recommendation and declaration of various places, five counties were selected as pilots of urban-village system plan; 17 towns were selected to conduct the township planning pilot work; 10 administrative villages were designated to conduct the village plan pilots.

The National Development and Reform Commission, the Ministry of Land and Resources, the Ministry of Environmental Protection and the Ministry of Housing and Urban-Rural

Development jointly released the *Notice on Carrying out the Pilots of "Multi Plans in One" in Cities and Counties*, on August 26. According to the *Notice*, 28 cities, counties and districts jointly conducted the pilot work of "*Multi Plans in One*". The *Notice* pointed out that, the pilots planning in cities and counties are urgently needed to solve the prominent problems such as independent system of city and county planning, content conflicts and shortage of coordination and guarantee the effective implementation of city and county planning; it is an important measure to intensify the governmental capacity of spatial control and realize the intensive, efficient and sustainable utilization of state-owned land, and also an important foundation to reform the governmental planning system and establish the spatial planning system with uniform engagement, complementary functions and mutual coordination; it has attached significance to speed up the transformation of economic development pattern, optimize the spatial development mode, unswervingly carry out the functional zoning system and promote the coordinated development between economic society and eco-environment. The mission of pilot is to explore the concrete ideas of "*Multi Plans in One*" that integrates the economic and social development plan, urban-rural plan, land use plan and eco-environment protection, rationally determine the deadline, objective and mission of the planning, research and propose the program of "*Multi Plans in One*" that can be copied and generalized.

(Ⅱ) Building "sponge city"

In recent years, "rain-triggered waterlogging" has been an important problem facing many cities in China. As to this problem, President Xi Jinping proposed that every detail of urban planning construction has to take account of the influences to the nature, avoiding the break in the natural system. While improving the urban drainage system, we must give top priority to retaining limited rainwater and draining water by nature, so as to establish a "sponge city" that is able to store, drain and purify rainwater by natural forces.

To protect and improve the urban eco-environment and promote the construction of ecological civilization, the Ministry of Housing and Urban-Rural Development released the *Technical Guidelines for Construction of Sponge City (Trial)*. The *Guidelines* specify contents, requirements and methods that have moderate or low impact on the process of urban planning, project design, construction, maintenance and management, and also present a part of implementation cases in China.

"Sponge city" refers to a city that has good "elasticity" in adapting itself to environmental changes and responding to natural disasters, just like a sponge. "Sponge city" may absorb, store, drain and purify rainwater when it rains and then "release" the stored water for urgent need. The construction process of "sponge city" shall make overall arrangement of the systematicness of natural precipitation, surface water and underground water, coordinate water supply, drain and all other links of water recycle, and take into account its complexity and long-lasting characteristics. The construction approaches of "sponge city" include: protection for original ecological system of a city and maximized protection of original rivers, lakes, wetland, ponds, drainage ditches and other water ecological sensitive region; ecological restoration and rehabilitation of damaged water body and other natural environment; rational control of development intensity based on development and construction concept with the minimized influence to the urban eco-environment. The construction of "sponge city" shall place stress on developing low-impact rainwater system, urban rainwater pipe system and runoff discharge system of over standard rainwater. These three aspects shall be complementary and interdependent.

The Ministry of Finance, the Ministry of Housing and Urban-Rural Development and the Ministry of Water Resources jointly released the *Notice on Carrying out the Construction Pilots of Sponge City Subsidized by the Central Finance*, on December 31. The Central Finance decided to allocate a special subsidy for construction pilots of "sponge city" for consecutively three years. The specific subsidy shall be determined and categorized by city scale. That is, the annual subsidy shall be RMB 600 million for a municipality, RMB 500 million for a provincial capital and RMB 400 million for other city. For a "sponge city" that reaches a certain percentage under the mode PPP, an additional incentive of 10% of the above subsidy will be granted. The pilot city shall build itself into a sponge that has the function to absorb, store, purify and drain water and also enhances its own ability of flood prevention, flood drainage and disaster reduction. These three ministries will conduct the regular performance appraisal on the pilot work and assign penalty and award in line with the results.

(Ⅲ) Shanghai launched a new round of urban master plan formation

On February 13, 2014, Shanghai Municipal People's Government released the *Opinion on Drawing up the New Round of Shanghai's Master Plan.* The future development orientation of Shanghai is: By 2020, Shanghai will strive to develop itself into a global city with the ability of global resource allocation, stronger international competitiveness and influence based on four centers (international economy, finance, trade and shipping) and socialistic modern international metropolis, so as to create the upgrading version of China's economy and contribute its bets to realizing the Chinese dream for great rejuvenation of the Chinese nation. Then, Shanghai will be a smart, safe and convenient livable city featured with sound ecological environment, social harmony and low carbon, a city suitable for various talents to grow up and start a business, a charming and desirable metropolis of international cultures and also one of core cities of world urban system. The term of new round plan will be accomplished by 2040.

There are some major problems in Shanghai's urban development as follows: *Shanghai's Master Plan* (1999 – 2020) requires that, the actual resident population in Shanghai will be around 16 million by 2020, but the total resident population has numbered 24.15 million in 2013, including non-native resident population of 9.90 million; the urban central areas are facing a heavy pressure in decentralizing population, the newly developed areas are inadequate in population agglomeration, the structure of construction land is not reasonable and the trend of contiguous extending the central areas outwards is not effectively stopped; in the central urban areas, the overall development intensity of residential land is too high, leading to the municipal ecological space near the rock-bottom and inadequate display of urban features and specialties; more improvements are badly needed in overall accessibility of civil infrastructures and the level of security; the implementation of master plan fall shorts of stable assessment mechanism and program design, continuously uniform planning objectives and indicators that can be assessed, reliable platform of basic data, engagement with specific departments in the formation of implementation policies and carrier for objectives and policy amendments, so the plan is hard to effectively link itself to dynamic maintenance and management.

In the formation of new round of Shanghai Master Plan, the emphasis is to enhance international competitiveness, sustainability and charms of Shanghai. For this goal, we shall consider the improvement of people's livelihoods as the starting point and foothold of urban development. Based on the orientation of building the world cities, enhancing the readjustment of industrial structure, the bottom line of resource and environment bearing capacity and the support of public services and infrastructure accessibility, we will optimize industrial structure, improve public policies and strengthen social management to comprehensively control the scale of urban development, strictly control the scale of population and land use to bring the scale of population under the moderate control, and continuously optimize population layout and structure; we will strictly observe the "ceiling" of land areas for construction purposes, implement the most strictest system of arable land protection and stinted and intensive system of land use, so as to meet the demands of land for urban development by relying on stock optimization, flow efficiency and quality improvement and also realize the "zero growth" in the total amount of construction land for urban development. Following the concept of organic decentralization, we shall strengthen the overall arrangement of urban-rural space and marine and overland resources and form the intensive, compact and network-based urban spatial layout that takes the basic ecological space as the bottom line, orients to the "multi-center and opening" spatial structure and related policy system. We shall hold that the concept of improving urban quality and cultural connotation run through the whole process of urban planning, construction and management, so as to enhance the heritage and innovation of urban cultures and strive for building the international metropolis featuring the "Shanghai style" cultural charms and urban quality with the global influences.

On May 6, Shanghai Municipality convened the sixth work conference of planning the land, where the new round of formation of urban master plan was officially kicked off and deployed in full swing. The meeting emphasized that the new round of master plan must adhere to "four transformations": Planning transformation shifting from scale expansion to borders under the binding constraints of resource environment; transformation from the pure planning centralized on economic development to the one targeting at comprehensive development of people; transformation from technical documents laying stress on formation of objectives to comprehensive public policies emphasizing the planning implementation; transformation from the static planning without changes upon the formation to the maintainable dynamic planning based on process control. "Six highlights" were set up: People-oriented development, development pattern focusing on regional integration, development bottom line focusing on ecological preference, development direction highlighting functional enhancement, development pathways to wise and farsighted growth, and development spirit of opening and inclusiveness.

Mr. Han Zheng, Secretary of the CPC Shanghai Municipal Committee, pointed out, "Planning work is a fundamental task crucial for generations to come. The formation of the plan shall be active and reliable. We shall do things that we commit and also leave a room for our generations. What we should hold shall remain unchanged, but we shall guarantee it within the bottom line. For the essential aspects, we must advance with the times and forge ahead to the future, but we shall leave enough room for our generations."

(Ⅳ) Beijing started to revise city master plan

According to the current *Beijing City Master Plan* (2004 – 2020), the actual resident population of Beijing shall be controlled around 18 million by 2020. However, by the end of 2013, the resident population in the city had reached 21.148 million, including the non-native resident population of 8.027 million. Along with excessive population growth, environmental pollution, traffic congestion and resource shortage, a variety of "urban diseases" have become increasingly prominent. On January 16, 2014, Mayor Wang Anshun proposed in the 2nd Session of the 14th Beijing Municipal People's Congress. He said, we will revise the city's master plan, advance the integration of economic development, urban-rural construction and land use plans, mark boundaries for urban development, and improve the functional and urban planning of urban and rural areas alike. We will stop urban sprawling and improve the quality of urbanization. Meanwhile, we will implement the national strategy for regional development and actively cooperate in the formulation of plans for developing the capital economic region; preparing special plans on urban planning, infrastructure, industrial development and ecological conservation; establish and improve coordination mechanisms for regional cooperation and development; take the initiative in the development of urban agglomerations comprising Beijing, Tianjin and Hebei Province.

On February 25 ~ 26, President Xi Jinping surveyed Beijing and chaired a symposium proposing five requirements for promoting the development and management of Beijing: first, we shall define the urban strategic position, persist on and strengthen the core functions of the capital as the national center of politics, cultures, international communication and scientific innovations, thoroughly implement the strategy of Green Beijing, High-tech Beijing and Humanistic Beijing and do our utmost to build Beijing into the world first-class harmonious and livable capital; second, we shall adjust and reduce the capital non-core functions, optimize the structures of primary, secondary and tertiary industries with a special focus on selecting industrial projects that characterize in high-end, service orientation, aggregation, integration and low-carbon, effectively control the population scale, boost the balanced distribution of regional population and promote the regional balanced development; third, we shall enhance the urban construction and infrastructure quality in particular, and form the interconnecting function system that gives moderate considerations to adapt to the need of future development, so as to contain the sprawl typed urban development and bring forth new ideas for the capital construction; fourth, we shall improve the urban management system, enhance the management level and attach special concerns to strengthening civil facility operating management, traffic control, environment control and emergency management, and push forward the modernization of objective, method and pattern of urban management; fifth, we shall increase the intensity of air pollution control. Responding to haze pollution and improving air quality, our primary mission is to control PM2. 5. To achieve this goal, we shall take major measures to strictly control vehicles, readjusting the industrial structure, intensify our management, fully implement the action plan for preventing and controlling air pollution and insist on the legal governance. Furthermore, we shall place stress on key fields, implement the rigorous index assessment, strengthen our supervision on environmental law enforcement and earnestly investigate accountability of concerned parties.

On June 5, Beijing Municipal Government asked for the instructions of the State Council on Revise Beijing City Master Plan. The revised planning period kept in line with the original, namely, end to the year of 2020. For the requirements of researches, however, appropriate long-term prospects could be made. The main concept for the revise city master plan is to embark on doing "subtraction" using the bearing capacity of population, resources and environment as the bottom line, with preference to decide urban, land, population and production by water resources. We shall clearly and definitely make an overall plan for objectives and tasks in terms of function decentralization, population control, land-use shrink, spatial optimization, ecological security and quality improvement, so as to lay a foundation for deepening and coordinating the governance of "urban diseases" and play a leading role in promoting the construction of the world first-class harmonious and livable capital and coordinated development of Beijing, Tianjin and Hebei.

On August 3, Capital Planning and Construction Commission convened the 33rd plenary session to research how to revise *Beijing City Master Plan.* Mr. Guo Jinlong, Secretary of the CPC Beijing Municipal Committee, proposed five requirements in allusion to revise the plan. First, place stress on "fitness but reduce scale". On the one hand, we shall resolve to adjust and control the capital non-core functions; on the other hand, we shall make fruitful achievements in developing the precise and advanced economic structure. Second, focus on the world first-class and strive to create the exquisite works of urban construction. In particular, we shall lower the development intensity and restrain the urban sprawl to enlarge the green space. Third, highlight cultural heritage. We shall handle properly the relationship between preservation of ancient capital features and modernized construction, extend the historical context and benefit the masses. Fourth, the construction of ecological civilization and urban environmental governance shall be included as important contents, and the urban spatial layout shall be further optimized. Five, emphasize reforms and innovations. After the amendment, the plan will better reflect the capital features, Beijing peculiarity and characteristics of the era.

Ⅵ. International Experiencing on Theory and Practice of Urbanization

(Ⅰ) The Seventh Session of the World Urban Forum

The Seventh Session of the World Urban Forum (WUF7) took place in the city of Medellín, Colombia, during April 5 ~ 11, 2014, sponsored by the UN-Habitat. The WUF7 organized around 500 partner activities and set up 110 exhibition booths. Totally 22 000 participants from more than 140 countries including the Chinese delegation presented themselves at the forum.

Theme of the WUF7 is Urban Equity in Development-Cities for Life. On the opening ceremony, UN Secretary-General Mr. Ban Ki-moon proposed, "We need inclusive development to eradicate extreme poverty." Mayor of Medellin Mr. Aníbal Gaviria appealed, "We want to face the creation of a more equitable city and we show that we can do it with innovation." Dr. Joan Clos, Executive Director of UN-Habitat, pointed out, "We must think urbanization. We must plan. It is not enough that only 20 countries of 193 have national urban development plans."

WUF7 featured six dialogue sessions, held each morning from 9 to 11 April. The topics of dialogues are: Equity in Urban Development Law; Urban Planning and Design for Social Cohesion; Innovative Financing Instruments for Local Authorities; Basic Services: Local Businesses for Equitable Cities; Raising Standards of Urban Resilience; and A Safe City as a Just and Equitable City.

WUF7 adopted the Medellin Declaration entitled Equity as a Foundation of Sustainable Urban Development. The Declaration states that, the participants of the WUF7—governments, private sector, international organizations, academia, professionals and civil society—reaffirm our commitment to integrate urban equity into the development agenda, employing all means and resources available to ensure that cities are transformed into inclusive, safe, prosperous and harmonious spaces for all. As a matter of urgency, we must take action, collectively and individually, to bring the benefits of sustainable urban development to all.

Participants of the WUF7 highlighted the need to promote a new urban agenda that can overcome the challenge of the lack of adequate legal framework and planning. The new urban agenda requires new technologies, reliable urban data and integrated, participatory planning approaches to respond both to present challenges and emerging needs of cities of the future. This agenda should promote an urbanization model that is people-centered, based on "Cities for Life" . We acknowledge that there are many models of urbanization that respond to countries' and cities' diverse cultural, institutional and social conditions. In this context, the new urban agenda should: Encourage governments to develop and use methods, such as national urban plans and policies, that link current urban development with future needs, and that are solidly grounded in the fundamental principles of equity, justice and human rights; advance greater social cohesion and break down social divides, promoting equity through empowering all segments of society, particularly women, youth and indigenous peoples. Promote participatory and inclusive local governance that empowers all inhabitants; recognize key contributions of various levels of government, including regional, sub-regional and municipal levels; strengthen formal coordination mechanisms; define joint responsibilities; and provide each level of government with the necessary resources and incentives to carry out their respective roles effectively. Promote sustainable urban development, based on urban planning that promotes youth participation, gender equality, balanced territorial development; strengthened resilience to climate change and natural disasters; the upgrading and prevention of slums; and provision of housing, basic services and land tenure security; access to safe, affordable, accessible, and sustainable transport; and access to safe public spaces and services for all.

(Ⅱ) Celebration for the First World Cities Day

Upon the proposal of Chinese government, the 2nd Committee of 68th UN General Assembly adopted the resolution on designating every October 31 as World Cities Day. This is the first time China promoted the establishment of an international day at the United Nation, which represents China's significant contribution to promoting the sustainable development of cities in the world. Upon the approval of the State Council of China and the permission of UN-Habitat, Shanghai has become the home city for series commemorative activities of the first World Cities Day. On October 31, the global opening ceremony of the World Cities Day was held in Shanghai Expo Center, jointly sponsored by the UN-Habitat, the Ministry of Housing and Urban-Rural Development and Shanghai Municipal Government.

Premier Li Keqiang, on behalf of Chinese government and people, extended his warm congratulations to the series activities of the World Cities Day in Shanghai. Li said that cities are important platforms for human civilization's advancement and various countries' economic and social development. Around the general theme "better city, better life" and this year theme of "urban transformation and development", it shows cities' functions and essence, and reflects people's thoughts on and actions for cities' development in the new period. As a largest developing country with a population of 1. 3 billion, China is advancing the new urbanization. The core is to follow the concept of people orientation, realize the harmonious and inclusive development of cities and towns, and enable new urbanization and agricultural modernization to complement each other. The international society shall strengthen exchange and cooperation in terms of green cities, smart cities, city governance and city cultures, facilitating cities to create a better future in the history.

With the decision by the United Nations General Assembly to establish World Cities Day, we now have an annual date on which to celebrate one of humankind's greatest and most complex creations, UN Secretary-General Ban Ki-moon said on World Cities Day. This new day is one of the legacies of Expo 2010 Shanghai, at which the international community explored urban best practices and concepts from all over the world. So it is fitting that Shanghai is hosting the main inaugural event of this new UN observance. The theme of this first World Cities Day— "Leading Urban Transformations" —highlights the pioneering power of cities. In a world where already over half the population lives in urban areas, the human future is largely an urban future. We must get urbanization right, which means reducing greenhouse emissions, strengthening resilience, ensuring basic services such as water and sanitation and designing safe public streets and spaces for all to share. Livable cities are crucial not only for city-dwellers but also for providing solutions to some of the key aspects of sustainable development. In 2016, the international community will come together for the third United Nations Conference of Housing and Sustainable Urban Development (Habitat Ⅲ). As we reflect on our urban future, let us seize all the opportunities cities offer to create a new and transformative urban agenda.

Shanghai's Mayor Mr. Yang Xiong said in his speech that the world is now advancing to the era of cities. City brings to human beings not only prosperity and convenience but also many challenges such as traffic jam, environmental pollution, resource strains and cultural conflicts. In responding to these challenges, cities of all countries shall join hands, use the advantages of each other for reference and search for the scientific and reasonable road of sustainable development. Shanghai, as the pioneer of World Cities Day, will work together with all countries to jointly create a more beautiful city and a better life.

(Ⅲ) APEC Meeting in Beijing

On November 5 ~ 11, APEC Economic Leaders' Meeting was held in Beijing. The meeting adopted two files, *Beijing Agenda for an Integrated, Innovative and Interconnected Asia-Pacific-The 22nd APEC Economic Leaders' Declaration* and *Statement on the 25th Anniversary of APEC: Shaping the Future through Asia-Pacific Partnership*, and approved the *Roadmap for APEC's Contribution to the Realization of the Free Trade Area of the Asia-Pacific* (*FTAAP*), the *APEC Blueprint on Connectivity*, and important cooperation proposal in the field of global value chain, supply chain and capacity building. Besides, the *APEC Accord on Innovative Development, Economic Reform and Growth* was adopted at the meeting.

At the meeting, we recognize that the Asia-Pacific is currently facing challenges and opportunities of urbanization. We realize that sustained and healthy development of urbanization is conducive to promoting innovative growth and realizing robust, inclusive and sustainable development in the Asia-Pacific; the meeting gives a high appraisal on the constructive work undertaken by APEC this year in promoting urbanization cooperation in the Asia-Pacific region, and adopts the *APEC Cooperation Initiative for Jointly Establishing an Asia-Pacific Urbanization Partnership*. The meeting undertakes to establish a cooperative network of sustainable cities in APEC economies, join hands to organize the cooperation projects of ecological cities and smart cities, generalize low-carbon demonstration projects of cities and towns, collectively promote cooperation projects, and to further explore pathways to a new urbanization and sustainable city development, featuring green, energy efficient, low-carbon and people-orientation. The meeting encourages members to facilitate the use of existing resources for research and capacity building on urbanization and support urbanization cooperation and urbanization-related projects, including by making voluntary contributions to establish a sub-fund within the APEC framework.

To safeguard the air quality around Beijing during the APEC period, Beijing, Tianjin, Hebei, Shanxi, Inner Mongolia, Shandong and Henan, as the key controlled areas to guarantee the air quality for the meeting, will thoroughly implement the guarantee measures, such as stopping work and production, synchronous limits on journey and reducing dust and emission, etc. The average concentration of PM2.5 in Beijing, Tianjin, Hebei and surrounding areas dropped by around 29%. According to the data of Beijing Municipal Environmental Monitoring Center, from November 1 ~ 12, the concentration of PM2.5, PM10, SO_2 and NO_2 in the air dropped by 55%, 44%, 57% and 31% respectively over the same period of previous year. With "Effort and Luck", Beijing air quality was excellent for 4 days and good for 7 days during the APEC meeting. The concentration of all pollutants reached the lowest level over the same period of the past five years. The statistics of the Ministry of Environmental Protection showed that all provinces and cities cumulatively sent 434 000 people times to inspect 61 000 industrial enterprises and 123 000 other pollution sources of all kinds; during the APEC meeting, 9 298 enterprises stopped production actually, 3 900 enterprises curtailed production and more than 40 000 construction sites suspended, which were respectively 3.6 times, 2.1 times and 7.6 times as much as that stated in the *Scheme of Safeguarding the Air Quality for the APEC Meeting* issued by the Ministry of Environmental Protection.

Ⅶ. Conclusion

As the time goes by, the years are shuttling ahead. The new year of 2015 will be a key year of comprehensively deepening the reform, a starting year of thoroughly advancing the law-based governance and also a perfect ending of fully completing the "Twelfth Five-year Plan". We must clearly realize that China is still in the primary stage of socialism and will remain a long way to go. The situation still remains harsh and complicated. To defuse problems and risks, avoid falling into the "middle-income trap", and achieve modernization, China must rely on development, and development must be scientific, sustainable and inclusive, respectively following economic laws, natural laws and social laws.

President Xi Jinping pointed out in his speech at New Year's party of the Chinese People's Political Consultative Conference, "Problem is the sound of our era and the people's will is the biggest politics. To advance all works of the Party and the country, we must hang on the problem orientation and listen to the people's call." "What we are undertaking now is an entirely new endeavor. On the way of forging ahead, we shall neither conformism or follow a stereotype routine nor ignore national conditions and to imitate awkwardly. We must be steady and unswerving to follow in our own footsteps."

(Author: Mao Qizhi, professor of Tsinghua University, Academician of International Eurasian Academy of Sciences)

2014年中国城市发展十大事件

2014年，是我国全面深化改革的开局之年，全面深化改革在重要领域和关键环节向纵深推进，一批重大改革方案稳步实施。中共十八届四中全会审议通过了《中共中央关于全面推进依法治国若干重大问题的决定》，提出要全面推进依法治国，建设中国特色社会主义法治体系，在法制轨道上推进国家治理体系和治理能力现代化，建设社会主义法治国家；国务院印发了《关于进一步推进户籍制度改革的意见》，明确提出了进一步推进户籍制度改革的指导思想、目标任务、政策措施和实现路径，标志着进一步推进户籍制度改革开始进入全面实施阶段；国务院印发了《关于建立统一的城乡居民基本养老保险制度的意见》，决定合并新型农村社会养老保险和城镇居民社会养老保险，建立全国统一的城乡居民基本养老保险制度，这是中国政府全面深化改革的一大举措，是在建立社会基本公共服务均等化方面迈出的坚实一步。

2014年，是我国政府着力推进制度建设之年，多项重要的政策法规和规划相继颁布实施。国务院发布了《不动产登记暂行条例》，建立不动产统一登记制度、整合不动产登记职责，是推进简政放权、减少多头管理的有效举措，对于保护权利人合法财产权，提高政府治理效率和水平，尤其在方便企业、方便群众方面，具有重要意义；国务院印发了《关于调整城市规模划分标准的通知》，对原有城市规模划分标准进行了调整，明确了新的城市规模划分标准，可更好地实施人口和城市分类管理，满足经济社会发展需要；中共中央、国务院印发了《国家新型城镇化规划（2014-2020年）》，这是中央颁布实施的第一个城镇化规划，规划明确了未来城镇化的发展路径、主要目标和战略任务，对于指导我国城镇化健康发展具有基础性和战略性作用。

2014年，我国在探索自贸区建设、区域协调发展、加强国际交流等方面取得重要成果。国务院批准在广东、天津、福建特定区域建立三个自由贸易园区，充分检验相关改革开放措施的实施效果以及复制推广的可行性，为全面深化改革、扩大开放进一步探索新途径、积累新经验；国家启动京津冀区域协调发展及城镇体系规划，京津冀协调发展是一个重大国家战略，对于实现京津冀优势互补、促进环渤海经济区发展、带动北方腹地发展具有重要意义；我国成功举办了2014年亚太经合组织（APEC）领导人会议，中国提出的多项议题得到会员国的广泛关注和认同，极大提升了中国在国际事务中的话语权和影响力，同时也广泛宣示了我国的国内外政策，赢得了更多的国际理解和支持。

2014 年年末，上海市黄浦区外滩陈毅广场发生严重踩踏事件。23 时 35 分，上海市黄浦区外滩陈毅广场东南角通往黄浦江观景平台的人行通道阶梯处发生拥挤踩踏，事件造成 36 人死亡，49 人受伤。这是一起对群众性活动预防准备不足、现场管理不力、应对处置不当而引发的拥挤踩踏并造成重大伤亡和严重后果的公共安全责任事件。这给城市安全敲响了警钟。

一、《国家新型城镇化规划（2014－2020 年）》出台

2014 年 3 月 16 日，中共中央、国务院印发了《国家新型城镇化规划（2014－2020 年）》（以下简称《规划》）。《规划》分为规划背景、指导思想和发展目标、有序推进农业转移人口市民化、优化城镇化布局和形态、提高城市可持续发展能力、推动城乡发展一体化、改革完善城镇化发展体制机制、规划实施共 8 篇 31 章。《规划》按照走中国特色新型城镇化道路、全面提高城镇化质量的新要求，明确未来城镇化的发展路径、主要目标和战略任务，统筹相关领域制度和政策创新，是指导全国城镇化健康发展的宏观性、战略性、基础性规划，也是中央颁布实施的第一个城镇化规划。

《规划》主要内容可以归纳为一条主线、四大任务、五项改革、六个创新。

一条主线：紧紧围绕全面提高城镇化质量，加快转变城镇化发展方式，以人的城镇化为核心，有序推进农业转移人口市民化；以城市群为主体形态，推动大中小城市和小城镇协调发展；以综合承载能力为支撑，提升城市可持续发展水平；以体制机制创新为保障，通过改革释放城镇化发展潜力，走以人为本、四化同步、优化布局、生态文明、文化传承的中国特色新型城镇化道路，促进经济转型升级和社会和谐进步。

四大任务：一是有序推进农业转移人口市民化，按照尊重意愿、自主选择，因地制宜、分步推进，存量优先、带动增量的原则，以农业转移人口为重点，兼顾高校和职业技术院校毕业生、城镇间异地就业人员和城区城郊农业人口，统筹推进户籍制度改革和基本公共服务均等化。二是优化城镇化布局和形态，根据土地、水资源、大气环流特征和生态环境承载能力，优化城镇化空间布局和城镇规模结构，在《全国主体功能区规划》确定的城镇化地区，按照统筹规划、合理布局、分工协作、以大带小的原则，发展集聚效率高、辐射作用大、城镇体系优、功能互补强的城市群，使之成为支撑全国经济增长、促进区域协调发展、参与国际竞争合作的重要平台；构建以陆桥通道、沿长江通道为两条横轴，以沿海、京哈京广、包昆通道为三条纵轴，以轴线上城市群和节点城市为依托、其他城镇化地区为重要组成部分，大中小城市和小城镇协调发展的“两横三纵”城镇化战略格局。三是提高城市可持续发展能力，加快转变城市发展方式，优化城市空间结构，增强城市经济、基础设施、公共服务和资源环境对人口的承载能力，有效预防和治理“城市病”，建设和谐宜居、富有特色、充满活力的现代城市。四是推动城乡发展一体化，坚持工业反哺农业、城市支持农村和多予少取放活方针，加大统筹城乡发展力度，增强农村发展活力，逐步缩小城乡差距，促进城镇化和新农村建设协调推进。

五项改革：一是推进人口管理制度改革，在加快改革户籍制度的同时，创新和完善人口

服务和管理制度，逐步消除城乡区域间户籍壁垒，还原户籍的人口登记管理功能，促进人口有序流动、合理分布和社会融合。二是深化土地管理制度改革，实行最严格的耕地保护制度和集约节约用地制度，按照管住总量、严控增量、盘活存量的原则，创新土地管理制度，优化土地利用结构，提高土地利用效率，合理满足城镇化用地需求。三是创新城镇化资金保障机制，加快财税体制和投融资机制改革，创新金融服务，放开市场准入，逐步建立多元化、可持续的城镇化资金保障机制。四是健全城镇住房制度，建立市场配置和政府保障相结合的住房制度，推动形成总量基本平衡、结构基本合理、房价与消费能力基本适应的住房供需格局，有效保障城镇常住人口的合理住房需求。五是强化生态环境保护制度，完善推动城镇化绿色循环低碳发展的体制机制，实行最严格的生态环境保护制度，形成节约资源和保护环境的空间格局、产业结构、生产方式和生活方式。

六个创新：一是强调以人为本，就是要有序推进农业转移人口市民化，首次提出了常住人口城镇化率和户籍人口城镇化率两个指标，这是与以往最大的不同，也是最大的进步。二是强调“四化同步”，就是要深入推动新型城镇化与新型工业化、信息化、农业现代化同步发展，这也是当今中国现代化建设的必然要求，“新四化”相辅相成，融合互动，从而推动现代化建设的进程。三是强调优化布局，就是要以城市群为主体形态，促进大中小城市和小城镇协调发展；要引领国土空间的均衡发展，东部地区需要调整优化转型升级，中西部地区要培育发展若干新的城市群，培育区域新的增长极。四是强调生态文明，就是要着力推进绿色发展、循环发展、低碳发展，要节约集约利用水、土地、能源等资源，强化生态修复和环境治理，推进绿色城市、智慧城市的建设。五是强调文化传承，彰显城市的特色和个性，要根据不同城市的自然历史文化的禀赋，体现差异性，倡导多样性，防止千城一面；要注重在旧城改造中保护历史文化遗产，注重在新城新区建设中注入传统文化元素。六是强调制度改革，形成有利于城镇化健康发展的体制机制，统筹推进人、地、钱等重点领域和关键环节的改革，逐步破除城乡二元结构及城市内部的二元结构，通过改革来释放城镇化的发展潜力，为新型城镇化注入活力和动力。

城镇化是人类社会发展的客观趋势，是国家现代化的重要标志。按照建设中国特色社会主义“五位一体”总体布局，顺应发展规律，因势利导，趋利避害，积极稳妥扎实有序推进城镇化，对全面建成小康社会、加快社会主义现代化建设进程、实现中华民族伟大复兴的中国梦，具有重大现实意义和深远历史意义。

中国城镇化大事记

•2002 年，党的十六大报告明确提出，要逐步提高城镇化水平，坚持大中小城市和小城镇协调发展，走中国特色的城镇化道路。

•2003 年，十六届三中全会正式提出了包括统筹城乡发展在内的“五个统筹”的发展观，要求加快城镇化进程，逐步统一城乡劳动力市场，形成城乡劳动者平等就业的制度。

•2004 年，中央经济工作会议指出，我国现在总体上已进入了以工促农、以城带乡的发展阶段。必须有效引导城镇化健康发展，妥善处理城乡关系，建立逐步改变城乡二元结构的机制。要注意保护和节约土地，维护农民的合法权益，合理把握城镇化进度。

• 2005 年，国家有关部门相继出台规定，要求将工伤、医疗保险逐步覆盖到进城务工人员。

• 2006 年，“十一五”规划纲要提出，坚持大中小城市和小城镇协调发展，提高城镇综合承载能力，按照循序渐进、节约土地、集约发展、合理布局的原则，积极稳妥地推进城镇化，逐步改变城乡二元结构。

• 2007 年，党的十七大报告指出，走中国特色城镇化道路，要按照统筹城乡、布局合理、节约土地、功能完善、以大带小的原则，促进大中小城市和小城镇协调发展。

• 2008 年，国务院出台的扩大内需 4 万亿投资计划中，有 9000 亿元用于保障性安居工程，加大对廉租住房建设支持力度，加快棚户区改造。

• 2009 年，我国制定保障性住房发展规划，计划 2009－2011 年解决 750 万户城市低收入住房困难家庭和 240 万户棚户区居民的住房问题。

• 2010 年，中央“一号文件”明确提出要加快城镇化步伐，提高城镇综合承载能力。当年，《国务院批转发展改革委关于 2010 年深化经济体制改革重点工作意见的通知》提出，深化户籍制度改革，加快落实放宽中小城市、小城镇特别是县城和中心镇落户条件的政策。

• 2011 年，“十二五”规划纲要提出未来五年我国将建设 3600 万套保障性住房，使其覆盖率达到 20%。同年，《全国主体功能区规划》发布，这是中国第一个国土空间开发规划。

• 2012 年，《国务院办公厅关于积极稳妥推进户籍管理制度改革的通知》发布，提出要分类明确户口迁移政策，继续探索建立城乡统一的户口登记制度。逐步实行暂住人口居住证制度。

• 2013 年，中央城镇化工作会议在北京召开，这是新中国成立以来中央召开的首个城镇化工作会议。会议讨论了国家新型城镇化规划，明确了推进城镇化的指导思想、主要目标、基本原则，提出了城镇化发展的六大重点任务。

• 2014 年，中共中央、国务院印发了《国家新型城镇化规划（2014－2020 年）》。

（参考资料来源：新华网）

二、国家启动京津冀协同发展及城镇体系规划

2013 年 5 月，国家主席习近平在天津调研时提出，要谱写新时期社会主义现代化的京津“双城记”。2013 年 8 月，习近平在北戴河主持研究河北发展问题时，又提出要推动京津冀协同发展。此后，习近平多次就京津冀协同发展作出指示，强调解决好北京发展问题，必须纳入京津冀和环渤海经济区的战略空间加以考量，从而打通发展的大动脉，更有力地彰显北京优势，更广泛地激活北京要素资源，同时，天津、河北要实现更好发展也需要连同北京发展一起来考虑。

2014 年 2 月 26 日，国家主席习近平在北京主持召开座谈会，专题听取京津冀协同发展工作汇报，强调实现京津冀协同发展，是面向未来打造新的首都经济圈、推进区域发展体制

机制创新的需要，是探索完善城市群布局和形态、为优化开发区域发展提供示范和样板的需要，是探索生态文明建设有效路径、促进人口经济资源环境相协调的需要，是实现京津冀优势互补、促进环渤海经济区发展、带动北方腹地发展的需要，是一个重大国家战略，要坚持优势互补、互利共赢、扎实推进，加快走出一条科学持续的协同发展之路。

习近平指出，北京、天津、河北人口加起来有1亿多人，土地面积有21.6万平方公里，京津冀地缘相接、人缘相亲，地域一体、文化一脉，历史渊源深厚、交往半径相宜，完全能够相互融合、协同发展。推进京津冀协同发展，要立足各自比较优势、立足现代产业分工要求、立足区域优势互补原则、立足合作共赢理念，以京津冀城市群建设为载体、以优化区域分工和产业布局为重点、以资源要素空间统筹规划利用为主线、以构建长效体制机制为抓手，从广度和深度上加快发展。推进京津双城联动发展，要加快破解双城联动发展存在的体制机制障碍，按照优势互补、互利共赢、区域一体原则，以区域基础设施一体化和大气污染联防联控作为优先领域，以产业结构优化升级和实现创新驱动发展作为合作重点，把合作发展的功夫主要下在联动上，努力实现优势互补、良性互动、共赢发展。

习近平就推进京津冀协同发展提出7点要求：一是要着力加强顶层设计，抓紧编制首都经济圈一体化发展的相关规划，明确三地功能定位、产业分工、城市布局、设施配套、综合交通体系等重大问题，并从财政政策、投资政策、项目安排等方面形成具体措施。二是要着力加大对协同发展的推动，自觉打破自家“一亩三分地”的思维定式，抱成团朝着顶层设计的目标一起做，充分发挥环渤海地区经济合作发展协调机制的作用。三是要着力加快推进产业对接协作，理顺三地产业发展链条，形成区域间产业合理分布和上下游联动机制，对接产业规划，不搞同构性、同质化发展。四是要着力调整优化城市布局和空间结构，促进城市分工协作，提高城市群一体化水平，提高其综合承载能力和内涵发展水平。五是要着力扩大环境容量生态空间，加强生态环境保护合作，在已经启动大气污染防治协作机制的基础上，完善防护林建设、水资源保护、水环境治理、清洁能源使用等领域合作机制。六是要着力构建现代化交通网络系统，把交通一体化作为先行领域，加快构建快速、便捷、高效、安全、大容量、低成本的互联互通综合交通网络。七是要着力加快推进市场一体化进程，下决心破除限制资本、技术、产权、人才、劳动力等生产要素自由流动和优化配置的各种体制机制障碍，推动各种要素按照市场规律在区域内自由流动和优化配置。

3月5日，国务院总理李克强在第十二届全国人民代表大会第二次会议上作新一届政府首份工作报告时提出，要“推进长三角地区经济一体化，深化泛珠三角区域经济合作，加强环渤海及京津冀地区经济协作。实施差别化经济政策，推动产业转移，发展跨区域大交通大流通，形成新的区域经济增长极”。

3月16日，中共中央、国务院印发了《国家新型城镇化规划（2014－2020年)》，提出将京津冀建设成为世界级城市群。

8月，国务院成立京津冀协同发展领导小组，组长由国务院副总理张高丽担任。作为顶层设计的京津冀协同发展规划也正在紧锣密鼓地编制。

9月4日，京津冀协同发展领导小组第三次会议在北京召开，国务院副总理、京津冀协同发展领导小组组长张高丽指出，要深化研究论证京津冀区域和三省市功能定位，科学合理确定在国家和区域发展大局中的“角色”和“职责”，合理分工，优化配置，并和环渤海地区发展协调衔接。要加快实施交通、生态、产业三个重点领域率先突破，着力推动网络化布局、智能化管理、一体化服务，构建安全可靠、便捷高效、经济实用、绿色环保的综合交通运输体系；着力推进绿色循环低碳发展，加强生态环境保护，发挥重点治理工程带动作用，节约集约利用资源，形成区域良好生态格局；着力实施创新驱动发展战略，促进产业有序转移承接，推动产业结构调整优化升级。要尽快完善协同发展规划总体思路框架，为编制总体规划奠定坚实基础。

12 月 26 日，京津冀协同发展工作推进会议在北京召开，国务院副总理、京津冀协同发展领导小组组长张高丽强调，京津冀协同发展的顶层设计已经取得阶段性成果，下一步要把工作重点从总体谋划转向推进实施，对确定的各项任务要狠抓落实、务求实效。要抓紧修改完善规划纲要，加快编制相关领域专项规划，确保在一个目标下协同、一张蓝图下推进。要深入研究体制机制改革、强化创新驱动、开展试点示范等重大问题，优先启动一批有共识、看得准、能见效的非首都核心功能疏解项目，加快推动交通一体化、生态环保、产业转移三个重点领域率先突破，抓紧确定 2015 年的重点工作和重大项目清单。

三、国家推行户籍改革，取消城乡“二元户口”

为深入贯彻落实党的十八大、十八届三中全会和中央城镇化工作会议关于进一步推进户籍制度改革的要求，促进有能力在城镇稳定就业和生活的常住人口有序实现市民化，稳步推进城镇基本公共服务常住人口全覆盖，2014 年 7 月，国务院印发了《关于进一步推进户籍制度改革的意见》(以下简称《意见》)，明确提出了进一步推进户籍制度改革的指导思想、目标任务、政策措施和实现路径，包括总体要求、进一步调整户口迁移政策、创新人口管理、切实保障农业转移人口及其他常住人口合法权益和切实加强组织领导五个部分，标志着进一步推进户籍制度改革开始进入全面实施阶段。

《意见》提出户籍制度改革的发展目标是，进一步调整户口迁移政策，统一城乡户口登记制度，全面实施居住证制度，加快建设和共享国家人口基础信息库，稳步推进义务教育、就业服务、基本养老、基本医疗卫生、住房保障等城镇基本公共服务覆盖全部常住人口。到 2020 年，基本建立与全面建成小康社会相适应，有效支撑社会管理和公共服务，依法保障公民权利，以人为本、科学高效、规范有序的新型户籍制度，努力实现 1 亿左右农业转移人口和其他常住人口在城镇落户。

《意见》提出，要进一步调整户口迁移政策。全面放开建制镇和小城市落户限制，在县级市市区、县人民政府驻地镇和其他建制镇有合法稳定住所（含租赁）的人员，本人及其共同居住生活的配偶、未成年子女、父母等，可以在当地申请登记常住户口。有序放开中等城市落户限制，在城区人口 50 万人至 100 万人的城市合法稳定就业并有合法稳定住所（含租赁），同时按照国家规定参加城镇社会保险达到一定年限的人员，本人及其共同居住生活的配偶、未成年子女、父母等，可以在当地申请登记常住户口。合理确定大城市落户条件，在城区人口100万人至300万人的城市合法稳定就业达到一定年限并有合法稳定住所（含租赁），同时按照国家规定参加城镇社会保险达到一定年限的人员，本人及其共同居住生活的配偶、未成年子女、父母等，可以在当地申请登记常住户口；城区人口300万人至500万人的城市，要适度控制落户规模和节奏，可以对合法稳定就业的范围、年限和合法稳定住所（含租赁）的范围、条件等作出较严格的规定，也可结合本地实际，建立积分落户制度。严格控制特大城市人口规模，改进城区人口500万人以上的城市现行落户政策，建立完善积分落户制度，按照总量控制、公开透明、有序办理、公平公正的原则，达到规定分值的流动人口本人及其共同居住生活的配偶、未成年子女、父母等，可以在当地申请登记常住户口。有效解决户口迁移中的重点问题，认真落实优先解决存量的要求，重点解决进城时间长、就业能力强、可以适应城镇产业转型升级和市场竞争环境的人员落户问题。

《意见》提出，要创新人口管理。建立城乡统一的户口登记制度，取消农业户口与非农业户口性质区分和由此衍生的蓝印户口等户口类型，统一登记为居民户口，建立与统一城乡户口登记制度相适应的教育、卫生计生、就业、社保、住房、土地及人口统计制度。建立居住证制度，公民离开常住户口所在地到其他设区的市级以上城市居住半年以上的，在居住地申领居住证，符合条件的居住证持有人，可以在居住地申请登记常住户口；以居住证为载体，建立健全与居住年限等条件相挂钩的基本公共服务提供机制。健全人口信息管理制度，建立健全实际居住人口登记制度，全面、准确掌握人口规模、人员结构、地区分布等情况；建设和完善覆盖全国人口的国家人口基础信息库，分类完善劳动就业、教育、收入、社保、房产、信用、卫生计生、税务、婚姻、民族等信息系统，逐步实现跨部门、跨地区信息整合和共享。

《意见》提出，要切实保障农业转移人口及其他常住人口合法权益。完善农村产权制度，加快推进农村土地确权、登记、颁证，依法保障农民的土地承包经营权、宅基地使用权；推进农村集体经济组织产权制度改革，探索集体经济组织成员资格认定办法和集体经济有效实现形式，保护成员的集体财产权和收益分配权；建立农村产权流转交易市场，推动农村产权流转交易公开、公正、规范运行。扩大基本公共服务覆盖面，保障农业转移人口及其他常住人口随迁子女平等享有受教育权利，完善就业失业登记管理制度，将农业转移人口及其他常住人口纳入社区卫生和计划生育服务体系，把进城落户农民完全纳入城镇社会保障体系，提高统筹层次实现基础养老金全国统筹，加快建立覆盖城乡的社会养老服务体系，完善以低保制度为核心的社会救助体系，把进城落户农民完全纳入城镇住房保障体系。加强基本公共服务财力保障，建立财政转移支付同农业转移人口市民化挂钩机制；完善促进基本公共服务均等化的公共财政体系，逐步理顺事权关系，建立事权和支出责任相适应的制度，中央和地方按照事权划分相应承担和分担支出责任；深化税收制度改革，完善地方税体系；完善转移支付制度，加大财力均衡力度，保障地方政府提供基本公共服务的财力。

进一步推进户籍制度改革，是涉及亿万农业转移人口的一项重大举措。《意见》要求各地区、各有关部门统一思想，加强领导，周密部署，敢于担当，按照走中国特色新型城镇化道路、全面提高城镇化质量的新要求，切实落实户籍制度改革的各项政策措施。同时，积极做好宣传引导，凝聚各方共识，形成改革合力，为进一步推进户籍制度改革营造良好的社会环境。

中国户籍制度改革历程

● 第一部户口管理条例出台

1951 年 7 月，公安部公布《城市户口管理暂行条例》，规定了对人口出生、死亡、迁入、迁出、“社会变动”（社会身份）等事项的管制办法。这是新中国成立后第一部户口管理条例，基本统一了全国城市的户口登记制度。

1955 年，《国务院关于建立经常户口等级制度的指示》的发布，统一了全国城乡的户口登记工作，规定全国城市、集镇、乡村都要建立户口登记制度，户口登记的统计时间为每年一次。

● “农”与“非农”二元格局确立

1958 年 1 月，全国人大常委会通过《中华人民共和国户口登记条例》，第一次明确将城乡居民区分为“农业户口”和“非农业户口”两种不同户籍，奠定了我国现行户籍管理制度的基本格局。

1964 年 8 月，《公安部关于处理户口迁移的规定（草案）》出台，集中体现了该时期户口迁移的两个“严加限制”基本精神，即：对从农村迁往城市、集镇的要严加限制；对从集镇迁往城市的要严加限制。

● 实施居民身份证制度，小城镇户籍逐步放开

1984 年 10 月，《国务院关于农民进入集镇落户问题的通知》颁布，户籍严控制度开始松动。通知规定，农民可以自理口粮进集镇落户，并同集镇居民一样享有同等权利，履行同等义务。

1985 年 7 月，《公安部关于城镇暂住人口管理的暂行规定》的出台标志着城市暂住人口管理制度走向健全，同年 9 月，作为人口管理现代化基础的居民身份证制度颁布实施。

1997 年 6 月，《国务院批转公安部小城镇户籍管理制度改革试点方案和关于完善农村户籍管理制度意见的通知》出台，规定已在小城镇就业、居住并符合一定条件的农村人口，可以在小城镇办理城镇常住户口。

1998 年 7 月，《国务院批转公安部关于解决当前户口管理工作中几个突出问题意见的通知》让户籍制度进一步松动。根据此《通知》，新生婴儿随父落户、夫妻分居、老人投靠子女以及在城市投资、兴办实业、购买商品房的公民及随其共同居住的直系亲属，凡在城市有合法固定的住房、合法稳定的职业或者生活来源，已居住一定年限并符合当地政府有关规定的，可准予落户。

2001 年 3 月，《国务院批转公安部关于推进小城镇户籍管理制度改革意见的通知》，标志着小城镇户籍制度改革全面推进。《通知》规定，对办理小城镇常住户口的人员不再实行计划指标管理。

2012 年 2 月，《国务院办公厅关于积极稳妥推进户籍管理制度改革的通知》指出，要引导非农产业和农村人口有序向中小城市和建制镇转移，逐步满足符合条件的农村人口落户需求，逐步实现城乡基本公共服务均等化。

• 新型户籍制度改革目标确立

2013 年 11 月，《中共中央关于全面深化改革若干重大问题的决定》指出，要“创新人口管理，加快户籍制度改革，全面放开建制镇和小城市落户限制，有序放开中等城市落户限制，合理确定大城市落户条件，严格控制特大城市人口规模”。

2014 年 7 月，《国务院关于进一步推进户籍制度改革的意见》正式发布。计划到 2020 年，基本建立与全面建成小康社会相适应，有效支撑社会管理和公共服务，依法保障公民权利，以人为本、科学高效、规范有序的新型户籍制度，努力实现 1 亿左右农业转移人口和其他常住人口在城镇落户。

（参考资料来源：新华网）

四、国务院调整城市规模划分，增设超大城市

2014 年 10 月 29 日，国务院印发了《关于调整城市规模划分标准的通知》（以下简称《通知》）（国发〔2014〕51 号），对原有城市规模划分标准进行了调整，明确了新的城市规模划分标准。

《通知》指出，改革开放以来，伴随着工业化进程加速，我国城镇化取得了巨大成就，城市数量和规模都有了明显增长，原有的城市规模划分标准已难以适应城镇化发展等新形势要求。当前，我国城镇化正处于深入发展的关键时期，为更好地实施人口和城市分类管理，满足经济社会发展需要，对城市规模划分标准做出调整十分必要。

《通知》明确，新的城市规模划分标准以城区常住人口为统计口径，将城市划分为五类七档：城区常住人口 50 万以下的城市为小城市，其中 20 万以上 50 万以下的城市为Ⅰ型小城市，20 万以下的城市为Ⅱ型小城市；城区常住人口 50 万以上 100 万以下的城市为中等城市；城区常住人口 100 万以上 500 万以下的城市为大城市，其中 300 万以上 500 万以下的城市为Ⅰ型大城市，100 万以上 300 万以下的城市为Ⅱ型大城市；城区常住人口 500 万以上 1 000万以下的城市为特大城市；城区常住人口1 000万以上的城市为超大城市。（以上包括本数，以下不包括本数）

与原有城市规模划分标准相比，新标准有四点重要调整：一是城市类型由四类变为五类，增设了超大城市。二是将小城市和大城市分别划分为两档，细分小城市主要为满足城市规划建设的需要，细分大城市主要是实施人口分类管理的需要。三是人口规模的上下限普遍提高。小城市人口上限由 20 万提高到 50 万，中等城市的上下限分别由 20 万、50 万提高到 50 万、100 万，大城市的上下限分别由 50 万、100 万提高到 100 万、500 万，特大城市下限由 100 万提高到 500 万。四是将统计口径界定为城区常住人口。城区是指在市辖区和不设区的市，区、市政府驻地的实际建设连接到的居民委员会所辖区域和其他区域。常住人口包括：居住在本乡镇街道，且户口在本乡镇街道或户口待定的人；居住在本乡镇街道，且离开

户口登记地所在的乡镇街道半年以上的人；户口在本乡镇街道，且外出不满半年或在境外工作学习的人。

《通知》要求，新标准自通知印发之日起实施。各地区、各部门出台的与城市规模分类相关的政策、标准和规范等要按照新标准进行相应的修订。

按照新的城市规模划分标准，城区常住人口 1000 万以上的城市为超大城市，分别是北京、上海、天津、重庆、广州、深圳、武汉 7 座城市；特大城市有成都、南京、佛山、东莞、西安、沈阳、杭州、苏州、汕头、哈尔滨和香港 11 座城市。

《通知》下发前我国城市规模划分标准是依据 1989 年制定的《中华人民共和国城市规划法》，《城市规划法》规定大城市是指市区和近郊区非农业人口 50 万以上的城市，中等城市是指市区和近郊区非农业人口 20 万以上、不满 50 万的城市，小城市是指市区和近郊区非农业人口不满 20 万的城市。但是，这部规划法已于 2008 年 1 月 1 日废止，而同时实施的《中华人民共和国城乡规划法》没有设定城市规模的条文。《通知》的下发从立法的层面对大中小等城市规模概念进行了定义。

五、上海外滩陈毅广场发生“12·31”踩踏事件

2014 年 12 月 31 日，上海市黄浦区外滩陈毅广场东南角通往黄浦江观景平台的人行通道阶梯处发生拥挤踩踏。22 时 37 分，外滩陈毅广场东南角北侧人行通道阶梯处的单向通行警戒带被冲破，大量市民游客逆行涌上观景平台。23 时 23 分至 33 分，上下人流不断对冲后在阶梯中间形成僵持，继而形成“浪涌”。23 时 35 分，僵持人流向下的压力陡增，造成阶梯底部有人失衡跌倒，继而引发多人摔倒、叠压，致使拥挤踩踏事件发生。事件造成 36 人死亡，49 人受伤。

事件发生后，习近平总书记、李克强总理等中央领导同志分别作出重要批示，要求上海市全力以赴救治伤员，做好各项善后工作，抓紧调查事件原因，深刻吸取事件教训，及时准确向社会发布信息。上海市迅速成立了市政府联合调查组，通过现场勘查、调查取证、专家论证、综合分析等，还原了事件过程，查明了有关应对情况，分析了事件原因，认定了事件性质，对相关责任人提出了处理建议，并针对事件原因及暴露出的突出问题，提出了加强城市公共安全工作的整改建议。

2015 年 1 月 21 日，上海发布“12·31”外滩拥挤踩踏事件调查报告。调查报告认为，这是一起对群众性活动预防准备不足、现场管理不力、应对处置不当而引发的拥挤踩踏并造成重大伤亡和严重后果的公共安全责任事件。

调查报告分析了拥挤踩踏的主要原因：①对新年倒计时活动变更风险未作评估。大量市民游客认为外滩风景区仍会举办新年倒计时活动，南京路商业街和黄浦江对岸的上海中心、东方明珠等举办的相关活动吸引了部分市民游客专门至此观看。对此，黄浦区政府在新年倒计时活动变更时，未对可能的人员聚集安全风险予以高度重视，没有进行评估，缺乏应有认知，导致判断失误。②新年倒计时活动变更信息宣传严重不到位。新年倒计时活动变更后，

主办单位应当提前向社会充分告知活动信息。但是，直至 12 月 30 日，黄浦区旅游局才对外正式发布了新年倒计时活动信息，对“外滩”与“外滩源”的区别没有特别提醒和广泛宣传，信息公告不及时、不到位、不充分。③预防准备严重缺失。黄浦公安分局未按照黄浦区政府常务会议要求，在编制的新年倒计时活动安全保卫工作方案中，仅对外滩源新年倒计时活动进行了安全评估，未对外滩风景区安全风险进行专门评估。黄浦公安分局仅会同黄浦区市政委等有关部门在外滩风景区及南京路沿线布置了 350 名民警、108 名城市管理和辅助人员、100 名武警，安保人员配置严重不足。④对监测人员流量变化情况未及时研判、预警，未发布提示信息。12 月 31 日 20 时至事件发生时，外滩风景区人员流量呈上升趋势。黄浦公安分局指挥中心未严格落实上海市公安局指挥中心每半小时上报人员流量监测情况的工作要求，也未及时向黄浦区委区政府总值班室报告。黄浦公安分局对各时段人员流量快速递增的变动情况未及时采取有效措施，未报请黄浦区政府发布预警，控制事态发展。对上海市公安局多次提醒的形势研判要求，未作响应。⑤应对处置失当。针对事发当晚持续增加的人员流量，在现场现有警力配备明显不足的情况下，黄浦公安分局只对警力部署作了部分调整，没有采取其他有效措施，一直未向黄浦区政府和上海市公安局报告，未向上海市公安局提出增援需求，也未落实上海市公安局相关指令，处置措施不当。上海市公安局对黄浦公安分局处置措施不当指导监督不到位。黄浦区政府未及时向上海市政府报送事件信息。

调查报告认为，黄浦区政府和相关部门对这起事件负有不可推卸的责任。①黄浦区政府对事件负有主要管理责任。黄浦区政府对新年倒计时活动场所变更后的风险预判不足；对包括黄浦公安分局、黄浦区市政委等相关部门落实黄浦区政府常务会议要求的情况未进行检查督促；未建立健全预警机制；未严格按照中办、国办的要求“严格执行 24 小时专人值班和领导带班制度”；事件发生后，未按规定及时向市政府报告。②黄浦公安分局对事件负有直接管理责任。黄浦公安分局未落实黄浦区政府常务会议提出的具体要求，未研究制定专门的应对方案；对 12 月 31 日监测到的人员流量变化情况风险评估不足，未及时提出预警；应对处置措施不到位；未及时向本级政府和上级主管部门报送突发事件信息；对上级主管部门的要求执行不力。③黄浦区市政委对事件负有管理责任。黄浦区市政委未落实黄浦区政府常务会议提出的具体要求。④黄浦区旅游局对事件负有管理责任。黄浦区旅游局作为历年新年倒计时活动以及 2015 年新年倒计时活动的承办方，对活动场所变更风险未充分评估，变更信息向社会公众告知不充分。⑤黄浦区外滩风景区管理办公室对事件负有管理责任。黄浦区外滩风景区管理办公室未具体落实黄浦区政府常务会议提出的工作要求，未依法制定外滩风景区域内相应的应急预案。⑥上海市公安局对事件负有指导监督管理责任。上海市公安局对黄浦公安分局落实上海市公安局“一点一方案”，制定周密的安保工作方案和应急处置预案，加强活动现场警力配置的要求监督检查不到位；对黄浦公安分局 12 月 31 日外滩风景区安全保障工作的检查指导督促不够。

调查报告提出，要切实落实安全责任制，加强对大人流场所和活动的安全管理，加强监测预警，加强应急联动，加强宣教培训。各级政府和领导干部必须时刻把人民群众生命财产安全放在第一位，不能有丝毫侥幸，不能有丝毫疏忽，不能有丝毫懈怠，必须以对党和人民极端负责的精神，不遗余力、竭尽全力、殚精竭虑，切实保护好人民群众生命财产安全，切实维护好城市运行安全，切实履行好党和人民赋予的神圣使命。

六、国务院设立广东、福建和天津自由贸易园区

中国（上海）自由贸易试验区于2013年8月22日经国务院正式批准设立以来，围绕外商投资负面清单管理、贸易便利化、金融服务业开放、完善政府监管制度等，在体制机制上进行了积极探索和创新，形成了一批可复制、可推广的经验做法。

2014年12月12日，国务院总理李克强在国务院常务会议上提出依托现有新区、园区，在广东、天津、福建特定区域再设三个自由贸易园区，以上海自贸试验区试点内容为主体，结合地方特点，充实新的试点内容。

广东自贸区涵盖广州南沙新区片区、深圳前海蛇口片区和珠海横琴新区片区，主要对准港珠澳，未来在高端金融服务业方面，可以有大的发展。首先，广州要充分利用两个港口的优势，大力发展空港经济区，真正推动兴起一批临空产业，包括现代物流、飞机维修、高端消费品制造、通用航空等。其次，空港与海港的辐射面较广，要跳出自贸区来布局产业和城市功能。如果发挥后发优势，广州在自贸区实践和探索中还可以赶上上海的发展势头，并为全国的复制和推广提供新的经验和范本。

天津自贸区涵盖天津港片区、天津机场片区和滨海新区中心商务片区，主要对准东北亚，大力发展航运，未来金融租赁业有优势。天津自贸区除了保留上海自贸区内可复制的方案外，还会以发挥融资租赁业务功能为重点，增加对内辐射效应。作为北方首个自贸区，天津自贸区融汇京津冀协同发展国家战略，必将为其提供巨大的助力。自贸园区落户天津，无疑会增强天津和滨海新区在京津冀发展中的资源整合能力和龙头带动作用。未来的天津自贸区会进一步放开金融管制和行政审批。在产业结构上，天津可能注意优化利用内外资结构，引导资金投向优势支柱产业、战略性新兴产业、现代服务业和节能环保等领域，加快推进金融、教育、文化、医疗、旅游等领域有序开放。

福建自贸区涵盖平潭片区、厦门片区和福州片区，主要是要发展台海贸易，促进对台合作的发展。福州学习上海自贸区成功经验，在海关监管、商事制度等方面已复制一些创新举措。2013年9月，福州保税港区率先实施“先进区、后报关”、“区内自行运输”、“保税展示交易”、“批次进出、集中申报”4项海关监管制度。2013年，福州开展商事制度改革、投资管理制度改革，复制推广上海自贸区14项监管创新制度和6项检验监管创新制度。在推进自贸区建设过程中，福州将积极融入“一带一路”建设，着力打造21世纪海上丝绸之路战略枢纽城市。创新两岸金融协作机制、深化两岸金融合作，将成为福州推进自贸区建设的一大特色。

在广东省、天津市和福建省，依托现有新区、园区再设3个自由贸易试验区，可以与中国（上海）自由贸易试验区形成互补试验和对比试验，充分检验相关改革开放措施的实施效果以及复制推广的可行性，为全面深化改革、扩大开放进一步探索新途径、积累新经验。

2014年12月28日，第十二届全国人民代表大会常务委员会第十二次会议通过《全国人民代表大会常务委员会关于授权国务院在中国（广东）自由贸易试验区、中国（天津）自由贸易试验区、中国（福建）自由贸易试验区以及中国（上海）自由贸易试验区扩展区域暂时调整有关法律规定的行政审批的决定》，决定授权国务院在中国（广东）自由贸易试验区、中国（天津）自由贸易试验区、中国（福建）自由贸易试验区以及中国（上海）自由贸易试验区扩展区域内，暂时调整《中华人民共和国外资企业法》、《中华人民共和国中外合资经营企业法》、《中华人民共和国中外合作经营企业法》和《中华人民共和国台湾同胞投资保护法》规定的有关行政审批。但是，国家规定实施准入特别管理措施的除外。上述行政审批的调整在三年内试行，对实践证明可行的，修改完善有关法律；对实践证明不宜调整的，恢复施行有关法律规定。

七、国务院发布实施《不动产登记暂行条例》

我国不动产登记制度长期缺失，使得产权保护在很多领域难以落到实处，给产权侵犯打开了方便之门。建立不动产统一登记制度是推进简政放权，整合部门职能职责、减少多头管理、逐步实现一个窗口对外，方便企业和群众、降低创业成本的有效举措。

2014年11月24日，国务院总理李克强签署第656号国务院令，公布《不动产登记暂行条例》（以下简称《条例》），自2015年3月1日起施行。《条例》分为总则、不动产登记簿、登记程序、登记信息共享与保护、法律责任和附则共6章35条。《条例》出台标志着不动产统一登记制度的正式建立。

《条例》落实了统一登记机构的要求，条例规定：一是明确由国土资源部负责指导、监督全国不动产登记工作，同时要求县级以上地方人民政府确定一个部门负责本行政区域不动产登记工作，并接受上级不动产登记主管部门的指导和监督。二是规定不动产登记原则上由不动产所在地的县级人民政府不动产登记机构办理，直辖市、设区的市人民政府可以确定本级登记机构统一办理所属各区的登记。三是规定跨县级行政区域的不动产登记，由所跨县级行政区域的登记机构分别办理、协商办理，或者由共同的上一级人民政府不动产登记主管部门指定办理。

《条例》对不动产登记簿的登记内容、登记形式、介质保管等作出明确规定，《条例》规定：一是明确登记内容，要求登记机构设立统一的不动产登记簿，将不动产的自然状况、权属状况、权利限制状况等事项准确、完整、清晰地予以记载。二是规范登记形式，要求登记簿原则上要采用电子介质，暂不具备条件的，可以采用纸质介质，登记机构要明确唯一、合法的介质形式。三是细化保管责任，要求登记机构建立健全相应的安全责任制度，永久保存登记簿；纸质登记簿要配备防盗、防火、防渍、防有害生物等安全保护设施；电子登记簿要配备专门的存储设施，采取信息网络安全防护措施，并定期进行异地备份；任何人不得损毁登记簿，除依法予以更正外不得修改登记事项；登记簿损毁、灭失的，要依据原有登记资料予以重建。

《条例》在登记程序方面体现了方便群众的原则，《条例》规定：一是稳定申请人预期，对申请人、申请材料、初审受理、查验要求、实地查看、办理期限等均作出明确规定。二是尊重申请人意思自治，规定登记机构将申请登记事项记载于登记簿前，申请人可以撤回登记申请。三是简化申请程序，强调当场审查的原则，要求登记机构受理后书面告知申请人，对不符合法定条件不予受理的，以及不属于本机构登记范围的，也要书面告知申请人，并一次性告知需补正内容或者申请途径；未当场书面告知申请人不予受理的，视为受理；登记机构原则上要自受理登记申请之日起 30 个工作日内办结登记手续，完成登记后依法核发权属证书或登记证明。四是减轻申请负担，规定登记机构能够通过实时互通共享取得的信息，不得要求申请人重复提交。

《条例》实现了登记信息共享与保护，关于信息共享的规定：一是建立信息管理基础平台，要求国土资源部会同有关部门建立统一的不动产登记信息管理基础平台，登记信息要纳入该平台，确保国家、省、市、县四级登记信息的实时共享。二是加强登记部门与管理部门的信息共享，要求登记信息与住房城乡建设、农业、林业、海洋等部门的审批信息、交易信息等实时互通共享。三是加强其他部门之间的信息共享，要求国土资源、公安、民政、财政、税务、工商、金融、审计、统计等部门加强不动产登记有关信息互通共享。关于登记资料查询的规定：一是查询主体，按照《物权法》的有关规定，把登记资料查询人限定在权利人和利害关系人，有关国家机关可以依法查询、复制与调查处理事项有关的登记资料。二是查询资料的使用，规定查询登记资料的要向登记机构说明查询目的，不得将查询获得的资料用于其他目的，未经权利人同意，不得泄露查询资料。

《条例》规定了严格的法律责任，督促登记机构依法履行职责：一是登记错误责任，规定登记机构登记错误给他人造成损害，要依法承担赔偿责任。二是不当履职责任，规定登记人员有虚假登记，损毁、伪造登记簿，擅自修改登记事项等滥用职权、玩忽职守行为的，依法给予处分；给他人造成损害的，依法承担赔偿责任；构成犯罪的，依法追究刑事责任。三是安全保密责任，规定登记机构、信息共享单位及其工作人员要对登记信息保密，涉及国家秘密的要依法采取必要的安全保密措施，违反规定泄露登记资料、信息，或者利用登记资料、信息进行不正当活动，给他人造成损害的，依法承担赔偿责任；对有关责任人员依法给予处分；构成犯罪的，依法追究刑事责任。

此外，《条例》对当事人提供虚假材料申请登记，伪造、变造、买卖、使用不动产权属证书、登记证明，违法泄露、非法利用查询的登记资料、信息等行为，也规定了相应的法律责任。

为维护物权稳定，保护不动产权利人合法权益，《条例》规定施行前依法颁发的各类不动产权属证书和制作的不动产登记簿继续有效，不动产权利人已经依法享有的不动产权利，不因登记机构和登记程序的改变而受到影响。

八、国务院推进改革城乡居民基本养老保险制度

2 月 7 日，国务院总理李克强主持召开国务院常务会议，决定合并新型农村社会养老保

险和城镇居民社会养老保险，建立全国统一的城乡居民基本养老保险制度。这是中国政府全面深化改革的一大举措，是在建立社会基本公共服务均等化方面迈出的坚实一步。

2月21日，国务院印发《关于建立统一的城乡居民基本养老保险制度的意见》（以下简称《意见》）。《意见》提出坚持和完善社会统筹与个人账户相结合的制度模式，巩固和拓宽个人缴费、集体补助、政府补贴相结合的资金筹集渠道，完善基础养老金和个人账户养老金相结合的待遇支付政策，强化长缴多得、多缴多得等制度的激励机制，建立基础养老金正常调整机制，健全服务网络，提高管理水平，为参保居民提供方便快捷的服务。到“十二五”末，在全国基本实现新农保和城居保制度合并实施，并与职工基本养老保险制度相衔接；2020年前，全面建成公平、统一、规范的城乡居民养老保险制度，与社会救助、社会福利等其他社会保障政策相配套，充分发挥家庭养老等传统保障方式的积极作用，更好地保障参保城乡居民的老年基本生活。

《意见》规定，年满16周岁（不含在校学生），非国家机关和事业单位工作人员及不属于职工基本养老保险制度覆盖范围的城乡居民，可以在户籍地参加城乡居民养老保险。国家为每个参保人员建立终身记录的养老保险个人账户，无论在哪里缴费，也无论是否间断性缴费，个人账户都累计记录参保人权益。个人缴费、地方政府对参保人的缴费补贴、集体补助及其他社会经济组织、公益慈善组织、个人对参保人的缴费资助，全部记入个人账户。个人账户储存额按国家规定计息。

《意见》规定，城乡居民养老保险继续实行个人缴费、集体补助、政府补贴相结合的筹资方式。个人缴费标准统一归并调整为每年100元至2000元12个档次，省级政府可以根据实际情况增设缴费档次，参保的城乡居民自主选择缴费档次，多缴多得；集体补助方面，在原有政策基础上增加了公益慈善组织的资助，以利于进一步拓宽筹资渠道，提高参保人员的待遇水平；政府补贴方面，对选择较高档次标准缴费的人员适当增加补贴金额，并明确规定对选择500元及以上缴费档次的补贴标准不低于每人每年60元，进一步强化了多缴多补的激励机制。

《意见》规定，城乡居民养老保险待遇由基础养老金和个人账户养老金组成，并支付终身。基础养老金由中央确定最低标准，并将建立正常调整机制；地方政府可根据实际情况提高当地基础养老金标准，对长期缴费的，可适当加发基础养老金，以鼓励长缴多得；城乡居民养老保险待遇领取人员死亡的，个人账户资金余额可以依法继承。

《意见》规定，参加城乡居民养老保险的个人，年满60周岁、累计缴费满15年，且未领取国家规定的基本养老保障待遇的，可以按月领取城乡居民养老保险待遇，城乡居民养老保险待遇领取人员死亡的，从次月起停止支付其养老金。参加城乡居民养老保险的人员，在缴费期间户籍迁移，可跨地区转移城乡居民养老保险关系，一次性转移个人账户全部储存额，继续参保缴费的，缴费年限累计计算。

《意见》规定，将新农保基金和城居保基金合并为城乡居民养老保险基金，完善城乡居民养老保险基金财务会计制度和各项业务管理规章制度；各级人力资源社会保障部门要会同有关部门认真履行监管职责，建立健全内控制度和基金稽核监督制度，对基金的筹集、上解、划拨、发放、存储、管理等进行监控和检查，并按规定披露信息，接受社会监督。

《意见》要求省级人民政府切实加强城乡居民养老保险经办能力建设，科学整合现有公共服务资源和社会保险经办管理资源，充实加强基层经办力量，做到精确管理，便捷服务。各地要加强信息化建设，大力推行全国统一的社会保障卡，方便参保居民持卡缴费、领取待遇和查询本人参保信息。

实施统一的城乡居民基本养老保险制度，有利于建立更加公平可持续的社会保障制度，城乡居民享受制度上无差别、水平大致相当的养老保障，在制度模式、筹资方式、待遇支付等方面将实现无差距对接，在养老保障方面消除了过去城乡二元户籍制带来的不公平。同时还有利于促进国内消费，统一城乡居民基本养老保险不仅有利于促进人口纵向流动、增强社会安全感，而且可以使群众对民生改善有稳定的预期，对于拉动消费、鼓励创新创业，具有重要意义。

九、北京成功举办亚太经合组织领导人会议

2014 年 11 月 5 日至 11 日，亚太经合组织（APEC）领导人会议周在北京举行，会议确定了构建面向未来的亚太伙伴关系、启动亚太自贸区进程，为亚太地区长远发展和共同繁荣勾画新愿景，指引新方向，注入新动力。

11 月 5 日至 6 日，亚太经合组织（APEC）第四次高官会在国家会议中心举行，拉开了 APEC 领导人会议周大幕，21 个成员经济体的高官出席了高官会，为会议周期间即将举办的部长级会议、领导人非正式会议做最后准备。2014 年 2 月、5 月和 8 月，第一、第二、第三次高官会分别在浙江宁波、山东青岛和北京举行，各成员高官围绕会议主题和重点议题进行了深入讨论。

11 月 7 日至 8 日，亚太经合组织（APEC）第 26 届部长级会议在北京召开，会议通过了《亚太经合组织第 26 届部长级会议联合声明》。会议围绕“共建面向未来的亚太伙伴关系”主题以及各项议题进行了深入讨论，达成六点共识：一是共同构建面向未来的亚太伙伴关系，实现亚太长远发展与共同繁荣；二是致力于建立亚太开放型经济格局，巩固亚太引领全球经济增长的引擎地位；三是坚持区域经济一体化方向，启动推进亚太自贸区建设，努力构建惠及太平洋两岸的区域经济新架构；四是同意探讨经济创新发展、改革与增长，就跨越中等收入陷阱、互联网经济、城镇化等新领域开展合作，为亚太经济挖掘新动力；五是高度重视亚太地区在基础设施与互联互通建设方面的巨大需求，提请领导人批准《亚太经合组织互联互通蓝图》；六是通过了《北京反腐败宣言》，成立 APEC 反腐执法合作网络，在亚太加大追逃追赃等合作，携手打击跨境腐败行为。

11 月 8 日至 10 日，2014 年亚太经合组织（APEC）工商领导人峰会在北京举行。峰会讨论并达成了诸多共识，与会工商界代表呼吁推进亚太自贸区建设，继续提升贸易投资便利化和自由化水平，共同构建良性互动、协调发展的开放型亚太经济格局；建议各经济体研究制定私营资本参与基础设施投资的相关政策，全面实现亚太互联互通和联动发展的宏伟蓝

图；希望各经济体支持建设亚太开放创新平台，促进全球价值链发展合作，充分发掘经济增长新动力，实现平衡增长。

11月10日，亚太经合组织（APEC）领导人与工商咨询理事会代表对话会在北京举行，对话会上，APEC成员领导人分组同工商咨询理事会代表进行对话，就各方高度关注的问题交换意见。

11月10日至11日，亚太经合组织（APEC）第二十二次领导人非正式会议在北京怀柔雁栖湖国际会议中心举行，会议主题为“共建面向未来的亚太伙伴关系”，在这个主题下有三个重要的议题：推动区域经济一体化，促进经济创新发展、改革与增长，加强全方位基础设施和互联互通建设。

会议通过了《北京纲领：构建融合、创新、互联的亚太——亚太经合组织领导人宣言》和《共建面向未来的亚太伙伴关系——亚太经合组织成立25周年声明》这两份成果文件，进一步明确了亚太地区经济合作的发展方向、目标、举措。

会议决定启动和推进亚太自由贸易区进程，批准《亚太经合组织推动实现亚太自由贸易区路线图》，这是朝着实现亚太自由贸易区方向迈出的实质性一步，标志着亚太自由贸易区进程的正式启动，这一成果将把区域经济一体化水平提升到新的高度，也将使太平洋两岸的经济体广泛受益，为亚太经济增长和各成员共同发展注入新的活力。

会议批准了全球价值链、供应链、能力建设等领域的重要合作倡议，发出了支持多边贸易体制、推动多哈回合谈判早日结束的强有力呼声。

会议通过了《亚太经合组织经济创新发展、改革与增长共识》，决定以经济改革、新经济、创新增长、包容性支持、城镇化作为五大支柱，加强政策协调和对话，推进务实合作、经验分享、能力建设，实现创新、改革、增长三者之间良性循环，进一步巩固亚太的全球经济引擎地位。

会议开拓了全新的合作领域，讨论了跨越“中等收入陷阱”、互联网经济、城镇化等重要新兴议题，各方决心通过合作来共同应对全球性挑战。会议决定大力推动亚太反腐败合作，建立亚太经合组织反腐败执法合作网络，携手打击跨境腐败行为。在蓝色经济、绿色经济、可持续能源、中小企业、卫生、林业、矿业、粮食安全、旅游、妇女与经济等领域加强合作。

会议批准了《亚太经合组织互联互通蓝图》文件，在2025年前实现加强硬件、软件和人员交流互联互通的远景目标，并完成具体指标，各国将按照蓝图构想，加大投入，构建全方位、多层次的复合型亚太互联互通网络，为实现亚太长远发展夯实互联互通的基础。

会议决定拓展基础设施投融资领域务实合作，推广公私合作伙伴关系模式，帮助本地区破解互联互通建设资金瓶颈；会议决定实施跨境教育、商务旅行卡、跨境旅游等新倡议，让太平洋两岸更多普通民众从中受益；会议决定共同应对大规模流行性疾病、恐怖主义、自然灾害、气候变化等全球性挑战，面对当前肆虐的埃博拉疫情，亚太经合组织领导人决心携手合作，帮助非洲国家有效应对和防控疫情，支持联合国在援助非洲和抗击疫情中发挥领导和统筹作用，支援疫区人民共渡难关，直至取得最终胜利。

21 个 APEC 成员怀着合作发展的愿望而来，带着携手共进的成果而归，世界见证了亚太承前启后、开创未来的重要时刻。APEC 领导人绘制了面向未来的亚太一体化发展蓝图，开创了互联互通的发展路径，为携手推进亚太命运共同体建设迈出历史性的关键一步，驱动 APEC 航船在辽阔的太平洋乘风破浪，驶向和平、发展、繁荣、进步的美好未来。

APEC 会议期间，北京碧空万里，“APEC 蓝”传遍神州。为确保空气质量达标，北京、天津、河北、山东、山西、内蒙古六省（自治区、直辖市）市采取了一系列“史上最严”措施，据初步测算，6 省（自治区、直辖市）在 APEC 会议期间实际停产企业 9298 家，限产企业 3900 家，停工工地 4 万余处。此外，北京市、河北省等机动车单双号限行。监测数据显示，11 月 1 日至 12 日期间，虽然经历了两次不利的气象扩散条件，但空气质量仅 1 天轻度污染，其余 11 天均为优良天；PM2.5 日均浓度值平均降低 30%，与 2013 年同期相比下降了 55%。

历届 APEC 峰会一览表

序号	时间	地点	主要内容
1	1993 年 11 月	美国 西雅图	发表《亚太经合组织领导人经济展望声明》
2	1994 年 11 月	印度尼西亚 茂物	通过了《亚太经合组织经济领导人共同决心宣言》(简称《茂物宣言》)
3	1995 年 11 月	日本 大阪	发表了《亚太经合组织经济领导人行动宣言》(简称《大阪宣言》),通过了实施贸易投资自由化和开展经济技术合作的《大阪行动议程》
4	1996 年 11 月	菲律宾 苏比克	通过了《马尼拉行动计划》和《亚太经合组织经济领导人宣言:从憧憬到行动》,批准了《亚太经合组织经济技术合作原则框架宣言》
5	1997 年 11 月	加拿大 温哥华	通过了《亚太经合组织经济领导人宣言:将亚太经合组织大家庭联合起来》
6	1998 年 11 月	马来西亚 吉隆坡	发表了《亚太经合组织经济领导人宣言:加强增长的基础》,通过了《走向 21 世纪的亚太经合组织科技产业合作议程》和《吉隆坡技能开发行动计划》
7	1999 年 9 月	新西兰 奥克兰	发表了《亚太经合组织经济领导人宣言:奥克兰挑战》,批准了《亚太经合组织加强竞争和法规改革的原则》和《妇女融入亚太经合组织框架》等
8	2000 年 11 月	文莱 斯里巴加湾	通过了《亚太经合组织经济领导人宣言:造福社会》和《新经济行动议程》
9	2001 年 10 月	中国 上海	通过并发表了《领导人宣言:迎接新世纪的新挑战》、《上海共识》和《数字亚太经合组织战略》等
10	2002 年 10 月	墨西哥 洛斯卡沃斯	通过了《亚太经合组织经济领导人宣言》等文件
11	2003 年 10 月	泰国 曼谷	通过了《亚太经合组织经济领导人宣言》,决定加强伙伴关系,推动贸易投资自由化与便利化
12	2004 年 11 月	智利 圣地亚哥	会议通过了《圣地亚哥宣言》,重申通过贸易和投资自由化促进发展
13	2005 年 11 月	韩国 釜山	发表《釜山宣言》、《亚太经合组织领导人关于世贸组织多哈发展议程谈判的声明》、《亚太经合组织流感大流行防控倡议》等
14	2006 年 11 月	越南 河内	通过了旨在实现茂物目标的《河内行动计划》,签署《河内宣言》

续表

序号	时间	地点	主要内容
15	2007年9月	澳大利亚 悉尼	发表《亚太经合组织领导人关于气候变化、能源安全和清洁发展的宣言》
16	2008年11月	秘鲁 利马	发表了《利马宣言》和关于全球经济的声明
17	2009年11月	新加坡	发表了《"倡导新的增长方式，构建21世纪互联互通的亚太"领导人声明》
18	2010年11月	日本 横滨	发表了《横滨宣言》、《成长战略》、《2010茂物目标评价》、《亚太自由贸易圈(FTAAP)》
19	2011年11月	美国 夏威夷	发表了《檀香山宣言——迈向紧密联系的区域经济》
20	2012年9月	俄罗斯 符拉迪沃斯托克	发表了《融合谋发展，创新促繁荣——APEC第二十次领导人非正式会议宣言》
21	2013年10月	印度尼西亚 巴厘岛	发表了《活力亚太，全球引擎——APEC第二十一次领导人非正式会议宣言》和《支持多边贸易体制和世界贸易组织第九届部长级会议声明》
22	2014年11月	中国 北京	通过了《北京纲领：构建融合、创新、互联的亚太——亚太经合组织领导人宣言》、《共建面向未来的亚太伙伴关系——亚太经合组织成立25周年声明》、《亚太经合组织经济创新发展、改革与增长共识》，批准了《亚太经合组织推动实现亚太自由贸易区路线图》、《亚太经合组织互联互通蓝图》

十、十八届四中全会部署全面推进依法治国

中国共产党第十八届中央委员会第四次全体会议于2014年10月20日至23日在北京举行，会议审议通过了《中共中央关于全面推进依法治国若干重大问题的决定》（以下简称《决定》）。《决定》立足于我国社会主义法治建设实际，明确提出了全面推进依法治国的指导思想、总体目标、基本原则，对科学立法、严格执法、公正司法、全民守法、法治队伍建设、加强和改进党对全面推进依法治国的领导作出了全面部署，是加快建设社会主义法治国家的纲领性文件。

全面推进依法治国，总目标是建设中国特色社会主义法治体系，建设社会主义法治国家。这就是指，在中国共产党领导下，坚持中国特色社会主义制度，贯彻中国特色社会主义法治理论，形成完备的法律规范体系、高效的法治实施体系、严密的法治监督体系、有力的法治保障体系，形成完善的党内法规体系，坚持依法治国、依法执政、依法行政共同推进，坚持法治国家、法治政府、法治社会一体建设，实现科学立法、严格执法、公正司法、全民守法，促进国家治理体系和治理能力现代化。

全面推进依法治国的重大任务是完善以宪法为核心的中国特色社会主义法律体系，加强宪法实施；深入推进依法行政，加快建设法治政府；保证公正司法，提高司法公信力；增强全民法治观念，推进法治社会建设；加强法治工作队伍建设；加强和改进党对全面推进依法治国的领导。

法律是治国之重器，良法是善治之前提。要把公正、公平、公开原则贯穿于立法全过

程，完善立法体制机制，坚持立改废释并举，增强法律法规的及时性、系统性、针对性、有效性。完善立法体制，加强党对立法工作的领导，完善党对立法工作中重大问题决策的程序，健全有立法权的人大主导立法工作的体制机制，依法赋予设区的市地方立法权。加强重点领域立法，加快完善体现权利公平、机会公平、规则公平的法律制度，保障公民人身权、财产权、基本政治权利等各项权利不受侵犯，保障公民经济、文化、社会等各方面权利得到落实。实现立法和改革决策相衔接，做到重大改革于法有据、立法主动适应改革和经济社会发展需要。

法律的生命力在于实施，法律的权威也在于实施。各级政府必须坚持在党的领导下、在法制轨道上开展工作，加快建设职能科学、权责法定、执法严明、公开公正、廉洁高效、守法诚信的法治政府。依法全面履行政府职能，推进机构、职能、权限、程序、责任法定化，推行政府权力清单制度。健全依法决策机制，把公众参与、专家论证、风险评估、合法性审查、集体讨论决定确定为重大行政决策法定程序，建立行政机关内部重大决策合法性审查机制，建立重大决策终身责任追究制度及责任倒查机制。深化行政执法体制改革，健全行政执法和刑事司法衔接机制。

公正是法治的生命线。完善确保依法独立公正行使审判权和检察权的制度，建立领导干部干预司法活动、插手具体案件处理的记录、通报和责任追究制度，建立健全司法人员履行法定职责保护机制。优化司法职权配置，推动实行审判权和执行权相分离的体制改革试点，最高人民法院设立巡回法庭，探索设立跨行政区划的人民法院和人民检察院，探索建立检察机关提起公益诉讼制度。推进严格司法，坚持以事实为根据、以法律为准绳，推进以审判为中心的诉讼制度改革，实行办案质量终身负责制和错案责任倒查问责制。保障人民群众参与司法，在司法调解、司法听证、涉诉信访等司法活动中保障人民群众参与，完善人民陪审员制度，构建开放、动态、透明、便民的阳光司法机制。

全面推进依法治国，必须大力提高法治工作队伍思想政治素质、业务工作能力、职业道德水准，着力建设一支忠于党、忠于国家、忠于人民、忠于法律的社会主义法治工作队伍。

党的领导是全面推进依法治国、加快建设社会主义法治国家最根本的保证。健全党领导依法治国的制度和工作机制，完善保证党确定依法治国方针政策和决策部署的工作机制和程序，加强对全面推进依法治国统一领导、统一部署、统筹协调，完善党委依法决策机制。各级人大、政府、政协、审判机关、检察机关的党组织要领导和监督本单位模范遵守宪法法律，坚决查处执法犯法、违法用权等行为。加强党内法规制度建设，完善党内法规制定体制机制，形成配套完备的党内法规制度体系。提高党员干部法治思维和依法办事能力，把法治建设成效作为衡量各级领导班子和领导干部工作实绩重要内容，纳入政绩考核指标体系。推进基层治理法治化，发挥基层党组织在全面推进依法治国中的战斗堡垒作用。深入推进依法治军、从严治军，紧紧围绕党在新形势下的强军目标，构建完善的中国特色军事法治体系，提高国防和军队建设法治化水平。依法保障“一国两制”实践和推进祖国统一，保持香港、澳门长期繁荣稳定，推进祖国和平统一，依法保护港澳同胞、台湾同胞权益。加强涉外法律工作，运用法律手段维护我国主权、安全、发展利益，维护我国公民、法人在海外及外国公民、法人在我国的正当权益。

全面推进依法治国，关系党执政兴国、关系人民幸福安康、关系党和国家长治久安。当前，全面建成小康社会进入决定性阶段，改革进入攻坚期和深水区，依法治国在党和国家工作全局中的地位更加突出、作用更加重大。必须坚定不移走中国特色社会主义法治道路，以建设中国特色社会主义法治体系为总抓手，在法制轨道上推进国家治理体系和治理能力现代化，建设法治中国。

改革开放以来历届四中全会一览表

序号	会议名称	核心议题及主要内容	历史意义
1	十一届四中全会（1979年9月25日至28日）	讨论通过《中共中央关于加快农业发展若干问题的决定》	对于统一全国人民的思想、加快农业的发展具有重要意义
2	十二届四中全会（1985年9月16日）	讨论并原则通过了《中共中央关于制定国民经济和社会发展第七个五年计划的建议(草案)》,讨论确定了关于进一步实现中央领导机构成员新老交替的原则	全会确定了关于进一步实现中央领导机构成员新老交替的原则,对保证党的政策的连续性具有重大意义
3	十三届四中全会（1989年6月23日至24日）	审议通过了《关于赵紫阳同志在反党反社会主义的动乱中所犯错误的报告》	对中央领导机构的部分成员进行了必要的调整
4	十四届四中全会（1994年9月25日至28日）	讨论了党的建设问题,并作出了《中共中央关于加强党的建设几个重大问题的决定》	指出党的建设面临的形势和任务;坚持和健全民主集中制;加强和改进党的基层组织建设;培养和选拔德才兼备的领导干部
5	十五届四中全会（1999年9月19日至22日）	审议通过了《中共中央关于国有企业改革和发展若干重大问题的决定》	确立国有企业改革和发展的主要目标和必须坚持的指导方针
6	十六届四中全会（2004年9月16日至19日）	讨论了“党的执政能力建设问题”,审议通过了《中共中央关于加强党的执政能力建设的决定》	全会确定了当前和今后一个时期加强党的执政能力建设的指导思想、总体目标、主要任务和各项部署
7	十七届四中全会（2009年9月15日至18日）	审议通过了《中共中央关于加强和改进新形势下党的建设若干重大问题的决定》	进一步研究和部署以改革创新精神推进党的建设新的伟大工程,深入贯彻落实科学发展观,有效应对国际金融危机冲击、保持经济平稳较快发展,夺取全面建设小康社会新胜利、开创中国特色社会主义事业新局面
8	十八届四中全会（2014年10月20日至23日）	审议通过了《中共中央关于全面推进依法治国若干重大问题的决定》	对全面推进依法治国做出了重大部署,标志着党对执政规律、社会主义建设规律、人类社会发展规律的认识和实践上升到新的高度

（参考资料来源：新华网、人民网）

（作者：邵益生，中国城市规划设计研究院研究员，国际欧亚科学院院士；周长青，中国城市规划设计研究院水务发展研究所所长，高级工程师）

2014年中国城市交通发展进程

在国家新型城镇化的指引下，我国城市交通持续快速发展。截至2014年年底，我国民用机动车保有量已超过2.64亿辆，其中汽车1.54亿辆，占世界汽车总量的15%，汽车数量仅次于美国，位居世界第二。全国35个城市汽车超过百万辆，其中北京、成都、深圳等10个城市汽车超过200万辆。全国机动车驾驶人数量突破3亿人，占全国总人口的22%，相当于每5个人或每3位适龄驾驶人（18至70周岁）就有1人持有机动车驾驶证，驾驶人数量稳居世界第一。回顾2014年，我国城市交通大发展，交通出行方式多样化，但交通运行状态反复波动的形势并没有改变，并处于趋坏与向好拉锯时期，城市中“行”的问题越来越成为新闻媒体和百姓关注的话题，城市交通变革、交通规划、交通管理及科技应用取得了新进步和新进展，但也面临着巨大挑战与考验。

一、新型城镇化发展下的城市交通一体化

（一）《国家新型城镇化规划（2014－2020年）》明确城市交通发展方向

2014年3月16日，中共中央、国务院发布《国家新型城镇化规划（2014－2020年）》（以下简称《规划》）。《规划》指出，近年来交通运输网络的不断完善，为进一步优化城镇化空间布局和形态，推动城镇可持续发展提供了有力支撑。而目前日益严重的交通拥堵问题已经成为“城市病”，影响了城市管理和服务水平的提升。为促进城市群协调发展，要统筹交通基础设施布局，建立城市群成本共担和利益共享机制，加快城市公共交通“一卡通”服务平台建设，完善交通枢纽功能，推进中心城区功能向1小时交通圈地区扩散。《规划》用大量篇幅就“完善城市群之间综合交通运输网络”、“构建城市群内部综合交通运输网络”、“建设城市综合交通枢纽”、“改善中小城市和小城镇交通条件”以及“优先发展城市公共交通”等内容做了详细阐述，凸显了城市交通在城镇化发展中的重要作用，为今后城市交通发展指明了方向。

（二）交通一体化在京津冀协同发展中发挥关键作用

2014年2月，习近平总书记明确提出，实现京津冀协同发展，是一个重大国家战略，

要加快走出一条科学持续的协同发展路子来。同时指出，要把交通一体化作为推进京津冀协同发展的先行领域，加快构建三地快速、便捷、高效、安全、大容量、低成本的互联互通综合交通网络。习总书记的讲话首次将京津冀协同发展上升到国家战略层面，而三地交通运输一体化发展率先取得突破，则为京津冀区域协同发展奠定坚实基础，为打造世界级城市群提供有力保障。为贯彻落实中央战略决策的实际举措，京津冀协同发展领导小组着手开展交通一体化中有关项目建设、规划制定、法规出台等方面的顶层设计工作；8 月，京津冀交通一体化领导小组和办公室成立，交通运输部部长杨传堂亲任组长；10 月，领导小组制定并着手实施推进《京津冀交通一体化率先突破工作方案》，拟尽快启动一批示范性强、作用显著的重大项目，加强城际铁路建设，完善高速公路网络，推动港口和机场协同发展，推进区域内交通基础设施互联互通和运输服务一体化进程，完善港口集疏运体系。

（三）重大交通基础设施建设助力城镇群交通协同发展

2014 年 12 月 15 日，国家发展改革委批复了北京新机场工程可行性研究报告，同意建设北京新机场，并要求努力把北京新机场建成代表新世纪新水平的标志性工程。根据批复，新机场工程将按 2025 年旅客吞吐量 7 200 万人次、货邮吞吐量 200 万吨、飞机起降量 62 万架次的目标设计，总投资达 799.8 亿元，项目工期为 5 年。此外，北京新机场还将建设 70 万平方米的航站楼、7.5 万平方米的货运站、3.5 万平方米的货运综合配套用房、7.4 万平方米的海关监管仓库。北京新机场的建设不仅是首都现代经济服务体系的重要支点，带动北京南部发展的重要引擎，也是京津冀协同发展总体布局下的交通一体化至关重要的一步。12 月 17 日，国家民航局发布《关于推进京津冀民航协同发展的意见》；12 月 22 日，京津冀签署三地机场协同发展战略合作框架协议，明确了三地机场在京津冀协同发展国家战略中的功能定位：首都机场将增强作为国际航空枢纽的中转能力，提升国际竞争力；天津机场将强化枢纽功能，大力发展航空物流；石家庄机场将积极发展航空快件集散及低成本航空。三地机场将科学合理分工，优化资源配置，完善机场布局，扩大航线网络，共同推动京津冀协同发展。

（四）全国 14 省市实现高速公路 ETC 联网收费

2014 年 3 月 7 日，交通运输部下发《关于开展全国高速公路电子不停车收费联网工作的通知》，要求依托京津冀鲁晋区域 ETC（电子不停车收费）清分结算系统建设全国 ETC 清分结算系统，全面推进全国 ETC 联网工作。2014 年 12 月 6 日，北京、天津、河北、山东、山西、上海、江苏、浙江、安徽、福建、江西、辽宁、陕西、湖南 14 个省（直辖市）的电子不停车收费系统正式联网运行，14 个省（直辖市）共建成 ETC 专用车道 6 659 条，发展 ETC 用户 909 万。联网区域内实行“一车一卡一标签”，车主可以凭借一卡畅行全国 14 个省（直辖市）高速，标志着我国综合交通体系的建设又向前迈进了一步。目前，全国共建成 ETC 车道7 600余条，用户超过1 300万。预计到 2015 年年底，ETC 联网将扩展覆盖到全国所有省（直辖市），实现全国范围内的互联互通。

（五）超大城市着力谋划新一轮城市交通发展战略

随着城镇化和机动化同步快速发展，超大城市的交通问题成为世界性难题，为顺应城市发展和居民出行需求变化，北京、上海等超大城市提出了未来交通发展目标和战略举措，对于构筑国际大都市综合交通体系具有重要指导意义。北京市编制完成了《北京交通发展纲要（2014－2030 年）》（征求意见稿），提出了要提升综合交通规划在城市总体规划中的地位，促使交通与城市发展的关系由被动适应转变为主动引导，从严控制中心城区建设增量、发挥产业调控作用，严格执行重大项目交通影响评价。北京将着力打造京津冀“一环六放射二航五港”的交通一体化体系，疏解城市功能和人口。同时，将强化交通需求管理和“城六区”的交通拥堵治理，研究利用经济杠杆减排和缓堵，积极探索车辆电子标识的使用推广。

2014 年 3 月，上海市正式发布新版《上海市交通发展白皮书》，明确提出上海未来十年交通发展的总体目标是构筑国际大都市一体化交通，形成以轨道交通为骨干、公共汽（电）车为基础、客运交通枢纽为衔接的城乡一体化公共交通体系，加快建成国际海空枢纽城市，着力打造绿色交通都市，实现交通的安全、畅达、高效、绿色和文明。同时，上海将进一步完善步行与自行车交通系统，继续严格控制小客车总量，研究并适时出台小客车额度有期限使用、限制转让、长期在沪使用的外省市号牌机动车管理、拥挤收费、车辆限行等政策。

2014 年 12 月，北京、上海、广州、深圳四个城市共同签署了《北上广深四市交通合作备忘录》，建立四市交通年会制度，每年轮流在四市举办，商讨应对特大城市交通发展问题。北上广深是当前中国城市交通问题比较集中的城市，同时也是应对经验丰富、交通理念先进、交通技术前沿的地区，共同举办交通年会将对中国城市交通发展带来深远影响。根据备忘录，四市将推动交通“政策互联、信息互通、经验互鉴、工作互动”，在交通政策制定、公交发展、治理交通拥堵、智能交通建设等方面加强交流合作，共同推动特大城市交通问题的解决。

二、绿色交通主导下的交通发展与实践

（一）城市轨道交通建设投资逐年增加

截至 2014 年，我国获批轨道交通建设规划的城市已达 37 个，全年全国城市轨道交通投资达2 200亿元，同比增加 400 亿元。2014 年，长沙、无锡、宁波相继开通运营城市轨道交通，全国开通运营轨道交通城市达到了 22 个。从 2005 年至 2014 年的 10 年间，中国拥有城市轨道交通的城市从 8 个发展为 22 个；运营线路数由 17 条增长为 83 条；运营线路总长由 381. 6 公里增长至2 699. 6公里，年均增长 231. 8 公里，运营车站数由 237 座增长至1 770座。2014 年，全国新增运营线路 9 条，新增运营线路长度 373. 6 公里、运营车站 251 座。目前，上海以 539. 2 公里的运营线网总长度名列第一（14 条线路）。2014 年 12 月 28 日，北京 4 条

轨道线路同时开通试运营，轨道交通运营里程再添62公里，以527公里名列第二（18条线路），广州（9条线路）、重庆（4条线路）、深圳（5条线路）分别以245.4公里、192.6公里、176.3公里名列第三、第四、第五名。

此外，2014年我国开通运营现代有轨电车线路的城市已达到8个，运营线路共计12条，运营线路总长172.6公里，运营车站共计192座。其中，新增开通运营现代有轨电车线路的城市有南京、苏州、广州，新增运营线路5条，新增运营线路长度83.7公里，新增运营车站58座。

（二）加快公共交通发展系列政策措施出台

2014年，各城市和相关部门制定并完善了城市加快公共交通发展的政策措施、相关规划及技术标准，为城市交通的科学发展提供了有力保障。

3月21日，宁波市政府常务会议审议通过了《宁波市城市公共交通发展规划（2012-2020)》（以下简称《规划》），该规划旨在有效整合公共交通资源，推动“公交都市”创建，提升宁波公共交通整体水平。该《规划》对宁波轨道交通及中运量公交的线网、场站做了详细规划，对出租车以及智能公交系统建设提出了发展要求。预计到2020年，中心城公交分担率将达到33%~35%，公交站点500米覆盖率达到90%以上，公交线路网密度超过3km/km^2，公交平均换乘时间缩短至5分钟以内，公交平均运营速度达到20km/h，城乡客运公交化覆盖率85%以上。

9月2日，北京市地方标准《公交专用车道设置规范》向全社会公开征求意见。该标准规定了公交专用车道的设置原则、设置条件、设置方法及相关设备的安装。首次提出了在城市快速路和承担城市交通功能的高速公路上设置专用车道的条件以及专用车道在交叉口连续的设置方法，为建立网络化、多层次的公交专用车道系统提供了依据，对于提升北京市公交服务水平具有重大意义。

11月19日，交通运输部印发了《城市公共交通规划编制指南》，为指导各地科学编制城市公共交通规划，推动建立城市公共交通支撑和引导城市发展的规划模式，保障广大群众基本出行需求的重要举措。该规划有利于实现城市公共交通资源的优化配置，提升城市公共交通服务能力和服务水平，最大限度地保障公众基本出行需求。

12月22日，北京市政府发布《关于加快公共交通发展提高服务和管理水平的意见》（以下简称《意见》），2007-2014年，北京市公共交通出行比例由34.4%增至48%，进入了公共交通主导城市交通时代。《意见》提出，预计到2017年年底，全市轨道交通运营里程达到600公里以上，公交专用道总里程达到480公里以上且形成网络，改善300公里人行步道、自行车道配套设施条件，全面提高公共交通的便捷性、安全性、舒适性的工作目标。《意见》明确了2015-2017年公共交通发展的工作思路、主要目标，围绕公共交通的发展水平以及服务水平和管理水平制定了提升地面公交运行效率、强化轨道交通运营保障、改善绿色出行条件、优化地面公交乘车环境、完善轨道交通乘车环境、提高公共交通换乘效率、提高科技信息服务水平、做好特定群体乘车服务工作、加强公共交通企业管理、保障公共交通乘车秩序、保障公共交通路权优先、做好社会车辆引导 12 个方面的 20 项工作措施。

（三）定制公交服务逐步推广并趋于完善

从 2013 年 9 月北京第一班定制公交（又称商务定制班车）运行以来，定制公交的运营线路和班次都在不断增长。全国多个城市在 2014 年也相继推出定制公交，或将其提上日程，成为全国公共交通服务模式改革的一大亮点。继北京推行定制公交后，2014 年，深圳、成都、天津、济南、哈尔滨、青岛、南京、郑州、大连、杭州等多个城市陆续开通了定制公交服务。“定制公交”由定制公交线路的发起、乘客征集、确定线路、座位预定、在线支付、乘车等环节组成。只要预定人数超过车辆座位数的一定比例，则可开行公交专线。定制公交采用一人一座的公交大巴，可以在公交专用道通行，采取大站停靠或一站直达方式，票价虽然比普通公交贵，但方便快捷。有的城市定制公交乘客还可享受免费 Wifi 服务。

（四）步行和自行车交通系统设计规范化

在城市步行和自行车出行环境日益恶化、出行分担率普遍下滑的背景下，住房和城乡建设部组织编制了《城市步行和自行车交通系统规划设计导则》（以下简称《导则》）。《导则》提出发展城市步行和自行车交通是预防和缓解交通拥堵、减少大气污染和能源消耗的重要途径，关系到人民群众的生产生活和城市的可持续发展。步行和自行车交通出行灵活、准时性高，在我国具有良好的发展基础，是解决中短距离出行和接驳换乘的理想交通方式，是城市综合交通不可缺少的重要组成部分。各地要充分认识加强城市步行和自行车交通系统建设的重要性和紧迫性，结合当地实际和《导则》要求，抓紧编制《城市步行和自行车交通系统规划》。7 月，住房和城乡建设部办公厅下发通知，确定北京市西城区步行和自行车交通系统示范项目等 94 个项目为第三批城市步行和自行车交通系统示范项目，其中安徽省为城市步行和自行车交通系统建设示范省。

（五）“APEC 蓝”呼吁民众践行绿色出行

2014 年 11 月，北京市举办亚太经合组织（APEC）第 22 次领导人非正式会议期间，为了确保不受雾霾天气的干扰，北京市及周边的天津市、河北省、山东省相继采取了工业企业停限产、施工工地停工、市民调休放假、机动车单双号限行等措施，在这些综合措施作用下，北京市自 11 月 1 日起，连续十几天保持良好空气质量，空气质量指数 PM2.5 平均浓度始终控制在 100 以下，APEC 期间，北京市民更多地选择了绿色出行，公共交通出行比例从 47% 增长到 56%，其中 11 月 3 日至 6 日（工作日），地面公交客运量全年首次，并连续四天突破1 500万人次，有效承载了小汽车转移的出行量。人们用“APEC 蓝”这一网络新词汇来形容 APEC 期间北京连续保持的蓝天，反映出广大北京市民内心对良好空气质量、良好人居环境的深切期盼，也说明只要痛下决心、综合施策，驱散雾霾让蓝天常驻并非是不可实现的目标。习近平总书记在 APEC 会议讲话中明确提出，要通过不懈的努力，使道路更加顺畅，让人们工作得更好，生活得更好，希望把“APEC 蓝”保持下去。人们也越来越意识到，必须不断改善公共交通服务，倡导集约化出行和绿色出行，才能看到不远将来可以预见的公交愿景。

三、行政与法治视野下的交通改革与治理

（一）小汽车“限购”示范效应持续升温

2014 年 3 月 25 日晚 7 时，杭州市政府宣布自 3 月 26 日零时起，在全市实行小客车总量调控管理，采取控制总量和“错峰限行”调整的双重措施。2014 年 12 月 29 日下午 5 时 40 分，深圳市政府举行新闻发布会，发布《深圳市人民政府关于实行小汽车增量调控管理的通告》，宣布从 18 时开始实施小汽车增量调控和指标管理，有效期暂定 5 年。与杭州不同的是，为避免机动车突击上牌，小汽车“限购令”突降后，深圳市由交通执法、国税局等联合组成的督查组对部分 4S 店要求清场停业，对所有店面的销售情况和库存情况进行核对整理。至此，继北京、上海、广州、贵阳、天津和杭州之后，深圳成为全国第 7 个小汽车限购的城市，中国大城市汽车“限购”示范效应持续影响着城市政府的决策和交通政策的走向，大城市交通拥堵综合治理体系面临困境。

（二）机动车辆管理改革拓展便民服务

2014 年 5 月 1 日，国家商务部、发展改革委、公安部、环境保护部颁布实施《机动车强制报废标准规定》，根据机动车使用和安全技术、排放检验状况，对达到报废标准的机动车实施强制报废，私家车 15 年必须强制报废生死线将被废除，取而代之的是 60 万公里后的“引导报废”。

5 月 16 日，公安部、国家质监总局两部委发布《关于加强和改进机动车检验工作的意见》(以下简称《意见》)，出台了一系列机动车检验新政，包括从 2014 年 9 月 1 日起试行 6 年内非营运轿车和其他小型、微型载客汽车免上线检测，推行异地年检、预约年检服务等。在此期间，每两年提供交强险凭证、车船税纳税或免税证明后，车主可直接向公安交管部门申领检验标志，并按规定粘贴。《意见》还鼓励简化机动车检验工作流程，创新检验工作便利设施，加强对检验机构监管、严格查处违法违规检验问题、推动政府部门与检验机构脱钩、鼓励社会资源加入检验机构建设。

（三）公车改革确定路线图和时间表

2014 年 7 月 16 日，国务院正式印发《关于全面推进公务用车制度改革的指导意见》和《中央和国家机关公务用车制度改革方案》，首次从顶层设计的高度为公车改革定下了路线图和时间表，标志着公车改革正式启动。按照改革方案，2014 年年底前，中央和国家机关力争基本完成公车改革；2015 年年底前，地方党政机关基本完成。我国取消副部级以下领导干部用车，取消一般公务用车，普通公务出行社会化，适度发放公务交通补贴。从 1994

年《关于党政机关汽车配备和使用管理的规定》出台起，公车改革已经探索了 20 年时间。2014 年，中央和国家机关率先推进车辆封存和补贴发放，让外界看到了中央带头改革、以上率下的决心，为各地的改革实践树立了榜样。地方实践需要因地制宜，按照中央确定的原则和目标想办法、抓落实，从改革方案到推进措施，同中央要求和社会关切进行有效对接。

四、移动互联网发展下的特色交通服务与探索

（一）高德发布城市交通拥堵指数引热议

2014 年，国内数字地图内容提供商高德地图公司连续按季度发布《2014 年中国主要城市交通分析报告》。作为首份由互联网企业发布的城市出行建议，高德以互联网众包的思路采集数据，将 3 亿高德地图导航用户作为数据蓝本，以浮动车数据为佐证，对全国主要城市的交通出行及拥堵情况做了分析。随着每一季度报告中发布的“堵城”的出炉，大数据治疗城市拥堵的话题成为社会热议话题，并引起地方政府及相关单位的关注，社会反响较大。高德地图发布的交通分析报告，是地图行业的首个基于大数据的产品，虽然该系列报告在数据处理以及计算方法上仍有待商榷，但其发布将交通参与者对交通拥堵的“感性认识”转变为“描述性统计”，直观、简单、易懂，促使社会公众越来越关注城市实际交通状况。《高德报告》也是全国首个基于大数据对城市交通拥堵进行评价和排名的专项公开报告，该报告对于进一步提高社会对城市交通拥堵的关注度、增强公众对城市交通拥堵基本理解、进一步挖掘交通运行数据价值等方面，具有重要的推动意义和导向作用。

（二）百度 LBS（基于位置的服务）服务展现

2014 年 1 月春节期间，百度地图基于 LBS（基于位置的服务）平台大数据的春节人口迁徙大数据正式上线，人们在网上可查询国内各大城市在过去 8 小时的人口迁出和迁入详细情况，并能统计当前春运热门线路，展现了交通大数据的魅力。12 月，继谷歌、苹果、诺基亚、Skyhook 和高德之后，百度 LBS 开放平台正式开放了全球定位能力，标志着用户在中国大陆以外的地区，都可以更好地使用到百度以及第三方 App 所提供的地图、LBS 类服务。得益于拥有近 4 亿用户的百度地图 App，百度 LBS 开放平台定位请求已经高达 100 亿次/天，同比增长一倍多。

（三）打车、专车软件备受争议

2013 年 12 月起，“滴滴打车”和“快的打车”相继推出打车补贴计划，补贴大战在 2014 年不断升级。据统计，截至 2014 年 9 月，我国打车软件用户数已达 1.54 亿，其中，“快的打车”和“滴滴打车”分别以 54.4% 和 44.9% 的占比位居前两位。目前，打车软件服务已覆盖全国 300 多个城市。2014 年 12 月，百度公司通过入股外企 Uber，也参加到打车市场的“争霸战”中。各地政府交通管理部门也陆续出台相应的管理措施。例如，北京禁

止了打车应用的竞价排名功能，上海早晚高峰禁用打车软件约车，杭州拟建统一的叫车平台。此外，成都交管局认定出租车驾驶员在驾车过程中，使用手机打车软件抢单，以及拨打接听手持电话，均属于违法行为。在传统出租车行业市场推出打车软件后，为开拓新市场，2014 年第三季度，滴滴、快的等企业又推出了定位于高端商务出行人群的“专车服务”，为用户提供更加多元化的出行。专车市场运行的同时，也暴露出很多问题，社会争议较大，如专车运营的合法性问题，专车在计价器、发票和乘客维权问题等。

五、智慧城市引领下的智能交通发展

（一）智能交通行业快速发展

自 20 世纪 70 年代我国智能交通开始发展以来，我国智能交通行业迅速扩张，大量从事智能交通的企业涌现。截至 2014 年，我国已经有2 000多家企业从事智能交通行业，其中有的企业已经进入资本市场，并成为我国智能交通行业的中坚力量。随着信息技术的不断发展以及机动化水平的不断提高，这些智能交通企业在营销网络、技术研发、人才积累、资金实力、品牌建设等方面都积累了大量的经验和竞争优势。作为智慧城市的重要组成部分，各地对智慧交通的投入力度也逐渐加大。此外，《国家新型城镇化规划（2014－2020 年）》出台，智能交通得到更多的政策扶持，我国智能交通市场前景向好，智能交通企业也将迎来新一轮的大发展。

（二）交通数据应用进一步深化

近年来，大数据的概念风靡全球。数据是智能交通的基础和命脉，交通系统的方方面面都产生大量的数据，这些数据都是亟待挖掘的宝藏，能够为解决交通问题带来极大帮助。2014 年，阿里巴巴集团与贵州省共同宣布面向全球启动“智慧交通算法大挑战”。贵阳市向参赛者开放了海量的脱敏交通数据，包括公交车 GPS 数据、出租车 GPS 数据、高德导航数据，逐步启动大数据商业开发。南京市则将大数据应用在交通事故理赔上，基于互联网大数据技术开发的交通事故快速处理综合应用平台。同一个驾驶人、同一辆车，甚至同一个手机号码，如果在短时间内多次出险报案，就会触发系统“报警”。该平台投入使用以来，交通事故理赔量明显下降，并已发现多起涉嫌骗保的案件，显示了大数据的威力。

（三）各地智慧交通实践遍地开花

2014 年，全国各地交通运营和管理部门紧跟时代步伐，大力推进信息化建设，为推动城市智能交通发展，进行了很多有益的尝试与实践。例如，山东青岛市交警部门选取部分公交线路安装了违法占用公交专用道自动抓拍设备，抓拍占用公交专用道交通违法行为，使得占用公交专用道的违法行为下降了八成多，公交专用道更加顺畅。广东佛山交警在国内首创通过使用视频语音进行“交通事故远程查勘处理”，使得轻微交通事故同比下降近 30%，有效地减少了因事故造成的交通拥堵。重庆警方在全市范围内启用“人行横道智能监测系统”，规范机动车在人流量不大、未安装红绿灯的人行横道前的驾驶，确保使用斑马线的行人能够安全、顺利地通过马路。杭州着力打造交通信息资源云平台，实现了交通、交警、城管、铁路、民航等单位和公交、地铁、水上巴士、公共自行车、出租车五位一体公交体系相关数据的接入和整合，为综合交通体系的优化和建设奠定了坚实基础。

六、交通文明下的文化建设

（一）第8个“9·22世界无车日”

“9·22世界无车日”是由法国在1998年发起的，旨在提倡绿色出行，降低城市空气和噪声污染，提高市民环保意识。迄今为止，全世界已有1480多个城市开展“无车日活动”，影响不断扩大。我国自2007年首次开展城市无车日活动以来，参与的城市逐年增加，目前已有154个城市参与，涉及超过两亿的城区人口。2014年的无车日以“我们的街道，我们的选择”为主题，重点关注交通对城市生活质量的影响，鼓励重新分配和设计街道及公共空间，促进多种交通方式在道路空间分配上的平衡。全国多个城市积极采取各项行动，开展无车日活动。如杭州市政府在当天采取临时交通管制措施，将整个杭州市的核心区作为交通管制区，禁止本地和外地的所有小型客车通行。交通管制区域内，提倡市民采用公交车、自行车、步行等绿色交通方式出行。

（二）第3个“全国交通安全日”

2014年12月2日，我国迎来第3个“全国交通安全日”，主题是“抵制七类违法，安全文明出行”，呼吁广大交通参与者自觉抵制超速、超载、酒驾、毒驾、闯红灯、占用应急车道和不礼让斑马线这七类违法行为。同时，在全社会树立法治意识、规则意识、安全自律意识、社会责任意识、文明礼让意识，促进形成“遵守交通法规光荣，违反交通法规可耻”的社会氛围。全国各地各级交管部门充分利用电视、网络、微博、微信等传媒手段，通过丰富多彩的影视作品、公益广告、“中国好交警”评选、展板等形式，深入社区、学校、企事业单位，开展交通安全日主题活动，举办交通安全文化周活动，组织交通安全公益活动，达到了良好的宣传效果。同日，我国首个全国性的交通管理和交通安全宣传专业网站“122交通网”（www.122.cn）正式上线，网民可获取各类交通安全知识、查询交通违法信息、咨询交通安全相关问题、学习交通安全法律法规、了解交通管理热点事件、参与交通管理话题讨论、与交管部门互动沟通。

（三）相关论坛、研讨会、博览会相继召开，助力城市交通发展

2014年，我国各地相继举办了多次与城市交通相关的论坛、研讨会、博览会，如2014年4月，以“新型城镇化与交通发展”为主题的中国城市交通规划2013年年会暨第27次学

术研讨会在北京召开；9月，以“大数据背景下的城市交通管理创新”为主题的第二届中国城市智能交通管理暨科技创新论坛在南京召开；10月，以“移动互联网，让公交更优先”为主题的第三届中国智能公交论坛在深圳召开；11月，以“智能化信息化引领综合运输发展”为主题的第九届中国智能交通年会在广州召开，相关的专家、学者、工程人员和政府人员齐聚一堂，共谋我国城市交通发展大计，从智力上支持城市交通发展。

七、结语

2014年是贯彻落实党的十八届四中全会精神、全面推进依法治国、全面实施新型城镇化建设的开局之年。在城市交通快速发展、交通运行态势复杂多变且人们对交通环境改善有期待、有要求的情况下，我国城市交通发展呈现出许多的新情况、新问题、新变化，各级人民政府和相关部门也尝试采取许多的新思路、新模式、新探索。虽然当前以及今后相当长的一段时期内，我国城市交通供需矛盾依然突出，交通系统科学化、智能化和法制化的任务依然严峻，交通发展与环境保护的矛盾依然存在，但是，在党中央、国务院的领导和支持下，在各级政府、相关部门的共同努力下，只要坚持改革创新、积极探索、顺应信息时代潮流，综合科学运用行政、经济、法律、教育等手段加以支撑完善并作为长期政策，持之以恒，久久为功，我国必将走向城市交通发展的“新常态”。

（作者：王静霞，国务院参事室特约研究员，住房城乡建设部城市交通工程技术中心，中国城市规划学会副理事长，教授级高级规划师；戴帅，公安部道路交通安全研究中心交通政策规划研究室副主任）

2014年中国城市信息化进展

2014年，智慧城市仍然是中国城市信息化的主题，全社会对智慧城市的认识进一步深入，智慧城市作为城市信息化的新阶段，其规划与建设是一个长期的过程，体现为：信息化、新型城镇化、工业化和农业现代化的深度融合发展；信息惠民工程有效整合孤立、分散的公共服务资源，强化多部门联合监管和协同服务，全面提升各级政府公共服务水平和社会管理能力；电子商务的发展与创新从市场层面推动城市信息化进程；政府和社会资本合作（PPP）模式开始改变城市信息化的投融资模式。总体而言，2014年，网络安全管理、智慧城市发展等信息化政策措施取得新进展；以移动通信、物联网、大数据、云计算、导航与位置服务等为代表的新一代信息技术的发展为城市信息化带来新活力；“多规合一”、不动产统一登记及社区服务管理等正成为城市信息化应用新方向。

一、城市信息化政策措施取得新进展

2014年，围绕城市信息化发展的网络安全、信息管理、资源整合、信息惠民、系统集成应用、智慧城市建设等主题，国家相继出台了多项政策措施，为城市信息化有序发展提供了重要保障。

（一）加强网络安全管理，保障城市信息化健康发展

以物联网、大数据、云计算等技术为代表的新一代信息技术对信息安全提出了新的要求。服务器虚拟化和数据集中部署显著地改变了传统网络应用模式，飞速增长的数据和业务不仅使网络架构变得非常复杂，同时也面临网络安全的巨大挑战。由于云计算应用的用户信息资源的高度集中，存在的风险以及带来的安全事件后果也较传统应用更高。

2014年2月，中央网络安全和信息化领导小组成立，中共中央总书记、国家主席习近平亲自担任领导小组组长。领导小组将着眼国家安全和长远发展，统筹协调涉及经济、政治、文化、社会及军事等各个领域的网络安全和信息化重大问题，研究制定网络安全和信息化发展战略、宏观规划和重大政策，推动国家网络安全和信息化法治建设，不断增强安全保障能力。领导小组的成立充分体现党和国家对网络安全与信息化的高度重视，同时也为信息化顶层设计和信息治理提供了管理体制的保障，有利于促进城市网络安全与信息化管理的制

度化。

4 月 8 日，OpenSSL 爆出严重安全漏洞 Heartbleed，被形容为致命的“心脏出血”。利用该漏洞，黑客坐在自己家里就可以实时获取约 30% 的 https 开头网址的用户登录账号密码，其中包括网民最常用的购物、网银、社交、微博、微信、邮箱等知名网站和服务，影响至少两亿中国网民。

11 月 24-30 日，首届国家网络安全宣传周启动。过去老百姓对于网络安全的认识是抽象的，通过网络安全周体验展示，让老百姓亲自看到网络安全跟自己的生活和利益都是密切相关的，使大家更关心网络安全。网络安全宣传周实现了网络安全宣传从概念到理念的跨越。

12 月 20-21 日，部署在阿里云上的一家游戏公司遭遇了全球互联网史上最大的一次 DDoS（分布式拒绝服务）攻击，该攻出主要利用合理的服务请求来占用过多的服务器资源，从而使合法用户无法得到服务器响应。本次攻击时长 14 个小时，攻击峰值流量达到每秒 453.8G。阿里云安全防护产品“云盾”，结合该游戏公司的“超级盾防火墙”，帮助用户成功抵御了此次攻击。本次攻击说明了网络安全在信息化时代的重要性，自主可控和安全可信应该是保障。

在国家高度关注及产业持续发展下，我国信息安全市场规模逐步扩大。2014 年 12 月，互联网数据中心（IDC）发布了 2014 年上半年中国网络安全市场分析报告，统计显示 2014 年上半年中国 IT 安全硬件市场规模接近 30 亿元，并预计全年可达 70 亿元，同比增长 18.8%。据 IDC 统计分析，防火墙硬件市场规模上半年超过 10 亿元，同比增 13.6%。随着全社会对网络安全的重视，发展自主可控、安全可信的核心基础软硬件，实现信息技术与产品的国产化成为我国信息化发展的必然趋势。

（二）颁布多项相关政策，引导城市信息化有序建设

2014 年国务院及相关部委发布的相关文件，对智慧城市和城市信息化建设多有引导，形成了有利于城市信息化发展的政策环境。在这些文件中，最为重要的是《国家新型城镇化规划（2014-2020 年）》和国家发展和改革委员会等八部委《关于促进智慧城市健康发展的指导意见》。

2014 年 3 月，《国家新型城镇化规划（2014-2020 年）》发布，在“推进智慧城市建设”一节中：“提出统筹城市发展的物质资源、信息资源和智力资源利用，推动物联网、大数据、云计算等新一代信息技术创新应用，实现与城市经济社会发展深度融合；促进跨部门、跨行业、跨地区的政务信息共享和业务协同，强化信息资源社会化开发利用，推广智慧化信息应用和新型信息服务，促进城市规划管理信息化、基础设施智能化、公共服务便捷化、产业发展现代化、社会治理精细化；增强城市要害信息系统和关键信息资源的安全保障能力。”在“开展试点示范”一章中指出，继续推进创新城市、智慧城市、低碳城镇试点。

8 月，国家发展和改革委员会、工业和信息化部等八部委联合印发了《关于促进智慧城市健康发展的指导意见》，提出智慧城市是运用物联网、云计算、大数据、空间地理信息集

成等新一代信息技术，促进城市规划、建设、管理和服务智慧化的新理念和新模式。指出：到2020年，建成一批特色鲜明的智慧城市，聚集和辐射带动作用大幅增强，综合竞争优势明显提高，在保障和改善民生服务、创新社会管理、维护网络安全等方面取得显著成效；实现公共服务便捷化、城市管理精细化、生活环境宜居化、基础设施智能化、网络安全长效化。该《指导意见》认为：建设智慧城市，对加快工业化、信息化、城镇化、农业现代化融合，提升城市可持续发展能力具有重要意义。

此外，2014年1月，国家发展和改革委员会、工业和信息化部等12个部门联合印发《关于加快实施信息惠民工程有关工作的通知》（以下简称《通知》），以解决当前体制机制和传统环境下民生服务的突出难题为核心，有效整合孤立、分散的公共服务资源，强化多部门联合监管和协同服务，构建方便快捷、公平普惠、优质高效的公共服务信息体系，全面提升各级政府公共服务水平和社会管理能力。《通知》要求围绕当前群众广泛关注的医疗、教育、社保、就业、养老服务等民生问题，选择信息化手段成效高、社会效益好、示范意义大、带动效应强的内容作为工作重点，增强信息服务的有效供给能力，提升信息便民惠民利民水平。信息惠民是从民生服务的视角来践行推动智慧城市非常重要的工作。

2月，国务院发布《关于推进文化创意和设计服务与相关产业融合发展的若干意见》，在"重点任务"中提出要加快数字内容产业发展。推动文化产品和服务的生产、传播、消费的数字化、网络化进程，强化文化对信息产业的内容支撑、创意和设计提升，加快培育双向深度融合的新型业态。深入实施国家文化科技创新工程，支持利用数字技术、互联网、软件等高新技术支撑文化内容、装备、材料、工艺、系统的开发和利用，加快文化企业技术改造步伐。大力推动传统文化单位发展互联网新媒体，推动传统媒体和新兴媒体融合发展，提升先进文化互联网传播吸引力。全面推进三网融合，推动下一代广播电视网和交互式网络电视等服务平台建设，推动智慧社区、智慧家庭建设。

6月，国务院办公厅印发《关于加强城市地下管线建设管理的指导意见》，针对我国地下管线建设规模不足和管理水平不高等状况，一些城市相继发生大雨内涝、管线泄漏爆炸、路面塌陷等事件，提出要切实加强城市地下管线建设管理，保障城市安全运行，提高城市综合承载能力和城镇化发展质量。推进城市电网、通信网架空线入地改造工程，实施城市宽带通信网络和有线广播电视网络光纤入户改造，加快有线广播电视网络数字化改造。建立和完善综合管理信息系统，满足城市规划、建设、运行和应急等工作需要；要求管线信息系统应按照统一的数据标准，实现信息的即时交换、共建共享、动态更新；推进综合管理信息系统与数字化城市管理系统、智慧城市融合。

11月，国务院发布《关于创新重点领域投融资机制鼓励社会投资的指导意见》，强调在公共服务、资源环境、生态建设、基础设施等重点领域进一步创新投融资机制，鼓励和引导社会投资，提高公共产品与服务的供给能力和效率，促进调结构、补短板、惠民生。12月，国家发展和改革委员会发布《关于开展政府和社会资本合作的指导意见》，进一步细化了政府和社会资本合作（PPP）模式的实施细则。12月，工业和信息化部发布了《关于向民间资本开放宽带接入市场的通告》，提出鼓励民间资本以多种模式进入宽带接入市场。政府和社会资本合作（PPP）模式将改变城市建设、运管及城市信息化的投融资模式。

二、移动通信与物联网促进城市信息化落地

2014 年，以 4G 为代表的无线通信及移动互联网迅速发展，推动移动应用成为城市信息化的新热点；以 RFID 为代表的传感器布设及传感网与物联网的建设，促进了车联网、智慧医疗、智能家居等多行业的智能化发展。

（一）无线通信发展推动移动应用新热点

工业和信息化部最新数据显示，自 2013 年年底发放 TD－LTE 4G 牌照以来，中国 4G 用户数已突破 9000 万，建成 4G 基站 70 万个以上。

2015 年 2 月 3 日，中国互联网络信息中心（CNNIC）发布第 35 次《中国互联网络发展状况统计报告》。该报告显示，截至 2014 年 12 月，中国网民规模达 6.49 亿，互联网普及率达到 47.9%，较 2013 年年底提升了 2.1 个百分点。其中，手机网民规模 5.57 亿，较 2013 年增加 5672 万人。网民中使用手机上网的人群占比由 2013 年的 81.0% 提升至 85.8%。2014 年，家庭 Wi－Fi 的普及情况已达到很高水平，比例为 81.1%；家庭 Wi－Fi 的使用对家庭中高龄成员上网具有较强带动作用，推动城市互联网普及率的进一步提升。

2014 年，在移动互联网的推动下，个人互联网应用发展整体呈现上升态势。即时通信作为网民第一大上网应用，在高使用率水平的基础上继续攀升，达到 90.6%；媒体功能凸显，使用率呈现回升态势；电子商务类应用依然保持快速发展，手机旅行预订应用表现突出。同时，网民对各项网络应用的使用程度更为深入。移动商务类应用在移动支付的拉动下，正历经跨越式发展，在各项网络应用中地位愈发重要。互联网金融类应用第一次纳入调查，互联网理财产品仅在一年时间内，使用率超过 10%，成为 2014 年表现亮眼的网络应用。

互联网降低了沟通和交易的成本，也营造了互惠分享的网络空间。本次调查显示，2014 年有 60.0% 的网民对于在互联网上分享行为持积极态度，其中，非常愿意的占 13.0%，比较愿意的占 47.0%。借助网络空间，网民在信息和资源方面互惠分享，不仅降低了交易成本，也创造了新的价值。截至 2014 年 12 月，手机即时通信使用率为 91.2%，较 2013 年年底提升了 5.1 个百分点。手机即时通信由于其随身、随时、拥有社交属性和可以提供用户位置的特点，自身定位逐渐从以前单一的通信工具演变成支付、游戏、O2O 等高附加值业务的用户入口，以其庞大的用户基数为其他服务提供了巨大的潜在商业价值。

2014 年，中国网民手机商务应用发展大爆发，手机网购、手机支付、手机银行等手机商务应用用户年增长分别为 63.5%，73.2% 和 69.2%，远超其他手机应用增长幅度。而长期处于低位的手机旅行预订，2014 年用户年增长达到 194.6%，是增长最为快速的移动商务类应用。截至 2014 年 12 月，我国网络购物用户规模达到 3.61 亿，较 2013 年年底增加 5953 万人，增长率为 19.7%；我国网民使用网络购物的比例从 48.9% 提升至 55.7%。综观 2014

年我国网络购物市场，呈现出普及化、全球化、移动化的发展趋势。

北京市交通信息中心自主研发的手机应用“北京实时公交 APP”，自 2013 年 10 月上线以来，到 2014 年 12 月，用户量累计超过 76 万，已实现北京市 241 条（含 37 条夜班线）公交线路的公交车实时运行位置、到站时间等动态信息及公交线路优化调整等静态信息手机查询，公众可以根据所关心的实时公交车位置和到站时间，合理安排出行。今后，还将通过扩展其他公交线路公交车的实时定位能力，提供更多的公交信息服务。

（二）物联网技术促进多行业发展智能化

2014 年 5 月，工业和信息化部发布了《工业和信息化部 2014 年物联网工作要点》，旨在贯彻落实《国务院关于推进物联网有序健康发展的指导意见》（国发〔2013〕7 号）和全国物联网工作电视电话会议精神，扎实组织实施物联网发展专项行动计划。要求各相关部门按照工作要点的部署安排，结合自身实际，切实做好相关工作，推动我国物联网产业快速有序健康发展。

9 月，作为中国物联网行业规格最高、规模最大的国家级会展活动，第五届中国国际物联网（传感网）博览会在无锡开幕。博览会以“体验助推应用，应用引领发展”为主题，参展企业达 311 家，特设智能工业、车联网、智能医疗、智能家居、智能农业等多个专题展区，集中展示了物联网领域最新技术成果和创新产品。会上公布的“RFID 医院智能护理系统”等物联网十大优秀应用案例引起与会者广泛关注。

物联网已成为无锡转型升级的强力引擎，全市物联网企业 794 家，就业人员突破 12 万人，建设物联网应用项目 160 多个，产业规模超过 1400 亿元，连续 3 年增幅超过 30%。同时，无锡一批物联网企业正在崛起，物联网企业涵盖设备制造、软件产品开发、系统集成、网络及运营服务四大类，基本形成了感知、网络通信、处理应用、关键共性、基础支撑在内的物联网产业链，其中智能传感系统产业集群被认定为全国首批，移动、联通、电信等运营商开始提供电力、交通、农业、环保等领域的物联网运营与服务，市场应用正在培育。截至 2014 年，无锡已集聚重点物联网研发机构 39 家，引进物联网高层次人才 2000 多人，承担研发项目近千项，获得物联网领域专利 1970 项，累计制订、修订物联网标准 49 项。自 2014 年以来，无锡国家传感网创新示范区加快集聚研发资源与创新要素，商业模式持续创新，市场运行机制不断完善。

2014 年我国物联网技术与产业发展呈现出新的特点与趋势：一是初步建立了较为完善的政策体系，包括国家物联网发展指导意见、行动计划、工作要点等顶层政策架构与一系列配套政策相继制定推出。二是产业高地加快崛起，产业协同全面推进，初步形成了涵盖芯片、元器件、软件、系统集成、电信运营、物联网服务等各产业环节、产业门类，较为完整的物联网产业体系。三是惠民应用不断深化，物联网与传统产业的融合进一步深化，工业云平台、工业大数据等基于物联网的创新技术已成为传统工业和实体经济转型升级的重要引擎。截至 2014 年 8 月，中国交通、物流、环保、医疗、能源、安防等领域的物联网应用市场规模已近千亿元。四是创新技术深度融合，智慧城市加快孕育。伴随物联网、云计算、大数据、移动互联网的融合发展，智慧城市加快发展，建设内涵全面深化。

三、大数据与云计算创新城市信息化模式

智慧城市作为城市信息化发展的新阶段，其规划与建设离不开大数据与云计算等技术的支撑。大数据与云计算技术的应用，为城市信息化提供了一系列创新发展模式，大数据应用可实现城市规划的理性化发展，云计算应用则创新了电子政务新模式。

（一）大数据应用提升理性化的城市规划

有观点认为：大数据是信息化时代的“石油”，开发大数据资源的能力将影响未来国家的核心竞争力。因此，大数据在城市信息化及城市规划领域中的应用也备受关注。2014 年，在全国各地举办了一系列有关城市规划大数据分析与应用的学术论坛，其中引起较大反响的论坛包括 9 月中旬的海口中国城市规划年会及 9 月下旬的长沙城市规划信息化年会。

2014 年 9 月，中国城市规划年会在海南省海口市召开。6000 多名来自全国各地的规划专家学者围绕“城乡治理与规划改革”的主题进行交流。由中国城市规划学会与清华同衡规划设计研究院联合主办的《大数据与城乡治理》自由论坛备受关注，十多位业界资深学者与十多位青年精英共同探讨大数据与城市信息化及城市治理的关系。大家认为：智慧城市建设为城市规划改革与城市治理现代化带来了新的契机，借助大数据可以实现以人为本的理性城市规划！

第一，智慧城市的规划建设催生了大数据的时代。大数据的时代意味着信息无所不在，使得规划师将有能力随时捕捉城市的人流、车流、物流，从而认识城市人的行为模式与城市社会的整体变化，应用于规划实践，制定理性的规划。正如规划界德高望重的崔功豪教授所言：虽然过去城市规划有很多的改革，包括定量化的改革搞了很长时间，但是没有解决对“人”的深入分析；而大数据能够分析人的行为，真正能够把以人为本的城市规划加以实现。

第二，智慧城市规划建设与大数据应用分析，在技术上可以把经济学、社会学、地理学、环境学等各专业分析方法集成应用，将经济社会发展规划、国土规划、城乡规划、环境规划等多种规划统筹到一个网络信息共享服务平台上，使得多规划融合成为可能，也可以说信息技术是融合各专业规划的重要途径。同时，可以期待新的信息平台与传统的规划相结合，对规划框架体系进行整体更新，使其更趋科学合理，同时推进多规融合，更好地为城乡治理服务。

第三，智慧城市规划管理信息系统的建设及大数据分析应用，将通过民众行为模式信息的分析应用及规划信息的可视化推广而实现参与式的规划，而各部门协同的信息平台将使城市规划有可能成为政府各部门、企业机构、民间团体、广大市民的共同作品，其中可视化是掌握现状、规划评价与规划合作的核心手法，相信参与式的规划成果更能体现理性思维、更能体现以人为本的理念。

（二）云计算应用拓展了电子政务新模式

2014年，在云计算发展的国家政策支撑下，相关企业积极探索应用服务方案，多个城市出台创新发展应用模式，特别是拓展了电子政务新模式。2014年11月15日，国务院总理李克强主持召开国务院常务会议，确定促进云计算创新发展措施，培育壮大新产业，催生基于云计算的在线研发设计、教育医疗、智能制造等新业态。会议认为，加快发展云计算，打造信息产业新业态，对于推动传统产业升级和新兴产业成长，具有重要意义。

5月，中国电信首次对外公布电信云服务6个方面的核心指标，重点在政务、教育、医疗、金融、园区5个方面打造云优势。7月，在2014可信云服务大会上公布了我国第一批通过“可信云服务认证”的名单，包括中国电信、阿里巴巴、腾讯、中国移动、华为等19家云服务商的35项云服务通过了认证，它将引导云服务规范化发展。8月，阿里云启动“云合计划”，拟招募1万家云服务商，为企业、政府等用户提供一站式云服务，其中包括100家大型服务商、1000家中型服务商，东软、中软、浪潮、东华软件等国内大型IT服务商，均相继成为阿里云合作伙伴。9月，中国联通在完成沃云SDN网络商用部署，并宣布正在部署廊坊、呼和浩特等十大云数据中心、31个省会城市云计算资源池、400个地市CDN（内容分发网络）节点的计划。9月，华为发布了一系列云产品，包括由业务驱动的分布式云数据中心架构SD－DC2、云操作系统FusionSphere5.0、数据中心统一管理软件ManageOne等。10月，腾讯公司对外公布腾讯云的连接计划，宣称未来两年内连接100万家传统企业，打造大的腾讯云生态环境。11月，中国移动苏州研发中心宣布正式开工，由中国移动注资31亿元，建设高水平的云计算服务平台。12月，金山软件董事长宣布金山软件未来3～5年内将会向云业务进行规模超过10亿美元的投资，金山云未来3年将执行“all in cloud”的战略。

2014年，阿里云推出智慧政务解决方案，其政务云应用模式是由社会、政府、政务云平台运营商、阿里云、应用集成商、独立软件开发商（ISV）多方共同参与的可持续运营的商业模式和生态系统，通过建设统一的政务云平台，支持政府管理和服务创新，提升工作效率、服务质量和决策水平。1月，国内首个“人社一体化信息系统”在阿里云平台上线，该系统包括浙江省淳安县社会保险、就业、执法、仲裁等几十个政府业务系统，承载着全县45万人民的社会保险信息以及超过3000家的参保单位信息，连接全县几十家医院和卫生院、100多家药店以及财政、银行、地税等单位，是当地政府部门最为复杂的民生应用信息系统。“社保云”的应用在一定程度上摆脱了对传统IOE（IMB、Oracle、EMC）的依赖，也论证了云计算在支持政府管理、服务创新和提升工作效率上的积极作用。

杭州市政务云、丽水智慧政务等，都是阿里云这种政务云模式的典型的应用。以杭州市政务云为例，采用三层结构，即互联网数据中心（IDC）＋云平台＋系统集成商（SI）这种合作模式，机房是部署在华数的IDC机房，中间层采用阿里云的飞天分布式系统，上层是SI、ISV等集成商提供的解决方案。从2013年6月到2014年7月，阿里巴巴已与海南、浙江、河南、河北等7个省级政府确立云计算和大数据合作关系，在发展电子商务的同时，布局电子政务，电子商务、电子政务、电子金融将在阿里云中和谐运转。

四、地理信息技术及产业支撑城市信息化建设

以遥感（RS）、地理信息系统（GIS）及全球卫星导航系统（GNSS）为主体的地理信息技术，是城市信息化重要的基础支撑技术。2014年，地理信息技术及产业发展取得积极进展，提升了城市信息服务质量，促进了城市信息化向纵深发展。

（一）地理信息技术发展提高城市信息服务质量

2014年6月，中国卫星导航定位协会主导的中国位置网服务联盟（简称中国位联）成立。中国位联将集结卫星导航与位置服务产业链龙头企业、科研单位、创新应用单位，以北斗系统应用为核心，以兼容其他卫星导航系统为补充，通过多种导航定位技术集成融合，推进导航定位应用，满足经济社会发展和大众对位置服务的需求。目前，联盟成员单位175家，工作重点是推进北斗地基增强系统建设和室内导航，提升位置服务精度。通过统筹整合区域北斗CORS网，形成覆盖全国的北斗CORS网，为行业用户和大众提供更高精度的北斗导航与定位服务。联盟成员单位开展的京津冀北斗CORS网一体化燃气管网精准服务项目、普适定位和室内导航示范应用项目已经启动。

8月19日，作为我国高分计划重要组成部分的高分二号卫星成功发射，顺利进入预定轨道，所获取图像的空间分辨率优于1米，同时还具有高辐射精度、高定位精度和快速姿态机动能力等特点，标志着中国遥感卫星进入亚米级“高分时代”，为城市信息化提供了新的国产数据源。

在航空遥感技术领域，倾斜摄影技术的迅速发展与应用，为城市三维数据采集提供了新的、实用的技术手段。倾斜摄影通过在同一飞行平台上搭载多台传感器，同时从一个垂直、四个倾斜等五个不同的角度采集影像，获取丰富的建筑物顶面及侧视的高分辨率纹理，不仅能够真实地反映地物情况，高精度地获取物体纹理信息，还可通过先进的定位、融合、建模等技术，生成真实的三维城市模型。国产SuperMap GIS软件在支持倾斜摄影三维数据上取得重大进展，可以直接加载OSGB格式倾斜摄影生成的三维数据，实现数据可视化和分析计算。

12月，国家测绘地理信息局在湖北武汉召开数字城市向智慧城市转型升级工作会，总结了2006年启动数字城市地理空间框架建设，推介智慧城市时空信息云平台，标志着测绘局主导以数字城市地理空间框架为核心的数字建设向以智慧城市时空信息云平台为核心的智慧城市转移。数字城市地理空间框架建设自2006年启动以来，已在全国333个（全部）地级市和380多个县级市开展，目前已有220余个地级市、100余个县级市完成了建设并投入使用，累计开发应用系统3600多个，涉及国土、规划、公安、环保、交通、卫生、旅游等众多领域。经过9年时间的不懈努力，数字城市建设的经济效益和社会效益日益显现。据不完全统计，国家测绘地理信息局主导的数字城市建设直接带动各级财政投入61亿元，节约

财政资金超过 100 亿元，拉动产值 300 多亿元。经过多年的积淀，已建立了国家、省、市三方共建共享的良好机制，为智慧城市时空信息云平台建设及城市信息化发展奠定了坚实基础。

（二）地理信息产业发展促进城市信息化的提升

2014 年 1 月，《国务院办公厅关于促进地理信息产业发展的意见》（以下简称《意见》）发布。《意见》指出，地理信息产业是以现代测绘和地理信息系统、遥感、卫星导航定位等技术为基础，以地理信息开发利用为核心，从事地理信息获取、处理、应用的高技术服务业。发展地理信息产业是实现科学发展的重要支撑，是维护国家安全的重要保证，是加快转变经济发展方式的重要手段，是保障和改善民生的重要内容。地理信息产业的不断发展，将促进物联网、智慧城市以及关联服务业的发展。《意见》强调在维护国家安全的前提下，积极推进地理信息公共服务平台建设，促进地理信息高效、广泛利用。地理信息产业的发展无疑为智慧城市建设为提供重要的技术与数据支撑，促进城市信息化发展。

11 月，《国务院关于创新重点领域投融资机制鼓励社会投资的指导意见》提出，鼓励民间资本参与国家民用空间基础设施建设。完善民用遥感卫星数据政策，加强政府采购服务，鼓励民间资本研制、发射和运营商业遥感卫星，提供市场化、专业化服务。引导民间资本参与卫星导航地面应用系统建设。中国科学院长春光机所已启动“吉林一号”民用高分辨遥感卫星研制工作，研制及发射计划总投资 4.5 亿元，预计 2015 年投入运行。智慧城市建设将是民营遥感卫星的主要市场。

2014 年，作为国家地理信息公共服务平台，天地图的建设与应用得到进一步发展，主要体现在：提升了主节点的服务效率与架构灵活性，实现各数据中心的全局负载均衡；进一步优化手机版地图，增强实用性和可靠性；推进天地图数据融合工作，实现各级节点数据资源的优势互补，提升天地图的整体数据质量与深度应用支撑能力；将智慧城市建设、地理国情监测等成果整合到天地图，并通过天地图涉密版、政务版、公众版面向不同对象发布数据和提供服务；推动天地图更好地贴近管理决策需要、满足社会民生需求，深化基于测绘地理信息业务的应用示范，重点为政府部门提供高效、稳定的在线地理信息服务。天地图的进一步发展，将为城市信息化提供更有力的支持。

五、城市信息化建设应用呈现新的趋势

2014 年，城市信息化发展呈现出若干面向新型应用领域的新趋势，诸如为城市“多规合一”提供多源信息与集成平台保障；为“不动产登记”提供多部门协作与数据库支撑；为“智慧社区”建设提供信息服务模式与智慧生活体验等。

（一）“多规合一”可成为城市信息化应用的新领域

2014 年 1 月，住房和城乡建设部下发《关于开展县（市）城乡总体规划暨“三规合

一”试点工作的通知》，提出全面推动城乡发展一体化，按照城乡一体、全域管控、部门协作的要求，编制县（市）城乡总体规划，实现经济社会发展、城乡、土地利用规划的“三规合一”或“多规合一”，逐步形成统一衔接、功能互补的规划体系。以城乡规划为基础、经济社会发展规划为目标、土地利用规划提出的用地为边界，实现全县（市）一张图，县（市）域全覆盖。全面优化城镇化布局和形态、合理确定城镇化发展的各项目标、积极推进基本公共服务均等化、明确全域空间管控目标和措施。

12月，由国家发展和改革委员会发布《关于开展市县“多规合一”试点工作的通知》，国家发展改革委、国土资源部、环境保护部、住房城乡建设部等部委联合开展市县“多规合一”试点工作，指出：开展市县空间规划改革试点，推动经济社会发展规划、城乡规划、土地利用规划、生态环境保护规划“多规合一”，形成一个市县一本规划、一张蓝图，强化政府空间管控能力，实现国土空间集约、高效、可持续利用。已选定辽宁省大连市旅顺口区等28个市（县）作为“多规合一”试点。“多规合一”需要信息平台的支撑，广东省广州市及福建省厦门市等，借助智慧城市建设的信息化基础，研发了“多规合一”的空间规划“一张图”平台，构建了全市统一的空间信息联动管理和业务协同平台，在初步实现了建设项目、规划、国土资源管理的信息资源共享共用基础上，将涉及用地空间行政审批的事项接入该平台，在行政审批系统内实现网络互通，变串联审批为并联审批，“跑部门”变成了平台上的部门内部协调，行政审批效率将由此大幅提升。

“多规合一”在城市发展中的龙头作用，将成为智慧城市应用的重要内容，也是城市信息化应用的新趋势之一。

（二）不动产统一登记可成为城市信息化服务新专题

2014年11月，国务院总理李克强签署国务院令，公布《不动产登记暂行条例》（以下简称《条例》），规定国家实行不动产统一登记制度，国务院国土资源主管部门负责指导、监督全国不动产登记工作，不动产统一登记将于2015年3月1日起施行。

《条例》规定：要明确登记内容，要求登记机构设立统一的不动产登记簿，将不动产的自然状况、权属状况、权利限制状况等事项准确、完整、清晰地予以记载。要规范登记形式，要求登记簿原则上要采用电子介质，暂不具备条件的，可以采用纸质介质，登记机构要明确唯一、合法的介质形式。要细化保管责任，要求登记机构建立健全相应的安全责任制度，永久保存登记簿；电子登记簿要配备专门的存储设施，采取信息网络安全防护措施，并定期进行异地备份。

《条例》规定：要建立信息管理基础平台，要求国土资源部会同有关部门建立统一的不动产登记信息管理基础平台，登记信息要纳入该平台，确保国家、省、市、县四级登记信息的实时共享。要加强登记部门与管理部门的信息共享，要求登记信息与住房城乡建设、农业、林业、海洋等部门的审批信息、交易信息等实时互通共享。要加强其他部门之间的信息共享，要求国土资源、公安、民政、财政、税务、工商、金融、审计、统计等部门加强不动产登记有关信息互通共享。

不动产统一登记的难点和重点将是房产登记，而房产登记可以与智慧城市的建（构）筑物数据库建设相结合，并且可以通过不动产统一登记实现多部门的共享。通过多部门共享形成新机制，带动城市信息化服务新发展。

（三）智慧社区服务管理成为城市信息化建设的落脚点

2014 年 5 月，住房和城乡建设部根据智慧城市试点工作的总体部署，为指导各地开展智慧社区建设，组织编制了《智慧社区建设指南（试行)》，表明智慧社区建设是智慧城市建设的重要内容。作为智慧城市的细分领域，智慧社区概念和愿景，正被国内各大房企所看重和寄予厚望。按不同功能模块划分，智慧社区提供的服务或业务一般可以分为四大类：基础网络服务，包括有线无线通信网、宽带网络接入、弱电强电等；物业管理服务，包括安防报警、电子巡更、门禁、照明等；智能家居服务，包括家庭监控、居家养老、远程控制、通信娱乐等；便民生活服务包括电子政务、电子商务、收费交易、医疗健康、邻里社交等。智慧社区以整合资源为手段，并通过大数据分析用户行为，最终实现提升用户体验。

5 月 22 日，京东在美国纳斯达克挂牌上市。9 月 20 日，阿里巴巴在美国纽约证券交易所挂牌上市。阿里巴巴和京东上市体现了中国电子商务的影响力，也标志着我国电子商务进入了一个新的阶段。2014 年“双十一”天猫交易量达到 571 亿元，相比 2013 年的 350 亿元增长 63.14%，反映我国电子商务快速发展。顺丰快递 2014 年正式在全国铺开名为“嘿客”的网购服务社区店，通过整合渠道资源，为顾客提供更灵活、更便捷、更智能化的线下社区服务体验，服务包括快递物流、虚拟购物、ATM、冷链物流、团购预售、试衣间、洗衣、家电维修等多项业务，店内的海报、二维码墙放置虚拟商品，可以通过手机扫码、店内下单购买，除试穿试用的样品外，店内不设库存。首批共 518 家，步入火热的 O2O（从线上到线下）市场，这一模式将对国内电商格局产生较大影响。

2014 年，从事社区便民服务的拉卡拉，将 O2O 商务模式与社区销售渠道有机结合，社区便利店的店主可以通过加盟拉卡拉、安装“开店宝”终端的方式开展电子商务，依托拉卡拉“开店宝”电子商务平台、社区通便民金融服务平台的软硬件设备，构建“拉卡拉小店”。拉卡拉已和中粮、国美等平台商和福临门、金龙鱼等品牌商建立合作关系，基于“B2b2c”的物流配送系统使供应商、物流公司、便利店、社区居民环环相扣，保证高效、低成本的配送，解决“最后一公里”问题。显然，社区电商成为 2014 年电子商务 O2O 模式发展的新趋势。

六、结语

2014 年，伴随着移动通信、智能终端、物联网、云计算、大数据、导航与位置服务等技术的发展与应用，智慧城市作为城市信息化的新阶段正在全国迅速发展，一大批智慧城市试点、规划、建设工作正在稳步推进，一些示范性应用成果已经发挥作用。它与国家的多项政策支撑密不可分，特别是《国家新型城镇化规划（2014-2020 年)》、《关于加快实施信息惠民工程有关工作的通知》、《关于智慧城市建设健康发展指导意见》、《关于加强城市地下管线建设管理的指导意见》和《关于创新重点领域投融资机制鼓励社会投资的指导意见》等。当然，网络安全及信息管理是涉及国家安全的大事，必须高度重视。

“多规合一”、“不动产统一登记”、“智慧社区”建设等众多城市管理服务业务的信息化，可以纳入智慧城市的典型应用的范畴。“多规合一”主要解决城市的规划问题，不动产统一登记是城市建设项目管理的最后一个环节，建设项目管理涉及规划选址、土地供应、规划审批、建设工程监管、项目验收、不动产登记等环节，实现这些环节的多部门协同，是政务信息化必须解决的关键问题；而智慧社区则是主要解决城市居民享用城市信息化的成果。

可以预期，当城市规划、建设与运行三大核心业务过程通过数字化、智能化手段实现协同，将使城市基础设施管理与维护进入信息化新时代，将智慧化贯通城市规划、建设、运行及其管理和服务的方方面面，使政府、企业、公众都能从中受益，真正实现智慧生活和智慧工作。

（作者：党安荣，清华大学建筑学院教授；王丹，建设综合勘察研究设计院有限公司研究员；梁军，北京超图软件股份有限公司总工程师、教授级高工；何建邦，国际欧亚科学院院士，中国科学院地理科学与资源研究所研究员）

论坛篇

气候变化对我国沿海城市安全的影响分析

一、引言

我国是个海洋大国，也是海岸线最长的国家之一，海域面积约470万平方公里，属我国管辖的约300万平方公里；大陆岸线全长18000多公里，岛屿岸线14000多公里。我国沿海地区是人口密集、经济发达的重要地区，涉及9省2个直辖市2个特别行政区（台湾未计入），下属52个沿海城市（香港特别行政区、澳门特别行政区未计入），200余个沿海区县[1]。沿海地区土地面积占全国的13.6%，人口占全国的43.8%，GDP占全国的60.1%[2]。沿海地区不仅布局了核电站等许多重大工程，还形成了环渤海、长江三角洲、东南沿海、珠江三角洲和西南沿海五大规模化港口群，是运输关系国计民生的煤炭、石油、铁矿石和集装箱等大宗货物的枢纽。

在快速推进城镇化和土地资源紧缺的大背景下，我国“面朝大海”的发展战略与格局趋于明显，并呈现出“区域发展沿海化”和“沿海城市临海化”的趋势[3,4]。但是，全球气候变暖和海平面上升，则有可能破坏海岸带生态系统，并威胁沿海城市及其设施安全。沿海城市“向海”发展的趋势必将与海平面上升发生冲突，因此，迫切需要针对未来气候变化对我国沿海城市可能造成的影响进行分析与预估，并提出相应的应对策略。

二、气候变化对海岸带的影响及其机理

全球变暖导致了海平面上升，加剧了风暴潮灾害、海岸侵蚀、咸潮入侵、海水入侵和土壤盐渍化等，破坏海岸带生态系统，威胁沿海基础设施安全，影响人们正常的生产和生活。全球变暖对沿海城市的影响的逻辑关系如图1所示。

全球气候变化最直接的影响是海平面上升。政府间气候变化专门委员会（Intergovernmental Panel on Climate Change，IPCC）第五次评估第一工作组的最新报告对全球海平面的历史数据进行了系统的回顾。报告表明，从1880年以来海平面基本上呈上升趋势，并且近年来上升的速度在加快。从1901年到2010年，全球平均海平面上升了0.19（0.17~0.21）m，平均每年上升1.7（1.5~1.9）mm。根据卫星数据观测，1993-2012年间平均速

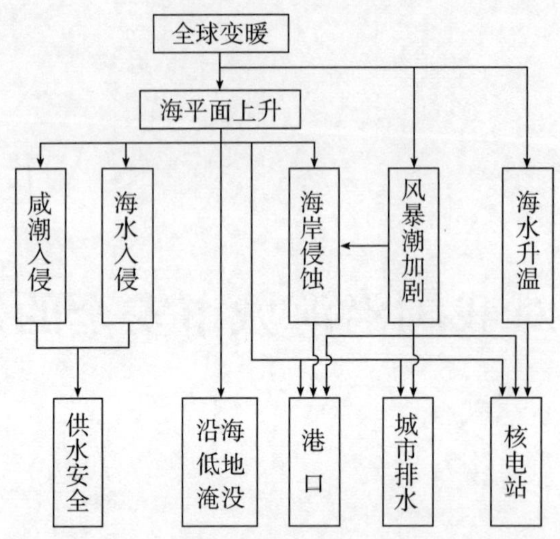

图1 全球变暖对沿海城市的影响的逻辑关系图

度则达到每年3.2mm[5]。据国家海洋局《2013年中国海平面公报》，1980-2013年，我国沿海海平面总体呈波动上升趋势，平均上升速率为2.9mm/年。2012年海平面为1980年以来最高位。2013年，我国沿海海平面为1980年以来的第二高位，较1975-1993年的平均值偏高95mm，较2012年偏低27mm[6]。

气候变化还会引发或加剧如下海洋灾害：①风暴潮。全球变暖将导致风暴潮、浪潮等海洋灾害的强度和频度逐步提高[7]。与海平面上升的影响相叠加，将极大增加风暴潮灾害的破坏性。②海岸侵蚀。随着海平面上升，海水向陆地入侵导致岸线后退、沿海平原低地的淹没和沼泽化，使近岸波浪作用增强。加之风暴潮强度和频度的增加，海岸侵蚀将会加剧。[7]③咸潮入侵。气候变化引起的降水异常、生产生活用水量的迅速增长以及跨流域调水会使入海径流减少，降低抵御咸潮入侵的能力。海平面上升将使河口盐水楔上溯，加剧咸潮入侵[7]，增加河口地区供水困难，对城市供水安全产生威胁。④海水入侵。沿海地区由于过量开采地下水，地下水位不断下降，低于海平面，使海水入渗至地下水。海平面上升会加重海水入侵和地下水盐渍化，影响人畜饮用水和生产用水，造成良田荒芜。[7]

三、气候变化对沿海城市的影响预估

（一）海平面上升预估

IPCC第五次综合报告预估，以1986-2005年统计数据为标准，2016-2035年全球平均气温很有可能上升0.3℃~0.7℃，2081-2100年全球平均气温很有可能上升0.3℃~4.8℃；2081-2100年全球平均海平面很有可能上升26~82cm[5]。

根据我国科学家的预估，到2050年和2100年，我国的平均气温将分别上升2.3℃~3.3℃和3.9℃~6.0℃，高于全球平均水平[8]；未来我国沿海海平面上升值的区域差异很大，相对于1990年，2050年将上升25～61 cm[9]~[11]，上升幅度最大的为长江三角洲和珠江三角洲，未来100年海平面上升最大值可能达到100 cm[7]。

（二）气候变化对沿海地区淹没影响

我国沿海地区的三大主要脆弱区，即珠江三角洲地区、长江三角洲及江苏和浙北沿岸地区、黄河三角洲及渤海湾和莱州湾地区，将承受着海平面上升的严重威胁。海堤虽然能对沿海低地进行一定程度的保护，但仍无法适应未来海平面上升所带来的威胁。在相关的沿海淹没面积估算[12]的基础上，测算出：到2050年，在我国平均海平面上升35cm、65cm、100cm的情景下，当百年一遇的高潮位出现时，三大脆弱区的淹没损失分别为5.3万亿元、17.3万亿元、30.8万亿元。在2050年海平面上升100cm的情景下，三大脆弱区的淹没损失相当于2010年全国GDP（40.15万亿元）的3/4。

如果在预估的情景中考虑到我国不同区域海平面上升的差异性，则当出现百年一遇的高潮位时，中国沿海2050年的可能淹没面积是9.83万km^2，约占国土总面积的1.02%，约占沿海地区面积的7.5%；2080年可能淹没面积10.49万km^2，约占国土总面积的1.09%，约占沿海地区面积的8.0%。其中三大主要脆弱区，2050年的可能淹没面积8.45万km^2，占中国沿海总淹没面积的86.0%，2080年的可能淹没面积9.02万km^2，占中国沿海总淹没面积的85.9%[13]。在此基础上，测算出三大主要脆弱区2050年的淹没损失为30.9万亿元（2010年价），2080年的淹没损失为68.6万亿元（2010年价），分别相当于2010年全国GDP的3/4和1.7倍。

随着沿海地区入海发展态势的继续，围海造田面积会不断增加，有可能淹没的国土面积将更大。由于沿海城市发展的临海化，经济重心将进一步向临海区域倾斜，有可能遭受的灾害和损失将更为巨大。围填海土地的地面相对松软，易发生地面沉降；大规模填海区也往往受经济成本所限，一再降低地面高程，增加了遭受灾害的风险。限于人类对自然的认知水平以及工程措施的局限性，再坚固的海堤在遭遇极端海洋灾害事件时也未必是万无一失，一旦海堤失守，后果将不堪设想。

（三）对沿海城市排水的影响

沿海城市由于地势和海潮的影响，特别容易遭受城市内涝的袭扰。在全球气候变化的背景下，城市降雨发生改变，尤其是可能导致的短历时强降雨的增加，与沿海风暴潮频率与强度的增加相叠加，将导致城市内涝灾害的发生更加频繁，强度更大。此外，当海平面上升之后，高潮潮位增高，由于下游水位顶托，沿海城市管网和泵站的排水能力将会被削弱，原有设计标准将降低，城市排水的难度将进一步加大。尤其当强降雨、强风暴潮和高潮位顶托三种因素同时叠加时，将会急剧地加大城市排水的压力，造成排水不畅，甚至是海水、河水倒灌，从而加剧城市内涝。

我国大部分入海河口（长江、珠江等大河除外）兴建了涵闸工程，这些工程一般都具有挡潮、排涝与蓄淡灌溉等综合功效。海平面上升，闸下潮位抬高，潮流顶托作用加强，将导致涵闸自然排水历时缩短、排水能力下降。我国很多沿海地区的城市雨水排除都是依靠泵排，海平面升高和城市降雨的增加，将使得泵的扬程需要增加，泵的设计流量也需要增大，会给社会经济发展带来一定的压力。

如果未来海平面上升50cm，上海市区的排水能力将被削弱20%，对上海市构成较大的威胁[11]；珠江三角洲的机电排水装机容量将至少增加15% ~20%，才能保证现有低洼地排涝标准不降低[14]；苏北滨海平原四个主要排水闸的一潮排水历时将平均缩短15% ~19%，一潮排水总量平均下降20% ~30%[15]。

（四）对沿海港口的影响

我国沿海的长江三角洲港口群、珠江三角洲港口群和环渤海地区港口群都位于主要的海平面上升影响的脆弱区内，因此，上述港口群势必受到海平面上升的影响。由于高程设计标准未考虑气候变化因素，海平面上升将影响某些港口的适航性。很多港口都处于极高的洪水风险区，这些港口往往都是在当地经济中占有重要分量的。随着气候变化，这些港口暴露于洪水中的风险将会进一步加剧。[16]

研究表明，海平面上升30cm，燕尾港、新洋港、大洋港百年一遇的风暴潮位将变为不到50年一遇；海平面上升53cm，小洋口百年一遇的风暴潮位也将变为50年一遇[17]。海平面升高抬升了风暴增水的基础水位，高潮位相应提高，风暴潮致灾程度加大。这些影响将破坏港口码头建筑物、防波堤、码头仓库、船舶和货物以及桥梁和港口集疏运通道等设施。

海平面上升破坏海岸区侵蚀堆积的动态平衡，改变海岸附近沙堆的分布，或导致泥沙的堆积逐渐占优，引起航道淤塞，使海港水深降低，妨碍其功能的正常发挥，甚至使其报废[18]。此外，气候变化引起的强风、强降水、高温、雷电等极端事件增加，也将对港口的正常运营产生较大的负面影响。

四、应对气候变化的策略建议

（一）总体应对策略

总体上，沿海地区应加强气候变化和海平面上升的影响评估和脆弱性区划，实施海岸防护、生态保育与适度开发并重策略。对于已开发利用区域，根据社会经济发展程度，采取防护、后退和顺应等适应性措施，并应以防护为主。对于未开发利用区域，应在风险评估的基础上，进行适度的开发与合理的避让。在保存相对较好的自然岸段和重要生态保护区海岸的滨海地区，合理布局，预留滨海生态系统后退空间，实现人与自然的和谐统一。

（二）加强海岸带规划与管理

在大力发展海洋经济的过程中，应通过加强海岸带的规划与管理，强化规划对海岸带开发活动的空间管控，使得沿海城市发展朝着正确的空间发展方向，控制向海洋发展的合理规模，形成合理的产业结构布局，实现科学、有序的发展。

应避免“过度临海化”和“过度工程化”的倾向。目前，我国沿海经济区对海平面上升问题的认识仍显不足，以经济利益为单一价值取向，过度侵占海岸空间，沿海生态控制退线不足等现象屡见不鲜。

目前，我国海岸带的管理主体众多，涉及国土部门、海洋部门、发改部门等，分头管理机制在应对全球气候变化导致的海洋灾害时显得应对不足。建议在宏观层面进行各部门间的协调，加强海岸带的规划与管理，以统一协调和管理海岸带开发建设、生态保护与应对自然灾害能力建设，引导沿海重点经济战略地区的永续发展，并保持长久竞争优势。

（三）沿海城市应对措施

1. 完善和提高海岸防护工程标准，包括海堤工程标准和沿海防护林标准

目前，我国海堤的设计标准相对较低，难以应对未来气候变化背景下海平面上升的挑战。建议针对我国海堤的现状，根据对未来全球气候变化及海平面上升的形势判断，结合社会经济发展状况，对现行海堤设计标准进行适当修订，重新确定海堤等级及划分依据，尤其对高风险的脆弱地区应大幅提高建设标准，以提高海堤防潮抗浪能力，有效应对气候变化。

针对沿海地区盐碱地、海岛等地区造林成本高、维护难度大等实际情况，以及低效防护林改造、红树木引种驯化、重大病虫害防治、高效防护林体系配置、滨海湿地恢复技术等问题，加强有关沿海防护林体系设计、建设、保护、监管等方面的标准制定，以降低防护林建设成本，提高防护林质量，充分发挥其应对海平面上升的重要作用。[7]

2. 加强海岸带和沿海地区的防护体系建设，包括堤坝防护工程和生物防护工程

加强沿海地区堤防建设。加高加固沿海大堤，使其能抵御海平面上升及风暴潮增水和波浪爬高的侵袭。在沿海平原地区，特别是河口三角洲地带，建设永久性的重大工程时还应提高其建筑基面，以免未来海平面上升被淹没。在城市地面沉降地区应建立高标准防洪、防潮墙和堤岸，并在需要的位置新建达标海堤，形成完善的工程体系。加高加固下游河口段标准较低的河堤，以防止未来受上升的海平面与高潮和风暴潮顶托而发生洪涝灾害。大力建设生态型海堤，以减少因海堤中断海陆水循环所带来的湿地退化、栖息地消失等生态环境问题。[7]

加强生物防护工程建设。充分发挥生物防护工程的自组织、费用低、使用寿命长等优势，积极建设和保护生物防护工程。鼓励植树造林，禁止砍伐原始林或次生林改种经济林，以有效保护海洋生态环境、涵养水源、保持水土、净化水质。沿岸一定范围内的林木或是水源涵养林，应当划为公益林，不得随意采伐。[7]通过推动沿海生物防护工程的建设，与沿海堤坝防护工程体系互补，构建坚固的海防线，保障人民的生命财产安全。

3. 加强地面沉降防治

对城市的产业结构布局及社会经济发展进行科学的规划，提高水资源的利用效率，以减少对水资源尤其是地下水资源的需求量。不断完善地下水资源的经济和政策管理体系，做好地下水资源的综合开发和利用，防止由于地下水的过量开采而导致地面过快沉降。

合理规划城市布局，控制地面沉降。减少在软土层、古河道、古海滩、工矿采空区和断裂带上建设重大工程项目，不允许布置密集的城市建筑，必要时打深桩加固地基，减缓地面沉降程度。在矿石采空区做好善后工作，用土石填埋或者加设支撑物，避免地面塌陷。在有条件的地方，对地下水进行合理的人工回灌，修复或防止地面沉降。[7]

4. 加强城市洪涝防治

在沿海城市的规划中，考虑气候变化和海平面上升因素，进行洪水风险评估，绘制洪水风险图。基于洪水风险评估和洪水风险图，在沿海地区开发建设时进行合理的避让，在城市规划中合理地进行场地和道路竖向设计。改造城市排水系统，对低洼地区进行整治和改造，提高城市抵御内涝的能力。推行低影响开发（LID）模式，在源头上削减降雨形成的地表径流，减小气候变化和海平面上升带来的城市内涝叠加效应。修建各类调蓄设施，增加对城市雨洪的调蓄能力。考虑气候变化和海平面上升因素，提高挡潮闸的建设标准和设计工程水位，提高沿海、沿江排水泵站的抽排水能力。

5. 建设监测预警体系

完善全国的海平面上升监测网络，加强和改善观测设施，改进观测方法，提高技术水平和观测精度，取得长时间序列的观测资料。监测内容包括沿海的海平面变化、地面垂直升降，以及海洋水文、湿滩湿地、海岸侵蚀、地下水位、咸潮入侵、海水入侵、土地盐渍化等。[7]

加强海洋灾害的监测预警，完善全国海岸带和相关海域的海洋灾害监测预警系统，构筑统一的信息平台，重点加强风暴潮、海浪、海冰、咸潮、海岸带侵蚀等海洋灾害的立体化监测和预报预警能力，强化应急响应服务能力。[19]

五、结论

本文分析了气候变化对海岸带的可能影响及其机理，并对未来气候变化对我国沿海城市将产生的影响进行了预估，最后提出一系列的应对策略与措施。主要结论如下：

（1）根据相关预测，2050 年、2100 年，我国的平均气温将上升 2.3℃ ~3.3℃ 和 3.9℃ ~6.0℃；未来我国沿海海平面上升值的区域差异很大，2050 年将上升 25 ~61cm，上升幅度最大的为长江三角洲和珠江三角洲，未来 100 年海平面上升最大值可能达 100cm。

（2）全球变暖将导致风暴潮、浪潮等海洋灾害的强度和频度逐步提高，与海平面上升的影响相叠加，将极大增加风暴潮灾害的破坏性。全球变暖和海平面上升还将加剧海岸侵蚀、咸潮入侵和海水入侵，威胁城市的供水安全。

（3）海平面上升对沿海城市最直接、最严重的影响是淹没沿海低地。我国沿海地区的三大主要脆弱区，为珠江三角洲地区、长江三角洲及江苏和浙北沿岸地区、黄河三角洲及渤海湾和莱州湾地区。预计当出现百年一遇的高潮位时，我国沿海 2050 年、2080 年的可能淹没面积分别占国土总面积的 1.02% 和 1.09%，占沿海地区面积的 7.5% 和 8.0%。三大主要脆弱区，2050 年、2080 年的可能淹没损失分别相当于 2010 年全国 GDP 的 3/4 和 1.7 倍。

(4) 全球气候变化对沿海城市的其他主要影响：城市内涝灾害的发生将加剧；现有港口的适航性将受到影响，暴露于洪水中的风险将加剧，航道可能因海岸侵蚀加剧而淤塞，甚至报废。

(5) 总体上，沿海地区应加强气候变化和海平面上升的影响评估和脆弱区划，实施海岸防护、生态保育与适度开发并重策略。通过加强海岸带规划与管理，强化规划对海岸带开发活动的空间管控，避免“过度临海化”和“过度工程化”的倾向。

(6) 建议沿海城市采取如下的应对措施：完善和提高海岸防护工程标准；加强海岸防护体系建设，包括海堤防护工程和生物防护工程建设；加强地面沉降防治；加强城市洪涝防治；加强监测预警体系建设。

(7) 建议港口等重点沿海工程采取如下的应对措施：对于现有工程，进行脆弱性分析和风险评估，提高防护的设计标准，并按标准进行加固。对于新建工程，除按修订后的设计标准进行修建外，首先应在选址上尽量避开海岸带的脆弱区和高风险区。

(8) 关于气候变化对沿海城市的影响，我国学术界未来可在气候变化的不确定性（包括模型的不确定性和观测的不确定性）及社会经济成本效益分析等方面作进一步的深入研究。

（作者：邹德慈，中国工程院院士；邵益生，中国城市规划设计研究院研究员，国际欧亚科学院院士；徐一剑，中国城市规划设计研究院副研究员）

参考文献

[1] 国家海洋局．中国海洋统计年鉴 2011 [M]．北京：海洋出版社，2012.

[2] 国家统计局．中国统计年鉴 2011 [M]．北京：中国统计出版社，2011.

[3] 邵益生，张泉．江苏沿海地区综合开发战略研究——城镇卷：江苏沿海地区城镇发展与空间布局研究 [M]．南京：江苏人民出版社，2008.

[4] 邵益生．浙江沿海及海岛综合开发战略研究——城镇卷：浙江沿海及海岛地区城镇发展与空间布局研究 [M]．杭州：浙江人民出版社，2012.

[5] Church，J. A.，P. U. Clark，A. Cazenave，J. M. Gregory，S. Jevrejeva，A. Levermann，M. A. Merrifield，G. A. Milne，R. S. Nerem，P. D. Nunn，A. J. Payne，W. T. Pfeffer，D. Stammer and A. S. Unnikrishnan，2013：Sea Level Change. In：Climate Change 2013：The Physical Science Basis. Contribution of Working Group I to the Fifth Assessment Report of the Intergovernmental Panel on Climate Change [Stocker，T. F.，D. Qin，G. - K. Plattner，M. Tignor，S. K. Allen，J. Boschung，A. Nauels，Y. Xia，V. Bex and P. M. Midgley (eds.)]. Cambridge University Press，Cambridge，United Kingdom and New York，NY，USA.

[6] 国家海洋局．中国海平面公报 [M]．北京：海洋出版社，2013.

[7] 秦大河，丁永建，穆穆，等．中国气候与环境演变（第二卷）：影响与脆弱性 [M]．北京：气象出版社，2012.

[8] 秦大河，丁一汇，苏纪兰，等．中国气候与环境演变（上卷）：气候与环境的演变及预测 [M]．北京：科学出版社，2005.

[9] 黄镇国，谢先德．广东海平面变化及其影响与对策［M］．广州：广东科技出版社，2000.

[10] 刘杜鹃．相对海平面上升对中国沿海地区的可能影响［J］．海洋预报，2004，21（2）：21-28.

[11] 施雅风，朱季文，谢志仁，等．长江三角洲及毗连地区海平面上升影响预测与防治对策［J］．中国科学（D辑），2000，30（37）：225-232.

[12] 杜碧兰，田素珍，沈文周，等．海平面上升对中国沿海主要脆弱区潜在影响的研究//杜碧兰．海平面上升对中国沿海主要脆弱区的影响及对策．北京：海洋出版社，1997.

[13] Yang Y Q，Zuo J C，et al. 2012. Cost-benefit Analysis of Adaptation to Sea Level Rise in Major Vulnerable Regions along the Coast of China. ISOPE-2012 conference. RHODES，Greece，1522-1528.

[14] 范锦春．海平面上升对珠江三角洲水环境的影响// 海平面上升对中国三角洲地区的影响及对策．北京：科学出版社，1994：194-201.

[15] 都金康，史运良．未来海平面上升对江苏沿海水利工程的影响［J］．海洋与湖沼，1993，24（3）：279-285.

[16] 吴喜德，纪龙．关于气候变化对我国港口影响及应对措施的探讨［J］．中国水运，2013，13（10）：116-119.

[17] 李加林，王艳红，张忍顺等．海平面上升的灾害效应研究——以江苏沿海低地为例［J］．地理科学，2006，26（1）：87-93.

[18] 董锁成，陶澍，杨旺舟，等．气候变化对中国沿海地区城市群的影响［J］．气候变化研究进展，2010，6（4）：284-289.

[19]《第二次气候变化国家评估报告》编写委员会．第二次气候变化国家评估报告［R］．北京：科学出版社，2011.

广州南沙区域规划

南沙地区位于广州的东南部，地处珠江出海口，是广州—香港—澳门“A”字形结构的顶端，也是连接珠江两岸城市群的通道，区位优势明显（见图1）。21世纪初，广州市政府编制南沙地区规划并按规划进行建设。在南沙地区构建广州市的临海新城区使广州从传统的沿江城市变成临海城市；南沙新港区改变了历史悠久的广州黄埔港的港口布局，从内河港变为现代海港，再进而利用这两者的潜能和优势建立一个临海工业区，将重构广州及珠江三角洲的产业布局，提升珠江三角洲地区整体竞争力。南沙规划建设是广州近百年来城市转型与重构的重要内容之一。

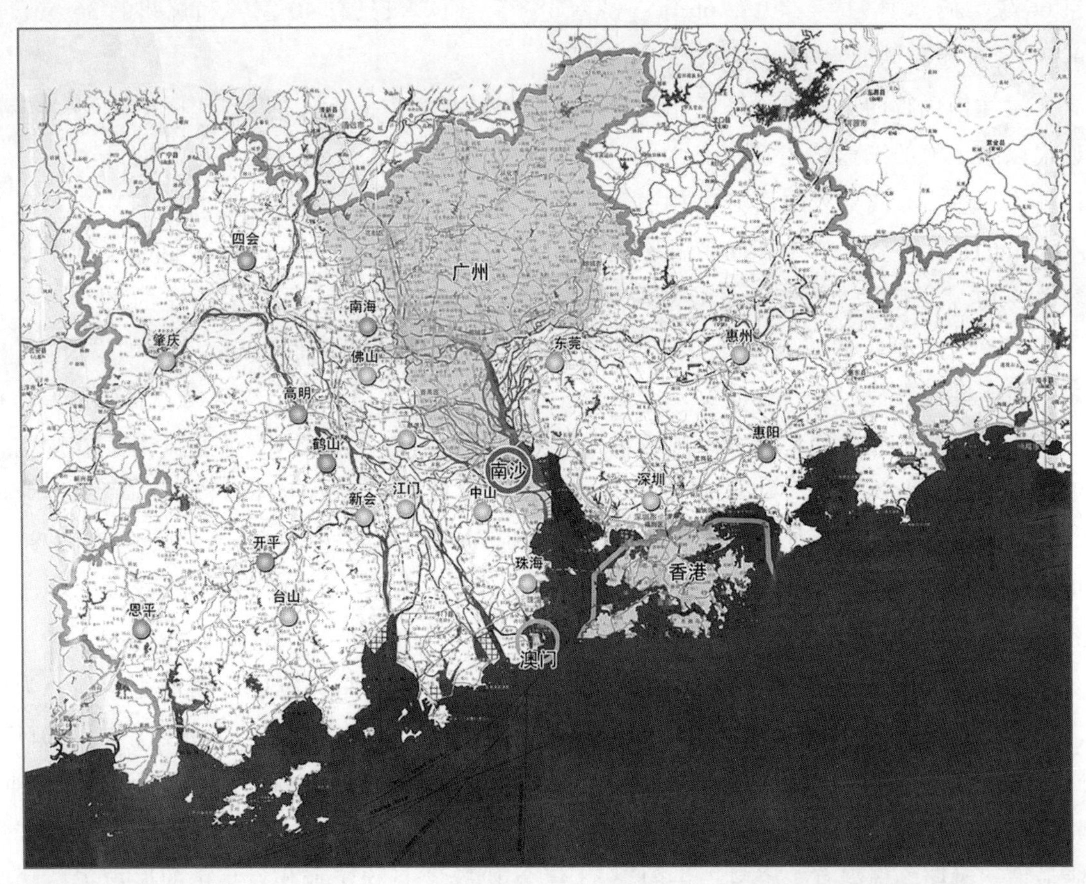

图1　南沙地区位置图

一、南沙规划建设的动因

四个概念促使广州市委、市政府在世纪之交对南沙进行大规模规划建设。

(一) 构建现代产业中心

近代“五口通商”后，相对于历史的辉煌，广州相当长一段时间一直不温不火，究其深层次原因有三：一是交通运输条件不便，经济腹地有限，使广州在“多口竞争”中处于不利地位；二是未能完成商贸定城向工商定城转化，未建立起与城市规模相适应的制造业基地，形成现代产业中心；三是社会的动乱不安改变了广州的贸易环境，迫使广州外贸、商业、航运业、金融业等向外转移。

中国的门户开放之后，“进口替代”成为工业投资的第一推动力。最初的产品是面粉、棉纺织品、火柴、卷烟、肥皂等生活用品，接着是橡胶、毛纺织品、水泥、电灯电器、化妆品，然后是化工原料、无线电、电机、铅笔、金笔等制造业。既然是“进口替代”，选择什么地方投资跟该地方的经济腹地、市场及流通条件就有极大关系。在对1895-1927年中国44个城市近代工业统计表中统计可知，近代工业企业上海537家、天津94家、武汉133家、北京66家、哈尔滨71家、无锡66家、济南48家，而广州只有40家，和杭州的36家、重庆的35家处于相同的水平[1]。

上海凭借优越的工业投资环境在开埠之后不久就成为中国近代的工业中心。不少学者认为近代以来上海的工业是建筑在三大强有力支柱之上的。所谓“三大支柱”是指：一是政治杠杆作用；二是工业发展所必需的各种要素（资金、原料、劳动力）之汇流；三是科学技术力量的强大优势。有个别学者甚至将“租界”这一鸦片战争及战后签订一系列不平等条约的产物，也视为“奇特的缩微型地球村”，在上海“营造了一个国际化的工业投资市场”，“相对安全稳定的城市社会环境”和广袤的经济腹地推进着上海近代工业的发展[2]。

相对于国内其他门户开放城市，工业企业在广州一直没有很突出的地位，也就是说，在近代，广州始终未能建立起与城市规模相适应的制造业基地，形成现代产业中心。在中国初始工业化时期，新式工厂开始在广州出现，但没有形成像上海、天津、汉口一样的产业中心。相反，甲午战争后，外国资本主义更进一步加强对广州以外贸投资为重点的经济渗透。1895-1991年间，在广州沙面开设的较有名望的洋行有13家，号称外资十三行（有别于鸦片战争前的华资十三行）。外资一如既往想延续发挥广州商贸业的“长处”。

20世纪30年代，陈济棠主政广东，提倡兴办工业，以广东具有优势的产业制糖业为中心，大力发展各项投资少、见效快的中小型“省营”工业，在珠江三角洲建了一批糖厂，在广州的西村、河南开辟了两个工业区，初步建立了以制糖业为中心，纺织、水泥、造纸、橡胶、化工等几个行业同时发展的工业化格局。这一时期，是中华人民共和国建立之前广州工业最发达时期。根据有关资料提供的1933年全国12个近代工业相对集中的城市工厂状况的统计，广州有工厂1104家，工人32131人，工厂资本32131千元，生产净值101569千元，资本和生产净值均次于上海居第2位[3]。但这样的辉煌时期没能保持多久，因为除了少数"省营"工厂稍具规模外，多数工厂依然是从属于进出口贸易的加工型小企业，他们的命运取决于进出口贸易的兴衰。30年代受世界经济危机影响，一下子几十家丝厂就倒闭了。其他生活消费品和生产资料像水泥、橡胶这些企业，因销售市场狭小，加上洋货竞争，也一步步走向衰落，终成不了气候，无法在广州形成现代产业中心。

构建广州现代产业中心，特别是南沙地区的重化工业基地，关系到整个珠江三角洲的竞争力。米高·因莱特（Michale J. Enright）在《香港与珠江三角洲经济互动》一书中有这么一些话："在历史上，与中国的其他地区相比，珠江三角洲地区的重工业、机械和化学工业相对落后。""作为一个人口稀少的农业地区，这里几乎没有重工业、机械制造和化工生产。传统上这些工业集中在北方的工业化地区，而且今天它们依然集中在北部地区。""汽车工业的发展和南沙的重工业设施投资计划，将对珠江三角洲地区此类工业的发展产生重要影响。"[4]

（二）构建珠江三角洲的临海工业区

日本战后新兴、新建的大量消耗原料的资源型工业，如炼油、石油化工、钢铁、造船等都分布在东京湾以南的沿海太平洋的带状工业地带上，且都是建造在填海造陆的土地上，形成巨大的临海型工业带。如日本新建的14个大型钢厂都建在临海区，占钢铁总产量的96%，石油化学工业百分之百地建在海岸工业地带的填海造陆区。大工业紧密结合港口布置配以最经济合理的工艺流程，许多工厂的生产流水线都是由船边进料，经过紧凑的自动流水生产线再到船边输出产品，整个生产过程都在港口上完成，使生产和运输融为一体。这就把周转过程减少降低到最低限度，既缩短了生产运转的时间，又节约了用地，具有极高的效率。在构建海岸工业带的同时组建大船队，正是有了庞大的港口群和大船队，使其拥有充分的能力利用世界上最优质最廉价的资源。一变资源贫乏的小国为利用世界资源的第一大国。远洋巨轮运输费用低廉，使工业原料成本大大降低，产品具有很强的竞争力，成为全世界最大的钢铁和其他重化工业产品出品国[5]。

欧洲在"二战"后经济恢复阶段，临港工业区在规模化、集约化方面发挥了重要作用，莱茵河三角洲地区是一个成功的典范。鹿特丹港位于莱茵河下游，从1958年开始，政府将城市建设与发展临海工业结合起来，在港口西部建立了石油化学和造船工业基地。首先在佩尔尼，随后在博特勒克（Botlk）建立新的港口工业带，引导工业从内陆向临港迁移，并于1961年在荷兰湾对岸开辟了可供最大油轮和散货进出的新港，解决了"大进大出"问题。与此同时，阿姆斯特丹、艾默伊登也相应地建立起钢铁联合企业，在荷兰境内完整地构建了以石油化工、钢铁、造船为主导产业的临港工业区。地处荷兰南部的比利时安特卫普也在斯海尔德河右岸建立重化学工业基地。欧洲的其他港口城市，如法国的马赛、西班牙的巴塞罗那、意大利的那不勒斯都利用港口原材料和成品运输成本低的因素建立起自己的临海工业区。

仿照日本和西欧临海工业区的做法，亚洲的韩国后来也在条件良好的临港地带建立工业区，以发展诸如钢铁、造船、石油化工以及汽车等重化工业的生产和出口的蔚山工业区，以钢铁为主的浦项工业区。素有“花园城市”之称的新加坡，在本岛南部7个小群岛上，用人工填海的方式连接成人工岛屿裕廊岛。在距离城市只有10公里的裕廊岛上，建成世界著名的石油化工专业区。2004年，裕廊岛石化工业总产值占新加坡制造业总产值的比例达28%，是全球第三大石油炼制中心，也是全球六大乙烯生产中心之一。

（三）构建现代化的海港

广州作为华南地区的中心城市，在历史上就是著名的港口城市。广州港对促进广州中心城市的形成，对带动广州市经济社会的发展，对扩大广州市的对外开放和我国及世界各地的贸易往来，对推动广州的对外文化交流，都起了十分重要的作用。可以说以港兴城，港以城兴，两千年来港城一直在良性互动，港就是市，市就是港。经济社会发展到今天，广州港面临新的挑战，对于以集装箱船运输为主要方式的现代港口来说，原来的广州港已走到了尽头。黄埔港是一个内河港，航道水深不够，集装箱船进不来，进不来就没有国际航线，成不了国际性的海港，最后的命运就只有萎缩。多年前，交通部的一位领导同志曾对广州市政府领导说过：广州要搞港口就到南沙去，黄埔港没什么前途，泉州港的今天就是黄埔港的明天。

（四）构建现代化的滨海新区

长期以来，受城市发展空间的局限，广州的城市建设呈现了L型摊大饼式的发展，生产力空间布局不够合理和舒展，制约了广州经济社会的发展。

番禺、花都撤县级市建区后，拓宽了生产力发展的空间布局。按照“南拓北优、东进西联”的城市空间发展布局构想，广州将依托南部地区丰富的空间资源，拉开城市建设，开辟新城区，发展新产业。

将南沙建设成为现代化的滨海新区，使广州由沿江城市向滨海新城转变。加快南沙开发建设，可以使广州在更大的空间范围内整合城市经济，优化城市空间结构，纾缓老城区工业布局密度高、配套设施不足、人口密度大、居民居住条件受限制以及交通拥挤等问题，加快建设适宜创业发展和生活居住的现代化中心城市。

二、南沙地区规划的核心是南沙港

20世纪90年代初，省有关部门认为，随着深圳盐田港和珠海高栏港的开发，广州港因为水深自然条件的限制可能没有什么发展前景。1994年，广东省制定《珠江三角洲经济区规划》时，给深圳港和珠海港做了一个很高的年均增长率预测（至2000年深圳港年均增长14%，珠海港年均增长27%），而给广州港做了一个很低的年均增长率预测（至2000年年均增长率2.9%），预测到2000年珠江三角洲港口货物吞吐量将达到3.69亿吨，其中广州港8 000万吨，深圳港6 600万吨，珠海港是5 700万吨；到2010年珠江三角洲港口货物吞吐量将达到 6.36 亿吨，其中广州港 1.2 亿吨、深圳港 1.5 亿吨、珠海港 1.15 亿吨。不甘于这样一种预测发展结果，广州人用自己的努力去改变这种状态。1995 年 6 月 14 日，十届政府第 50 次常务会议，作出了疏深广州港航道的决定。航道疏深改变了 6 年前预测的结果。2000 年广州港货物吞吐量已达到 1.11 亿吨，2001 年达到了 1.28 亿吨，提前 10 年实现了亿吨大港的目标。而深圳港、珠海港分别只有 5 697 万吨和 1 252 万吨。实践证明，广州依然是华南的物流中心。应该指出，港口集装箱吞吐量虽有增长，但没有实质性突破。1996 年 55.7TEU（Transmission Extension Unit，是国际标准箱单位）、1997 年 68.7TEU、1998 年 84.1TEU、1999 年 117.7TEU。因此，为适应现代物流运输发展的需求，广州港的唯一出路是到珠江口去搞深水码头，变内河港为海港；到珠江口去搞南沙港区。广州市政府当时面临两大挑战：其一，工程可行性。因为“小南沙”的概念出现在先，因此，有人把南沙深水港视为“计划动议与建设开工之间间隔短暂，缺乏成本效益分析，似乎不太合逻辑的计划”[4]。其二，政治可行性。为了保证香港国际航运中心的地位，只允许香港人到盐田、到内地其他地方搞集装箱港，而不想让广州建设深水泊位的集装箱码头。已初具规模的盐田港，也不希望珠江口再出现一个竞争对手。

对于工程可行性，一般认为珠江口伶仃洋东侧的大亚湾、大鹏湾和香港九龙的港湾，水深岸陡，是优良的深水港。珠江口伶仃洋西侧到崖门、黄茅海，则为珠江口泥沙大量淤积的海滩，形成大片滩涂。由于潮流和涂流偏西，形成稳定而较强大的西向沿岸流，直至台山、广海一带才稍变疲弱，故水深日渐减少。在这些地方建港，必然淤积得很快，每年峻深花费很大[6]。有研究表明，珠江河口伶仃洋最大混浊带洪季、枯季日平均悬移质泥沙淤积量为 55930 吨和 29047 吨，为了保持广州港航道，伶仃洋西槽每年挖泥量都处在百万立方米级的水平[7]。作为多泥沙港口，必须谨慎勘查，选择优良位置构造新的港湾工程。

中交第四航务工程勘察设计院在珠江口左、右岸线中选择了海鸥岛、南沙岛、龙穴岛围垦区及万顷沙围垦区四段岸线作为比选港址（见图 2）。四个港址按回淤情况看，南沙岛最小，龙穴岛、万顷沙相对较大，但综合各种条件比选，最终还是选择了龙穴岛围垦区。

龙穴岛围垦区陆域主要是 20 世纪 70 年代以来的人工围垦区，现有围垦面积约 47.9 平方公里，北面隔凫洲水道与南沙经济技术开发区相邻，西面隔龙穴南水道与万顷沙围垦区相对，东西隔珠江与东莞、深圳相望。该围垦区具有丰富的可开发利用岸线资源和临海陆域资源，在未来，还可以结合邻近的万顷沙地区进行全面的开发建设，发展潜力难以估量。其地理位置位于虎门以外，离国际主航道最近，离已有一定基础的南沙经济技术开发区也较近。规划时龙穴岛围垦区陆域还未与大陆相连，但规划的南横大桥跨凫洲水道与番禺南沙岛相连将改变这一状态。由于番禺区已形成较完备的路网，龙穴岛与岛外的集疏运条件将得到满足。因此，从各个方面的条件来看，龙穴岛围垦区岸线是建设大型集装箱深水作业区的首选[8]。

龙穴岛港区按起步工程 $-15.5m$ 方案，港池及引航道淤积量约为 $115 \sim 120m^3/a$，这是一个可行的方案。设计单位还收集了国内一些已营运多年的港口的回淤情况对“预可”时数模实验结果进行对比分析。上海外高桥港是上海港集装箱作业区之一，其港池水深

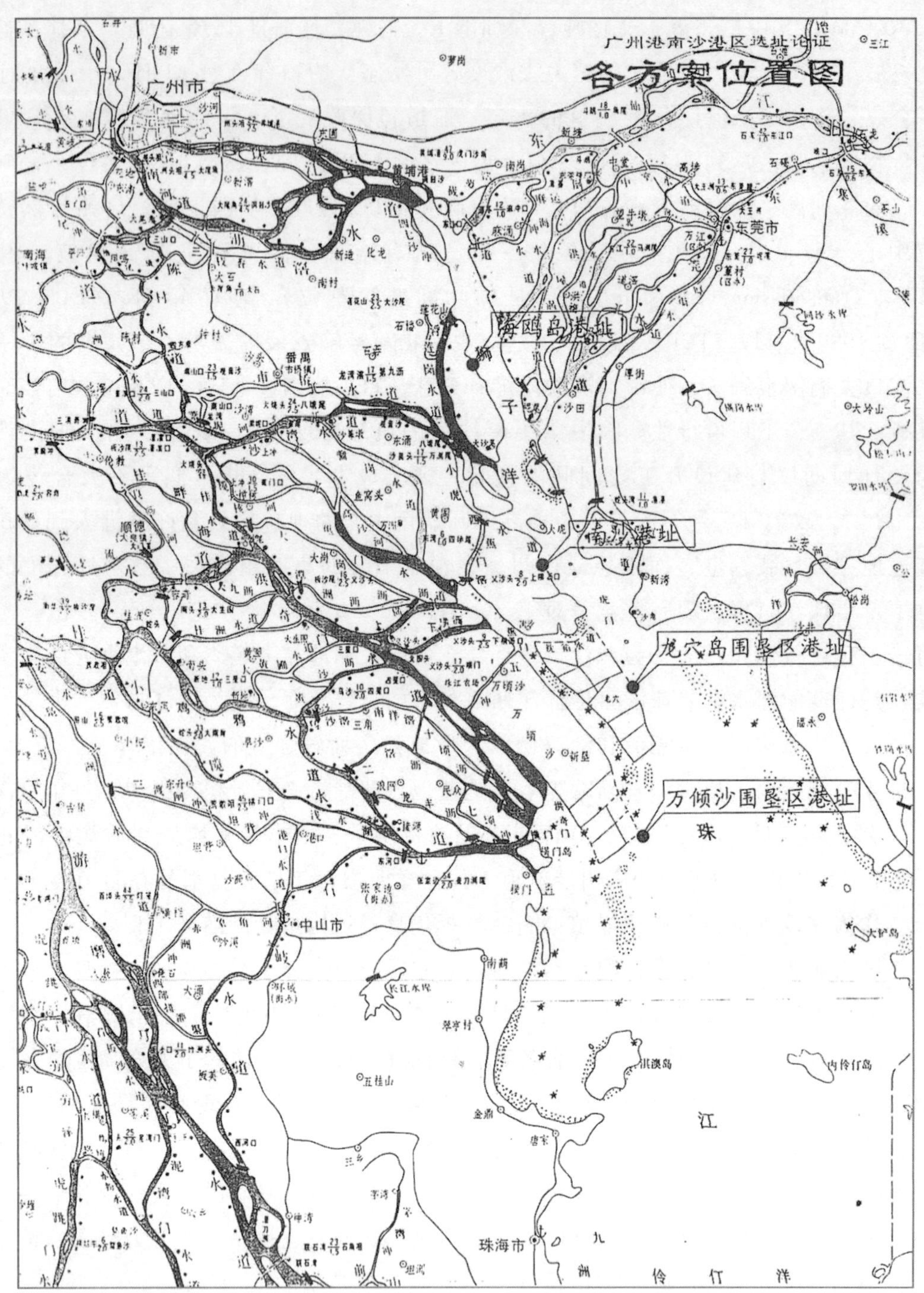

图2 各方案位置图

-12.5m，平均淤强 1.42m/a；广州港新沙一期工程 10 个 3.5 万吨级泊位，港池水深 -10.0m，平均淤强 0.6~0.7m/a。南沙港区淤强和新沙港区同一数量数，比上海外高桥要优。天津港 1959 年只有 9 个万吨级泊位时，其港池水深为 -8.0m~-10.0m，平均淤强 4m/a，但发展到 1996 年，共有 44 个万吨级泊位，港池水深达 -10.0m~-15.0m，此时的平均淤强为 0.93m/a，从天津港的发展过程可以看出，建港初期的回淤强度较大，但随着港口向规模化发展，其回淤强度会逐渐降低，这也与南沙港区起步工程及后期发展阶段的数学模拟结果吻合[9]。

对于政治可行性，主要是阐明南沙港区建设对香港构不成“影响”，只是广州自己发展的需要，其理由是：

（一）广州港的快速发展是全省以及华南地区经济社会发展对增强广州中心城市服务功能提出的客观要求

珠江三角洲港口群吞吐量由1990年的0.47亿吨发展到2000年2.43亿吨，年均增长17.9%。1979-2000年，广州国民生产总值年均增长14.2%，广州总人口不足全省的十分之一，经济总量却占全省的四分之一强，工业增加值超过全省的五分之一，服务业增加值占全省的三分之一，实现税收占了全国的十七分之一。广州作为广东省乃至华南地区的中心城市，随着经济持续快速增长，城市功能不断完善并在逐步增强；以港口城市著称的广州不可能不发展自己的港口。广州港的发展取决于其优越的地理位置，便利的集疏运条件，珠江三角洲经济区的快速发展和良好的港口配套服务能力，这是不以人的意志为转移的客观现实。今后广州港的继续发展仍是大势所趋，它绝不会被其他港口的发展所代替，也不会阻碍其他港口的发展，整个珠江三角洲港口群将继续呈现互相促进、竞相发展的格局。

（二）珠江三角洲地区经济的迅速发展需要珠江口港口群的共同支持

世界经济和港口发展的历史表明，在高度发达的经济区域需要有多个枢纽港共同支持其发展。广东省的经济总量已占全国经济总量的九分之一，经济发展迅速，这种庞大的经济总量产生了巨大的货物运输需求，集装箱运输的增长尤为突出。这是迫使本区域港口群中港口功能转换的客观因素。原来只经香港中转的集装箱转运功能逐步过渡到香港和其他港口共同转运，并朝着多个枢纽港的方向发展，这也是符合经济发展要求和世界港口群发展规律的。

在世界经济全球化的今天，珠江三角洲经济区迫切需要通过降低生产经营成本，提高其国际竞争力。香港的营商成本已成为亚洲地区最昂贵的城市之一，这与降低区域营商成本、发挥区域经济的比较优势、在国际分工中不断提高竞争力的要求是不相适应的。不同功能的港口组成的港口群布局，通过优势互补，在竞争中共同发展，有利于提高本地区的综合竞争力，从而从更高层次上促进香港的繁荣和稳定。

（三）影响香港集装箱运输货运量增长的主要因素不是广州港

集装箱吞吐量：香港从1990年510万TEU发展到2000年1 810万TEU；深圳从1990年3.2万TEU发展到2000年399万TUE，2001年达506万TEU；广州港从1990年11万TEU发展到2000年143万TEU，2001年广州港达到174万TEU，其中内贸为71万TEU，外贸为103万TEU。与1998年（香港回归第一年）相比，广州港内贸箱增长达511%，而外贸箱只增长47%。可见，广州港集装箱运输近几年的增长主要是内贸箱。广州港已逐步发展成为我国最大的内贸集装箱枢纽港。今后随着经济发展和运输方式的变革，预测广州港内贸箱的发展潜力还将不断增大，外贸箱喂给香港也将继续增长，这不但不会对香港国际航运中心的地位造成影响，而且还将对其起到巩固和加强作用。

深圳港的集装箱运输则以外贸远洋航线为主，特别是港商投资经营的盐田港，远洋航班已经发展到每月 197 班，2000 年远洋货运量占外贸集装箱总量的 71%，直接分流了香港的集装箱吞吐量，影响了香港远洋航线运量的增长。

据香港政府 2001 年第二季度统计资料显示，香港海运集装箱量同比下降 4%，而河运量同比增长 10%。这也说明影响香港集装箱运输量的主要因素不是广州港。

（四）广州港南沙港区的建设主要是服务于南沙的开发

加快南沙开发是番禺、花都撤县级市建区后，广州城市布局战略调整的需要，它的开发将有利于解决广州、珠江三角洲乃至广东省近期发展后劲不足的问题，有利于创建和提高广州市和广东省的国际竞争力。

南沙开发建设将从产业发展起步，将作为广州基础产业和原材料工业转移安置的一个临港工业区，加上高新技术产业和港口加工工业，必将产生以原材料、出口加工产品为主的大物流。为物畅其流，促进南沙地区的开发建设，必须加快规划建设交通基础设施，尤其是港口设施，这是南沙开发建设的重要前提，同时对发挥广州中心城市的辐射作用，连接珠江三角洲东西两翼和港澳地区也具有十分的重要意义。现在，珠江下游东岸经济发展比较快，在西岸启动南沙地区的基础设施建设，将会有力带动包括番禺、中山、江门等珠江干流西岸地区的经济发展，并为广东省增创新一轮经济发展的环境新优势打下基础。

（五）选择南沙作为广州港的新港区是在交通部的主持下经过充分论证确定的

2000 年以来，广州市组织全国著名的科研设计单位对广州港南沙港区的开发建设进行了大量的勘察论证，先后 4 次召开了包括中国工程院院士、国家级设计大师参加的专家论证会。经论证认为，选择南沙建港是必要和可行的。

2001 年 8 月，交通部会同广州市人民政府组织召开了南沙港区选址论证会，论证认为：

（1）为了完善珠江三角洲地区港口布局，改善集装箱运输格局，增强港口适应能力，拓展港口发展空间，适应广州市城市产业空间南拓的发展需要，在珠江右岸开辟南沙港区十分必要，是广州市实施城市“南拓”战略的重要举措。（见图 3）

（2）南沙具有较丰富的可供开发利用的港口岸线，港区陆域开阔，可延伸至万顷沙，具备建设集疏运通道和外部配套设施的条件，靠近伶仃洋西航道，离国际航线较近，选择南沙建港是适宜的。

（3）预测的起步工程和远期发展阶段港区泥沙回淤量和回淤强度的数量级基本可信，是可以承受的。建议结合起步工程港池航道的试挖开展泥沙回淤观测研究。

（4）将南沙港区的规划纳入广州港的总体布局规划，结合总体布局规划编制工作，深入论证港区开发的总规模，完善港区功能分工和总平面布置方案。

附图GZHG-10广州港南沙港区规划图
沙仔岛
小虎岛
东
莞
市
N
南沙
大角头岛
川鼻岛
沙角
伶
仃
航
道
万顷沙
横门岛
说明：
1、本图根据交通部安全监督局1997年海测图、当地陆域地形图、和有关规划图绘制；
2、图中尺寸以米计；
3、高程系统从当地理论最低潮面起算。
图例
规划
水域
陆域
现状
在建

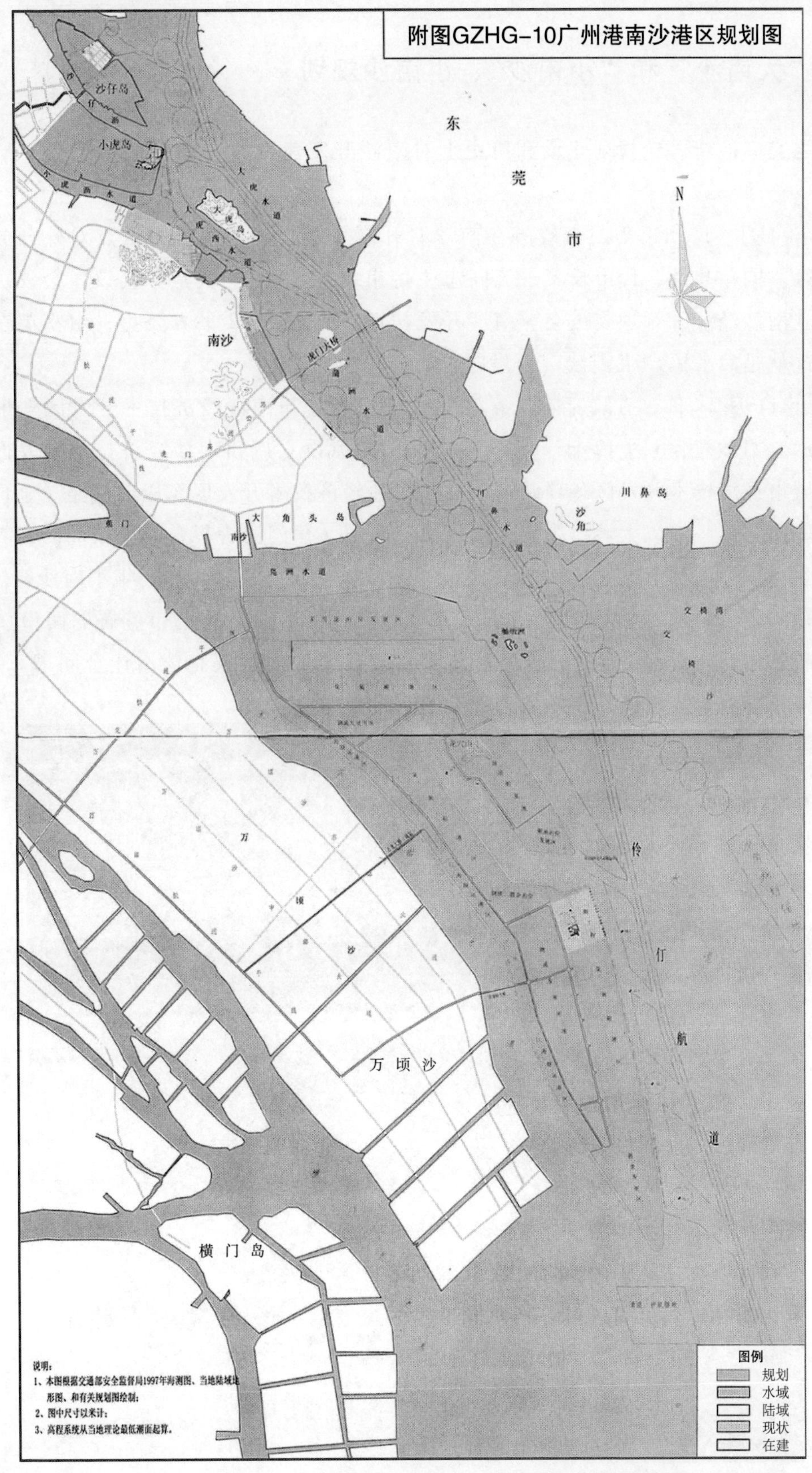

图3　南沙港布局图

三、“大南沙”和“小南沙”、小南沙规划

世纪之交南沙新一轮规划建设和历史上对南沙开发建设的差别在于“大南沙”和“小南沙”。

1990年4月，广州市委、市政府在南沙召开现场会，确定南沙为重点对外开放区域和重点开发区。同年8月，代市长黎子流同志主持市政府九届79次常务会议，会议决定开发南沙，成立南沙经济区管理委员会。南沙开发初期规划面积22平方公里，由霍英东先生投资建设。这就是后来搞“大南沙”开发时称的“小南沙”。

1992年11月21日，省政府向国务院呈报《关于广州南沙经济技术开发区选址和规划面积的请示》，1993年5月12日，国务正式批复同意设立广州南沙经济技术开发区，享受沿海开放城市经济技术开发区各项政策。广州南沙经济技术开发区东以金沙路、金珠路、合成桥、金岭路为界，南以大岭村为界，西以蕉门水道、蕉门河为界，北以小虎沥为界，面积9.9平方公里。同年7月8日，南沙经济技术开发区挂牌。图4为1987年小南沙航摄图。

霍英东基金会根据1991年1月9日及1992年6月28日和番禺市签署的两份《预留土地协议》、1993年5月5日签订的《南沙经济开发区土地使用权有偿出让合同书》，拥有南

图4 1987年小南沙航摄图

沙东部约22平方公里土地的开发权，如图5所示。分界线将小南沙划分为东部和西部，西部占地32平方公里，东部占地22平方公里。

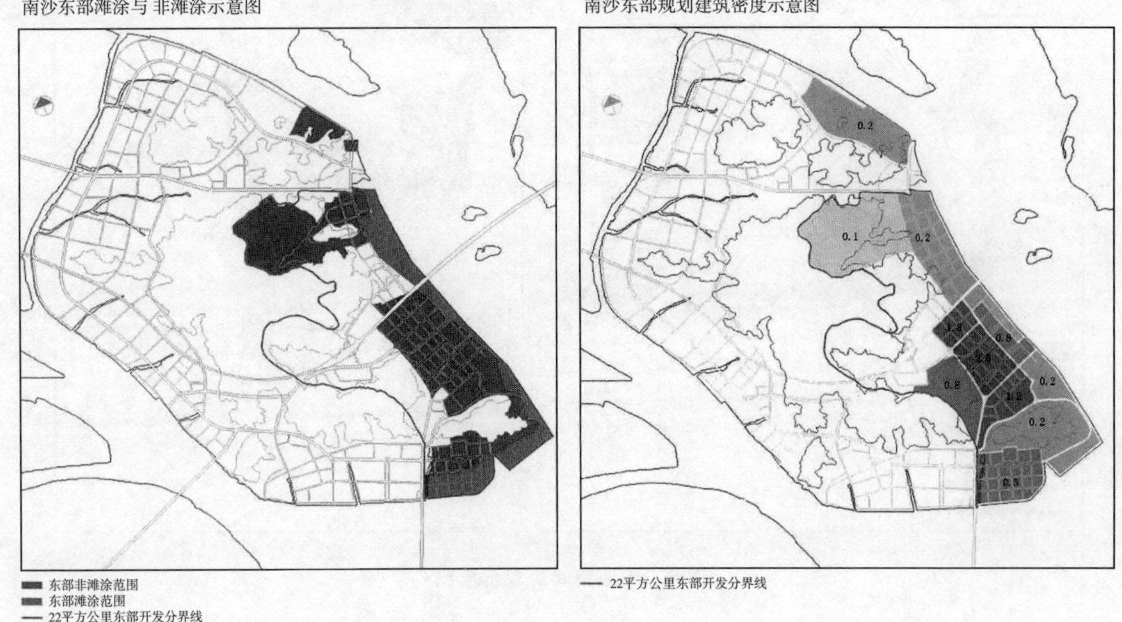

图5　小南沙开发轻度示意图

1993年，西班牙著名建筑规划师里卡多·波菲尔对南沙54平方公里作了初步较为全面规划，提出了《南沙新城总纲图可行性研究》。在此基础上，1997年，南沙经济技术开发区管委会与安徽省城乡规划设计研究院，编制了《广州南沙经济技术开发区总体规划》。霍英东基金会南沙设计部2001年根据以上两份材料，编制了《广州南沙新城东部总体规划·城市设计研究》[10]（以下简称《研究》）。

《研究》按人均建设用地指标120平方米，按环境容量法测算，南沙东部城市人口终极规模为18万人，由于经济技术开发区的特点，总人口其中40%为常住人口，60%为暂住人口或流动人口，流动人口中包括有购置产业和假期来度假的省港澳人士。

总体规划依据地形地貌，规划建设建筑组团和群落布局，尽可能地保留原地段自然风貌和利用良好的景观资源，把自然山、水融于南沙新城之中。同时补充近代园林景点和大面积绿化带。风景优美的海滨大道沿海岸线而建，大道两侧绿化带和棕榈林与商贸中心的现代化高层楼宅相互辉映，营造了南沙海滨新城的形象主题（见图6）。

新城的布局规划，采用中国传统中轴对称和两则平衡的原则，并按此原则指导部分建筑群落的城市设计和建筑设计。

按《研究》规划，新城还将拥有一个大型的多功能城市中心，其中包括由高层商业楼宅组成的商贸中心、五星级酒店、蒲洲商贸购物中心、医院、科学馆和影剧院等文化休闲设施。规划中除已建成的南沙高尔夫球会外，还将建设颇具规模的体育馆（见图7）。

新城规划中的居住小区将坐落在风景优美的地段，为适应不同阶层的需求，营造不同档

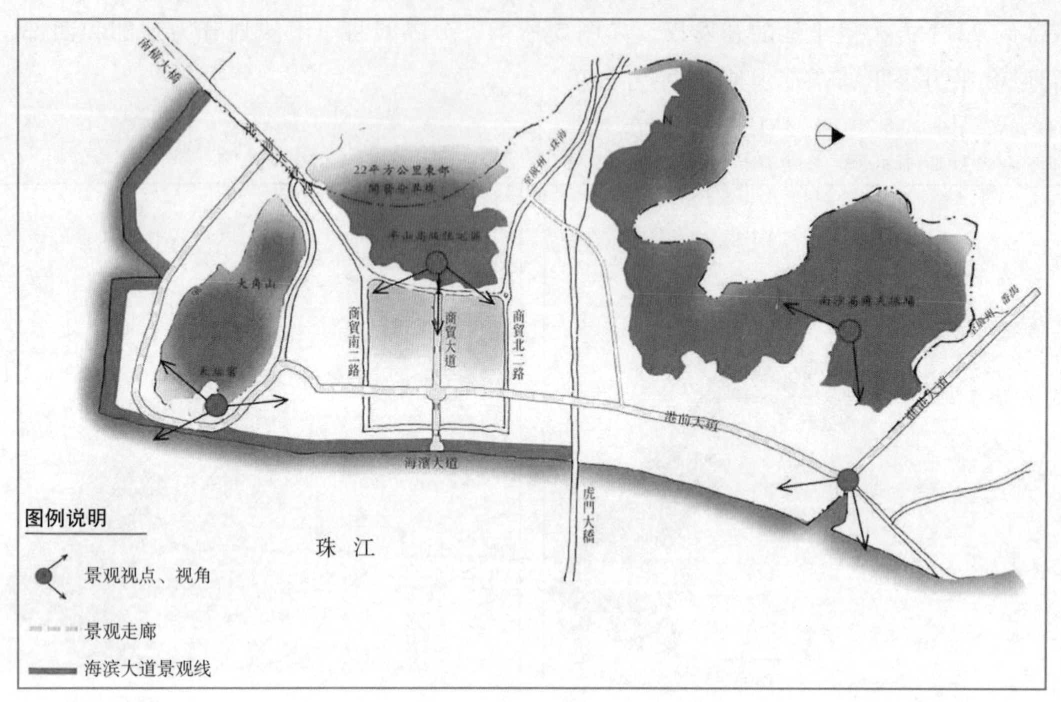

图6　南沙空间景观示意图

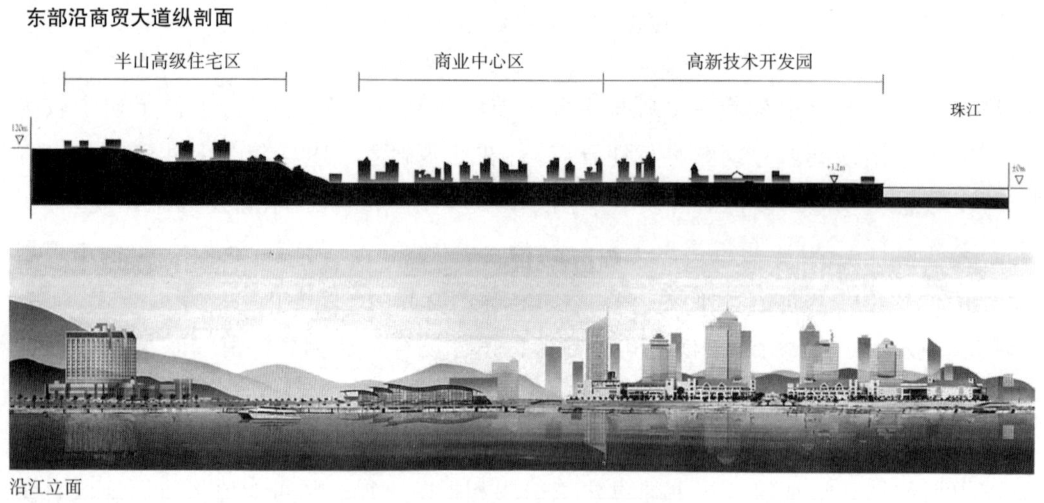

图7　东部沿江天际轮廓示意图

次的楼宅。

货运区和资讯科技园区这些无污染的工作区域将分布在新城南北沿海两端。这些产业发展可为新城创造各种就业机会，使区域的产业结构和人群结构和谐。

南沙是中国历史上鸦片战争的主要战场，有不少历史遗址，连同有关有价值的文物，在总体规划中都给予了保留（图8）。

1998年后，广州对番禺沙湾水道以南的“大南沙”开发的空间布局和功能定位安排时，市政府明确指出：霍英东先生在“小南沙”已开发了近十年，投入了数十亿，他想建设的

图8 虎门炮台

南沙新城就是想作为香港的后花园，和“大南沙”的发展策略和整体规划并不矛盾，两个积极性比一个积极性好，只能帮忙而决不干预霍英东先生在“小南沙”的一举一动，我们可以在“小南沙”的南边搞大港口、搞临港工业区，在“小南沙”的北面搞制造业，中间“小南沙”作为新城的中心搞服务业、高科技产业。“大南沙”的总体规划大体上就是按照这个思维从2001年7月着手编制的。

四、南沙地区规划

（一）基本思路和基本原则

1. 基本思路

（1）南沙地区规划要有利于优化城市空间布局。按照《广州城市建设总体战略概念规划纲要》，广州市将沿珠江重点向南拓展，形成“山、城、田、海”的生态城市架构。南沙一带将建设成为广州未来新城市重要组团之一。将南沙规划建设成为现代化的滨海新区，使广州实现由沿江城市向现代化滨海新城转变。

（2）自古以来，广州就是一个港口型城市。城市的形成发展与港口的兴衰息息相关，呈现出强烈的“港城互动效应”。时代的进步，生产力的发展，作为内河港的黄埔港（广州港）已濒临危机，广州港的唯一出路是到珠江口去搞深水码头，变内河港为海港。南沙规划首先要实现这一历史性的转变。

（3）作为发展中的城市广州，保持相当长一段历史高速发展，是广州自身发展的需要，也是城市之间竞争的需要。南沙规划要有利于形成新的经济增长点，促进广州产业的发展。南沙规划要充分考虑其得天独厚的区位优势，优越的自然条件，突出发展大交通、大工业、大港口、大物流，使其成为新世纪广州经济发展的新增长点。

2. 基本原则

一是“生态优先”原则。南沙地区水网密布，湖塘众多，自然环境优美，北部大多为农田耕地，南部入海口地区多为围垦填地，现状建设量小，自然生态要素保持良好。规划应坚持“生态优先”，注重环境保护和建设理念。南沙地区“城”融于由“山”、“田”构成的绿色生态系统和由“江”、“海”构成的蓝色生态系统交织而成的生态网中，延续了广州“山、城、田、海”城市自然空间结构的基本特征。

二是新兴产业和基础产业、传统产业共同发展。因为所有产业都能运用高科技，所有产业都可以是知识密集产业。所以，传统上把经济体区分为高科技与低科技，或制造业与服务业，并没有太多意义，因为所有产业都能以最先进的技术和熟练的技能，达到更高水平的生产力[11]。作为广州经济新的增长点，南沙必须要使新兴产业和基础产业、传统产业共同发展，才能保持珠江三角洲整个经济的竞争性。

三是南沙开发要为整个珠江三角洲协调发展和产业整合做出贡献。广州与珠江三角洲各市要形成整体优势，通过南沙规划进一步整合。基础设施建设要相互配合，发挥群体优势。如港口建设，枢纽港和喂给港要成为体系，不搞低水平的重复建设。利用南沙深水港和地理优势建设石化、钢铁、汽车、造船及其他重型成套设备等产业基地，将有利于珠三角各产业组团的整合和提升。南沙大力发展包括物流、商流、资金流、信息流为重点的现代服务业也将为珠三角的经济腾飞提供更有力的保障。

（二）空间结构

2002 年 4 月广州市城市规划局编制的第五版《广州南沙地区规划（初稿）》给出的规划空间结构分为三个层次：规划区（沙湾水道以南所有地区）总面积约 797 平方公里，其中陆域面积约 575 平方公里；规划控制区总面积约 536 平方公里，其中陆域面积约 330 平方公里；近期重点发展区的 319 平方公里，其中陆地面积约 212 平方公里[12]。规划控制区陆地面积只占规划区陆地面积的 57.4%，如图 9 所示。

之所以这样安排就是为了符合“生态优先”的原则。生态城市不希望把城市的任何地方都变成人工建造的空间容器，希望有更多的地方保留原有的自然生态。广州南沙区域规划做到了这一点，最大限度保留不开发的农地和湿地。南沙地区湿地占总辖区的 89.2%。其中，近岸与海岸湿地占湿地总面积的 96.1%，河流水域、库塘湿地和其他类型湿地分别占湿地总面积的 3.3%、0.2% 和 0.4%。河口水域面积占南沙湿地面积的 47%，三角洲冲积平原是南沙地区面积最大的湿地类型，占湿地总面积的 47.9%[13]。南沙湿地是其城市化进程中难以再生且不可多得的宝贵资源，保持建设区湿地生态类型的多样性，修复建设中受损的滩涂和水域，避免出现由于大规模开发建设导致的湿地生态系统的严重破坏，自始至终是南沙规划注意的一个问题。规划临港工业基地的建设并未占用重点保护湿地，钢铁基地和石化基地所处位置属于三角洲冲积平原，其面积占湿地面积的 2.4%[13]。

詹姆斯·拉伍洛克（J. Lovelock）认为，生命是大量能量流动的许多过程中的一种，其

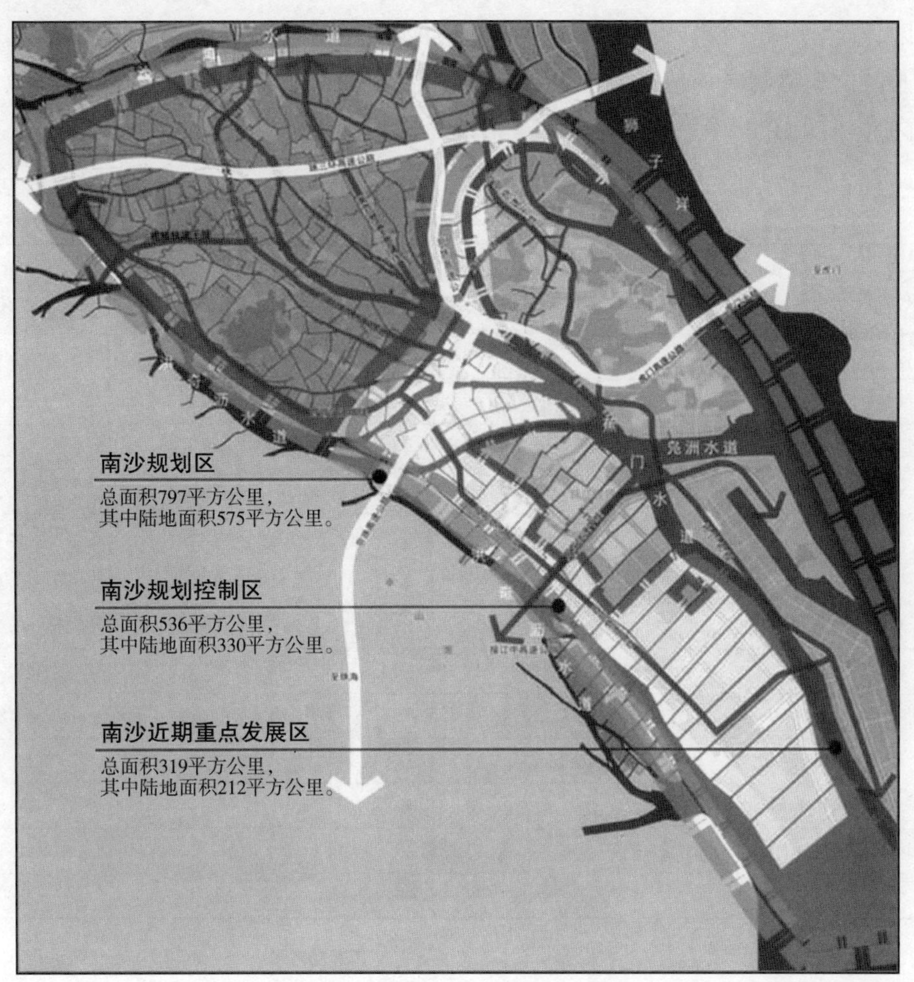

图9　南沙规划空间层次示意图

特点在于它具有在消耗自身的同时塑造自身的趋势。但是，这样做时，它必须一直向周围环境排泄低等产物[14]。从这个角度理解，人是最大的污染源。为了保持城市生态可持续发展及城市发展与生态支持系统承载能力相协调，必须保持适度人口规模。按照最适宜生活居住的环境目标，规划按环境容量预测，南沙地区规划人口规模宜控制在约100万人；南沙开发区规划人口规模则宜控制在约60万人。

用地布局方面，南沙地区规划城市建设用地约366平方公里，占全区总用地的46%，其中南沙开发区建设用地约292平方公里，占开发区总用地的54%。特殊用地除外，涉及八大类城市建设用地（见表1）。

居住用地集中分布于中部中心组团，主要有黄阁老镇区、蕉门河两岸地区、进港大道沿线地区、虎门大桥桥头周边地区、南沙老镇区、横沥、珠江管理区。公共设施用地主要集中在蕉门水道和蕉门河交汇的多岸地区，是服务全区的一级公共服务中心，其余还有三个次一级的副中心，分别是：位于黄阁大道与市南路交汇地区的黄阁综合工业组团综合服务次中心；位于南沙岛东南部的休闲商务次中心；位于蕉门水道西岸临港工业区内的综合服务次中心。工业用地主要分布于三个地区：黄阁北部综合工业园区，含小虎岛石化储运区和沙仔岛临港工业区；南沙经济技术开发区的东北部和南沙经济技术开发区、珠江管理区；南部万顷沙临港工业区。仓储物流用地主要集中在龙穴岛港，另外还有横沥岛中部少部分地区和沙仔岛北部地区（见图10）。

表1 南沙地区规划用地平衡表

类别	类别代码	类别名称	用地面积（万平方米）	占城市建设总用地面积比例	占总用地面积比例
城市建设用地	R	居住用地	3 187.61	8.72%	4.00%
	C	公共服务设施	2 036.12	5.57%	2.55%
	M	工业用地	5 212.77	14.25%	6.54%
	W	仓储用地	1 228.22	3.36%	1.54%
	S	道路广场用地	5 453.42	14.91%	6.84%
	T	对外交通用地	2 896.32	7.92%	3.63%
	U	市政公用设施用地	269.61	0.74%	0.34%
	G	绿地	16 259.12	44.53%	20.40%
	小计		36 575.55	100%	45.84%
非城市建设用地	E	水域 E1	22 711.35		28.49%
		其他用地	20 421.50		25.62%
	小计		43 132.85		54.11%
规划总用地			79 708.40		100%

（三）交通网络规划

主骨架路网规划由高速公路、快速路、主干道构成，总长约1 200公里，整体上呈以南沙地区为中心的环形放射式路网格局。道路系统规划充分强化地区对外交通联系，依托“五纵五横”的高快速道路将地区路网与广州乃至珠江三角洲地区路网融为有机整体，同时进一步理顺道路功能分级，满足内部交通需要，确保各种交通活动的有序性。(见图11)

南沙地区的轨道交通系统包含国有铁路和城市快速轨道交通两个系统。国有铁路主要用于满足大区域的长途客、货运输需求；城市快速轨道交通将为城市及城际中短途客流提供大容量、快速、准时的运输服务。

规划南部铁路北接规划中的新京广铁路快线，向南经南海进入番禺区，沿番禺西部南下、于万顷沙西北部向东转折，顺万龙快速干线进入港区，并在港区预留远期跨珠江口向东接广深铁路的通道。线路经万顷沙编组站后，预留衔接未来广珠铁路线通道。

规划广州地铁3号线延长线由市桥向东延伸至广州新城（规划）与地铁4号线交汇后，再向南延至南沙国际客运港。南沙地区通过地铁3号线与机场快轨线在广州东站衔接换乘，可直达广州新白云国际机场。

此外，意向中的穗港特快线，环南沙岛轻轨线，环大南沙地区轻轨线，珠江三角洲城际

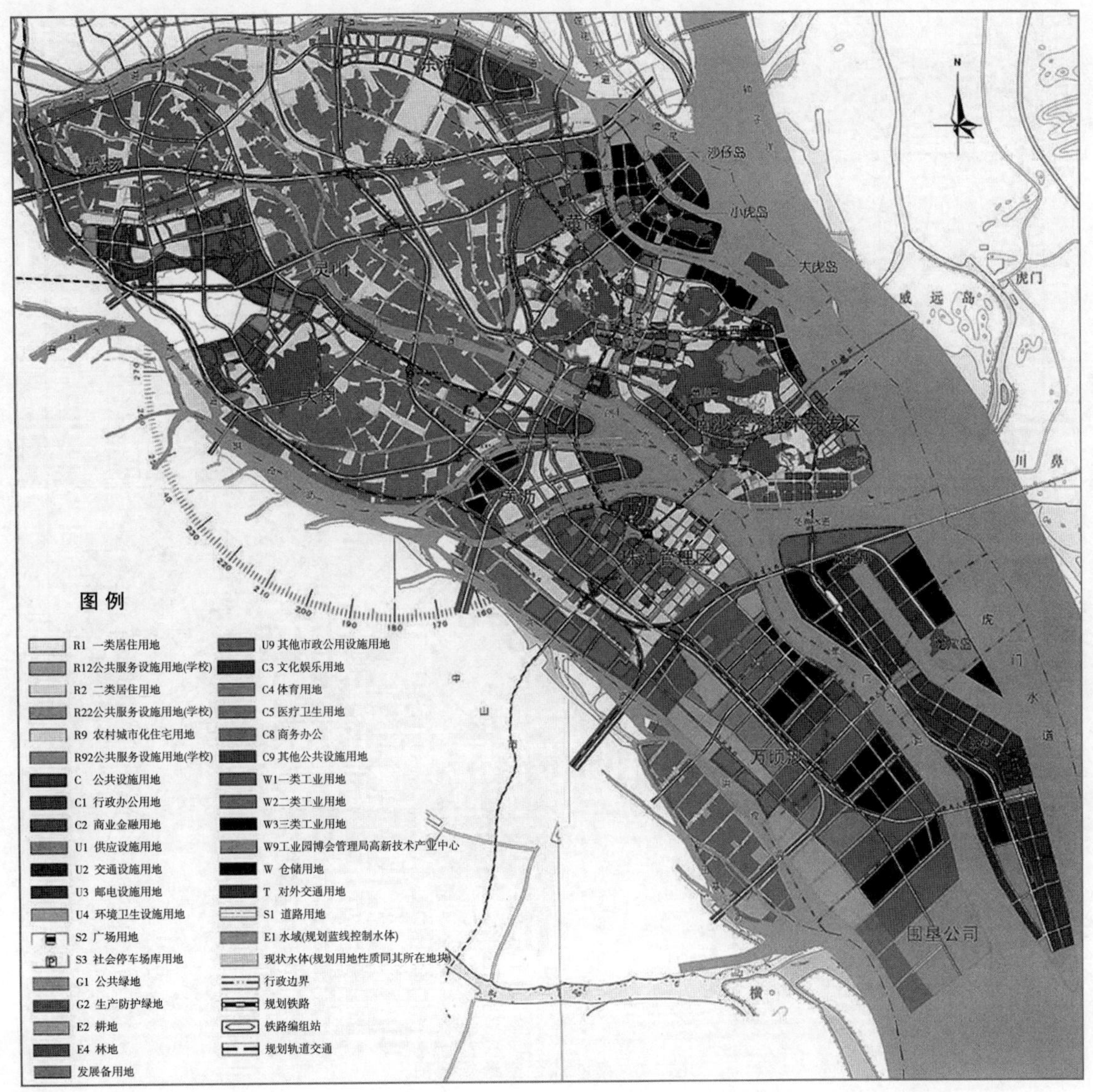

图10　南沙地区土地规划图

快轨等将进一步充实，完善未来南沙地区轨道客运交通系统。

南沙地区未来将结合港口、产业发展、用地布局规划设置8个大型客货运中心。其中，结合南沙东南客运港设置的国际客运中心，将通过建立水路运输与公路、轨道等方式换乘联运，打通粤港第二通道，实现穗港的直接联系，建成现代高效的客运中心。

（四）石化和钢铁项目

构建珠江三角洲重工业中心必须包括石化和钢铁，而在南沙新建石化和钢铁项目的关键是对环境的污染。

同样是詹姆斯·拉伍洛克的观点，污染并不像人们经常所说的那样是道德堕落的产物，而是生命运转的结果。只有当我们无法找到令人满意的极好方法消除这一问题并把它转向有利一面时，批评才是合理的[14]。生态城市建设不可能杜绝污染，关键是减少污染物排放，

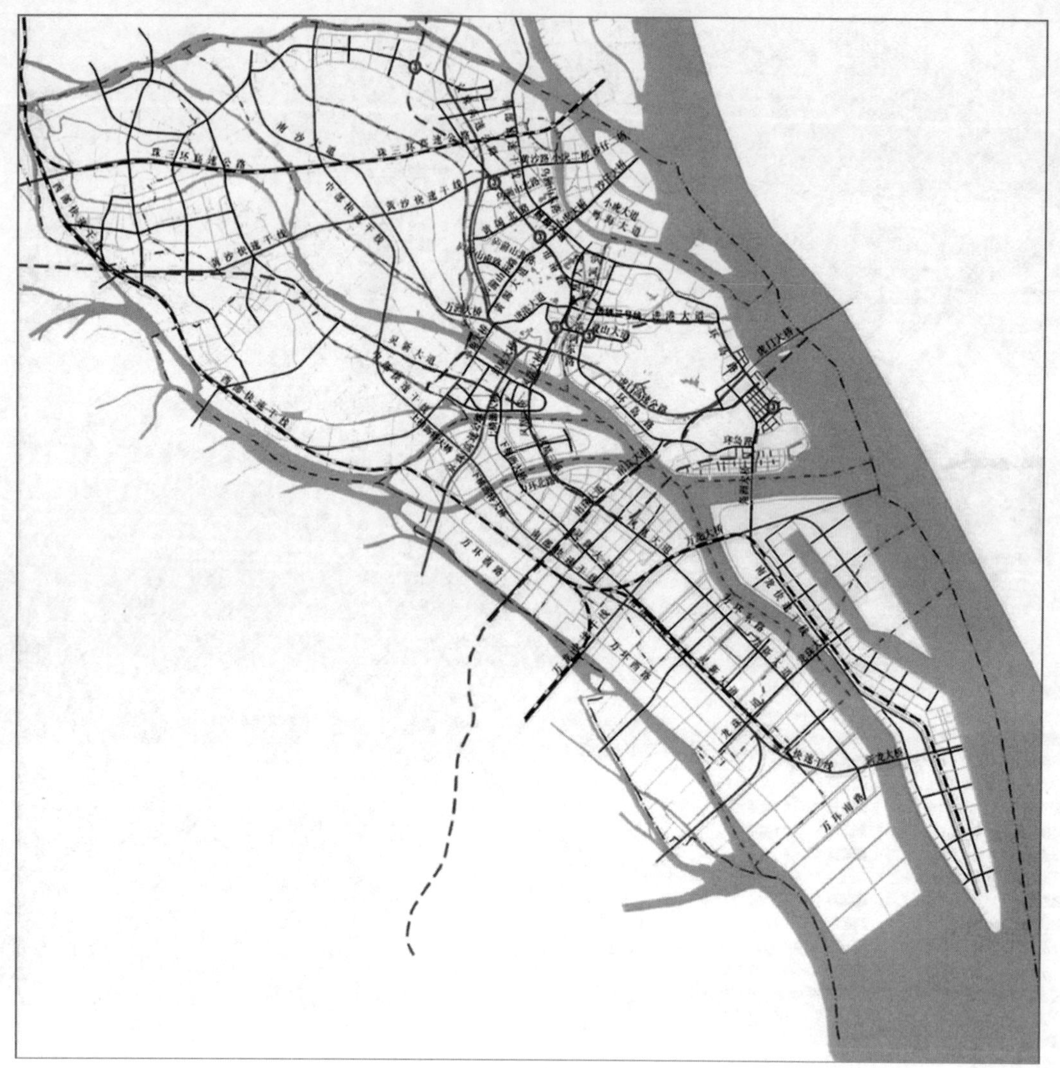

图 11　南沙综合交通规划图

处理和环境允许容量的控制。由北京师范大学、广州市环境保护科学研究院 2008 年 9 月编制的《广州南沙地区发展规划环境影响评价技术报告》采用 A 值法测算（本底浓度采用国家环境空气质量一级标准，即 SO_2 为 0.02mg/m^3；NO_2 为 0.04mg/m^3；PM_{10}为 0.04mg/m^3），南沙区理想的环境容量为：SO_2 排放 3.34 万 t/a，NO_2 为 3.35 万 t/a，PM_{10}为 5.02 万 t/a。

按照以下三种情景分别预测主要大气污染物排放总量。情景 1：1 500万吨炼油 +100 万吨乙烯 +500 万吨全流程钢铁（焦化、烧结、炼铁、炼钢、冷轧）。情景 2：1 500万吨炼油 +100 万吨乙烯 +500 万吨钢铁（炼钢、冷轧）。情景 3：1 500万吨炼油 +100 万吨乙烯 +500 万吨钢铁（冷轧）。三种情景规划项目主要大气污染物排放总量预测见表 2。

2006 年，南沙区大气主要污染物排放量为：$SO_2$2.39 万 t/a，$NO_2$1.44 万 t/a，PM_{10}1.43 万 t/a。保持这一基数、叠加石化、钢铁项目运行后情况，大气主要污染物 NO_2 和 PM_{10}不是规划环境的限制因子，SO_2 在采用国内先进工艺时，情景 1、情景 2 环境利用率超过 100%（达 119.5%、100.9%），即超过环境容量。2007 年，南沙区大气主要污染物排放量为：

$SO_2$1.18 万 t/a，$NO_2$1.44 万 t/a，PM_{10}1.43 万 t/a[15]。SO_2 在采用国内先进工艺时，情景 1、情景 2 环境利用率降低至 83.4% 和 64.7%，也就是说，三种建设情景在南沙区规划建设都是许可的。

表 2　钢铁和石化规划项目主要大气污染物排放总量预测

单位：t/a

排放情况	污染物类型	石化				钢铁				合计	
		1 500 万吨炼油		100 万吨乙烯		首期 300 万吨		二期 200 万吨			
		国内先进	国际先进	国内先进	国际先进	国内先进	国际先进	国内先进	国际先进	国内先进	国际先进
情景 1	SO_2	5 850	3 000	150	120	6 000	3 000	4 000	2 000	16 000	8 120
	NO_2	4 560	3 600	672	608	3 030	2 400	2 020	1 600	10 282	8 208
	PM_{10}	3 000	1 350	210	180	6 000	3 000	4 000	2 000	13 210	6 530
情景 2	SO_2	5 850	3 000	150	120	2 280	1 140	1 520	760	9 800	5 020
	NO_2	4 560	3 600	672	608	909	720	606	480	6 747	5 408
	PM_{10}	3 000	1 350	210	180	2 280	1 140	1 520	760	7 010	3 430
情景 3	SO_2	5 850	3 000	150	120	960	480	640	320	7 600	3 920
	NO_2	4 560	3 600	672	608	484.8	384	323.2	256	6 040	4 848
	PM_{10}	3 000	1 350	210	180	960	480	640	320	4 810	2 330

事实上，根据南沙区节能减排计划，南沙区 2010 年 SO_2 排放量消减到 0.6 万 t/a，这种情况的环境容量利用率见表 3。

表 3　节能减排后及叠加重点项目排放量后环境容量利用率分析

生产水平	环境容量（万 t/a）	节能减排排放量（t/a）	钢铁、石化项目污染物排放（t/a）			SO_2 环境容量利率（%）		
			情景 1	情景 2	情景 3	情景 1	情景 2	情景 3
国内先进	3.34	0.6	1.6	0.98	0.76	65.87	47.31	40.72
国际先进	3.34	0.6	0.81	0.5	0.39	42.22	32.93	29.64

值得注意的是，南沙区环境空气质量不仅受本地污染源的影响，同时还受周围地区大气污染源的影响。南沙区现状虽然有剩余环境容量，但 2006 年万顷沙地区 SO_2 和 NO_2 年均浓度超过二级标准限值，超标率分别为 21% 和 11%。从地理位置上看，万顷沙地区位于珠三角地区常年主导风的中轴线和区域污染物传输通道上，处于众多的电厂群包围之中：北面的珠江电厂有限公司、粤华发电有限责任公司、恒运电厂；东北面约 16 公里处的沙角电厂群，东南面的深圳妈湾电厂；南面的珠海电厂；西面的中山市中山火力发电厂、中山发电厂；西北面的佛山市南海新田电厂。此外，对南沙区环境空气质量影响较大的污染源还包括佛山的陶瓷厂群和肇庆地区的水泥厂群。

北京师范大学、广州市环境保护科学研究院对 SO_2 排放预测是国内先进工艺 0.6 万 t/a，国际先进工艺 0.312 万 t/a。中国石化集团洛阳石油化工工程公司所做的《中科合资广东南沙炼油化工一体化项目环境影响报告书》，对具体项目对污染物排放分析为 $SO_2$0.43 万 t/a[16]。介于国内先进工艺和国际先进工艺之间。预测和具体测算一致。南沙区的珠江电厂 2007 年上半年脱硫装置投入使用之前，SO_2 排放量为 2 万 t/a。沙角电厂在 2006 年 11 月 27 日脱硫设施投入使用之前，SO_2 排放量为 11.46 万 t/a。虽然石化项目对大气污染物排放只有这些电厂的几十分之一或几分之一，但这些电厂项目当初建设和随后长时间运行都没有多大的风波，人们是否可以从中思考出一些问题。

事实上，珠三角地区脱硫工程的潜力还是很大的，在那一个阶段，改善包括南沙在内的珠三角各市的空气质量状况的主要矛盾，不在于钢铁、石化项目是否建设，而在于各自认真地做好减排工作，因为三角洲各市 SO_2 排量和石化项目相比是以百倍计。表 4 是 2005 年、2006 年珠三角各市 SO_2 排放量。

表 4　珠三角地区各市 2005 年、2006 年 SO_2 排放量（万 t/a）

地区	2005 年	2006 年
广州	14.9	12.9
深圳	4.3	4.2
珠海	3.8	3.0
佛山	14.9	14.5
江门	3.7	3.7
肇庆	2.6	2.6
惠州	1.1	2.3
东莞	17.7	14.0
中山	3.2	2.8
合计	66.2	60.0

（五）物流中心

珠江三角洲作为中国经济最发达的地区之一，拥有全世界加工制造业的各个门类，全世界十分之一的消费品在这里制造，产业群落云集，第二、第三产业发达，已步入世界新兴发达地区的行列。南沙地区位于珠江三角洲的地理几何中心，方圆 60 公里范围内，有十几个大中城市；100 公里范围内，珠江三角洲城市群网络中，人口超过 4 000 万人。

充分利用南沙区的陆域优势和岸线资源，建设现代化港口及其配套的服务设施、仓储服务、物品包装，形成现代化的物流产业基地。围绕港口的开发，将“大进、大转，大出、快递”作为物流业的主题，发展货物运输、装卸、保税、仓储、包装，代办理货、配送以及信息咨询、商业贸易、金融保险等服务，形成立足珠江三角洲、辐射华南、面向世界的物流中心。

物流中心用地主要集中在龙穴岛。龙穴岛物流中心主要由广州港南沙港区和物流产业区两大功能组成，用地规模约 65 平方公里。其中，广州港南沙港区包括集装箱码头、散货码头、各种专业码头；物流产业区规划建设保税加工，贸易服务、仓储服务、物流配送等现代物流业的各种功能设施，如图 12 所示。

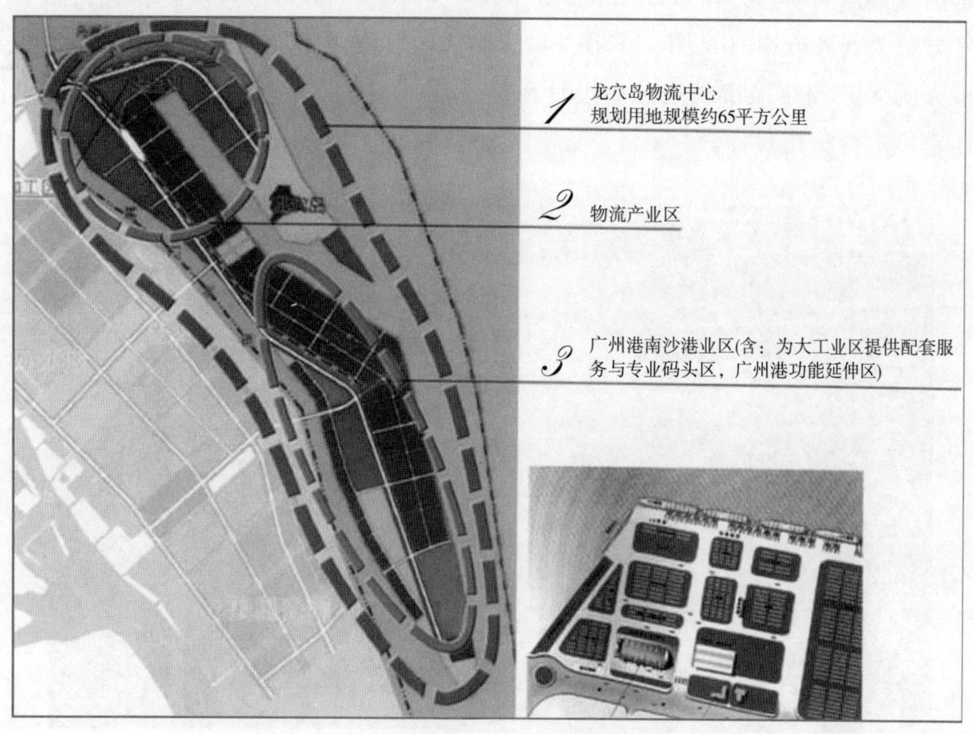

图 12　龙穴岛功能分区图

（六）城市设计国际竞赛

南沙节点是城市南拓中关键的一颗棋子，做好南沙规划与建设具有双重意义，它既可树立一个创造两个适宜的典范，又能为确定城市格局，落下决定成败的一子，因此，南沙规划得到了高度重视，重要项目均用用国际竞赛或招标形式完成。

南沙地区的区位独特，来自周边城市的影响错综复杂，南沙的发展涉及周边城市和整个珠江三角洲大城市带的发展，城市发展过程中将有许多不确定的因素对其产生影响。南沙的发展需要积极推进，但同时需要经过较长时间的协调研究，应加强城市发展和周边地区城市带发展的系统研究，才能达成共识。根据广州市政府的要求，开展了“广州南沙地区整体城市设计与重要节点城市设计国际竞赛”。竞赛分两部分内容：一是地区整体城市设计，对南沙地区 536 平方公里（含水域 206 平方公里）的城市空间进行宏观、概念性整体城市设计，提出地区总体空间布局的整体构思；二是在地区整体城市设计的基础上，对虎门大桥桥头及南沙岛东南角、蕉门河沿岸、灵山及横沥岛类、龙穴岛港区等主要城市节点（总面积 1 500万平方米，其中陆域面积1 300万平方米）进行中微观的、具体的城市设计，并提出城市设计导则。

“广州南沙地区整体城市设计及重要节点城市设计国际竞赛评审会” 于 2002 年 11 月在

广州城市规划展览馆召开，评审委员会由国内城市规划与城市设计、建筑、生态、环境、交通、经济等领域的知名专家组成。评审委员对参赛设计成果进行了认真研究和充分讨论与比较，选定由香港泛亚易道公司（EDAW）& Kohn Pedersen Fox Associates PC（美国 KPF）设计的3号方案为优胜方案（见图13、图14），由法国巴内瀚建筑、城市规划与景观设计联合建筑师事务所 & 广州市城市规划勘测设计研究院设计的2号方案为第二名。决定由优胜方案的设计单位进行深化设计。

图13　南沙虎门大桥桥头及南沙岛东南角城市设计图

图14　南沙灵山和横沥的滨水区城市设计图

由广东省政府转报国务院的《广州市城市总体规划（2001-2010）》文本中关于南沙规划的表述是：

南沙重点发展区分为三个功能组团：

1. 南部龙穴岛组团，空间上可划分为广州港南沙作业区及物流中心区、蕉门水道西岸新垦临港工业及配套生活服务区、横沥物流配送区以及万顷沙生态农业综合发展区。

（1）广州港南沙作业区及物流中心区包括鸡抱沙、龙穴岛和孖沙围垦区的全部地区，以集装箱为主的港口货物运输、物流中心为主导功能，发展保税加工、仓储配送、修船等与港口运输货物相关产业。

（2）新垦临港工业及配套生活服务区包括蕉门水道以西的新垦、万顷沙和围垦公司的部分地区，主要发展临港产业、仓储、散货码头以及港区的生活居住配套服务设施。

（3）横沥物流配送区包括横沥岛、灵山镇东南角的部分地区以及珠江农场的北部地区，发展物流储运配送业，满足港区对内、对外的物资集散要求。

（4）万顷沙生态综合发展区包括蕉门水道西岸万顷沙、新垦、珠江管理区和围垦公司的大片地区，建设绿色农产品生产基地，综合发展生态都市农业、渔业和以此为基础的生态旅游业。

（5）在万顷沙地区，建设以炼油和石油化工为龙头，以石化产品深加工和精细化工、新材料化工为主的现代化临港石油化工工业基地。并依托广州港南沙港区，在万顷沙或孖沙地区建设大型钢铁工业基地。

2. 中部南沙组团，空间上可划分为地区服务中心区、休闲商务区和资讯产业区。

（1）地区服务中心区包括黄阁南部和南沙岛北部沿东湾滘水道两岸地区，发展集行政办公、商贸金融、文化体育、医疗、教育、居住等功能于一体，形成服务于整个南沙区配套设施完善的地区性综合服务中心。

（2）休闲商务区包括南沙岛滨江的东岸地区及中部山地东侧，主要功能为商务会展、旅游服务、体育休闲等。

（3）资讯产业区包括南沙岛西岸南部（西部工业区）和南岸地区（粤港资讯产业园），发展以资讯科技产业为主导，集研发、生产、出口加工、教育培训、高科技工业、居住于一体的综合功能。

3. 北部黄阁组团在空间上可划分为临港工业园区和生活服务区。

（1）临港工业园区主要由黄阁北部工业区、小虎岛石化工业区、沙仔岛造船工业区、南沙岛东北部沿岸工业区构成。

（2）生活服务区位于黄阁镇南部，主要功能有居住区和地区公共服务中心区。黄阁组团以小虎岛石化工业、沙仔岛造船工业为基础，重点发展石化、造船、原材料等大型基础性工业，形成黄阁临港工业园区及石化储运基地。

国务院于2005年12月22日以国函〔2005〕105号文批复广东省政府《关于广州市城市总体规划（2001－2010）的请示》，原则同意修订后的《广州市城市总体规划（2001－2010）》。

（作者：林树森，全国政协港澳台侨委员会）

参考文献

[1] 瑰瀛涛．中国近代不同类型城市综合研究［M］．成都：四川大学出版社，1998，12.

[2] 陈正书．租界与近代上海工业的三大支柱［J］．史林，2002（3）．

[3] 严中平．中国近代经济史统计资料选辑［M］．北京：科学出版社，1955.

[4] 米高·恩莱特（Michael J·Enright），等．香港与珠江三角洲经济互动［Z］.2003.

[5] 田汝耕．港湾建设是日本创造奇迹的基本成因［J］．港口科技动态，1989（12）．

[6] 谬鸿基，沈灿燊，黄光耀，等．珠江三角洲水土资源［M］．广州：中山大学出版社，1988，9.

[7] 中山大学地理系《珠江三角洲研究丛书》编辑委员会．珠江三角洲自然资源与演变过程［M］．广州：中山大学出版社，1988，7.

[8] 中交第四航务工程勘察设计院．港址比选综合分析报告［Z］.2001，6.

[9] 中交第四航务工程勘察设计院．广州南沙港起步工程预可行性研究报告（初稿）（2），2000，11.

[10] 霍英东基金会南沙设计部．广州南沙新城东部总体规划，城市设计研究（Z）.2001.

[11] 迈克尔·波特著，竞争论［M］．高登第，李明轩，译．北京：中信出版社，2003.1.

[12] 广州城市规划局．广州南沙地区规划（初稿）［Z］.2002.4.

[13] 北京师范大学，广州市环境保护科学研究院．广州南沙地区发展规划环境影响评价技术报告［R］．2008年9月．

[14] ［英］詹姆斯·拉伍洛克·盖娅：地球生命的新视野［M］．肖显静，范祥东，译．上海：上海人民出版社，2007.6.

[15] 北京师范大学，广州市环境保护科学研究院．环境影响报告书［R］.2009.4.

[16] 中国石化集团洛阳石油化工工程公司．中科合资广东南沙炼油化工一体化项目环境影响报告书［Z］.2009.3.

关于“京津冀城市群协调发展规划”课题的几个核心问题

京津冀地区集中了我国最高等级和最大规模的人力资源，由于环渤海有大量的盐城滩地可作为城市发展用地（不占耕地来推进城镇化），更为重要的是，该地区是继珠三角、长三角之后更有发展潜力的超级经济引擎。与此同时，该地区也正面临最为紧迫的大气污染、水污染及水资源短缺、特大城市规模失控、中小城市发育不良、地区和城乡居民之间收入差距过分悬殊等问题。

以“有机疏散、协调发展”来破京津冀的困境，打造助推中国腾飞的“第三极”有着特殊的战略意义。研究此课题有几个方面特别值得关注：

一、强化背景研究

背景分析要涉及以下几方面的内容：

第一，城市群关系到国家竞争力。全球化与城镇化是相互影响、相互融合的。全球化时代是以城市群作为竞争单元融入国际竞争的新阶段。国家竞争力是以城市群整体依托的企业集群为主体来体现的，而不是单个城市或企业。这一背景变化给我们提出了非常重要的课题，即京津冀地区城镇化如何与全球化深度衔接和融合。如果不能以城市空间、基础设施和服务功能合理布局的城市群为梯队迎接全球竞争、融入世界城市网络并成为重要节点，那么，我国最重要的经济引擎在今后的全球化竞争中就有可能会被边缘化。一旦城市群被边缘化，意味着这个国家和地区的经济竞争力会因边缘化而衰退。这个问题已经非常紧迫地摆在我们面前。

第二，城市群是产业升级的龙头。“中国制造”曾助推我国经济腾飞，但要适时走向“中国创造”。现代经济体的持续繁荣并跨越“中等收入陷阱”本质上是由越来越多的企业家和一般民众积极投身于创新创意过程的产物，要有一系列社会文化和制度的创新来激励。这种氛围不可能是全国平均形成或由各地同步进行的均衡结构转型，而要由人力资本最为富集的京津冀城市群率先发动并引领“中国制造”向“中国创造”转变。我国产业结构调整的三大“高地”与现在经济的发动机的地理空间是重合的。由于历史遗留问题的积累，京津冀地区钢铁、水泥、煤电、石化等重污染高能耗产值约占全国半壁江山，结构转型升级的任务尤为繁重。正因为资源环境约束的劣势和人力资本的优势，本应后发的京津冀城市群作为新发动机进行先创先试，最先引领中国经济向“中国创造”转变。

第三，城市群是生态文明示范区。传统粗放型城镇化、工业化模式转向为绿色可持续发展模式具有紧迫性。比如该地区城市人口多少、人均消耗能源多少、人均 GDP 和专利数多少等，都应该有数据支撑和国际比较。京津冀地区人口密度、开发强度、能源消耗、可用资源都极其有限，资源、能源和生态环境的约束和治理形势也最为紧迫，有必要也有条件进行生态文明城区的先行先试，可将其分为新城区和既有城区生态化规划建设两个部分。前者可以充分借鉴“中新天津生态城”的经验。5 年前，该项目落户天津新区盐碱地上，也是为打造在北方缺水的地区引进水循环利用的试验区并在非耕地上建造“可复制”的低碳生态城。目前，有条件在整个京津冀地区进行推广复制。

第四，首要的问题是协同环境污染治理。京津冀地区已经到了一个区域环境共同治理的新阶段。以前对环境协同治理并不太重视，上游排污、下游治，城市治、城郊排，但现存的问题不能由单个城市解决，只能由城市群政府统一规划整体齐心协力地去解决。无论是水污染或空气污染，京津冀城市群都是重灾区，都已成为世界瞩目的紧迫性问题，规划编制必然要重视整个华北地区气象参数如主导风向、降雨量、地面风速等长期的变化趋势（气象数据显示：近几十年来每隔几年华北地区地面风速就降低 10%，这一趋势要引起重视）。在此基础上，污染治理和生态修复问题必须以城市群为单元来统一协调解决、刻不容缓。

第五，“四化同步”必先从城市群始。新型城镇化的几个同步发展是地区社会经济均衡健康发展的前提，促使新型城镇化、新型工业化、绿色机动化、信息化、农业现代化同步，也必须从这京津冀城市群最先开始实践协同推进。这些同步会形成系统效应和扩散示范效应。这就需要管理者和规划师具有广宽的背景思维和科学务实的态度。现在是到了系统研究和治理城市群问题的新阶段，有后发优势的京津冀城市群能否健康发展从某种意义上将决定国家整体竞争力。

二、合理界定城市群范围

要研究如何科学界定城市群的范围和对城市群进行分类。城市群种类要科学划分，要有几大原则。第一，可以从不同的角度，如地理屏障、开发强度、历史文化、发展水平、物流、人流、资源和污染物扩散路径等方面的关联性，或从生产力发达程度、经济关系或文化认同等原则来测算和划定城市群的空间范围，要有大数据支撑。第二，要讲基本服务功能。我国要建立面向全球化的第一梯队城市群和未来参与全球化的第二梯队城市群和国家级的城市群，实现梯度化融入全球化。第三，区位性。城市群要有明确的辐射服务范围，其分类标准是什么，标准是否可行等，都需要深入讨论研究。

三、创建协同机制

京津冀城市群能否健康发展，归根结底是协同机制的创新。城市群内部需要重建协同机制。这至少涉及五个方面：

第一，世界城市群的协同机制的经验和教训是什么？我国的特色优势是行政区划的可调整，这是国外没有的，也是我们的制度优势。作为经济和科技创新的大引擎如何加足马力推进结构升级和生态环境治理？如何进行分步合理调整行政管理模式和范围？而且，调整出于什么理由，如何减小阻力，等等，都要进行系统研究。

第二，扁平化的城市群协调机构与机制如何建立？城市不分大小在城市群中都应是平等协作的伙伴关系，如何按资源共享、环境共保、基础设施共建和支柱产业集群共树的互利互惠原则及合作共赢机制，利益共同方如何协调制度和组织管理模式等问题都应深入研究。

第三，专业化协同规划的编制与实施。当前，最紧要的是如何提炼出影响城市群协调健康发展的关键问题。只有这样，才能“有的放矢”科学编制专业性协同规划。国际上较有效率的专业协同机制案例之一是多瑙河的水污染协调模式。产生了水污染，主要是下游国家吃亏，所以在规划实施中，下游国家话语权就较大。我国缺乏这类基础性协调规划和成功案例，要突破部门分割进行编制。

第四，协同机制创新要由几个方面入手。一是协同机制必须建立在专业性协同规划和制度之上，再逐步形成整体协同机制。由此可见，城市群规划编制顺序十分重要。这些规划都要基于专业化的区域分析之上。专业性核心规划先编制，区域协同规划的创新就易水到渠成（这其中城市群空间布局规划的修编尤为重要，因为其他专业规划都是为合理的城市空间构建服务的）；二是城市群的协同模式建设必然涉及一些利益机制分配问题，比如联建城际轨道交通、防治污染措施、资源共同开发、分流首都重叠功能、追求可达性、统一 TOD（以公共交通为导向的开发）建设模式创新等，都要善于从问题导向来务实创新；三是资源类保护模式的创新。在城市群中，空间开发强度和人口密度高，不可再生的自然文化遗产、生态等资源最易破坏，如何通过绿道网建设和“四线管制”来强化系统保护，通过协同保护监督机制等来解决问题。此类资源保护有规律可循。经验表明，寺庙、塔类文物比深山坟墓类文物较容易获得妥善保护，因为经常有人来往。通过绿道建设形成的可达性转变为稀缺资源保护机制，把可达性改善与文化遗产、自然遗产保护紧密结合起来，这是绿道网提供的额外的资源保护功能。

第五，城市群规划和实施应做好时序和空间上安排。对主城区人口规模超过 200 万人的中心城市都应尽快制订有机疏散规划，在京津冀城市群内形成 500 万人口的核心组团、200 万～300 万人口的中心组团、100 万～200 万人口的卫星城群、10 万～30 万人口的卫星城以及星罗棋布的绿色小城镇，构成类似于金字塔结构的城镇群空间布局。新建卫星城应编制生态新城规划，老城则应进行生态改造。农村也要同步进行生态保护和修复，形成与城镇互补协调的发展模式。国际经验表明，生态有机疏散、生态新城建设、老城改造、农村生态保育、绿色有机农业等方面都应有一系列新的规划建设模式的创新和管理创新与之相适应。

四、制定健康发展评价标准

评价标准是城市群健康发展的轨道之一，应基于先行城镇化国家的经验进行科学编制，从而形成城市群中各城市合理竞争的公平环境。此类指标一般不应以人口或 GDP 等总量为单位，而应以人均或单位 GDP 为计量单元，每个区域建立健康发展指数，鼓励城市群内部和外部的平等竞争。因为城市群内部各城市之间竞争非常激烈，如果盲目竞争，攀比上产业项目和基础设施，不仅浪费极大，资源环境保护也会成为空谈。

重要的是推行生态补偿方式的创新。如减少同样单位的 PM2.5 空气污染，北京城内投资成本远比河北高，但由于现行财政体制的原因，北京财政不愿意帮河北治理，这就涉及生态补偿模式创新问题。生态合理补偿是复杂的计算和具体的讨价还价过程，而不是直接划定某几种功能区域就可实施补偿的。国际经验表明，涉及城市群内部各方面、各利益主体之间复杂的利益分配和具体谈判过程是必需的。

五、强化对城市群发展机制的研究

这类机制从系统论角度来看有几个部分。首先是结构，城市群空间结构有多种模式，比如单中心、多中心、大中小嵌套模式等多种模式，结构合理与否将对城市群整体长期发展产生重要影响。其次是节点，城市群中大中城市作为主要的资源集聚点及它们之间的关系和共享的利益机制是否建立。最后是通道，这包括交通、物流、金融、信息、人力资本等方面的流动通道。例如，已进行高铁建设的城市，实际就具有地理空间紧缩效应，对城市群协调发展和人口空间布局会产生全新的影响。

六、开展城市群“弹性”机制的研究

没有弹性的系统往往是僵化的、脆弱的。21 世纪以来，国际规划界流行的“弹性城市”(Resilient City) 正基于此原理。京津冀城市群的研究首先应把全国健康城镇化规律研究明白，再移植到城市群中去。京津冀城市群实际上是新型城镇化整体战略规划的缩小版，其城市群协同发展规划则是全国城镇化体系规划的试验版。宏观方面的规划如能避免大的错误，微观尺度的设计就肯定能减少细节错误。只要不出现房地产市场进入“明斯克”危机态、土地私有化、大中小城镇布局失误、生态和文化遗产资源受到毁灭性破坏等“底线”式错误，公平竞争和“市场机制”一般可自动修正一般性错误和提高普通资源配置的效率。在全国范围内必须由政府行政力量推动的工作，在京津冀城市群中可由市场机制来推动，城市群内部的市场化程度事实上比其他地区更高，但空间布局、生态环境治理、重大基础设施等都必须靠政府规划这一“有形之手”来调控。城市群是信息化、城镇化、工业化、全球化、市场化、机动化等的多因子混合作用体。

增加京津冀城市群协同规划的“弹性度”应遵循以下的原则：

第一，多样性。多样性是任何一个自适应系统以多种方式应对变化和干扰的能力表征。事实上，产业、文化、自然资源、人力资本等方面的多样性越丰富，城市群越能实现可持续发展。富有弹性的城市群规划能为全球投资者提供多样化的选择、为地方政府提供多样化的政策工具，以满足百姓的民生和创业需求及千差万别的市场机会。

第二，灵活性。具有弹性的系统能承受和利用形势和需求的变化，而不是硬性的对抗和控制。传统的城市群规划为什么失效，原因之一就是试图沿用行政手段强行扼制百姓民生需求和市场的变化，或力求用“一刀切”的政策去应对千差万别的城市社会经济发展水平和市场主体的需求。合理的城市群规划应充分调动群内每个城市政府和市场主体的积极性与创造性，主动参与公平竞争。只要这种竞争的轨道是“绿色、低碳、智能、集约”的，此类富有创造力的竞争过程就会丰富系统的灵活性。

第三，模块化。富有弹性的政策集一般是由不同的模块构件组成的。每项调控措施既具有相对独立性，又能相互协同作用。相互依赖过密的政策集更容易受到外部干扰而趋于低效，而具有独立协同性的模块化政策工具，在城市群协同发展调控的过程中能从下而上创新性地生成某些有效的新模块。这方面可以肯定的是：将生态新城建设和旧城区生态化改造作为整个京津冀城市群主要模块是合适的。这也符合“风尚从上而下、创新从下而上”的规律。

第四，管理慢变量。具有弹性的系统必然具有应对慢变量的敏感性和实时调控能力，从而控制那些跨越阈值的突然变量，避免“温水煮青蛙”式的毁灭。例如，京津冀地区空气污染、房地产市场风险、地面沉陷等方面正在遭遇前所未有的慢变量。又如，错误的经济发展观、独生子女政策、对城镇化终结的错误判断和人口快速老化等，都会影响该地区经济社会发展的可持续性。对慢变量的敏感，可使系统能承受更多的外部干扰，从而有利于城市群整体能从未来可能来临的国际金融危机等强烈干扰下适时恢复过来，从而避免经济崩溃。

第五，适时反馈。任何弹性系统都必然具有适时的反馈机制。作为具有弹性的城市群经济社会复合系统必须强化中央政府与京津冀城市群地方政府、城市与农村、企业及民众之间的反馈机制。任何重大政策的出台都应在征求各方意见的过程中倾听不同利益方尤其是弱势群体的呼声。2008 年的金融危机使人们痛彻地觉悟到：一旦全球化和资产证券化使得反馈机制变得十分松弛，就会引发全球性或全局性的危机。

第六，协同作用。具有弹性的系统应促进子系统之间的信任和协作，充分发挥社会成员、市场主体间交流网络的作用。实现城市群协同发展尤其需要各方面的协同作用并具有优先的次序安排，如“能由市场机制自行调整的，就不用政府出政策‘越俎代庖’”；“能由下级政府主动应对的，就不必由上级政府出台‘一刀切’的政策”；“能用经济杠杆调节的，就不必用行政手段来强行干预”等。增强协同性既能克服各方的摩擦及错位调控所产生的相互抵消，而且还能增强“举国体制”的优势，有效应对外部干扰的能力。

第七，权力叠加。富有弹性的系统必然拥有“冗余”的调控机制。对于快速变化的全球化和城镇化时代，城市群协同发展的政策及其调控机构应具有多种重叠的响应方式。足额冗余的结构能增加系统反应的多样性与灵活性，也能加强跨尺度影响的调控意识和质量。一个自上而下没有角色冗余的政策体系可能在短期内具有高效率，但是一旦外部形势或周边环境发生突变，就有可能出现 20 世纪 80 年代日本房地产那样的雪崩式溃败。史实已经证明，那些看似“混、杂”的多层政府复合调控结构更能在突变的环境中有效削减危机。

以上七个方面“弹性度”的要求是京津冀城市群协同发展规划编制和实施的重要原则。

总之，城市群规划研究要突出借鉴和创新性。编制我国京津冀城市群协同发展规划主要应以问题为导向来展开研究，解决问题的关键在于科学规划空间结构和协同机制创新，特别是不同的专业规划之间的协同和总体规划的深化与可实施性。要将有限的行政协调资源用到关键处，将历史经验导向、问题导向和理论导向三方面结合起来进行系统研究，这样才能创造出高质量的规划编制与实施成果。

（作者：仇保兴，国务院参事，中国城市科学研究会理事长，住房和城乡建设部原副部长）

我国城市噪声环境的现状及挑战

一、引言

噪声污染和大气污染、水污染并列为三大污染，但是噪声污染却远远不如后两者那样受到重视。相反，噪声污染问题往往被忽略。世界卫生组织近些年就全世界的噪声污染情况进行了调查，结果显示，美国等发达国家的噪声污染问题都呈现出越来越严重的发展态势。世界卫生组织进行的全世界噪声污染调查认为，噪声污染已经成为影响人们身体健康和生活质量的严重问题。

首先，噪声对人体最直接的危害是听力损伤。如果人们长期在强噪声环境下工作，听觉疲劳不能得到及时恢复，内耳器官就会发生器质性病变，形成永久性听阈偏移，又称噪声性耳聋。若人突然暴露于极其强烈的噪声环境中，听觉器官会发生急剧外伤，引起鼓膜破裂出血，迷路出血，螺旋器从基底膜急性剥离，可能使人耳完全失去听力，即出现爆震性耳聋。

其次，噪声污染还会给人体其他系统带来危害。由于噪声的作用，会产生头痛、脑涨、耳鸣、失眠、全身疲乏无力以及记忆力减退等神经衰弱症状。长期在高噪声环境下工作的人与低噪声环境下的情况相比，高血压、动脉硬化和冠心病的发病率要高2～3倍。噪声也可导致消化系统功能紊乱，引起消化不良、食欲不振、恶心呕吐，使肠胃病和溃疡病发病率升高。此外，噪声对视觉器官、内分泌机能及胎儿的正常发育等方面也会产生一定影响。在高噪声中工作和生活的人们，一般健康水平逐年下降，对疾病的抵抗力减弱，诱发一些疾病。

除此之外，噪声还会干扰人的谈话、工作和学习。实验表明，当人受到突然而至的噪声一次干扰，就要丧失4秒钟的思想集中。据统计，噪声会使劳动生产率降低10%～50%，随着噪声的增加，差错率上升。由此可见，噪声会分散人的注意力，导致反应迟钝，容易疲劳，工作效率下降，差错率上升。噪声还会掩蔽安全信号，如报警信号和车辆行驶信号等，以致造成事故。

噪声污染的危害不仅仅对人，对动植物、仪器设备和建筑的影响也不容忽视。它使多数动物食欲不振、繁殖能力下降。此外，道路交通噪声还直接影响到了路面周围的土地价值。韩国建立了特征价格模型用以评估交通噪声对韩国首尔土地价值的影响，发现交通噪声每增加1%，土地价格就会下降3%，每年每千米道路由于交通噪声而产生的费用为34.7万美元。有研究表明，各个国家每年因道路交通噪声污染都会不同程度地导致经济损失，我国为216亿元，芬兰为2.8亿美元，美国为51亿美元，瑞士为6.8亿美元，德国为10.6亿美元。

二、我国城市的环境噪声现状

（一）我国城市环境噪声现状综述

近些年来，随着噪声污染问题的扩大，我国对城市环境噪声状况的关注越来越重视。据《中国环境状况公报》2009年的数据显示，监测的354个城市当中，区域环境质量好的城市仅仅占5.9%，受噪声轻度污染的城市占到了24.3%，受中度噪声污染的占1.1%。环境保护重点城市区域声环境质量处于轻度污染的占到了23.0%，中度污染的占0.9%。

根据《中国环境状况公报》公布的数据，汇总2007－2011年的声环境监测结果，得到了我国城市声功能区监测点位的达标率分布情况，见表1。

表1　2007－2011年我国城市声功能区监测点位达标率

单位:%

功能区类别	0类		1类		2类		3类		4类	
	昼	夜	昼	夜	昼	夜	昼	夜	昼	夜
2007年	59.4	32.8	81.2	60.3	84.5	69.4	95.4	79.3	83.0	54.6
2008年	53.8	46.2	84.8	75.9	86.4	80.0	92.6	86.8	86.4	60.8
2009年	58.4	53.2	84.1	75.7	86.7	80.7	93.9	88.1	87.5	46.8
2010年	60.1	54.4	85.7	77.2	87.5	82.4	94.4	89.8	89.5	48.1
2011年	58.9	46.8	85.5	85.5	89.5	75.9	96.7	86.3	89.5	39.5

从表中可知，城市声功能区中，4类区的夜间达标率是逐年下降的。根据《声环境功能区划分技术规范》中对4类区的划分办法，了解到4类区是沿着城市道路并根据道路的规模以及道路两旁的环境而划分的，所以，以上分析可以归结为，我国城市噪声污染最严重的环节，是道路交通噪声。在城市化的进程中，各种各样的建筑设施的建设、道路桥梁的施工、工厂设备的生产运行，都给人们带来越来越多的噪声污染，但是通过合理的规划布局，严格的管理以及一些隔声降噪措施，都可以把噪声污染降低到较低的水平，0类、1类、2类、3类区的达标情况越来越好就是一种表现。

（二）城市环境噪声类型

城市环境噪声主要包括交通噪声、工业噪声、施工噪声和其他噪声。

1. 交通噪声

目前，交通噪声已经成为影响最广泛的一种环境噪声。随着城市规模不断扩大和城市间交通的日渐繁忙，道路交通噪声污染也越来越严重。有关国外交通噪声的统计数据比较少。

在我国，根据国家环保总局报告的中国声环境状况，在道路交通噪声方面，统计的401个城市中，13个城市属重度污染，占3.2%；21个城市属中度污染，占5.2%；50个城市属轻度污染，占12.5%。141个城市交通声环境质量较好，占35.2%。176个城市声环境质量好，占43.9%。47个环保重点城市中，5个城市属轻度污染，24个城市交通声环境质量较好，18个城市交通声环境质量好。

中国328个市（镇）中，167个城市道路交通噪声环境质量好，占50.9%；109个城市道路交通声环境质量较好，占33.2%；32个城市为轻度污染，占9.8%；14个城市中度污染，占4.3%；6个城市重度污染，占1.8%。47个重点城市道路交通环境质量，16个城市道路交通声环境质量好，占34.0%；29个城市较好，占61.8%；1个城市轻度污染，占2.1%；1个城市中度污染，占2.1%。

从全国城市道路交通噪声调查结果分析，目前全国有16%的居民住在道路两边，受影响的人群约3 400万人；其中80%的人群，约2 700万人，白天在平均噪声级超过70分贝，夜间超过55分贝的高噪声干扰下生活。自20世纪80年代以来，我国社会经济获得了巨大的发展。随着城市化进程的日益加快，城市交通设施迅猛发展，机动车数量与日俱增，城市交通噪声污染也日益加剧。在影响城市环境的各种噪声源中，交通噪声约占30%，是仅次于社会生活噪声的第二大噪声源。

2. 工业噪声

随着工业技术的发展，相关部门和越来越多的人开始关注工业噪声所带来的危害。工业噪声会对人们的生活和健康带来不利影响。我国相对于欧美发达国家而言，对于工业噪声的控制起步较晚。我国对于工业噪声控制和治理方面的研究主要开展于近几年，随着我国现代工业的迅速发展，越来越多的人开始重视工业噪声所造成的危害，并开始研究工业噪声的治理方法。由于我国劳动人口众多，发达地区人口相对密集，而且工业发展水平相对于发达国家较弱，因此，我国的工业噪声治理更加重要，也更加困难。通过对工业噪声的特点进行分析，企业或生产单位对噪声进行控制时，比较有效的方法是在工业生产中控制噪声源或阻隔工业噪声的传播途径。从企业的发展角度讲，对工业噪声进行有效治理，不但可以防止工业噪声对工作人员和周边居民的身体健康造成伤害，还有利于提高企业的形象和工作效益。

3. 施工噪声

伴随着经济的飞速发展，城市房屋开发建设呈现快速上升的势头。但诸多施工现场的出现造成了一系列环境问题，最严重的就是施工产生噪声，经常造成大量群众上访投诉，而作业场地狭小、设备颁布无序、作业时间随意常常成为噪声扰民的主要原因。

施工噪声的来源主要包括四个方面：一是施工机械设备工艺老化，适应不了现代化建设的需要，产生高噪声污染；施工单位不淘汰或不更换新型设备，使得一些机械“带病”运转，产生高声级噪声污染环境。二是施工场地布局不合理，大多数露天施工，往往不设置隔声、吸声、消声等声屏障，使得建筑施工噪声直接向周围环境排放，产生强烈的建筑施工噪声污染。三是在施工过程中，噪声监测与工程监理的作用得不到发挥，不能保证对建筑施工噪声的有效监督管理。四是一些施工单位唯利是图，法律、法规意识淡薄，一味追求利益，无视法律，不分时段，随意施工，产生超标施工噪声，严重干扰周围人们的正常生产、生活。

4. 其他噪声

城市噪声除交通噪声、工业噪声和施工噪声以外，主要是社会生活噪声。随着城市文化娱乐产业和商业的兴旺发达，众多营业性文化娱乐和商业场所的开设日趋增多；在丰富群众休闲娱乐生活和日常生活的同时，歌厅、酒店营业和商业经营活动等音响设备噪声也给周边的居住、教育、办公等环境带来了诸多不利影响，城市社会生活噪声污染成为群众反映的热点问题。社会生活噪声主要有以下三个方面的特点：社会生活噪声的声源种类繁多，声学的频率特征中低频声成分丰富；社会生活噪声分布面广，并呈立体分布，主要分布在居民集中的市中心区；社会生活噪声的影响时段在夜间比较严重。

三、噪声图技术与应用

（一）噪声图技术的发展状况

噪声图技术源于欧洲，早在20世纪60年代，德国、捷克等欧洲国家就开始使用类似噪声地图的声级分布图来反映城市的噪声影响。1994年，西班牙马德里市则是利用4395个监测点的数据来绘制城市噪声分布图，并因此获得欧洲环保大奖，成为“走在欧盟前头的城市”。欧盟城市区域级战略噪声地图绘制的大规模开展源于其颁布的环境噪声指令（END，Directive2002/49/EC）（EU 2002），该指令要求各成员国绘制交通、工业等主要声源噪声影响地图，并基于噪声地图的结果编制噪声行动计划，加强环境噪声管理，规划实施噪声削减措施。亚洲的噪声图技术运用稍晚于欧洲，目前日本、韩国、中国香港等均建立了本地区的噪声图技术。

中国香港、台湾等地区已通过相关政策法规要求实施了噪声地图，成功通过该技术来控制环境噪声，并应用于城市规划、公众参与等方面。台湾的台南市建立起不同性质用地上的噪声地图，且分为夏季和冬季的早、中、晚三个时段，以体现噪声在不同用地和不同季节的分布情况。

近年来，国家环境保护部要求对全国主要城市进行环境噪声动态管理，努力降低城市环境噪声日趋严重污染现象，提出了在“十二五”期间对全国重点城市开展城市噪声地图的建立工作，科学、动态、直观地反映城市环境噪声污染特点、污染原因、污染趋势以及污染控制要点，为城市环境噪声管理、治理以及预警预报提供科学手段与方法。所以，在我国大力推行噪声图技术是实现环境噪声控制的必然要求。

（二）噪声图技术系统介绍

噪声地图是一种以不同颜色表示某一地区声环境水平状况的数据地图，一般由地理信息系统结合声学仿真模型软件绘制，并通过实测数据检验校正（见图1）。噪声地图以数字与图形的方式显示了噪声污染在城市区域范围内的分布状况，可以从空间和时间维度上较为全面地对噪声的影响进行判断和区分，使噪声控制更为有效，也有利于公众更为直观地了解整个城市区域和其所居地的声环境状况，并参与管理和监督；同时也可以为城市总体规划、交通发展、噪声污染控制提供科学决策依据。

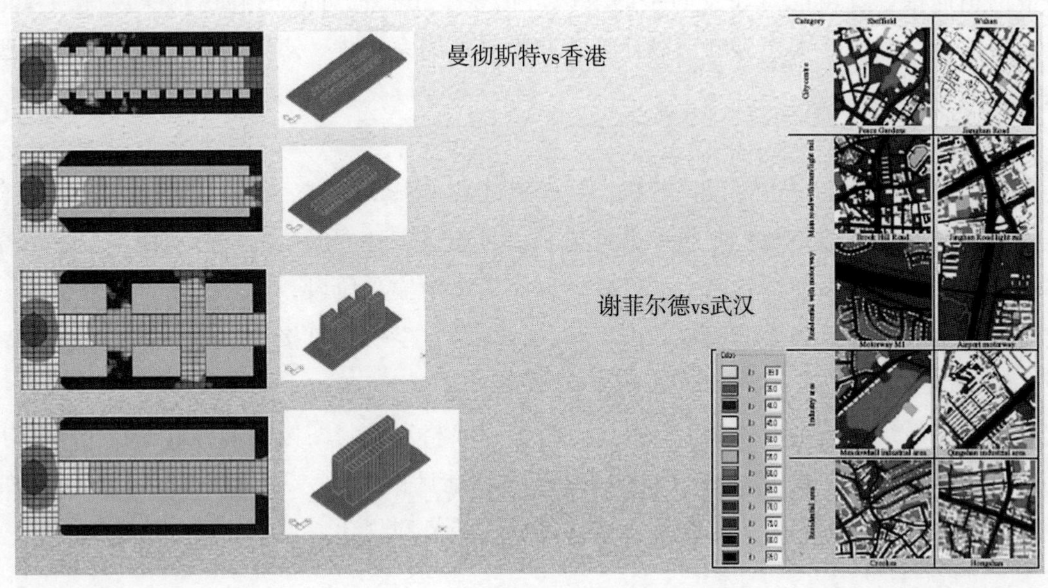

图1　噪声图技术示例

噪声地图系统可由地理信息系统（GIS）、声学模型系统、显示系统和校验系统4个子系统组成。地理信息系统主要用于建立区域地理模型；声学模型系统是将地理模型通过一定方式定义为声学模型，并进行声学计算的过程，也是整个系统的核心部分；显示系统用于将计算结果以各种形式直观地显示出来；校验系统主要用于系统误差分析。噪声地图的建立分为五个步骤：

1. *地理建模*

建立噪声地图系统的首要任务是区域地理模型的建立，即地理信息和相关建筑的输入。在噪声地图系统的地理建模中，主要输入内容包括：①城市道路、铁路和地面轨道交通的平面和立体分布；②相关建筑物位置及高度；③地形高差；④声屏障等降噪构筑物。噪声地图系统地理模型的主要特点在于，模型需突出其声源特性，对于道路、铁路、轨道交通等声源位置应重点关注，并明确它们与周围建筑之间的空间关系。

2. *声源定义*

声源定义过程的实质是将地理模型转变为声学模型的过程。在所建立的区域地理模型中，识别声源是主要的研究内容，识别声源又包括定义声源的地理属性和声源的流动特性。以道路声源为例，声源的地理属性主要包括红线宽度、车行道宽度、高程、坡度等；声源的流动特性则包括小时车流量、车型、车速等。

声源定义阶段必须明确区域的噪声特点、声源分布以及控制措施情况。一般而言，交通噪声（即道路、铁路、轨道交通等流动源产生的噪声）是城市区域的主要声源，也是系统重点考虑的对象，应予以明确识别。

3. 声学计算

在地理建模和声源定义后，需进行声学计算，计算原理遵循声波在空间传播规律，并考虑声源的指向性以及声能量在空间中的衰减等因素。主要的计算内容包括噪声源强度的计算、声传播计算和交通噪声影响声级计算。在噪声地图系统中，声学计算是通过声学模型软件来完成。

4. 结果校验

校验的目的是对系统进行误差分析。对于已建成的城市区域，校验主要通过计算点实测验证的方法，对计算结果和实测结果进行比较。对于噪声地图系统的实际应用应提出可靠的误差接受范围。在噪声地图系统中，校验结果应反馈给输入阶段，通过误差分析对建模、声源定义或参数输入进行必要的调整，进行再次计算，直至误差可接受。

5. 输出显示

噪声地图系统的输出以图像形式为主，可辅以表格形式。图像显示可以根据不同需求输出 2D、3D 或者动态图形，2D 显示一般可用于声功能区的管理，3D 显示可以判断声场的空间立体分布，动态显示则可用于表示区域噪声变化趋势和规律。

（三）噪声图技术的功能

噪声地图之所以在欧美发达国家广泛采用，是因为其在城市环境噪声管理方面具有优势。对城市大规模的环境噪声管理，传统监测技术就显得力不从心，其主要表现在运营成本高，受外界影响严重，同时对数据的统计和分析难度较大。噪声地图与传统的方法相比较，在噪声管理、工作效率和运行成本上具有较明显的优势，特别是在噪声污染的管理方面，由于噪声地图综合地融入了地理信息系统，使噪声地图在数据的采集与编辑、信息的统计分析等方面的功能得到更大的发挥。其主要功能有以下几方面：

（1）定性识别和定量分析噪声污染范围及程度，对城市范围内噪声污染严重的地区给予直观快速的展示和定位。

（2）分析环境噪声的发展趋势，预测未来噪声发展方向。对环境噪声情况的预测是噪声地图的重要功能之一。根据已有的噪声数据，结合交通等声源的发展趋势预测未来几年的环境噪声情况。环境噪声受周围环境情况的影响，如道路交通的新建、扩建及道路交通车流量的变化等都会使原有的区域环境噪声情况发生变化，而利用噪声地图，掌握相关的规划方案和声源方面的数据，就能对未来的噪声情况进行预测，以了解该区域若干年后的环境噪声情况。

（3）提供城市规划、道路变通规划的客观标准和依据。

城市规划是否合理，道路交通的规划是否合理，通过噪声地图的预测功能判断规划是否可行的标准和依据。城市、道路交通等建设规划除了满足相关领域的标准要求外，噪声也将是一个重要的衡量指标。利用噪声地图对拟规划的城市、道路交通建设进行模拟分析，预测建设完成后的建筑周围的环境噪声情况。如噪声超过标准，可对噪声严重的地方进行方案的修改或提前采取措施进行控制。

(4) 为环境决策者提供环境噪声利关的信息。

噪声地图能提供丰富的噪声信息，公众可通过噪声地图了解居住区的噪声信息，而环境决策者可利用噪声地图提供的信息进行决策或制定控制目标。

(5) 针对噪声严重的社区或区域，制定更加经济或有效的控制和减少噪声的措施。

通过噪声地图识别噪声较为严重的社区或区域，通过采取工程技术措施或相应的管理措施，并考虑措施引起的经济成本，综合各因素选择控制噪声的措施。

(6) 利用噪声地图研究噪声与投诉、烦扰度、失眠及其他指标的相关问题。

噪声是很多事件或现象的诱因，如噪声投诉事件，居民烦扰、失眠等现象，但是这些事件并不跟噪声的大小成简单的正比关系，还涉及噪声频谱、居住环境等因素。利用噪声地图，结合详细的地理信息，分析这些事件或现象跟噪声的关系。

(7) 噪声地图还具有检验噪声污染防治技术措施（如声屏障）和规划控制措施（如交通改道）有效性的功能。

基于噪声地图，可以通过调整输入数据来预测所采用措施能否达到预期效果，也可以将不同设计方案下的噪声预测结果进行比较，并结合其他因子（如成本等）选择最优的设计方案。

四、声景设计及运用

（一）声景简介

如今，人们对声环境舒适度的要求在不断提高，然而，噪声源的持续增加使得噪声控制技术的发展远远比不上声环境的恶化。随着研究的深入，人们发现降低声压级不一定能提高城市中的声舒适度。当声压级低于一定数值时，人们的声舒适度评价就不再取决于声压级，而是噪声类型、个人的特点以及其他因素起重要作用。

与传统的噪声控制不同，声景重视感知，而非仅物理量；考虑积极正面的声音，而非仅噪声；将声环境看成是资源，而非仅“废物”。综合物理、工程、社会、心理、医学、艺术等多学科的声景研究给环境声学领域带来了革命性的进展。研究的重点也不再是单纯地以降低声压级为目标的噪声控制，而是注重各个声音之间的平衡以及声音与环境、与人的和谐。声景观研究借鉴了心理学、社会学、生态学等方面的理论，注重听觉和非听觉因素在人对声音环境感知上的作用，力图通过声音环境的设计来提高整体环境的舒适度。声景设计为噪声控制提供了新的方法，同时也更突出了人的感受在环境优化中的作用。

（二）声景评价

声景观的评价是复杂的系统工程，与许多学科有关，如声学、生理学、社会学、心理学和统计学等。声景评价比较复杂，涉及不同声源之间的相互作用，也涉及声与其他因素之间的相互作用。

声景观在很多时候又被称为声生态学，主要研究声音、自然和社会之间的相互关系。声景观是一门涉及物理声学、环境科学、建筑学和生态学等多个领域的交叉学科，与环境心理学、环境影响评价等紧密结合，同时还从社会学、哲学、音乐学等一些全新的角度来看待和分析声音。声景观是多种学科相互渗透的结果，因此，对于声景观的评价量应该是包括其各方面特性的综合评价量。

声景观的定量评价量分为客观评价与主观评价两种，客观评价量主要是指由声音观引起的愉悦度，决定愉悦度主要因素包括：声音的物理属性、视觉景象、人文价值和个体特性。主观评价主要是在现场实验室的虚拟现实场景进行问卷调查，通过排序法、评分法、语义细分法、成对比较法等方法，得出对声景观的评价量。

（三）声景设计

声景设计不是简单的声音设计，更不是简单的电声系统集成，而是更高层次、内在的、综合的、带有很强“责任感”、能动地保护和创造美的声音生态环境的行动，是在创造生活环境的过程中，把声音作为一个要素，使之在改善我们的生活环境中发挥美的作用和价值。

近年来，以声景思想为基础的设计、施工的事例显著地增多，积极、有效地开展声景设计变得越来越热门。

声景设计的基本思想是取舍声音，不仅仅是听觉要素，还有视觉效果。在整个视野内，由于受到各种各样因素的影响，在某种程度上捕捉声音就不那么容易了。在360°的任何方向上，都有声音传来，既不能被遮断，也不能挑选和逃避。也就是说，声音是具有强制约束力的多媒体要素。仅仅这一点，可想而知它对环境的影响力有多大。所以，我们的责任重大。即使有好的设计方法，在应用时也要格外小心和慎重，不能主观想象，要有相当的责任感。

（四）声景观设计

声景观设计是运用声音要素，对空间的声音环境进行全面的设计和规划，并加强声环境与总体景观的协调。在传统的声学设计中，一般以人工声为主，而声景观的设计理念扩大了声音要素的范围，涵盖了自然声、城市声、生活声，也通过场景的设置，唤醒记忆声或联想声等内容，是声要素上一种思想的革新。

声景观的设计手法可分为以下几个方面：

（1）由于声景观包含了自然声、人工声以及人文声等多种因素，因此，在声景观的设计中，可以根据对象景观类型和使用功能的不同，结合景观设计对象的特征、定位、功能和使用特性，选定构成要素，协调各组成要素之间的关系。

（2）根据声景观的定位，针对不同情况运用正、负、零三种设计方法对声景观进行设计。正设计就是在原有的声景观中添加新的声要素；负设计去除声景观中与环境不协调、不必要、不被希望听到的声音；零设计是对声景观按原状保护和保存，不做任何更改。

（3）由于城市空间使用目的和功能分区各不相同，基于声景观全面、综合的理念，在公共空间设计中进行多样化的声景观设计，以此来与公共空间的功能分区相协调。

五、结论

伴随着我国经济的快速发展和人民生活水平的日益提高，噪声污染问题得到了更为广泛的关注，环境噪声与经济发展、人体健康和环境质量都有密切的关系。本文通过对我国城市环境噪声状况的综述和对噪声图技术及声景设计的介绍，总结了目前我国城市环境噪声的现状和挑战，指出了噪声图技术和声景设计的功能和优势。

噪声图技术的优势包括：①通过对比不同周期的噪声地图，掌握环境噪声的发展趋势，制订科学合理的噪声污染防治战略政策；②通过区域声环境影响预测，为城市建设规划和规模噪声控制措施规划提供重要信息和技术支撑；③通过直观展示声环境质量状况，为环境管理部门和公众提供更畅通有效的交流平台。

声景设计是环境噪声控制的新方法，它从声、环境和听者的角度出发研究声环境的组成、结构和功能，从审美和人文的角度出发研究听者在特定的环境中对声音的认识和评价，从自然、社会和文化的角度出发研究声音的环境效应，并在此基础上研究声景的规划、保护、设计、施工和记录的理论和方法。声景概念的提出为景观设计师提供了一个研究城市景观的新方向，以声景理论为基础，以声音为切入点研究城市空间则是建筑设计师或者城市规划师新的理论研究点。

面对我国城市环境噪声逐步恶化的现状，噪声图技术和声景设计方法应当被大规模和大范围地进行推广和运用。

（作者：陈勇，中国工程院院士，中国科学院广州能源研究所；康健，苏州中科院全周期绿色建筑研究院；宋蕾，苏州中科院全周期绿色建筑研究院）

参考文献

［1］Ballas，JA. Common factions in the identification of an assortment of brief everyday sounds［J］. Journal of Experimental Psychology：Human Perception and Performance，1993.

［2］Henrik K. The acoustic environment as a public domain［J］. Soundscape，2000，1（2）：10－13.

［3］KANG，J.，1996，Acoustics in long enclosures with multiple sources. Journal of the Acoustical Society of America，99，985－989.

［4］KANG，J.，1988，Noise at the year 2000. Proceedings of the 5th International Congress on Noise as a Public Health Problem，Stockholm.

［5］KANG，J.，1996，Modelling of train noise in underground stations. Journal of Sound and Vibration，195，241－255.

[6] KANG, J., 1996, Reverberation in rectangular long enclosures with geometrically reflecting boundaries. Acustica united with Acta Acustica, 82, 509-516.

[7] KANG, J., 1996, Sound attenuation in long enclosures. Building and Environment, 31, 245-253.

[8] KANG, J., 2000, Sound field resulting from diffusely reflecting boundaries: comparison between various room shapes. Proceedings of the 7th International Congress on Sound and Vibration, Garmisch-Partenkirchen, Germany.

[9] KANG, J., 2005, Numerical modeling of the sound fields in urban squares [J]. J. Acoust. Soc. Am. 117 (6).

[10] KANG, J., 2007, Urban Soundscape, Journal of South China University of Technology (Natural Science Edition) [J]. Vol35: 12-16.

[11] Kang, J. and BROCLLESBY, M. W., 2003, Apllication of micro-perforated absorbers in developing novel windows system for opimum acoustics, ventilation and daylighting performance. Proceedings of the Institute of Acoustics, Oxford, UK.

[12] Kang, J. and BROCLLESBY, M. W., 2004, Design of acoustic windows with micro-perforated absorbers. Proceedings of the 18th International Conference on Aountics, Kyoto, Japan.

[13] Kang, J. and BROCLLESBY, M. W., 2004, Feasibility of applying micro-perforated absorbers in acoustic window systems. Applied Acoustics. 66, 669-689.

[14] Kang, J. and Li, Z., 2006, Numerrcal simulation of an acoustic window system using finite element method. Acustica united with Acta Acustica.

[15] KANG, J., GRASBY, P., DERRICK, M., FRANKS, L., WILLIAMS, P., FLINDELL, I., and HARSHAM, K., 2001, Environmental Performance: Noise and Acoustic Management Engineering-Group Guidelines. BP report, London.

[16] Kang-Ting Tsai, Min-Der Lin, Yen-Hua Chen. Noise mapping in urban environments: A Taiwan study [J]. Applied Acoustics, 2009, 70 (7): 964-972.

[17] Phil Turner, lain McGregor, Susan Turner etc. Evaluating Soundscapes as a Means of Creating a Sense of Place [C]. Proceedings of the 2003 International Conference on Auditory Display, Boston MA, USA, 6-9, July2003.

[18] Schulte-fortkamp, B. The quality of acoustic environments and the meaning of soundscape [C]. Proceedings of the 17th International Congress on Acoustic (ICA), Rome, Italy, 2001.

[19] 陈克安，闫靓．环境声质量的主观与客观评价［A］．2003 全国环境声学电磁辐射环境学术会议论文集［C］．2003：1-6.

[20] 国家环保总局．中国 2003 年环境状况公报［Z］．2004.

[21] 葛坚．城市景观中的声景观解析与设计［J］．浙江大学学报（工学版），2004（8）.

[22] 葛坚，城市开放空间声景观形态构成及设计研究［J］．浙江大学学报（工学版），2006.

[23] 葛坚，卜菁华．关于城市公园声环境及其设计的探讨［J］．建筑学报，2003（9）.

[24] 李国棋．声景研究和声景设计［D］．北京：清华大学，2004.

[25] 刘磊，户文成．噪声地图技术的发展及应用实践［A］．2010 年全国声学设计与噪声振动控制工程暨配套装备学术会议［C］．2010.

[26] 林晶．声景研究［D］．武汉：华中科技大学，2008.

[27] 李迅，刘俊肖．完善中国噪音污染防治立法的思考［J］．资源与产业，2006，8（6）.

[28] 康健. 城市声环境论 [M]. 北京：科学技术出版社，2011：126-131.
[29] 康健，杨威. 城市公共开放空间中的声景 [J]. 世界建筑，2002，(6)：76-79.
[30] 康健. 声景：现状及前景 [J]. 新建筑，2014 (5).
[31] 宋剑玮. 声景观综述 [J]. 噪声与振动控制，2012，10 (5).
[32] 夏丹. 城市噪声地图系统研究及试验性应用 [J]. 噪声与振动控制，2011 (4).
[33] 夏丹，周裕德，祝文英. 噪声地图应用于声环境管理研究 [J]. 噪声与振动控制，2013 (4).

城市公共安全综合风险评估与评价指标体系

一、前言

公共安全是国家安全和社会稳定的基石，是人民安居乐业的基本保证，是构建和谐社会的重大战略性问题，也是涉及国计民生的重大公益性问题。当前，我国处于经济高速发展阶段，也正处于经济社会转型期，公共安全形势严峻。汶川大地震、南方雨雪冰冻、SARS/禽流感疫情、新疆暴力恐怖袭击事件等公共安全突发事件频发，严重影响着国民经济和民生的全面协调可持续发展。据统计，每年由自然灾害、事故灾难、公共卫生、社会安全等公共安全突发事件造成的损失从2005年的6 000亿元人民币上升到2012年的9 000亿元人民币，造成非正常死亡超过20万人，伤残超过200万人。大幅提升公共安全保障能力已刻不容缓、迫在眉睫。

公共安全的重点在城市。当前，世界的城市化平均水平已经超过50%，世界已经进入城市社会时代，我国也已进入加快城市化进程的阶段。党的十八届三中全会《中共中央关于全面深化改革若干重大问题的决定》中提出“推进以人为核心的城镇化”。《国家新型城镇化规划（2014-2020年）》中指出：“城镇化是现代化的必由之路。”截至2013年，我国城市达到658个，其中100万人口以上的城市140个，500万人口以上的城市16个，全国建制镇达到20113个。城市是所在地区的政治、经济、文化、交通的中心，人口密集、财富集中、建筑物密度高，基础设施和生命线工程发达且密集。城市突发事件往往造成严重的人员伤亡和经济损失。城市人流量大、交通和信息技术发达、媒体传播迅速的特点使突发事件极易演变为社会危机并迅速扩散。如果应对不当，危机极有可能变成区域性甚至全国性的社会危机。在城市安全问题日趋复杂、城市安全保障受到政府、社会和公众的普遍与高度重视的当前，我国政府提出了“预防为主、关口前移”的应急管理方针，《突发事件应对法》明确规定了“突发事件应对工作实行预防为主、预防与应急相结合的原则”，对突发事件风险评估工作给予高度重视。城市公共安全综合风险评估研究已成为当务之急。

二、公共安全三角形理论模型

风险评估是人们认识风险并进而主动降低风险的重要手段，是风险管理的重要基础。风险评估就是估算、衡量风险，通过运用科学的方法，对所掌握的统计资料、风险信息及风险的性质进行系统分析和研究，进而确定各项风险的频度（发生可能性）和强度（后果严重程度），为选择适当的风险处理方法提供依据。

长期以来，国内外在突发事件风险理论与方法方面开展了大量的研究，大致可分为以下三个发展阶段。第一阶段是致灾因子论阶段。致灾因子论学者认为，影响突发事件风险大小的主要因素来自于致灾因子的危险性，侧重于根据致灾因子强度阈值刻画灾害等级。第二阶段是承灾载体论研究阶段。承灾载体面对致灾因子表现出来的脆弱性受到学者们的极大关注。突发事件风险研究也由传统的致灾因子成灾机理分析及统计分析发展为与人类社会分析紧密结合，即不仅关注致灾因子分析，也注重承灾载体的脆弱性分析，其中承灾载体脆弱性的研究是重点。第三阶段是综合研究阶段。随着致灾因子论和承灾载体论学者从各自的研究领域对突发事件风险研究的深入，学者们开始从综合的角度考虑突发事件的风险，研究将致灾因子论和承灾载体论相结合的基于灾害系统的风险。

综观突发事件从发生、发展到造成灾害性作用直至采取应急措施的全过程，范维澄院士提出了“公共安全三角形”理论模型，诠释了公共安全的多主体、多目标、多层级、多类型的复杂体系。该模型将公共安全体系分为突发事件、承灾载体和应急管理三大组成部分，通过物质、能量和信息三个灾害要素将三者联系起来，形成一个有机整体，这对我们深入地认识和分析公共安全体系具有重要的指导意义。突发事件是灾害事故本身（如地震、台风、暴雨等），承灾载体是突发事件作用的对象（如城市构筑物、基础设施、人等），应急管理是采取应对措施的过程（如预防准备、应急响应、恢复重建等）。公共安全问题需要研究突发事件的孕育、发生、发展到突变的演化规律及其产生的能量、物质和信息等风险作用的类型、强度及时空特性；研究承灾载体在突发事件作用下和自身演化过程中的状态及其变化，可能产生的本体和（或）功能破坏，及其可能发生的次生、衍生事件；还需要研究在上述过程中如何施加人为干预，从而预防或减少突发事件的发生，弱化其作用；增强承灾载体的抵御能力，阻断次生事件的链生，减少损失；避免应急不当可能造成的突发事件的再生及承灾载体的破坏以及代价过度。

从公共安全体系架构的角度出发，我们构建了一个全面考虑突发事件、承灾载体和应急管理的系统性的城市公共安全综合风险评估模型，即以公共安全三角形理论为基础，从突发事件危险性、承灾载体脆弱性和应急能力三方面构建城市公共安全综合风险评估模型（见图 1）。该体系全面考虑了公共安全问题的主要因素，为城市公共安全综合风险评估奠定了良好的基础。

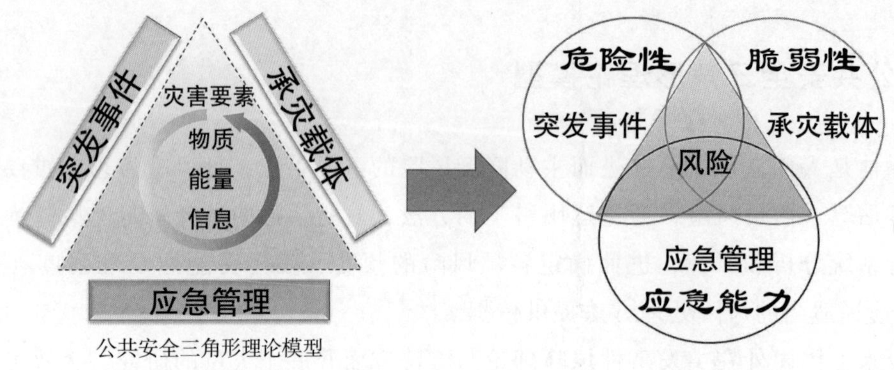

图1 基于公共安全三角形理论的城市公共安全综合风险评估模型

三、城市公共安全综合风险评估

对城市公共安全开展综合风险评估主要有基于事故分析的风险评估方法、基于指标体系的风险评估方法和基于突发事件演化动力学的风险评估方法等。我们主要介绍基于指标体系和基于突发事件演化动力学的评估方法。

（一）基于指标体系的城市公共安全综合风险评估方法

基于指标体系的评估方法一般包括如下几方面的要素：

（1）评估指标：对于基于指标体系的评估方法，指标是评价的依据。由于影响风险的因素往往非常多且复杂，通常需要建立一套指标体系，从整体上反映风险。每个指标都从不同的侧面刻画影响风险的某种特性。

（2）权重系数：对于不同的风险评估对象，评估指标之间的相对重要性是不同的，评估指标之间的这种相对重要性的大小，可以用权重系数来表示。每个指标对应于一个权重系数，反映出该指标对总风险的影响程度。权重系数确定得是否合理，关系到评价结果的可信程度。

（3）数学模型：对于已经建立好的评估指标体系，需要通过一定的数学方法将多个指标的评估值“综合”成为一个整体的评估值，这就是所选择的模型。可用于“综合”的数学方法很多，通常根据评估对象的特点和评估的需求选取适当的方法。常用的基于指标的风险评估方法主要有层次分析法、模糊综合评估法、基于灰色理论的综合评估方法等。

以台风灾害为例，以基于公共安全三角形理论的城市公共安全综合风险评估模型为基础，通过文献调研、致灾因子数据挖掘、专家商讨等方法，并根据统计数据，建立了一套台风综合风险评估指标体系。指标体系从致灾因子危险性、承灾载体脆弱性及应急能力三个方面对台风综合风险评估指标进行构建。如图2所示，致灾因子危险性包括台风发生频率、最大风速、最大24小时降雨量三个二级指标；承灾载体脆弱性包括地势高度、房屋抗风能力、农林牧渔业比例、人口密度及弱势群体比例五个二级指标。应急能力包括人均GDP、应急避难所数量、公路线密度和医疗水平四个二级指标。基于该指标体系，通过历史数据统计分析，可以对城市区域的台风灾害风险进行评估，并基于 GIS（地理信息系统）数据，绘制台风灾害风险地图。

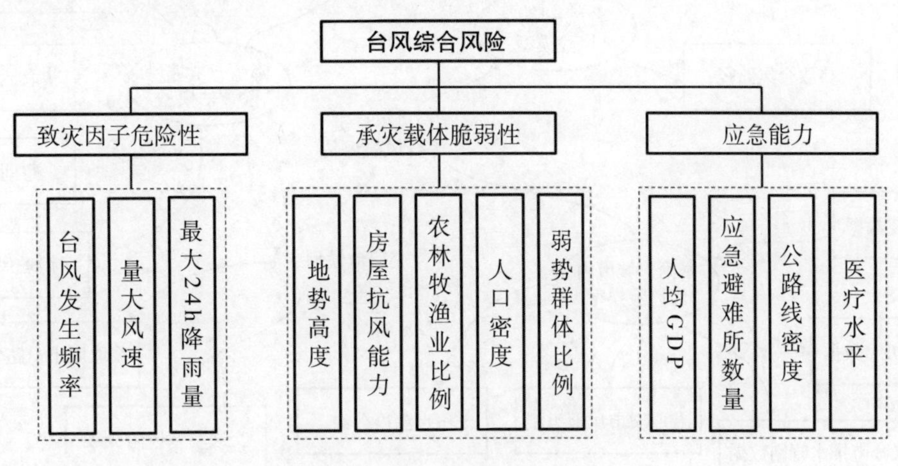

图2　台风风险综合评价指标体系

（二）基于突发事件演化动力学的城市突发事件链综合风险评估方法

近年来，城市公共安全突发事件呈现出典型的次生衍生特点。如地震引发滑坡、泥石流、火灾、危化品泄漏等，台风引发暴雨、内涝、滑坡等。我们将某一初始突发事件发生时，可能诱发一连串的次生、衍生突发事件发生的现象称为突发事件链。突发事件链已经成为威胁人民生命财产不容忽视的重要因素，对可能出现的突发事件链进行综合的定量风险分析对于提高应对突发事件链的风险管理水平有重要意义。

基于突发事件演化动力学的风险评估方法通过对可能发生的突发事件链的演化过程的模拟，分析其可能影响的范围和程度，考查该影响范围内人的生命所面临的风险、可能的经济损失、环境破坏等，从而计算总的风险值。

同样以台风为例，建立了基于突发事件演化动力学的城市台风突发事件链综合风险评估方法。对台风引发降水、降水引发城市内涝、降水影响区域性滑坡、内涝引发交通堵塞等的突发事件链式过程进行模拟、分析。集成了台风热带气旋风场模型、台风引发降雨模型、降雨径流模型、交通流模型等，对突发事件的强度和时空特性进行模拟。之后，基于承灾载体的脆弱性分析获得影响范围、经济损失等风险后果，具体流程如图 3 所示。该方法突破了以往基于指标体系的相对静态的风险评估模式，可以对突发事件进行时间和空间上的动态风险评估。

基于上述研究方法，研发了城市多灾种综合风险评估系统，由综合风险地图、动态风险评估、应急能力分析、事件风险管理、查询统计分析等子系统组成，已在宁波、龙岩等城市应急管理部门使用，取得了良好效果，为城市综合风险评估工作提供了有效的分析和管理工具。

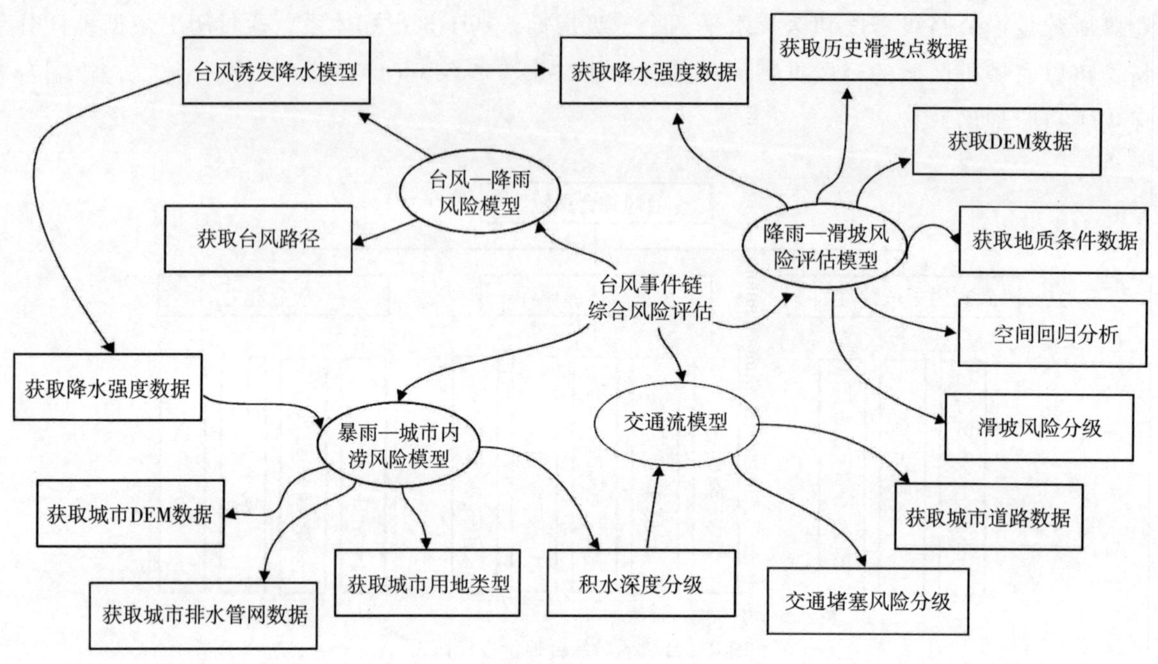

图3　台风突发事件链综合风险评估

四、安全保障型城市评价指标体系

日益加快的城市化进程给公共安全提出新问题，其核心是城市规划建设与城市安全综合评价等技术体系脆弱性的矛盾，这些问题为城市安全评价提出新需求。安全保障型城市的评价指标体系与评价系统可为我国安全保障型城市的综合评价提供技术手段和标准支撑，一方面，通过深入研究城市安全状况，可为推进创建安全保障型城市工作提供有效管理工具和评价依据，促进社会的安全发展、和谐发展；另一方面，通过评价指标体系的实施和对比分析，及时发现薄弱环节，采取针对性改进措施，以评促建，逐步提升城市安全水平和社会治理水平。

安全保障型城市评价涉及自然灾害、事故灾难、公共卫生、社会安全等多种类型的突发事件，又涉及对城市公共安全的历史状况的回顾评价、公共安全现状评价以及对未来应对突发事件的能力评价等时间因素，同时还体现了城市运行系统对城市公共安全状况所做出的反应。因此，在构建安全保障型城市评价指标体系时，需要考虑领域范畴、影响范围、时间跨度三个维度。在领域维度方面按照公共安全突发事件分类方法分为自然灾害、事故灾难、公共卫生、社会安全四个方面。在影响维度方面借鉴公共安全体系三角形模型，分为致灾因子、承受能力、防控管理、后果状态四个方面。在时间维度方面，按照时间顺序分为过去、现状、将来三个时间段。

基于影响维度的安全保障型城市评价指标体系（如图4所示），以问卷调查等形式，通过征求城市管理部门、社会公众、公共安全专家等不同人员的意见，在对相关意见汇总分析

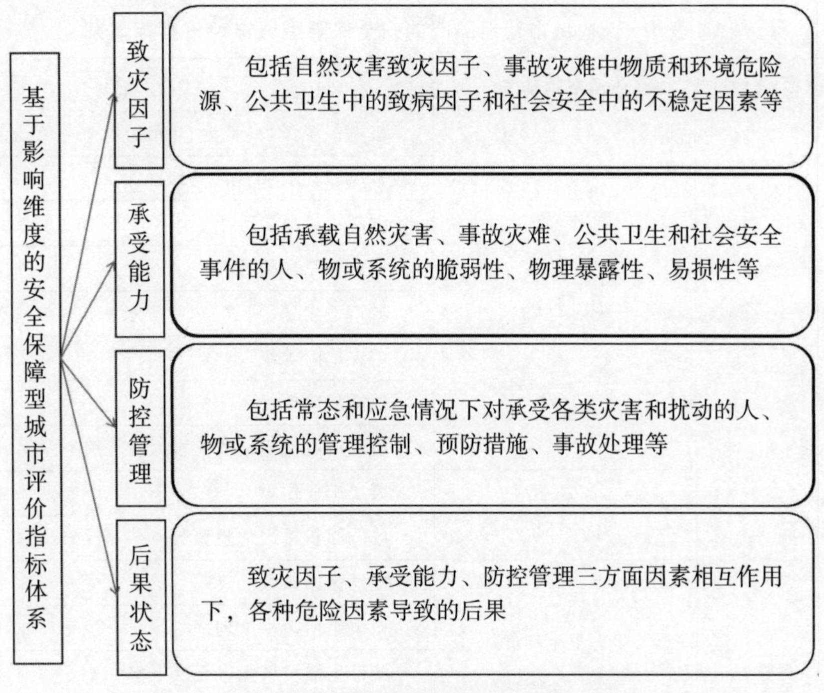

图4　基于影响维度的安全保障型城市评价指标体系

的基础上，并考虑获取数据的可能性，形成包括四大方面12项二级指标47项三级指标的《面向城市管理部门的安全保障型城市评价指标体系》（见表1）。为了让社会公众能够直观、快速地对城市的公共安全状况进行评价，广泛收集社会公众对安全保障型城市评价的意见和认识，在北京、上海、海口、合肥、阜新、遵义等35个城市进行拦截访问和问卷调查的基础上，形成包括10个指标的《面向社会公众的安全保障型城市评价指标体系》（见表2）。在此基础上，形成国家标准《安全保障型城市评价指南（送审稿）》。

安全保障型城市的评价系统是基于上述的评价指标体系，以地理信息为载体，收集和整合试点城市各部门、各区县数据资源，建立在面向安全保障型城市评价的数据资源体系的基础上，通过收集评价城市对指标的选择等反馈信息，研发具有开放性和适应性的软件系统。主要功能由运行监测、运行仿真、运行评估、安全评价等模块构成。运行监测模块通过政务专网采集涉及城市运行的给排水、供电量、供热量、气象、垃圾量、环保、安全生产、公共卫生等多个职能部门日常数据及相关视频数据，并进行综合分析和趋势预测，形成城市运行监测指标周报。运行仿真模块主要涉及描述单一基础设施网络在正常工况及故障条件下运行状态的单一网络运行仿真，推演基础设施网络相互影响的基础设施网络关联仿真，以及推演城市中各种能动主体相互影响的城市运行模拟仿真等功能。运行评估系统是针对城市运行相关事件，按照各级应急管理工作常态和非常态需要，日常接报各地、各有关单位城市运行事件信息和预测预警信息，进行风险分析和综合研判等。安全评价模块是基于上述评价指标体系进行综合评价的软件系统，包括面向管理部门、面向社会公众、历史评价结果、评价地图配置、评价指标管理、评价指标分配等功能模块。

表1　面向城市管理部门的安全保障型城市评价指标体系

一级指标	二级指标	三级指标
(A)致灾因子	(A1)自然环境	极端气温天数(低温、热浪)
		台风(风暴潮)风险等级
		洪涝灾害风险等级
		城市干旱风险等级
		城市沙尘暴(风灾)风险等级
		雪灾风险等级
		地震风险等级
		滑坡泥石流等地质灾害风险等级
	(A2)生产环境	第二产业比重
		单位面积重大危险源数
	(A3)生态卫生环境	空气污染指数优良率
		城镇生活污水处理率
		城市生活垃圾无害化处理率
	(A4)社会经济环境	恩格尔系数
		城乡居民收入差距比值
		城镇登记失业率
		城市流动人员比例
		万人刑事案件立案数
(B)承受能力	(B1)人口脆弱性	人口密度
		人口年龄结构指数
	(B2)结构脆弱性	建筑物密度
		单位面积地下管线长度
		三级及以下公路占公路总长度的比例
	(B3)经济脆弱性	单位面积 GDP
(C)防控管理	(C1)预防保障	气象观测站密度
		建筑物抗震设防等级
		重大危险源监控率
		突发公共卫生事件报告及时率
		刑事案件破案率
		基本社会保险覆盖率
	(C2)应急处置	人均避难场所面积
		人均道路面积
		万人消防人员数
		万人卫生技术人员数
		万人医疗卫生机构病床数
		万人人民警察数

续表 1

一级指标	二级指标	三级指标
(C) 防控管理	(C3) 安全投入	公共安全财政支出占 GDP 比重
		社会保障财政支出占 GDP 比重
		医疗财政支出占 GDP 比重
		教育财政支出占 GDP 比重
(D) 后果现状	(D1) 人口伤亡	自然灾害受灾人口比重
		亿元 GDP 生产安全事故死亡率
		甲乙类法定传染病十万人死亡率
		万人刑事案件死亡人数
	(D2) 财产损失	自然灾害直接经济损失占 GDP 比重
		万人因灾受损、倒塌房屋数量
		生产安全事故直接经济损失占 GDP 比重

表 2　面向社会公众的安全保障型城市评价指标体系

评价方面	评价指标
(A) 孕育环境	典型自然灾害风险等级
	单位面积重大危险源数
	空气污染指数优良率
	万人刑事案件立案数
(B) 安全防控保障	基本社会保险覆盖率
	110、119、120(999)到达现场的平均时间
	人均避难场所面积
	公共安全财政投入占 GDP 比重
(C) 历史灾害影响	突发事件人员伤亡率
	灾害直接经济损失占 GDP 比重

上述成果在重庆市应急管理办公室、重庆市长寿区应急管理办公室和规划局，吉林市应急管理办公室，长治市安全监督管理局进行示范应用，取得了良好的效果，均评价系统技术先进、稳定可靠、高效实用、操作方便，为完善城市公共安全治理体系、全面提升城市公共安全治理能力提供了重要手段和科技保障，具有很好的推广价值。

五、结语

随着城镇化进程的加快，城市公共安全突发事件更加复杂化、多样化，总体形势严峻。“预防为主、关口前移”是我国政府应急管理的基本方针，开展有效的城市公共安全风险评估是预防和减轻突发事件损失的重要途径。基于公共安全三角形理论的城市公共安全综合风险评估模型全面地考虑了公共安全体系的主要因素，为城市公共安全综合风险评估奠定了良好的基础。指标体系和事件演化动力学相结合是城市公共安全综合风险评估的主要方法。安全保障型城市评价指标体系为城市安全评价提供了科学的依据。研发的城市公共安全综合风险评估系统为城市风险管理和安全评价提供了有效的分析和管理工具。着眼平时保障，加强风险评估，重视科技研发，为实现科学有效的城市公共安全保障提供有力支撑。

（作者：黄弘，清华大学公共安全研究院教授；翁文国，清华大学公共安全研究院教授；范维澄，中国工程院院士，清华大学公共安全研究院院长、教授）

关于协调区域与城乡发展的政策建议

2014年12月，习近平总书记在论述“四个全面”的战略布局时指出：“中国已经进入全面建设小康社会的决定性阶段。实现这个目标是实现中华民族伟大复兴的关键一步。”他所指的全面小康，就是要使不同人群，不同地域的城乡居民全都实现小康。他认为，要实现这一目标，“当前最艰巨最繁重的任务在农村，特别是在贫困地区”。如何实现上述战略目标，就自己所从事的专业角度，提出协调区域与城乡发展的若干政策建议。

一、我国经济社会发展到现阶段，应在逐步缩小区域间、城乡间的相对贫富差距方面加大力度

国外有人把中国特色的社会主义道路，诬称为中国共产党领导的资本主义，对此应据理予以驳斥。他们将市场经济完全等同于资本主义。的确，若听凭市场经济无任何约束导向的盲目自由地发展，必将导致资本主义。我国实行的是社会主义的市场经济。在当前深化改革的过程中，既要让市场这只看不见的手在资源配置中起决定性作用，通过市场竞争提高效率，尽量把经济产出这块蛋糕做大；又要让代表全国最广大人民根本利益的中国共产党领导的政府这只看得见的手，在规划引导、宏观调控、市场监管和收益分配的社会公平方面更好地发挥作用，尽量把经济收益这块蛋糕分好，使其不偏离走向共同富裕的社会主义道路。

在我国经济社会的发展进程中，始终存在着经济效率与社会公平这对矛盾。在经济开始崛起的高速增长期，主要追求经济效率。在社会物质生活条件普遍有所改善的同时，地区间、城乡间、群体间贫富差距的拉大，是一时难以避免的不争事实。现今我国已进入中等收入国家行列，经济的发展已由以往追求GDP的高速增长，转向提质量、增效益、调结构的新常态。提质增效应兼顾经济、生态和社会效益，使发展具有可持续性。调结构应包括产业结构和地域结构。调产业结构要重视转型升级，改以创新为重要驱动力。调地域结构要促进区域间、城乡间更协调和谐地发展，要为相对缩小区域间、城乡间的贫富差距和在全国各地全面建成小康社会，制定更合理有效的政策和更有力的改革措施。

二、区域政策应由协调东部与中、西部地区及东北地区的发展，进一步向协调发达或较发达的核心地区与其外围欠发达或贫困地区之间的发展深化

改革开放以来，我国的区域政策主要侧重于协调东部地区与中、西部地区的发展。在我国确实存在着长期历史开发过程所形成的由沿海向内地，由东部向中部、西部地区较明显的发展水平递降的梯度差，需通过协调促进其共同发展。后来为振兴东北老工业基地，又划出一块东北地区，变成四大板块区域的协调发展。但最近一二十年来，随着市场经济的快速发展，地域间贫富差距的拉大，并不主要体现在四大板块之间，而是体现在以大都市或城市群所在地区为核心的发达、较发达地区与其外围的农村为主的欠发达或贫困地区之间。若只看四大区域板块的平均值，地区间的差别不是很大，而且还在逐步缩小。如以东部地区2000年和2012年的人均GDP指数各为1，则中部地区2000年为0.49，2012年为0.56；西部地区2000年为0.41，2012年为0.54；东北地区2000年为0.80，2012年仍为0.80。同在东部地区的河北省，实为京津都市区外围的欠发达省，其与京津地区发展水平的差距，大于西部地区与东部地区的平均差距。具体到冀北、冀中地区，以及东部其他省的鲁西、苏北、浙西南、闽西、粤东北等地区，则其发展水平与京津、长三角、珠三角等东部核心地区的差距高出西部地区与东部地区平均差距约一倍左右。在中、西部地区也有一些较发达的以大都市为核心的地区，其发展水平略低于东部核心地区而高于整个东部地区的平均水平。东部核心地区与中西部的有些贫困地区的平均收入差距则超出10倍以上。因此，有必要以县（市、区）域为单元，按不同的人均GDP或人均收入水平，划分出发达、较发达、欠发达、贫困等不同类型区域，以利于制定有区别对待的区域政策。同时通过市场运作和政府推动，在不同类型区域间发展不同层次、相互交叉、互联互通、以强带弱、协调配合、互利共赢的都市经济圈。

三、发展城市群只能作为人口密集的发达地区城镇化的主体形态，不宜作为全国城镇化的主体形态

大都市作为一定区域经济社会发展的核心，其空间演化存在着以下几种布局形态：一为大都市中心区不断摊大饼式向外空间扩张，形成单一的特大、超大城市。二为在大都市周围发展卫星城和相对独立的中小城市，形成众星拱月的都市圈。三为与邻近较大的都市和众多不同规模的城市组成相互紧密联系的城市群。

城市群所在地区一般均指城镇化水平和城市发育程度较高的大中小城市分布较密集的核心地区。在人口密集的发达地区，发展城市群的空间布局形态，肯定优于单中心独大的空间过度膨胀，也优于众星拱月式的都市圈。然而，并不是所有地区在经济发达后都能形成城市群。只有在人口密集、区位和资源环境优势明显的核心地带，通过长期发展和规划引导，才

能形成高度城市化的多中心、较密集的城市群。有些发达的核心地区，因早已形成一城独大的格局，为改善其空间布局，只宜在其周围发展培育众多中小城市的都市圈，已无可能亦无必要发展成为多中心的城市群。若任意将彼此相距遥远，间隔有广大农村地区甚至大片草原牧场的多个中心城市捆绑在一起，圈成城市群，则将失去城市群的真实含义，难以合力发挥城市群作为核心地区的强大对外辐射影响作用。

在我国适宜于发展城市群或都市圈等核心地区的地域面积毕竟只占全国广大国土面积的较小比重。故不宜将发展城市群作为全国城镇化的主体形态。城镇化的国土空间开发，一般都要经历由点、轴到网络的逐步推进过程。在对全国具有巨大影响力的东部三大城市群中，长三角和珠三角城市群发育已较成熟，已基本上实现了由点轴到网络的空间开发全过程。京津冀城市群尚处在进一步发育阶段。为改变以往过于突出京津两大都市的局面，正通过京津冀的协同发展，加速对毗邻京津的河北省境内的轴网开发，使其多数城市也能融入京津冀城市群。为加强我国中西部地区的开发，仍有必要沿长江经济带和丝绸之路经济带国内段的主要发展轴，培育若干新的城市群或都市圈。然而当前在中西部地区新培育城市群，已不具备像改革开放初期那样培育沿海城市群的难得机遇和特殊优惠条件。只能在规划引导下，顺其自然推动其逐步发展，不能揠苗助长，急于求成。总之，我国发展到现阶段，已不能将城镇化的重点主要放在发展核心地区的城市群，应同时加大关注城市群外围地区的城镇化。后者空间布局的主体形态，将是以中小城市为主的广域分布的城镇网络体系。

四、因地制宜，着力发展广大农村地区的县域经济，推进以产业化为基础的部分农村人口在县域内就近城镇化

要使全国各地全面实现小康，必须着力发展欠发达和贫困地区的县域经济。要使我国现有的贫困人口迅速脱贫，除采取针对贫困户和贫困乡村的精准扶贫措施外，还要重视发展当地的县域经济，否则将难以巩固已取得的脱贫成果。在我国县域经济发展较好的地区早已实现了全面小康，遇有少数困难户或贫困乡村，当地政府可依靠雄厚的财力轻易帮助他们脱贫致富。

县是我国历史延续已两千多年的行政管辖基本地域单元。历来就有“郡县治，天下安”之说。我国有些县域面积甚至还大于欧洲的小国。所以，要在全国全面建成小康社会，必须发展各县的县域经济。发展欠发达地区和贫困地区的县域经济已成为当前的难点和重点。

现有的欠发达县或贫困县多以从事农业生产的农村地区为主，当地城镇的非农产业基础相当薄弱，主要依靠大量农民外出打工挣钱以增加当地居民的收入。故要发展欠发达和贫困地区的县域经济，首先应在深化农村经济体制改革的基础上，引进资金和技术，大力推进农业生产现代化和产业化的规模经营，发展主要农牧产品由生产、储运、加工到市场营销的一条龙产业链，发展以中小企业为主、有当地资源和产品特色、有市场需求的加工制造业。同时可积极创造条件，争取从发达地区引入某些因其产业结构转型需向外转移的加工企业或其主要产业链需进一步向外拓展延伸的企业。要大力发展为当地生产和生活服务的包括部分现

代服务业在内的第三产业，尤其是根据社会基本服务均等化的政策要求，需在各县大力加强医疗、教育、文化、体育、卫生、养老、休闲、公共交通等各种现代社会服务业。为此还必须同时加大基础设施建设和生态环境建设的力度。县域内非农产业的发展和各项开发建设工程的进展，必将为吸纳县域内部分农村人口的就近城镇化创造条件。

城镇化离不开城镇建设，但切忌本末倒置。企图大搞小城镇建设来推动农村地区的城镇化，其结果只能出现城镇住房空置率很高或迫使被拆迁农户进城住楼房等尴尬局面。一定要在积极发展县域经济，大量增加非农就业岗位，对城镇住房的市场需求不断增大的基础上，推进城镇建设和房地产开发，才能使其也成为共同繁荣县域经济、促进城镇化健康发展的重要环节。

我国各县在地理与交通区位、自然条件与资源环境、人口构成与分布密度、经济与社会文化基础等诸多方面，存在着明显的差别。因此，发展县域经济必须特别注意因地制宜。要在发展能充分体现当地特色的县域经济方面下大功夫。在位于生态严重脆弱地区的县域或按《全国主体功能区规划》大部分属禁止开发区或限制开发区的县域，应在鼓励和妥善安排当地过多人口外迁就业定居以减轻生态压力的基础上，发展对当地生态有益无害的产业。应把对生态的修复和保护也列为重要产业，其所创造的生态效益，将受惠于广大地域的人民。专职从事生态修复和保护的人员应由国家和地方的财政收入及发达地区的生态补偿保证其收入。为了使留守在生态脆弱地区的人民也能过上享受现代文明的幸福生活，应重视在县域内进行有选择的点状开发建设，在若干城镇发展能就近提供现代社会公共产品的非农产业。

五、新农村建设只有与县域内部分农村人口就近城镇化密切结合，才能最终实现缩小城乡差别的城乡一体化

进入新世纪以来，在我国广大农村地区已大力加强新农村建设，使农村基础设施与农村面貌已有不同程度的改善。但有些地区只是孤立地抓新农村建设，没有将其与发展县域经济和部分农村人口就近城镇化密切地结合起来，致使在提高农村生活质量和缩小城乡差距方面收效不很明显。可以作这样的设想：如果在广大农村地区只注重新农村建设，不就近发展现代化的中小城市和小城镇，农村居民就难以就近享用现代城市文明所代表的优质社会服务，就不可能最终实现真正意义上的城乡一体化。

以农村地区城镇化替代农村城镇化，以就近城镇化替代就地城镇化，可避免将城镇化简单地视作把农村变为城镇的误解。即使在未来一二十年内全国都已基本实现城镇化，散布在广大地区的农村也不会消失。只是一部分农村人口远距离转移进入大都市和城市群，一部分农村人口就近转移进入中小城市和小城镇，一部分留在新农村的人口也能过上类似城镇的文明生活。

不能把新农村建设片面理解为拆旧建新，变旧村为新村。对有些具有较高历史文化价值和能充分体现当地特色的古村落，应尽快列入严加保护名单，只能在修旧如旧基础上改善其

生活设施。但也要防止出现对现有村落一律不准拆建动迁的另一极端。随着农业现代化的进展，以及因大量农民外迁而出现众多村落的空心化，有必要进行适当的并村定点，由此可腾出不少建设用地。要允许供农民使用的农村宅基地的产权可在县内城镇购房中转让作价。如果对现有的已空心化的农村宅基地都不能替换耕地，那么县内城镇化需要扩大的城镇建设用地面积势必均将占用大量宝贵的耕地，这显然不符合我国的基本国情。

需要对县域内的经济社会发展、产业布局、城乡建设、基础设施、生态环境和土地利用进行统筹规划，将众多欠发达县和贫困县建设成为城乡融合、全面小康、山川秀丽、社会和谐的美好家园。这样才能有效缓解因过多农村人口向少数大都市、都市圈和城市群不断集聚而引起的巨大生态压力和社会困境。

六、改革现行行政区划的设市体制，允许在众多县域内设立一个或多个副县级市

按一般规律，随着国家城镇化的进展，设市的城市应越来越多，但在我国却出现了不增反减的现象。如在1997年全国有设市城市667个，2014年却降至653个。日本的国土面积还不及我国的一个云南省，却设有700多个市，我国的总人口数高出日本的10倍，而现有的设市总数还少于日本。存在上述问题，其根源在于我国现行的行政区划设市体制。

改革开放初期，我国行政区划的设市工作仍多采取传统的“切块设市”模式。即从县域范围内切割出城市化水平较高的城区及其近郊区单独设市，形成市、县并存，城乡分治，县包围市的空间格局，加深了城乡之间的分离和矛盾。故自20世纪80年代中期开始改为采取“撤县设市”模式，即将整县改为市。但由于1986年民政部制定的设市标准明显偏低，一般县城非农业人口已达10万以上，全县常住人口中农业人口不超过40%的即可撤县设市。致使在1986-1997年期间全国出现了撤县设市的高潮，全国设市城市由324个猛增至667个。撤县设市后，易把整县视为城市，其实真正的城市地域只占其中的很小比重。而且照此发展势头，用不到几年我国绝大多数县都可达到撤县设市标准，将会使我国历史悠久的县制趋向消失。因此，国务院于1997年做出在全国冻结撤县设市工作的决定。直到近年，只在边境地区因特殊需要新设了少数几个市，整个设市工作基本上尚未解冻。与此同时，几乎所有地级市都实行与地区合并。有些地级市为把城市做大，把不少原有相对独立的县级市改为市辖区，致使全国设市的城市数不增反减，而且还呈现出鼓励大城市膨胀和限制小城市发展的不合理趋向。

当前我国已有许多县的县城及某些中心镇已集聚了一二十万以上的城镇人口，受镇的行政编制束缚，已严重影响小城市和县域经济的正常发展。因此，建议对现行的设市体制进行必要改革，将“撤县设市”改为“县内设市”，将县内新设市定为副县级，仍归县管。这样既可避免“切块城市”导致县市分治，又可避免“撤县设市”导致模糊城市与县域的不同概念。要保护县制的基本稳定。只允许少数已高度城市化的县域撤县设市。不要以我国宪法未载明县下可设市为由，拒绝进行县下设市的改革试验。我国现有的设市城市分为省级市、

副省级市、地级市、县级市，也均非宪法所载明的。我国台湾各县都设有县辖市，在桃园和嘉义县内还不止一个县辖市。如果在我国大陆也能允许县下设市，将会很快涌现出一大批富有活力的中小城市，可有效地带动县域经济的发展，推进广大农村地区的就近城镇化。

七、加大国家和省级财政向贫困县和欠发达县的转移支付力度，在加强县级领导班子的基础上向县放权

为缩小地区间、城乡间的相对贫富差距，必须逐步加大国家和省两级财政向贫困县和欠发达县的转移支付力度，一般贫困县或欠发达县的基础设施建设，尤其是能体现社会基本公共服务均等化的现代社会服务设施的建设和营运，有相当部分要靠外来财政转移支付的支持。下拨的各专项资金，特别是扶贫开发资金，应尽可能减少中转环节，直接下拨到县。

我国的行政区划体制，原只分为省、县、乡三级。地区行署不是一级政权，只作为省的派出机构，协助省处理地区内有关各县的行政事务。然而现今我国已普遍实行地区与设有政权机构的地级市合并，由地级市管辖若干县，在省与县之间增加了地区一级政权。在发达地区由经济实力强大的地级市管若干县，尚有助于带动各县的发展。在贫困地区和欠发达地区的地级市，因其本身经济实力较弱，不仅无力带动所辖各县的发展，而且还有可能占用各县的资源以发展自身这个地区中心城市。所以应坚持省直管县，向县放权。地级市政府对所辖各县（市），只能起如同地市合并前地区行署那样代省协调处理区内各县（市）相关事务的作用。

要想全面建成小康，首先要抓好县这个承上启下面向基层的重要环节。应下大力选拔、配备和加强县级领导班子。只有在廉洁奉公、关注民生、求真务实、敢于担当、集思广益、奋发图强的领导班子的坚强领导下，才能充分调动广大人民群众的积极性，迅速改变贫困县和欠发达县的落后面貌。

八、鼓励发达地区的城市群和都市圈的资金、人才、技术、信息等要素向欠发达的农村地区流动，倡导先富市县帮带贫困县脱贫致富

东部沿海的城市群和某些内地省的都市圈，都是利用其区位优势和国家赋予的各种特殊优惠政策，以背离市场的低地价或零地价，以来自广大农村的大量廉价劳动力，广泛招商引资，占尽国家改革开放前期的先机，才导致今天这样的发达和富裕。故而理应饮水思源，富不忘本，重视向其外围广大农村地区的反馈。应鼓励发达地区的资金、人才、技术、信息等各种生产要素向都市经济圈辐射影响所及范围的欠发达县和贫困县流动。鼓励企业家去欠发达县和贫困县创业，鼓励优秀的医生、教师和科技文化工作者抽出一定时间去农村地区的城镇工作，轮流换岗，帮助当地提高社会基本服务水平和科技文化水平。倡导发达市县与贫困市县之间的长期结对帮扶，将扶贫成果也列入发达市县的重要政绩。

加大发达的核心地区对外围边缘欠发达和贫困地区的经济辐射和援助，不是单向的付

出。欠发达和贫困地区发展的加速，可以有效地扩大我国的内需市场，为核心地区开拓更为广阔的发展空间，使全国顺利地跨越“中等收入国家陷阱”，实现伟大中国的复兴梦。

（作者：胡序威，中国科学院地理科学与资源研究所研究员，原经济地理部主任，中国城市规划学会原副理事长）

观察篇

2014年全国"两会"城乡规划建设与管理热点问题综述

2014年是我国全面建成小康社会的攻坚之年，是贯彻落实党的十八大精神的关键之年。本届政府按照十八大确定的经济社会发展的框架，制定了2014年中国经济社会发展的具体路线图。作为我国社会主义民主政治的重要舞台，第十二届全国人大第二次会议和全国政协十二届第二次会议（以下简称"两会"）分别于2014年3月5日至3月13日和3月3日至12日在北京隆重召开。2014年的"两会"是承前启后的大会，5 000余位与会的人大代表和政协委员积极建言献策，为我们国家提出迎接挑战的韬略及克服危机的良策，为指引国家未来一年乃至更远的发展提供了强大的智力支撑。

全国"两会"召开前夕，人民网就公众关注的21个热点话题展开网上调查。从2月10日至3月2日，该调查已吸引近340万人次投票。截至3月3日零时，"社会保障"问题获51万余票，占总票数的15%，蝉联排名第一位；"反腐倡廉"排名第二位，获得超过45万余票；紧随其后的是"食品药品安全"问题，以42万余票排名第三。另外，入选热点排行榜前十名的还有"收入分配"、"干部作风"、"计划生育"、"环境治理"、"教育改革"等。与去年相比，"干部作风"、"计划生育"、"环境治理"、"教育改革"、"新型城镇化"为新入选的热点话题。

对本届代表委员们的提案、议案和建议等进行梳理、分析，具体呈现以下主要特点：一是议案、提案聚焦法治和深化改革，推进国家治理体系和治理能力现代化；二是围绕反腐败

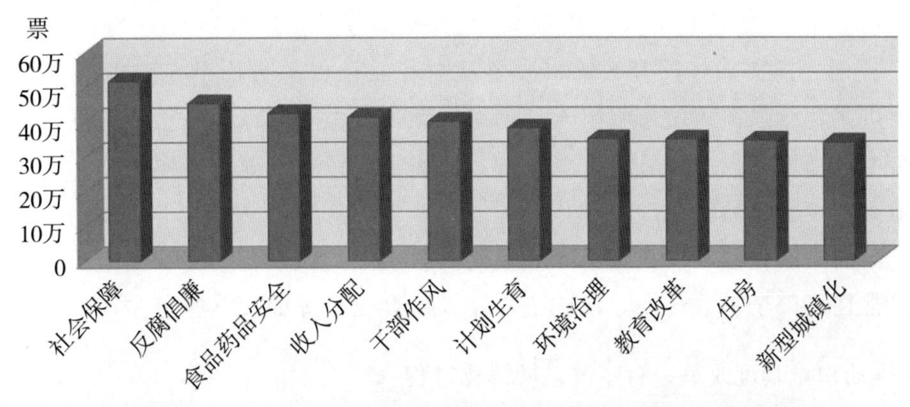

"两会"受网民关注程度的话题排行及得票数

以及作风建设，代表委员们提出了许多独到的见解；三是围绕社会保障、收入分配、科教文卫、养老问题、食品安全等事关民生的重要问题，代表委员们积极出谋划策，为许多重点难点问题提出了针对性很强的解决方案。

在2014年“两会”的提案和议案中，城乡规划建设话题依然是代表委员们关注的“热点”。与往年相比，2014年“两会”城乡规划建设的提案和议案数量更多，质量更高，而且“亮点”频现，呈现以下三个典型的特征：一是在新的发展形势下，以往的一些热点，如住房问题、农业现代化问题持续升温，城镇化上升为国家战略层面，被认为是中国经济未来的最大动力，也是今年政府工作报告重点强调的工作之一；二是随着居民生活质量的不断提升，民生问题依然是最主要的“热点”之一，关注热点则从城乡硬环境建设向城乡软环境建设逐步过渡；三是如何将当下各种新兴信息技术融入新型城镇化的建设之中，实现中国的现代化，成为新的热点话题，很多代表委员们对此提出了宝贵的建议。

基于提案、议案和建议对城乡规划建设与管理热点的关注程度，本文重点从六个方面进行综述，即：新型城镇化建设；保障性住房建设与房地产市场调控；城乡生态环境建设；保障和改善民生，关注城乡软环境建设；农业现代化建设；区域协调与发展。

一、新型城镇化建设

如何积极稳妥地推进新型城镇化发展，城从哪里来？人往哪里去？近年来一直是各界关注的热点话题。《国家新型城镇化规划（2014-2020年）》提出，要以人为核心，着重解决好既有“三个1亿人”问题，即拆除隐形“篱笆墙”，落实以人为本；降低圆梦“高门槛”，实现共享文明；抹平东西部经济鸿沟，力求区域发展均衡。

在推进以人为核心的新型城镇化建设的过程中，不能单纯追求速度和数量上的提升，必须从实际出发，提高城镇建设水平。就如何实现新型城镇化，许多代表、委员给出了“良方”。

（一）以人为本，健全城镇化发展体制机制

李铁委员认为，若要让进城农民早日共享城镇化发展成果，当务之急是尽快将“三个1亿人”的目标细化，根据城市人口规模和综合承载力，合理设定任务指标，以早日形成“硬约束”。同时，还需做好配套政策，既要从财税、社保等方面健全农业转移人口市民化成本的分担机制，增强流入城市吸引人口定居的动力，也要从产业政策、基础设施建设等方面着手，给中西部地区、中小城镇更多支持，让更多农民实现就地城镇化。

辜胜阻委员表示，城镇化涉及“人、业、钱、地、房”五大要素，“人”是城镇化的主体与核心。当前城镇化亟须从偏重土地城镇化向重视人的城镇化转变，基本公共服务由户籍人口独享向常住人口全覆盖转变。让城市常住人口享受平等的公共服务是市民化的关键。

（二）推动户籍制度改革，有序推进城镇化进程

要在未来一个时期内，有序推进农业转移人口市民化。对于应如何具体落实，孟晓苏委

员认为，推动户籍制度改革，把有能力、有意愿并长期在城镇务工经商的农民工及其家属逐步转为城镇居民，这恰是数据统计的我国城镇化率是52.5%和实际户籍人口仅是35%中间差别的17.5%的内涵所在。让已进城的农民工转为城镇居民，让他们在城市中工作生活，不仅可以有效推进城镇化的发展，而且可以有效提高这批农民的收入水平，同时促进消费。

汪玉凯委员认为，政府工作报告中提出的居住证制度，从长远发展来看，有可能使城乡二元户籍制度向构建一个统一制度的方向发展。要通过建立一些产业门槛，来疏散大城市的人口。所以，户籍制度的改革会加快步伐，但是不同规模的城市的政策是有差异性的，这个政策和对户籍的整体调控政策是一致的。

民革中央认为，提高城镇化质量的核心在于有序推进农业转移人口市民化，并以此为优化经济结构，扩大内需创造条件。并就此提出建议：第一，扩大户籍制度改革范围，进一步加快农业转移人口的“市民化”进程；第二，以土地制度改革为重点，给农业转移人口“定心丸”；第三，以产业为支撑，为农业转移人口提供更多的就业机会；第四，以统筹安排为思路，分层、分批地推进农业转移人口市民化。

（三）加快就地城市化步伐，不断促进中西部新型城镇建设

汪玉凯委员认为，提出加强中西部新型城镇建设，重点通过中西部小城镇就地城市化等方式，避免扎堆儿到东部、北部的一些大城市。此外，还要发展相关配套的设施和就业机会，这部分人口只有在小城镇完成了就业，才能在这里居住生活，因此，打造宜居宜业的新型城镇是疏解农业转移人口的一个非常重要的方向。

（四）优化城镇交通体系，保障交通和谐发展

随着新型城镇化建设的加速推进，汽车社会的和谐发展也成为其建设内容的一个重要领域。王凤英代表针对促进新型城镇化建设与汽车社会的和谐发展的议题，提出以下建议：一是提前做好功能区划规划，政府应科学利用政策规划和审批手段，逐步引导合理布局，化解交通压力；二是提前做好路网规划、注重交通管理，新型城镇路网规划应与功能规划相协调，落实城市公交优先策略，推行绿色出行；注重交通管理，提高交通效率；三是完善道路停车设施规划，增加公共区域停车设施规划，缓解停车供需矛盾；四是完善新型城镇的汽车配套服务体系规划与建设，为新型城镇化进程中的汽车社会实现可持续良性运转提供保障。

考虑中心城市交通体系可持续运行的长久、治本之策，在借鉴国际经验和结合我国各地情况的基础上，贾康委员特提出如下意见建议：一是必须下最大决心，在我国北京、上海、广州、深圳、南京、武汉等一批中心城市，加快建成如纽约、东京、莫斯科、慕尼黑等城市那样的四通八达、密度足够的蛛网状轨道交通系统，首先在中心区要发展为蛛网状，并对接停车场和立体化联通体系；二是相关的一些配合事项和对策要领，亟须认真研究和合理设计、掌握，抓紧付诸实施。

（五）控制大城市发展规模，积极推进中小城市及小城镇新型城镇化建设

我国城镇化的快速发展为经济发展做出了重大贡献。但以大城市及沿海发达地区为中心

的城镇化同时也带来了诸多问题。宗庆后代表建议严格控制大城市发展规模，积极推进产业下乡，让2.6亿农民工回家乡就业，实现就近转移，同时带动教育医疗文化和人才下乡，并在此基础上规范土地流转，推动农业集约化发展。

胡葆森委员认为中小城市及小城镇在获得重大发展机遇期的同时，也面临着诸多发展问题，建议从以下几个方面着手推进中小城市及小城镇新型城镇化建设：一是突出政府规划职能，发挥规划对中小城市及小城镇新型城镇化建设的引领作用；二是放宽市场准入，发挥民间资本在城镇化建设中的作用；三是改革用地制度，支持中小城市及小城镇承接产业转移；四是加快财税体制改革，构建合理的城镇化成本分担机制；五是加快户籍制度改革，促进人口向中小城市及小城镇转移；六是加强公共基础设施建设，增强中小城市及小城镇吸引力。

二、保障性住房建设与房地产市场调控

住房是我国当前最大的民生话题。当前我国房地产调控正处于关键时期，如何提供更好的住房保障，促进房地产市场平稳健康发展依然是本届“两会”的热点话题之一。关注重心包括如何扩大城市住房保障覆盖面，对房地产分类调控以及完善不动产登记等一系列问题。

（一）完善顶层设计，扩大城市住房保障覆盖面，构建多层次住房供应体系

张泓铭委员表示，政府工作报告中提到的扩大城市保障住房，应该涵盖外来人口，要保障人民群众居住的需要。保障性住房需借助一部分市场进行集资；保障房应该建立退出机制，保障房的建设供应，不要集中在某一地区，避免形成一种新的城市分化，从中长期来看，还是要在技术、规划、建造方面，很好地解决这个问题。

蔡继明代表指出，政府要构建以市场为主导的多层次需求的住房供应体系。在房地产市场调控中，政府将更多依靠市场手段，同时加大保障房供应，加快解决中低收入群众基本住房问题。

为及时有效地解决城镇化进程中的住房保障问题，闫小培代表提出了四点建议：首先，建立公平效率兼顾的住房保障体系。合理建构住房供给模式，有机结合政府、市场、社会等多元主体。其次，与新型城镇化政策相协调，推进工业化、城镇化、农业现代化同步发展。探索建立“城镇群—大城市—中小城市”多级土地开发权转移的区域统筹机制。再次，创新土地制度，多渠道增加保障房供给。最后，完善保障住房管理机制。加快社会保障性住房信息系统建设，建立统一的住房管理信息库；加强居民信息管理系统建设，整合相关部门信息，以有利于核定住房保障对象居住、收入和财产情况。

（二）注重房地产分类调控，探索共有产权住房试点工作

姜伟新委员表示，继续抓好房地产市场调控和监管工作，同时传递出三个政策信号：更加注重分类指导、探索发展共有产权住房和强化市场监管。

齐骥委员表示，一是对房地产分类调控，即对热点城市继续增加供应，加快建设和开发节奏，限制政策不退出。对高库存城市，控制住宅用地规模，调整新建住房上市结构，通过必要的经济手段，消化库存。二是增加普通商品房住房供应，同时继续采取调控措施，包括差别化的信贷和税收政策。对高库存城市要控制住宅用地规模，调整新建商品房上市的结构，通过必要经济手段来支持当地居民合理住房需求，消化库存。三是开展共有产权房试点。对于供需矛盾比较突出、房价上涨压力仍然很大的城市，今年将选择一部分城市作为推进共有产权住房的试点工作。

（三）完善不动产统一登记制度，优化房地产税制结构

闫冰竹委员建议，建立完善不动产统一登记制度，要加快修订和完善相关法律法规，尽快起草和颁布《不动产统一登记条例》，建立并完善不动产统一登记制度，明确不动产登记信息管理平台建立的时间表。同时，加快修订和完善现行的《税收征管法》、《房产税暂行条例》等法律法规，建立相应的自然人税收征管机制，明确自然人纳税的义务、税款征缴方式、税收保全措施等问题，在法律框架内赋予地方政府一定的税收立法权限。

同时，在优化房地产税制结构方面，闫冰竹还指出，要合并减少与房地产行业相关的税费种类，提高税收征收效率，实现综合治税。开征房地产持有环节税收必须与减少开发流转环节税费相平衡。

对于备受关注的房产税问题，李稻葵委员建议应该适时推出，至少在一部分地区应该先推出，比如房地产有上涨空间的地区，意义在于给地方政府比较稳定的、可以和百姓形成良性互动的税种，交给最基层的政府使用，直接用于业主住房大环境的改善，诸如治安、基础设施建设以及城市环境治理。他认为房产税的比例应该是低于1%，短期内也不可能成为地方税收的主要来源。至于房产税如何收，李稻葵的观点是税率要低，而且是普世的，人人都要交，而不是一部分人交。同时强调机制建设，纳税人要问责，要对税收使用者问责。

（四）综合治理房地产问题，切实提高城乡居民住房需求

解决房地产问题不能局限于房地产本身，民工党中央认为，要从系统的角度进行综合治理。为此建议：第一，以新型城镇化为契机下沉经济与社会资源，用产业转移和社会资源转移引导人口从大城市向下转移；第二，切实引导资金流向实体经济，资金流入实业，才能创造真实财富，推动经济持续增长，消化房地产虚拟财富增值带来的经济空洞；第三，鼓励发展民间金融引导资金到实体经济；第四，通过预期管理引导购房者需求的理性回归，应对民众心理预期进行舆论引导与舆情应对；第五，做好危机预警与应对准备，必须直面房地产泡沫的潜在风险，以积极的姿态做好危机的应对准备，将可能造成的危害减到最低限度。

三、城乡生态环境建设

党的十八大把生态文明建设提高到新高度，提出要优化国土空间开发格局，全面促进资

源节约，加大资源生态系统的环保力度，加强生态文明政治建设，把生态文明制度化、法制化、规范化。而环境问题一直是国家普遍关注的问题，越来越多地关注近段时间来出现的雾霾问题，雾霾天、极端自然灾害的频繁出现为生态环境敲响了警钟。

（一）多措治污减少雾霾，加强城乡生态文明建设

多位政协委员表示，治理雾霾可以采取建林带、用核电等措施，在发展经济的同时要考虑长远未来。杨铿委员认为，应出重拳整治雾霾，建议2014年内全国重点城市全面实施国五汽柴油标准及汽车排放标准。杨铿提出，整治雾霾天气应上升到国家战略。他建议，以2020年实现全国空气质量达标为目标，公布各城市的降霾时间表，纳入政府的政绩考核。同时，完善立法，建立环保执法警察队伍，对违法违规企业重罚。全国政协委员杨伟也表示，应加强对环境污染等社会重点、热点问题的科普力度。冯丹藜委员表示，治理雾霾，需要在发展经济的同时重视长远发展，周全考虑，而不能以牺牲环境的代价一味追求经济的快速发展。

孙太利委员认为四大要素造成了大气污染：一是机动车排放问题日益突出；二是工业污染以及燃煤排放体量巨大；三是城市复合型污染严重；四是有关大气保护相关的法律法规的缺失。为此，他建议：一是各地政府应摆正发展与治理的关系，真正树立绿水青山就是金山银山的发展理念；二是大气污染治理，必须要优化法规；三是大气污染治理要与经济战略转型相结合，加快经济改革；大气污染治理，必须从源头治理抓起，应把降低能源消耗，降低污染排放，提高能源利用效能，作为经济转型的重大战略目标；四是大气污染治理要把“科技治污”贯穿全过程；五是建议中央政府安排专项资金治理大气污染；六是加强大气污染治理监管力度，推行网格化管理。

（二）大中城市拆墙透绿通风散霾，改善城市自净化能力

许韓委员指出，很多大中城市人口超载，规模超过了环境自净化能力，城市规划中在高大楼宇布局时未留足好通风主道，单独小区高墙壁垒私密不透风在很大程度上阻碍了大中城市雾霾消散。建议从国家层面倡导大中城市开展拆墙透绿工作，鼓励拆墙透绿等亮化城市、改善城市通风能力的行动。制定拆墙透绿等提高城市通风散霾能力的鼓励政策，将拆墙透绿列为生态宜居城市建设考量的一项内容。还可选择一些城市作为示范样点，先行开展拆墙透绿，总结经验，形成可学可仿的样板。同时，严格限制在建和待建小区四周完全被铺面或墙体围死，要留出足够的透气通道，用通透围栏替代围墙。待建城区在规划建筑物布局时，要充分考虑当地主要气流风向和风力，为通风散霾留出足够的通道。

（三）做好顶层设计和部门协调，政策层面给予大力引导和支持

随着工业化和城镇化快速发展，我国生态环境问题日益突出。农工党中央为此建议：一是建立健全与我国基本国策相匹配的国家红线管控体系；二是划分并严守生态红线是完善生态文明制度、全面深化改革的要求；三是要密切关注民生问题，对影响老百姓身体健康、区

域生态安全和关系社会稳定的优先划为生态红线；四是规范生态红线管理技术支撑体系；五是要确立生态红线的法律地位，建立健全红线管理法律法规体系；六是推行生态红线的奖励和惩罚机制。

民建中央建议国家从经济社会生态发展全局出发，在政策层面给予大力引导和支持。在大力发展环保产业的提案中建议，《中华人民共和国环境保护法》修订草案应该尽快推出，进一步明确环保产业在环境保护、生态文明建设中的地位和作用；加大金融机构信贷力度；采用政府贴息等方式，鼓励银行业金融机构投资环保产业。在促进清洁能源发展的提案中建议，从国家可持续发展和能源安全的战略高度优先发展清洁能源，适时修订《可再生能源法》、《电力法》等相关法律法规。完善对清洁能源的项目支持、财税和价格补贴、成本与风险分摊机制等优惠政策并保持相关政策的延续性，研究扩大清洁能源的补贴范围。

四、保障和改善民生，关注城乡软环境建设

近年来，中国的民生成绩单亮点频现，但从全面建成小康社会的角度看，民生领域一些体制性弊病仍然严重，公共服务领域欠账不少，“看病难、就业难、上学难”这老三难还没抖清楚，“养老难、入托难、出行难”的“新三难”又摆在前面，城乡软环境的建设迫在眉睫。

在 2014 年“两会”期间立案的提案中，围绕保障和改善民生提案数量最多，共有 1484 件，其中涉及教育科技事业发展的提案 606 件，占民生提案近 4 成。主要建议包括合理调整农村中小学布局，加快民族地区职业教育发展，完善高校自主招生制度等。

（一）完善社区居家养老模式，加快发展健康养老服务

农工党中央认为社区居家养老是适合我国国情的新型社会化养老服务模式，建议：一是进一步完善社区居家养老服务法规政策体系；二是加强社区居家养老人才和队伍建设；三是提高社区居家养老服务质量和水平；四是鼓励社会力量参与社区居家养老服务；五是探索建立长期照护保险制度。

2013 年《国务院关于加快发展养老服务业的若干意见》（国发〔2013〕35 号）提出一系列政策要求，为贯彻实施好这一意见，民革中央建议：一是确立“居家为基础、社区为依托、机构为辅助”的养老模式。应进一步明确居家养老和社区养老将是适合我国国情的主要养老模式。二是加大对养老用地的支持力度，实现应保尽保。在摸清底数的基础上，将养老建设规模和布局、养老用地总规模和年度安排，体现在城市规划、土地利用总体规划和土地利用年度计划中。三是加快研究制定养老用地的具体支持政策，包括明确养老用地的适用范围、土地用途和年期、供应计划安排、供地方式，鼓励租赁使用养老用地，降低养老服务设施建设成本等，同时，加强养老用地监管，禁止改变用途搞商品房开发。

（二）提高义务教育覆盖面，加强区域教育资源的配置

农工党中央认为为适应城镇化发展的需求，应进一步整合城乡教育资源，加大教育投入

特别是义务教育阶段学校投入，尤其是重点加大城区基础设施投入，合理规划布局城镇学校校点，改善办学条件，提高教育质量，合理配置城镇化区域教育资源。

王麒代表提出，针对目前公办、民办幼儿园，城、乡幼儿园比例失调问题，建立公办、民办并举的双轨教育体制，努力构建覆盖城乡、合理布局的学前教育公共服务体系。其中，鼓励实施以政府为主导，社会参与，公办民办并举的举措，加大对学前教育基础设施的建设力度，完善各项基本工作，保障适龄儿童能够接受基本的、有质量的学前教育。另外，可将幼儿园纳入房地产开发项目、厂区建设、社区建设等规划指标中，不仅有利于解决财政支出困难，同时还能增强企业社会责任感。

五、农业现代化建设

中央提出新型城镇化的核心之一是实现农业现代化。但是目前，大部分关注点还是在城镇，对城乡发展一体化、城镇化联系的另一端——乡村，关注还是不够多。农业现代化建设不仅是解决农业、农村、农民问题，也是推动区域协调发展的有力支撑，是扩大内需和促进产业升级的重要抓手，对全面建成小康社会、加快推进现代化意义深远。因此，农业现代化逐渐成为代表们热议的话题。

（一）支持耕地修复保护，发展生态友好型农业

钱克明委员表示，我国三大传统粮仓都面临资源环境压力大的问题。典型问题是：南方有的水稻产区重金属污染；华北地下水漏斗扩散；东北黑土层有机质流失。而同时，消费者对食品安全的要求不断提高。所以，要促进农业可持续发展，重点是耕地修复保护。

胡汉平委员表示，目前当务之急是要深入推进农业发展方式转变；大力发展绿色农业，推进标准化、清洁化生产，国家和地方加快建立一批高标准、高起点的绿色优质的农产品基地，加大管理力度；要有制度和政策来保证。

车黎明委员也指出，今后农业发展必须走“生态、环保、可持续”之路；支撑农业发展的各个生产要素都要科学合理。

（二）加强顶层设计，用改革思维拉长农业现代化短板

目前在乡村的规划建设过程中：一缺资金，二缺人才，三缺技术，四缺法规。周岚代表表示，法规是基础性和制度性的，要厘清在建设过程中，农民的责任，政府怎么帮助农民发展的责任，对农民建房技术指导的责任，还有政府建设项目怎么管理。在人口动态变化过程中，又该怎样来配置公共资源、乡土文化怎样保护，建设美丽乡村，要有一个顶层设计来鼓励各地的创新。

吴沛良代表也认为，要拉长农业现代化短板，激发农业现代化内生动力，就必须坚定不移地走深化改革的道路，通过新一轮改革激发动力、释放红利，拉长农业现代化短板。一是加快推进农村土地确权登记颁证，让农民成为土地的主人；二是加快农村产权交易市场建

设，让农民成为交易的主体；三是加快农业科技体制改革，让农民用上质优价廉的国产品种；四是加快农业经营方式和体制机制创新，让农民收入最大化、农业效益最大化、土地产出最大化。

（三）加大龙头企业优惠政策，农村产业调整不宜全国一刀切

王勇代表认为，目前农村要实现农业现代化有三个问题：一是土地的规模经营，二是机械化作业，三是有知识的新型农民。为此，他建议依托农产品的产业链，加大对农业产业化的龙头企业的优惠政策。国家可以利用农村产业化的龙头企业，吸引农村的剩余劳动力，向乡镇集中。这就将劳动力向小城镇集中，当人口开始集中，城镇化逐步形成，剩余劳动力也可以合理安排。

张萍委员建议，农村改革以及农村产业调整需要根据当地特色进行，考虑地区差异，不宜在全国统一推进。农村建设需要产业支撑，而产业结构调整需要考虑到东西部地区差异，不宜采取一刀切方式推进。西部地区发展程度不及中东部地区，统一让农民上楼方式会导致农民失去产业支撑。

六、区域协调与发展

区域协调与发展问题仍是本届“两会”的讨论焦点。如何实现区域协调与发展，关系到全国能否实现全面建成小康社会的宏伟目标。许多代表委员在区域发展和区域政策方面提出了创新性的建议。

（一）区域发展

杜宇新委员建议，请国务院支持将“在黑瞎子岛设立国际公路客货运输口岸”纳入中俄首脑会晤内容并达成共识，以推动黑瞎子岛这一中俄国际大通道的建设步伐。

陈求发委员建议，尽快出台专门扶持政策，推进武陵山片区区域发展与扶贫攻坚的先行先试；进一步加大投入，加快谋划推进重点项目建设；进一步建立和完善协调机制。

陈际瓦委员建议，广西要创建世界长寿养生旅游特区；加快交通为重点的基础设施建设；制定政策助推长寿养生旅游产业发展。

王明方委员建议，国家批准安徽省为新型城镇化建设试点省，支持安徽在城市规划建设管理、产城一体化、要素配置、公共服务、社会管理、城镇化推进机制等方面进行探索、先行先试、率先突破，为全国新型城镇化发展积累经验、提供示范。

（二）区域政策及机制

杨松委员建议，建立健全补偿机制。加快推进片区生态安全保护区、生物多样性保护区、水源涵养保护区和国家级生态文明示范区建设；同时，建议将湖北省十堰市作为全国生态补偿先行区。

罗正富委员建议，建立国家层面的示范区建设协调机制；进一步支持云南民族工作先行先试；加大对云南开展兴边富民工程的支持力度；强化对云南特困民族的重点扶持；设立示范区建设中央专项资金。

栗甲委员建议，要强化政府责任；完善农村环境保护的法律、法规；提升农民环保意识，建立市场化运作与农民自筹相结合的农村环保投入机制；大力推进农业面源污染和生活污染防治；统一规划、合理布局，严控工业企业污染。

除了上述六个方面外，“两会”提案、议案和建议还涉及历史文化遗产保护、城乡防灾减灾规划、可持续发展等话题。虽然这些话题的代表性不及前文所述的几大方面，但也反映了代表、委员对城乡规划建设和管理的深入观察和思索。

在历史文化遗产保护方面，邹建平代表建议相关部门加强历史文化遗存对城市发展影响的研究，对历史文化遗存的文化价值、经济价值、社会价值进行科学、综合、全面的评估，考察其可能对城市就业和地区发展产生的影响，更好地发掘其潜在价值。通过政策制度的联动实施，让更多的产权所有人通过自我维护的方式实现对建筑遗存的改善更新。通过政府和市民合力，逐步实现人居环境改善和历史文化复兴。

在城乡防灾减灾方面，宇如聪委员建议，强化气候可行性论证，提高防灾减灾和应对气候变化的能力。开展城市规划、重点建设工程、重大区域性经济开发项目和有关气候资源开发利用项目的气候可行性论证，一方面能通过分析、评估或者预测规划和建设项目的气候条件适宜性、自然灾害风险性以及可能对局地气候环境产生的影响，有效避免或者减轻规划和建设项目实施后遭受气候灾害的不利影响；另一方面有利于从促进城镇、重大基础设施布局合理均衡的角度，避免建设规划不当对气候资源环境造成破坏，提高资源利用效率，减少投资浪费。

在可持续发展方面，刘汉元委员建议提高应用比例，强化可再生能源战略地位。一是制定刚性措施，确保实现可再生能源消费目标；二是加大支持力度，适度提高可再生能源的发展目标；三是提高战略定位，有效开展可再生能源的长期发展研究。

（作者：廖远涛，广州市城市规划勘探设计研究院城市与建筑设计所副所长，高级工程师；陈婷婷，香港理工大学博士；钱前，南京大学建筑与城市规划学院；魏宗财，香港中文大学博士）

处在十字路口的中国土地城镇化

——土地有偿使用制度建立以来的历程回顾及转型展望[①]

中国的城市化无论总体规模还是发展速度，都堪称前所未有。1981-2013年30多年间，中国的城市化率由20.1%提高到53.7%，总计增长了33.6个百分点，城镇人口总量由1.99亿提高到7.31亿，净增加了5.32亿，超过美国总人口的1.5倍多。在高速城市化进程中，无论是产业结构调整、人口集聚，还是基础设施建设，都离不开土地空间载体和土地资源的重新配置。"土地城镇化"是指由于城镇化的推进，土地利用属性由农业用地转变为城市建设用地以及土地产权属性由农村集体土地转为国有土地的过程（吕萍等，2008）。1988年土地有偿使用制度的建立，使土地收益成为提高政府财政收入和增加城市建设资金的重要来源，启动了"土地资本化"驱动城镇化的加速阶段（黄爱东，2011）。过去20多年来快速的城镇化进程，亦伴随着可利用土地资源的逐步枯竭，以及人口城镇化速度远低于土地城镇化速度带来的社会问题，使得城镇化快速发展所依赖的资源低成本模式在新时期的发展面临重大挑战。随着土地、劳动力、环境等资源的成本逐渐上升，未来土地城镇化的转型已迫在眉睫。

一、有偿使用制度建立以来我国土地政策和土地市场的变迁

1949年新中国成立以来，在我国不存在所谓的土地市场。随着1979年改革开放，市场要素逐步被引入农业、制造业、住房和其他领域。土地使用的制度改革，和其他领域的改革一样，采取了渐进式改革的方式。1987年12月1日，深圳通过拍卖方式出让了一块土地。此后，土地批租逐步在全国推广开来。1988年4月，七届人大第一次会议通过了《宪法修正案》，将《宪法》第十四条第四款改为"任何组织或个人不得侵占、买卖或者以其他形式非法转让土地。土地的使用权可以依照法律的规定转让"，明确了土地使用权可以依照法律的规定转让，也正式确立了土地有偿使用的法律框架。综观1988年以来我国土地政策和土地市场的变迁，大致可以划分为三个阶段：

① 国家自然科学基金委项目（批准号：51108325；51222813）、"中央高校基本科研业务费专项资金"（批准号：0100219117）和国家"十二五"科技支撑课题（批准号：2012BAJ22B03）联合资助。

（一）土地有偿适用制度确立阶段（1988－1995年）

1988年土地有偿使用制度确立后，房地产市场也随之发育。20世纪90年代早期，无论就投资的增长速度还是就开发商的利润而言，中国的房地产市场都达到了顶峰。尽管缺乏官方的统计数据，人们普遍认为房地产开发商的利润十分惊人。根据海里亚（Halia，1999）对几家新加坡房地产投资商的访谈，它们在20世纪90年代早期的利润率高达450%，20世纪90年代末期利润下降，但仍保持在100%左右。1991－1993年期间，银行、企业乃至私人开发商全部投入到房地产市场，对土地的需求大大增加。既然土地出让已成为扩大政府财政收入的重要来源，而廉价的土地又成为吸引投资的有效手段，一些政府领导常在开发部门追求高额利润的压力下做出让步，以致无节制地批出土地，等待土地收益滚滚而来。与土地无节制的供应相比，房价的涨幅相当惊人。例如，1991年初深圳市的市区平均房价为每平方米3000元，到年末就上涨至每平方米4000元。1992年6月，海南省的平均房价和前一年同期比较，上涨了100%，珠江三角洲的平均房价上涨了60%。全国性的房地产过热，一方面造成了土地闲置炒卖现象严重，国家土地资产大量流失，耕地锐减；另一方面刺激了房地产业的大量投入，"房地产泡沫"的直接后果就是高级商品房和办公楼的高空置率；最后，土地批租的失控直接导致了城市的无序蔓延①，导致交通阻塞、环境污染等问题进一步恶化，影响了城市的发展。1993年6月，中央宣布紧缩过热的房地产市场、改革银行系统等一系列措施。宏观经济政策的调整冷却了过热的房地产市场，但由于政策调整与实施结果之间的时滞性，这些政策调整对土地市场的影响直至1995年才显示出来。

（二）土地市场机制完善及土地储备制度形成（1996－2003年中）

20世纪90年代早期的房地产热导致了全国的经济过热。1997年，经营性用地的供应叫停，为1998年修订的《土地管理法》的出台提供缓冲空间。通过对《土地管理法》的修订，中央政府加强了对土地管理的控制。土地出让方式的变化对土地市场也有着重要影响。90年代末期，为了减少协议出让方式带来的土地市场不透明、腐败、土地资产流失等问题，规范国有土地使用权出让行为，优化土地资源配置，建立公开、公平、公正的土地使用制度，部分沿海发达地区城市如上海、广州、深圳等地逐渐引进招标、拍卖、挂牌等方式而非协议方式出让土地。2002年3月，国土资源部发布国土资发〔2002〕11号令，《招标拍卖挂牌出让国有土地使用权规定》，规定自2002年7月1日起，商业、旅游、娱乐和商品住宅等各类经营性用地，必须以招标、拍卖或者挂牌方式出让。之后，又连续发文明确经营性土地必须停止采用协议方式，由此逐步确立了土地交易的市场方式。

同时，20世纪90年代末期也伴随着土地储备制度的建立与发育。自1996年上海建立全国第一家土地储备机构以来，据不完全统计，全国的土地储备中心已超3 000家。与西方土地储备制度较为成熟的发达国家如瑞典、荷兰等相比，我国土地储备的出发点有所不同。在

① 据统计，1990－1995年间，城市人口增加了21.6%，而城市的面积却增加了90.4%。

这些国家里，土地储备最重要的职能是平抑房价，提高居民购买住房的能力。具有反讽意味的是，我国实行土地储备制度以来，政府在土地出让上的收益增加了，然而房价却节节上扬。开发商的利润没有受到影响，而广大市民不得不承受住宅价格上涨的成本。住房和城乡建设部的统计数据表明，2002 年上半年，当土地储备在全国推行以后，平均房价比 2001 年同期上涨了 10%。以杭州市为例，1997 年土地储备中心成立以来，政府的土地收益以每年 56% 的速度上涨，房价上涨的速度亦同样惊人。1997 年全市平均房价为 2 700 元/m^2，至 2004 年涨至 5 565 元/m^2，在 7 年时间里上涨了 1 倍多。虽然房价的上涨不能完全归因于土地储备制度，然而土地储备的实行无助于房价的平抑却是不争的事实。

（三）土地政策作为国家宏观经济调控手段（2003 年下半年至今）

21 世纪初期以来，中国经济迈入了新一轮高速发展的轨道。以高投资、高产出为特征的汽车、石化等产业的发展对土地、能源、电力、原材料及其他产品的需求大幅度上涨，并催生了新一轮投资热潮。政府不得不采取一系列政策来抑制过热的中国经济，包括提高利率、提高存款准备金、控制信贷规模、调整贷款结构等手段。针对局部地区出现的房地产投资增幅过大、土地供应过量、价格增长过快等现象，2003 年 9 月，国务院宣布，将土地政策上升到国家宏观调控的战略高度，同货币政策、财政政策一起，构成国家宏观调控的重要手段，并全面开展对土地市场的治理整顿。2006 年，国务院对土地市场的调控由总量调控转变为结构调控，国务院相继出台“国六条”、“国十五条”，对住房供应结构、税收、信贷、土地、廉租房和经济适用房建设等进行规定。要求各城市在 2006 年 9 月底前公布普通商品房、经济适用房和廉租房建设目标，其中“7090”政策（套型在 90 平方米以下的住宅比率必须达到开发面积的 70%）对房地产市场影响巨大，税收和信贷等政策进一步紧缩。土地交易方面，保障性住房用地将单列，全面清理别墅用地等。

然而，花样繁多的调控措施并未遏制房价的快速上涨。尤其是伴随着 2008 年全球性金融危机的蔓延和 4 万亿元政府资金的入市，房地产业再次担负起力挽经济狂澜的角色。全国工商联房地产商会发布的《2009－2010 年度中国房地产报告》显示，2009 年商品房房价涨幅 24%，平均每平方米上涨 813 元，创出历史新高。高房价引起民怨沸腾，危及民生，2010 年 9 月 29 日国家有关部委出台“新国五条”，被称为“最严厉楼市调控措施”的“限购令”在一线城市实行，之后逐步推开，房价节节上涨的趋势方得以遏制。

二、土地城镇化进程回顾及其双刃剑效应

（一）土地供应、房地产投资和国家宏观经济

1988 年土地有偿使用制度的建立对中国的城市发展具有里程碑式的意义。土地有偿使用催生了“土地财政”这一最为重要的预算外收入来源，地方政府获得了更大的财政自主权和更多的权力，从而有更雄厚的财力投资基础设施，为城市的发展和经济的增长注入了活

力和动力。1988年以来，房地产市场的发展对促进消费、扩大内需、拉动投资、改善居民居住条件和城镇面貌、带动建筑建材等相关产业发展，促进宏观经济发展，发挥了重要的作用。1988-2013年间，房地产的投资增加了335倍，远高于GDP增长的38倍（见图1）。因此，可以判断，房地产投资增长给我国带来的GDP增长相当可观，对我国20多年来的宏观经济增长发挥了重要作用。

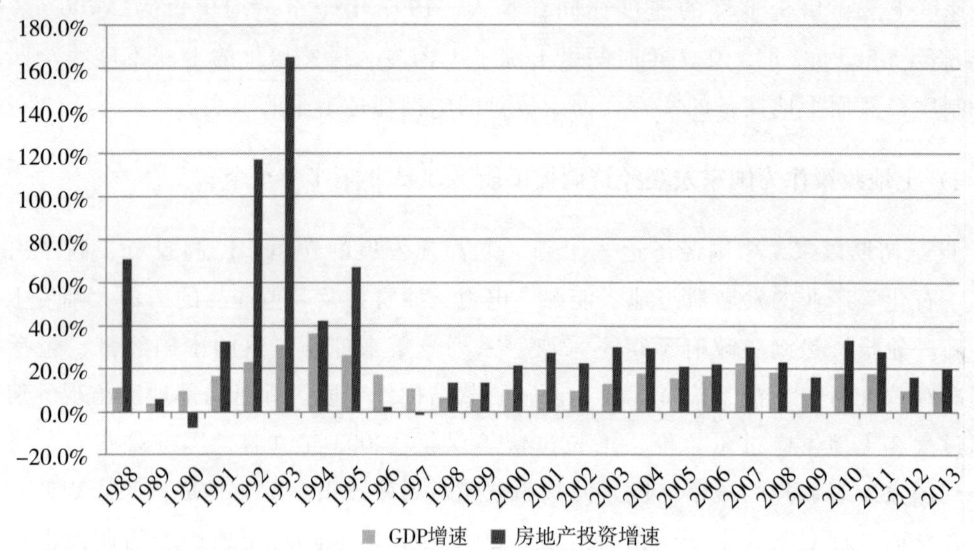

图1 1988年以来我国房地产投资和GDP增速比较

数据来源：中国统计年鉴

（二）土地城镇化与城市建成区面积扩展和人口增长

我国土地城镇化的速度远高于人口城镇化的速度，30多年间土地城镇化增速为人口城镇化的两倍。据统计，全国城市建成区面积由1981年的7438 km^2 增加到2013年的47900km^2，年平均拓展速度为6.01%，远高于同期城镇人口的年增长速度4.14%和城镇化的年增长率3.12%。与此同时，建成区人口密度却呈现不断下降的趋势（见表1），而城镇化的空间形态呈现低密度蔓延的特点。国土资源部副部长胡存智2012年3月25日指出：要警惕城市发展中土地扩张过快的现象，土地城镇化速度和人口城镇化速度应该有一个合理的比值，也就是约在1~1.12之间的范围①，以保证土地的集约和高效利用。

同时，我国的地均GDP和国外大城市相比明显偏低。即使土地集约度较高的上海中心城区与发达国家城市相比，地均GDP② 只有纽约辖区地均GDP的1/2，上海辖区只有纽约辖区地均GDP的1/44，差距显著（见图2）。这些都和我国人多地少的国情相悖。伴随着未来城市人口的进一步增加，我国的人地矛盾将进一步尖锐。

① http://xuzifang.i.sohu.com/blog/view/209741092.htm，2013/03/30.

② 地均GDP均以行政辖区为统计范围，其中巴黎指大巴黎地区，上海数据均为2007年。

表 1 我国 1981 年以来城市建成区面积和人口密度变化

年份	城市建成区面积（km^2）	城镇人口（万人）	城镇化水平	建成区人口密度（人/ km^2）
1981	7438	19970	20.12%	26849
1985	9386	25094	23.71%	26736
1990	12856	30191	26.41%	23484
1995	19264	35174	29.04%	18259
2000	22439	45906	36.22%	20458
2005	32521	56212	42.99%	17285
2006	33660	58288	43.90%	17316
2007	35470	60633	44.94%	17094
2008	36295	62403	45.68%	17193
2009	38107	64512	46.6%	16929
2010	40058	66978	49.7%	16720
2011	43603	69079	51.27%	15843
2012	45566	71182	52.57%	15622
2013	47900	73111	53.73%	15263

资料来源：中国城市建设统计年鉴，中国统计年鉴。

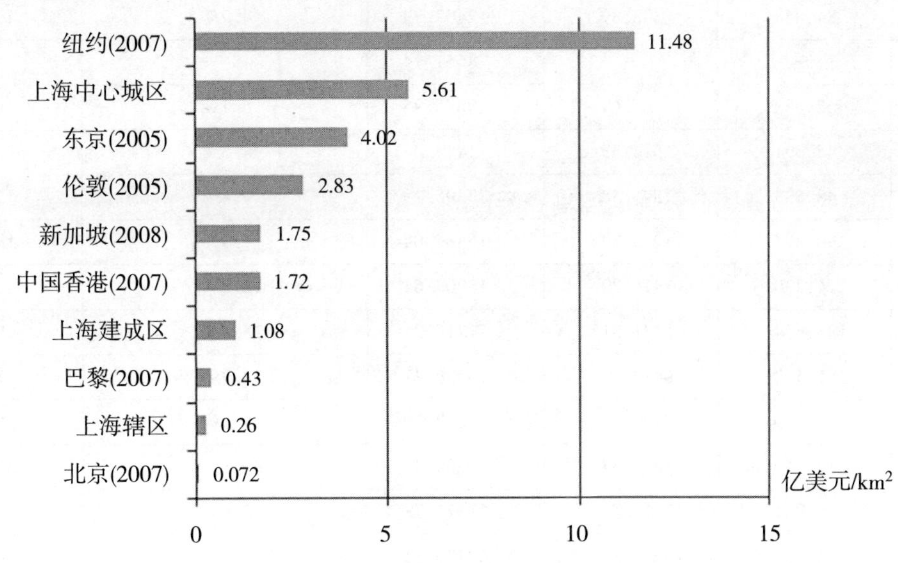

图 2 国际大城市地均 GDP 比较

数据来源：田莉，姚凯，王伟，董衡苹．世界著名大都市规划建设与发展比较研究［M］．北京：中国建筑工业出版社，2010.

(三) 土地资本化与地方财政和基础设施建设

土地有偿使用制度的建立启动了“土地资本化”的序曲，进而加速了城镇化的进程。城市土地批租使各级地方政府掌握大量预算外收入，成为城市基础设施建设最重要的资金来源。20世纪年90年代以来，以“土地资本化”为主要驱动力的城镇化，日益演变成为各级政府的“土地财政”（黄爱东，2011）。“土地财政”包括和土地有关的税收（如房地产企业营业税、土地增值税等）及与土地有关的政府非税收入（如土地出让金、耕地开垦费等）。其中土地出让金占据了土地财政的绝大部分，属于预算外收费，又称第二财政。1993-2013年20年间，土地出让金收入占政府财政收入的比例从9.7%飙升到32.5%（见表2）。在部分城市，土地财政所创造的收益甚至超过预算内收入。伴随着土地出让金的大幅增加，地均土地出让金也显著上涨。1993-2013年，土地出让面积增加为原来的6.4倍，而土地出让金收入增加至99.8倍，地均土地出让金上涨15倍多（见表2），土地价格日益高涨。

表2 土地出让金和政府财政收入

年份	土地出让面积(ha)	土地出让金收入(亿元)	政府财政收入(亿元)	土地出让金收入占政府财政收入的比例	地均土地出让金(元/m²)
1993	57,338	420.78	4349	9.7%	73.4
1994	49,432	637.95	5218.10	12.2%	129.1
1995	43,092	387.52	6242.20	6.2%	89.9
1996	34,048	348.89	7407.99	4.7%	102.5
1997①	—	—	8651.14	—	—
1998	62,058	507.69	9875.95	5.1%	81.8
1999	45,391	514.33	11444.08	4.5%	113.3
2000	48,633	595.58	13395.23	4.4%	122.5
2001	90,394	1295.89	16386.04	7.9%	143.4
2002	124,230	2416.79	18903.64	12.8%	194.5
2003	193,604	5421.31	21715.25	25.0%	280.0
2004	181,510	6412.18	26396.47	24.9%	353.3
2005	163,200	5883.82	31649.29	18.6%	360.5
2006	232,500	8077.64	38760.20	20.8%	347.4
2007	234,961	12216.72	51321.78	23.8%	519.9
2008	165,860	10259.8	61330.35	16.7%	618.6
2009	209,000	15910.2	68518.30	23.2%	761.3
2010	291,500	30108.93	83101.51	36.2%	1032.9

① 1997年国务院停止营利性用地的出让，以整顿土地市场，为修订后的1998年《土地管理法》出台奠定基础。

续表 2

年份	土地出让面积(ha)	土地出让金收入(亿元)	政府财政收入(亿元)	土地出让金收入占政府财政收入的比例	地均土地出让金(元/m²)
2011	335,085	31500	103874.43	30.3%	940.06
2012	322,800	26900	117253.52	22.9%	833.33
2013	367,000	42000	129143	32.5%	1144.41

注：2010 年数据来源于财政部，其他数据来自于中国统计年鉴。

土地资本化带来的收益在基础设施建设投资中发挥了重要作用。以广州为例，1992 年土地收益和基础设施建设投资的比例为 108.7%。之后，随着基础设施投资额的增加，仅仅依靠土地收益不足以全部支付基础设施建设的投资，然而它仍然扮演着重要角色。1992－2006 年间，土地收益在广州基础设施建设投资的比例介于 38% 和 108% 之间。总体平均水平为 68.3%，土地收益成为基础设施建设投资的最主要来源。

（四）土地财政、房价上涨与住房保障

我国住房制度改革 20 多年来，城镇家庭的居住条件显著改善，人均住房建筑面积从 1978 年的 6.7 平方米增加到目前的超过 30 平方米。伴随着人均居住面积的提升是房价过快上涨。在土地财政的激励下，地方政府和开发商形成“联盟”，成为高房价和高地价的直接受益者。普通居民面对日益高涨的房价只有“望房兴叹”。以北京为例，2003 年，北京楼市商品住宅的成交均价是 4456 元/平方米，8 年后，北京楼市商品住宅的成交均价是 21929 元/平方米。8 年间，虽然由于调控政策的作用，楼市成交量出现了明显的涨跌，房价水平也随之出现过阶段性的调整，但北京房价总体涨势未改——8 年，上涨 4.92 倍①，同时段内居民可支配收入上涨 2.37 倍（北京统计年鉴，2012）。以三口之家购买一处 90 平方米的房子计算，需要 20 年的时间。由复旦大学住房政策研究中心和上海同策咨询研究中心联合发布的上海均质住房价格指数显示，上海商品住房自 2004 年以来 7 年间实际上涨了 253%，同期上海城镇居民家庭人均可支配收入上涨约 1.9 倍，收入增长速度远落后于房价上涨速度。

（五）土地城镇化与流动人口的“半城镇化”

我国人口城镇化进程明显落后于土地城镇化。据统计，打工的农民工群体接近两亿在城市，面临着“市民化”的困扰。城镇化本质上应是农村人口在城市的一种社会融合，但大量的流动人口在经济体系、社会体系、文化体系及制度体系等方面均难以融入城市，在行动、生活方式等方面与城市居民存在明显的区隔，处在“半城镇化”状态，这对中国社会发展提出严峻挑战，这对中国社会结构的转型和变迁相当不利（王春光，2006）。对地方政府而言，土地城镇化可以带来大量的“土地财政”，而“人口的城镇化”却会给地方财政带

① 张晓蕊，新京报，2011－11－11。

来基础设施、公共服务设施、社会福利等方面的财政负担，直接导致地方政府对“土地城镇化”的偏好而漠视“人的城镇化”。

三、土地城镇化进程中的利益分配和运行机制

（一）土地城镇化进程中的利益主体

错综复杂的利益主体对土地城镇化进程发挥着这样或那样的影响。总体而言，相关利益主体主要包括：中央政府、地方政府（市、县、镇乡、村）、农民/城市居民、开发商/企业（见图3）。不同的主体所拥有的土地权利和从土地开发中获得的利益不同，很多时候处于利益冲突的状态：农民和城市拆迁户希望获得较高的补偿标准；开发商希望征地补偿标准越低越好；高度依赖土地财政的地方政府，希望压低征地和拆迁补偿标准，并抬高土地出让价格，以获取土地利益的最大化；对居于顶层的中央政府而言，确保18亿亩耕地红线，集约利用土地，同时确保社会稳定才是最重要的①。目前，在土地一级市场由政府垄断的情况下，中央政府和地方政府扮演了主导者的角色。

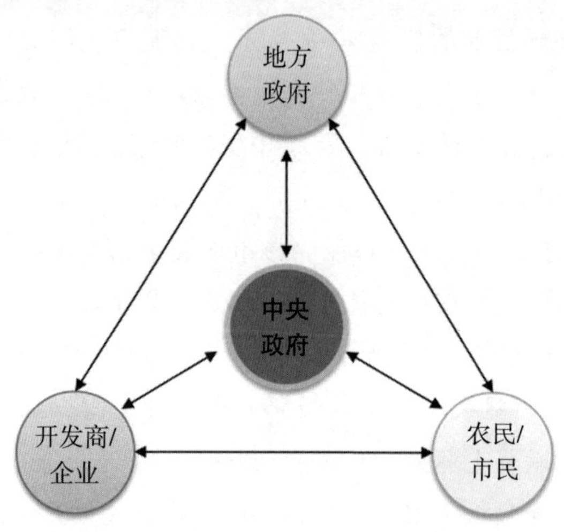

图3 土地城镇化进程中的利益主体

（二）土地城镇化进程中的中央—地方博弈

土地城镇化进程中，中央和地方政府的博弈贯穿始终，突出体现在土地目标和土地收益的博弈上。

1. 土地目标之博弈

中央政府土地政策的目标是多重的，首先是保护18亿亩的耕地生命线，确保粮食安全；

① 经济观察：让土地相关利益主体公平博弈［N］. 新京报，2006-10-23。

其次是维护农民利益和保持社会稳定，在此前提下，适当增加建设用地，保持经济稳定增长。其中，粮食安全主要是国家目标，地方政府、开发商和农民对此并不关注（张曙光，2008）。对地方政府来说，土地政策的目标是扩大建设用地，加速本地区的工业发展和经济增长，增加地方收入和地方融资规模。因此，从土地政策目标的取向来说，中央政府和地方政府之间存在矛盾和冲突。两者的关系是经济学意义上的委托人与代理人的关系。抽象的土地国家所有权中，地方政府是土地事实上的代理人，对土地的使用和控制最终是通过地方政府来实现的。虽然中央政府可以定期不定期地发布土地政策和控制管理办法，包括自上而下地划定基本农田，审批土地利用总体规划和年度计划，给各地分配新增建设用地指标等，但最终的实施效果仍然取决于地方政府。因此，土地城镇化的进程控制与其说取决于中央，不如说取决于地方——既要看中央目标和地方目标的一致性，也有赖于中央的控制能力和地方的意愿与执行力度（张曙光，2008）。

2. 土地收益之博弈

在土地出让金的分成比例上，中央、地方之间也经历了多次变迁。1988 年 5 月，国务院发出《关于加强国有土地使用权有偿出让收入管理的通知》，规定国有土地使用权出让的收入中，40% 上缴中央财政，60% 留归地方财政。1992 年 9 月，财政部出台《关于国有土地使用权有偿使用收入征收管理的暂行办法》，把中央对土地出让金的分成比例缩小为 5%。

1994 年年底实行分税制改革后，土地出让金全部划归地方政府，使土地出让金彻底成为地方政府的预算外“小金库”和地方政府的“第二财政”。地方政府因此有了足够的“土地冲动”，这期间建设用地总量增长过快、工业用地过度扩张、违法违规用地、滥占耕地等现象相当突出。为了保护耕地，充分利用经济机制引导土地合理利用，国务院 1997 年发布了《关于进一步加强土地管理切实保护耕地的通知》，规定“农地转为非农建设用地的土地收益，全部上缴中央”；1998 年修订《土地管理法》时，又调整为“新增建设用地的土地有偿使用费，30% 上缴中央财政，70% 留归有关地方政府所有，都专项用于耕地开发”。

从 2007 年 1 月 1 日起，土地出让收支全额纳入地方基金预算管理。收入全部缴入地方国库，支出一律通过地方基金预算从土地出让收入中予以安排，实行彻底的“收支两条线”。在地方国库中设立专账，专门核算土地出让收入和支出情况。中央各部门要求地方政府从土地出让净收益中提取 10% 用于保障房建设、10% 用于教育投入、10% 用于水利建设，加上 2004 年规定计提 15% 用于农业土地开发，目前已有 45% 的土地出让净收益被中央指定了用途。

综观中央政府参与分成的土地收益，总是在出现之初，所有收益归地方政府。随着该类收益在全国范围的大面积推广，中央政府会出台有关收益分成分享的政策。但收益分享政策无一不受到地方政府的抵制，中央政府又不得不逐步下调分成比例，中央政府仅得到象征意义的收益，但其政策意图仍难以实现（李明月等，2005）。目前我国的税制设计下，中央政府和地方政府的财力与事权不对称。中央和省级政府不断提高制造业、工商业税收等的分成额度，造成地方政府财政收入比重较大幅度下降，但事权没有相应减少，引发地方政府对土地财政依赖的恶性循环。实践中如何切实抑制地方政府“以地生财”的冲动，仍需疏堵结合，为地方财政开辟新的税源，减少对“土地财政”的依赖。

（三）土地城镇化的主要推手——发展型地方政府

利奥（Liew，1995）将中国渐进式经济改革的成功归因于强势的政府和基层的充分参与。在中国现行的官员考核机制下，GDP 和城市形象是两项重要的政绩指标。随着 1994 年分税制的实行，地方政府成为有自身经济利益的利益集团，为了增加地方财政收入，它具有发展经济的强烈动机，称为“发展型政府”。在制造业税收大部分被中央政府分享的情况下，土地财政成为地方政府财税收入的最主要来源，这也直接导致了城市的快速扩张。在这种情况下，地方政府和企业的利益是一致的。新旧体制共存的渐进式改革为地方政府和开发商的“联盟”创造了条件，使房地产热和城市扩张持续升温。

我国土地城镇化速度之所以明显超过人口城镇化，农民工之所以难以转化为市民，关键在于公共产品的供给问题。由于缺乏中央层面的财政转移支付制度和地方政府职能的缺位，对外来人口的公共产品和公共服务，全部由进城农民工自掏腰包，大大超过了其承受能力。相关资料显示，要把深圳市的农民工全部转变为市民，与市民平等享受公共服务，所需要的投入相当于深圳市 2009 年地方财政收入的 10 倍（黄爱东，2011）。而这样巨大的成本，由一地政府来承担显然并不现实，亟须中央政府的制度变革。

四、处在十字路口的土地城镇化：何去何从

毋庸讳言，土地资本化对 20 世纪 90 年代以来我国城镇化进程的快速推进，城市形象和投资环境的改善发挥了重要作用。如今时时为人诟病的“土地财政”，也曾一度作为“城市经营”的成功经验予以推广。然而时过境迁，伴随着可利用土地资源的捉襟见肘和房价一路高歌，传统的“土地城镇化”方式转型已迫在眉睫。

（一）土地资源的日益短缺和土地成本的日益高涨促使土地城镇化转型

改革开放 30 多年来建设用地的粗放式扩张和城镇人口的持续增加，使得我国的可利用土地资源日益紧缺。随着未来城镇化水平的进一步提升，越来越多的人口将继续进入城镇，给建设用地供给带来巨大的压力。同时，随着市场经济的发展，不同利益群体对于自身权利的保护，尤其是房屋产权的保护意识逐步增强。个体在思想意识上由被动服从向维护自身权利的转变，将导致城市扩张成本的提高和城市增长速度的放缓。进入城镇化成熟期，土地的稀缺程度加剧，“寸土寸金”现象越来越明显，促使人们把更多的资本、技术投入到土地上，土地城镇化方式的转型不可避免。未来，城市尤其是大城市的开发重点，将由“绿地（Greenfield）”转向“棕地（Brownfield）”。未来，提升建成区人口密度、使人口增加与土地扩张保持合理比例应成为我国土地城镇化进程的主要任务之一。城乡规划部门应制定人口密度约束性指标（下限），对不同规模的城市、县城、乡镇等建成区的人口密度进行指导。

（二）政府职能转变的影响：由“土地城镇化”偏好转向“人的城镇化”

如果说东亚、东南亚新兴工业化国家的崛起，使得强势的发展型政府的作用被作为成功经验而得到强调，那么，金融危机的爆发、区域发展不平衡、收入差距过大、资源和环境压力增加等问题，使发展型政府陷入前所未有的困境。在社会主义市场经济体制已初步建立的新历史条件下，中国政府必须适时实现角色的转型，由发展型政府转变为公共服务型政府，将对“土地城镇化”的痴迷转向对“人的城镇化”的重视。其中，失地农民工的市民化是未来我国城镇化进程中需要关注的核心问题。通过逐步提供和市民同等的教育、医疗、社会保障等公共服务给予那些在城市中具有稳定职业的农民工及其家庭成员，使他们逐步融入城市，脱离“半城镇化”状态。同时，可以借鉴城乡建设用地挂钩的办法，建立“人地”挂钩机制，即根据吸纳农民工人口定居的数量，每年增加一部分用地指标用于解决农民工市民化后的用地问题（中国发展基金会，2010）。在中央层面上，对于解决进城农民“市民化”标准的地方政府，应将人口流出地的公共财政转移至人口输入地。此外，每年的建设用地储备出让计划中，必须将保障性用地的出让作为硬性指标，以解决城市中低收入阶层的住房问题，充分体现土地的福利功能特征。

（三）破解中央与地方的“土地博弈”困局，摆脱“土地财政”依赖

“土地财政”与地方政府垄断建设用地供应是一套共生的制度安排。破解中央与地方的“土地博弈”困局，只有从改变地方财政收入的结构入手，建立财权与事权相适应的制度，才能避免地方政府沉迷于“土地财政”，充当“低价征地、高价出让”的土地经营者的角色。在切断“卖地财政”的同时，应借鉴发达国家的经验，建立和完善房产财产税的年税制度，使之成为地方政府可以常年分享的财政收入重要而稳定的来源。只有这样，才能使地方政府摆脱“土地财政”的依赖，而逐步转向其主要应承担的公共服务的职能。

（四）重构土地收益分配关系，完善土地治理结构

土地城镇化进程中出现的种种问题，核心根源在于土地增值收益分配的不公平。宋敏（2006）等对浙江省的一项调查表明，以征地成本价为 100 % 计算，被征土地收益分配的格局大致是：地方政府 20 % ~30 %，村级组织 25 % ~30 %，开发企业 40 % ~50 %，农民仅享有 5 % ~10 %。由于土地开发所产生的土地巨额增值收益，大部分被中间商或地方政府所获取。这也直接刺激我国城市在低成本的基础上大肆扩张，并衍生土地利用绩效偏低、征地过程中的社会动荡、贫富差距过大等一系列问题。

合乎公共利益的优良的土地制度，应让各个利益主体都享受到土地增值带来的发展机会。在我国未来的城乡发展中，首先，进一步明晰农村集体土地产权，明确土地收益受益主体，使得集体组织和农民获得与其权益相匹配的收益，共享城镇化的果实。其次，改变以 GDP 和城市形象为标准的考核制度，规范国有土地出让收入分配，严格界定国有土地出让收入的支出范围，强化土地的福利功能。最后，与土地相关的其他利益主体，尤其是农民、

城市居民，在打破地方政府与开发商之间的“利益同盟”方面也可以发挥重要作用，这也是我国更为广泛的政治经济改革进程的一部分。

（作者：田莉，同济大学城市规划系教授，博士生导师）

参考文献

[1] 邓宏乾．公共财政视角下的土地收益分配改革［J］．江海学刊，2007（3）：64-69.

[2] 黄爱东．分税制改革引发的土地财政与土地城镇化之反思［J］．湖南行政学院学报，2011（3）.

[3] 李明月，胡竹枝．分权体制下的中央政府土地收益分享安排［J］．财经论丛，2005（2）：62-65.

[4] 吕萍，周滔，张正峰，田卓．土地城镇化及其度量指标体系的构建与应用［J］．中国土地科学，2008，22（8）：24-28，42.

[5] 宋敏．城镇化与土地收益分配［J］．安徽农业科学，2006，34（7）：1471-1474.

[6] 田莉．我国城镇化进程中喜忧参半的土地城镇化［J］．城市规划，2011（2）：11-13.

[7] 王春光．农村流动人口的“半城镇化”问题研究［J］．社会学研究，2006（5）.

[8] 张曙光．如何破解中央与地方“土地博弈”困局［N］．南方周末，2008-06-04.

[9] 中国发展研究基金会．中国发展报告2010：促进人的发展的中国新型城镇化战略［Z］．2010.

[10] Haila, A.. “Why is Shanghai Building a Giant Speculative Property Bubble?”［J］. International Journal of Urban and Regional Study, 1999, 23（3）：583-588.

[11] Liew, L. H.. “Gradualism in China's Economic Reform”［J］. Journal of Economic Issues, 1995, 29（3）：883-895.

[12] Tian Li, MaW.. Government Intervention in City Development of China: A Tool of Land Supply［J］. Land Use Policy, 2009, 26：599-609.

[13] Zhu, J. M.. “Local Developmental State and Order in China's Urban Development during Transition”［J］. International Journal of Urban and Regional Research, 2004, 28（2）：424-447.

我国新城新区的理性建设与科学发展

我国正处在城镇化发展的快速成长阶段，在新型城镇化背景下，未来我国将走高效、低碳、生态、环保、创新、智慧、平安的新型城镇化道路，但城镇化进程将面临日益严峻的供地压力。在这种情况下，一些地方将新城新区开发作为争取城镇化用地的重要手段。自浦东新区开发建设以来，各地纷纷效仿建设新城新区，出现了新城新区规划与开发热潮。我国新城新区建设取得了可喜成绩，但也暴露出不少亟待解决的现实问题。全国新城新区建设已过多过大，即便如此，各地还是鼓足了劲，酝酿借新型城镇化之机推动新一轮“新城新区新扩新建”的热潮，以获取更多的城市建设用地和土地财政收益。在我国新城新区建设缺乏顶层规划设计、空城空区频出的情况下，不少地方政府仍在打着推进新型城镇化的旗号，不顾当地条件，不顾实际需要，不顾自身财力，盲目再造新城新区，其合理性和必要性实在令人担忧，建议从国家战略高度科学引导新城新区的适度有序建设。

一、新城新区建设取得的巨大成就

自上海浦东新区成功开发建设 20 多年来，我国新城新区建设取得了举世瞩目的巨大成就，对加快我国工业化和城镇化进程做出了重大贡献。具体表现在：

（一）新城新区建设吸纳了大量人口居住就业，改善了城市人居环境

新城新区建设吸引了大量的人口就业，增加了城市住房面积，缓解了城市居住压力，维护了职住平衡，改善了城市人居环境。据统计，2013 年重庆两江新区已经集聚了全市 297 万人居住就业，未来全市 50% 以上的人口将集聚在两江新区；上海浦东新区集聚了 545.2 万人就业居住，占上海市总人口的 22.9%，成为上海人口最多的一个区；天津滨海新区集聚了 255 万人口居住就业，占全市的 18.2%。相对于老城而言，这些新城新区由于建设起点高，标准优，显著地改善了城市人居环境。

（二）新城新区推动了城市产业转型升级，提升了城市发展质量与效益

上海浦东新区、天津滨海新区、重庆两江新区等多数新城新区都是城市经济发展和空间布局的新增长点，成为国家战略性新兴产业、高科技产业、先进制造业和现代服务业集中

区、自主创新示范区和自由贸易实验区，是国家和城市经济发展的新门户、新基地、新试区和新引擎，对推动国家经济发展和城市经济转型做出了重要贡献。尤其是上海浦东新区2013 年 GDP 占到了全市经济总量的 30%，增长速度比全市快 2.6%，进出口总额占全市的 56.6%，增长速度比全市快 2.9%；天津滨海新区 2013 年 GDP 占全市经济总量的 55.8%，增长速度比全市快 5.0%，进出口总额占全市的 69.6%；重庆两江新区 GDP 占全市经济总量的 13.03%，增速比全市快 3.7%。不少新区在国家和城市经济社会发展中担当了“排头兵”的重要作用。

（三）新城新区建设有效地疏解了城市功能，缓解了日益严重的城市病

在经济全球化和快速城镇化背景下，我国不少特大城市在发展过程中暴露出来的交通拥堵、住房紧张、污染严重等城市病进入高发高危期，亟须建设新城，以治顽疾。实践证明，通过新城新区建设，成功疏解了母城承载不了的人口和城市功能，外溢了母城的部分生产要素，与母城形成了互补的产业联动与功能联动关系，实现了母城中受限的经济结构转型升级，减轻了主城超负荷的承载压力，缓解了日益严重的城市病，推动了城市可持续发展。

（四）新城新区建设拓展了城市发展空间，优化了城市空间结构

新城新区建设在吸纳人口、增加就业、疏解功能、提升质量的同时，还拓展了城市发展空间，优化了城市生态空间、生产空间和生活空间，使城市生态空间更加优美秀丽，生产空间更加集约高效，生活空间更加宜居舒适。通过新城新区建设，优化了城市空间形态与结构，完善了城市基础设施和公共服务设施，改变了城市建设面貌，提升了城市形象和美誉度。

二、新城新区建设过多过大的问题十分突出

（一）新城新区过多过大，缺乏科学规划与合理引导

新城新区是城市空间扩张的一种形式，是中国改革开放后城镇化进程的重要支撑和空间表现。据不完全统计，截至 2014 年 12 月底，全国在建的各类新区达 105 个（见图 1、表 1），其中国家批准的新区 15 个，省级政府批准的 38 个，其余为市级政府批准的；按照规划面积划分，超过 1000 km^2 的新区 21 个，500～1000 km^2 的新区 10 个，100～500 km^2 的新区约40 个。

就国家级新区来说，2010 年之前近 20 年只批准了 3 个，即上海浦东新区（1992 年）、天津滨海新区（2006 年）和重庆两江新区（2010 年），此后于 2011 年批建了舟山群岛新区，2012 年批建了兰州新区和南沙新区，2014 年批建了西咸新区、贵安新区、青岛西海岸新区、大连金普新区和成都天府新区。就省级新区来说，中部地区的河南省最为典型。2010 年 2 月至 2013 年 1 月，不足 3 年先后在河南全省 18 个地级市范围内批准成立了 14 个省级新区。再加上已有的郑州新区和洛阳新区，目前共有 16 个城市新区，总面积达 5047 km^2。

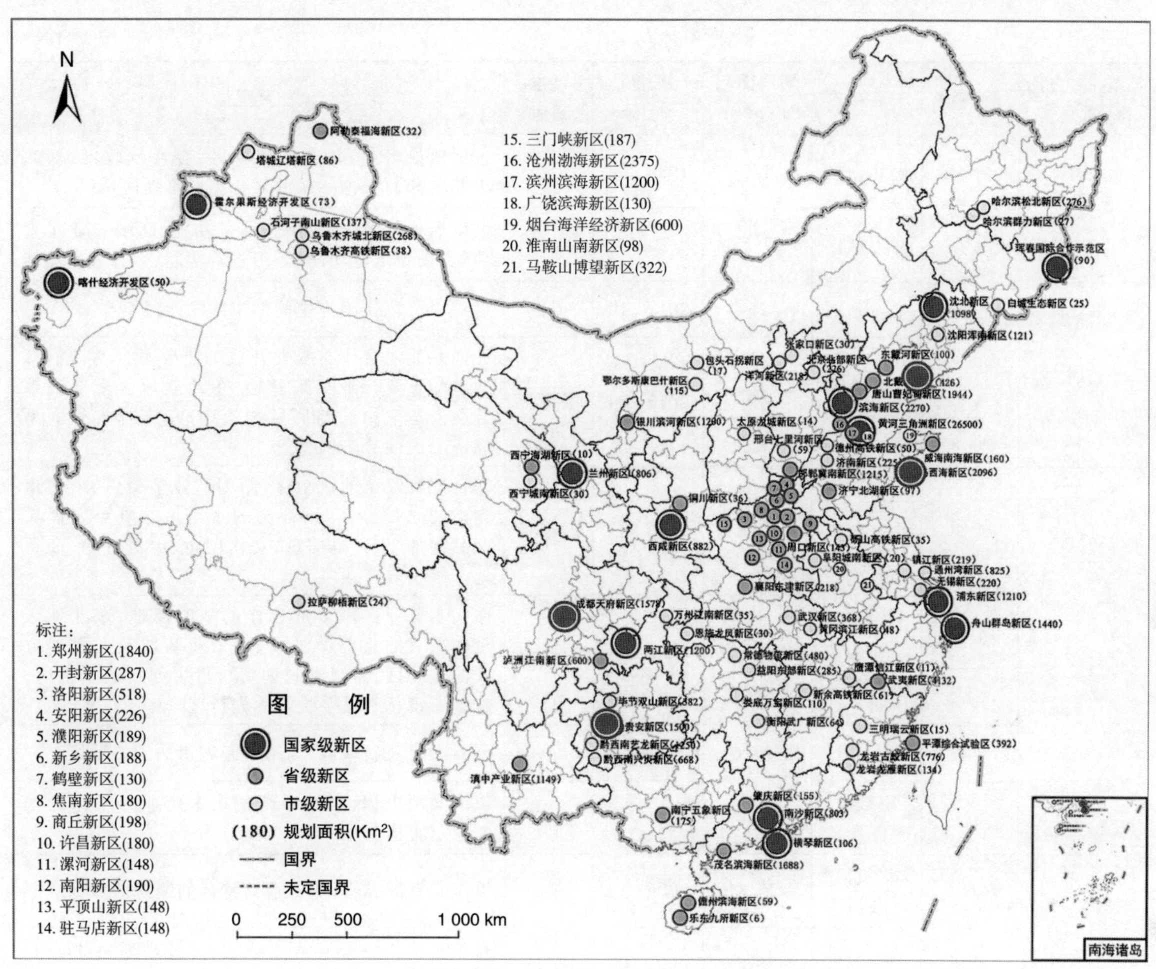

图 1　中国新区建设现状分布示意图

表 1　中国新区建设现状与发展定位比较分析一览表

所在省、自治区、直辖市	所在地	名称	规划面积（km^2）	批准时间	批准级别	发展定位
上海	上海	浦东新区	1210.40	1992.10	国家级	围绕上海市的战略定位（国际经济中心、国际金融中心、国际贸易中心、国际航运中心），建成为科学发展的先行区、“四个中心”的核心区、综合改革的试验区、开放和谐的生态区
天津	天津	滨海新区	2270	2006.05	国家级	中国北方对外开放的门户、高水平的现代制造业和研发转化基地、北方国际航运中心和国际物流中心、环境优美的宜居生态型新城区
重庆	重庆	两江新区	1200	2010.05	国家级	统筹城乡综合配套改革试验的先行区，内陆重要的先进制造业和现代服务业基地，长江上游地区的金融中心和创新中心，内陆地区对外开放的重要门户，科学发展的示范窗口
	万州	江南新区	34.75	2003	省级	万州区重要的文化新区、活力新区和宜居新区
北京	北京	北部新区	226	2006.11	省级	重点发展软件与信息网络技术、新材料、新能源与环保、生物工程与新医药等产业

续表 1

所在省、自治区、直辖市	所在地	名称	规划面积(km²)	批准时间	批准级别	发展定位
黑龙江	哈尔滨	松北新区	276	1998.06	市级	包括风景名胜区、文化体育区、教育行政区、新兴工业区和商贸金融区的复合型城市新区
		群力新区	27.33	2005	市级	城市居住新区,具有中央商务功能、高端产业集聚功能、创新示范功能、休闲旅游功能、生态宜居功能
吉林	白城	生态新区	25	2012.10	市级	形成以文化休闲为主的都市滨湖园区
	珲春	国际合作示范区	90	2012.04	国家级	面向东北亚合作与开发开放的重要平台与图们江地区的重要产业集聚基地,东北亚地区重要的综合交通运输枢纽与商贸物流中心,吉林省外向型经济发展的战略增长极
辽宁	沈阳	沈北新区	1098	2006.03	国家级	综合配套改革的试验区、新型产业集聚区、生态市建设的先行区、和谐社会的示范区。重点发展农产品深加工、光电信息、文化创意、生命健康、商贸地产等主导产业
	大连	金普新区	2299	2014.07	国家级	面向东北亚区域开放合作的战略高地,东北地区全面振兴的重要增长极,老工业基地转变发展方式的先导区,体制机制创新与自主创新的示范区,新型城镇化和城乡统筹的先行区
	沈阳	浑南新区	120.6	2001	市级	创新型科技新城区,国家中心城市的中心城区
	绥中	东戴河新区	100	2011.03	省级	以人文历史为内涵、以高新技术产业为主体的滨海生态宜居新城
河北	秦皇岛	北戴河新区	425.81	2006.12	省级	以生态宜居、新型服务业为特色的滨海新城区
	沧州	渤海新区	2375	2007.03	省级	石油化工和装备制造业基地、区域性航运中心和物流基地,河北沿海地区新的经济增长极
	邯郸	冀南新区	1215	2010.10	省级	冀南地区重要的经济增长极、晋冀鲁豫四省交界区最大的现代物流枢纽、重要的装备制造业基地、产业与生态相融合示范区
	邢台	七里河新区	58.8	2010	市级	滨水新区、生态新区、文化新区、休闲旅游新区
	唐山	曹妃甸新区	1943.72	2008.10	省级	能源及铁矿石等大宗货物的集疏港,新型工业化基地,国家级循环经济示范区,生态宜居的滨海新城
	张家口	张家口新区	30	2012.08	市级	张家口市未来的行政、文化和商贸中心
	张家口	洋河新区	218	2000	市级	集大众、娱乐、健身运动和自然生态绿化于一体的滨河生态宜居新区
山东	济南	济南西区	225		市级	济南西部新城区,区域性现代服务业中心
	青岛	西海岸新区	2096	2014.06	国家级	国家海洋科技自主创新领航区,深远海开发战略保障基地,海洋经济国际合作先导区,陆海统筹发展试验区
	滨州	北海新区	1200	2010.09	省级	重要的盐化工、石化、高分子原材料基地,山东省北部重要的港口物流中心,生态宜居的滨海新区
	威海	南海新区	160	2009.10	省级	以蓝色经济和高端产业为主的生态型经济新区

续表 1

所在省、自治区、直辖市	所在地	名称	规划面积（km^2）	批准时间	批准级别	发展定位
山东	烟台	海洋经济新区	600	2012.02	市级	现代化海洋经济新城、高端海洋产业集聚区、国家级海洋科研成果转化示范区、面向东北亚经济合作重要承载区、滨海生态宜居新城区
	德州	高铁新区	50	2012.07	市级	德州市域新型产业集聚区和外向型功能拓展区，宜居的新城区
	济宁	北湖新区	97	2008	省级	行政商务中心、科教文化基地、休闲度假胜地、生态宜居新城
	东营	广饶滨海新区	130	2011	市级	海洋化工和新兴产业基地，现代物流基地，生态宜居新区
江苏	无锡	无锡新区	220	1995	市级	先进制造业和高技术产业基地，研发及物流等现代服务业基地，生态宜居新区
	镇江	镇江新区	218.9	1998	市级	先进制造业基地，高技术产业研发孵化及生产基地，生态宜居新区
	南通	通州湾新区	825	2011.10	市级	战略性新兴产业国际合作区，国际自由贸易大港，江海联动试验区，长三角北翼高端制造业与现代服务业基地，国家海洋创新发展示范区与海洋生态度假基地
	徐州	徐州新区	60		市级	徐州市的行政中心，区域性商务及金融、文化中心
浙江	舟山市	舟山群岛新区	1440	2011.06	国家级	国家陆海统筹发展先行区、海洋综合开发试验区、重要的现代海洋产业基地、海洋海岛科学保护开发示范区、长江三角洲地区经济发展的重要增长极、浙江省海洋经济发展的先导区
广东	广州	南沙新区	803	2012.09	国家级	粤港澳全面合作及优质生活圈和新型城市化示范区，以生产性服务业为主导的现代产业新高地，社会管理服务创新试验区
	珠海	横琴新区	106.46	2009.12	国家级	粤港澳合作新模式的示范区
	茂名	滨海新区	1688	2012.04	省级	区域性航运物流中心，重要的石化装备制造、信息产业基地。广东海洋经济和海洋产业集聚发展示范区，国家级滨海旅游度假区，粤西地区的经济核心区和新兴增长极，现代化国际化滨海新城
	肇庆	肇庆新区	115	2012.10	省级	未来肇庆的行政中心，文化、体育和城市公共生活中心，小企业总部基地和重要的会展商务旅游目的地
河南	郑州	郑州新区	1840	2009.07	省级	中原城市群“三化”协调科学发展先导示范区，国家综合交通枢纽、物流中心，先进制造业和高技术产业基地，以金融、商务、会展为主的现代服务业基地，科教基地、生态宜居新区
	焦作	焦南新区	180	2010.02	省级	焦作市“三化”协调发展先导区、老工业基地振兴和资源型城市转型示范区、现代化复合型功能区、城乡统筹发展先行区和对外开放示范区
	新乡	平原新区	188	2010.02	省级	农业硅谷，科技新城，产业基地，休闲之都
	许昌	许昌新区	180.4	2010.02	省级	重要的输变电装备制造业基地，许昌市经济社会发展的核心增长极，现代生态宜居新区
	开封	开封新区	287	2010.02	省级	郑汴一体化的核心增长极之一。以产业集聚为基础，融居住办公、科研教育、旅游休闲、商贸物流于一体的现代化生态型复合型新城区

续表 1

所在省、自治区、直辖市	所在地	名称	规划面积（km^2）	批准时间	批准级别	发展定位
河南	洛阳	洛阳新区	518		省级	集办公、文化、商业、体育、休闲娱乐和居住为主要功能的生态型复合型新城区
	南阳	南阳新区	190	2010.12	省级	城乡一体化先行区、现代化复合型功能区、对外开放示范区、豫鄂陕结合部综合交通枢纽和物流中心
	平顶山	平顶山新区	295	2011.12	省级	城乡一体化先行区、产业转型升级先导区、对外开放示范区、豫中南综合交通枢纽和物流中心
	安阳	安阳新区	226	2011.07	省级	城乡一体化先行区、现代化复合型功能区、对外开放示范区、产业转型升级先导区、豫晋冀交界地区综合交通枢纽和区域物流中心
	商丘	商丘新区	198	2011.07	省级	包括中央商务区、智慧信息区、物流商贸区、文化科教区、生态宜居区等功能完备的新城区
	漯河	漯河新区	148	2012.05	省级	城乡一体化先行区、现代化复合型功能区、对外开放示范区、豫中南综合交通枢纽和区域性商贸物流中心
	三门峡	三门峡新区	187	2012.08	省级	生态宜居现代复合型新区、对外开放示范区、产业转型升级引领区和豫陕晋黄河金三角地区综合交通枢纽和商贸物流中心
	鹤壁	鹤壁新区	130	2012.08	省级	市域城乡一体化先行区、现代生态宜居区、对外开放示范区、产业转型升级先导区
	濮阳	濮阳新区	189	2012.08	省级	市域城乡一体化先行区、对接环渤海开放合作示范区、生态宜居示范区、豫鲁冀区域的交通枢纽和物流中心
	驻马店	驻马店新区	148	2012.10	省级	承接产业转移示范区、现代生态宜居区、区域性农产品加工贸易基地
	周口	周口新区	143	2013.01	省级	城乡一体化发展先行区、对外开放示范区、现代生态宜居区、豫鲁皖苏接合部综合交通枢纽和区域商贸物流中心
山西	太原	龙城新区	14	2009	市级	以居住生活为基本功能，以商务、金融、办公、科教、物流等为发展重点的城市南部功能复合的新型城市综合性片区
湖北	武汉	武汉新区	368	2004.02	市级	辐射长江中游的先进制造业基地、生产性服务中心、文化旅游中心，以滨江滨湖为特色的现代生态宜居新区
	黄冈	小池滨江新区	48	2012.10	市级	湖北长江经济带开放开发的示范区，体制机制创新的试验区，湖北跨越式发展的经济特区
	恩施	龙凤新区	30	2012	市级	集商住小区、商业娱乐、休闲购物于一体的现代化城市综合体
湖南	益阳	益阳东部新区	285	2008.5	市级	“两型”社会建设示范区、全国知名的文化体育产业新基地和文化旅游目的地，生态宜居新城
	常德	常德物流新区	480	2011	市级	以第三方物流作为重点，具有一定集聚和辐射能力的现代商贸物流基地
	衡阳	武广新区	64	2010	市级	城市副中心，湖南南部重要的交通枢纽，生态宜居新区
	娄底	万宝新区	110	2010.08	市级	区域性商贸物流中心，新型城市示范区、两型产业聚集区、城乡统筹样板区、生态文明先导区

续表 1

所在省、自治区、直辖市	所在地	名称	规划面积（km^2）	批准时间	批准级别	发展定位
安徽	合肥	滨湖新区	196	2006.11	省级	现代化滨湖大城市建设的重要组成部分和示范区
	马鞍山	博望新区	322	2011.02	市级	重要的新兴产业集聚区，对接南京禄口空港的门户示范区，绿色宜居的现代化副城区
	阜阳	城南新区	20	2011	市级	集政务办公、商务金融、文化体育、教育医疗、会展旅游、商业居住为一体的现代化阜阳新城
	淮南	山南新区	98	2005	市级	具有淮南山水特色的现代化南部新城区
	宿州	砀山高铁新区	35	2012.02	市级	集生产、居住、商贸、物流、休闲、文化、娱乐等功能于一体的综合新区
江西	新余	高铁新区	61	2012	市级	区域性交通枢纽，宜居生态新城区
	鹰潭	信江新区	11.28	2010	市级	未来鹰潭主城区的核心区
福建	福州市	福州新区	2050	2014.01	省级	台海两岸交流合作先行区、新型城市化示范区、扩大对外开放新门户、海西经济区现代产业高地和城乡统筹改革试验区
	武夷山市	武夷新区	4132	2012.07	省级	国际性文化与自然旅游目的地，宜居宜游宜业的生态新城，闽浙赣交界区域重要中心城市
	龙岩	古蛟新区	766.18	2012.03	市级	国家级旅游度假区、国家级循环经济示范区、革命老区城乡一体化示范区、国家级文化产业园区
	龙岩	龙雁新区	134	2012.03	市级	闽台经济合作的先行区、区域经济发展的示范区、生态工贸新城
甘肃	兰州	兰州新区	806	2012.08	国家级	西北地区重要的经济增长极、向西开放的重要战略平台和承接产业转移示范区，特色鲜明、功能齐全、产业集聚、服务配套、人居环境良好的现代化产业新区
贵州	贵阳、安顺	贵安新区	1500	2014.01	国家级	内陆开放型经济示范区、特色装备制造业基地、区域性商贸物流中心和科技创新中心
	毕节	双山新区	382	2011年	市级	毕节市未来的商业、文化、教育和居住中心
	黔西南	义龙新区	1250	筹建	市级	生态文化旅游功能区，新兴产业集聚区，区域性商贸物流中心
	黔西南	兴贞新区	668	筹建	市级	重要的煤电化工、新型建材、冶金、农特产品加工、制造业新区，集工业、商贸、物流、仓储、休闲、居住为一体的现代化生态宜居新区
陕西	西安	西咸新区	882	2014.01	国家级	西安主城功能新区和生态新城，内陆型经济开发开放的国家级新区；国际文化交流的重要基地；新兴产业集聚区；城乡统筹发展的示范区
	铜川	铜川新区	35.8	1993.11	省级	铜川市新的政治、经济、文化中心，现代宜居新区
内蒙古	呼和浩特	呼东新区	103	2011.08	市级	功能完善、生态宜居、充满活力的现代化新城区
	包头	石拐新区	16.6	2012	市级	资源枯竭型城市转型发展示范区
四川	成都	天府新区	1578	2014.10	国家级	以现代制造业为主、高端服务业集聚、宜业宜商宜居的国际化现代新城区，西部经济发展高地
	泸州	江南新区	600	2012.05	省级	宜居宜业宜商的现代化“中国酒城”新区，核心功能概括为“一极三区”

续表 1

所在省、自治区、直辖市	所在地	名称	规划面积（km^2）	批准时间	批准级别	发展定位
云南	昆明、玉溪、楚雄	滇中产业新区	1149	2012.11	省级	国家级重点开发区之一，推动云南省经济跨越发展的核心区
广西	南宁	五象新区	175	2006	省级	区级商贸中心，宜居的城市新区
青海	西宁	西宁城南新区	30	2001	市级	青藏高原科学发展示范型新区和生态文明建设示范型新区
	西宁	海湖新区	10.46	2009	省级	集商贸金融、科技文化、旅游服务、行政办公、居住休闲为一体的现代化生态新城区
宁夏	银川	滨河新区	1200	2013.02	省级	先进制造业与高技术产业和现代服务业新区，特色文化休闲旅游区
新疆	塔城	辽塔新区	85.8	2011.11	市级	中国向西开放的重要门户、东西合作的示范区、新疆沿边地区新的经济增长极、兵地融合发展示范区
	乌鲁木齐	城北新区	268	拟建	市级	金融、物流、科技、文化等现代服务业基地，新兴产业基地，生态宜居新城区
	喀什	喀什经济开发区	73	2011.10	国家级	面向中亚地区的国际化大都市，向西出口加工基地和商品中转集散基地
	伊犁	霍尔果斯经济开发区	50	2011.10	国家级	中国与哈萨克斯坦国际合作贸易中心，向西开放的战略高地，向西出口加工基地和商品中转集散基地
	乌鲁木齐	高铁新区	37.7	拟建	市级	区域性交通物流中心，现代化产业和现代生态新城
	石河子	南山新区	137	2012.01	市级	面向中亚地区的高端制造业、研发设计基地，天山北麓经济区的产业金融集聚区、低碳产业示范区
	阿勒泰	福海新区	32	2010.08	省级	区域性商贸、旅游服务区，生态新城
西藏	拉萨	柳梧新区	24	2007.11	市级	集金融、商贸、房产地、旅游等产业为一体的现代化新城区
海南	乐东县	九所新区	6.18	2001.12	省级	乐东县政治、经济、文化以及物流与信息中心
	儋州	滨海新区	59	2009.01	省级	面向东南亚的对外开放门户和新兴城市

资料来源：根据各省政府及各地政府相关文件整理而成。

不仅直辖市、计划单列市和省会城市建设了新城新区，而且多数地级城市和部分县级市甚至县城也在规划和建设新城新区。实地调研得知，规划面积806平方公里的兰州新区刚批建不到一年，就提出要求增加建设用地。由于缺少科学规划和合理预判，新城新区建设遍地开花、市市有新城，县县有新区，甚至不少城市同时有多个新城新区。结果导致新城新区建设供过于求、配套不足，除了催生房地产泡沫、加重地方对土地财政依赖外，还过度消耗了有限的土地资源。部分新区建设过于超前，圈而不建或建而不用，导致新城新区沦为城市空心化、产业空心化、人口空心化的“空城”、“烂区”，新城新区产业基础薄弱，难以有效支撑新区经济增长。

（二）新城新区建设面积不断扩大，已建新区谋划扩容

全国范围内城市新区建设不仅表现在数量的增多，目前已建新区还在谋划扩容，致使新建区规模越建越大。据不完全统计，全国新区规划总面积达到4.64万平方公里。截至2014年年底，中国已有29个新区的单体面积超过400平方公里，而面积超过1 000平方公里的城市新区也已达到21个。其中面积前十位的分别为：福建省武夷新区（4 132平方公里）、福州新区（2 050平方公里）、河北渤海新区（2 375平方公里）、大连金普新区（2 299平方公里）、天津滨海新区（2 270平方公里）、青岛西海岸新区（2 096平方公里）、唐山曹妃甸新区（1 944平方公里）、郑州新区（1 840平方公里）、茂名滨海新区（1 688平方公里）以及成都天府新区（1 578平方公里）。在面积超过1 000平方公里的21个新区中，东部沿海地区占了12个，西部地区有5个，中部地区仅有1个，表明当前中国的新区建设主要集中于东部地区，中西部地区所占份额还较小。

（三）新城新区建设过快过急，"倒逼返修"城市总体规划使其合法化

由于新城新区建设普遍过大过快，不少新城新区建设用地面积大大突破了原来已批的城市总体规划和土地利用规划中的城市建设用地控制指标，不少地方政府采取了"返修"城市总体规划的做法，一方面确保新城新区建设所需的足够建设用地面积，另一方面使得新城新区建设合法化。这种情况导致新城新区面积大于老城，极大地浪费了城市土地资源。调查发现，大同御东新区（42平方公里）建设等导致城市建设用地面积实际已达到180平方公里，远超出了国务院批复的到2020年大同主城区建设用地控制在127平方公里以内的标准，2011年该市通过"返修"城市总体规划将到2020年的城市建设用地调整到195平方公里。采取"返修"城市总体规划确保新城新区建设足够面积并实现合法化的城市屡见不鲜。

（四）新城新区建设体制错综复杂，与主城及原行政区之间存在矛盾冲突

整体上看，新城新区的开发建设一般采用的开发管理模式为：由政府控股的城市开发投资公司作为投资主体，成立党工委和管委会作为政府派出机构进行管理，并给予土地征收、银行信贷、财政税收等方面的优惠和扶持政策。实际上，具体的管理方式多样，新城新区与主城及行政区的关系错综复杂，大多数新城新区的设立都打破了原有行政区划，增加了行政区划的复杂化和政府协调难度，某种程度上激化了新区与老区之间的利益冲突和管理矛盾。从区位上看，中国现有的城市新区多数毗邻城市主城区，与主城区保持密切的联系和功能分工；但也有远离主城区的"飞地"型新城新区，如鄂尔多斯康巴什新区、兰州新区等，主要原因是主城区周边缺少可利用的土地资源。从行政区划关系上看有几种模式：一种是"合一"模式，如浦东新区、天津滨海新区、舟山群岛新区等；一种是"内含"模式，新区位于行政区内部的特定区域，如郑东新区、铁西新区等；一种是"整合"模式，新城新区跨相邻几个行政区的特定区域，如两江新区跨重庆江北、渝北、北碚3区；西咸新区和天府新区都跨多个县、市、区。

（五）新城新区盲投盲建，加大了地方政府的负债风险

新城新区的建设涉及全方位的基础设施建设，包括土地征收、房屋拆迁、道路交通、水电气热供给、信息网络、污水垃圾处理、生态绿化等，会产生巨大的投资需求；同时，不管是新上产业项目，还是传统产业项目的改造升级，都需要大量的资金投入，这对新城新区所在城市投融资提出更高的要求。一些城市新城新区开发建设的投资需求动辄几百亿元乃至数千亿元，远远超出多数中小城市的投融资能力，迫使所在城市竞相通过地方政府融资平台公司举债融资，导致地方政府融资平台公司数量膨胀，负债规模急剧攀升，地方债务性风险不断加大。据相关研究统计，截至 2010 年年底，全国共有地方政府融资平台公司多达万家，地方政府性债务余额超过 10 万亿元。新城新区建设涉及的重大项目往往投资回报周期较长，部分行业和领域负债规模较大，一些地方政府在财政收入、资产变现等方面偿债能力弱；还有一些地方政府的债务偿还严重依赖土地出让收入，甚至存在借新债还旧债的现象，进一步增加了地方政府性债务风险隐患。

调查发现，不少地方政府将经营土地、负债发展的中国式城市发展模式运用到了极致，一些政府领导不懂投资，项目未经科学论证就盲目上马，造就了不少“拍脑袋”的新城新区，新城建设中卖地造城建区成了一种常见的开发模式。但由于新城新区建设需要投入巨额资金，单靠卖地不足以满足巨额资金保证，于是进行贷款和融资，结果加大了地方政府负债风险。据审计部门公布的截至 2010 年年末政府性债务数据显示，多个省份的债务率可能已超过 100%。2011 - 2012 年间，有 9 个省会城市本级政府负有偿还责任的债务率已超过 100%，最高达 189%，远远超过了审计署和国际惯例规定的 20% 警戒线。其中，大同市政府因新城建设导致政府负债率达到 200%，西安曲江新区负债率达到 66%，唐山曹妃甸新区负债总额至少 600 亿元，导致许多大型在建工程被迫停工。地方债总量扩张可能引发的危机使紧绷的资金链随时有断裂的危险，需要引起高度重视。

三、新城新区建设失控的原因分析

（一）权威评估监管机制缺失导致新区新城建设自由裁量空间过大

为什么很多新城新区规划粗放、浪费严重，却仍然得以顺利推进，至今没有放慢脚步？原因之一就是我国目前还没有一个权威的关于各类新城新区建设的评估监管机制：到底哪些城市需要建新城新区？应该建多大？建在哪里？哪些地方需要建国家级新区？哪些地方需要建省级市级新区？建多少个新区？诸如此类问题没有权威机构来回答、管控。由于缺乏权威的监督评估与管控机制，各地新城新区建设很大程度上是自己说了算，任建随扩的自由裁量空间很大，这导致新城新区要建多大就能建多大，想建多少就能建多少。

（二）规划失控失效导致新城新区建设贪多求大

在地方政府强势推动下，不少规划设计部门听命于长官意志，基本按照政府事先划定的新城新区建设范围做规划设计，而没有科学分析新城新区建设的可行性、必要性、合理性和科学性，新城新区到底建多大是合理的规模，能吸纳多少人口，承载多少经济总量，有无相应的资源环境承载能力等，对于这些问题在规划阶段因政府不关注而被大大忽视了。在规划设计过程中，政府不断改变规模范围，不断强加个人意图，结果造成科学规划被政府主管意志绑架，导致规划失控失效，造成新城新区越建越多、越建越大。

（三）土地财政的路径依赖加速了新城新区建设

调研发现，在现行财政体制下，地级城市财政收入的30%～35%、县级城市和县财政收入的50%～70%来源于土地出让和房地产开发收入，这是一种典型的土地财政。一旦停止政府供地，政府就可能被“断奶”，财政就难以持续。为避免财政危机，政府就会千方百计地通过多种途径出让土地。而老城区可出让的土地不断减少，开发新城新区就成了各地共同的选择，这客观上加速了新城新区建设。土地财政依赖与债务危机之间形成的恶性循环是新城新区越建越多、越建越大的主要动因。

（四）监管漏洞的路径依赖催生了新城新区建设

国家新型城镇化规划提出到2020年全国城镇化平均水平达到60%，这对低于这一水平的不少省区、城市和县来说，60%成了其奋斗的标杆。要提升省域、市域或县域城镇化水平，就必须引导农民进城，农民进城就要新增建设用地。增加建设用地有两种途径：第一种途径是采用修编城市总体规划的方式，这种方式受《城乡规划法》约束，要通过系统评估后才能允许修编，即便同意修编，也因修编周期长、速度慢、总量增加有限（一般地规划期内新增的建设用地面积不能超过现状建成区面积的20%～30%）而望而却步，很少采用这种形式。第二种途径就是绕过《城乡规划法》等法规约束，通过政府常务会议形成纪要的形式，以会议纪要为依据，决定开建各类新城新区，不需要评估，更不需要审批，一切都是“自己说了算”。这种先圈地、后招商、再生产、最后补建设用地报批手续的“先斩后奏”的做法，正是无序催生各类新城新区的主要根源。新城新区建设的评估、监管、审批由谁来负责监管，这个管理漏洞不堵住，就堵不住新城新区的盲建盲扩。

（五）政绩考核冲动与形象工程的惯性思维助推了新城新区建设

很长一段时间以来，我国干部政绩考核、职务升迁主要以经济数据、经济指标论英雄，受这种考核机制的驱动，政府主导突击造城建区的惯性思维根深蒂固，不少领导干部敢拍板，一味贪大求快，甚至陷入盲目造城扩区的“怪圈”中不能自拔。同一级别行政区域的各县市之间在新城新区建设中，竞相比大小、比体量，把新城新区建设视为政府的形象工程、“一号工程”，视为“政治任务”。这导致不少新城新区建设严重脱离了实际，造成了土地资源和财力的严重浪费。

四、新城新区适度理性建设的科学路径

新城新区建设是推动新型城镇化的一种重要手段，但不是唯一手段，对于新城新区建设要从国家战略层面做好顶层设计、科学引导和合理布局，中国各地城市建设差异很大，不平衡性非常突出，因此，新城新区建设既要禁止搞“一刀切”，也要禁止放任自流，随报即批。

（一）建立新城新区建设的国家综合评估审查机制，严把审批关

从国家经济社会发展的战略安全角度，做好统一的国家新城新区建设规划和顶层设计，从全国一盘棋的角度提出到底需要建设多少个多大规模的国家级新区？建设标准到底有多高？新区到底承担着国家和地区什么样的功能？为此建议建立国家新城新区建设的评估审查机制，成立国家新城新区建设综合评估审查委员会，对各地拟提议建设的新城新区的必要性、合理性和可行性等进行严格科学的综合评估，提出哪些新城新区必须建、哪些新城新区不该建的判断。通过评估，确定出国家级新区建设的目标导向、建设规模、战略布局与资金投向；各省相应成立新城新区建设的评估机构和省级新城新区建设综合评估委员会，在国家新城新区总体建设规划宏观指导下，确定省级新城新区建设的目标、合理规模、科学布局和资金投向。只有这样，才能避免新城新区建设的拍脑袋决策、拍胸脯蛮干、事后拍屁股走人的“三拍”现象再度发生。同时，要吸取曹妃甸新区建设的教训，确保国家级新城新区建设有管有控。

（二）制定可行措施，整改规范在建和规划建设的各类新城新区

面对全国不少地区正在掀起的新一轮“新城新区新扩”和“新城新区新建”倾向，建议以国家新城新区建设综合评估审查委员会评估结果为基础，及时采取措施，清理整顿各地在建和规划建设的各类新城新区，根据城市建设和产业发展需要，立足当地资源环境承载力，科学定位“新城新区”发展功能，提出各类“新城新区”科学合理的建设规模和主导产业，明确产业发展方向与重点，并严格按照《土地管理法》和《城乡规划法》的规定，纳入土地利用规划和城市总体规划之中，确保“新城新区”建设范围与城市总体规划建成区面积精准衔接，对已经超标建设的“新城新区”建议限期整改，对即将超标建设的“新城新区”必须立即停止建设。对于不顾资源与生态环境承载能力，肆意扩大城市建设范围、随意占用基本农田或变相调整基本农田为一般农田再占用的相关责任人做出严肃处理。从确保国家18亿亩耕地这一红线不可逾越的战略高度出发，建议各级城市规划和国土管理部门严把城市用地报批关和盲目扩张关，依法继续实施最严格的土地管理制度，严防部分领导借城乡一体化和践行科学发展观之名，变相圈地造城，越位撤县改区，剥夺基层地方政府的发展权，严防出现新城新区“建而不营、占而不用”的屯地现象发生。

进一步统一和明确城市新城新区的界定和类型，从严管理各级城市随意设立、自称或改名为城市新城新区；制定设立城市新城新区的科学流程和审批程序，加强对设立城市新城新区的评估论证和公开公示；加强上级政府对于设立城市新城新区的审批和监管，原则上应只有国务院和省级政府拥有设立城市新城新区的审批权限，其他各级政府和部门不得审批设立城市新城新区，从制度上严控新城新区的数量；实行同级政府规划、国土、环保、产业、发改等相关部门的协商会签制度，加强同级人大、政协、社会组织、新闻媒体等机构的监督，不断提高城市新城新区设立的规范性和民主性，从而提高新城新区建设的质量。

（三）科学规划新城新区，量需而动，量力而行，量地而置

坚持“量需而动，量力而行，量地而置”的原则，一方面，建议国家编制国家级新城新区建设总体规划，完成新城新区建设的顶层设计，合理界定并严格控制新城新区建设规模和数量；另一方面，在国家规划指导下通过综合评估审查机制选出确需建设新城新区的城市，然后高标准做好新城新区建设的科学规划，正确处理好新城新区与旧城在产业外溢对接、功能疏解互补、交通对接、人员分流、基础设施和公共服务设施配套等方面的相互依存关系，协调好新城新区与主城及原有行政区划存在的错综复杂关系，防止出现“建了新城空老城、建了新城变空城”等不良现象再度发生。

把新城新区建设作为协调区域发展规划、土地利用规划和城市总体规划“三规关系”的重要试验平台，逐步缓解长期以来中国土地利用总体规划、城市总体规划和经济社会发展规划（主体功能区规划）“三规”之间不协调的现象发生，努力协调好目标、坐标和指标“三标”之间的关系，探讨三规协同指导城市新区建设的途径和技术路径，不断提高新城新区建设的产业集中度和用地集约度。

（四）合理运用土地增减挂钩机制，优化新城新区建设用地

土地增减挂钩机制本来是推进城乡用地协调发展、提高城乡土地利用效率、缓解城市建设用地的一种有效手段，但这种手段被一些地方政府用于建设新城新区、随意扩大新城新区面积的重要机制。一些地方采用这种增加挂钩机制，把从县城、乡镇中腾退出来的建设用地全部集中于城市的新城新区，在某种程度上诱导了新城新区建设的用地条件。建议合理运用土地增减挂钩机制，为新城新区建设提供适度的用地保障，通过增减挂钩的新增建设用地要在城市市区、县城、乡镇、农村社区之间合理进行重新配置，不可过分集中于城市新城新区。

针对城市新城新区土地经营粗放、空间积聚程度偏低的问题，在新城新区规划中应整合破碎、分散的各类用地功能。在城市新城新区空间布局上应体现适度分散、相对集中的原则，利用公共交通引导城市开发，强调土地的混合使用和密集开发策略，集中紧凑规划城市建设用地，形成精明增长的城市发展模式。在新城新区开发中应充分利用城市存量空间，加强对现有建成区的再开发，以减少基础设施和公共服务设施建设的成本，保护空地。通过整合城市各类用地，建设紧凑新城新区，提高新城新区土地集约利用效率。

（五）将新城新区建成“产城一体”的产业功能区和城市功能新区

长期以来，以产业发展为目的形成的各类开发区，普遍缺乏人性化的服务和居住功能，难以满足人们全面发展的需要，也不利于土地资源的集约节约利用。新城新区不是开发区，新城新区走的是城镇与产业、安居与乐业相结合的道路，注重城市功能与产业功能的协调发展，实现新型城镇化和新型工业化共同推进。从国外经验看，产业对城市发展的支撑作用日益为人们所重视。伦敦、东京、香港、巴黎等大都市新区都在政府的规划指导下发展成为具有产业功能的新城新区。城市新城新区开发要迅速产生城市综合性社区的功能，核心是促进城市的产业成长。因此，必须培育城市新城新区产业集群，从而产生集群效应，构筑起城市新城新区发展的核心区域。城市新城新区应当致力于培养房地产、金融、保险、现代咨询等在内的第三产业，同时大力发展高新技术产业，推动原有产业的升级，打造城市新的经济增长点。

（六）树立科学政绩观，遏制“催生”新城新区建设的政绩冲动

长期以来，在以经济数据、经济指标论英雄的片面政绩观和考核机制驱动下，政府主导突击造城建区的惯性思维和做法仍未破除，为遏制盲目建设新城新区、一味贪大求快之风，陷入盲目造城扩区热中而不能自拔。建议改革现行政绩考核体系，结合当前正在进行的群众路线教育实践活动和各级领导干部的专题民主生活会，切实转变领导干部的政绩观，把政绩冲动的负效应，转化为促进科学发展、改善民生的正能量。正确认识“以人为本”新型城镇化的本质内涵，以科学理性的思维合理引导新城新区的适度有序建设，逐步化解新城新区建设给地方政府带来的负债风险，不断提升城镇化发展质量，使新城新区建设真正发挥对推动国家新型城镇化的重要作用。

（作者：方创琳，中国科学院地理科学与资源研究所研究员，博士生导师，区域与城市规划设计研究中心主任，中国地理学会人文地理专业委员会主任。）

参考文献

[1] 方创琳．中国新型城镇化发展报告［R］．北京：科学出版社，2014：35－59.

[2] 朱孟珏，周春山．改革开放以来我国城市新区开发的演变历程、特征及机制研究［J］．现代城市研究，2012（9）：80－85.

[3] 朱孟珏，周春山．我国城市新区开发的管理模式与空间组织研究［J］．热带地理，2013，33（1）：56－62.

[4] 方创琳，马海涛．新城新区，如何让城市更美好［N］．光明日报，2014－07－01.

[5] 王浩．基于快速城镇化背景下城市新区建设的探讨［J］．工程与建设，2011，25（4）：451－453.

[6] 方创琳，马海涛．新型城镇化背景下中国的新区建设与土地集约利用［J］．中国土地科学，2013，27（7）：4－10.

[7] 高国力．科学管理和引导城市新区的开发建设［J］．中国发展观察，2012（12）：36－39.
[8] 阎炎．量需而行，量地而制——中国科学院研究员方创琳谈新城建设［J］．中国土地，2010（8）：11－14.
[9] 王青．以大型公共设施为导向的城市新区开发模式探讨［J］．现代城市研究，2008（11）：47－53.
[10] 高波，葛扬，黄贤金．城市新区开发的对策与政策建议［J］．南京社会科学，2002（11）：13－18.

食品质量安全的问题与对策

一、我国食品质量安全的现状、问题与面临的形势

（一）我国食品质量安全的现状

我国高度重视食品安全工作，国务院成立了食品安全委员会及其办公室，加强了对食品安全的组织领导。在各地区、各有关部门和全社会的共同努力下，食品安全监管力度不断加大。尤其是2009年《中华人民共和国食品安全法》实施以来，食品安全各项工作取得了明显成效，全国食品安全形势总体稳定并保持向好趋势，产品质量稳步改善，产品总体合格率不断提高。目前，23大类3800多种加工食品质量国家监督抽查批次抽样合格率由2005年的80.1%提高到2010年的94.6%，提高了14.5个百分点，出口食品合格率一直保持在99%以上。2010年，食品投诉案件34789件，较2006年下降17.4%。截至2010年年底，已完善了1800余项国家标准、2500余项行业标准和7000余项地方标准及企业标准，公布新的食品安全国家标准176项，为保障食品安全奠定了良好基础。

（二）我国食品质量安全存在的问题

我国食品质量安全存在的主要问题是食品安全保障体系不够完善。食品安全事件时有发生，消费者对食品安全仍较担心。早些年，食品容易在添加剂、农药残留和兽药残留等方面出现问题，但随着我国对食品中农药残留、兽药残留和食品添加剂等使用的监管力度不断加强，食品中这类有害化学物质的污染率不断下降。相反，由于生态破坏和环境污染、食品生产模式及饮食方式的改变、食品流通的日益广泛、新的病原体的不断出现、细菌耐药性的生产等，使食品，尤其是动物性食品，被病原体及其毒素污染的可能性越来越大。不仅如此，企业违法生产、加工食品现象不容忽视。一方面，少数不法分子违法使用食品添加剂和非食品原料生产加工食品，掺假制假，影响恶劣；另一方面，我国现有食品行业整体素质仍处于较低水平，卫生保证能力差的手工及家庭加工方式在食品加工中占相当大的比例，有的从业人员甚至未经健康体检，农村和城乡结合部无证无照生产加工食品行为屡禁不止，给食品安全造成重大隐患。而且，这些微小规模的食品企业在食品收购、储藏和运输过程中，过量使

用防腐剂、保鲜剂，直接或间接造成的食品安全隐患持续不断。此外，我国食品质量标准体系尚不完善，食品卫生标准、食品质量标准、农产品质量安全标准和农药残留标准等标准体系有待进一步整合，不同行业间制定的标准在技术内容上存在交叉矛盾。技术保障能力尚难以满足食品安全监管需要，检测技术相对落后，仪器设备配置不足，部分检验设备严重老化；基层检验机构和人员数量偏少，检测能力亟须加强。食品安全监管机制还不够健全，食品安全责任追溯制度尚不完善。一些企业主体责任不落实，自律意识不强，诚信缺失。

（三）食品质量安全面临的形势

从国际上看，食品质量安全受到空前关注，安全保障难度加大。食品安全问题作为一个全球性的基本公共卫生问题，已经受到世界各国和国际组织的普遍重视，对食品安全投入不断增加，发达国家基本都建立了较为完善的食品安全监管体制和科学的管理模式，发展中国家食品安全保障能力也正在加强。然而，全球食品安全形势仍然不容乐观，食品产业链的全球化增加了食品安全保障难度，工业发展和环境破坏导致食品的化学危害趋于严重。受经济发展水平的制约，发展中国家和不发达国家食品安全保障能力仍然较低，每年都有大量的食源性疾病发生，不发达国家甚至每年约有 220 万人死于食源性腹泻，发达国家每年仍约有 1/3 的人感染食源性疾病，食品安全事故时有发生。保障食品安全已经成为世界各国面临的共同难题。

从国内看，食品安全风险广泛存在，食品质量安全已成为全社会高度关注的焦点。随着食品相关领域认知水平的提高，特别是检测技术和医学的发展，对农药兽药残留、抗生素以及非法添加物等物质的危害性研究的深入，影响食品质量安全的风险因素不断被认知；同时新材料、新技术、新工艺的广泛应用使食品安全风险增大，使得越来越多与食品安全相关的问题时有发生，对食品安全风险分析与控制能力、检验检测技术和监管方式提出了新的要求。随着人们生活水平的提高和健康意识的增强，对食品安全与营养提出了更高要求，而食品工业在产品标准、技术设备、管理水平和行业自律等方面还有较大差距。

二、国外发达国家食品安全问题的应对

食品安全问题是各国需要长期面对的严峻挑战，发达国家和地区已将其上升为国家战略层面，美国、欧盟等发达国家和地区，不仅不断完善标准体系，在食品质量安全控制技术领域更是注重包括农产品原料在内的过程的管控，降低危害物污染的风险，同时大力开发检测技术，强化追溯体系建设，普遍采用了最大残留限量（MRLs）标准体系。

（一）美国、日本、澳大利亚和新西兰等发达国家食品中污染物限量规定

1. 美国食品中污染物限量规定

美国农药登记与农药 MRLs 的制定由美国环境保护局（USEPA）负责。美国是世界上农药管理制度最完善、程序最复杂的国家，建立了一整套较为完善的农药残留标准、管理、检

验、监测和信息发布机制。为了确保食品安全，维护消费者利益，美国制定了详细、复杂的农药 MRLs，共涉及 380 种农药约 11 000 项，大部分为在全美登记的农药并根据联邦法规法典（CFR）制定的农药 MRLs，其余为农药在各地区登记中制定的农药 MRLs、有时限或临时的农药 MRLs、进口农药 MRLs 和间接残留的农药 MRLs 等，还列出了豁免物质或无须农药 MRLs 的清单，提出了“零残留”的概念。

美国农药 MRLs 中有时限或临时性的农药 MRLs 约有 600 项，涉及 100 种农药，1998-2008 年已撤销了 400 多项有时限的农药 MRLs，2010 年撤销了 27 种农药的 114 项有时限的农药 MRLs。列出了约 165 种豁免物质清单，包括柴油、增效醚、除虫菊（酯）、鱼藤酮、藜芦碱等农药活性成分，部分收获后使用和用于特殊处理的农药（如溴甲烷作为移栽前的土壤熏蒸剂，碘化钾作为香蕉叶面处理剂等），其余绝大部分为非活性成分（如助剂）。美国根据需要，对国内没有登记的部分农药/作物组合制定了少量的进口农药 MRLs。

2. 日本食品中污染物限量规定

日本农药 MRLs 的建立分为 3 个部分，毒理学评估、理论摄入评估以及暴露评估。其中动物试验是风险评估中风险鉴定的一部分，ADI、ARfD 和推荐 MRLs 则成为风险表征。日本《食品卫生法》于 2003 年修订并公布，此后厚生劳动省制定了食品中农药化学品肯定列表制度。肯定列表制度所涉及的农药中“不得检出（Not Detected，ND）”的农药（包含现行标准和暂定标准）约占 1%；现行标准和一律标准都使用的农药约占 11%；现行标准、暂定标准和一律标准都适用的农药约为 32%；暂定标准和一律标准都适用的农药约 55%；同时现行标准涉及的农药约占总数的 46%。

2006 年 5 月 29 日之后“肯定列表制度”在 700 多种农药范围内，凡是根据 codex 标准已建立最大残留限量的，或者日本已经登记过的，或者按照其他科学评估结果而设立过暂定标准的化合物，按照其设定的 MRLs 监控，凡是超过 MRLs 的一律禁止在日本销售流通；对于规定的 65 种豁免物质，已经有充足的数据和结论证明其对人类健康无不良影响，不在肯定列表制度限制范围内；对于一律标准（没有建立 MRLs，且不在豁免物质之列的其余 400 多种化合物的统一标准）范围内的农产品中一旦检出高于 0.01mg/kg 水平的残留量，一律严格按照法律条文要求，禁止其销售流通。

3. 澳大利亚和新西兰食品中污染物限量规定

澳大利亚的农药登记与农药 MRLs 制定由其农药和兽药管理局（APVMA）负责。2008 年 10 月，APVMA 发布了新的农药 MRLs 标准，新标准由 5 个附表组成：一为 500 多种农药的共 4000 多项 MRLs；二为食品和动物的分类，该分类参考了 CAC 的食品和动物分类；三为残留定义；四为动物中的 MRLs，共涉及 184 种农药的 570 项 MRLs；五为豁免物质清单，该清单详细列出了不需要制定 MRLs 的农药的各种前提条件。新西兰的农药登记和农药 MRLs 制定由其食品安全局负责，新西兰目前共制定了约 2 900 项 MRLs。

（二）污染物限量（MRLs）标准制定的特点及趋势

1. 标准体系化

欧盟各国、美国等发达国家和地区在大批量制定农药 MRLs 标准前均要出台或修订相关食品安全管理法规。这些国家依靠其先进的科学技术及强大的国力，积累了大量农药毒理、残留、环境等方面的基础数据，其农药 MRLs 标准几乎涉及所有的农产品和食品，一种农药在不同的作物包括很多小作物上都有详细规定，并制定了一系列与农药 MRLs 标准配套的技术规范。其法律依据充分，标准和规范数量庞大，指标具体，体现了标准的权威性和可操作性，加上标准制定、实施和技术支撑的协调统一性，从而形成了一个有机的标准体系和有效的监管机制，确保避免因农药残留超标引起的食品安全问题。

2. 制定农药 MRLs 时重视风险评估

国际食品法典委员会（CAC）、欧盟各国、美国等国际组织和发达国家在制定农药 MRLs 标准时日益强调风险评估，并在风险评估中突出了对弱势群体如儿童、育龄期妇女的保护。风险分析已被认为是制定食品安全标准的基础，在其 4 个组成部分中，风险评估是整个风险分析体系的核心和基础，也是 CAC、欧盟各国、美国等国际组织和国家目前和将来工作的重点。在国际上，农药残留风险评估的目的就是制定农药 MRLs，风险管理的结果就是决定农药能否获准登记，而农药 MRLs 的制定水平直接反映了农药登记管理和风险评估的水平，并直接影响到消费安全与食品和农产品国际贸易。

3. 标准制定中的协调性和工作分工

农药残留限量标准制定中的协调性及工作分工主要体现在：一是在制定农药 MRLs 中，国际组织间、国际组织与国家间以及各国家之间均加强了协调与工作分工。如农药残留联席会议（JMPR）加强了与经济合作与发展组织（OECD）的合作与工作分工，OECD 制定了与农药 MRLs 相关的指导文件和准则，如农药在植物中的代谢准则、轮作作物田间试验准则、残留定义准则、农药残留试验准则、作物田间残留试验模板和家畜饲料表等。JMPR 和 OECD 共同制定了尽可能多的、具体的准则和规范，以确保制定农药 MRLs 时所需资料的质量以及农药 MRLs 的协调一致。

4. MRLs 标准越来越严格和具体

为了确保食品安全及保护各国的贸易利益，欧盟各国、美国和日本等国在制定农药 MRLs 时力求覆盖所有农产品和食品，标准指标越来越严格，主要体现在所有未经过风险评估的农药 MRLs 值都定为临时标准，以方法的检测限或一律标准（0.01mg/kg）为限值，或者定为“零残留”或“不得检出”。在标准制定中不仅考虑农药母体，还考虑农药的异构体、代谢物和手性结构毒性，同时为避免因缺乏标准可能产生国际贸易问题，对可能检测不出的农药残留，也有可能制定残留限量标准。

（三）控制技术方面

发达国家特别重视对食品生产、加工过程质量安全控制技术的研究，是在透彻研究危害物形成机制的基础上，在不影响食品感官和品质的前提下，采用物理、化学或生物的方法控制危害物的形成过程。尤其是采用微生物的方法替代传统食品加工中可能产生潜在危害因子的物质。例如，开发优良乳酸菌，将复配后的乳酸菌添加于肉制品中替代传统的亚硝酸盐呈色作用，可以避免亚硝酸盐潜在的致癌性。

（四）检测技术方面

以欧美为例，由于其整体食品安全管理机制较为完善，农药、兽药、重金属的污染物残留相对较少，所以就检测技术而言，在注重化学性危害检测技术研究、严把进口食品及食品原料质量关的同时，越来越注重对生物性危害的检测技术开发。这也与其社会食品供应体系发达，直接进入家庭的食品半成品乃至即食食品消费量快速增长密切相关。因为已经经过初步加工的肉食、蔬菜等半成品和干酪、沙拉等即食食品，最大的危害风险往往来自于食源性致病微生物。因此，食源性致病微生物鉴定与检测技术在其研究中所占比重越来越大。其技术发展趋势，可为我国相关领域研究指引方向。

（五）追溯控制技术方面

日本的食品可追溯体系（Food Traceability System）于1997年开始建立，是最早实施食品质量安全追溯体系的国家之一。要求所有食用农产品和农产品成分具有可追溯性，供应链上的所有企业要记录、公开和保管产品的履历信息。消费者购买产品时，可以查询到所购买产品在生产、加工、流通、销售各个环节的相关资料。2011年3月日本福岛核泄漏事故发生后，日本农产品管理中“可追溯体系”发挥了作用。日本很多餐馆公布其食材来源等信息，把食物原材料的来源公之于众。超市中出售的本土产品均能做到溯源，消费者用手机便可以查到这些食品的生产、包装和流通过程的详细信息。其追溯体系主要依托于传感网及数据处理、RFID及无线应用、数据库与并行计算等技术的应用。研究日本农产品可追溯体系的建设，对于我国具有借鉴意义。

三、国外发达国家食品安全问题应对给我们的启示

我国近年来虽然非常重视食品质量安全领域的研究，并在某些方面取得了较好的进展，但整体食品质量安全技术与管理水平与发达国家相比仍处于相对落后的水平。针对我国具体国情，并适应我国食品工业的变化，我国食品质量安全在管理与技术领域需要借鉴一些发达国家或地区的经验。

（一）加快农药残留限量标准制定工作

一是全面清理整合相关标准。根据《食品安全法》有关规定，食品安全国家标准是强制执行的标准。除食品安全标准外，不得制定其他食品强制性标准。当前涉及农药残留标准的有国家标准（GB）、农业行业标准（NY）等，涉及农药残留检测方法的标准有国家标准（GB）、农业行业标准（NY）、水产行业标准（SC）、出入境检验检疫行业标准（SN）、烟草行业标准（YC）等。因此，应按照《食品安全法》要求，会同有关部门整合现行有效的食品农药残留相关标准，提高标准的统一性。重点是对现行的约300多项农药残留农业行业标准进行梳理整合，统一公布为食品安全国家标准。二是将国际食品法典委员会（CAC）

标准转化为国家标准。鉴于CAC是联合国粮食及农业组织（FAO）和世界卫生组织（WHO）联手创建的，CAC标准又是世界贸易组织卫生与植物卫生措施协议（WTO/SPS）和世界贸易组织贸易技术壁垒协议（WTO/TBT）认定的标准，且CAC标准也较其他国际标准科学、客观，又鉴于我国尚有一批食品安全标准处于空白状态，一时难于完全补缺。根据我国农药登记情况，结合我国膳食结构特点，对CAC已制定的2300项农药残留限量标准进行研究，必要时进行风险监测，在可接受风险的前提下，争取转化为国家标准。三是加大农药残留试验力度，加快国家标准制定。借鉴农药临时登记超过有效期限产品清理的经验和做法，对没有残留数据等资料的农药作物组合，进行残留试验，补充残留试验数据。同时利用我国已开展并积累的农药残留试验所取得的试验数据，根据风险评估原理，加快农药MRLs标准的制定。四是采用国际通用的方法，拓展标准制定范围。参照国际通用的农药残留限量标准类推的原则，在研究、建立我国农产品分类的基础上，结合我国农药登记残留试验作物分类的相关规定，对已制（修）订的限量国家标准进行类推，必要时可做验证残留试验，拓展制定标准范围。如：豆类蔬菜，如已有扁豆标准，则可类推到豇豆、豌豆、荷兰豆等；同时参照国际通用方法，加大对饲料、肉、蛋、奶、果汁等产品中农药残留限量标准制定工作。五是制定豁免限量标准和一律限量标准农药名单。根据我国农药管理相关规定，参照国际上相关国家的通常做法，按照相关程序，建立我国豁免残留限量和一律限量的农药名单。

（二）加大高通量及便捷检测技术研究

在保障食品安全方面，现代检测技术是不可或缺的。发达国家的农产品安全检测技术呈现出快速化、系列化、精确化和标准化的特征。高通量多残留分析方法在发达国家已经得到广泛应用。美国多残留方法可检测360多种农药，德国多残留方法可检测325种农药，加拿大多残留方法可检测251种农药。因此，紧跟国外发展趋势，开展高通量检测技术的研究。

此外，便捷检测技术灵敏度高，特异性高，适用范围较宽，检测的费用低。目前，国外以公司为主体，开发了大量的便捷检测技术和产品，广泛应用于世界各国食品质量安全的日常监管之中。由于我国政府及食品企业对食品安全的日益高度重视，在检测方面投入越来越大，导致目前每年大量的国外检测技术及产品（仪器装备、试剂盒、试纸条等）进口，我国急需自主技术及产品，因此，应大力开发便捷检测技术及产品。

（三）加大生物性危害防控技术研究

目前我国对于危害物的检测多针对化学性危害物，而发达国家特别重视生物性危害的防控技术。一些发达国家建立了致病菌遗传物质的DNA指纹图谱鉴定技术，可以确定食源性疾病患者排泄物中所分离的细菌与可疑中毒食品中分离的细菌的同源性。对病原微生物的检测，目前我国多采用PCR类检测技术，该技术在食品检测中检测敏感性较低、时效性和准确性差，因而无法进行危险性分析和快速应对。发达国家特别重视基于核酸扩增和基于芯片的高通量检测技术，该技术可以从众多致病菌或致泻性病毒中筛选出病原，除了具有可以多重定量检测的优点之外，还能达到准确定位和溯源的效果。

(四) 加大对战略性食品质量安全控制技术的研究

鉴于我国目前的发展阶段，应加大粮油、畜产、果蔬等战略性食品质量安全控制技术的研究。在相对全面兼顾的同时，应着力加强某些影响面大、关注度高的食品的检测、溯源和控制技术的研究。以乳品为例，由于其涉及的产业链较长，质量安全问题除了营养指标外，还包括致病微生物及其毒素、管道清洗消毒剂、重金属污染物、兽药农药残留等。2013 年爆发的恒天然肉毒杆菌事件也说明了世界各国在乳品质量安全方面仍然普遍存在薄弱之处，因此，可以以此类食品为突破口，研究开发一批具有国际水平的、基于检测及追溯手段实现的食品质量安全控制技术，打破发达国家食品质量安全方面的技术和产品的壁垒，以技术的支撑和保障提升消费者的信心。

(五) 加强食品真伪鉴别和产地溯源技术研究

食品真伪鉴别和产地溯源技术是农产品与食品质量安全控制中的新兴研究热点和重要研究内容，迫切需要高技术的引领和支撑。目前，不法分子在食品中的掺假方式越来越多、范围越来越广、内容越来越复杂，主要包括掺兑、混入、抽取、假冒、粉饰等手段。掺假范围涉及粮油、肉类和加工制品、乳制品、果蔬、糖及糖制品、饮料类以及高附加值食品等各领域。如新大米中掺入陈米；面粉中混入滑石粉；食用油中掺兑地沟油及其他非食用油（如桐油、蓖麻油等）等。

除了原料品种造假，另外一个比较严重的问题是产地造假。例如，冬虫夏草被称为“软黄金”，价格十分昂贵。真正具有营养价值的是西藏和青海原产的冬虫夏草，每千克能卖到 22 万元以上，而现实中不法分子多用亚香棒虫草和凉山虫草冒充。这些假虫草不仅缺乏营养价值，而且可能带来健康风险。据报道某些地区的假虫草达到市场的 50%。这就需要对不同的食品进行产地溯源，产地溯源技术主要是探寻表征不同地域来源食品的特异性指标，包括同位素含量与比值、元素含量、化学成分含量、动物遗传图谱、微生物图谱、感官特性、挥发性成分等。

随着科技迅速发展，掺假的手段和花样也是不断翻新，对鉴伪技术的各项指标和发展速度提出很高要求。从传统的经验判断、感官鉴别到经典的生化分析，到现代仪器方法，再到分子生物学技术，食品检测从表观形态学发展到生化学，再到基因水平，一方面准确性、灵敏度和稳定性越来越高，另一方面，反映了食品从简单的农产品到复杂加工品的转变对检测或鉴别技术的解读能力提出更高的要求。食品真伪鉴别技术主要分为物理方法、化学方法和生物学方法，具体包括以 PCR、实时荧光 PCR、基因芯片、SSR、RFLP、基因测序等技术为代表的 DNA 检测技术，以聚丙烯酰胺凝胶电泳、双向电泳、酶联免疫、生物质谱等技术为代表的蛋白质分析技术，以红外光谱、核磁共振、表面荧光等为代表的光谱分析技术，以气相色谱、高效液相色谱为代表的色谱分析技术，以稳定同位素、电耦合等离子体质谱等为代表的质谱分析技术，以及以电子鼻、电子舌、电子眼为代表的智能感官仿生技术等。

（六）加快食品安全溯源技术系统的集成与示范应用

食品安全溯源技术是重要的食品安全监管技术，通过溯源技术可以快速应对食品安全突发事件，同时也可以从源头上准确控制食品安全风险。但是，目前我国食品安全溯源技术在适用性和易用性方面还存在一些瓶颈问题，造成溯源技术难以推广应用。针对与食品安全溯源相关的检测技术、信息追踪技术、信息管理技术等进行目标化集成，形成适合我国食品生产、流通特点同时又能够满足市场需求的、可以示范应用的成熟技术。通过该项技术的应用，可以有效提高我国对于食品安全事件的快速应急反应能力和源头管控能力。

（作者：黄蔚霞，中粮营养健康研究院食品质量与安全中心副主任，技术总监）

参考文献

［1］Hon-Ming Lam，Justin Remais，Ming-Chiu Fung，Liqing Xu，Samuel Sai-Ming Sun. Food supply and food safety issues in China［J］. The Lancet. 2013，381：2044－2053.

［2］Edward I. Broughton，Damian G. Walker. Policies and practices for aquaculture food safety in China［J］. Food Policy. 2010，35：471－478.

［3］Food safety in China：a long way to go［J］. The Lancet. 2012，380：75.

［4］Guoxue WEI，Jikun HUANG，Jun YANG. The impacts of food safety standards on China's tea exports［J］. China Economic Review. 2012，23：253－264.

［5］http：//www. businessinsider. com/chinese-rice-cadmium-contamination-2013-5.

［6］Peter Ho，Eduard B. Vermeer and Jennifer H. Zhao. Biotechnology and Food Safety in China：Consumers' Acceptance or Resistance［J］. Development and Change. 2006，37：227－25.

2014 年中国市长协会舆情观察

一、舆情综述

2014 年，通过中国市长协会舆情监测系统共监测到 16 126 123 条相关信息，相较 2013 年信息量减少约 15%。其中，网络新闻 11 373 733 条，论坛帖子 3 393 629 条，博客 963 513 条，平媒 395 248 条。相较 2013 年，新闻信息量减少了约 15%，博客减少了约 10%，论坛减少了约 20%，平面媒体有较大幅度的增长，增长了约 30%。年初的 1 月信息量最高，但与排名第二的 12 月信息量相差幅度极小。

如图 1 所示，2014 年，舆情走势较为平稳，信息量最高月和信息量最低月相差幅度远低于 2013 年，最低的 4 月信息量约为最高月 1 月的 70%，而 2013 年则约为 40%。

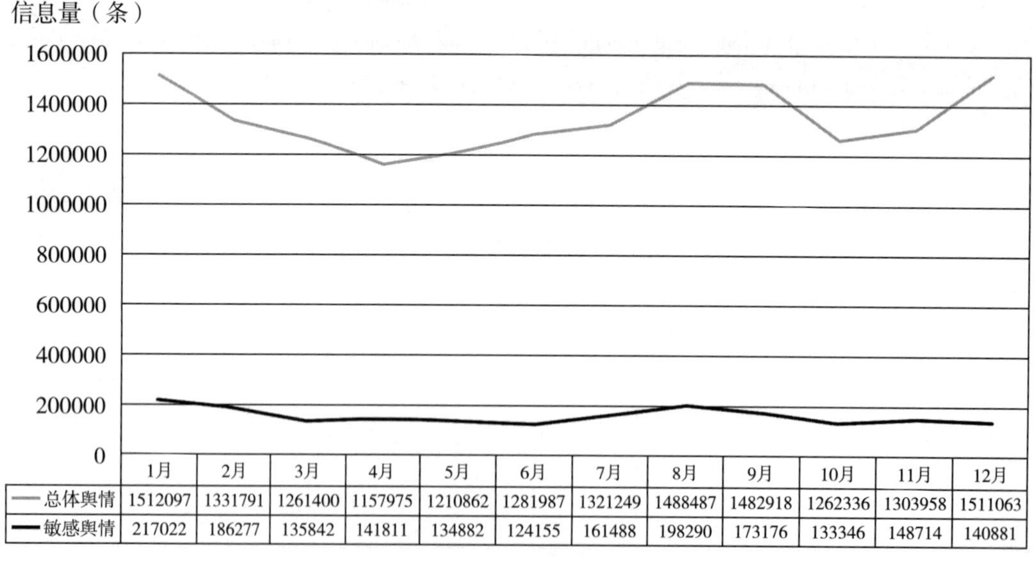

	1月	2月	3月	4月	5月	6月	7月	8月	9月	10月	11月	12月
总体舆情	1512097	1331791	1261400	1157975	1210862	1281987	1321249	1488487	1482918	1262336	1303958	1511063
敏感舆情	217022	186277	135842	141811	134882	124155	161488	198290	173176	133346	148714	140881

图 1　2014 年舆情走势

2014 年农历新年前的 1 月信息量全年最高，农历新年所在的 2 月信息量排名第六，这与 2013 年 2 月、1 月信息量全年排名倒数第一、第二形成鲜明反差。2014 年网络在农历新年前后对于时政反而更加关注，具体原因值得玩味。

2013 年，随着 3 月“两会”的召开，网络对时政的热情迅速上升，在 4 月信息量达到一个峰值，2013 年全年第二。而新的 2014 年却恰恰相反，“两会”召开的 3 月信息量排名倒数第三，“两会”过后的 4 月和 5 月排名倒数第一和倒数第二，2014 年“两会”召开时期网络对时政的关注大为降低，“两会”召开过后，网络对时政的关注度更是降低到了全年的最低点。

而后，6 月到 8 月信息量逐步上升，在新学年开学前后的 8 月和 9 月信息量达到一次高峰，8 月和 9 月信息量排名 2014 年第三和第四。国庆长假和十八届四中全会所在的 10 月信息量有所下降，排名第九。而后信息量迅速放大，到 12 月，信息量达到 2014 年第二高的位置。

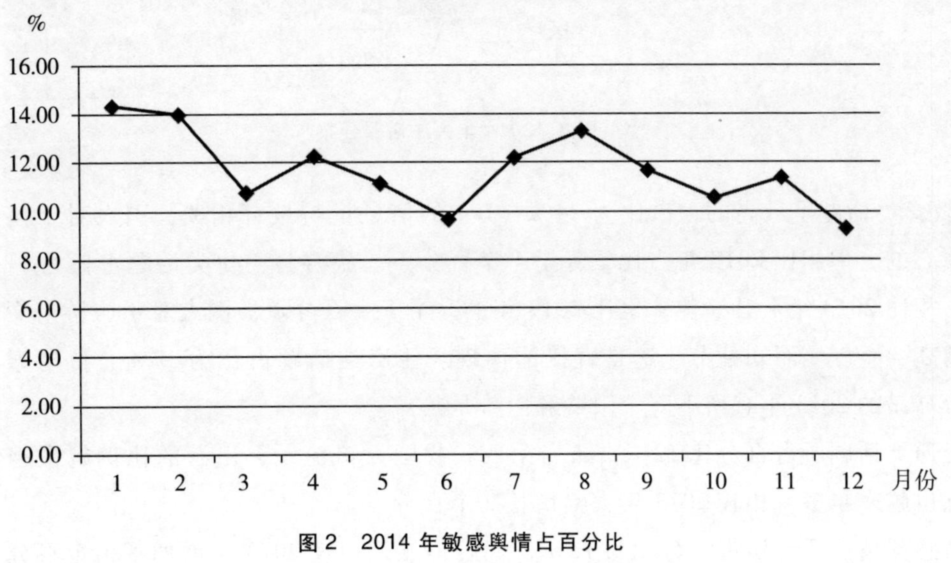

图 2　2014 年敏感舆情占百分比

2014 年，敏感舆情占总体舆情量的 12%，相较 2013 年增加了 1 个百分点。如图 2 所示，2014 年敏感舆情所占百分比整体走势为平缓下降趋势，但下降幅度相对 2013 年要较小一点。

在农历新年前后的 1 月和 2 月所占比全年最高，为 14%。“两会”召开的 3 月敏感舆情所占百分比有较大幅度的降低，达到全年倒数第四的 10.7%，之后有所上升。暑假所在的 8 月敏感舆情占总体舆情量的百分比达到一个峰值，达到全年第三的 13.3%。之后一路下降，在年底的 12 月达到全年最低，为 9.3%。

二、话题分析

2014 年，在我们横向比较的 12 个关注话题中，每个话题得到的关注度依旧表现出了较为明显的差别。“教育”、“旅游与文化”、“住房”依旧得到了更高的关注度，排名前 3 位，合计占比高达 58%，与 2013 年相一致，但三项具体百分比小有增减，原先排名第二的“住房”下降一位，现排名第三，而原先排名第三的“旅游与文化”上升一位，现排名第二。

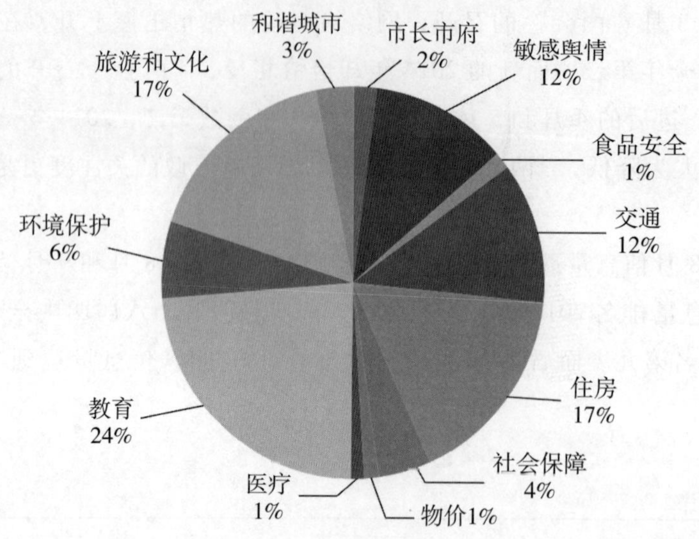

图 3　2014 年关注话题分布

教育类话题是最高的，占比为 24%，1/4 的信息量与教育相关，国人对于孩子的教育是最关心的，但相比 2013 年占比下降了 1 个百分点。旅游与文化类话题占比为 17%，跃居第二，相比 2013 年上升一位，也比 2013 年上升了 1 个百分点。国人对于旅游与文化的热情越来越高，仓廪实而知礼节，这是直接的体现。住房类话题占比为 17%，位居第三，但比较房价高昂的 2013 年有所下降，限购和限价是热点。

交通类话题所占百分比 12%，跃居第四，我国人口流动，出游的比例越来越大，相关的信息也越来越多，相较 2013 年大幅增长 2 个百分点。

敏感舆情类话题所占百分比为 12%，位居第五，相较 2013 年增加了 1 个百分点，新一届政府正在大力推进党风和廉政建设，敏感舆情所占百分比的增加也恰当其时。

环境保护类话题所占百分比为 6%，位居第六，与 2013 年相一致。对于直接影响我们

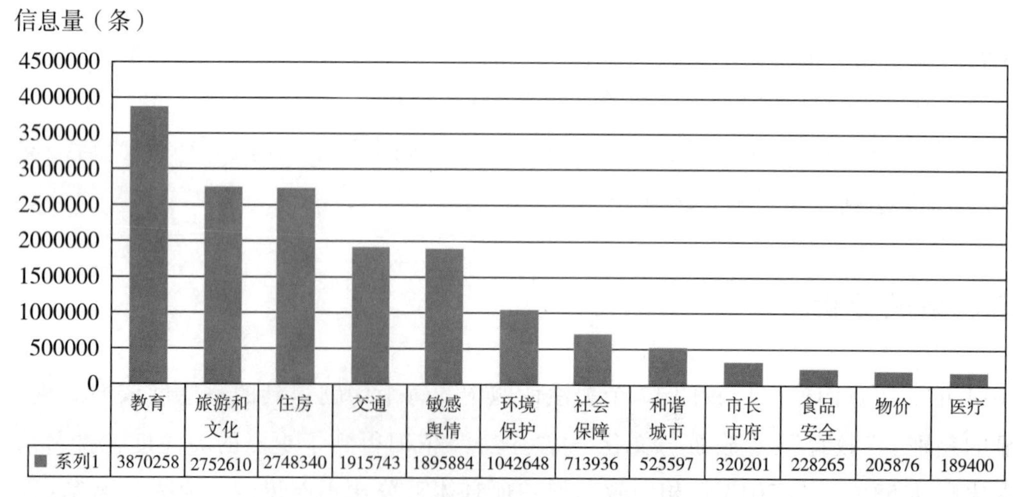

	教育	旅游和文化	住房	交通	敏感舆情	环境保护	社会保障	和谐城市	市长市府	食品安全	物价	医疗
■ 系列1	3870258	2752610	2748340	1915743	1895884	1042648	713936	525597	320201	228265	205876	189400

图 4　2014 年关注话题排行

健康的环境问题，关注度一直较高。

社会保障类话题所占百分比为 4%，名列第七。

和谐城市类话题所占百分比 3%，名列第八，所占百分比相较 2013 年降低 1 个百分点。

市长市府类话题，所占百分比为 2%，位居第九。

食品安全、物价和医疗类话题位居后三位。食品安全和物价类话题所占百分比相比 2013 年均有所下降，医疗依然是国人最少关注的话题。

三、教育类舆情分析

（一）舆情走势

由图 5 可见，教育类舆情在 2014 年信息量起伏较大。与 2013 年形成鲜明对比的是，农历新年和学生寒假前后的 2014 年 1 月和 2 月信息量不是全年的最低谷，反而在 1 月达到了全年的最高点，这与 2013 年同期完全不同。

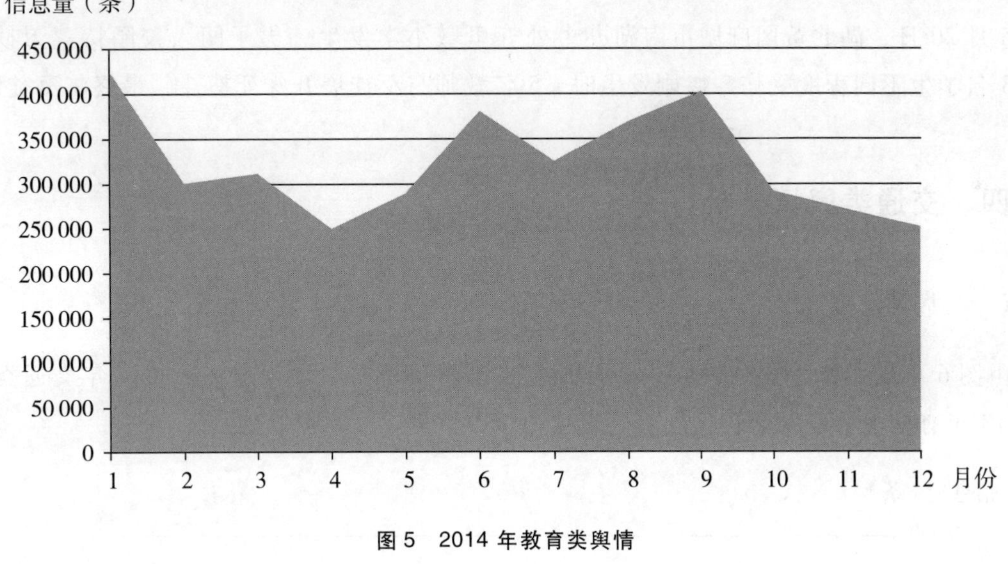

图 5　2014 年教育类舆情

新学年开始的 2014 年 9 月信息量第二高，2013 年 9 月则是全年最高，高考所在的 6 月信息量第三。

（二）2014 年重点话题事件

1. 山西五台学校流行做法事，学生被要求课间叠元宝

监测数据：共监测到 15 632 条相关数据。

事件背景：

五台县位于山西省忻州市境内，因有著名的佛教名山五台山而得名。山西省忻州市五台县校园内盛行举办“谢土”仪式，校领导焚香点蜡，甚至下跪祭拜。逢每年一度的这种仪

式前，老师要凑份子，自备纸元宝送到学校。多名当地中学生称，学校“谢土”前，老师还会给学生发纸，让他们在下课期间叠纸元宝。

对此，多所学校校长表示，“谢土”旨在祈求师生平安。五台县宣传部工作人员则称，尽管“谢土”仪式含一定的迷信色彩，但作为当地的一种风俗，学校、单位甚至政府部门都会办。

2. 河南高考替考事件

监测数据：共监测到 15 541 条相关数据。

事件背景：

6 月 17 日，央视曝光高考枪手替考利益链，有人组织武汉在校大学生“枪手”前往河南杞县等高考考点替考，组织者称给枪手 5 万元可考上重点本科。此事曝光后，教育部派工作组赶赴河南省、湖北省指导督办调查，并请公安部指导有关地方公安机关立案侦查。河南省招生办公室发布情况说明称，查实违规违纪考生 165 人，其中替考 127 人。

3. 湖北麻城小学砍人事件

监测数据：共监测到 7 721 条相关数据。

事件背景：

5 月 20 日，湖北黄冈麻城市南湖办事处五里墩小学发生一男子闯入校园持菜刀砍人事件，8 名学生不同程度受伤。惨剧发生时，5 名教师与歹徒展开殊死搏斗，最终将歹徒制伏。

四、交通类舆情分析

（一）舆情走势

由图 6 可见，交通类舆情在 2014 年信息量基本保持平稳增长态势。2014 年交通类舆情较 2013 年有较大幅度的增长，排名也超越敏感舆情类舆情跃居第四。

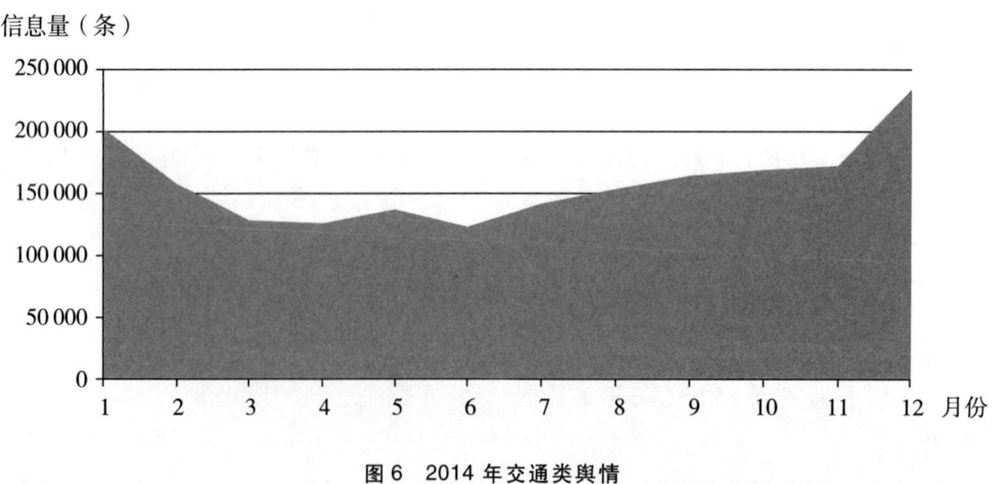

图 6　2014 年交通类舆情

最低谷是 6 月，与最高峰的 12 月相差较大。年初的 1 月信息量第二。

（二）2014 年重点话题事件

1. 多地大雪，69 条高速局部封闭，近百趟高铁列车晚点

监测数据：共监测到 9 231 条相关数据。

事件背景：

2 月 5 日，我国中东部地区普遍出现雨雪天气，部分地区出现大到暴雪，对春运返程交通运输造成较大影响。受降雪影响，69 条高速公路局部路段封闭，路面结冰致高速路事故频发；京广、京沪高铁降速运行，近百趟高铁列车晚点。

2. 晋济高速致 40 死危化品燃爆事故 33 人被控制

监测数据：共监测到 35 241 条相关数据。

事件背景：

3 月 1 日 14 时 45 分许，位于山西省晋城市泽州县的晋济高速公路山西晋城段岩后隧道内，一辆山西铰接列车追尾一辆河南铰接列车，造成前车装载的甲醇泄漏，后车发生电气短路，引燃周围可燃物，进而引燃泄漏的甲醇，并导致其他车辆被引燃引爆，共造成 40 人死亡、12 人受伤和 42 辆车烧毁，直接经济损失 8 197 万元。6 月 10 日晋济高速公路山西晋城段岩后隧道“3·1”特别重大道路交通危化品燃爆事故调查报告，由国务院批复并向社会全文公布。

3. 交通运输部公布 2013 年全国收费公路统计公报

监测数据：共监测到 6 518 条相关数据。

事件背景：

12 月 23 日国家交通运输部网站消息，国家交通运输部根据《政府信息公开条例》的有关规定，将 2013 年全国收费公路统计汇总结果发布公报。2013 年度，全国收费公路通行费收入为 3 652 亿元。2013 年度，全国收费公路支出总额为 4 313 亿元。2013 年度，全国收费公路收支平衡结果为负 661 亿元，即整体亏损 661 亿元。

五、和谐城市类舆情分析

（一）舆情走势

由图 7 可见，和谐城市类舆情在 2014 年信息量基本保持平稳。信息量峰值位于 1 月，其他 11 个月份的信息量比较接近，且都远低于 1 月，约为 1 月的 50%。和谐城市类舆情 2014 年所占百分比为 3%，相比 2013 年下降了 1 个百分点。

相较而言，“两会”召开的 3 月信息量稍高，与 2013 年“两会”召开期间信息量大幅增长形成对比。暑假期间的 8 月信息量稍高。而四中全会所在的 10 月信息量没有明显的增长。

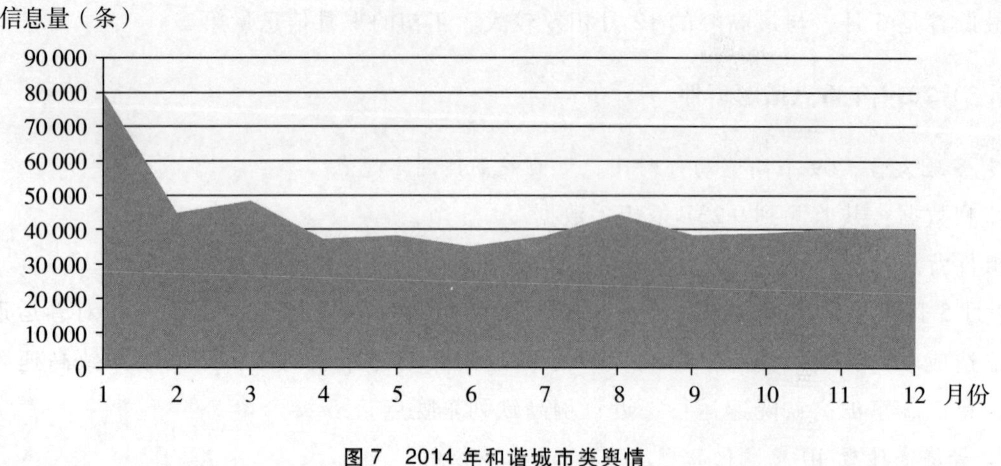

图7　2014 年和谐城市类舆情

（二）2014 年重点话题事件

1. 2013 年三公经费降 10.2%

监测数据：共监测到 2 892 条相关数据。

事件背景：

2014 年 3 月，国务院要求 98 个中央部门公开“三公”数据。截至 4 月 21 日，已有超过 90 家中央部门公开其 2013 年“三公经费”预算执行情况和 2014 年预算安排。财政部公布数据显示，2013 年中央部门“三公经费”预算执行数与年初预算相比，下降 10.2%，兑现了国务院总理李克强“三公经费只减不增”的承诺。

2. 干部培训频现“天价学费”，多超官员工资支付水平

监测数据：共监测到 1 782 条相关数据。

事件背景：

不少以“干部培训”为关键词的招生广告中，收费标准从数万元起步，到数十万元不等。对于各类干部培训班，不少培训班的收费已大大超出了官员的工资支付水平。“天价”干部培训之所以市场火爆，源自官员、高校、企业的三方需求。此类培训学费动辄几十万元，普通官员的收入并不足以应付这笔开支。这种情况下，一方面，一些企业会主动为干部出资，建立往来。另一方面，高校既是平台的提供者也是受益者，天价学费是其不可忽视的创收。由此看来，此类培训价格虚高、水分巨大却依旧生源火爆便不足为奇。

一方面是一些干部本身参加教育培训的动机和目的不纯，把参加干部教育培训班当成获取文凭的平台，想以此为跳板谋求升官发财，且与企业达成某种默契与交易；另一方面是对干部教育培训机构管理不严，在从事教育培训时，很多培训机构并未取得教育部门的行政许可，属于违法经营，最终使得干部教育培训的管理制度形同虚设。

3. 中国正啃最硬一块“三公”骨头：公车改革

监测数据：共监测到 5 878 条相关数据。

事件背景：

7月16日，中共中央办公厅、国务院办公厅印发的《关于全面推进公务用车制度改革的指导意见》和《中央和国家机关公务用车制度改革方案》向社会公布，其中的一系列改革方案，如取消一般公务用车等，因为力度大且直指现实弊端，甫一推出，广受赞誉。

六、社会保障类舆情分析

（一）舆情走势

由图8可见，社会保障类舆情在2014年信息量起伏不大。年初的1月信息量第二大，随后信息量一路下降，在5月达到低谷，而后信息量一路上升，在年底的12月信息量达到一年中的峰值。

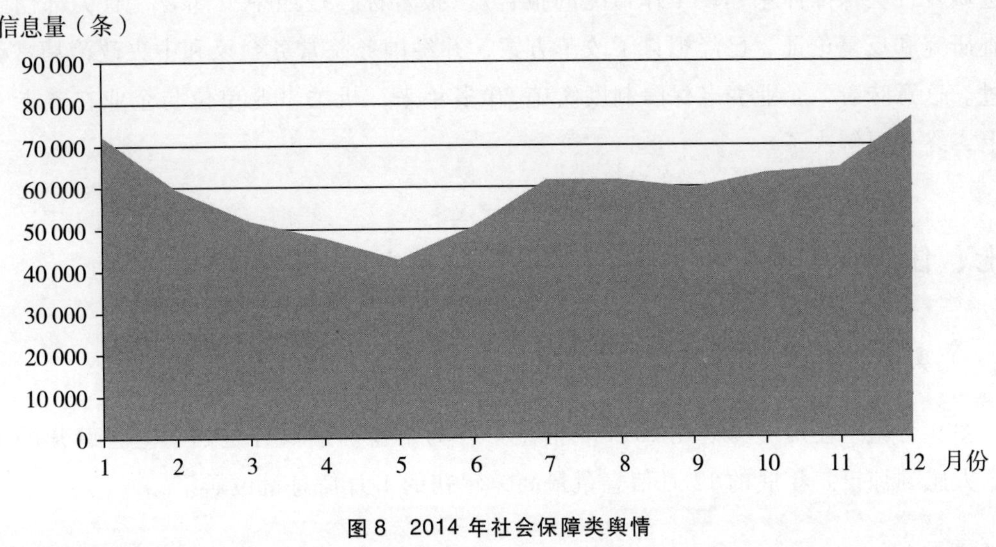

图8　2014年社会保障类舆情

“两会”所在的3月，四中全会所在的10月，社会保障类舆情信息量都没有明显的变化。而2013年“两会”和三中全会对于社会保障类舆情信息量却有巨大的提升作用。

（二）2014年重点话题事件

1. 公积金监控联网爽约3年，部分公积金成政府小金库

监测数据：共监测到1 365条相关数据。

事件背景：

早在2011年年底的住房和城乡建设部年度工作会上，时任住房和城乡建设部部长的姜伟新提出，到2012年年底，要实现全国100个主要城市住房公积金联网监控。但直至2014年，由于地方利益博弈，联网推进十分艰难，全国联网监控连续3年爽约。

2. 社科院报告：中国城乡人均养老金水平相差24倍

监测数据：共监测到2 761条相关数据。

事件背景：

1月社科院发布的报告显示，2012年城镇职工人均养老金水平达2.09万元，新农保为859.15元，两者养老金水平相差24倍之多，这成为阻碍城镇化进展的关键因素。城市靠离退休金养老的占2/3，而农村只有4.6%。2012年中国城镇化率达到52.57%，但只实现了35%的户籍人口城镇化率。这意味着，还有2.5亿左右的农民工难以享受到城镇基本社会公共服务。

3. 中央通过养老金并轨方案

监测数据：共监测到28 549条相关数据。

事件背景：

“千呼万唤始出来”的养老金并轨改革，终于在2014年年底有了眉目。

12月23日，国务院副总理马凯向第十二届全国人大常委会第十二次会议做了《关于统筹推进城乡社会保障体系建设工作情况的报告》。报告称，按照中央部署，有关部门经过广泛调查研究和反复论证，已经拟订了改革方案，并经国务院常务会议和中央政治局常委会审议通过。这意味着，企业养老保险制度实施20多年来，机关事业单位与企业在养老双轨制问题上，终于要解决了。

七、住房类舆情分析

（一）舆情走势

由图9可见，住房类舆情在2014年信息量较为平稳。最低谷是四中全会召开的10月，这很令人感到惊讶。年底的12月信息量最高，年初的1月信息量位居第二。

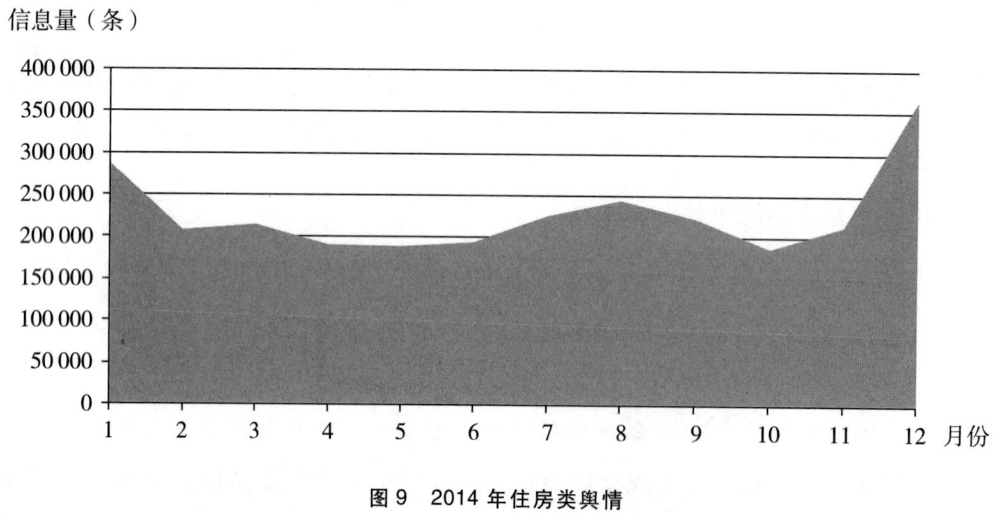

图9 2014年住房类舆情

2014年住房类话题信息量所占比为17%，所占比退居第三，较房价高昂的2013年有所下降。

（二）2014 年重点话题事件

1. 广州回应 39 平方米三居公租房：满足三代同住需求

监测数据：共监测到 5 418 条相关数据。

事件背景：

1 月，广州市首批 2000 多套公租房迎来市民踩点。其中，位于天河区珠吉村安厦花园的“三室一厅”户型在市民中引发不少争议，这类户型的房屋建筑面积 49.26 平方米，使用面积 39.4 平方米，最小的一间不到 4 平方米，遭到一些市民吐槽：“只能摆下一张床。”

2. 5 月 300 城土地出让金骤降近四成，土地市场遇冷

监测数据：共监测到 12 451 条相关数据。

事件背景：

4 月，在楼市成交量下滑的影响下，多地频频出现土地流拍现象，土地出让金均价和总量锐减，同时房地产相关税收大幅下滑，地方财政在两大财源“双降”的重压之下，处境不易且难言乐观。

土地市场的低迷现状，不仅出现在二线、三线城市，一线、二线城市也未能幸免。其中，广州、南京等地即使有土地成交，也多为底价成交。而上海计划推出的两幅地块因无人竞拍而延期出让。

除了土地出让金下滑，与房地产相关的税种收入也出现锐减。财政部公布的 4 月份公共财政收支数据显示，房地产营业税环比锐减 102 亿元。地方税收收入、土地出让金“双降”，房地产因素拖累地方财政收入已成不争的事实。

3. 不动产登记局正式挂牌成立

监测数据：共监测到 18 541 条相关数据。

事件背景：

5 月 7 日，国土资源部办公厅下发《关于在地籍管理司加挂不动产登记局牌子的通知》，在国土资源部地籍管理司加挂不动产登记局牌子。地籍管理司是国土资源部负责组织和指导土地调查、统计、确权、登记、遥感监测、权属争议调处的职能部门。国土资源部的不动产登记职责还包括会同有关部门起草不动产统一登记的法律法规草案，推进不动产登记信息基础平台建设。

不动产登记局挂牌成立标志着统一的不动产登记机构正式组建，不动产登记“四统一”工作（登记机构、登记簿册、登记依据和信息平台）迈出重要一步。

八、食品安全类舆情分析

（一）舆情走势

由图 10 可见，食品安全类舆情在 2014 年信息量起伏较大。最低谷是 4 月，农历新年所

在的2月相关信息数量为第二少。

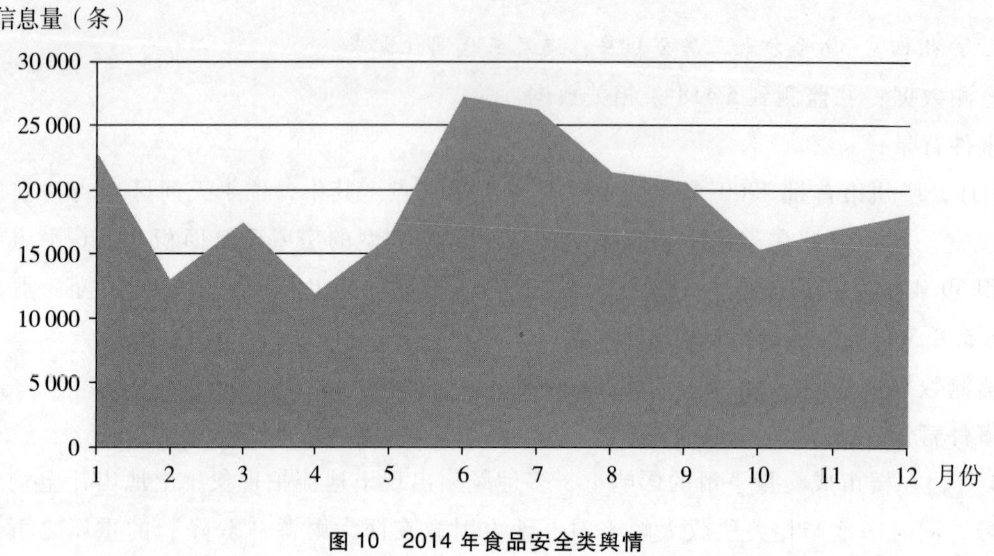

图10 2014年食品安全类舆情

相较而言，自国务院通过食品安全法修订案建立最严处罚制度的5月开始相关食品安全类舆情信息量大幅上升，6月、7月信息量全年最高。

2014年食品安全类话题所占百分比1%，所占百分比相比2013年的2%有所下降。食品安全类话题在网络中受到关注越来越少。

(二) 2014年重点话题事件

1. 沃尔玛被曝“特批”三无食品进店

监测数据：共监测到2 513条相关数据。

事件背景：

1月，央视报道，一些不具备完整资质和证照的食品企业却能得到沃尔玛的“特批”进店销售，其中包括假冒飞天茅台等产品。24日，沃尔玛发声明解释“特批”一事，但对关键问题只字未提。央视报道称，记者在采访中看到近200份经过特批的入场通行证，涉及年份从2006年到2013年。这些“特批”食品有的没有食品生产许可证，有的没有QS生产许可标识，有的没有检验报告，有的没有食品流通许可证等。而依照国家相关法规，存在上述情况的商品均不得进入市场销售。

2. 农村市场成问题食品卸货场，假冒伪劣品扎堆横行

监测数据：共监测到1 653条相关数据。

事件背景：

就在人们将目光还聚焦在城市食品安全问题的当下，中国农村正以惊人的速度成为问题食品的“卸货场”。过期食品翻新登场、假冒伪劣食品扎堆横行，一些在大城市里几乎无处遁形的问题食品，却在农村市场上明目张胆、遍地开花，令人担忧。

3. 国务院通过食品安全法修订案，建最严处罚制度

监测数据：共监测到7 539条相关数据。

事件背景：

国务院总理李克强5月14日主持召开国务院常务会议，讨论通过《中华人民共和国食品安全法（修订草案）》，《食品安全法（修订草案）》23日提请第十二届全国人大常委会第九次会议审议。草案总体思路是：更加突出预防为主、风险防范；建立最严格的全过程监管制度；建立最严格的各方法律责任制度；综合运用民事、行政、刑事等手段，对违法生产经营者实行最严厉的处罚，对失职渎职的地方政府和监管部门实行最严肃的问责，对违法作业的检验机构等实行最严格的追责；实行食品安全社会共治。

九、物价类舆情分析

（一）舆情走势

由图11可见，物价类舆情在2014年信息量非常稳定。除农历新年前的1月信息量高峰外，其他11个月的信息量相差较小。

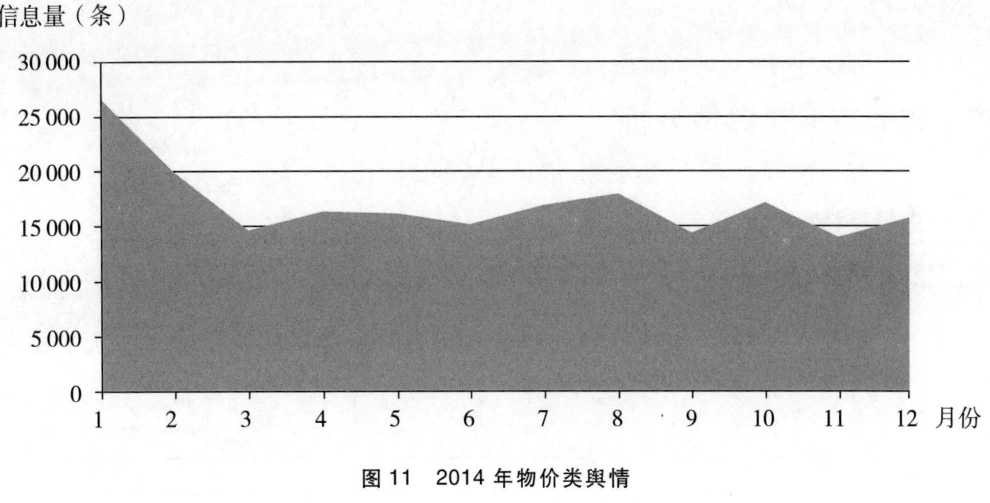

图11　2014年物价类舆情

物价类舆情在2014年信息量非常稳定，信息量基本稳定在1.5万条左右，相比2013年有较大幅度的降低，降幅约为40%。这源于2014年的物价涨幅远小于2013年的物价涨幅。2014年物价类话题所占百分比为1%，所占百分比相比2013年有所下降。

（二）2014年重点话题事件

1. 五部委：CPI涨幅连续3月超3%将给困难民众发价格补贴

监测数据：共监测到2 031条相关数据。

事件背景：

国家发展和改革委员会1月30日宣布，国家发展和改革委员会、民政部、财政部、人力资源社会保障部和国家统计局日前下发通知，要求各地在2014年3月底前完成完善社会救助和保障标准与物价上涨挂钩的联动机制。这意味着数千万困难群众在物价上涨达到一定幅度和时间后将得到政府的临时价格补贴。

2. 中国人民银行：56%的居民认为中国物价高将难以接受

监测数据：共监测到752条相关数据。

事件背景：

中国人民银行调查统计司6月25日发布的一份例行调查显示，有56.5%的居民认为当前中国物价“高，难以接受”，这一比例比上季度上升0.7个百分点。相应地，居民对当期物价满意指数为23.2%，比上季度略有降低。

3. 国家统计局：多地11月CPI涨幅创新低，8省份物价逼近零增长

监测数据：共监测到3 512条相关数据。

事件背景：

国家统计局12月公布的数据显示，2014年11月份全国CPI同比上涨1.4%，涨幅较10月份回落0.2个百分点，创下5年来新低。多地11月CPI涨幅创出新低，8个地区CPI涨幅跌破1%，逼近零增长。工业品的出厂价格环比、同比降幅都有所扩大，11月份同比下降2.7%，环比下降0.5%。

十、市长市府类舆情分析

（一）舆情走势

由图12可见，市长市府类舆情在2014年信息量较为稳定。最低谷是5月，四中全会所在的10月相关信息数量为第二少。相较而言，“两会”所在的3月信息量较大，排名第二，

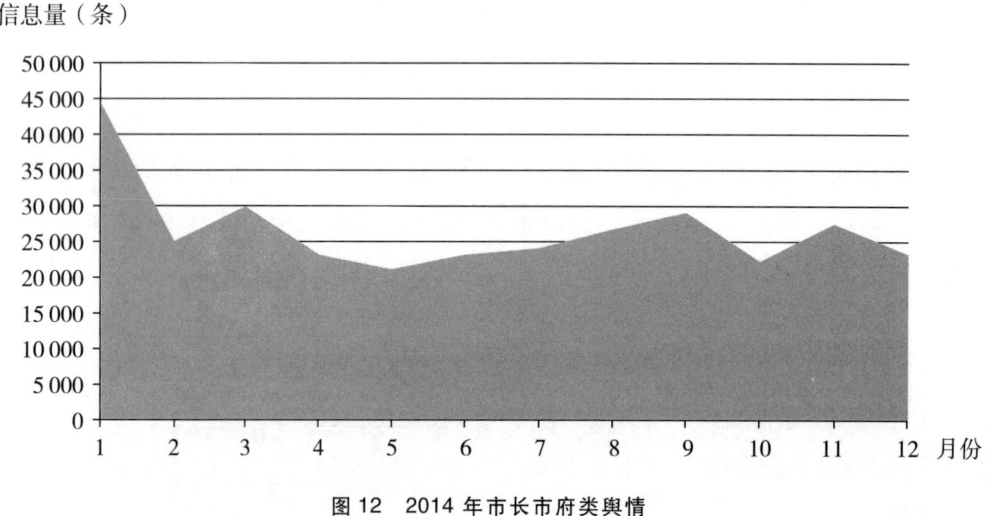

图12 2014年市长市府类舆情

农历新年年前的 1 月信息量最高。

市长市府类舆情在 2014 年信息量较为稳定，除信息量最高的 1 月外，其他 11 个月的信息量都分布在 2 万～3 万条之间，差距不大。相比 2013 年有一定幅度的较低，约为 25%。与 2013 年有明显区别的是相关负面信息居多。

（二）2014 年重点话题事件

1. 湖南临湘农民不满征地补偿，将市长告上法庭

监测数据：共监测到 1 538 条相关数据。

事件背景：

因对征地补偿有异议，湖南临湘市横铺乡三个村的村民将市政府和市长龚卫国告上了法庭。5 月 22 日，这起民告官案件在岳阳市君山区人民法院开庭审理，临湘市长龚卫国没有出现在被告席上，临湘市派出了法制办工作人员出庭，并未当庭宣判。

2. 官方确认洛阳市副市长郭宜品失联

监测数据：共监测到 16 531 条相关数据。

事件背景：

9 月 14 日，百度有网友发帖称："洛阳市副市长郭宜品带着当地一房地产公司老总三人跑路。"网帖还称，"当地专案组正组织人员满世界找人"，并曝光了一份《"8·5"专案排查提纲》和一些疑似警方排查照片。

尽管当地警方早已掌握郭宜品的失联信息，但直到排查照片被传到网上，这一消息才被外界所知。洛阳市委宣传部在追问下回应："副市长失联"情况属实，公安正在调查。

郭宜品大约在 8 月 5 日前后失联。"可能知道要被查，所以提前就跑了。"郭宜品失联后，警方排查了其家庭，发现郭的孩子早在国外，其妻也不见踪影。在郭宜品失联后，公安部门将其列为网上追逃人员。

3. 大同原市长耿彦波调离，125 项工程停工

监测数据：共监测到 9 835 条相关数据。

事件背景：

每个地方的市长都有自己的施政风格，引发一些争议在所难免。但没有想到，耿彦波在大同所引发的争议持续发酵，即使 2013 年 2 月调离大同之后，至今仍是最受争议的市长之一。

10 月月中，大同市委书记丰立祥被调查，市民长期的不满找到了宣泄的出口，终于导致了 10 月 18 日近千人聚集，请愿要求耿彦波回大同，让其收拾"烂摊子"。

其实，这反映了部分民众存在两种不满：一方面不满意耿彦波大拆大建让自己的生活陷入困顿；另一方面则不满意"新官不理旧政"。尽管大同官员承诺"新官理旧政"，但 125 项工程被叫停却是事实。所以，老百姓希望耿彦波回来收拾"烂摊子"。

十一、医疗类舆情分析

（一）舆情走势

由图 13 可见，医疗类舆情在 2014 年信息量起伏较大。最低谷是 6 月，信息量最高的是 1 月和 12 月，约为最低月 6 月的 2.5 倍。相较而言，“两会” 所在的 3 月信息量第三，且与最高的 1 月和 12 月信息量相近。

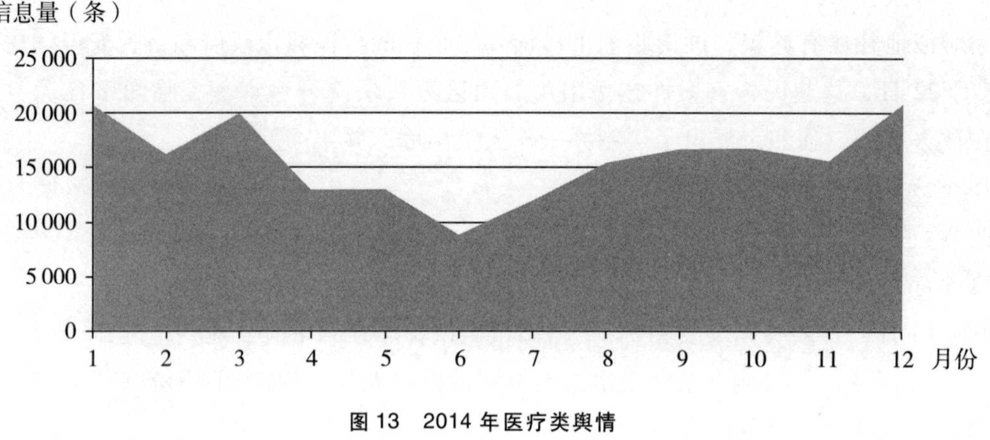

图 13　2014 年医疗类舆情

医疗类舆情依然是 12 个舆情类目中最少的，且 2014 年信息量较 2013 年又有所下降，但其下降幅度小于总信息量的下降幅度。

（二）2014 年重点话题事件

1. 人社部谈医保结余数千亿：不存在结余过多花不出去

监测数据：共监测到 1 498 条相关数据。

事件背景：

人力资源和社会保障部 1 月 24 日召开 2013 年第四季度新闻发布会，介绍 2013 年第四季度人力资源和社会保障工作进展情况。人社部新闻发言人李忠回应“中国医保结余数千亿”时表示，真正医疗保险统筹基金结余大概是结存数里的 40% 多一点。

人力资源和社会保障部公布的《2012 年度人力资源和社会保障事业发展统计公报》，数据显示，全国医保结余7 644亿元，其中统筹基金累计结存4 947亿元，个人账户积累结存2 697亿元。针对这个数据，李忠表示，医保基金结余的问题，老百姓非常关注。

2. 医保卡变身购物卡已成公开秘密

监测数据：共监测到 1 969 条相关数据。

事件背景：

我国新医改推行以来，由职工医保、居民医保和新农合这三项制度构成的基本医疗保障制度，对普惠民生贡献很大。然而，以地域为单位“分级分灶吃饭”的医保模式，使各地医保资金在归集和使用上存在差异且漏洞多。挂床骗保、冒名报销、刷卡套现或购物等行为，正在疯狂侵蚀医保资金。医保卡变相套现，则是城市医药经营领域套取“救命钱”的常用手法。医保卡变身购物卡已成为公开的秘密。牙膏、毛巾、护肤品、烟、酒、茶叶、巧克力等大小商品均可在药店刷医保卡购买，部分商品刷医保卡还可享受9折优惠。

3. 2015年基本实现省内异地就医

监测数据：共监测到2 879条相关数据。

事件背景：

人力资源和社会保障部、财政部、卫生计生委12月25日联合发布了《关于进一步做好基本医疗保险异地就医医疗费用结算工作的指导意见》。到2015年年底，我国异地就医住院费用将实现省级“漫游”。据测算，医保地级市内“漫游”可以解决60%左右的异地就医问题，而省级“漫游”则可解决将近90%的异地就医问题。但医保全国“漫游”仍难一蹴而就。

十二、敏感舆情类舆情分析

（一）舆情走势

由图14可见，2014年敏感舆情信息量走势较有起伏。年初的1月和2月信息量较大，排名第一和第三。而后敏感舆情信息量随着3月“两会”的召开反而一路下降，到6月达到一个低点，后信息量上升，在8月相关信息量达到又一个高点。

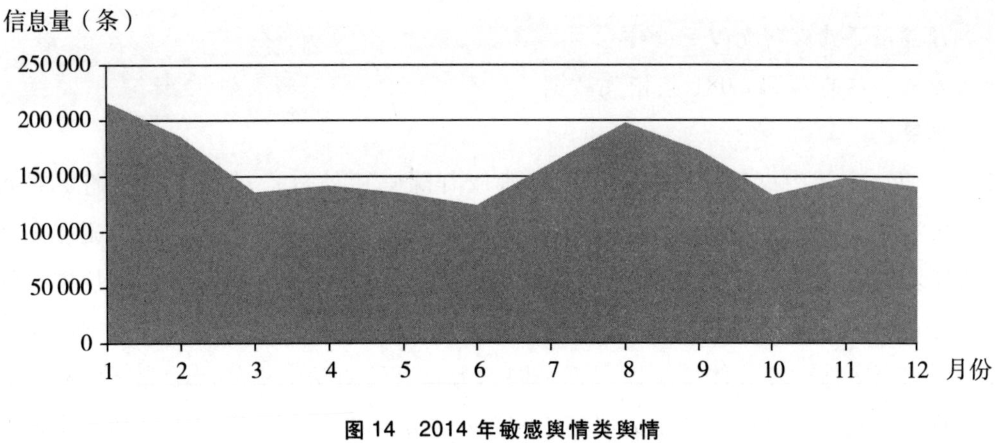

图14　2014年敏感舆情类舆情

2014年，敏感舆情占总体舆情量的12%，相较2013年增加了1个百分点。新一届政府正在大力推进党风和廉政建设，敏感舆情所占百分比的增加也恰当其时。但需要注意的是2014年敏感舆情所占百分比整体走势为平缓下降趋势，尤其是在年底的12月敏感舆情所占百分比更是降到了全年的最低点9.3%。

（二）2014 年重点话题事件

1. 东莞扫黄

监测数据：共监测到 33 851 条相关数据。

事件背景：

“色情行业”是许多人对东莞的印象，甚者有人给这座城市贴上了“性都”、“春城”的标签。但 2 月，东莞的色情行业似乎一夜之间销声匿迹，“扫黄”行动也成为大街小巷的热点话题。2 月 9 日央视曝光东莞市多个娱乐场所存在卖淫嫖娼等违法行为后，东莞市公安局迅速成立专案组，对中央电视台曝光的 12 间涉黄娱乐场所进行了查处，依法查封上述 12 间涉黄娱乐场所。东莞市共出动 6 525 名警力，对全市娱乐场所开展统一清查行动。随着官方严查幕后“保护伞”的态度，以及一批官员与相关部门人员被处分，许多人开始认为，此轮“扫黄”目的在于反腐，是一项大的反腐行动，由“扫黄”引起的“官场大地震”才刚刚开始。

2. 云南晋宁征地冲突

监测数据：共监测到 13 582 条相关数据。

事件背景：

10 月 14 日，云南省晋宁县晋城镇发生一起当地泛亚工业品商贸物流中心项目建设方人员与富有村部分村民因矛盾纠纷引发暴力违法犯罪行为，共造成 8 人死亡和 18 人受伤严重后果的群体性突发事件。

非法扣押人员、投掷自制燃烧瓶……这场发生在云南省晋宁县的冲突事件细节触目惊心，引起各界的强烈关注。除了事件的惨烈外，有关围绕该项目征地和拆迁补偿等话题也引起广泛关注。

3. 割除腐败毒瘤深得党心民心

监测数据：共监测到 2 081 条相关数据。

事件背景：

12 月 5 日，中共中央政治局决定给予周永康开除党籍处分，对其涉嫌受贿犯罪问题及线索移送司法机关依法处理；最高人民检察院经审查决定，依法对周永康涉嫌犯罪立案侦查并予以逮捕。决定公布后，社会各界反响强烈。广大干部群众纷纷表示坚决拥护中央的处理决定，认为这一决定彰显了中国共产党从严治党、惩治腐败的坚定意志，深得党心民心。

查办周永康案件，充分体现了以习近平同志为总书记的党中央从严治党、励精图治的历史担当和政治勇气，充分体现了中央坚定不移维护党的团结统一、坚定不移惩治腐败的坚强意志和坚决态度，充分体现了我们党坚持党纪国法面前人人平等、反腐没有禁区的原则。

十三、环境保护类舆情分析

（一）舆情走势

由图15可见，环境保护类舆情在2014年信息量非常稳定，呈平缓下降趋势。农历新年之前的1月相关信息数量最大，“两会”期间和过后的3月、4月信息量有所提升，而后一路下降，在9月和10月达到全年低点。

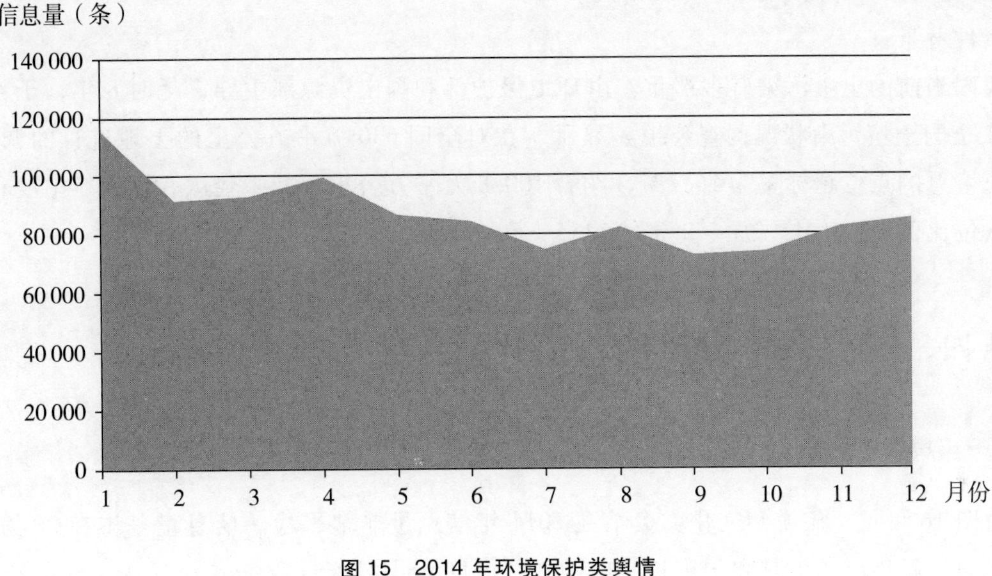

图15　2014年环境保护类舆情

环境保护类话题所占百分比为6%，位居第六，与2013年相一致。对于直接影响我们健康的环境问题，网络关注度一直较高。但相关信息量较2013年有所降低。

（二）2014年重点话题事件

1. 腾格里沙漠遭工业污染：黑色管道直接插入沙中

监测数据：共监测到10 561条相关数据。

事件背景：

“腾格里”在蒙古语里的意思是“天”，用以描述沙漠“像天一样浩渺无际”。然而9月，就在这片浩渺无际的沙漠深处，记者却看到了一片“天”一样大的污水处理坑。“天”一样大的污水处理坑源于内蒙古和宁夏分别在腾格里沙漠腹地建起了内蒙古腾格里工业园和宁夏中卫工业园，引入了大量的化工企业。

2. 兰州水污染

监测数据：共监测到15 218条相关数据。

事件背景：

4月10日，兰州市威立雅水务公司检测发现其出厂水苯含量超国家标准20倍，兰州市政府宣布该市自来水24小时内不宜饮用。兰州威立雅水务集团副总经理闫晓涛表示，威立雅早在4月2日就对水质进行了取样检测，但完整的检测和全分析过程需要时间，至4月10日正式确认自来水苯超标并采取措施，在前后8天时间里，兰州市民“有可能已经饮用了苯超标的自来水”。4月13日，兰州市政府通报，污染事故直接原因是水厂自流沟中出现了含油污水，原因是自流沟附近的中国石油天然气公司兰州石化分公司曾发生泄漏事故，致一些渣油和消防污水渗入地下。

3. 0.5亿亩耕地因污染已不再适于耕种

监测数据：共监测到6 513条相关数据。

事件背景：

我国当前的土壤污染有多严重？由环境保护部和国土资源部主导，耗时8年，于4月发布的《全国土壤污染状况调查公报》显示，在对全国630万平方公里的土地进行的调查中，全国土壤总的点位超标率为16.1%，约合100.8万平方公里。其中轻微、轻度、中度和重度污染点位比例分别为11.2%、2.3%、1.5%和1.1%。

十四、旅游和文化类舆情分析

（一）舆情走势

由图16可见，旅游和文化类舆情在2014年信息量非常平稳。信息量基本在20万到25万条之间。新年前的1月和国庆长假前的9月信息量最大。

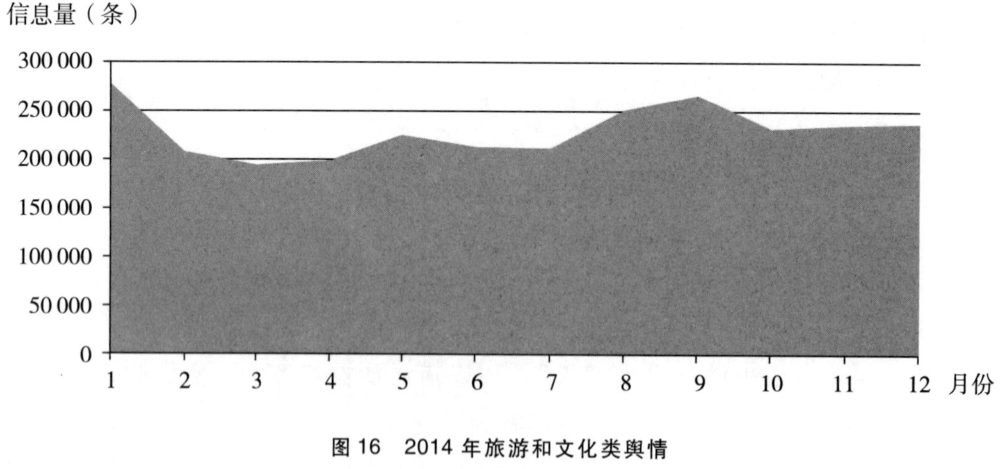

图16　2014年旅游和文化类舆情

2014年，在我们横向比较的12个关注话题中，旅游与文化类话题所占比为17%，跃居第二，相比2013年上升一位，相比2013年上升了1个百分点。我们的生活越来越富裕，对于旅游与文化的热情越来越高。

（二）2014 年重点话题事件

1. 海南小学春游大巴侧翻致 8 人死 32 人伤

监测数据：共监测到 7 658 条相关数据。

事件背景：

海南文昌市委宣传部 4 月 10 日下午向媒体通报称，10 日上午 10 点 30 分，在该市公坡镇水北墟往东阁镇宝芳墟 1 公里路段处发生一起交通事故，造成澄迈县老城镇欣才学校 8 名学生当场死亡，4 人重伤，28 人轻微伤。

2. 习近平文艺座谈会讲话

监测数据：共监测到 26 398 条相关数据。

事件背景：

在 10 月 15 日召开的文艺工作座谈会上，习近平总书记指出，要高度重视和切实加强文艺评论工作，运用历史的、人民的、艺术的、美学的观点评判和鉴赏作品，倡导说真话、讲道理，营造开展文艺批评的良好氛围。

（供稿：中国市长协会。技术支持：北京一飞科达软件有限公司）

专题篇

从美国的三次债务危机看我国地方政府债务的新常态

一、引言

地方政府债务有多少？地方债务风险有多高？地方政府危机有多大？这是一个中国经济的迷局，被人们争论了不下五年。

我们分四个问题论述此题：

第一个问题是研究美国历史上的三次地方政府债务危机与四种新常态化解法，由此找到研究问题的国际坐标。

第二个问题是研究区域经济不平衡发展的规律与地方政府的五色债务生态，由此找到分析问题的理论依据。

第三个问题是研究中国地方债务的三分结构与地方融资平台四大基本特征，由此找到观察问题的基本数据。

第四个问题是研究中国经济的五重再造与五种政府债务风险的全方位化解，由此找到解决问题的系统对策。

二、美国历史上的三次地方政府债务危机与四种新常态化解法

美国220多年的发展史表明，一部美国的发展史，就是国债产生、发展的成长历史，美国经济史学家约翰·戈登就认为国债对美国具有极其重要的战略意义①。

美国历史上在19世纪40年代、19世纪70年代、20世纪30年代分别爆发过三次地方政府债务危机，其严重程度是我们现在无法想象的。在这三次债务危机和借债运作过程中，美国地方政府形成了一套解决债务危机的方法。

---

① 参见《汉密尔顿的赐福：美国国债的兴衰史》，约翰·戈登著，1997年。“18世纪70年代，国债帮助我们赢得独立；18世纪80年代-19世纪60年代，国债为美利坚赢得最高的信用评级，欧洲资金得以滚滚流入美国，协助美国经济快速成长；19世纪60年代，我们凭借国债拯救合众国；20世纪30年代，我们凭借国债拯救美国经济；20世纪40年代，我们凭借国债拯救全世界。”

(一) 19世纪40年代的州政府危机：联邦自治负债与市场解债模式

美国第一次大规模的地方政府债务危机发生在19世纪40年代，当时涉及阿肯色、伊利诺伊、印第安纳、路易斯安那、马里兰、密歇根、密西西比、宾夕法尼亚8个州和佛罗里达领地。[①] 引发债务危机的起因是，州政府将绝大部分债务资金划拨给州银行，用于支持私人风险项目或私人交通公司投资运河、铁路和公路等项目。由于产出效率低下，债务到期时项目大都没有建成，在既没有项目收入又得不到新贷款的情况下，大面积的债务违约出现。

陷于拖欠危机中的8个州极力游说联邦政府对其进行财政援助。美国国会认为，如果就此开启联邦对地方紧急援助的先例，必然会纵容未来更多的赤字和拖欠，最终导致地方政府的软约束和低效运行。为此，国会和联邦政府坚决拒绝了对州政府的紧急援助，明确告诉他们"此路不通"，只能依靠地方政府自身解决债务危机。

于是，一种新的债务化解手段——市场解债应运而生，即通过中介金融机构介入并出资购买低价债券。比如，摩根财团就是在为地方政府和铁路发债、救债过程中发展起来的。当时他们为美国地方政府在英国伦敦发售的债券作担保，与英国进行谈判，为此摩根财团与政府之间形成了千丝万缕的联系[②]，甚至渗透到政府的权力结构之中，而危机过后，贬值的州政府债券再次付息又使他们获取了巨大的商业利益。由于中介金融机构的介入，债务危机得以缓解。

但是，这一时期的美国州政府，也有很多拒绝市场化解决的，就像罗恩·彻诺在《摩根全传》[③] 中所说的，一些州政府联合起来拒绝还债，直到今日，密西西比州仍然拖欠这笔债务。

(二) 19世纪70年代的地市危机：政府举债立法与政府破产解债

在19世纪70年代，州以下地方政府债务违约现象大范围蔓延。除战争外，引发这次地方债务危机的主要原因是，地方政府将债务资金主要用于战后土地开发项目和铁路建设等投机性投资，并主要依靠土地升值后的特别房产税等收入来偿债，在1873年经济萧条导致大量投资项目失败后，过分依赖土地收入还债的模式顿时难以为继。这次地方债务危机和中国的情况十分相近，都是对土地财政过于依赖，也就是通过土地升温获取财政收入，土地降温

---

① 资料来源：《美国地方政府债务危机处理》，财政部预算司课题组，《经济研究参考》，2009年第43期。

② 资料来源：《摩根财团：美国一代银行王朝和现代金融业的崛起》，（美）罗恩·彻诺著，中国财政经济出版社，2003年。

③ "在19世纪40年代早期的大萧条中，也就是所谓饥饿的40年代，美国州政府的债券价值每美元跌到50美分。当美国5个州——宾夕法尼亚、密西西比、印第安纳、阿肯色以及密执安——和准州佛罗里达不能按期支付利息时，最糟糕的局面出现了。一些美国的州长联合起来，组成了最早的债务人卡特尔，拒绝还债。直至今日，罪孽深重的密西西比州仍无耻地拖欠着。"——《摩根全传：向生意之王学做生意，胜过读商学院》，（美）罗恩·彻诺著，重庆出版社。

则引发地方债务危机。

这次危机以后，为加强对地方政府债务管理，美国所有的州都通过了限制地方政府举债的法律，通常是限定债务占地方税收能力的比例。在危机发生之后，各州也坚持“不救助原则”，让地方政府进行破产来解决债务危机。后来这一手段还通过《破产法》构建了其独具特色的地方政府债务破产清理程序。

美国关于地方政府破产法规则的许多设计都来源于其独特的政治架构（联邦主义）以及将政治问题转化为法律问题和奉行司法裁决终局性原则的一贯法治理念，但美国经验至少提供了一种通过法制手段化解地方债危机的借鉴。因此，在中国学习借鉴的过程中必须准确把握中美政治生态的差异以及一系列风险的规避。

（三）20 世纪 30 年代的全面危机：凯恩斯主义[①]盛行与转移支付解债

20 世纪 30 年代又出现了一波市级政府的债务拖欠。大量州政府债务问题急剧恶化，又因为美国三级分制的独特体制，大量地方政府选择拖欠债务不还，或采用变相赖账[②]（延期支付、利用通货膨胀、增发货币、提高金价等）的方式推脱债务。

从 1920 年到 1930 年间，美国地方政府通过债券募集资金使其资本投资的水平增长了近 1 倍，并以房产税收收入作为担保。1929 年到 1933 年的“世纪经济大萧条”爆发后，地方政府房产税税收急剧降低，与此同时，用于低收入家庭服务和失业抚恤的资金大量增加，市级政府债务拖欠呈爆炸式恶化。1932 年，有 678 个地方政府发生债务拖欠，到 1935 年年底，超过 3200 个政府资不抵债。

于是，为了真正意义上缓解债务危机，刺激经济成为当时美国政府的首选。以刺激经济为目的的凯恩斯主义经济理论流行于罗斯福新政，1933 年，罗斯福总统采纳了凯恩斯主义的主张，采用政府财政和金融刺激手段调节经济，用赤字手段刺激经济成为一种主导性的趋势并使之长期化、经常化。新政推动之下的经济刺激，最终避免了债务违约和国家信用的丧失。

所以，我们可以说通过赤字财政政策扩大总需求的凯恩斯主义就是在这次危机和衰退中盛行起来的。在赤字财政思维的主导下，美国进入财政赤字快速增加时代，截至 2014 年 11 月 30 日，美国的债务总额已超过 18.01 万亿美元，历史上首次超过该国年度国内生产总值（GDP）的规模。而刺激经济作为一种转移解债和变相国家救助的形式成为缓解债务危机最有效的措施与手段之一。

最后，尽管美国中央政府在处理地方政府债务危机时惯用“不救助原则”，但是，联邦政府可能会对州和地方政府提供部分救助。纵观美国历史，当地方政府面临财政危机时，除

① 1936 年，英国经济学家凯恩斯出版了《就业、利息和货币通论》一书，该书对国家干预经济的实践进行了理论总结，形成了凯恩斯主义。凯恩斯主义主张政府对经济的积极干预，突出了政府赤字支出对总需求的扩张作用，认为在总需求不足，即经济陷入产出水平远远低于潜在产出水平的状况下，如果政府增加其购买量，总需求就会增加。

② 1788 年生效的美国宪法第六条规定：“本宪法生效前所负的一切债务和所签订一切契约在本宪法生效后对合众国仍然有效，其效力一如邦联时代。”所以 1788 年后直接的赖账行为是违宪的。

1997 年的华盛顿危机外，联邦政府基本一直坚持拒绝援助的立场。但是不可否认，政府直接救助（除刺激经济外）确实也是解决地方债务危机的一种手段。

结论：这三次危机之后，1993 年和 2008 年美国又出现两次地方债务问题，但是都没有形成危机，究其原因，地方政府负债已经成为常态，怎么解决已发生的地方债务问题已经形成一套系统方法，而从美国的经验看，基本有以上 4 种较为常见（破产保护、市场化债务转换与债务拖延滞后偿还以及政府直接或间接救助），而债务赖账则是特定时期的特例。

三、区域经济不平衡发展的规律与地方政府的五色债务生态

产业经济学与区域经济学都研究市场竞争中的债务风险，但两者的区别却十分明显。

产业经济学研究产业发展趋势、产业升级方向、产业竞争态势与产业重组模式，这四个层次的产业走向，都意味着产业内大批企业的兴衰存亡，其债务风险比比皆是。

从产业发展趋势角度看，一个产业因市场需求萎缩甚至消失而走向衰亡，一定会伴随整个产业的崩溃和全行业的债务危机。这时，行内企业的退出时机和转型方式，都会决定企业负债的风险程度，突如其来的产业灾难一定会造成错位者的债务危机与破产风潮。中国改革开放之初，排浪式的消费导致“老三大件”和“新三大件”的消费浪潮，然而，近年来，受市场需求萎缩以及各项生产因素成本上升影响，缝纫机械行业景气指数一直在过冷区间徘徊，行业盈利能力下降，近 1/5 的规模以上企业处于亏损状态，一哄而上的企业后来都被市场所淘汰了。

从产业升级方向角度看，一个产业因技术颠覆与产品升级根本再造，一定会伴随整个产业的巨变。这时，行内企业的机会判断和升级方式，都会决定企业负债的风险程度，风云变幻的产业变局一定会造成落伍者的债务危机与破产风潮。中国电池产业的升级令人眼花缭乱，由于污染阴影的影响，铅蓄电池行业受到环保部门大规模整顿，似乎走到了生命的尽头，然而铅蓄电池喊了多少年还是没有消亡，镍氢电池技术刚刚成熟并一哄而上建了一大批工厂时，最被看好未来前景的锂电池洪流就铺天盖地滚滚而来，无数镍氢电池厂还没开工就已关门。

从产业竞争态势角度看，一个产业因规模、管理、品牌、业态等种种因素的深度改变，一定会伴随不同企业的分化。这时，行内企业的资源不足和能力缺失，都会决定企业负债的风险程度，竞争激烈的市场博弈一定会造成失败者的债务危机与破产风潮。同是国务院确定的全国 520 家重点企业、同是中国名牌、同是地处中原的肉类加工企业，在发展初期，春都集团从各方面都处于绝对优势。春都火腿风光无限时，它把双汇当鸡鸣狗盗。但是结果，双方各自走向了相反的极端，短短几年后，双汇迅速崛起成了同行业的排头兵，而春都却走向了衰败。

从产业重组模式角度看，一个产业因资本热度与人才结构导向变化，一定会伴随重组整合的冲击。这时，行内企业的资本结构和并购技巧，都会决定企业负债的风险程度，巨额资本的收购兼并一定会造成失误者的债务危机与破产风潮。三九集团曾经势如破竹地收购国有

企业，资产在短短两年内增长一万倍，最终因债务危机而破产重组。

总之，产业经济学主要研究产业竞争力，其结果一定涉及企业的债务风险。但是，因为这种风险完全由企业承担，人们往往把它当产业发展的常态，即便整个行业烟消云散也没有人大惊小怪。

而对于区域经济学，目前学术界则主要存在着四派理论，都是在研究生产要素在区域之间的转移规律，成功的区域迅速发展，失败的区域就是当地企业与地方政府的共同灾难，地方政府的债务危机因此而产生。

农业成本区位论是进行单一的成本比较，自然资源、劳动力成本和政府的优惠政策都可以吸引投资和拉动产业转移。这时的地方政府，不会有大量的环境改造投入，债务风险相对较小。20 世纪 20 年代，国际薄荷产品市场主要为巴西所控制，90 年代我国成本优势显现并曾大面积种植，一举超过巴西处于领先地位。从 90 年代末期开始，印度薄荷产业一年两季成本极低，中国的农民迅速退出。

工业配套区位论是进行工业系统能力的完善，政府需要对公共设施和配套条件进行投入，辅之以不同类型配套企业的招商引资，实现企业集群的进入。这种发展模式不仅要靠政策与体制，而且要进行中等规模的融资投入，引导区域招商引资的税收产出，如果招商引资进程滞后，就一定会产生还债的暂时压力，必须等待区域经济升温的良性循环。20 世纪初，美国五大湖区利用矿产资源及临河地理优势，首先得到了开发建设，随着政府对城市建设和公共设施的系列投入，大大增强城市的吸引力和竞争力，形成了五大湖工业基地，一度成为全球最重要的制造业基地之一。但由于产业出现转移、衰退，流域生态环境更加恶化，五大湖地区甚至在 20 世纪 80 年代还被人们称为“铁锈地带”①，部分老工业城市遭遇了产业衰退和人口减少，城市转型非常困难，地方政府的债务风险急剧加大。

产业领袖区位论是研究行业领袖的区域发展功效，地方政府要吸引领袖企业投资，拉动产业上下游企业跟随进入，形成产业在区域内的全球竞争力。这种发展模式需要地方政府大投入，为大公司进入牺牲大量地方利益，并加大投资配套创造投资环境，才能引来产业竞争力位移的大产出。这时的地方政府融资投入，是为大公司投资进行的定制融资，其风险相对较小。在整个 20 世纪，汽车制造业一直是美国最重要的支柱产业。20 世纪 70 年代以后，美国汽车接连受到来自日本自下、德国自上、韩国自右、中国自左的冲击。日本汽车企业到美国本土设厂生产，为避开工会势力而远离底特律，到美国南方和西部地区设厂。结果，一旦美国汽车三巨头竞争失利并相继申请破产保护，以美国汽车制造中心闻名的底特律必然出现连锁反应，诸多汽车工厂倒闭，失业率高，人口锐减，政府财政恶化，地方政府因债务危机而必然破产。

城市功能区位论是中心城市与卫星城的区域布局理论，要把区域的产业发展与城市的功能发育互动运作，建立城市圈的房地产能力提升。这种发展模式是在经营城市，是将工业房

---

① 资料来源：《美国制造业带发展的历史经验与启示》，中国社会科学院工业经济研究所叶振宇，《中国发展观察》，2014 年第 11 期。

地产与城市功能房地产协同开发，政府为此将收获从产业发展到地产升值的多重产出。上海浦东新区的成功主要体现在功能区的作用发挥上。但是，天津滨海新区经济结构和产业布局不合理，中心城市的载体功能和集聚辐射效应较弱，制造业规模大，服务业规模小，城市服务功能不强，新区快速发展的持续性和动力不强，政府与政府投融资平台的债务风险随之加大。

总之，区域经济学主要研究经济要素在区域间的转移力，其结果一定涉及区域企业与区域政府的双重债务风险。用区域经济学四种理论看地方政府负债，我们认为单纯地用二元论去判断地方债务风险是不够的。

于是，我们尝试找寻一种分析模型并用以区分出不同类型地方政府所处的五种不同的债务生态，并尝试用区域经济不平衡发展的常态思维来解决不同债务生态下的不同债务问题。

具体而言，我们按照不同区域的发展属性，将地方债务生态划分为五种类型，并用五种颜色对其进行形象的表述，即：

（1）衰退产业城市处于黑色债务生态中，其传统产业全面衰败，地方政府按当年兴盛期正常负债，一旦传统产业低迷，必然进入黑色债务生态，形成死亡债务为主的“黑色债务风险”。

（2）落后乡镇政府处于灰色负债生态中，其大量负债不是银行负债，而是政府通过关系找富户借债，由于这些地区农业产业凋零，无法产生政府税基，没有房地产基础，导致这些乡镇政府收入来源很差，但又不会产生债务纠纷，从而进入灰色债务生态，形成隐性债务为主的“灰色债务风险”。

（3）新兴工业城市处于红色负债生态中，其最大的特点是，一些新兴工业城市在没有税基、没有现金流量、没有人流量的情况下，政府大规模投资基础设施，寄希望于尽快招商引资，能够形成产业群，而一旦招商失败，就进入红色债务生态，形成巨额债务为主的“红色债务风险”。

（4）旅游中心城市处于黄色负债生态中，相当数量的旅游人群进入这些地区之后，并没有产生很强的税收基础，导致虽然有旅游人流流入，但是大量的基础投资、形象工程建设、景点投入等无法很快进入良性循环，城市进入黄色债务生态，形成拖延债务为主的“黄色债务风险”。

（5）大型国际都市处于“白色债务生态”中，其产业基础、服务业基础、税收能力等各方面都非常良性，但是传统负债已经达到极限，而重大的转型机会亟待大规模投资，很多空白信用空间需要挖掘，包括互联网金融的很多手段必须使用，对周边卫星城和产业辐射力的金融支撑处于白色债务生态，形成创新债务为主的“白色债务风险”。

结论：用区域经济学的方法看地方债务问题，地方政府债务没有不变的平衡点，永远与地方经济的发展周期对立统一，时高时低地波动发展。因此，我们要把地方债务问题当作区域经济发展的新常态来看待，并制定不同的策略解决不同颜色的债务生态，使之从不平衡的五色债务生态转化为相对平衡的绿色债务生态。

四、中国地方政府债务的三分结构与地方融资平台四大基本特征

中国地方政府债务风险，应该说与2008年的全球经济危机与2009年的4万亿元经济刺激计划直接相关，同时，大量不良债务的产生，又是地方政府融资平台一刀切清理政策的必然结果。

2008年，美国次贷危机爆发，雷曼兄弟破产、美林转手，全球经济持续动荡，经济危机肆虐全球。而中国同样在外部环境恶化和国内政策调整的双重压力下，经济增长经过6年的上升后进入调整周期，宏观经济开始进入经济周期的下行区间。

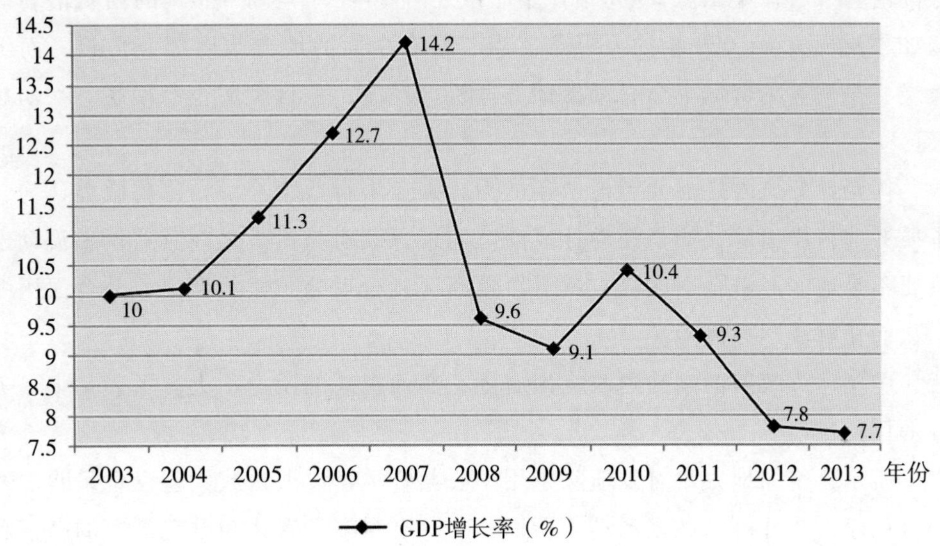

图1　2003-2013年中国GDP增长情况

为了应对金融危机对中国的影响，实现中国经济的软着陆与平稳发展，2008年11月9日，政府宣布了4万亿元的投资计划，以刺激经济。但4万亿元刺激政策有明显的行政摊派色彩，在总额为4万亿元的财政刺激计划中，除1.2万亿元为中央投资外，其余2.8万亿元资金都由地方配套，地方的压力可想而知。4万亿元经济刺激方案公布一周之内，各地政府便纷纷宣布大规模投资计划，据统计，投资总额在一周内已经超过10万亿元。

而在债务结构分配上，地方政府债务根据主体结构的不同可以一分为三：一是地方政府的直接负债，二是政府融资平台的多种负债，三是大型产业公司的各种负债。其中，融资平台公司举债的占比超过50%，是主要的举债主体。

下面，我们分三部分具体分析债务的风险程度。

（一）政府直接的负债，从总量到结构，从直接负债到或有负债都不存在大面积的债务风险，这与近年来中央政府对地方财政的管制密切相关

分析地方政府直接负债的风险性要从以下几个方面入手：

首先，根据国家审计署2013年12月30日公布的《全国政府性债务审计报告》。报告显示：中国地方政府债务近年来增长迅速，地方政府债务总额（直接+或有）2010年年底为10.7万亿元；2013年6月底为17.9万亿元；两年半增长67.3%。从地方债的总量来看，中央和地方政府的债务规模占GDP的比例，控制在40%以内，这仍处于国际货币基金组织确认的60%债务率控制标准参考值范围之内。

其次，判断地方债务风险的依据应是地方政府的债务偿还能力。我国国民经济和财政收入已保持了30多年的快速增长，2001-2013年间，我国GDP、财政总收入、地方财政收入的年平均增长率分别为10%、20%、20%左右，无论是中央还是地方政府综合财力的强劲增长势头并未减弱。北京大学国家发展研究院教授、前世界银行副行长林毅夫甚至认为：从后发优势的潜力来看，中国从2008年开始应该还有20年平均每年8%的增长潜力。也就是说，中国如果出现美国1929年的大萧条，当然会有全面的地方政府债务危机，而经济持续下滑，煤炭、钢铁等集聚城市会有局部债务危机。反之，一旦经济企稳回暖，一切焦虑都是杞人忧天。

再次，衡量债务风险还需要考虑偿还能力，兴业银行首席经济学家鲁政委认为，中国地方债的本质并非信用风险，而是流动性风险。而地方政府与银行之间具有调整流动性的谈判优势，只要不是地区经济全面崩盘，就可以重新谈判合理分布偿债期限，并全面压缩政府其他预算，从而化解流动性风险。

最后，中国地方政府的刚性财政支出有限，全面提高的压力不大。下表是中、美国债与地方债务的用途比较。

如表1所示，美国地方政府发债除了用于公共资本建设项目或大型设备采购之外，还有很大一部分用于支持并补贴私人活动。所以，一直有众多学者认为欧美国家的高福利政策导致了其债务危机的加剧。而反观中国政府，基础设施投资一直是地方政府举债的重要投向，可收缩调节的余地很大。

中、美国债与地方债务的用途比较

国债用途		地方债务用途	
中国	美国	中国	美国
1. 弥补财政赤字	1. 筹措军费	1. 城市基础设施投资	1. 公共资本建设项目或大型设备采购
2. 筹集建设资金	2. 应对经济危机	2. 应对经济危机	2. 支持并补贴私人活动
3. 调节经济	3. 到期债券清偿		3. 为短期周转性支出或特种计划提供现金
	4. 向联邦政府所属企业和机构提供资金		4. 偿还旧债

所以，就总体而言，在不对经济健康造成较大损失和对经济增长速度造成较大的不利冲击的条件下，中国可以处理好政府直接负责的银行负债。总体上，其风险是完全可控的。

（二）融资平台的多种负债，是中国国有经济的一大创举，创造了多种形式的负债模式，并且与地方财政有着天然的债务防火墙

1994年中国实行财政分权以后，大部分财政税收收入划归中央政府，而大部分公共事业和经济建设任务却留给了地方政府。这就大大强化了地方政府兴建“融资平台”大举借债的经济动力。为此，分析这类负债，我们必须看到这类地方政府负债与纯粹的地方政府债务的区别。

（1）多数政府融资平台的信用基础为优良，有大量的资产并且投向是有现金流量收入的基础建设项目，包括土地、建筑、交通等。2011年6月27日，国家审计署首次公布的《全国地方政府性债务审计结果》显示，至少有72.48%的资产是优质资产。如果再加上未投入使用的11 044.47亿元货币资产，则优质资产至少达到82.79%。2013年12月30日，国家审计署再次公布的《全国政府性债务审计结果》指出，从债务资金投向看，主要用于基础设施建设和公益性项目，不仅较好地保障了地方经济社会发展的资金需要，推动了民生改善和社会事业发展，而且形成了大量优质资产，大多有经营收入作为偿债来源。

（2）以目前中国的现状而言，地方政府债务规模仍低于资产规模。此前多家市场机构曾经估计，中国地方国有资产规模至少有30万亿~40万亿元，目前接近17万亿元的地方政府负债，仍然低于资产价值。

（3）这些政府融资平台目前仍是地方的举债主体，部分债务与政府或有债务交叉，有些在由政府直接偿还。2013年，地方融资平台在政府负有偿还责任的债务中占据38%，在全部债务中占比39%。根据中金公司预计，30%~40%的融资平台贷款项目能够依靠自身现金流偿还贷款本息，余下大约60%~70%的贷款也仅需要土地开发权、地方政府财政安排等第二还款来源解决。只要融资平台资金链不断裂，是能够在经济发展中自行动态化解风险的。

目前，我国地方政府的投融资平台在向市场化过渡过程中仍存在一系列问题，部分政府为了政绩举债建设，却忽略了融资平台公司的监督与管理，这些问题是不容回避的。但是我们需要注意的是，地方融资平台的改革方向是推动其继续市场化转型，使其真正成为产业性控股与金融性投资的商业机构。

（三）产业公司的各种负债，是产业扩张式的负债，如果经济发展的大势继续向好，这些国企的资源与资产价值连城。但是，经济一旦全面下滑，那才是地方政府无力回天的债务危机

中国的国有企业在2009年的4万亿元刺激政策投入中高歌猛进，不仅央企受益极大，地方的资源与能源企业、大型房地产公司和著名的国有控股公司都在出手抢夺这场银行低息放款的盛宴，全面加大负债，成为影响地方政府负债的重要组成部分。因为，这些国有企业原来是地方政府财政收入的重要组成部分，从税收到利润上交再到行政摊派。一旦经济全面下滑，一旦行业出现危机，不仅地方政府收入会受到严重影响，而且地方政府融资平台的大量担保也会落空。

以煤炭产业为例，据煤炭协会的一份内部数据显示，目前煤炭企业亏损面超过70%。不光小煤矿掀起倒闭潮，大中型煤炭企业的日子也每况愈下，甚至到了破产的边缘。2014年4月前后，山西最大民营煤企联盛集团债务危机爆发，负债近300亿元，最终破产重组，目前仍在进行中。2014年8月18日，河南四大煤炭企业均陷入亏损泥潭，现金流极度紧张。

通过以上数据，我们不难看到，这类掌握资源的企业如果在整体经济上行的环境里，资源需求量增大，导致价格上涨，则可以推动资源迅速升值，企业收入与利润可以实现快速攀升，从而带动地方经济快速发展，地方债务问题自然迎刃而解。但是，可怕的是，一旦在经济下滑加上整体行业危机的双重压力下，带给这些企业的冲击是灾难性的，甚至可能像鄂尔多斯一样，致使城市整体陷入债务与经济危机，这才是地方政府最需要关注的难点与困境。

从这一意义上讲，中国的地方政府债务危机是个子虚乌有的命题，其本质是一个中国经济刺激政策大起大落带来的发展停滞，地方政府不仅是经济衰退的受害者，而且成了这场错误的替罪羊。因此，中国地方政府债务风险的化解之道要从治标与治本两个层面来研究，前者是解决地方政府以及政府融资平台化解债务的技术问题，后者是解决中国宏观经济政策的大战略问题，靠结构调整的刺激政策再造中国经济。

因此，我们反对经济紧缩政策。

结论：解决地方政府债务风险问题，要从治本入手，通过分析中国经济，再造战略系统设计——五色地方政府债务风险的化解方案。

五、中国经济的五重再造与五种政府债务风险的全方位化解

中国地方政府债务风险的化解之道要从治标与治本两个层面来研究，前者是解决地方政府以及政府融资平台五色债务生态向绿色调整的技术问题，后者是解决中国宏观经济政策的大战略问题，靠结构调整的刺激政策五重再造中国经济。

下面，我们从治本问题入手，通过分析中国经济的五重再造，系统设计五色地方政府债务风险的化解方案。

4万亿元经济刺激政策生效以后，铁道部的巨额负债与地方政府的满身债务吓坏了中国学者和书生气十足的政府官员，2011年以后就马上收手重回紧缩之路，当时的政策注定了今天的经济下滑，特别是清理政府平台公司的举动，不仅夭折了大批在建的投资项目，而且放大并加剧了所谓的地方政府债务危机。

十八大以后，习近平提出的民族复兴中国梦震动全球，唱响中国成为新一代领导的主旋律。李克强总理开始制订40万亿元的城市化投资刺激方案，让全国各行各业与各地政府翘首以待新政府的新政策。

但是，以城市化为中心的大规模刺激政策如果缺少产业基础，各地空城、“鬼城”的前

车之鉴一定不可回避。于是，40 万亿元的大手笔一拖再拖，而后，就是不可避免的经济下滑，新常态的理论应运而生。

何为新常态？就是适应放慢经济发展速度的新态势，在经济波动中看准产业结构的调整方向，把中国经济的五重再造与地方政府五色负债生态变色结合起来，为中国经济重回高速发展快车道奠定基础。

（一）丝绸之路复兴计划的“金政策”再造全球市场需求，解决低迷产业城市的黑色债务风险，加速重化工业的升级与转型，重建衰败城市的政府金融信用

所谓“金政策”特指资本集聚量，就是全球经济互动的推进政策，即，丝绸之路复兴计划的 4 万亿美元聚焦投入，再造全球互动的市场需求，输出中国的过剩产能，在高涨的经济环境下完成过剩产能的再转移与再转向。

2013 年 12 月，我们为蒙古与俄罗斯的“北水南调”研究美国的马歇尔计划，探索 4 万亿美元的投资模式。在我们看来，中国应该借鉴美国 1949 年的马歇尔计划，动用 4 万亿美元的国家外汇储备，推进全球经济的互动。依据十分简单：

其一，今天中国的产能过剩，不是 1929 年的美国而是 1949 年的美国，表面看因战争需求戛然而止，经济衰退严重，而事实上全球恢复战争破坏的需求潜力巨大，只欠东风。于是，美国推出马歇尔计划，一旦巨额美元贷款撒向欧洲，全球需求井喷而至，不仅带动美国过剩产能走向世界，而且造就了一大批统治世界的跨国公司。这时，欧洲没落的贵族企业家才认可了美国企业家的领袖地位。

其二，今天中国资本的过剩，超越 1949 年的美国，4 万亿美元的外汇储备是政府拥有的无债主债权，可以市场化地进行新兴国家的基础设施建设投资，推动全球经济的互动发展，拉动中国过剩产能的大规模输出。

但是，习近平新政推出的丝绸之路复兴计划，超出世人想象，不仅设立起亚洲基础设施投资银行和丝绸之路基金，并且在北京 APEC 会议上提出基础设施互联互通大战略，震动了世界各国。全球经济互动的投资战略，已经被习近平经济学提升到丝绸之路复兴计划的层次，其“金政策”的质与量，都远远超越了美国马歇尔计划的境界。

中国的全球基础设施资本金投资以“一带一路”为载体，以金砖国家开发银行和亚洲基础设施投资银行为平台向外输出资本。根据亚洲开发银行的预测，未来 10 年，亚太地区约有 8 万亿美元的基础设施建设资金需求，金砖银行初始资本为 1 000 亿美元，亚洲基础设施投资银行资本金 1000 亿美元，通过金融杠杆放大 5 ~ 10 倍，将能撬动 5 000 亿 ~ 10 000 亿美元的资金支持规模，这对中国钢铁、水泥等过剩产能的拉动，对中国黑色债务生态区的影响不可低估。试想，一旦 4 万亿美元投向全球，带动 20 万亿美元其他资本进入投资项目，其一半采购中国过剩产能，中国外汇储备将继续大规模增长，丝绸之路复兴计划会良性扩张，全球经济会加速度互动发展。这时，地方政府的黑色债务生态区，会发生巨大的两极分化，因为：中国的过剩产能有两种情况，其中一种是有竞争力而缺少市场，“金政策”的投入将会迅速拉动城市衰退产业的复苏，带动这些城市走出黑色债务生态，从根本上解决黑色债务风险。这时，政府应该利用金融信用恢复的机会，加速传统产业的技术升级，提升全球竞争力，搞好城市的节能减排。

但是，丝绸之路复兴计划将大大加速中国经济全球化的进程，使中国没有竞争力的产业加速死亡。以煤炭产业为例，中国周边国家有大量煤矿成本奇低，低于中国煤价的几倍，中国资本涌入各国并投资煤炭，我们本国产业的贸易保护政策很难持续，从而会加剧黑色债务风险，甚至迫使这些城市必须进行债务重组与城市再造，全面推进城市的产业转型。

黑色债务生态向绿色转换的经典案例，是德国最大的工业区鲁尔工业区。鲁尔工业区从19世纪中叶开始发端，一直以采煤、钢铁、化学、机械制造等重工业为核心。由于自身产业结构单一，同时受到外部环境新技术革命的冲击，到20世纪80年代末期，整个鲁尔工业区陷入了严重的结构性危机。为此，北威政府出台了一系列措施进行鲁尔工业区的经济转型和产业改革。经过几十年的努力，鲁尔区成功再生，成为既有强大传统工业作基础、又有新兴产业为增长点“双轮驱动”的新型综合工业区①。

中国黑色债务生态区不应该回避政府债务的破产，地方政府的破产重组应该成为中国经济的新常态，美国有史以来申请破产的最大城市底特律经过一年的努力逐渐走出了破产阴霾，重现生机。为此，死亡政府与企业的主体再造，是靠破产重组债务，进行死亡区域的治标之举，重组后的政府与企业还是要进行产业转型再造，实现黑色债务生态向绿色债务生态转换。

结论：丝绸之路复兴计划的“金政策”再造全球市场需求，解决低迷产业城市的黑色债务风险，加速重化工业的升级与转型，重建衰败城市的政府金融信用。

（二）农民收入倍增计划的“水政策”再造中国内需市场，解决农村乡镇政府的灰色债务风险，加速农业基础的改革与改造，培育农村城镇的政府金融信用

所谓“水政策”特指加速双重的“水流动”，一是银根放松向零利率趋近的刺激政策，二是用农田水利建设的大投入推进中国农村创富计划，即，再造农田水利、农业流通和补贴模式，形成农民收入倍增而消灭农民工现象，在小城镇良性发展的环境下完成内需市场的再扩容与再扩展。

在十八大上，习近平新政提出居民收入倍增问题，让我们再次聚焦日本的农业产业化经验，研究从农业入手的扩大之策。

今天中国的内需问题，不是2000年的日本而是1960年的日本，日本1960年的国民收入倍增是从农民收入倍增开始的，靠三步并举的改革得以推进：其一，农产品价格大幅提高，水稻价格高于国际市场近三倍；其二，农产品流通规范入市，严格农产品市场的统一管控；其三，强势农协的垄断运作，进行农业周期调节和国际市场谈判。三招过后，日本农村经济出现了根本性变化。一是农村居民收入开始高于城市居民收入（到1975年农民收入已超过城市居民14.5%左右，农村家庭超出城市家庭收入37%左右）；二是刺激了农民的消

① 资料来源：《工业重镇鲁尔的转变发展方式之路》，李江涛，《学习时报》，2010年11月8日。

费，并且消灭了所谓的“农民工”现象，导致内需迅速扩张；三是加速了城镇化建设，推动了小城镇的迅速发展，由此导致城乡差距急剧缩小，城乡差别基本消失。

今天中国的农业潜力同时面临三大亟待解决的问题：一是从20世纪80年代中后期卖粮难开始，全国农民深陷农业周期带来的价格周期，农民的收益没有保障，忽高忽低；二是20世纪90年代末大批农村强壮劳动力进城打工，用农民工微薄的收入补贴农村，留守老人耕种乏力，土地开始随意半荒或低价转租；三是政府补贴无效运作，腐败与寻租开始滋生蔓延。

为此，我们只有再造农业的盈利能力和产业基础，才能消灭农民工现象，进而推动城乡共同消费，才能拉升农民的平均收入超过城市居民，推动我国经济转向内需拉动的轨道。这时，大都市2.69亿农民工必将迅速分化，“80后”与“90后”将因家庭土地收入上涨转而读书深造并留在大城市上学工作，而“70后”农民工会有强大的动力回归乡土，在当地就业，从而为传统制造业向中西部转移创造人力资源条件。

但是，中国的农业问题十分复杂，与美国相比，我们的农民太分散，与日本、欧洲相比，我们的国土面积太广阔，直接学习欧美日的经验都有很多不现实的成分。这时，习近平新政结构性放松银根的政策一出，让我们找到了解决农业再造问题的钥匙，即，从农田水利建设的投资入手，一揽子解决农民致富、土地流转、消化过剩产能、拉动农村消费、发展小城镇经济等的多重难题。

现代农业的物质基础是现代农业设施的投入与土地规模的扩大，并在农业产业收益增长的条件下，最大限度地发挥农业技术服务的功效。但是，我国农村承包制长期分割分散土地资源，农田水利设施30年欠账，使农业只能靠劣质化肥增产，土地与食品质量双重下降。

根据2013年第二次全国土地调查，全国耕地20.3亿亩，其中有灌溉设施的9.2亿亩，占比45.1%，无灌溉设施的11.1亿亩，占比54.9%。一半多的耕地靠天吃饭。近40%的水库病险问题严重，近40%的灌溉设施已经损坏，近80%的灌溉耕地只能抗御一般性干旱灾害。为此，我们应当从9亿亩有灌溉条件的农田起步，搞4亿亩滴灌大项目、4亿亩喷灌大项目，再向8亿亩无灌溉条件的土地进军，先上水泥渠修建大项目，形成农田水利建设的万亿元投资工程。

中国农田水利建设投资只有成本投入一端，而没有收益获利的另一端，完全靠财政投入，不仅有政府财力不足的问题，而且会滋生腐败，流失全民资产。因此，我们主张引入农业水资源“水权交易机制”，用民营官助的市场化方式运筹万亿元水利建设投资工程。据调查，每年中国用水的65%~70%是农业用水，而农业用水中80%以上是灌溉用水。在中国，生产1公斤粮食耗水量高达800公斤。这足以表明灌溉用水的浪费程度，也足以表明节水的巨大空间。

在这里，“水政策”的两个方面要互通互动，倾斜的银行低利率与水权流通的法律保护并行，两者缺一不可。同时，“水政策”还要与“木政策”联动，把农业补贴转换到两个方向，一是贴息加速改造和加大投入流量，二是降低滴灌水价和补贴溶水化肥。

如前所述，我国落后乡镇政府处于灰色负债生态中，其大量负债不是银行负债，而是政府通过关系找富户借债，由于这些地区农业产业凋零，无法产生政府税基，没有房地产基础，导致这些乡镇政府收入来源很差，但又不会产生债务纠纷，从而进入灰色债务生态，形成隐性债务为主的"灰色债务风险"。因此，一旦"水政策"全面投入，中国农业会发生根本性的变化，乡镇政府会因此而得到大量税源，从而彻底解决灰色债务风险。

结论：农民收入倍增计划的"水政策"再造中国内需市场，解决农村乡镇政府的灰色债务风险，加速农业基础的改革与改造，培育农村城镇的政府金融信用。

（三）工业集聚内迁计划的"土政策"再造传统制造能力，解决新兴工业城市的红色债务风险，加速传统工业的集聚与提升，恢复新兴城市的政府金融信用

所谓"土政策"特指沿海传统制造业内迁转移的扶植政策，由此推进传统制造业的集聚内迁再造计划。这一政策的关键是新兴工业城市如何吸引沿海产业聚焦性内迁，即，形成制造能力和布局结构的系统再造，在中小城市和新兴城市发展的环境下完成设备市场的更替与更新。

在新兴工业城市的发展战略上，我们在借鉴美国20世纪50年代至70年代制造业集聚内迁的经验，在中国制造业世纪之交的民企再造基础上，把沿海传统制造业集聚内迁当作工业再造计划来推进，靠三大政策再造三大能力。

一是运用贴息贷款政策，再造我国工业的设备与硬件能力，再造传统制造业的国际竞争力；二是倾斜集聚内迁政策，再造我国工业的物流与软件能力，再造传统制造业的国内布局力；三是重点地区优先政策，再造地方债务转化与转换能力，再造传统制造业的政企互助力。

推出沿海传统制造业内迁再造计划，靠区位优势和政策倾斜拉动传统产业集聚转移，再造中国的制造业与物流业并加快中国的城市化进程，是习近平新政的第三大战略举措，并在调整落实方式。

中国沿海发达地区，特别是中心城市与旅游城市的传统制造业危机，是人所共知的普遍现象。中部地区与西部地区各城市，为了招商引资不惜血本地制定优惠政策，并大规模进行基础设施投资，很多城市因此而债台高筑，进入了红色债务生态而产业集群转移并没有真正实现。

当今中国的重大的问题，是怎样阻止东部大都市的传统产业全面外流，怎样靠政府的积极作为推动新兴城市及中西部中小城市的产业集聚。这不仅对中国保持和提升制造业的全球竞争力意义重大，而且是解决地方政府债务危机的唯一出路。

今天中国传统制造业的基本能力与全球信誉堪称一流，2013年，中国制造业净出口居世界第一位，制造业增加值在世界占比超过1/5。按照国际标准工业分类，在22个大类中，中国在7个大类中名列第一，钢铁、水泥、汽车等220多种工业品产量居世界首位。

同时，我们的工业装备制造业的水平与能力也进入世界前列，2013年中国装备制造业产值规模突破20万亿元人民币，占全球装备制造业的比重超过1/3，稳居世界第一，多数装备产品产量位居世界第一。为此，中国沿海制造业的内迁过程，应该成为产业集聚转移与升级再造的过程，重新打造许许多多个工业集约化发展的新兴城市。

传统产业内迁过程不仅是中国新兴城市的城市化过程，而且是新兴城市解决债务危机的实现过程。这就是说，高负债城市一般都是基础设施投资超前的红色债务生态城市，高负债的地方政府，大多是在基础设施上过度投资。为此，从传统制造业的转移定位上看，债务越高、基础设施越好的城市，越该优先集聚转移。但是，这些城市由于负债较重，其他的优惠与补贴难以倾斜，需要国家运用积极的财政政策给予全力的支持。

中国地方政府的红色债务生态区，主要是沿海卫星城市、中部新兴城市和西部中心城市。这些地方政府的债务危机不是城市衰败后的黑色负债区，而是过度负债而招商引资明显滞后的红色负债区，科学的产业发展规划与有力的政府倾斜助力，是实现红色债务生态向绿色转换的两大支点。

所谓科学的产业发展规划，就是制定地区、城市、工业开发区的发展战略。为了推进产业集聚转移，这种发展战略应该与行业协会，与行业龙头企业共同研究，并一起争取中央与省级政府的认可。

所谓有力的政府倾斜助力，就是推动中央与省级政府进行土地指标与贴息贷款的扶助。为了推进产业集聚转移，这种政策公关应该与设备商协会，与专业工程龙头企业，与银行财团共同研究，并一起争取中央与省级政府的支持。

结论：工业集聚内迁计划的“土政策”再造传统制造能力，解决新兴工业城市的红色债务风险，加速传统工业的集聚与提升，恢复新兴城市的政府金融信用。

（四）全球创新人才计划的“木政策”再造创新创意产业，解决旅游中心城市的黄色债务风险，加速服务产业的升级与延展，创造移居新城的政府金融信用

所谓“木政策”特指快速生长力，就是对旅游热点城市和创新产业集聚城市高新技术产业和互联网创新的倾斜政策，即，聚焦新经济增长点的弯道超车计划，引导全球人才的流动方向，系统地投入技术创新、文化创意与互联网革命，完成超越世界的创新创意产业再造。

2014 年 2 月，我们与国家创新与发展战略研究会会长郑必坚合作研究中国和平崛起，第一篇报告就聚焦在技术创新与万点股市的互动。但是，三中全会的决议一出，让我们茅塞顿开，研究方法急转。不管是金融改革，还是技术创新，以及互联网革命，都被习近平提升到国家治理能力的层次，其“木政策”的范围，都远远超越了股市拉动的单一视野，聚焦到了以下三种创新能量。

其一，全面提升金融运作能量。三中全会以后，我们开始研究国家金融治理能力的系统提升，并把 4 万亿美元外汇储备（绿票子）的全球投资与 30 万亿人民币（红票子）的引导使用结合起来，系统提高国家金融治理能力，全面提升金融运作能量。

今天，我们面对丝绸之路复兴计划投向世界的 4 万亿美元和循环增加的 10 万亿美元，我们的红票子增发将超过 100 万亿元，如何应对利率大幅度下降后的资本流向，是对国家金融治理能力的重大考验。我们要充分重视互联网金融创新，让低利率时代的资金冲出银行牢

笼而进入高效运营的创新、创意和创业领域。

其二，全面提升技术创新能量。2014 年 11 月，习近平总书记到福建考察期间，第 21 次登上平潭岛，指出平潭面临的机遇，不是百年一遇而是千年一遇，平潭综合实验区是全国独创，要继续努力探索，真正把平潭建设成为两岸同胞的共同家园。1 个月之后，平潭企业家科学家创新论坛在福建平潭综合实验区举行，众多著名企业家和科学家共聚一堂，探讨两岸互动科技创新。在这次论坛上，我就全球科技创新的五种模式提出了我对平潭综合试验区的五大对策思考。

其三，全面提升互联网革命能量。惊爆马云上市震惊全球，我们的智库研究群的四场激辩，聚焦于四个时代的讨论：一是中国互联网时代开始了，二是资本主义旧时代逐步结束了，三是股东民主投票的时代刚想开始就被结束了，四是已经结束了的“文革”时代又有重新开始的危险了。

这一政策是借鉴 20 世纪 30 年代苏联的全球人才吸纳计划与 20 世纪 50 年代美国的全球人才争夺计划，推进全球人才流动的第三潮向中国集聚，形成中国创新与创意经济的三大能量（高新技术创新能量、互联网革命能量、金融运作能量）。

中国改革开放以来，出现过三次技术创新潮，从第一波的海归人才梦，到第二波的二板投资热，目前处于产业升级的第三波，全球资源和资本在向中国聚合，中国后发优势的弯道超车将在这里最后冲刺。

目前，全球的创新人才、创新项目以及各种骗子都云集中国，紧盯中国的资本、市场和制造能力。现在，不管是传统产业的升级，还是新兴产业的培育，以及高端服务的运作，或是互联网业的创新，也包括以“互联网模式”开展的传统产业的革命化改造等，都必须借助于股市资本的强力助推甚至疯狂催动。为此，我们寄巨大希望于这波股市，并全力推动股市资本聚焦全球人才的新一轮聚合。

中国农业再造并在一定程度上解决农民工问题之后，新兴旅游城市的服务产业价值会显性化并升值化，必然挤压促使这些城市的服务业税收急剧增长，从而走出黄色债务风险区。这时，中国新兴旅游城市的重大任务，是在于全面乃至全球广泛招揽人才，把传统的旅游产业与创新、创意和创业结合起来，推动城市的产业升级。

结论：全球创新人才计划的“木政策”再造创新创意产业，解决旅游中心城市的黄色债务风险，加速服务产业的升级与延展，创造移居新城的政府金融信用。

（五）都市价值升值计划的“火政策”再造虚拟经济财富，解决大型国际都市的白色债务风险，加速虚实经济的结合与外延，创新国际都市的政府金融信用

所谓“火政策”特指超大型都市的价值增值热浪区，就是都市服务业、房地产与股票市场的撬动政策，这一政策的核心是大都市实体经济与虚拟经济的同步增值计划，即，形成服务业收入和国民财富总量倍增，完成高端市场再提升与再提振。

单纯从地方负债的角度看问题，中国谈得上国际大都市的城市只有京沪广深四个超大都市，其债务总量巨大，但债务风险微乎其微，其城市功能和资源的价值增值速度，远远高于

其表面上的负债率。与京沪广深相比，其他各大城市都没有这种体量和底气，都有可能陷入黄色甚至红色的债务生态。

但是，京沪广深的城市负债率存在较大差别，四大都市的下属区县同样存在政府债务风险。因此，推高超大都市的产业价值和财富价值，并在此基础上推动政府金融创新，不断打破传统金融信用的白色警告，把白色债务生态向绿色债务生态转换。

中国房地产政策的争论由来已久，我们从来站在唱响派一边，认为解决平民住房问题根本不是打压大都市房价，而是加大卫星城土地供给和轨道交通投入。为此，我们 2013 年的研究局限于房地产低迷的救市问题，认为京沪广深等大都市的房地产发展根本不是限购打压而是放开市场，靠大幅度提高容积率进行旧城改造，并靠卫星城和高铁解决社会问题。

但是，伴随我们对习近平新政“水政策”的研究不断深入，解决农民工问题与利率趋近零对都市房地产的影响会无限放大，波及服务业的显性化与升级化，也会影响房市、股市等各种虚拟经济的价值大增值。这时，习近平新政提出一系列改革举措，包括户籍制度大改革、银行信贷政策放松、股市全面启动……使我们的研究转向更宽泛的“火政策”，并借鉴我国台湾 20 世纪 90 年代传统产业外移与都市经济升级的经验，以汇率、利率与股市联动为龙头，推动都市经济的多重升值。

一是大都市没有农民工后劳动力价格必升，导致服务业收入显性化与品质全面升级，GDP 倍增毫无悬念。

二是大都市地产业两极化，中心区房价继续强势上涨促都市财富大增值，不仅催化都市财富的全球化投资，而且推动低端产业外移与都市人口向卫星城转移，大都市与卫星城地产的两极化加剧。

三是大都市空心化迫使人们高度重视产业升级，而股市热潮是大都市高端产业的加速器，万点股市必定倾斜发展高端产业与升值产业。

四是中心城区的房地产价值暴涨，会大大提升大都市人群的财富价值总量，并刺激投资冲动的倍增，使基金投资与股市走高联动，最终实现股市冲高万点的梦。

总之，我国大都市的升级发展，虚实产业的价值要同步提升，特别是现代服务业与高新技术业的实体经济产业升级，靠大都市房地产与股票市场的持续增值，因为，虚拟经济的财富价值是城市投资能力的体现，与高端实体产业发展有密切的互动关系。以纽约为例，市中心与长岛的房地产价值奇高，代表着城市的财富总量，就像东京的地产价值能够买光全球的股票一样，纽约的地产暴跌就是城市竞争力的衰落。

至于现代股市的股价，是高新技术产业和互联网新经济的助推器，其最大的受益者既不是安逸的小城镇，也不是传统工业主导的中小城市，而是大都市中的高新技术产业和互联网拉动的现代服务业。

发展中国家解决了农民与农村问题，一定会带来内需大涨、大都市房价与生活指数大涨、高端服务业市场大涨与高新技术产业机会大涨，于是，股市的涨跌就成为高端服务业与新兴产业群发展状态的风向标。

中国地方政府的白色债务生态区，主要是在京沪广深四大都市，这些地方政府的债务问题往往是形式上的浅红色（有过度负债的指标），实际上的灰白色（也有加大负债的巨大潜力），被我们概括成白色负债生态区，需要通过债务转化（把融资平台公司转化成金融投资公司和产业集团公司）与金融创新（用互联网金融的方式创造新的金融信用），以实现白色债务生态向绿色的转换。

结论：都市价值升值计划的“火政策”再造虚拟经济财富，解决大型国际都市的白色债务风险，加速虚实经济的结合与外延，创新国际都市的政府金融信用。

（作者：李肃，和君创业咨询集团首席合伙人）

我国省级公共安全综合评价指标体系研究

一、导论：问题的提出和研究的重要意义

近年来，由于人类社会生态环境的破坏和自然环境的持续恶劣发展，在全球范围内，以人为和非人为表现的各种灾害现象明显增加。我国也一样，除了每年多发自然灾害外，一些人为灾害事故也频繁发生，并有不断上升的趋势，造成了许多不应有的损失，给人民群众的生命安全造成重大危害，公私财产也因此受到巨大的损失。

当前，我国的城乡安全面临着新的严峻挑战，自国家战略提出城镇化建设之后，城镇规模的扩大意味着一系列安全问题数量的上升。从社会的发展规律看，人均 GDP 在 1 000～3 000美元这个阶段，既是经济快速发展期，又是社会矛盾的集中期，城乡安全问题的凸显是这个阶段的典型现象。因此，各级政府对城乡安全工作的重视和建设，是社会城镇化发展的新的要求。虽然我国城镇化发展速度较快，但城乡安全保障系统还很不完善，全国灾害事故总量年均增长 6.28%，最高增幅达 22%。所以，构建公共安全的理论和公共安全的保障机制，是城乡转换发展过程中的重中之重。

我国每年因公共安全问题造成的经济损失高达 6 500 亿元，约占 GDP 总量的 6%。其中，生产事故引发的损失约为 2 500 亿元；社会治安事件造成的损失约为 1 500 亿元；自然灾难造成的损失约为 2 000 亿元；生物侵害导致的损失约为 500 亿元。每年因公共安全问题被夺去生命的约有 20 万人。全国需要防洪的城市达 642 座，但只有 177 座达到了国家的防洪标准，占总数的 28%，未达标的城市占 72%；城市中应建消火栓 31 万个，但实际只有 15 万个，缺口达 52%（以上均为 2012 年数据）。一些老城市的排水系统还是清代所建，因此城市的公共安全隐患很严重。现代的公共安全事故，除了传统的消防、交通和生产安全外，还涉及能源、生态环境、水资源、恐怖袭击、信息网络、流行病、食品药品、人口及城市建设等非传统安全问题。其涉及范围之广、影响程度之深、牵涉因素之多、突发能量之大，是任何其他社会经济问题均无法与之相比的。因此，仅有党和国家以及科技界的高度重视还不够，还应该把其纳入国家中长期经济和科技发展规划中，并切实推动省市县各级政府的具体落实。

我国政府对公共安全工作一直非常重视，尽管高度重视，各级政府也不断强调防灾安全工作的重要性，要求减少灾害事故的文件和法规每一届政府都不断出台，但灾害事故多发的势头仍然得不到有效扼制。其中一个重要原因，就是防灾安全的管理体制上存在政出多门的状况。现在每级政府都有十多个甚至数十个部门涉及公共安全工作，并且相互掣肘、各自为政，使有限的行政资源形成不了合力，重复建设、设备闲置、人员交叠和效率低下等现象比比皆是。这不但造成资源浪费、法律滞后、各行其是、虚报瞒报的现象，而且摁下葫芦起来瓢，火灾、交通、矿难、环境、暴恐等事件交替发生，加上各类自然灾害，致使各级政府为此伤透脑筋，因此，公共安全事件已经成为中央和地方政府面临的一大顽症。

近年来，发达国家对公共安全的评价研究开始兴起，甚至提高到“国家安全”的高度来进行。我国一些地方政府在加强法治建设的进程中，也开始对部分项目进行了评价体系的考核。例如，《广东省政府法治建设指标体系（试行)》2012 年发布，并于 2013 年 6 月 1 日起施行。这个体系既有具体要求，又有量化标准，其考评的对象主要针对政府行为。国内一些高校和研究机构也纷纷展开了对单项性公共安全评价指标体系的研究，这些都是政绩考评的内容和方式上的重大进步。但对囊括城乡整个区域，即对各省、自治区、直辖市区域的安全状况的综合性评价体系之研究，依然是一项空白。

已有的实践告诉我们，防灾减灾和公共安全工作是一个系统化工程，要从根本上解决问题，除了要形成社会公共安全管理的合力外，还应该对一个地方的公共安全指数进行综合性评价。否则，一个地方明明下大气力抓了公共安全工作，却因为在某一个节点上突然发生了重大灾难事故，结果被“一票否决”，甚至被追究某些领导的责任，这是很不科学的。因此，我们希望通过各省级政府之间的良性比较，一则可加大政府对所属防灾安全各部门之间的统筹管理，二则可探索省级及省级以下政府在防灾安全管理方面的综合性机构改革措施，以从根本上减少各种人为或自然灾害造成的损失。因此，这套评价体系既是对我国公共安全工作进行科学评估的客观需要，也是对各地方政府政务公开、定期公布实事求是的事故灾害统计数字的有力促进。

二、公共安全的基本概念、相关理论及研究方法

所谓公共安全，是指公众性的社会安全。关于公共安全的理论，国外在 20 世纪 60 年代开始提出，它属于国家行政管理的范畴。西方社会学认为，国家行政管理必须为公众提供公共产品，它是向社会公众提供的一种保障性公开性产品。公共产品是私人产品的对称，指的是在社会消费过程中不具备占有性和排斥性，没有价格、没有市场、不准自由买卖而只能由国家提供和调配的物质、教育或劳务；对此，每个公民享有同等的权利或强制性义务。

公共产品中包括公共安全产品，而公共安全是从公共安全产品中引申出来的外延性概念，它比产品的概念广泛得多，将所有社会公众涉及的安全问题全部概括在内。公共安全也有狭义和广义之分。狭义仅仅是指社会治安方面，但这里的治安不单是治安管理，而是整个社会秩序治理的安全；广义则除了私人领域外，相对的公共领域无所不包。

我国省级公共安全综合评价指标体系是为了综合反映和说明省一级公共安全状况而专门设计的评估系统，它具有平衡处理公共安全各项指标、科学反映公共安全指标内在联系的作用。它的目的是综合考察省一级政府对公共安全破坏力与控制力的动态状况，是客观发生指数与主观要求指标的科学统一，理论上具有比较科学的计量性和平衡性特征。但它的评价结果是否真实的前提是各类公共安全部门提供的统计数字必须真实可靠、准确无误。相关公共安全部门提供的数据越多，其科学的评估比较结果就越真实合理。同时必须说明，我们的评估结果是一个不断接近事实真相的过程，其真实并不是绝对的。

鉴于目前国家部委机构和各地公布的灾害事故统计数字具有较大的差异，且口径不一，有些部门甚至不定期或干脆不公布相关数字，致使本课题专家组搜集的数字呈碎片化状态。我们经过两年的模拟测试，目前只能择取6项指标进行初步的评价，虽然这里提供的安全指标评价体系在理论和框架上是科学的，但其得出的结果肯定会有一定的偏差，因此，目前的结果只具有参考意义。

需要指出的是，各地区发生的灾害事故虽然看上去是局部的、偶然的，但是从整体来看，灾害事故的发生还是有一定规律的。一个地方经济越发达，科技越先进，人口越密集，发生灾害事故的可能性就越大。同时，一个地方对安全管理越重视，措施越严密，投入越到位，其发生灾害事故的可能性就越小。这个在理论上成立的正比关系，在实际上却往往不一定能体现，因为这其中涉及许多复杂的因素。既有数据的可靠性因素，又有评估的科学性因素，还有灾害事故发生的偶然性因素。我们设计的评估方法和内容，就是紧扣这些目前难以把握的因素，希望通过科学的方法论，不断接近事实的真相，同时促进对公共安全工作的结构性改革。

现在的有利条件在于，现代社会的信息化程度越来越高，一旦发生灾害事故，隐报瞒报的可能性越来越小，特别是重大事故，基本上隐瞒不了。数字虚报也一样，虚报隐瞒了真相，同时也就隐瞒了隐患，这样会致使事后吸取的教训不足，整改也难以彻底，结果往往酿成更大的灾难；数字实报反映了真实情况，虽一时难看，但问题搞清楚了，就能够找到事故根源，促使整改到位、警钟长鸣，以此做到真正的防范。本课题的一个重要目标，就是能够促进各地对灾害数字如实公布，而对那些不愿意公布或有意公布虚假信息的地方政府，我们设计的评估方法是要以科学的坐标体系让他们得不偿失。这种方法运用统计学原理是不难做到的。

任何指数和实际情况总是有差距的。指数用以体现经济社会变化和发展的程度，可拿来作横向或纵向比较，对于指数的编制和发布，其专业能力和科学态度缺一不可。编制指数的过程中必然包含人为的数据处理过程。要得到真实反映客观实际的指数，必须坚持科学精神，使用科学方法。指数编制和发布要提升科学性，必须保证其调研对象、采用标准和基础数据的可信性、稳定性和一致性。公共安全的评价方法有多种，大体可分为定性分析方法、半定量分析方法和定量分析方法三大类。定性分析方法是对分析对象的危险状况进行系统、细致的检查，根据检查结果对其危险性做出大致的评价。半定量分析方法则是将对象的危险状况表示为某种形式的分度值，从而区分出不同对象的危险程度。而定量分析方法是对具体的数量进行对比后，用一个合理值的概念对其进行分析和比较，严格的定量分析应当以基于统计方法的事故概率计算为基础。

每个评价方法都有其各自独特的适用范围，有独特的优点和缺点。在选择公共安全评价方法时，专家组认为应不求精深，而求简洁适用，可操作性强，以减少评价的主观性，增加客观性，以原始数据为基础，克服因素权重由专家打分的弊端，使选择的评价方法适合省、自治区、直辖市的安全评价，评价结果能够客观反映省级区域的安全现状。

根据“问题选择方法，而不是方法选择问题”的原则，充分考虑了各省、自治区、直辖市安全评价的特点，由于城乡是一个复杂、开放的动力学系统，对其整体安全性进行评价，涉及的安全因素众多。因此，必须建立一套能从总体上反映对象本质的指标体系，并能将各指标综合成一个总体上可以衡量各省、自治区、直辖市安全状况的有效指数，专家组在认真研究以后，最后选择了以层次分析法和半定量分析法相结合的方式。

三、国内外公共安全指标体系设计文献

近年来，发达国家对城市安全的评价研究开始兴起，甚至提高到“国家安全”的高度来进行。国际上把能够带来安全问题的灾害按组成系统的致灾因子归为三类，即自然原因、人为原因、环境原因。在联合国开展的十年减灾活动和美国“9・11”事件之后，学术界广泛地认识到安全领域的重要性，并积极地将视野投向许多非传统领域，特别是严峻的人口与环境、经济与文化等民族之间的冲突问题。一些国家基于监测、描述和解释国际公共安全问题的需要，在研究和实践中设计了一系列公共安全评估体系，为人类秩序和国际社会的安全提供了必要的参照和警示。美、英、法、德、日等发达国家已经针对不同的城市做了大量的评估预警工作，这方面我们必须奋起直追。

西方专家认为，城乡公共安全体系主要包括6个方面：城乡公共安全的规划设计；城乡灾害风险的预测和评估；城乡应急救援能力的评价和落实；城乡应对突发事故的公共安全保障措施；城乡公共安全体系的优化研究；政府和社会组织为城乡公共安全提供的市场化运作方案。现在关于城乡公共安全的评价问题，英美学术机构认为需要考虑两个层面的问题，一种是“压力释放”模型，另一种是“致灾途径”模型。第一种模型说明，灾害是脆弱性承灾体与致灾因子相互综合作用的结果。由于改变致灾因子是困难的，所以减灾的关键是降低承灾体的脆弱性，增加其抗灾能力。第二种模型是对第一种模型中的主要因素进行深入分析，即对人类脆弱性根源与致灾因子相互作用进行分析，也就是对经济和政治的进展过程中如何产生脆弱性的分析。它说明，要降低脆弱性就必须改进预防灾害和受灾恢复的能力。除自然灾害学方面的专家外，社会科学等其他领域的专家也指出了类似的评价角度，将社会发展观作为公共安全评价的出发点。

国际上，公共安全评价方法的种类很多，大体可分为定性分析方法、半定量分析方法和定量分析方法三大类。定性分析方法对分析对象的危险状况进行系统、细致的检查，根据检查结果对其危险性做出大致的评价。半定量分析方法则将对象的危险状况表示为某种形式的

分度值，从而区分出不同对象的危险程度。引进“量”的概念是进行分析和比较的基础，严格的定量分析应当以基于统计方法的事故概率计算为基础。

本课题参考的国外主要文献如下：

（1）Saaty T. L.，Tran L. T.. On the invalidity of fuzzifying numerical judgments in the analytic hierarchy process. Math Compute Model，2007，46：962－975.

（2）Saaty T. L.，Shang J. S.. Group decision-making：Head-count versus intensity of preference. Social Econ Plan Sci，2007，30（6）：52－54.

本文介绍的主要方法也来自其中。

四、我国省级公共安全评价指标体系的现状和问题

2006 年，公安部消防局提出，要对各地消防安全工作进行综合评估体系的研究和探索，并委托上海市消防局牵头组织。上海市消防局于 2008 年拿出了一个初步方案，但在论证中遇到了许多问题，最终没能实施。当时有领导指出，这种课题最好由社会机构来做，由政府部门做是非常困难的。

我们认为做这种课题是防灾安全研究机构的特长，因此，专门组织了国内相关的权威专家学者，成立了课题攻关专家组，在对多种方案进行比较后，上海防灾安全策略研究中心根据当前公共安全领域存在的现实问题，最后采用了目前所做的对各省级区域的事故灾害指数进行综合评价的方案。

2013 年 5 月，课题组完成了对 2011 年“各省、自治区、直辖市的公共安全评价指标体系”的初评，此后在听取了各方面意见的基础上，又进行了重大修改，2014 年年初再次完成了 2012 年“各省、自治区、直辖市的公共安全评价指标体系”的课题，从形式到内容都有所提高。作为一项区域性的安全指标综合研究，我们这个课题是开放性、吸纳性的，希望经过多次的实践检验，能够逐渐接近社会公共安全评价的实际情况。

我国自 2003 年“非典”之后，开始重视城市公共安全的应急管理。2006 年 1 月 8 日，国务院发布了《国家突发公共事件总体应急预案》（以下简称《预案》），将突发公共事件进行了分类、分级，将公共安全事件从传统的自然灾害、事故灾难扩展到公共卫生事件、社会安全事件，并按照各类突发公共事件的性质、严重程度、可控性和影响范围等因素，将其分为四个等级。同时，《预案》还明确提出了应对各级各类突发公共事件的工作原则和各级政府部门的职责。在城市化过程中，人们对资源浪费、环境污染这两大问题认识得较早，宣传也较多，但在城市公共安全的防范和应急管理方面则相对薄弱。

如今，城乡公共安全的预防与应急系统建设已逐渐得到重视。不管是理论研究、法制建设、管理体系建设或规划应用层面都在加强，并取得了一些成绩。但也应该清醒地认识到，对于城乡公共安全建设，还有许多亟待加强的方面，如缺乏综合协调、灾害种类考虑不足、管理体系不健全等，本课题也是希望在这方面作一些探讨。

本课题专家认为，我国的区域性安全评价工作不能只围绕着城市进行。因为随着互联网

(物联网)的普及，城乡差距将会迅速缩小，公共安全问题也不是只有城市才有，而物联网的推广不仅仅是各种物质设备的智能化，更重要的体现是监控手段的无孔不入（从安全角度说，可以在监控方面作一篇大文章，限于篇幅，这里不能展开)。我国目前的统计体系是以行政区域为主的，单独的城市统计数据非常难搜集，而且在城乡一体化的过程中，所谓的城市数据也是很不精确的，因此，我们必须在一开始就以城乡区域为统一的评价基数（坐标)，从发展的角度看，这也是比较科学的。

归纳以上所说，我们所进行的省级公共安全评价指标体系是非常重要的跨学科领域的综合性研究课题，旨在通过分析我国城乡事故灾害统计数字的基础上，找出各地现有的城乡安全治理的薄弱点，以推动和改进对公共安全资源的整合和治理模式，加大各地对公共安全薄弱环节的投入，探索完善我国城乡公共安全管理的路径与方法，为我国城乡公共安全的监管实践提供指导性意见。

我们相信，省级公共安全综合评价指标体系的推出本身也是一个不断完善的过程，只要它能够引起各级政府的重视，那就一定会得到有关政府方面的认可和支持，一定会有越来越多的公共安全数据进入这个体系，其发展前景毋庸置疑，是有生命力的。

五、如何构建我国省级公共安全指标框架体系

安全环境，从理论上讲应当是没有危险，市民不受威胁，生产、生活不出事故，群众普遍有安全感的城乡环境。但在城镇现代化建设加快的现阶段，经济和社会结构的变革，利益关系的不平衡和贫富差距拉大，以及各种思想和价值观念的矛盾冲撞，许多新的犯罪诱因不断产生，各类违法犯罪案件的上升将是不以人们意志为转移的客观存在。因此，只要保障社会治安秩序稳定的控制力控制住危害社会治安秩序的破坏力，且破坏力的幅度控制在社会和群众能够承受的范围之内，那么城乡社会治安就是平稳的、安全的，即为安全城乡。这是目前国际、国内犯罪学研究的共识。

（一）评价指标

关于安全，就其本质而言，即：没有危险，不受威胁，不出事故；从人们最关心的方面看，莫过于人身安全和财产安全。安全又有广义和狭义之分：广义上的安全应涵盖政治、经济、社会、环境等一切因素；而狭义上的安全，主要指治安方面的安全。我们评价的自然是广义上的安全，但并非涵盖全部的广义上的安全，而是着重于社会、环境等可分析、可量化的技术指标评价。

科学界定省级区域公共安全状况的评价范围，是科学评价省级区域达到最安全目标的前提。从我国国情和现有条件出发，对省级区域公共安全的评价，范围和涵盖面都不宜过大，否则内容繁多又不易量化；但也不能太小，仅限于对构成公共安全状况的某一方面进行评价，涉及面窄，难以得出比较全面、系统的结论。

例如，过去经验式评价社会治安是否安全，常用违法犯罪案件发案数的高低这一单一指

标进行分析，发案数上升了，就认为社会治安变坏了；发案下降了，就认为社会治安好转了。事实上，社会治安状况的发展变化并非如此。当保证城市治安秩序稳定的控制力与对城市治安秩序和公共安全构成威胁的破坏力适应或基本适应时，城市治安状况就稳定或基本稳定，市民就感到安全；当控制力小于破坏力，不能有效地控制和消除违法犯罪对城市治安秩序的冲击时，城市治安状况就会不稳定，市民就感到不安全。这就是为什么美国等西方发达国家虽然犯罪率大大高于我国，而城市治安状况仍较稳定、市民仍有较高安全感的原因所在。

因此，对省级区域公共安全状况的评价应当取适中的范围，界定在可以量化的、具有可比性的、较为稳定的、对城市治安安全影响较大的三个方面，即：危害公共安全秩序的主要破坏力指标、维护城镇公共安全秩序的控制力指标以及公众安全感这一主观社会指标。只有将描述客观现象的破坏力、控制力指标，同反映公众安全感状况的主观社会指标有机结合起来，互相印证，才能科学评价省级区域公共安全状况，反之则不然。

评价指标不宜拘泥于拟定术语的绝对准确和严谨，否则陷入纯学术之争，不能自拔；主要在于科学界定其边界条件，保持公正性和可操作性。

（二）评价指标体系

省级公共安全综合评价指标体系，是为综合反映和说明省级区域公共安全状况而设计的一组具有内在联系的社会指标，它应该处于能综合考察省级区域公共安全状况破坏力与控制力的动态平衡状态，是客观指标与主观指标的统一，具有可计量性和可比较性的特征。

本指标体系评价方法采用加权综合评分法，即各指标均以三级计分法测评，再确定各指标在体系中的权重，最后将各指标按权重所得评分加总，得出总分。

1. 确定三级指标权重排序

基于“安全第一，以人为本”理念，三个层次三级指标及其排序的基本原则是以人为本的价值体系，物质损失其次的价值观。

为了便于计算，总的权数确定为100%。再根据各项指标在评价指标体系中的重要性，确定各级指标。

1）目前一级指标排序（见表1）

表1　目前一级指标排序

序号	一级名称	排序说明
1(准则层)	生存环境	任何人,任何时候都要在生存环境中生活和工作,须臾离不开,可谓息息相关,首要条件
2(准则层)	治安	任何人,任何时候都直接接触或间接感受自身乃至周围环境治安状况,关注度居次位
3(准则层)	交通	除了少数老弱病残不便户外活动者,绝大多数人都或多或少直接接触交通状况,关注度居第三位
4(准则层)	火灾	绝大多数人无直接接触火灾史,但人们都高度关注火灾,防患于未然

续表 1

序号	一级名称	排序说明
5(准则层)	自然灾害	由于自然要素(气象、水文、地质)的变化引发的自然灾害从天而降,除了不谙人事的婴幼儿外,绝大多数人都深切关注
6(准则层)	生产事故	虽然发生在局部环境,或少数人受害,但牵动全社会神经和人心所向

2) 目前二级指标遴选(见表2)

表2 目前二级指标遴选

一级指标	二级指标(要素层)名称	说明
生存环境	自然环境	囊括城镇和乡村的原生态环境
	工业化环境	城镇工业化环境变迁,衍生诸多问题
治安	刑事案件	刑事案件在治安事故中居首位,对人们生命安全潜在危险大
	经济案件	经济案件使人们财产损失,社会关注度大
	反社会秩序案件(含暴恐)	反社会秩序案件与日俱增,对社会稳定破坏力大
交通	铁路交通	由于铁路、航运、航空交通跨省际甚至国际,不受属地管理,且无各地数据,因此,不列入地方量化统计分析
	航运、航空交通	
	道路交通	其事故频发,生命损伤巨大,全社会关注度高
火灾	死亡人数	大小事故频发,物质损失巨大,生命损伤较大
	经济损失	直接接触不多,间接感受很大,全社会关注度高
生产事故	各类事故死亡人数	事故频发,生命损伤大,社会关注度大
自然灾害	地质灾害	地质性灾害、气象灾害和其他自然灾害属不可抗拒力,但全社会关注的是环境保护和应急救援工作。政府作为社会综合管理机构,应在环境保护、应急预案和善后工作方面有所作为
	气象灾害	
	其他灾害	

3) 目前三级指标细分及评分(见表3)

表3 目前三级指标细分及评分(总分400分)

序号	一级指标(准则层)	二级指标(要素层)	三级指标(指标层)	权重(分值)
1	生存环境(108分)	自然环境(28分)	空气(4分)	0.008929
			废水(4分)	0.008929
			废物(4分)	0.008929
			绿化(4分)	0.008929
			生态(8分)	0.017857
			土壤(4分)	0.008929

续表 3

序号	一级指标（准则层）	二级指标（要素层）	三级指标（指标层）	权重（分值）
1	生存环境（108 分）	工业化环境（80 分）	水（4 分）	0.009375
			电（4 分）	0.009375
			气（4 分）	0.009375
			排水（4 分）	0.009375
			电梯（8 分）	0.01875
			楼（8 分）	0.01875
			路（12 分）	0.028125
			桥（4 分）	0.009375
			食品（保健品）（16 分）	0.0375
			药品（8 分）	0.01875
			突发公共卫生事件（8 分）	0.01875
2	治安（96 分）	刑事案件（36 分）	杀人（8 分）	0.018519
			伤害、殴打他人（4 分）	0.009259
			抢劫、盗窃（8 分）	0.018519
			强奸（4 分）	0.009259
			诈骗、敲诈勒索财物（4 分）	0.009259
			贩毒（8 分）	0.018519
		经济案件（32 分）	伪造票券、证件、文书（4 分）	0.010417
			经营性网络犯罪（8 分）	0.020833
			贪污（4 分）	0.010417
			挪用（4 分）	0.010417
			受贿（4 分）	0.010417
			行贿（4 分）	0.010417
			走私（4 分）	0.010417
		社会秩序案件（28 分）	扰乱工作、妨碍公务及公共秩序（4 分）	0.011905
			结伙斗殴、寻衅滋事（4 分）	0.011905
			赌博（4 分）	0.011905
			卖淫、嫖娼（4 分）	0.011905
			虚假信息网络犯罪（4 分）	0.011905
			恐怖袭击与破坏（4 分）	0.011905
			群体性事件（4 分）	0.011905
3	火 灾（60 分）	死亡人数（36 分）		0.1
		经济损失（24 分）	生产经营（16 分）	0.033333
			其他（8 分）	0.016667

续表 3

<table>
<tr><th>序号</th><th>一级指标
(准则层)</th><th>二级指标
(要素层)</th><th>三级指标
(指标层)</th><th>权重
(分值)</th></tr>
<tr><td rowspan="4">4</td><td rowspan="4">陆上交通
(76 分)</td><td rowspan="2">铁路交通
(本文不做评价)</td><td>生产经营性铁路交通</td><td>0</td></tr>
<tr><td>其他铁路交通</td><td>0</td></tr>
<tr><td rowspan="2">道路交通
(76 分)</td><td>经营性交通(40 分)</td><td>0.1</td></tr>
<tr><td>其他——代步行车(36 分)</td><td>0.1</td></tr>
<tr><td rowspan="3">5</td><td rowspan="3">生产事故
(40 分)</td><td rowspan="2">各类事故死亡人数(24 分)</td><td>工矿商贸死亡人数(12 分)</td><td>0.033333</td></tr>
<tr><td>其他(12 分)</td><td>0.033333</td></tr>
<tr><td>事故起数(16 分)</td><td>较大事故起数(16 分)</td><td>0.033333</td></tr>
<tr><td rowspan="3">6</td><td rowspan="3">自然灾害
(20 分)</td><td rowspan="3"></td><td>地震、泥石流(8 分)</td><td>0.02</td></tr>
<tr><td>雷击、暴雨(8 分)</td><td>0.02</td></tr>
<tr><td>台风、海啸(4 分)</td><td>0.01</td></tr>
</table>

4）指标权重说明

构成自然环境各要素中——空气、废水、废物、绿化、生态和土壤，其中生态较重要，因为保护生态环境，功在千秋万代，故权重分值较高，其他五要素权重同等。

在工业化环境（城镇）中，（供）水、电、气（燃气和北方取暖热气）与排水均为居民必需品，故权重分值同等；然而（公共设施和住宅）电梯投入运行量与日俱增，与前者四要素不同，一旦停用带来诸多不便，而后者将是一个潜在的风险源，出现故障将与生命攸关，故权重分值较高。

以上属建筑内设施要素，而公共环境（城镇）中，楼、路和桥因各种因素造成倒塌和塌陷事故迭起，防不胜防，政府作为社会管理机构负有不可推诿的责任，故权重分值较高于上述属建筑内设施要素；而这三者中也是轻重不一的，按其破坏力和事故发生率综合排序则为路、楼和桥。路倒塌和塌陷事故最多，桥倒塌和塌陷事故次之，楼倒塌和塌陷事故最少，如上海一栋高层建筑民宅竣工未投入使用前整体倒塌事故，虽损失不大，但社会负面影响极坏。

食品（含保健品）安全事故和隐患层出不穷，成为全社会关注度极高的热点，也是影响我国在国际上持续崛起为强国形象的顽症。本着“以人为本，生命至上”宗旨，“民以食为天”，在工业化环境这种二级指标中，食品（含保健品）这一项三级指标分值最高，也远高于自然环境这种二级指标分值，即使在生存环境诸多三级指标中，它的分值是最高的。

药品安全事故和隐患迭起，因其直接危害人的生命安全和健康，成为全社会关注度很高的热点之一。因此，其分值次高，也远高于自然环境这种二级指标分值，即使在生存环境诸多三级指标中，它也是分值次高的。

突发公共卫生事件，严重危害人的生命安全和健康，也成为全社会关注度很高的热点之一。如 2003 年的“非典”大流行，但后几年发生的“禽流感”就被有效地遏制。因此，其分值较高，但事故发生率低、稀少，故其分值低于药品安全。

在治安一级指标中，刑事案件作为其主要的也是传统的二级指标，其分值仍旧最高。在这个二级指标中，“杀人”直接危害人的生命安全，自然是分值最高的；而“贩毒”，直接危害和摧残人的生命安全，也是罪大恶极的，则分值与“杀人”同等并列最高。实际上，它们都列为司法判决死刑的重大犯罪行为，并且是与国际司法理念与执法一致的。

其他刑事案件中，“伤害、殴打他人”、“强奸”和“诈骗、敲诈勒索财物”都是常见的一般刑事案件，其分值同等；而“抢劫、盗窃”也是常见的刑事案件，但属于控制力与破坏力博弈显性指标，当控制力小于破坏力时，不能有效地控制和消除它，这类犯罪活动倍加猖獗，市民就感到很不安全。作为考核政府执政能力和作为的显性指标，其分值高于一般刑事案件。

过去，经济案件与刑事案件不可同日而语；现在，经济案件不断攀升，逐渐接近后者。如上海市公安局“经济侦查总队”与“刑事侦查总队”大楼并坐而起、比肩而立，规模不相上下。作为公职人员常见的“贪污”、“挪用”和“受贿”，非公职人员常见的“行贿”与“伪造票券、证件、文书”，其分值同等；后者以往为数不多，现今经济社会呈上升态势；作为“IT时代”的负面衍生物——“经营性网络犯罪”纷纷出笼，属于现代社会中高智商犯罪，尽管还未泛滥成灾，但必须早期铲除，同样属于控制力与破坏力博弈显性指标，其分值高于一般经济案件。

“走私”是常见的传统经济案件，我国与国际社会都严惩不贷，但其分工职责主要不由各省、自治区、直辖市政府独立承担，而是由中央有关部门直接领导，纵向主管反走私活动，地方政府配合进行，且内地省份的“走私”远不如沿海省份猖獗，不在“同一条起跑线”上，不便各省份之间大权重的比较。因此，“走私”其分值取一般。

过去，社会秩序案件远少于刑事案件，也少于经济案件。当今社会矛盾错综复杂，社会秩序案件呈上升态势；其中结伙斗殴、寻衅滋事、赌博和卖淫、嫖娼等常见案件频繁发生，而以往少见的扰乱工作、妨碍公务、破坏公共秩序、恐怖袭击和群体性事件不时出现，且作为“IT时代”的负面衍生物——虚假信息网络犯罪也浮出水面。与上述的“经营性网络犯罪”不同，虽然二者都是属于现代社会中高智商犯罪，但是，经营性网络犯罪目的在于谋求不正当的经济利益，而虚假信息网络犯罪出于破坏正常社会秩序的政治目的。如近期出现两起“诈弹”事件，通过网络造谣生事，迫使多个航班客机中途返航，性质恶劣；还有通过网络造谣地震信息，制造混乱。

火灾造成大伤亡和财产损失，同样，本着“以人为本，生命至上”宗旨，火灾死亡其分值高于经济损失；而经济损失按火灾起因分为生产经营和其他两类，前者是从事创造物质财富过程中产生的，后者是非创造物质财富过程中出现的，如生活、休闲、文化娱乐等，以事故发生率和造成损失出发，前者分值高于后者。

交通主要分为水陆空三大类，水上交通又分为市内航运、江河航运和海上航运，市内航运在交通大类份额很小，且各省、自治区、直辖市差异悬殊，不便比较；江河航运和海上航运跨省际或跨国际，由交通运输部掌管，故本文也不做评价。陆上交通又分为铁路和道路大类，前者又分为生产经营性铁路交通和其他铁路交通，但跨省际，由国家铁路局主管、中国铁路总公司经营，故本文也不做评价。值得评价是道路交通，它又分为经营性道路交通和其他道路交通，后者为非经营性道路交通，如自驾汽车、助动车、各种代步行车等。经营性道路交通属性是公共交通，过去远大于非经营性道路交通。随着社会进步，后者发展迅速，尤其是在大城市的自驾汽车的拥有量早已超过公共交通车辆，因此，其他道路交通分值略低于经营性道路交通。

生产事故中，选取事故死亡人数和事故起数两个主要特征参数，同样，本着“以人为本，生命至上”宗旨，事故死亡人数重于事故起数，故前者分值高于后者，其中工矿商贸死亡人数与其他死亡人数分值同等；事故又分为较大事故与一般事故两类，后者频频发生，几乎防不胜防。而较大事故属于控制力与破坏力博弈显性指标，作为考核政府执政能力和作为的显性指标，因此，就以较大事故起数表征事故起数取分值。由此深入探讨，若直接选取生产事故死亡人数与事故起数作为三级指标欠妥，因与各地区经济发展程度（如 GDP）、人口等诸多因素有关。而国家有关部门下达生产事故死亡人数与事故起数全年控制指标百分比时，已充分考虑上述诸多因素并对各地区之间差异作出权衡，选取其占全年控制指标百分比作为指标权重，则更合理。

自然灾害大类中，选取地震、泥石流一类，雷击、暴雨一类和台风、海啸一类，其中前两类是各省、自治区、直辖市都面临的自然灾害，后一类则是沿海省（直辖市）面临的自然灾害，显然，前两类其分值同等且高于后一类。

（三）层次分析法

层次分析法（Analytic Hierarchy Process，AHP），在 20 世纪 70 年代中期由美国运筹学家托马斯·塞蒂（T. L. Saaty）正式提出。它是一种定性和定量相结合的、系统化、层次化的分析方法。由于它在处理复杂的决策问题上的实用性和有效性，很快在世界范围得到重视。它的应用已遍及经济计划和管理、能源政策和分配、行为科学、军事指挥、运输、农业、教育、人才、医疗和环境等领域。

1. 层次分析法简介

层次分析法可分为五个步骤，即：①建立层次结构模型；②构造判断矩阵；③层次单排序及其一致性检验；④层次总排序；⑤层次总排序及其一致性检验。

结合城市安全指数的案例，对上述步骤分别简单说明如下：

1）建立层次结构模型

在专家深入分析各城市安全风险的各项因子后，将其重要性划分为不同层次：目标层、准则层、要素层、指标层。可用表格及框图形式说明层次的递阶结构与因素的从属关系。

2）构造判断矩阵

判断矩阵元素的值反映了人们对各因素的相对重要性（优劣、偏好、强度等）认识，一般采用 1 ~ 9 表示其重要性等级，这些数值及其倒数作为标度构成判断矩阵。在构造时，当相互比较因素的重要性能够用具有实际意义的比值说明时，判断矩阵相应元素的值可以取出比值。在城市风险案例中，由专家对城市风险的各个因素重要性进行评分，由表格或框图可知不同的各个层次以及每个层次的各项因素具体评分。根据专家评分，对各因素之间的重要性用 1 ~ 9 及其倒数进行标度，组成不同的判断矩阵。

3）层次单排序及其一致性

对已知判断矩阵 A，可以通过 $AW = {}_{max}W$ 解出判断矩阵 A 的特征根${}_{max}$和特征向量 W，经归一化后即为同一层次各因素对于上一层次主因素的重要性的排序权值（即权重向量），这一过程称为层次单排序。

为进行层次单排序（或判断矩阵）的一致性检验，需要计算一致性指标 $CI = \dfrac{\lambda_{max} - n}{n - 1}$ 以及平均随机一致性指标 RI 的值。当随机一致性比率 $CR = \dfrac{CI}{RI} < 0.10$ 时，认为层次单排序的结果有满意的一致性，否则需要调整判断矩阵的元素取值。这里，${}_{max}$为判断矩阵 A 的特征根；n 为判断矩阵 A 的阶数；RI 为平均随机一致性指标，其值是由经验所得。

4）层次总排序

层次总排序是指计算同一层次所有因素对于最高层（总目标）相对重要性的排序权值。这一过程是最高层次到最底层次逐层进行的，若上一层次 A 包含 m 个因素 A_1，A_2，$\ldots A_m$，其层次总排序权值分别为 a_1，a_2，$\ldots a_m$，下一层次 B 包含 n 个因素 B_1，B_2，$\ldots B_n$，他们对于因素 A_j 的层次单排序权值分别为 b_{1j}，b_{2j}，$\ldots b_{nj}$，（当 B_k 与 A_j 无联系时，$b_{kj}=0$），则 B 层次总排序权值为 $B_i = \sum^{m} a_j b_{ij}$，其中 $i=1, 2, 3, \ldots n$。

5）层次总排序及其一致性检验

这一步骤也是从高到低逐层进行的。如果 B 层次某些元素对于 A_j 单排序的一致性指标为 CI_j，相应的平均随机一致性指标为 CR_j，则 B 层次总排序随机一致性比率为 $RI = \dfrac{\sum_{j=1}^{m} a_j CI_j}{\sum_{j=1}^{m} a_j CR_j}$。

类似地，当 $RI<0.10$ 时，认为层次总排序结果具有满意的一致性，否则需要重新调整判断矩阵的元素取值。

2. 中国各省、自治区、直辖市安全指数

在专家对各省、自治区、直辖市的风险因素进行重要性评分后，根据层次分析法取得相应的权重，结合各省、自治区、直辖市的相关统计数据，就可建立各省、自治区、直辖市安全指数。

3. 建立各层次因素权重

根据对各风险因素的重要性进行的评分，构造了图 1。

各省、自治区、直辖市安全因子层次结构模型分层图如图 2。

图 3 ~ 图 6 分别为生存环境分层图、治安分层图、火灾及交通分层图、生产和自然灾害分层图。

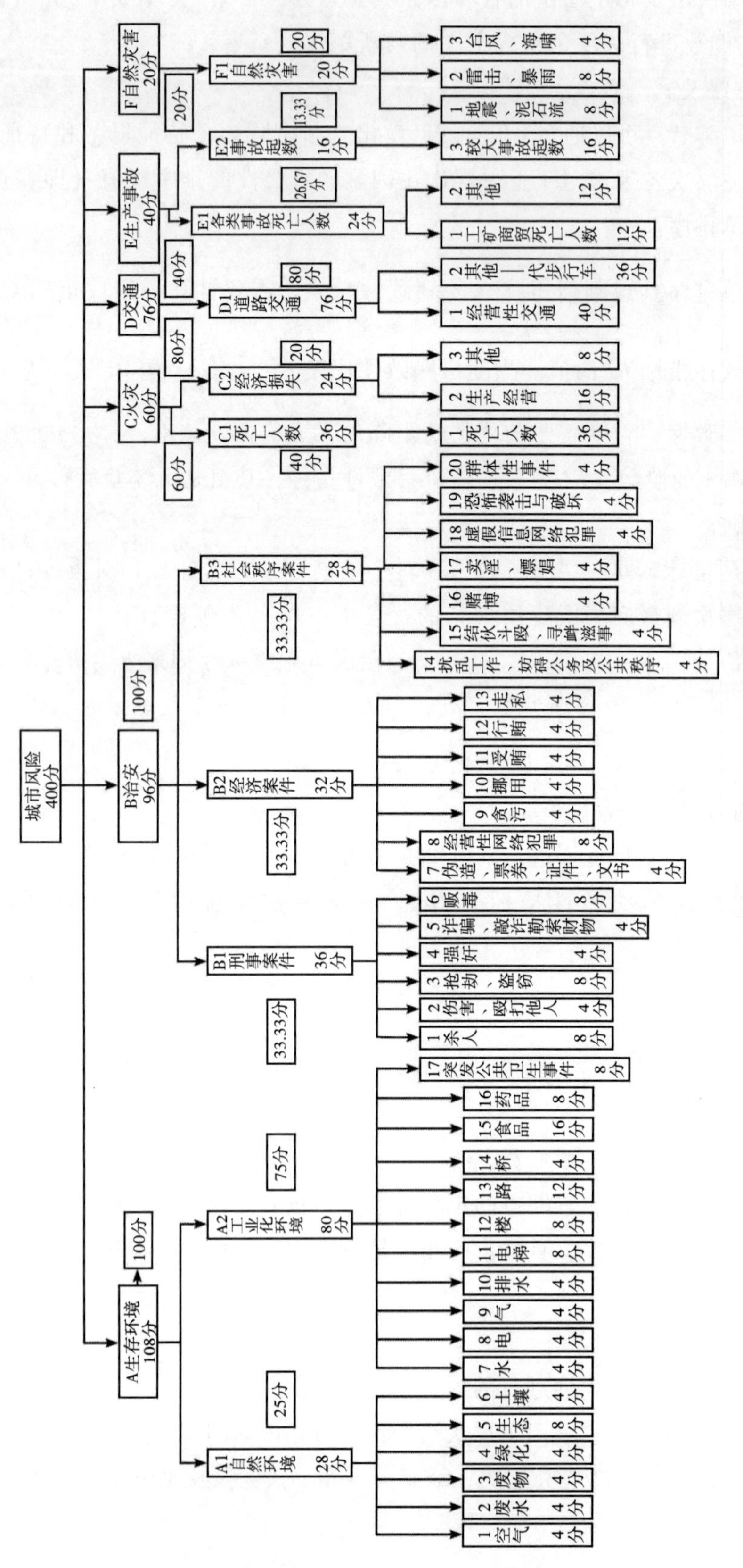

图1 各省、自治区、直辖市安全因子层次结构模型

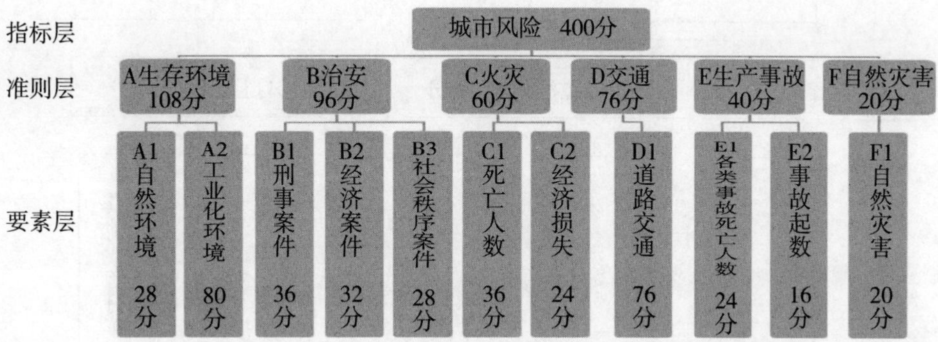

图2 各省、自治区、直辖市安全因子层次结构模型分层图

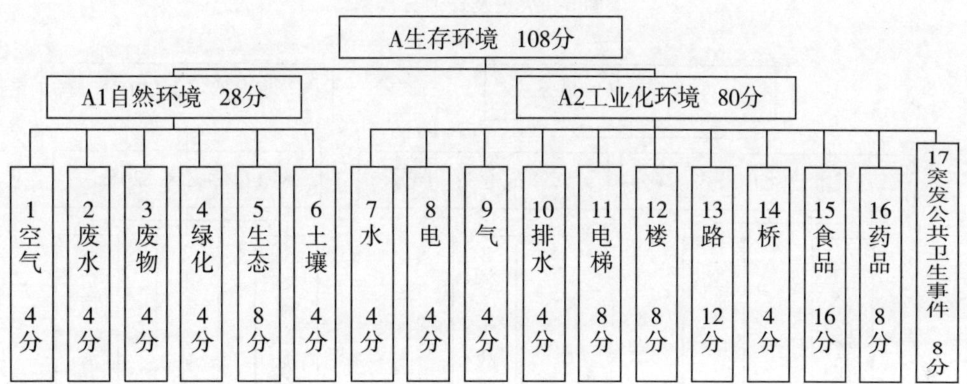

图3 生存环境分层图

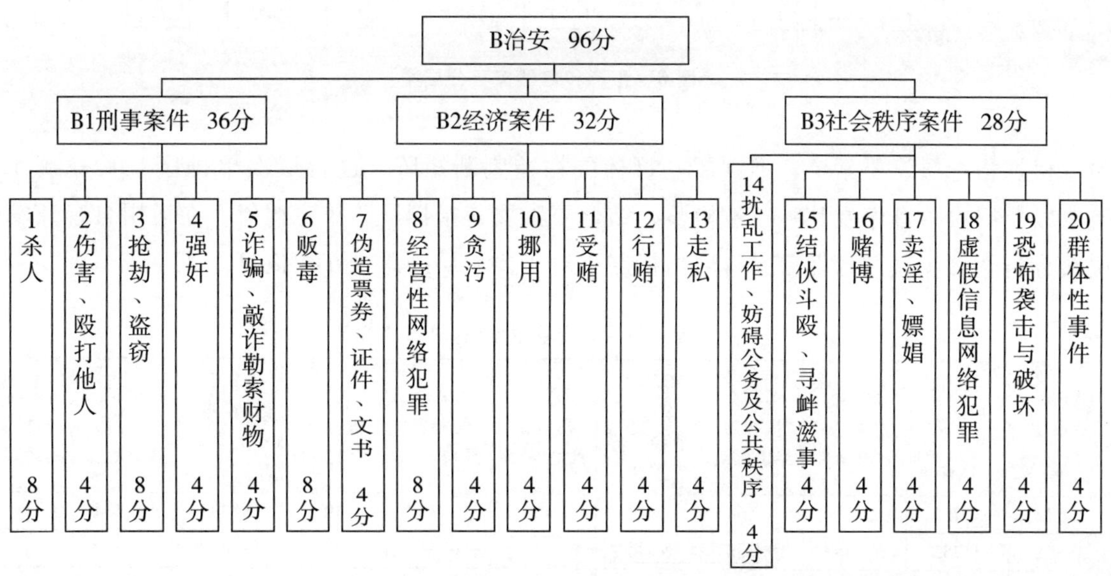

图4 治安分层图

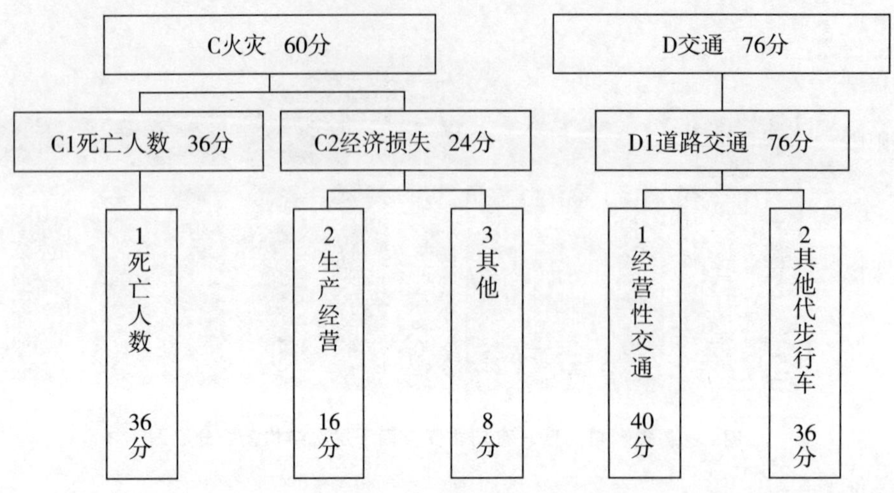

图5 火灾及交通分层图

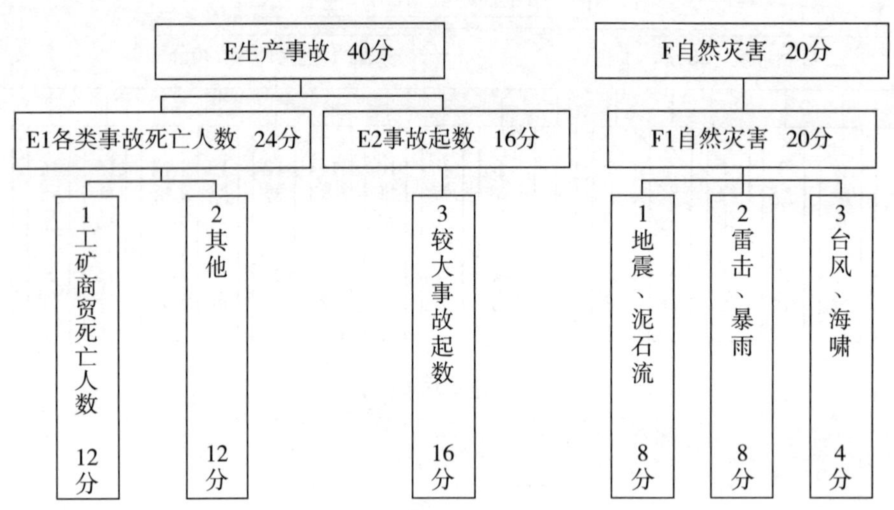

图6 生产和自然灾害分层图

根据指标层、要素层、准则层、目标层构造判断矩阵，进行层次单排序及其一致性检验，以及层次总排序及其一致性检验，结合要素层与指标层总排序权值，在运用自行开发的层次分析法计算软件计算后，得到指标层相对于要素层的总排序权值见表4。

表4 指标层相对于要素层的总排序权值

A1项 指标层 自然环境	A2项 指标层 工业化环境	B1项 指标层 刑事案件	B2项 指标层 经济案件	B3项 指标层 社会秩序案件	C1项 指标层 死亡人数	C2项 指标层 经济损失	D项 指标层 道路交通	E1项 指标层 各类事故死亡人数	E2项 指标层 事故起数	F项 指标层 自然灾害
3.572	3.752	7.408	4.168	4.76	40	13.332	40	13.333	13.334	8
3.572	3.752	3.704	8.332	4.76		6.668	40	13.333		8
3.572	3.752	7.408	4.168	4.76						4
3.572	3.752	3.704	4.168	4.76						
7.144	7.5	3.704	4.168	4.76						

续表 4

A1 项 指标层 自然环境	A2 项 指标层 工业化环境	B1 项 指标层 刑事案件	B2 项 指标层 经济案件	B3 项 指标层 社会秩序案件	C1 项 指标层 死亡人数	C2 项 指标层 经济损失	D 项 指标层 道路交通	E1 项 指标层 各类事故死亡人数	E2 项 指标层 事故起数	F 项 指标层 自然灾害
3.572	7.5	7.408	4.168	4.76						
	11.252		4.168	4.76						
	3.752									
	15									
	7.5									
	7.5									

由此得到层次分析法后，对图 3 ~ 图 6 各个图的加权分层图如下：

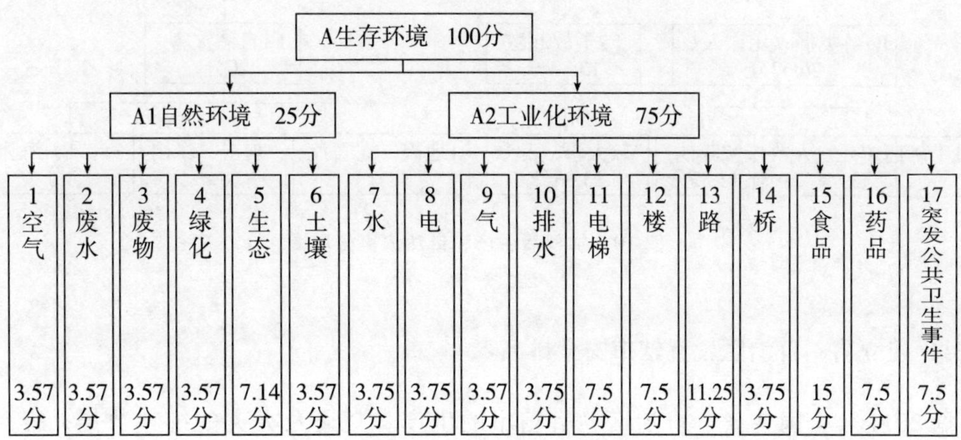

图 7 加权后生存环境分层图

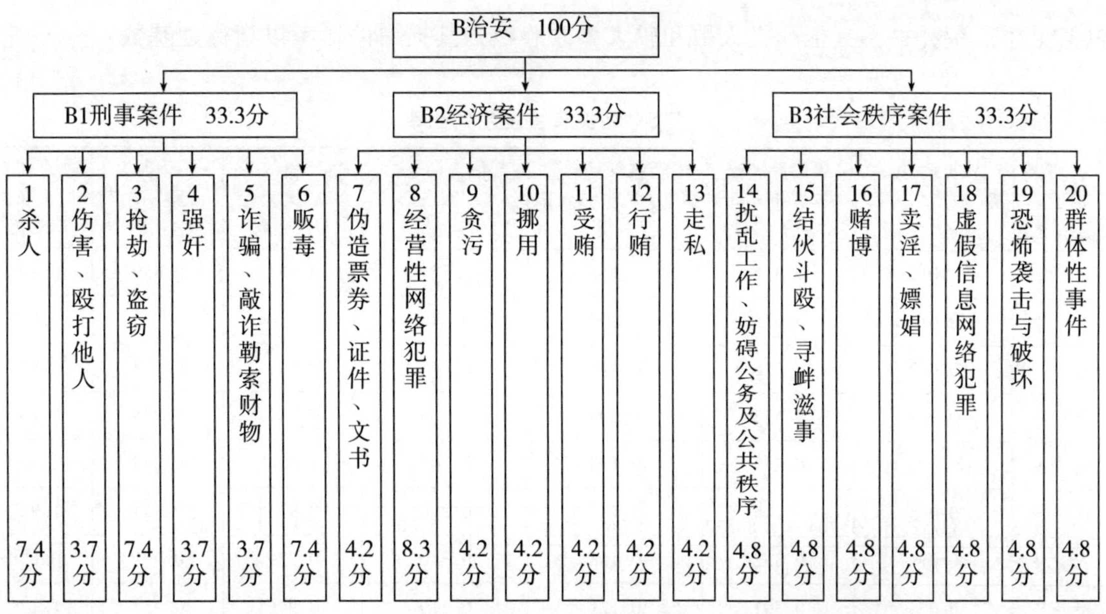

图 8 加权后治安分层图

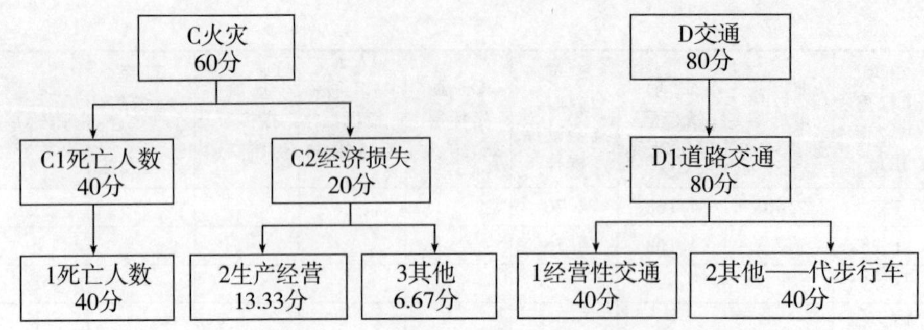

图9 加权后火灾及交通分层图

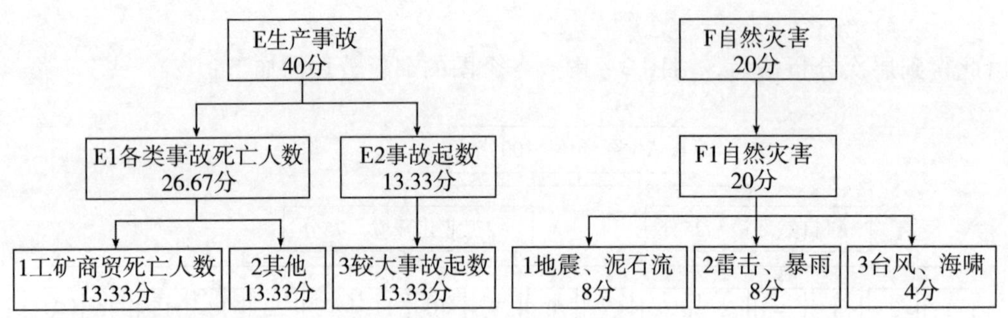

图10 加权后生产和自然灾害分层图

（四）建立省、自治区、直辖市安全排名表

根据2011年全国各省、自治区、直辖市的生产、交通及火灾的统计数据，得到如表5所示的各类灾害发生的比率。其中，火灾包括火灾死亡人数及火灾经济损失，交通事故包括生产性及其他交通死亡人数，其损失的比率以各省市的总人口或总GDP为基数，生产事故包括工矿商贸死亡、其他死亡人数和较大事故起数，其损失的比率以指标为基数。

表5 各类灾害发生的比率

省、自治区、直辖市	火灾死亡人数/城市总人口（万分之一）	火灾经济损失/城市GDP（万分之一）	生产性交通死亡人数/城市总人口（万分之一）	其他交通死亡人数/城市总人口（万分之一）	生产事故工矿商贸死亡人数指标	生产事故其他死亡人数指标	生产事故较大事故起数指标
北 京	0.015	0.310	0.107	0.351	0.644	0.889	0.792
天 津	0.013	0.075	0.294	0.376	0.900	0.943	0.800
河 北	0.002	0.275	0.140	0.220	0.997	0.977	0.800
山 西	0.004	0.413	0.309	0.333	0.551	0.945	0.800
内蒙古	0.020	0.433	0.170	0.342	1.074	0.925	0.959
辽 宁	0.008	0.725	0.183	0.294	0.975	0.984	1.222
吉 林	0.011	0.352	0.168	0.350	0.739	0.991	0.938
黑龙江	0.004	0.301	0.121	0.219	0.946	0.937	1.123

续表 5

省、自治区、直辖市	火灾死亡人数/城市总人口（万分之一）	火灾经济损失/城市 GDP（万分之一）	生产性交通死亡人数/城市总人口（万分之一）	其他交通死亡人数/城市总人口（万分之一）	生产事故工矿商贸死亡人数指标	生产事故其他死亡人数指标	生产事故较大事故起数指标
上　海	0.018	0.573	0.115	0.287	0.832	0.941	0.688
江　苏	0.009	0.219	0.212	0.408	0.979	0.989	0.769
浙　江	0.016	0.188	0.316	0.642	0.980	1.001	1.058
安　徽	0.006	0.411	0.213	0.249	0.958	0.976	1.031
福　建	0.012	0.397	0.252	0.468	0.894	0.963	0.983
江　西	0.006	0.717	0.156	0.180	0.950	0.943	0.973
山　东	0.002	0.171	0.148	0.264	1.129	0.936	1.140
河　南	0.002	0.130	0.074	0.104	0.573	0.920	1.071
湖　北	0.008	0.320	0.149	0.183	0.949	1.011	0.786
湖　南	0.007	0.379	0.121	0.188	0.881	0.953	0.780
广　东	0.012	0.406	0.189	0.370	0.991	0.956	0.896
广　西	0.010	0.495	0.181	0.311	0.960	0.990	1.038
海　南	0.007	0.565	0.166	0.373	0.913	0.973	0.800
四　川	0.005	0.485	0.119	0.229	0.864	0.964	1.083
贵　州	0.016	1.162	0.115	0.179	0.844	0.891	1.152
云　南	0.011	0.828	0.142	0.248	1.106	0.974	0.959
西　藏	0.033	0.875	0.888	0.158	0.667	0.742	1.067
重　庆	0.016	0.434	0.139	0.199	0.994	0.979	1.000
陕　西	0.006	0.753	0.221	0.285	0.984	0.978	1.310
甘　肃	0.002	1.075	0.257	0.330	0.934	1.003	0.914
青　海	0.011	3.618	0.440	0.544	1.000	0.983	1.158
宁　夏	0.002	0.113	0.288	0.382	0.922	0.958	1.167
新　疆	0.015	0.783	0.340	0.562	0.997	0.977	1.145

根据2011年全国各省、自治区、直辖市的交通及火灾的统计数据，结合以上由层次分析法得到的权重，得出如表6的区域安全风险排名，以权重最大为最不安全。

表6　2011年各地安全风险排名表

不安全排名	省、自治区、直辖市	权重（以400为总分）
1	青　海	154.0357453
2	新　疆	93.94600137
3	西　藏	92.78288517
4	浙　江	83.25410388

续表 6

不安全排名	省、自治区、直辖市	权重(以 400 为总分)
5	甘　肃	83.07127101
6	陕　西	79.15237037
7	辽　宁	76.29888377
8	福　建	75.09518674
9	云　南	74.57805322
10	贵　州	71.5412585
11	广　西	69.82584191
12	宁　夏	69.74402516
13	内蒙古	69.38112106
14	海　南	68.95235697
15	广　东	68.89243637
16	安　徽	66.47315011
17	江　西	66.23516691
18	江　苏	66.05594039
19	山　西	64.71944409
20	天　津	64.03494771
21	吉　林	63.7901432
22	四　川	63.58278407
23	重　庆	63.56164341
24	山　东	62.7349456
25	上　海	61.09619557
26	黑龙江	59.84820721
27	河　北	56.93703432
28	湖　北	56.58978115
29	北　京	56.09159108
30	湖　南	55.06871084
31	河　南	43.97207257

由排名可见，西部地区由于天气干燥、现代化发展进程较慢，导致在火灾、交通以及生产事故风险相对较大，西部有 7 个省（自治区）风险得分排在全国前十，有 4 个省（自治区）排在全国前五，可见这些地区风险之大。

2012 年全国各省、自治区、直辖市有关统计数据，在 2013 年第四季度已公布。同理，按上述方法可得到如表 7 的各类灾害发生的比率。

表7　各类灾害发生的比率

省、自治区、直辖市	火灾死亡人数/城市总人口(万分之一)	火灾经济损失/城市GDP(万分之一)	生产性交通死亡人数/城市总人口(万分之一)	生产事故工矿商贸死亡人数指标	生产事故其他死亡人数指标	生产事故较大事故起数指标
北　京	0.014498	0.165996	0.136761224	0.6875	0.964582357	0.739
天　津	0.029013	0.367826	0.236351414	0.9474	0.966785409	0.696
河　北	0.002196	0.342939	0.132281122	0.9293	1.002056926	0.938
山　西	0.003323	0.504085	0.283868252	0.8537	0.987576395	0.877
内蒙古	0.013655	0.637968	0.165471816	0.9898	0.922183038	0.708
辽　宁	0.007063	0.223964	0.16404648	0.9646	0.977156166	0.54
吉　林	0.001091	0.227695	0.150887144	0.9709	0.9743548	0.742
黑龙江	0.004695	0.395688	0.09989567	0.8740	0.944679361	0.782
上　海	0.016384	0.343083	0.107123503	0.9118	0.978512215	0.846
江　苏	0.00947	0.220061	0.204040919	0.9770	0.994277511	0.8
浙　江	0.015702	0.188814	0.274420303	0.9200	0.970400179	0.6
安　徽	0.005845	0.419526	0.19238477	0.8957	0.992250205	0.8
福　建	0.011473	0.410435	0.223052295	0.9269	0.944284739	0.864
江　西	0.006439	0.564728	0.130996646	0.8780	0.927667849	0.873
山　东	0.002065	0.175154	0.142385573	0.7831	0.965139302	0.909
河　南	0.002445	0.18469	0.068466936	0.7345	0.99819439	1.114
湖　北	0.002769	0.239442	0.124589029	0.9954	0.95728858	1
湖　南	0.006778	0.76473	0.109957478	0.6964	0.983071054	0.76
广　东	0.012365	0.383201	0.164243912	0.9827	0.961303689	0.939
广　西	0.009611	0.384462	0.157197779	0.9892	0.982035651	0.988
海　南	0.006768	0.649719	0.13874006	0.9342	0.973352396	0.813
四　川	0.004705	0.537888	0.112552933	0.8725	0.984268507	0.966
贵　州	0.008898	0.751175	0.090985543	0.5286	0.908833542	0.67
云　南	0.010947	0.436104	0.133290406	0.9429	0.992255072	0.889
西　藏	0.019505	0.872145	0.386840908	0.2222	0.766773193	1.5
重　庆	0.016299	0.225862	0.133106961	0.8592	0.978540367	0.694
陕　西	0.007727	1.118947	0.181716932	0.8481	0.974719393	1
甘　肃	0.003104	0.776043	0.196698415	0.9949	0.973560171	1.091
青　海	0.008723	0.757153	0.338468517	0.9518	0.949747855	0.905
宁　夏	0.001545	0.208048	0.270399728	0.8941	0.948983092	0.778
新　疆	0.01478	1.277269	0.300522219	0.9248	0.997487917	0.967

2012年排序，其中生产性交通死亡人数权重加倍。根据2012年全国各省、自治区、直

辖市的交通及火灾的统计数据，结合以上由层次分析法得到的权重，得出如表 8 所示的地区安全风险排名，以权重最大为最不安全。

表8 2012 年各地安全风险排名表

不安全排名	省、自治区、直辖市	权重(以 400 为总分)
1	新疆	88.70268
2	西藏	82.35697
3	青海	79.99022
4	陕西	74.86298
5	甘肃	72.17365
6	山西	69.16723
7	福建	62.98147
8	天津	62.22721
9	内蒙古	61.47591
10	宁夏	60.80275
11	海南	60.63848
12	广西	60.10584
13	安徽	59.85473
14	广东	59.73855
15	浙江	59.56332
16	江苏	58.05419
17	江西	57.74807
18	四川	57.58664
19	云南	57.47887
20	湖南	56.88899
21	河北	55.78756
22	湖北	54.2355
23	上海	52.57057
24	吉林	52.49896
25	辽宁	50.97562
26	黑龙江	50.76872
27	贵州	50.75698
28	山东	50.40572
29	重庆	49.57408
30	河南	47.2255
31	北京	46.72181

比对2011年与2012年排序表，可见全国各省、自治区、直辖市的安全风险排序名次有所变化，即处于动态平衡中，这是遵循科学发展观精神，也符合事物发展规律（见表9）。

表9　2011年和2012年风险排序变化表

排序	省、自治区、直辖市	2012年	2011年	排序变化
1	新　疆	1	2	-1
2	西　藏	2	3	-1
3	青　海	3	1	+2
4	陕　西	4	6	-2
5	甘　肃	5	5	0
6	山　西	6	19	-13
7	福　建	7	8	-1
8	天　津	8	20	-12
9	内蒙古	9	13	-4
10	宁　夏	10	12	-2
11	海　南	11	14	-3
12	广　西	12	11	+1
13	安　徽	13	16	-3
14	广　东	14	15	-1
15	浙　江	15	4	+11
16	江　苏	16	18	-2
17	江　西	17	17	0
18	四　川	18	22	-4
19	云　南	19	9	+10
20	湖　南	20	30	-10
21	河　北	21	27	-26
22	湖　北	22	28	-6
23	上　海	23	25	-2
24	吉　林	24	21	+3
25	辽　宁	25	7	+18
26	黑龙江	26	26	0
27	贵　州	27	10	+17
28	山　东	28	24	+4
29	重　庆	29	23	+6
30	河　南	30	31	-1
31	北　京	31	29	+2

（五）结语

目前有关全国及各省、自治区、直辖市的统计年鉴中，有关数据都是上一个年份的，即2012年的统计年鉴公布2011年的有关数据，2013年的统计年鉴公布2012年的有关数据。由于各省、自治区、直辖市安全统计的相关数据相当匮乏，严重地限制了城乡灾害风险评估的准确性和可操作性。我们拟订的一级指标六大类中仅有两大类指标齐全，一大类指标基本齐全。其他三大类指标大多缺失或参差不齐。当然，我们不能因数据匮乏就望而却步，这些指标是早晚要健全的，因此，我们就指标基本齐全的三大类先行纳入，其他三大类指标待逐步齐全后再分步纳入。

在其他三大类指标中，我们计划只要有半数以上的省、自治区、直辖市公布其中某一大类指标，就将其纳入总体指标体系进行评价，对缺失的省市指标项，且按最低指标值植入，这也是为了促进缺失指标的省市尽早公布，一旦有补充指标值，我们一定予以修正。

本项课题具有创新性，科学评价各省、自治区、直辖市的公共安全状况，通过比较鉴别，既促进政府工作，又提高民众公共安全意识。当然，我们的评价指标体系还处于动态改进中，在实践运行的过程中，须不断修订和完善，以期达到科学性与可操作性更强的中长期目标。

值得强调的是，本课题专家组是由上海防灾安全策略研究中心组织的。中心主任王瑚作为本课题策划人，最早提出创意，并由其出资委托花铁森组织实施，历经两年时间才得出目前的成果。林贤光和廖光煊两位教授作为国家公共安全领域的资深专家，为本课题的完善做出了重要贡献。吴凡副教授作为“海归”专家，在权重分类和计算公式上起了关键性作用。王松盛、严伟康、陆培德3位高级工程师，在制定框架、查阅提供资料和分析研究、深入讨论的每一个环节中，都付出了大量的心血。韩新博士作为上海同济大学社会防灾安全专家，也对本课题提出了宝贵的意见。肖修昆博士对全文进行了修饰，并提出了重要的修改意见，这些意见将作为今后进一步提高完善的基础。而王涛作为专家组秘书，帮助查阅整理资料等，也付出了许多辛劳。还需要指出的是，上海防灾安全策略研究中心理事长柳晓川和常务副理事长陈彪等领导同志也一直关注和支持课题组的工作进展，多次在中心理事会上对本课题作出指示。因此，本课题研究所取得的初步成果与领导的支持是分不开的。对于上述参与、参加和关注支持本课题的领导、专家和骨干人员，在此一并表示谢意！

（主要作者：王瑚，上海防灾安全策略研究中心主任；林贤光，清华大学建筑工程学院教授；花铁森，上海防灾安全策略研究中心高级工程师；廖光煊，原中科大国家火灾重点实验室执行主任；吴凡，上海交通大学经济管理学院副教授；肖修昆，广州中科院工业技术研究院研究室执行主任，博士；王松盛，上海石化消防工程有限公司高级工程师）

附：我国省级公共安全综合评价体系课题专家组名单

序号	姓名	单　位	职　务	责　任
1	王　瑚	上海防灾安全策略研究中心	主　任	本课题策划人、课题审核
2	林贤光	清华大学建筑工程学院建筑自动化专业、 民政部老专家委员会	教　授 副主任	专家组荣誉组长、成果审定
3	花铁森	上海防灾安全策略研究中心 核物理专家、安全报警器专家	理　事 高级工程师	专家组组长 执笔、成果审定
4	廖光煊	原中科大国家火灾重点实验室 中科大苏州城市公共安全重点实验室	执行主任、博导	专家组副组长 课题审定
5	吴　凡	上海交通大学经济管理学院	副教授	权重公式计算 评估坐标设计
6	肖修昆	广州中科院工业技术研究院	研究室执行主任、博士	课题审定
7	王松盛	上海石化消防工程有限公司	高级工程师	统计专家、资料查询
8	严伟康	上海华钟咨询服务有限公司	高级工程师	统计咨询、查询、一校
9	陆培德	中科院上海技术物理研究所	高级工程师	查询、二校
10	韩　新	同济大学防灾减灾研究所副所长	顾　问	三校意见修改
11	王　涛	上海防灾安全策略研究中心	办公室副主任	资料整理查询

参考文献

[1] 花铁森，吴凡，王松盛，严伟康，陆培德，著．中国各省（直辖市）公共安全评价体系初探［J］．防灾与安全·建筑机电工程，2013（5）：23.

[2] 刘爱华，欧阳建涛．城市安全评价体系基本框架的构建研究［C］．International Conference Management Science and Engineering，2010.

[3] 郭金玉，张忠彬，孙庆云．层次分析法的研究与应用［J］．中国安全科学学报，2008，18（5）：148－153.

[4] 高小平．中国特色应急管理体系建设的成就和发展［J］．中国行政管理，2008（11）．

比较视角下的中国公立医院管理效率研究

一、引言

基于经济发展的视角，2014 年注定是划时代的一年。根据世界银行以及国际货币基金组织等权威研究报告，按照购买力平价（Purchasing Power Parity）计算，2014 将是美国称雄全球经济长达一个世纪的最后一年，中国经济总量取而代之。尽管中美两国的人均收入水平还有近半个世纪的落差，中国步入中等收入国家的行列已是不争的事实。对于中国而言，当下最急迫的任务是如何转变经济发展方式，应对 30 多年后发优势的高速增长之后必然回归的“新常态”，关键挑战在于是否能够实现向内需经济的有效转型。

比较中国当前和其他发达经济体的结构不难发现，中国实现内需导向的经济转型具有相当巨大的潜力，其中包括至关重要的两点。第一，发达国家的现代服务业对宏观经济的贡献高达 70%，全球平均在 60% 之上，中国当前仅在 40% 上下。根据美国芝加哥大学诺贝尔经济学家罗伯特·福格尔（Robert Fogel）对欧美人群长达百年的消费行为研究，医疗服务的收入消费弹性高达 1.6，高居人们吃穿用住的常规消费之首。第二，各国从中等收入迈向高收入的发展路径必然伴随社会保障制度的完善，其中医疗保障是其增长最快、持续最长的组成部分。目前，经济合作与发展组织（OECD）国家的医疗服务占 GDP 的平均比重为 10%，美国则高达 19%。大多经济学家更进一步预测，长期而言，伴随人类收入水平的持续增长与期望寿命的不断提高，医疗服务将不可避免地成为未来全球经济的主导产业。因此，中国如果能够判断明确，抓住目前的优势机遇，因势利导，以医疗健康服务为龙头，大举推进新兴现代服务业的发展，必将助推实现转变经济增长方式与完善医疗保障制度的双重目标。

由于长期计划经济的历史原因，中国现行医疗服务体系基本以医院为中心，自上而下进行人财物的资源配置和服务安排，导致了长期的大医院拥堵不堪、社区诊所门可罗雀的状况。因此，近期的国家医改把公立医院改革作为重中之重的目标，并积极推进了包括多元化办医、医生多点执业、促进社区服务平台等措施。尽管如此，由于中国医疗卫生资源长期集中在大型公立医院，卫生资源浪费、医师资源配置扭曲、医疗质量与医院效率低下等众多问题非常严重（Yip 等，2012），积重难返，公立医院改革和管理水平的提高必须同步进行，并且是改革和发展要长期面临的重点和难点，关乎中国医疗改革的成败。

为提高医院运行效率，提升医疗服务质量，有必要建立现代医院管理制度，全面、持续地提高医院“软实力”，即管理水平。而现代医院管理制度的建立和完善，需要依托对中国医院管理的深入了解，进而针对其存在的漏洞与不足进行个性化改善。现行的中国医院评审制度和国际 JCI[①] 认证体系，均旨在直接评价医院的服务质量与绩效水平等结果指标，对于医院管理水平的评价目前仍是空白。除此之外，现有的医院评审制度和认证体系都是基于双方知情、督导评估等干预条件下开展的评审调查，这在相当程度上难以反映自然状态下医院的真实行为与管理水平。

2013 年 11 月，由北京大学牵头，联合清华大学、斯坦福大学、伦敦政治经济学院等多家研究机构启动的《全球医院管理研究——中国部分》，基于现代管理学的理论基础，采用《全球管理调查》（World Management Survey，WMS）[②] 针对机构调查的双盲访谈方法，从标准化运营、绩效监督、目标管理、员工激励四个维度，对自然状态下中国医院的管理水平进行科学、客观、准确地衡量，同时对中国医院管理水平进行全球范围内的系统定位与比较分析，进而为公立医院改革、现代医院管理制度的建立提供科学、实证依据。

二、国内外医院管理研究综述

由于世界各国医疗费用的不断增长，医疗服务效率的提升成为关注的焦点。面对日益增长的医疗服务需求以及更加激烈的市场竞争，医疗机构试图通过优化其内部管理来提高效率，如精益管理、平衡计分卡、六西格玛等。多个实证研究发现，改善医院管理可以成为提高医疗机构的运行效率、生产力、绩效等的一种有效手段（Bloom 等，2010；Mazzocato 等，2010；Kaplan 等，2011）。Shortell 等（1994）发现在 ICU 部门中，专业化分工、员工之间沟通的增加会显著降低住院时间，减少护士流动率，提高医疗服务质量。Bradley 等（2012）研究发现，在心内科，定期复审急性心肌梗死病例，鼓励医生进行创新，保证医生随时在岗等管理策略，可以显著降低死亡率。2010 年，Bloom 等首次应用 WMS 调查工具，对美国 147 家医院与英国 100 家医院进行调查，发现管理水平与急性心肌梗死死亡率、等待时间、患者满意度、财务收入显著相关。

国内学者的研究多数关注医疗服务质量管理和医院绩效管理。研究通过分析医疗质量标准化管理的方式，提出各种标准在中国的适用性。国际上质量标准主要有 ISO 标准、JCI 标准、英国 NICE 标准等，这些标准运用流程管理思想和 PDCA 循环[③]，促进医院持续提高医

---

① JCI 是国际医疗卫生机构认证联合委员会（Joint Commission on Accreditation of Healthcare Organizations，简称 JCAHO）用于对美国以外的医疗机构进行认证的附属机构。目前 JCI 已经给世界 40 多个国家的公立、私立医疗卫生机构和政府部门进行了指导和评审，13 个国家（包括中国）的 78 个医疗机构通过了国际 JCI 认证。

② http：//worldmanagementsurvey. org.

③ PDCA 的含义如下：P（Plan）——计划；D（Design）——设计（原为 Do，执行）；C（Check）——检查；A（Act）——修正，对总结检查的结果进行处理，成功的经验加以肯定并适当推广、标准化；失败的教训加以总结，未解决的问题放到下一个 PDCA 循环里。

疗服务质量（孙丁，李幼平，2006；鲍玉荣，李林，2013）。同时，很多学者积极探索构建医院绩效评价指标体系，但是评价标准和评价方法不一，侧重点不同，主要包括组织维度、资源配置、医疗服务质量、财务经营、患者费用及满意度等几个维度（李国红，胡善联，2002；姚岚，金新政等，2004）。然而，关于医院管理水平与医院绩效之间关系的研究相对较少，主要是对医院管理质量的描述性分析，鲜有研究通过计量经济学的方法全面、系统、科学地分析医院管理水平与医院绩效的相关关系。

三、《全球医院管理研究——中国部分》

（一）理论与方法

2003 年，斯坦福大学的尼古拉斯·布鲁姆（Nicholas Bloom）教授和伦敦政治经济学院的约翰·范雷南（John Van Reenen）教授总结了麦肯锡的实务管理经验——机构的核心运营管理措施是监督、目标设定与员工激励，认为这三者是机构的最佳实践（Bloom 等，2007，2010，2012）。由于产业性质不同，最佳实践的具体形式会有不同，但其核心精神——监督、目标与激励是不变的。在此基础上，两人提出了一种新的定量方法，即《全球管理调查》（World Management Survey，WMS），旨在通过一种跨国、跨产业通用的调查问卷来定量衡量机构的管理水平。《全球医院管理研究——中国部分》对 WMS 问卷进行汉化，形成针对中国医院的调查问卷，包含 21 个管理实践，涉及管理的四个维度：标准化运营、绩效管理、目标管理、人才管理（见图 1）。

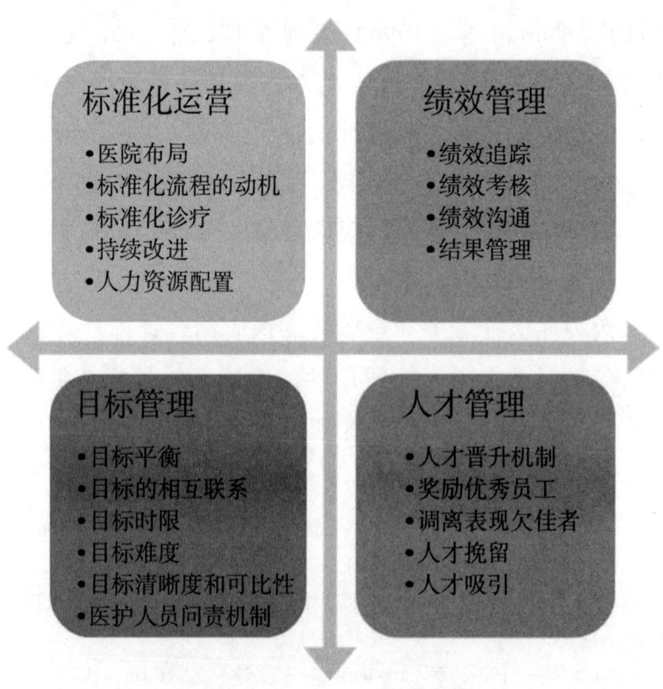

图 1 《全球医院管理研究——中国部分》四个管理维度

WMS 采用双盲访谈法[①]，对受访机构的中层管理人员进行电话访谈，每个管理实践通过 3～5 个开放式问题收集信息。问卷在量化管理水平时，通过检验一个组织在多大程度上切实执行了这些措施，对每个管理实践给予评分（1～5 分），1 分最低，5 分最高。采访过程中，由两名采访者根据受访者的回答进行独立评分，确保评分客观、公平、可信。WMS 针对医疗机构的特点，在通用问卷的基础上，开发了适用于测量医疗机构管理水平的问卷，并已在美国、英国、法国、德国、加拿大、意大利、瑞典、印度、巴西 9 个国家的 2000 多家医院完成调研。

（二）中国部分研究概况

2013 年 11 月，由北京大学牵头，协同清华大学、斯坦福大学、伦敦政治经济学院联合推动开展《全球医院管理研究——中国部分》的研究。采用 WMS 提出的管理实践访谈指南，结合中国医院的实际情况，开发了一套针对中国医院的调查问卷，通过双盲、电话访谈的形式，了解中国医院管理的现状。

2014 年 1 月，课题组完成了对全国 12 个省（黑龙江、吉林、辽宁、山东、江苏、福建、广东、河北、陕西、贵州、甘肃、青海）和 2 个直辖市（北京、重庆）共 20 家三级甲等公立综合医院的预调研工作，共采访了 39 名医护人员。受访者主要是医院心内科、骨科的主任、医生及护士，也有少数来自神经科、内分泌科等，其中包括 20 名医生，19 名护士（如图 2 所示），在医院的平均工作时间为 13.9 年。

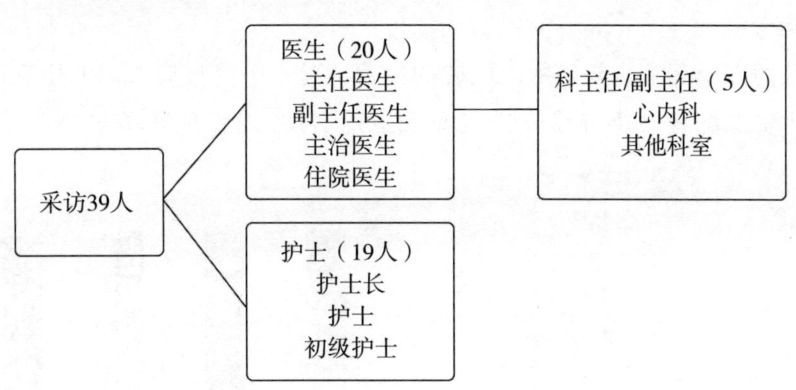

图 2　预调研访谈对象职称及职位分布

（三）医院管理水平评分

2014 年 10 月开始进行全国调研工作，计划覆盖全国 31 个省、自治区、直辖市的 400 家代表性医院。目前访谈数据还在陆续收集中，本文仅报告预调研的主要结果。

---

① “双盲”此处指采访者在采访前并不了解受访者的相关信息（例如：职位、业绩、所在医院），因此，可消除对受访者先入为主的观念；同时，受访者也不知晓采访者的容貌、背景、问卷内容以及评分，仅被告知采访用于学习了解医院管理的相关情况，可避免受访者由于各种原因而改变回答的内容和语气。

中国大型公立医院的管理总平均分为 2.86 分，标准化运营分数最高，人才管理分数最低（见图 3）。与其他国家同类医院的管理水平比较发现，中国医院管理的平均得分高于其他很多 OECD 国家且仅次于美国（见图 4）。由于预调研的 20 家医院均为公立医院分级体系中最高的三级甲等医院，结果可能在一定程度上高估了中国整体的医院管理水平。

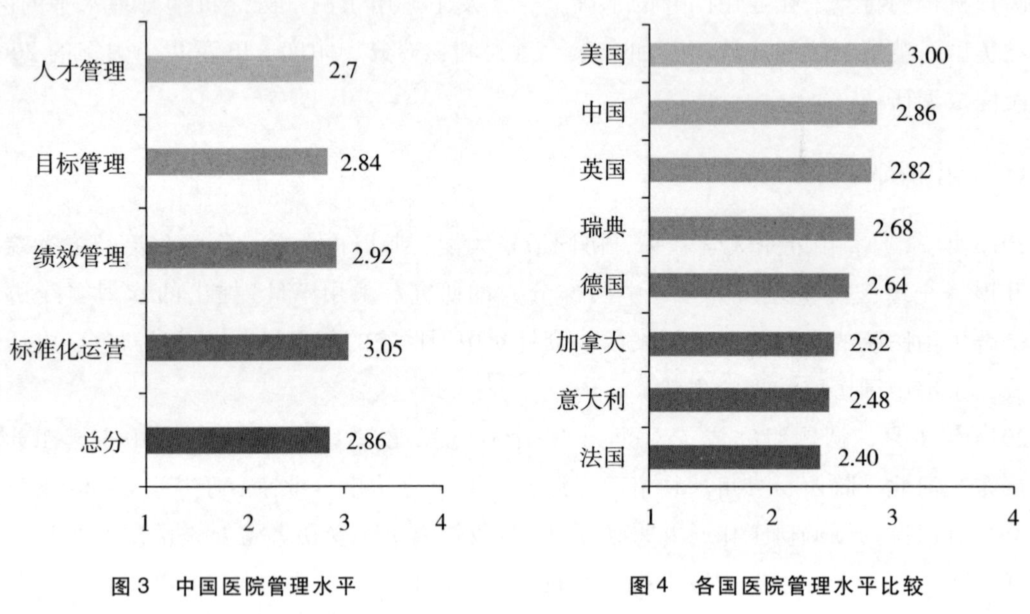

图 3　中国医院管理水平

图 4　各国医院管理水平比较

1. 标准化运营

从管理实践的五个环节来衡量中国医院的运营情况：医院布局、标准化流程的动机、标准化诊疗、人力资源配置以及持续改进（见图 5）。各常规管理环节详情汇总如下（见图 6）。

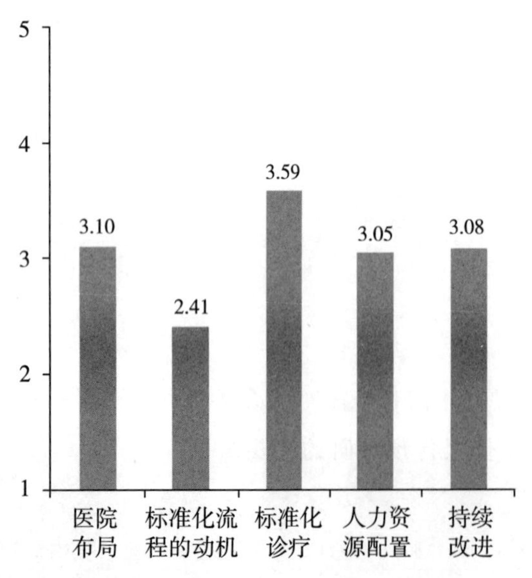

图 5　标准化运营各管理实践水平

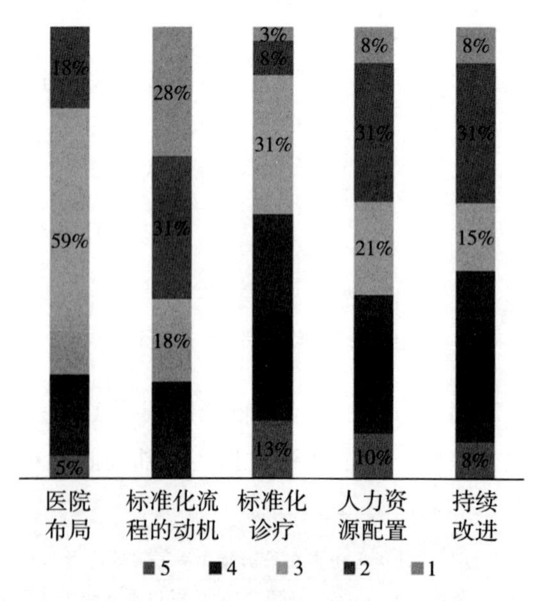

图 6　标准化运营各管理实践水平分布

（1）医院布局：半数以上（59%）的医院取得了3分的平均分。说明医院整体布局基本能够方便患者就诊，这可能因为在中国医院等级评定方面，已经有多项布局相关的要求，医院必须满足这些要求才能被评为三级。然而，医院一般不会超越卫生与计划生育委员会的相应规定，定期检查和及时调整工作场所的布局并非常态。

（2）标准化流程的动机：这是得分最低的一个管理实践。多数受访者表示临床路径是由卫生和计划生育委员会自上而下强制要求的，且只提供给符合特定要求的患者。医院在这方面的自主性不强，积极性不高，而且权力不足，许多医院都没有广泛施行临床路径管理。

（3）标准化诊疗：这一管理实践得分最高，89%的医院得分在平均水平以上。说明中国医院相当重视标准化以及临床操作的监督工作，各家医院的标准化操作规程一般会通过网页、公告板或印刷手册的方式公告给医院职工。然而，监督工作仅局限于检查患者病历记录和病房巡查，监督检查的职责仅限于科室主任和护士长。许多管理者都表示自己基本不清楚是否所有医护人员都能遵守操作规程。

（4）人力资源配置：此项评分差异较大，41%的医院得分在平均水平以上，39%的医院则低于平均水准。部分医院已经制定有效的人力资源配置体系，有的则没有制定相应的规程。由于专业上的划分，医生一般不能在科室之间调动。医院在很大程度上只能依赖于护士之间的工作协调，而且还要考虑人员的专业、能力和个人性格。得分较高的医院掌握有机动性应急护士小组，可以从欠繁忙区域调派到繁忙区域。

（5）持续改进：此项评分差异较大，46%的医院得分在平均水平以上，39%的医院则低于平均水准。得分差异在于，医院是否制定常规章程让医院职工及时发现和解决问题、及时在问题出现前进行妥善处理。得分较高的医院中，科室主任每月会和医生定期召开质量改善会议，并探讨有关问题及解决办法。大部分医院都要求护士长一天监督并检查护士工作至少3次，主要为核对患者病历记录和病房巡查。得分较高的医院中，患者会填写满意度调查表或在出院后收到电话回访。

2. 绩效管理

从管理实践的四个环节来衡量中国医院的绩效管理：绩效追踪、绩效考核、绩效沟通和结果管理（见图7）。各常规管理环节详情汇总如下（见图8）。

（1）绩效追踪：这一管理实践得分最高，超过85%的医院评分高于平均水准。由于卫生与计划生育委员会规定医院报告特定的绩效和质量指标，医院都会设立单独的信息或医疗服务部门监督数据收集，每月记录门诊数量、手术数量、平均住院时长、病床周转率、院内感染率等。得分较高的医院绩效指标达成情况会通过多种途径传达给员工，包括非正式会议、公告板通知或网页公告等。

（2）绩效考核：这一管理实践得分最低，半数以上（54%）的医院得分低于平均水准。多数医院缺乏针对绩效指标的定期考核会议，基本上只关注达成或者未达成，从而与科室和个人奖金挂钩，不会制订正式的、结构化的后续改进计划以促进绩效和质量的提升。

（3）绩效沟通：26%的医院得到最低的1分管理评分，而另外28%的医院则得到3分的平均分。这种得分上的差距主要是因为医院制度性地举行了各类评估会议或者根本没有举行过评估会议，不会使用根因分析方法寻找根本原因，并制订持续改进计划。

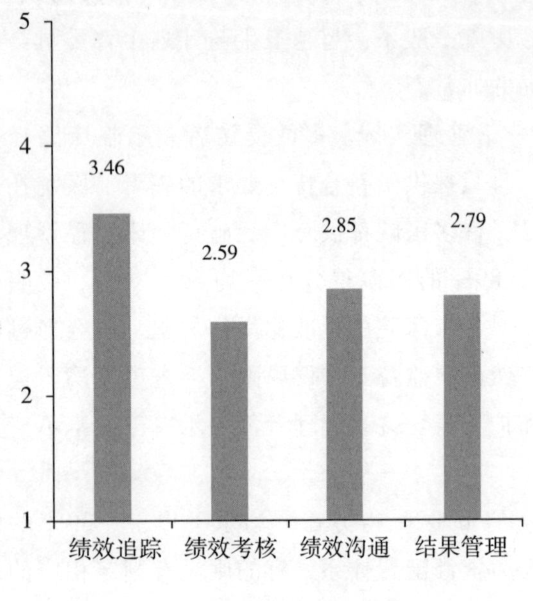

图7 绩效管理各管理实践水平

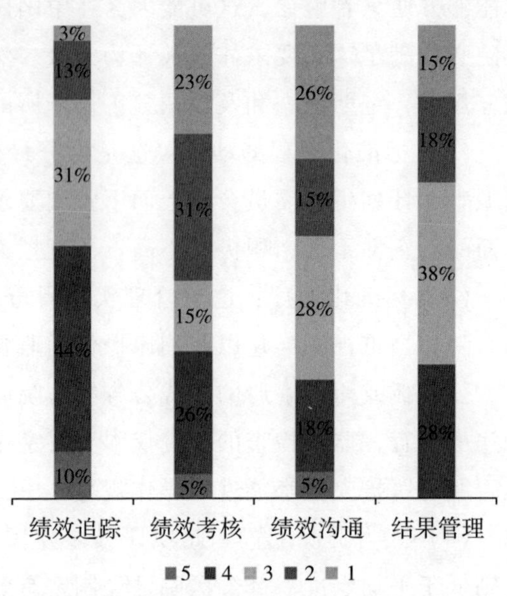

图8 绩效管理各管理实践水平分布

（4）结果管理：66%的医院得分在平均水平及以上。得分较高的医院设立有单独的医疗服务部门来监督整改计划的执行情况，并通过移动资源或培训等手段协助科室按计划执行。

3. 目标管理

从管理实践的六个环节来衡量中国医院的目标管理：目标平衡、目标的相互联系、目标时限、目标难度、目标清晰度和可比性以及医护人员问责机制（见图9）。各常规管理环节详情汇总如下（见图10）。

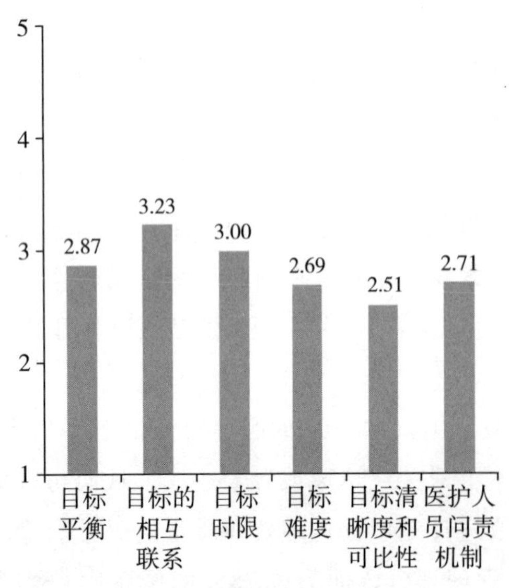

图9 目标管理各管理实践水平

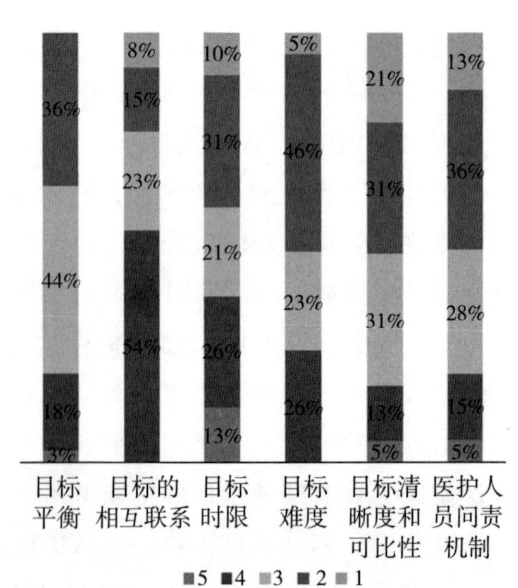

图10 目标管理各管理实践水平分布

（1）目标平衡：44%的医院都有较为均衡的目标，包括运营、财务、质量和满意度，评分为3分。评分较低的医院没有财务平衡或成本控制目标，只专注于医疗质量和科研目标，且目标设定通常旨在满足卫生和计划生育委员会的要求。

（2）目标的相互联系：半数以上（54%）的医院得分高于平均水准。医院目标由高层管理者探讨并通过周会形式下达给科室主任，再通过非正式途径下达到具体的医院职工。科室主任通常会向医生分配个人任务而不会明确传达医院目标，许多医生都表示自己不太清楚医院的目标，只了解自己个人的任务。

（3）目标时限：60%的医院得分在3分及以上，说明多数医院设定有长期与短期目标，但是都单独设定。短期目标（≤1年）仅限于满足卫生部的报告要求、完成临床任务、提高质量和科研目的。长期目标（3~5年）多为吸引人才、提高声誉或满足等级评定目标。

（4）目标难度：半数（51%）医院得分低于平均水准。医生在目标达成上存在挫折感，表示绝大多数目标都很难达成，而且在制定目标时根本没有有效征求医护人员意见的途径，医护人员只是被动地接受并努力达成这些目标。

（5）目标清晰度和可比性：近半数（49%）的医院得分低于平均水准，因为目标的设定没有经过充分沟通，且医护人员很难清楚理解。各科室目标的难度也存在很大差异，有些科室的目标特别容易达成，而有些科室则压力非常大。

（6）医护人员问责机制：半数以上（52%）的医院得分低于平均水准，因为医院只对临床质量有问责机制，医护人员只关注医疗服务的提供和保证医疗质量和患者安全。绝大多数医院没有成本节约要求及医疗费控制目标。而且，医生在实现各自目标时缺乏领导和责任心，只是被动地完成目标。

4. 人才管理

从管理实践的六个环节来衡量中国医院的人才管理：奖励优秀员工、调离表现欠佳员工、提拔优秀员工、人才管理、人才保留以及人才吸引（见图11）。各常规管理环节详情汇总如下（见图12）。

（1）奖励优秀员工：半数以上（61%）的医院在这一环节的得分低于平均水平。医生薪资构成分为基本工资和奖金，虽然有奖励体系，奖金取决于医生在医院中的职务和职称，但通常看重工作量而非工作质量或个人绩效。非奖金奖励包括培训机会和学术研究机会。

（2）调离表现欠佳员工：大多数医院会采取措施把表现欠佳的员工调到不太重要的岗位或者重新接受培训。考虑到卫生和计划生育委员会的评级要求和工作量压力，医院方面实际上不希望解雇医生。况且医生大多数具有编制，都是终身全职员工，解雇一名医生的难度非常大。

（3）提拔优秀员工：41%的医院得分在平均水准，41%的医院则低于平均水准。在绝大多数医院，资历是提拔升迁的基本要求，其次医院委员会才会考虑临床绩效、工作量、学历背景和科研经验。评分较高的医院都有供自我选择的晋升流程，让医生在规定时间内申请晋升，只要医生自认为个人绩效达到要求。

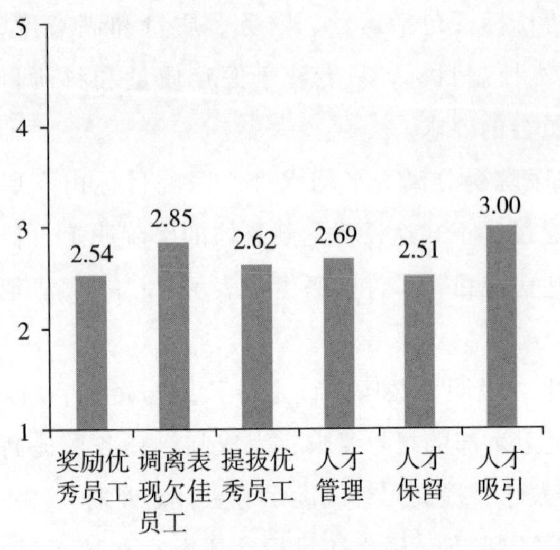

图 11　人才管理各管理实践水平

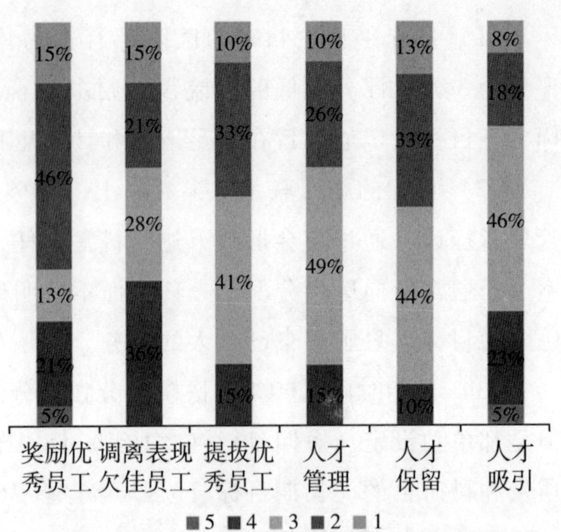

图 12　人才管理各管理实践水平分布

(4) 人才管理：近半数（49%）的医院得分在平均水平。绝大多数医院管理者认识到人才管理的重要性，但却没有手段激励管理者改善人才管理工作。医院管理者并不负责吸引、挽留或发展员工，或者在这一方面没有任何考核评估。

(5) 人才保留：这一管理实践分数最低，评分差异在于医院留住人才的力度。中国医院没有足够的自主权和主动性采取正式有效的方法留住顶尖人才，管理者通常只是通过谈话了解原因，挽留也多数只是一个形式。虽然多数医院都有强有力的财务激励体系来进行绩效管理，但管理者在人力资源管理方面应当获得更多的培训和给予更有力的激励措施。

(6) 人才吸引：46%的医院得分在平均水平。绝大多数医生表示自己的医院并没有独特的优势或价值主张吸引人才加入，与其他同类医院基本一样。因为在中国绝大多数医院只通过等级、声誉和学术影响力就能吸引到顶尖人才，而并不倚重具有竞争力的福利待遇。

(四) 政策建议

根据中国医院管理研究预调研的结果，我们对医院管理提出以下具体建议，希望可以对接下来的公立医院管理及改革提供一定支持。

1. 医院运营管理

医院运营管理的目的是提高医院流程的效率，尽量消除浪费，增加提升价值的活动比例，而价值则应以患者获得的服务来衡量。随着精益管理在医院中的应用，如何真正从患者的需求出发，提供高效的服务流程成为医院运营管理的重点。医院管理者应当根据患者需求及医院实际情况来调整医院布局、就诊流程及人力配置。在医院布局过程中应从方便患者就诊及医务人员工作两方面考虑，尽量避免移动、运输及时间浪费；流程管理避免过程及库存浪费，而标准化诊疗的建立可以减少过度生产浪费和重复工作浪费，同时合理的人力配置可以最大可能减少人力及重复工作浪费。另外，医院布局应当根据患者的要求而非政府要求来进行优化，医院管理者应当掌握更多样的手段，以便独立监督并定期改善经营状况。

2. 更加重视绩效及人才管理

随着医疗市场的竞争日趋激烈，医院间的竞争实质上就是医疗技术和服务的竞争，归根结底就是医疗技术人才的竞争。要想使医院在竞争中始终立于不败，能够为就医者提供安全、优质、满意的服务，就要求医院必须以人为本，重视人才的开发、引进与管理。薪酬绩效考核制度作为人才管理的一个重要组成部分，需要得到更多的重视。在奖励机制中，个人绩效表现占比应该高于职务和资历。奖金结构应该更好地体现医生的个人绩效，且应当根据个人绩效指标来设置奖金。同时，医院应当鼓励医院管理者更有效地管理表现相对优秀的医生。另外，管理者应当采用更多的手段来发展和培养优秀人才，为其提供职业发展机会。医院应当提供除医院等级和声誉之外的更多竞争优势，独特的员工价值理念才是医院构建人才库的关键所在。

3. 给予科室更大的自主权

科室是构成医院的基础和功能单位，各科室管理水平直接决定了医院管理水平。科室的医疗质量、人才培养、社会经济效益在一定程度上取决于科主任的管理水平。科主任既是学科带头人，集技术与管理工作于一身，同时又对提高全科医务人员的医疗、教学、科研等方面的技术负有领导和培训的责任。作为医院主要业务的执行者，科主任在管理自己科室方面应当拥有更大的自主权，包括开除和聘用人员、新增床位以及预算编制和投资。在人才管理方面，医院管理者需要给予医生更大的自主权来设定个人目标。医院目标的设定需要拓展到更多的职工群体，以便让目标变得更合理、更统一。

四、结语

国务院医改“十二五”规划以及国家卫生和计划生育委员会等多部委等联合下发的《关于公立医院改革试点的指导意见》（卫医管发〔2010〕20号）指出：将改革医院管理体制、运行体制、监管体制作为公立医院改革的重点。同时，我们也发现良好的医院管理水平是医院服务质量和效率的保障。因此，医院管理水平的提升应作为公立医院内部管理体制改革的重要组成部分。医院管理者应当积极引进标准化运营及精细化管理，以减少医疗服务过程中的浪费；加强绩效管理，跟踪、考核多维度的绩效指标，同时制度化强调根本原因分析、制订后续改进行动计划；关注目标管理，从实际出发，制定符合医院、科室、员工的发展目标，并监督目标完成情况，以期按时、按量达成目标，推进医院发展。另外，医院应当重视人才管理，努力吸引和留住优秀员工，为医护人员提供合适的职业发展机会，使员工与医院共同成长。

此外，政府决策者应当重视当地医院发展和医护人员生存状态，在医院经营管理、人力资源、薪酬体制等方面给予医院更大的自主权；切实评估中国医生和护士的劳动价值，调整现行的薪酬体系以匹配目前医护人员的工作量负荷。政府通过积极优化医疗服务资源配置，鼓励城市医院转型，引进社会资本办医等多种改革方式，合理布局、积极发展医疗卫生业，以医疗卫生业的发展撬动整个健康服务业，整合区域医疗、预防、保健、养老等资源，使健康服务业发展成为推动城市经济可持续发展的重要力量。

（作者：刘国恩，北京大学国家发展研究院经济学教授，北京大学中国卫生经济研究中心主任；孙艳坤，北京大学中国卫生经济研究中心；尤雪丹，北京大学中国卫生经济研究中心）

参考文献

[1] Yip W C M, Hsiao W C, Chen W, et al. Early appraisal of China's huge and complex health-care reforms [J]. The Lancet, 2012, 379 (9818): 833-842.

[2] Nicholas Bloom and John Van Reenen. Measuring and explaining management practices across firms and countries [J]. Quarterly Journal of Economics, 2007, Vol CXXII.

[3] Nicholas Bloom and John Van Reenen. Why Do Management Practices Differ across Firms and Countries [J]. Journal of Economics Perspectives, 2010 (24): 203-224.

[4] Nicholas Bloom, G. Genakos, R. Martin, and R. Sadun. Modern Management: Good for the Environment or Just Hot Air? [J]. Economic Journal, 2010, 120 (544): 551-572.

[5] Kaplan R, Porter M. How to solve the cost crisis in health care [J]. Harvard Bus Rev, 2011 (9): 47-64.

[6] Mazzocato P, Savage C, Brommels M, et al. Lean thinking in healthcare: a realist review of the literature [J]. Qual Saf Health Care, 2010 (19): 376-82.

[7] Stephen M. Shortell, Jack E. Zimmerman, Denise M. Rousseau, et al. The Performance of Intensive Care Units: Does Good Management Make a Difference? [J]. Medical Care, 1994, 32 (5): 508-525.

[8] Nicholas Bloom, Carol Propper, Stephan Seiler, and John Van Reenen. The Impact of Competition on Management Practices in Public Hospitals [J]. NBER Working Paper, 2010, w16032.

[9] Nicholas Bloom, C. Genakos, et al. Management practices across firms and countries [J]. Academy of Management Perspectives, 2012, 26 (1): 12-33.

[10] 鲍玉荣，李林，何宇，等．医院管理标准化的国际经验借鉴 [J]. Chinese Hospitals, 2013, 17 (8).

[11] 李国红，胡善联．上海市不同级别医院绩效评价 [J]．上海医科大学学报，2001 (11): 10-12.

[12] 孙丁，李幼平，周荣乐，等．从国内外医院质量评审体系对比看中国医院评审改革 [J]．中国西部科技，2006, 17 (1): 1-4.

[13] 姚岚，金新政，舒展．广东省中医院绩效评价 [J]．卫生软科学，2004, 18 (5): 221-224.

[14] 中华人民共和国国务院．国家经济与社会发展十二五规划 (2011-2015) [Z].

基于大数据开展规划决策支持的技术方法探讨

一、引言

中国正处于快速的城市化进程，中国的大部分地区尤其是大城市，都经历了显著的城市用地增长过程，城乡规划在促进城市物质空间和社会的可持续发展中起着十分重要的作用（龙瀛，毛其智，2010）。近 20 年来，在我国，支持城乡规划编制和评估的规划支持系统（Planning Support Systems，PSS）引起了学者和决策者的广泛关注。“规划支持系统”的概念最初由哈里斯（Harris，1960）提出，被认为是计算机辅助规划技术的最新形式（Geertman and Stillwell 2004；Klosterman 1997；Saarloos 2006）。近年来，一些关于 PSS 的研究相继问世（Rugg 1992；Chan 1997；Brail and Klosterman 2001；Geertman and Stillwell 2003；Geertman 2006；Brail 2008；Geertman and Stillwell 2009；Mao et al. 2008；Saarloos et al. 2008），其应用主要体现在空间规划（Geneletti 2008；Kammeier 1999；Long et al. 2011）、城市环境改善规划（Edamura and Tsuchida 1999）、政策制定（Ballas et al. 2007）和土地利用规划（Klosterman 1999；Veregin 2007；Sante-Riveira et al. 2008；Sun et al. 2009）等方面。

近年来，计算机的软硬件水平得到了长足的发展，信息和通信技术（Information and Communication Technologies，ICT）发展迅速，社会经济活动产生的数据突飞猛进，这样的“大数据（Big Data）”规模超大，以至于超过了传统的软件工具获取、存储、管理、共享、分析和可视化的能力。这些数据为建立规划支持系统提供了较好的机遇，对具体建立规划支持系统的技术也提出新的要求。要分析在大数据时代如何开展决策支持，需要回过来先看大数据的特点，其主要包括几个方面：一是作为个体层面的数据，大数据一般反映了人或物的空间位置和联系（主动贡献 volunteer 或非主动贡献 volunteered），例如，公交卡数据对应每个持卡人的不同时刻的空间位置，特别地，古德柴尔德（Goodchild）突破了传统的光学传感器思想，较早地提出将人作为传感器（Human as Sensors）以获取空间和社会信息的设想（Goodchild，2007）；二是覆盖面广，一般能够覆盖区域或城市内的较大比例的个体，规模巨大（遍布，ubiquitous），例如手机数据一般能够对应一个城市内大量的手机用户；三是数据质量较高，具有较细的空间分辨率和时间分辨率以及客观的个体反馈。因此，本文将对大数据时代如何开展规划支持的技术方法进行系统探讨。

二、基于大数据开展规划决策支持的技术路线

（一）规划数据资源的积累和准备

1. 规划基础数据积累

传统城乡规划数据资源的来源主要依靠权威部门提供官方数据，如规划编制部门生产的用地现状、用地规划、专项规划等数据，规划审批部门生产的规划项目审批和行政许可数据，测绘部门提供的基础地理信息数据，统计部门提供的中宏观尺度的人口、就业、经济等数据，以及各委办局提供的相关专题数据等。经历多年的积累，形成海量的规划数据资源综合数据库，其建设和管理的思路是遵循规划体系，摸底规划资源，梳理协同关系，建立数据框架，以确定数据库建设的目标和分工。这里面需要制定数据库建设的相关技术规范，包括数据制作流程规范、数据质量检查控制标准、元数据标准、符号库标准、数据更新流程与办法等，建立健全的更新机制，保障综合数据库的持续发展。

随着信息技术在日常生活中的广泛应用，产生了大量微观尺度的城市空间信息和人类城市活动信息。这些信息被大量集聚在互联网、移动互联网和传感器网络中，形成了极为丰富的数据资源，即“大数据”。当前，大数据已然成为城乡规划编制与规划研究中必不可少的数据补充，其获取、建设与应用是规划数据资源扩展的新方向。

2. 多源规划数据获取

多源规划数据泛指通过非官方渠道获取的规划信息资源，主要是指利用信息技术和计算机技术主动获取的官方小数据和自媒体方式的各类大数据，包括权威部门和数据生产商等社会力量通过互联网公开发布的开放数据，以移动互联网和传感器网络为载体的社会化数据等。多源规划数据获取的实现是切实拓宽数据获取渠道，打通数据瓶颈，丰富规划资源的有效方法和有益尝试。

多源规划数据获取的途径主要基于互联网。以城乡规划空间数据资源体系内容框架为引导，分析和评估互联网信息资源可用度，明确各类数据的获取途径。如空间位置地理信息数据来源于百度地图、谷歌地图、MapBar等网站；企业法人信息主要来源于阿里巴巴企业网、新浪企业黄页板块；社会活动信息数据来源于微博数据，如新浪、腾讯等。多源规划数据获取的技术方法是以网络爬虫技术为核心，依托火车头数据采集平台实现数据抓取。网络爬虫是一个自动提取网页的程序，为搜索引擎从万维网上下载网页，是搜索引擎的重要组成。多源数据获取成果一般是记录空间信息和专题属性信息的表格，后续还需跟进地址匹配、数据清洗、属性整理等一系列工作，保证多源数据科学合理地融入城乡规划综合数据库的建设与管理中。

（二）综合数据库建设方法与实践

在城市规划行业管理和应用大数据，除面临诸如海量存储管理、数据清洗与集成、云计算等大数据应用共性技术挑战外，还需面对规划行业特定的大数据处理与建库方法、综合数据库建设模式等问题。

1. 大数据处理与建库方法

面向大数据实时处理与计算需求，需要建立分布式、面向云计算的规划信息综合数据库。首先，分布架构下每个节点不论是数据内容还是对外提供服务能力都是一个完整、独立的数据库，并可随着规划业务内容、信息资源容量和单位组织架构变化，在节点数量上动态增加或减少，具有相当的灵活性。其次，分布式数据库平台利于将云计算理念引入数据库系统。通过在网络环境中动态配置服务器、存储、应用软件、服务等方法，整合网络后台各个数据库资源，为规划项目提供数据库资源访问、发现、整合等多方面应用服务，对于提高计算机和网络等资源利用率、节省硬件购买和维护成本、安全保护数据资源、充分利用数据库系统服务等具有重要意义，尤其适用于大数据时代规划行业构建以大量查询、统计为基础、面向规划分析和决策的应用信息系统。

传统数据库建设大都面向事务性业务处理，对企业内部日常发生的业务型数据进行采集、入库，做一般性查询和统计分析应用。但在面向规划分析决策上，大数据环境下的数据库建设方法，需要面向规划业务主题进行数据的再处理和组织。这里面需要将来自不同领域的相关数据按照规划预定的分析主题转换成统一的格式，集成、存储在一起，实现空间和非空间的联机分析操作，然后借助各种专业模型、通过数据挖掘技术从数据中发现知识，为辅助决策提供支持，使得综合数据库成为在大数据时代开展数据分析与数据挖掘的基础平台设施。

我们针对北京市政交通一卡通（Beijing Municipal Administration & Communication Card）数据进行了数据处理和建库的尝试。该数据是北京市民使用市政交通一卡通在乘坐公交、地铁和城铁上下车时于读卡机上进行刷卡的记录数据，包含卡信息、出行交易信息、线路和站点信息等，数据量巨大，仅一日交易量就超过千万条记录，具有典型大数据特征。研究中通过对一卡通刷卡数据集进行抽取、转换和聚集，形成面向规划主题的分析提炼信息，如每日刷卡记录数，每日完整出行人次数，各站点和线路某日全天、早高峰时段（7:00～9:00）、晚高峰时段（17:00～19:00）刷卡交易总量，各站点和线路某日全天、早晚高峰时段的分进、出的交易量；两两站点间每日全天、早高峰时段、晚高峰时段的出行人次数与平均出行时间等汇总信息。

2. 综合数据库建设模式的改变

目前，各规划单位数据库内容获取和管理主要依托信息技术部门，充分发挥该部门在新技术掌握和应用上的能力优势，统一对规划信息资源加工处理，使其数字化、标准化，然后通过入库环节，使用数据库对其进行存储和管理。这在新技术刚引入规划行业初期以及各规划单位规划信息资源尚不丰富、以内部加工制作数据为主要信息来源的阶段是合适的。大数据时代，面临内容丰富、数量巨大、来源多样的规划信息资源归集和管理任务，单靠某一部门难以胜任，必须实现由单部门独立建设管理转变为多部门协同建设管理。

大数据时代，规划信息资源更新来源于规划设计人员对城市各专题信息的长期持续跟踪，随着规划工作经验不断积累，其对信息资源内容敏感程度、分析能力等均有很大变化。因此，仅依靠信息技术部门在规划信息资源判定、获取、生产加工、应用等环节上能够发挥的作用有限。需要规划单位将行政管理中已建立的职责分工和专业内容分工，运用到规划信息资源数据库建设管理中，各司其职，发挥各自特长，共同参与。这样，业务部门和信息技术部门协同工作，工作内容均为各自最为熟悉部分，可确保数据完整性、准确性和动态更新，实现整个规划单位的信息资源共享和应用。

基于前述研究思路，北京市城市规划设计研究院提出了如图 1 所示的大数据时代规划综合数据库整体构建框架。在该框架下，目前行政体制管理中的二级业务部门共同参与规划综合数据库的建设、运行和管理。各部门对规划业务需求进行全面研究和细致梳理，形成院级统一信息资源组织结构和内容视图，将整个综合数据库划分为院级基础数据库和各部门的专业数据库，各个数据库搜集、归集和管理维护的数据内容与各部门日常专业工作开展密切结合，充分利用规划设计人员在规划工作开展过程中对信息资源不断接触、观察、理解、跟踪和积累形成的经验优势，通过网络、项目交流、调研与调查等手段不断拓展大数据获取渠道。

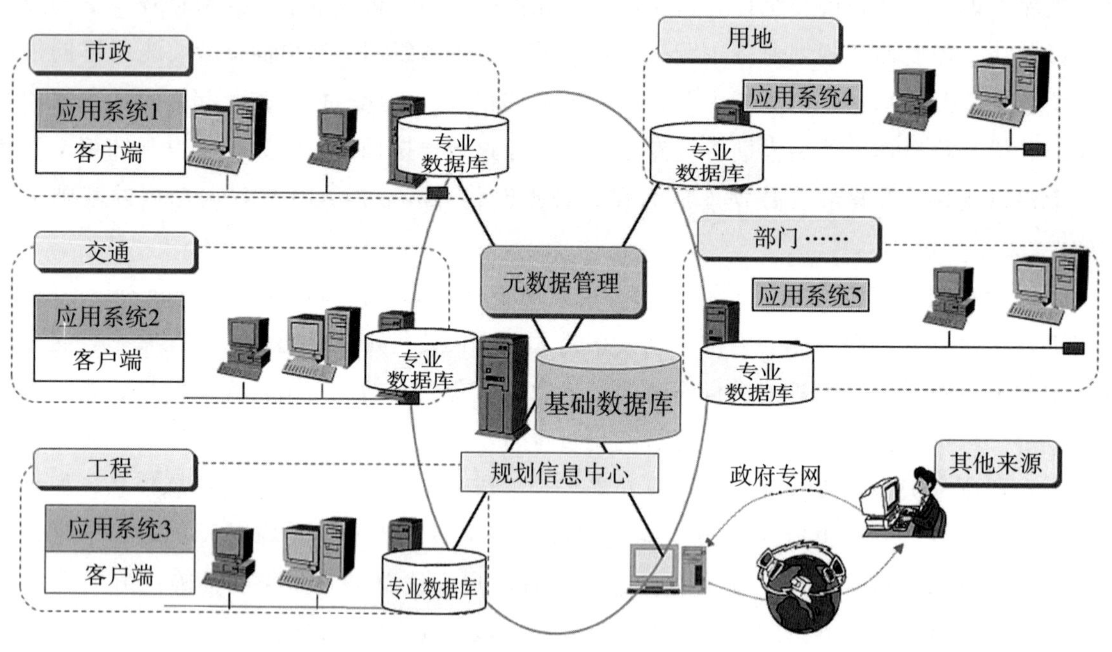

图 1　规划综合数据库总体架构

（三）基于大数据的规划决策支持技术路线探索

1. 技术框架体系

基于大数据和大量的开放数据开展规划支持，我们建议的总体思路是建立大量规划支持模型。北京市城市规划设计研究院于2007年开始零星的规划支持模型的研究与探索，2012年完成课题《规划支持系统框架体系及典型应用研究》，完善了规划支持系统基础理论，提出规划支持系统框架体系，从方法、软件、模型三个方面进一步研究确定了规划支持系统框架体系的具体内容（见表1）。项目共研究确定了128个方法、59个软件和58个模型，并将规划模型归纳为基础综合模型、专业综合模型、专业独立模型三个层次，提出优先建设用地现状综合分析模型和城乡空间发展模型、统筹建设专业综合和专业独立模型的实施方法，以便首先夯实规划支持系统建设的基础。

表1 PSS框架示意

<table>
<tr><th colspan="2">规划层次</th><th>规划内容</th><th>方法</th><th>软件</th><th>模型</th></tr>
<tr><td rowspan="18">总体规划</td><td rowspan="8">现状分析</td><td>基础地理（地形地貌、高程、坡度、坡向等）</td><td>坡度等</td><td>ArcGIS(3D analyst)</td><td></td></tr>
<tr><td>基础条件、区位特征分析</td><td>灰色理论</td><td>规划信息发布系统、CH规划数据管理工具</td><td>现状综合分析模型</td></tr>
<tr><td>用地适宜性分析</td><td>栅格代数运算</td><td>ArcGIS</td><td>用地适宜性分析模型</td></tr>
<tr><td>城市建设用地演变分析</td><td>OVERLAY</td><td>ArcGIS</td><td></td></tr>
<tr><td>城镇体系评估</td><td></td><td></td><td>现状综合分析模型</td></tr>
<tr><td>城镇建设用地规模与布局影响因素分析</td><td>线性回归、系统动力学、主成分分析</td><td></td><td></td></tr>
<tr><td>公共服务设施现状分析与评估</td><td></td><td></td><td>现状综合分析模型、公共服务设施综合模型</td></tr>
<tr><td>产业发展现状分析</td><td>投入产出分析</td><td></td><td>现状综合分析模型</td></tr>
<tr><td rowspan="4">社会经济</td><td>预测城市人口规模</td><td>回归分析、时间序列分析、贝叶斯预测、小波分析、情景分析、趋势分析</td><td>SPSS、SAS</td><td>人口模型（如马尔萨斯人口模型、Logistic 人口模型、Leslie人口模型、刘易斯二元经济模型、托达罗人口流动模型、人口再分布理论等）</td></tr>
<tr><td>就业岗位预测</td><td>情景分析、系统动力学</td><td></td><td></td></tr>
<tr><td>人口承载力分析</td><td>情景分析</td><td></td><td>人口承载力分析模型</td></tr>
<tr><td>人口空间分布模拟</td><td>密度核分析，空间插值</td><td>ArcGIS，GeoDA</td><td></td></tr>
<tr><td rowspan="6">空间布局</td><td>城市发展方向制定</td><td>多属性分析、基础地形分析、流域分析、OVERLAY</td><td>ArcGIS</td><td>区位模型、用地适宜性分析模型</td></tr>
<tr><td>城市空间结构</td><td>空间相互作用</td><td>ArcGIS</td><td>BUDEM</td></tr>
<tr><td>空间形态评价（城市重心、紧凑度、离散度等）</td><td>多属性分析</td><td>ArcGIS</td><td>Fragstats</td></tr>
<tr><td>地块方向评价（评估城市肌理变化）</td><td></td><td>ArcGIS</td><td>PARCTION</td></tr>
<tr><td>路网评价</td><td>空间句法</td><td>AxWoman</td><td></td></tr>
<tr><td>制定城市增长边界</td><td>元胞自动机</td><td>CH规划数据管理工具</td><td>城市增长模型BUDEM</td></tr>
</table>

2. 决策支持技术方法

大数据背景下决策支持技术方法可分为基础层面、复杂层面和综合层面三个层面，为不同内容、不同深度的规划任务提供服务。

基础层面主要是基本数据计算与汇总统计。该层面利用一般性商业软件、共享软件、免费软件或经过简单定制的计算机工具，通过数学计算、透视分析等方法对城市自然地理、人口和社会经济、土地利用、土地使用、土地规划、建设强度等的现状情况进行分析，并以专题图件、汇总表格等形式加以表达，为规划设计人员了解城市自然资源、历史沿革、空间布局、基础设施、人口和社会经济的空间分布等方面现状情况提供基础而又翔实的信息。

复杂层面主要是多元数据叠加与规划评估分析。该层面利用 GIS、SPSS、MatLAB 等专业分析软件以及规划编制系统、城市三维分析系统等专门开发的软件系统，通过多属性联合分析、空间分析、多元回归分析、相关性分析、视域分析等方法，将多元数据面向规划研究内容进行关联和融合，对城市区位条件、用地适宜性、用地空间结构特征、公共服务及市政交通设施、生态与环境等方面内容进行评估分析，提炼规划发展的有利因素、限制条件以及实施中的问题。

综合层面主要是复杂规划模型与城市发展判定。该层面运用元胞自动机、地租理论、区位理论等方法，使用 AgentAnalyst、What If、Cube 等商业软件和专门研发的决策支持系统，通过城市空间形态结构评价、生态敏感性评价模型、限建区规划模型、交通和土地使用整合模型、市政设施承载力分析模型和低碳城市规划模型等专业综合模型和专业独立模型，分析不同历史阶段城市扩张的驱动力，对城市不同约束条件下的发展进行情景分析，对不同的城市发展策略和政策影响进行预判，为实现城市理性增长，综合协调并确定基础设施的合理规模和布局，确保城市低碳发展提供分析和决策支持。

（四）基于大数据的规划决策支持技术平台建设方法

基于大数据的规划决策支持技术平台（Urban Planning Support System，UPSS）需要以城乡规划对规划信息资源和规划决策支持技术的复杂性、多变性需求为牵引，既要实现对已有的规划数据资源简单的发布、查询和调用，也要实现以不同方式进行大数据的获取和处理，它更强调的是提供面向规划需求的统计、分析和决策支持手段的共享和调用。平台需实现对各类规划支持服务资源的网络化管理和共享应用，为规划师、大数据 UPSS 平台建设和规划应用模型快速建设提供信息技术支持。

大数据 UPSS 平台的框架体系如图 2 所示。平台框架体系主要包括以下内容：建立城乡规划支持服务资源库，实现对面向城乡规划需求的各类规划支持服务资源元数据的管理；要建立服务资源建设规范和构建技术，以支撑不断提出的各类模型、分析工具等计算资源的开发建设，并能够在不同的网络环境中运行，进一步规范规划数据资源的标准，实现计算资源对数据资源的调用；要建立城乡规划决策支持平台，实现资源的注册、管理和发布，为资源调用支撑城乡规划提供技术支持。

在该框架体系中，既包含了辅助城乡规划的各类数据服务资源，也包含了基于数据开展辅助决策支持的各类数据获取、数据处理、空间分析、规划模型等计算服务资源。需要以城乡规划数据管理平台为基础，通过规划决策支持平台提供灵活的规划支持资源共享渠道，实现规划支持资源快速调用。

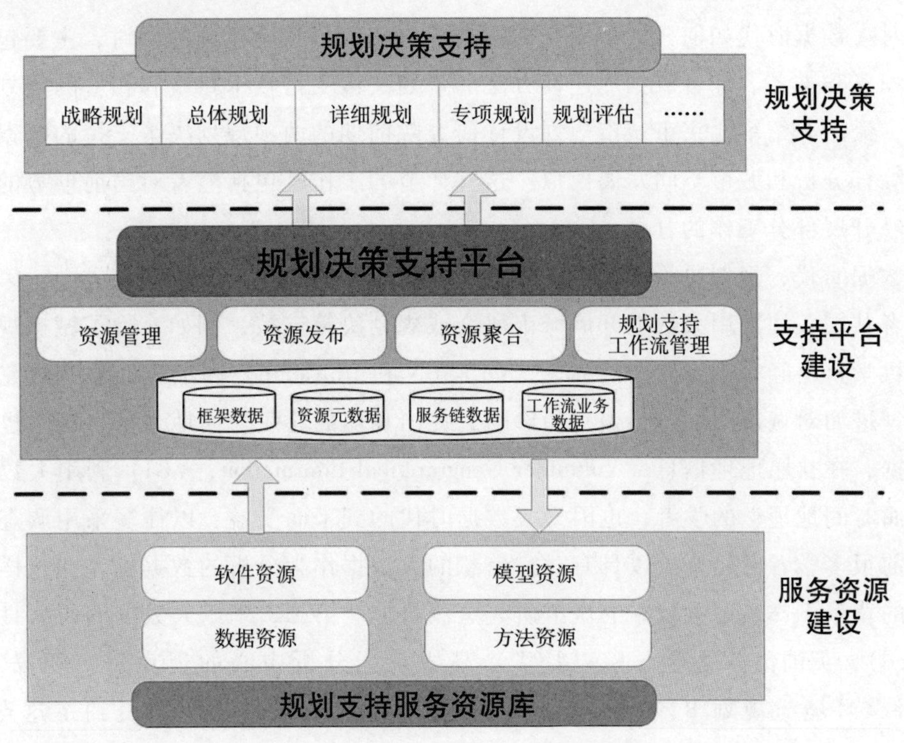

图2　大数据 UPSS 平台的框架体系

在服务资源数据库中，规划支持服务资源主要包括：支持规划业务工作的各类基础规划数据服务、规划分析成果数据服务和指标数据服务，即规划数据资源；基于规范标准开发建设的、在网络上能够运行的规划计算服务资源；可以在用户端独立运行的 UPSS 资源聚合系统以及在 UPSS 系统中运行的计算包等软件资源；还有支撑规划工作的理论方法等知识资源。开展城乡规划辅助决策支持，需要建立面向城乡规划需求的快速反应机制，利用规划支持技术积累，快速搭建规划支持模型和统计分析工具，并利用 UPSS 平台实现对计算方法的快速集成和调用，实现计算模型与规划数据的对接。

总体上，城乡规划支持服务资源构建涉及当今最先进的信息技术和软件构建方法，它不是各种信息技术在规划领域的简单应用，而是将规划自身的基础理论以专业模型的形式融入最为先进的信息技术中；大数据 UPSS 平台中的技术服务资源不是用于替代目前规划师所采用的软件工具的全新的技术，而是一个辅助规划的、可以按照规划工作流程进行集成的技术体系。对于大数据 UPSS 平台而言，它不是只支持数据获取、处理、分析和表达应用的静态的封闭的系统，而是一个实现规划师、软件专家、公众、政府、行业、社会之间快速进行信息和技术沟通的桥梁，以实现快速的城乡规划支持。

三、结论与讨论

本文对大数据时代如何开展规划支持的技术方法进行系统全面的探讨，主要包括规划数据资源的积累和准备、综合数据库建设方法、规划决策支持技术路线和相应的规划支持平台建设思想，最后介绍了北京市城市规划设计研究院前期的两项规划决策支持的探索性研究工作、现状综合分析和城市空间发展模拟。这些环节的工作既包括笔者对当前形势的思考，又包括对已经开展部分工作的分享。

在大数据时代，规划决策支持工作面临的新形势，主要体现在以下几方面：第一，多个领域的学者共同关注利用大数据开展城市研究或规划决策支持，例如，除了城市规划领域本身，计算机学科已经有很多专门的会议（如 LSBN 和 UbiComp）和主流的学者研究大数据挖掘的算法，进而对城市问题进行识别和诊断，提出相应的建议。而地理信息科学也将目光关注到大数据，在自愿地理信息（Volunteer Geographical Information，VGI）利用大数据进行城市研究。而时间地理学的学者，也因为大数据时代的到来而受益，以往多采用调查方法获得日志，目前很多学者已经开始以具有时空信息的大数据作为分析的数据源。在这样的多学科百花齐放的背景下，基于大数据的城市研究蒸蒸日上。第二，基于大数据的研究日趋破碎化（fragmented），英国伦敦大学学院（UCL）高级空间分析中心的迈克尔·巴蒂（Michael Batty），在《环境与规划 B》（*Environment and Planning B*）一文中提到了这点（Batty，2012），即这些研究往往侧重于城市现象的某一个局部方面，而鲜有综合的分析，这点可能在于大数据广、精和深的特点，适合专业分析和挖掘。而传统的城市模型，则基于来自多个渠道的数据，实现较为综合的分析。第三，大数据分析算法趋于简单化，甚至有观点声称“大数据本身就是模型”，即通过对大数据简单的时间、空间和属性层面的统计分析，就可以得到有趣（surprising）的分析结果（龙瀛等，2012）。

（作者：黄晓春，北京市城市规划设计研究院，教授级高级工程师；龙瀛，北京市城市规划设计研究院，高级工程师；何莲娜，北京市城市规划设计研究院，高级工程师；喻文承，北京市城市规划设计研究院，高级工程师；程辉，北京市城市规划设计研究院）

参考文献

[1] Ballas D，Kingston R，Stillwell J，Jin J. Building a spatial microsimulation-based planning support system for local policy making［J］. Environment and Planning A，2007，39（10）：2482 – 2499.

[2] Batty M. Smart cities，big data. Environment and Planning B：Planning and Design，2012，39：191 – 193.

[3] Brail R K（ed）. Planning support systems for cities and regions. Lincoln Institute of Land Policy，Cambridge，MA，2008.

[4] Brail R K，Klosterman R E（eds）. Planning support systems：Integrating geographic information systems，models and visualization tools［M］. ESRI Press，Redlands，CA，2001.

[5] Chan S. The development of planning support system by integrating urban models and geographic information systems: a framework and implementation [D]. University of Pennsylvania, the United States, 1997.

[6] Edamura T, Tsuchida T. Planning support system for an urban environment improvement project [J]. Environment and Planning B: Planning & Design, 1999, 26: 381-391.

[7] Geertman S, Stillwell J (eds). Planning support systems best practice and new methods [M]. Springer, Berlin, 2009.

[8] Geertman S, Stillwell J (eds). Planning support systems in practice. Advances in spatial science [M]. Springer, Berlin, 2003.

[9] Geertman S, Stillwell J. Planning support systems: An inventory of current practice [J]. Computers, Environment and Urban Systems, 2004, 28: 291-310.

[10] Geertman S. Potentials for planning support: a planning-conceptual approach [J]. Environment and Planning B: Planning and Design, 2006, 33 (6): 863-880.

[11] Geneletti D. Incorporating biodiversity assets in spatial planning: Methodological proposal and development of a planning support system [J]. Landscape and Urban Planning, 2008, 84: 252-265.

[12] Goodchild M F. Citizens as sensors: The world of volunteered geography [J]. GeoJournal, 2007, 69 (4): 211-221.

[13] Harris B. Plan or projection: An examination of the use of models in planning [J]. Journal of the American Institute of Planners, 1960, 26: 265-272.

[14] Kammeier HD. New tools for spatial analysis and planning as components of an incremental planning-support system [J]. Environment and Planning B: Planning & Design, 1999, 26: 365-380.

[15] Klosterman R E. Planning support systems: A new perspective on computer-aided planning [J]. Journal of Planning Education and Research, 1997, 17: 45-54.

[16] Klosterman R E. The What if Collaborative planning support system [J]. Environment and Planning B: Planning and Design 1999, 26: 393-408.

[17] Long Y, Shen Z, Mao Q. An urban containment planning support system for Beijing [J]. Computers Environment and Urban Systems, 2011, 35: 297-307.

[18] Mao F, Yu W, Zhou W, He G. An urban-rural spatial development planning platform using GIS [C]. Geoinformatics 2008 and Joint Conference on GIS and Built Environment: The Built Environment and its Dynamics, 2008.

[19] Rugg R D. A feature-based planning support system [J]. Computers, Environment and Urban Systems, 1992, 16 (3): 219-226.

[20] Saarloos D, Arentze T A, Borgers A W J, Timmermans H J P. A multi-agent paradigm as structuring principle for planning support systems [J]. Computers, Environment and Urban Systems, 2008, 32 (1): 29-40.

[21] Saarloos D. A framework for a multi-agent planning support system [D]. Technische Universiteit Eindhoven, the Netherlands, 2006.

[22] Sante-Riveira I, Crecente-Maseda R, Miranda-Barros D. GIS-based planning support system for rural land-use allocation [J]. Computers and Electronics in Agriculture, 2008, 63 (2): 257-273.

[23] Sun Z, Deal B, Pallathucheril V G. The land-use evolution and impact assessment model: a comprehensive urban planning support system [J]. Journal of the Urban and Regional Information Systems Association, 2009, 21 (1): 57-68.

[24] Veregin G. Integrating planning support system technologies in a rural land planning application [M]. University of Wyoming, the United States, 2007.

[25] 龙瀛，毛其智．城市规划支持系统的定义、目标和框架 [J]．清华大学学报（自然科学版），2010，50（3）：335-337.

[26] 龙瀛，张宇，崔承印．利用公交卡刷卡数据分析北京职住关系和通勤交通形态 [J]．地理学报，2012，67（10）：1339-1352.

[27] 甄峰，王波，陈映雪．基于网络社会空间的中国城市网络特征 [J]．地理学报，2012，67（8）：1031-1043.

绿色建筑的发展路径研究

一、我国绿色建筑的发展历程和绿色建筑的本质

（一）绿色建筑的发展历程

我国绿色建筑是从建筑节能起步的，从20世纪80年代开始，我国逐步意识到建筑能耗在经济和社会发展中的重要性，开始逐步推行建筑节能。以1986年颁布的《北方地区居住建筑节能标准》为开始，建筑节能更关注能耗的降低，注重建筑的保温隔热，提高建筑的气密性。自2006年国家颁布《绿色建筑评价标准》以来，我国的绿色建筑发展，由关注建筑节能、产品与能效技术、节能科技建筑，发展至对绿色建筑设计（建造）应用方法、成本及运营效果的重视。截至2013年12月底，我国已获得《绿色建筑评价标准》认证的绿色建筑项目共1 179个，公建项目557个、住宅项目622个，可绝大多数为设计标识。所以，更深层次地理解绿色建筑的真正内涵，对我国绿色建筑的发展有着重要意义。

（二）绿色建筑的深度与广度（绿色建筑与人居环境）

绿色建筑的发展反映了技术进步对人居环境改善的影响，也反映了改善人居环境的历程对技术和经济进步的促进作用。深层的绿色建筑是一个相互关联的微循环系统（4P），这个系统把“人”对绿色建筑的感受作为一个重要的评价因素，在全寿命周期内同时满足“成本”、“性能与能效”、“环境”的协调统一，即在一定的经济成本与能源消耗范围内，通过新技术的集成运用来创造更高的建筑性能和健康的人居环境。同时，在居住环境的建设中尽可能保护和合理利用自然环境，让人接近自然，与自然共生。

绿色建筑的广度更是一个宏观的涵盖经济、社会、生态环境、能源的城市可持续发展系统（4E），城市的可持续发展离不开建筑行业在内的相关行业的转型升级，而由绿色建筑推动的产业转型升级，也直接促进了地方经济的转型与发展；在经济转型的带动下，绿色建筑创造了更好的城市空间，提高了人民的生活水平。同时，在相关技术应用的过程中对城市环境的改善以及城市能源的消耗与节能减排有着直接的促进作用，进一步提高了城市的综合竞争力。所以，发展绿色建筑产业是城市可持续发展的全局判断，也是未来发展的必由之路。

二、我国绿色建筑发展的问题

目前，我国绿色建筑发展的起步阶段已经基本完成，正在向快速发展的阶段迈进。基于此前大量相关调研与文献收集，在这个时期中，绿色建筑的发展有两个核心的问题：一个是以政府政策为核心的政策问题；另一个是以技术产业化为核心的技术问题。当然，除此之外还有一些其他制约因素，例如，开发商的认知、公众的绿色建筑消费需求、设计院的绿色建筑设计能力和成本问题。

（一）政策和市场问题

在推动绿色建筑发展的进程中，我国已经在法律、行政法规和部门规章等不同层面上制定了多项相关政策，也积极制定了一系列的经济激励政策来推动绿色建筑发展。但是，目前我国在推广绿色建筑方面所采取的政策措施还远远不够，政策和规范的配套性、可操作性也存在许多不足。

1. 绿色建筑立法的缺失

法律层面上，绿色建筑的政策法规缺乏明确的法律依据，主要体现在三个方面：①缺乏针对绿色建筑的专门立法；②缺乏明确的法律责任与处罚措施；③操作性法规的层次较低，法律效力不大。目前，我国没有专门对绿色建筑领域的立法，且相关的法律中也缺少绿色建筑的具体操作内容，而行业主管部门和地方政府颁布的规范性文件、办法和规定等在实际运用中很难产生法律效力，约束能力较低。

2. 绿色建筑激励措施不足

绿色建筑的财税激励措施还有待完善，主要包括税收优惠和财政补贴两个方面。目前我国主要是通过财政补贴的方式来促进绿色建筑的发展，但是补贴的覆盖面还是相对较窄，政策落地的难度较大，真正获得补贴的绿色建筑项目所占的比率相对较低。同时，我国针对绿色建筑的税收优惠十分零散，且大多力度不够。此外，我国对绿色建筑有关的税收优惠政策还很不完善，发达国家采用的环境税对绿色建筑的发展有极大的推动作用，而我国现行的绿色建筑环境税还有待制定。

3. 政策对绿色建筑消费的引导力度不够

我国绿色建筑产业的市场竞争机制还没有形成，绿色建筑市场的发展还处于初始阶段，绿色建筑在很大程度上还没有得到消费者和开发商的认可。对开发商而言，面对成本和市场需求的双重压力，进行绿色建筑开发的动力严重不足，绿色建筑市场难以形成规模效应；对消费者而言，缺乏绿色消费理念、缺少对绿色建筑的切身体验都是抑制市场需求增长的关键因素。目前的市场还不能有效地解决这种供需之间的差异，此时就需要依靠政策的引导来对市场进行调节，尤其是对绿色建筑消费需求进行刺激，但是目前却缺乏相关的政策和措施。

4. 相关部门监督和管理的力度不够

绿色建筑法规和政策的实施需要相关部门的监督和管理。虽然目前，无论是在国家层面还是在地方层面都已经出台了许多绿色建筑相关的政策和规定，但是由于监管和审核制度的不健全，很多规章制度并没有真正地得到实施。

（二）技术问题

我国绿色建筑是从建筑节能起步的，但是，对建筑节能的单一追求也带来了一系列的问题，尤其是对人和自然环境的忽略。目前，我国的绿色建筑更趋向于高科技建筑或者说是技术综合建筑，表现为大量先进技术的堆砌和高额的增量成本。一方面，这类绿色建筑虽然体现了节能环保的绿色理念，但是却欠缺可推广性和实用性。高额的增量成本使开发商望而却步，技术的简单堆砌和叠加并不能有效地提高建筑性能和发挥技术优势，往往在建筑的运营和维护中还会带来新的问题，增加新的成本。另一方面，建筑商对于绿色建筑技术掌握得不够及时与充分，将使得该类技术应用不到位，从而影响绿色建筑的建造。目前，我国的绿色建筑技术发展主要暴露了四个方面的问题：

1. 基于“以人为本”的绿色建筑技术与建筑设计的融合不够

目前，对于绿色建筑技术的集成不仅局限于技术之间的耦合，也包括技术和建筑设计的耦合，同时成本和其他一些社会学因素也应逐步被囊括到绿色建筑的设计和评价当中。随着技术和设计理念的发展，一方面技术将逐步成为绿色建筑发展的手段，另一方面以人与自然的和谐为核心，注重绿色建筑给人的体验，在建设和使用的全周期过程中，科学有效地利用资源和高新技术成果，使建筑物对资源的消耗及对环境破坏的冲击降到最低限度，建造一个满足人类居住的室内环境，强调建筑的健康舒适，实现绿色人居建筑才是其发展的方向和追求。但是，由于绿色建筑是近几年才开始真正走向实践，国内普遍缺乏绿色建筑设计经验，同时绿色建筑所要求的整合设计理念也对传统的专业合作机制提出了新的要求，而在这些方面，我国的建筑设计机构的发展还普遍滞后。

2. 技术集成相对落后，技术的产业化还处于起步阶段

绿色建筑是一个综合的技术集成体系，它包括节能、节水、保温、隔热等诸多方面的技术，只有有效地实现这些技术的耦合和叠加才能实现真正的绿色建筑。如今国内绿色建筑技术的推广往往集中于单一的技术或单一的建筑主体，成熟的绿色建筑技术体系还相对较少，技术的产业化刚刚起步，还有很多问题亟待解决。

3. 缺乏技术评价和运行的参照标准及数据

绿色建筑技术自身的效率和运行情况受到诸多因素的影响，因此，在建筑的使用后评估中，监测建筑的运行状况和各项技术的运行性能是十分有必要的，获取相关的数据并制定技术运用的参照标准，有利于提高绿色建筑技术的运行效率。

4. 相关的基础性研究滞后

全生命周期理念要求对于建筑的研究不仅局限于目标建筑本身，同时涉及材料的生产、运输、建筑的废弃与再利用。这对于建筑基本信息的需求有了质的变化，更大量的基础性数据成为需求的重点。这也是绿色建筑技术从理论走向实践过程中首先需要面对的难题。

三、我国绿色建筑发展的政策建议

面对当前我国绿色建筑发展所暴露的政策和市场问题，相关法规政策的制定和实施是解决这些问题的关键。

（一）立法和相关标准的制定

首先，国家应当出台绿色建筑相应的强制性法规和政策，把绿色建筑上升到法律的层次，明确法律责任和处罚措施。绿色建筑的发展需要进一步完善建筑和能源领域的法律、法规建设，将绿色建筑的各个环节纳入法律法规之内，对新建和现有建筑制定明确和具体的能效标准，使法律法规更具有操作性。其次，国家和政府应当完善与绿色建筑相关的标准和规定，建立绿色建筑标准体系，即包括绿色建筑的设计、施工、验收、检测、运行等各方面标准。最后，在政绩考核方面需要引导各级政府树立可持续发展的政绩观，将绿色建筑相关内容作为政绩考核来推动绿色建筑的发展。

（二）扩大经济激励政策

相对于促进绿色建筑发展和推广的强制性政策，经济激励政策强调的是加强市场在解决绿色建筑发展问题中的作用，鼓励通过市场来影响政策对象使之做出行为决策。国家和各级政府应当建立和实施有效的经济激励政策，通过税收优惠、资金支持、财政补贴等措施促进绿色建筑的发展。针对我国推动绿色建筑中的经济激励政策不足，政策实施状况不佳的现状提出如下建议：①试行绿色建筑税收优惠；②扩大绿色建筑财政补贴，确保补贴落地；③绿色建筑其他经济奖励政策：扩大绿色建筑政府采购比例；增加绿色建筑工程示范与奖励。

具体来说，首先，政府还应该简化绿色建筑在规划和建设中的行政许可和审批手续，为绿色建筑工程项目提供便利，减少其行政成本。其次，政府可以给予绿色建筑开发商贷款利率的优惠，对于进行绿色建筑开发的用地，政府可以根据获得的不同星级认证，来进行相应比例土地出让金的减免，同时可以对开发商在绿色建筑上的收入进行相应的增值税和所得税的减免；对消费者而言，可以在其购买房屋时减免相关房产税与土地增值税，以及给予贷款利率的优惠等。

（三）加大绿色建筑行业的监管和审核的力度

绿色建筑的监管和审核力度应该从三个层面上来加强。首先，加强对评价标识部门、专家和咨询团队的监管；其次，健全监管和审核制度，在绿色建筑的规划和设计阶段进行严格的审核，真正做到把绿色建筑的规划和设计与规划许可证和施工许可证的获取进行直接关联，在施工、竣工和运行阶段进行严格的监管和验收，制定奖惩措施；最后，还应当加强舆论、行业和社会的监督，对绿色建筑项目和相关责任人进行公示。

综上，绿色建筑发展的政策问题和对策可总结如下，见表1。

表 1 绿色建筑发展的政策问题和对策

绿色建筑发展的政策问题	对 策
绿色建筑立法的缺失	①出台绿色建筑相应的强制性法规 ②完善与绿色建筑相关的标准和规定，建立绿色建筑标准体系 ③将绿色政绩考核作为政绩考核的内容
绿色建筑激励措施不足	①试行绿色建筑税收优惠 ②扩大绿色建筑财政补贴，确保补贴落地 ③绿色建筑其他经济奖励政策：扩大绿色建筑政府采购比例；增加绿色建筑工程示范与奖励
政策对绿色建筑消费的引导力度不够	
绿色建筑行业的监管机构和机制设立不健全	①加强对评价标识部门、专家和咨询的监管 ②健全监管和审核制度，把绿色建筑的规划和设计与规划许可证和施工许可证的获取进行直接关联 ③加强舆论、行业和社会的监督

四、绿色建筑的发展路径和技术对策

（一）绿色建筑的发展路径——全周期绿色建筑

全周期绿色建筑项目不再局限于传统建筑设计的常规工作，而是将触角延伸到绿色建筑全生命周期的各个阶段。首先，在回顾以往绿色建筑使用后评估研究发现的基础上，归纳总结不同设计策略的优缺点（包括不同技术集成方法所能带来的节能减排效果以及对使用者的影响等多方面因素），以之作为辅助设计决策的科学依据。在此基础上，在项目初期就对设计策略做出综合的考量，然后通过加强全周期项目管理与跟踪研究，确保在合理的增量成本范围内，实现设计阶段拟定的节能减排目标，同时保证建筑建成后使用者的满意度、工作效率等指标也如预期的得到显著改善。最后对项目的后续研究发现进行分析和整理，并将相关成果和经验反馈回循证数据库，用以指导下一阶段的同类建筑策划与设计。（图 1）

（二）我国绿色建筑发展的技术对策

1. 绿色建筑的整合设计路线

早期的绿色建筑相关研究指出（图 2），要在建筑的全周期中取得理想的节能减排效果，并将相关的增量成本控制在合理范围内，需要在项目初期就为相应的设计策略做出全盘的考量。所以，在全周期绿色建筑的思想中，建筑设计过程是十分关键的，该阶段将以项目的前期策划为依据，综合采用主动式和被动式的绿色建筑技术，并以计算机模拟结果为参照，对设计进行优化和调整。在此基础上，把循证设计的思想引入设计过程，可以构建出一条完整的绿色建筑设计路线（图 3），这条路线把建筑设计和绿色建筑技术进行了整合，突出了性能化设计的重要性，同时强调从成本的视角对建筑方案进行评估。

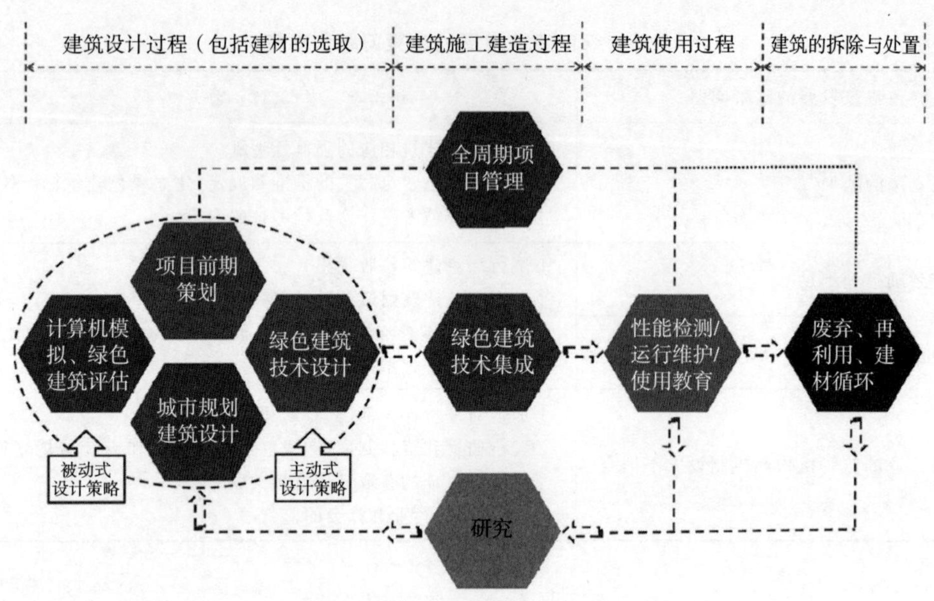

图1　全周期绿色建筑发展路线图

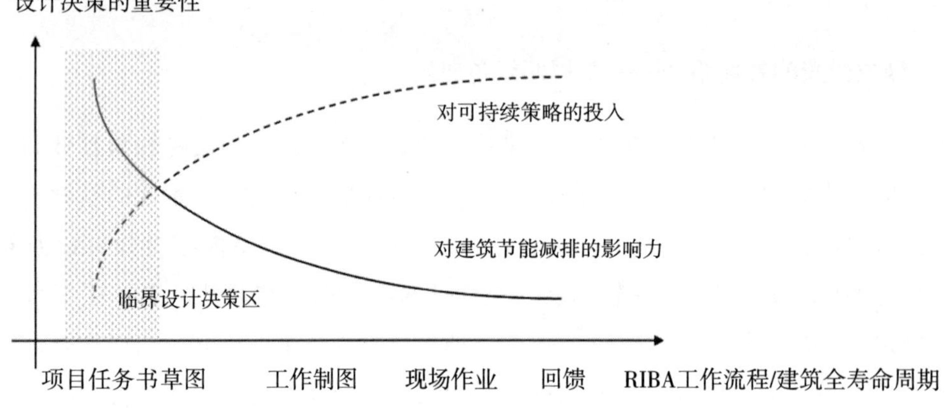

图2　在建筑全周期不同阶段，可持续设计策略对建筑综合节能减排效果的影响以及相关策略对应的增量成本之间的关系

2. 绿色建筑技术集成

绿色建筑的性能指标涉及多个方面，如能耗、节水率、风、光、热、声环境等；人居环境也包含了对多方面因素的考量，例如舒适度、智能化程度、垃圾处理方式及交通与绿化状况等。在绿色人居建筑的打造中应当综合考量绿色建筑和人居环境的相关指标，注重技术的耦合和集成，并且在集成过程中关注以下四个方面的综合表现：①人对居住空间的需求和感受；②系统的耦合效率与能效；③资源的综合利用和环境保护；④成本（图4）。

人对居住空间的需求和感受强调的是绿色人居建筑应当注重把“以人为本”的绿色建筑技术和建筑设计进行融合；系统的耦合效率和能效关注的是在能耗上限下，通过技术创新，提供优质的居住空间；资源的综合利用和环境保护强调的是对环境资源的优化组合和循环利用，并且进行环境保护式的开发；成本突出的是绿色建筑的性价比，强调把低增量成本

项目前期策划
主观因素
(甲方、SWOT)
客观因素
(气候、场地)
绿色建筑
(设计目标)
项目定位
预期设计成果
案例
弹性设计
设计控制
指标
性能指标
循证设计
工具
循证设计
数据库(EBD)
用研究成果
指导下一轮
的建筑设计
建筑方案A
建筑方案B
建筑方案C
集成技术方案1
集成技术方案2
集成技术方案3
综合方案A1
综合方案A2
综合方案A3
综合方案…
综合方案C2
综合方案C3
增量成本评估模型
方案Ⅰ
方案Ⅱ
方案Ⅲ
计算机
模拟
方案对比及细节设计调整
社会学视角评估
方案定稿
设计自评
绿建评估
BIM全周期管理
建筑性能监测&
使用后评估POE
完善EBD数据库
设计结果的比较
设计方法的改进

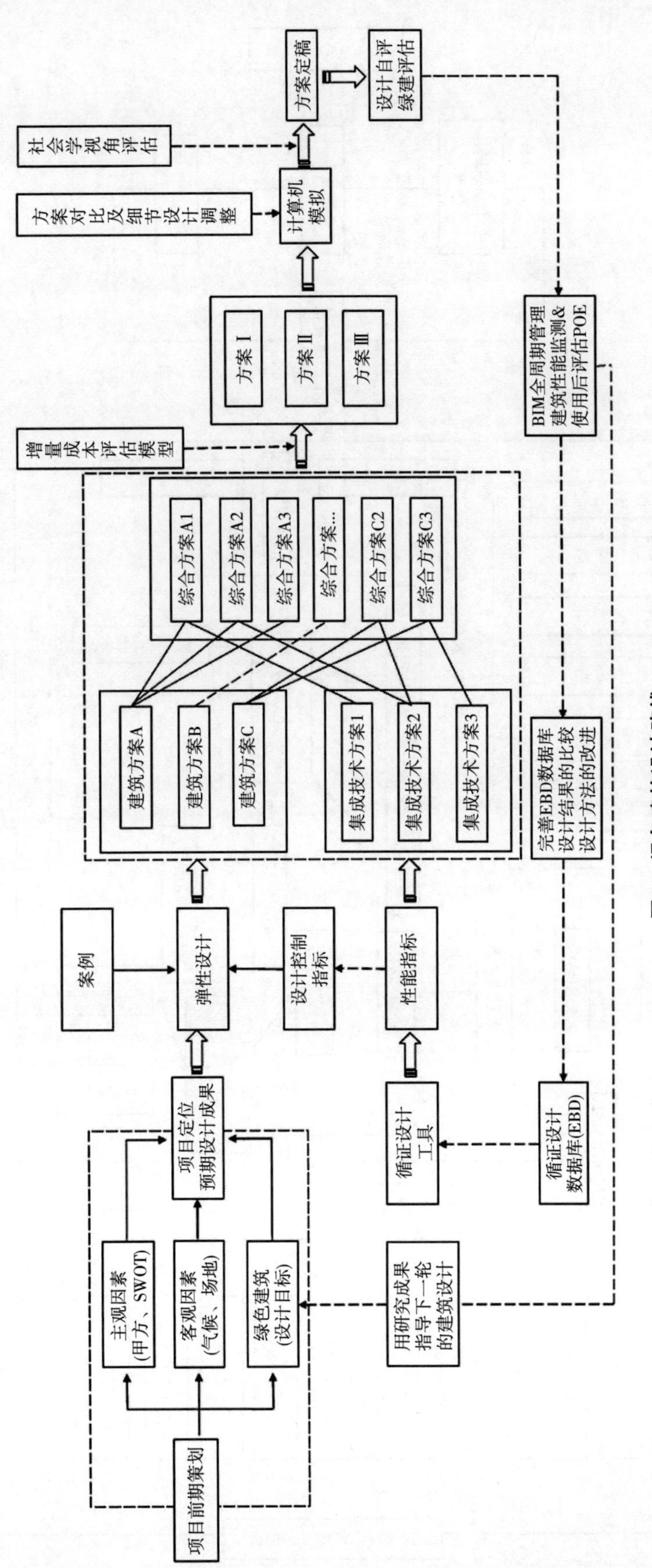

图3　绿色建筑设计路线

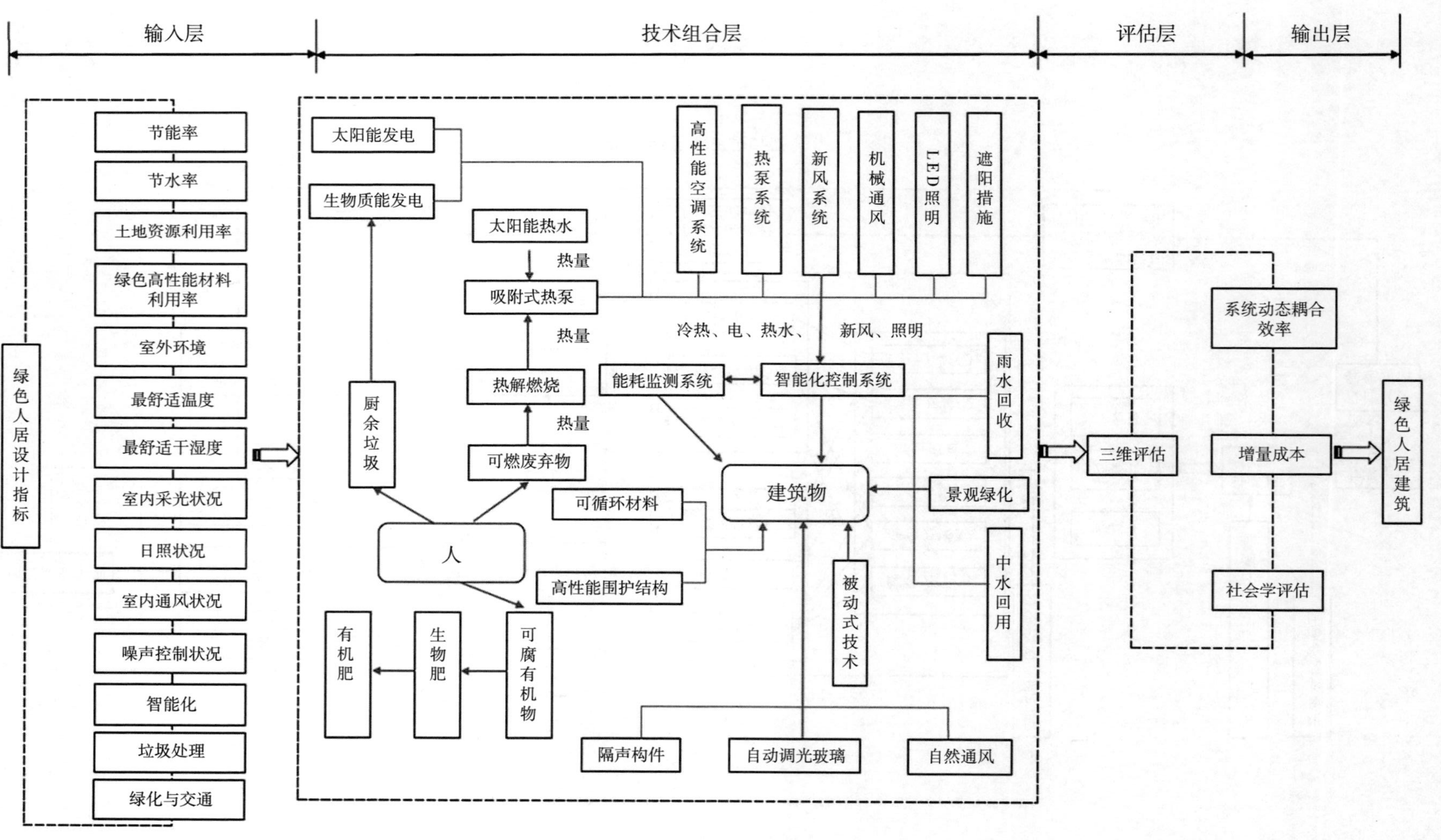

图4 绿色人居建筑技术路线图

作为参照标准来进行技术的筛选和组合。

3. 建筑和技术的使用后评估

通过建筑使用后评估可以对建筑与规划的预期目的与实际使用情况加以对照、分析，并收集反馈信息，为将来同类建筑与环境的规划、设计和建筑决策提供可靠的客观依据，同时也为绿色建筑技术的评价、推广和改进提供数据支持。绿色建筑的使用后评估不仅要以建筑的总体表现为视角，还要以每一项绿色建筑技术的表现为对象，监测其全生命周期的表现和效益。因为本项工作的复杂性和长期性，所以必须引入一个建筑信息集成的平台，也就是BIM技术。BIM平台可以高效地实现绿色建筑信息的记录、存储、修改、变更和调用，从而提高使用后评估工作的效率和效果。

五、结论与展望

绿色建筑的最终追求是实现全生命周期内的绿色人居建筑。绿色人居建筑的发展将会进一步带动绿色建筑技术的发展和整合，并且有利于推进绿色建筑产业的发展，拉动相关领域的经济增长。

目前，我国绿色建筑的发展仍处在以政策为引导的阶段。政府方面，首先，应该制定专门的绿色建筑法律法规与相关标准，通过法律的形式强制绿色建筑的推广，并进行全面的监督和审查；其次，政府应当推进和确保绿色建筑激励措施的实施和落地，可以考虑在下一阶段的发展过程中制定相关的税收减免政策，实施刺激绿色消费的调控手段；同时还应加大宣传力度，提升开发商与消费者的绿色建筑意识；提供经济激励、拓展企业融资渠道，解决开发商建造绿色建筑成本过高的问题；设立技术指导、健全指标体系，使企业发展绿色建筑的方向明晰化。企业方面，应与高校进行产学研的联合，进行技术上的创新，多参与绿色建筑项目，提升其行业竞争力；并以发扬自身社会责任感为己任，严格按照评价标准及法规要求建造绿色建筑，促进行业发展。

除此之外，绿色建筑产业的发展也要与时俱进，注重与当今建筑发展趋势和信息发展趋势的结合，例如BIM技术和云计算技术，从而解决绿色建筑基础性研究滞后的问题。实际上，全周期绿色建筑的发展是不可能脱离信息技术支撑的，例如建筑的后评估过程和性能表现的监测过程。从全周期绿色建筑的视角出发，综合运用BIM和大数据平台，完成绿色建筑资源的共享和整合，进而形成针对全周期绿色建筑、循环反复的“研究—设计”闭合路径。当然，在市场上推广该模式，不可能靠一己之力完成，所以需要政府的引导来打造“政、产、学、研”结合的平台，鼓励不同专业、不同领域的合作与互动，并在以BIM为基础的数字化平台上进行相关数据和资源的共享和整合。再以此为基础，在市场上孕育“研究—设计”交融的绿色建筑研发环境，辅助政府和企业进一步落实《绿色建筑行动方案》，同时通过大数据平台，对绿色建筑技术的运用和表现进行评价，形成可推广的技术集成体系和性能化设计策略；对市场的最新动向进行及时反馈，修正和完善现行的绿色建筑相关政策、法规和规范，进而推动建筑市场的健康有序发展。

（作者：陈天地，苏州中科院全周期绿色建筑研究院；尹金秋，苏州中科院全周期绿色建筑研究院；陈勇，中国工程院院士，苏州中科院全周期绿色建筑研究院，中国科学院广州能源研究所）

参考文献

[1] 陈冰，SODAGAR B.，KING B.，CHISHOLM P. 运用虚拟现实技术辅助可持续建筑参与式设计［J］. 建筑师，2012（5）：18－22.

[2] 陈柳钦. 从人文视角深化对绿色建筑的理解［J］. 新能源与绿色建筑，2010，237（38）：27－32.

[3] 姚润明，等. 绿色建筑的发展概述［J］. 暖通空调，2006，36（11）：27－32.

[4] 陈天地. 全周期绿色建筑设计理论与实践［C］//苏州中科院全周期绿色建筑研究院论文集，2014.

[5] 高升. 绿色建筑的发展趋势探讨［J］. 沈阳建筑大学学报（社会科学版），2010，12（3）：296－299.

[6] 高升. 论美国和欧盟促进绿色建筑发展的策略［J］. 山东科技大学学报（社会科学版），2010，12（3）：57－62.

[7] 林波荣，肖娟. 我国绿色建筑常用节能技术后评估比较研究［J］. 暖通空调，2012（10）：20－25.

[8] 隋红红. 推动我国绿色建筑发展的政策法规研究［D］. 北京：北京交通大学硕士论文，2012.

[9] 尹金秋，陈天地. 性能化导向的低增量成本绿色建筑集成技术选择方法［C］//苏州中科院全周期绿色建筑研究院论文集，2014.

[10] 尹金秋，陈天地，陈冰. 基于神经网络的绿色建筑增量成本评估模型［C］//苏州中科院全周期绿色建筑研究院论文集，2014.

[11] 杨元华. 绿色建筑发展制约因素分析与建议［C］//第九届国际绿色建筑与建筑节能大会论文集，2014：1－7.

[12] 张建国，谷立静. 我国绿色建筑发展现状、挑战及政策建议［J］. 中国能源，2012，34（12）：19－24.

案例篇

实施型村庄规划编制探索

——以广州市白山村美丽乡村规划为例

广州于2011年在市域范围全面启动新型城市化战略，核心内容包括两大方面：一是建设创新型的国家中心城市；一是建设若干“美丽乡村”，推动城与村的和谐发展。新型城市化是以城市建设为中心环节，以缩小农村发展差距、推动地区社会经济发展为目的的全面型城市化战略，因此，实现城乡统筹发展是其核心内容。在此背景下，广州市于2012年开展了“美丽乡村”建设行动，以促进规划实施为导向，切实发展村庄经济、提升村民收入，系统解决村庄在功能、用地、建房、设施以及景观等方面的规划建设，突出岭南村落特色，要求规划能够落地实施。白山村被选为“美丽乡村示范村庄”，探索实施型村庄规划的编制方法体系。

一、广州历次村庄规划编制特点及问题

（一）编制历程及特点

广州市村庄规划编制探索始于20世纪90年代中期，大致经历了农村居民点规划、新增分户规划、社会主义新农村规划、宜居村庄规划以及北部山区帮扶规划5个阶段。各阶段村庄规划由于关注重点问题的差异，呈现出不同的编制特点（图1）：

（1）“目标导向”的农村居民点规划。始于20世纪90年代中后期，广州在经历了若干年的快速城镇化发展后，农村地区在环境和设施等方面和城市存在较大的差距（王冠贤，2012）。为提升农村的生产生活质量，广州市依据国家颁布试行的《村庄与集镇规划建设管理条例》（1993）和《村镇规划编制办法》（2000），尝试对人口较为密集的农村居民点编制村庄规划，重点整治村庄环境、规划市政基础设施。但这一时期村庄规划编制方法体系尚未成熟，大多直接套用城市规划的技术路线，而且缺少相应的用地保障和实施路径。

（2）“问题导向”的新增分户规划。从2003年开始，针对大量符合新增分户政策的村民无处建房的严峻形势，广州市开展了以解决村民住房问题为导向的村庄规划，但由于关注点较为单一，对其他如村庄基础设施建设、村庄经济发展等多方面则缺乏统筹考虑。

（3）“政策导向”的社会主义新农村规划。党的十六届五中全会提出要按照“生产发

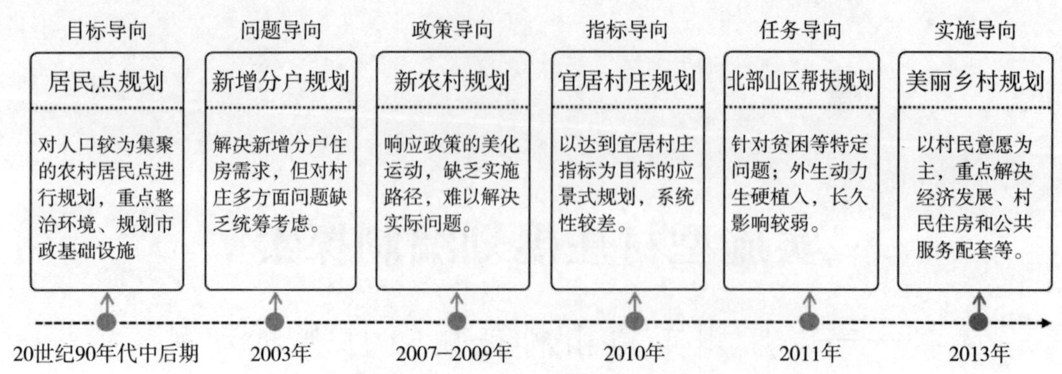

图 1　广州市村庄规划编制发展历程

展、生活宽裕、乡风文明、村容整洁、管理民主”的要求，扎实推进社会主义新农村建设。为响应国家政策号召，广州从 2007 年至 2009 年全面铺开了社会主义新农村规划编制运动。这一阶段以土地指标整理为核心，采用了“城乡建设用地增减挂钩”的方法，推进农村土地的集约节约建设，促进农民上楼，并规划建设了大量的新农村社区。其本质上是属于响应政策的美化运动，由于与农村地区的生产生活实际存在矛盾，因此，规划成果并未得到广泛实施。

（4）“指标导向”的宜居村庄规划。2010 年，广州市要求按照《广东省宜居城镇、宜居村庄、宜居社区考核指导指标（2010－2012）》确定的 4 类 12 项指标开展村庄规划，以达到宜居村庄指标为目的。这轮村庄规划在一定程度上满足了改善村庄环境的目标，但对指导村庄实现自我发展方面仍显不足。

（5）“任务导向”的北部山区帮扶规划。2011 年开始，广州市各区政府职能部门开展了为期 3 年的对口扶贫工作，对广州北部 8 个山区镇的 116 个贫困村开展对口帮扶，并编制了以实现扶贫目标为导向的村庄规划。该规划偏重于解决贫困等特定问题，对农村经济有一定的探索。但部门帮扶的痕迹较重，大多为“输血式”经济项目，外生动力生硬植入，对村庄资源的挖掘和村民的发展意愿了解不足，规划落地实施效果不佳。

（6）“实施导向”。“实施导向”的美丽乡村规划。2013 年开启的新一轮村庄规划，以村民意愿为主，重点解决经济发展、村民住房、公服配套等问题。

（二）问题检讨

广州市历次村庄规划对推动农村地区的发展建设起到了积极的作用，各阶段的规划要求、关注重点有所差异，但整体上还存在着操作性和实施性不足的问题：

（1）有规划、无策划。村庄规划需注重实施的可操作性，要求规划设计成果对村庄的建设有较强的指导性，因此，规划成果内容应能够以科学指导规划实施为主要目的（叶斌，等，2010）。策划实质是针对地区资源禀赋、运用各方面的利好条件，对地区在发展方向、功能主题、产业发展、经济提升等方面进行的系统性战略规划，最大化发挥地区的比较优势。农村地区要实现“自我造血”发展，策划本应是很重要的一个环节，但目前策划多是应用于城市地区，村庄规划少有涉及，导致村庄规划成为城市规划的翻版，难以解决村庄的发展问题，特色不突出，千村一面的规划现象经常发生。

（2）碎片式、体系弱。广州历次村庄规划多是一种基于单个事件的“碎片式”的规划编制，规划内容偏向于环境整治、农房建设或是设施建设，或是一种“大而全”的规划编制，缺乏针对村庄在功能、用地、建房、设施和景观等方面的系统性特色分析。

（3）重空间、轻建设。广州市历次村庄规划往往是落实上位政策或解决问题的被动式指南，关注的问题基本集中在完善村庄配套设施以及整治村庄环境等方面，缺乏对村集体经济发展的有效引导。虽然在一定程度上改善了村庄的环境，但这种“外部植入式”的规划理念过分依赖于政府的资金投入，没有建立起一套完善的区分政府与市场分工协作的“项目库”来指导村庄建设，因此，难以有效解决村集体经济的发展问题，也不能对村民的收入增长带来实质性的影响。

（4）重编制、轻实施。村庄规划与上位规划脱节，缺乏保证规划落地的实施机制，原因在于以往村庄规划在不同程度上没有有效衔接上位规划（主要是城市总体规划、城市控制性规划和城市土地利用总体规划）。没有充分调动村民“自己编规划”的积极性，反观国外，已经采用了“多回合的村民座谈会”等方式，来提高村民参与村庄规划的积极性（有田博之，2002）。在当前国家强调村民自治的大背景下，规划成果只有得到村民的全面认可，才能解决村民自治所面临的外部环境问题以及内部机制问题，建立更为完善的村庄规划实施体系。

二、面向实施的白山村村庄规划编制探索

（一）白山村基本情况

白山村位于广东省广州市白云区太和镇，紧邻国家4A级帽峰山景区。村域面积1016.65公顷，村建设用地37.24公顷，城市建设用地15.32公顷，农林用地和水域等非建设用地964.09公顷，村内绿化覆盖率高达90%，是典型的“青山、秀水、生态村”。村产业薄弱，以农业种植为主，由于白山村地处帽峰山景区控制范围，没有村办工业。2012年村集体收入约14万元，村民年均收入7865元，仅为广州市农民人均收入水平（14818元）的53.1%。

白山村的区位资源条件及上位规划要求决定了不能走传统珠三角地区“家家点火、户户冒烟”、“先污染、后治理”的乡村工业路径，而要按照新型城市化发展的基本要求，充分发掘白山村的比较优势，以提升村集体经济和村民收入为核心，切实推动村庄规划成果落地实施，建设成为宜居、宜业、宜游的美丽乡村。

（二）实施型村庄规划的路径构建

以往村庄规划虽然在解决村庄的空间发展问题上做出了诸多努力，但从效果上来看，在

挖掘村庄特色、指导村庄产业经济发展以及保障规划落地实施等方面相对缺乏。实施型村庄规划针对以往村庄规划存在的不足，从解决村庄发展（策划）、空间问题（规划）、建设行动（计划）、实施保障4个方面出发，全面推动村庄规划的实施（图2）。

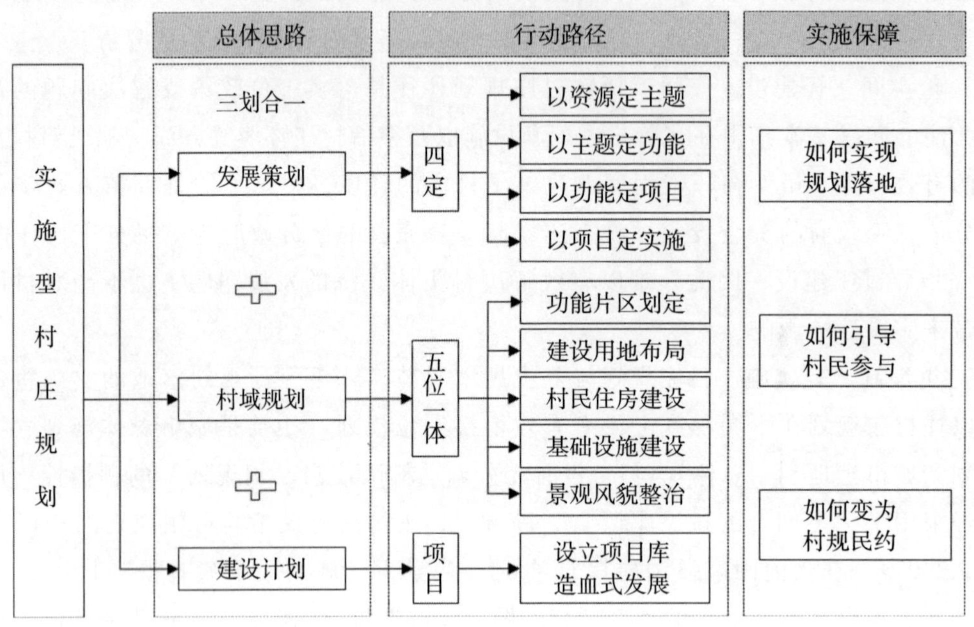

图2 广州市白山村实施型村庄规划路径构建

（三）总体思路——“三划合一”指导村庄规划建设

在深入挖掘“青山、秀水、生态村”内涵的基础之上，以“策划、规划、计划”三划合一的思路指导村庄规划建设。具体而言，发展策划运用“以资源定主题、以主题定功能、以功能定项目和以项目定实施”的思路进行层层推进；村域规划主要包括村域的功能片区划定、建设用地布局、村民住房建设、基础设施建设及景观风貌整治5个方面的内容；建设计划则是具体落实近三年的建设行动。

（四）发展策划——“四定”谋划村庄整体发展

以往的村庄规划，基本都是以空间规划、景观整治为主，很少关心村庄的发展问题，鲜有针对村庄特色和资源条件进行的发展策划。白山村美丽乡村规划按照“四定”思路，对村庄定位、产业、项目以及资金来源等进行了系统的发展策划（图3）：

（1）以资源定主题：通过整合资源优势，连通“青山、秀水”，打造以生态旅游、农业观光、休闲度假为特色，体现客家和广府村落风貌的“美丽白山村”。

（2）主题定功能：基于“青山、秀水、生态村”的主题定位，规划提出“支撑、生态、文态、业态、形态”五位一体的功能策划。

（3）以功能定项目：基于功能策划，规划旅游支撑项目、生态保育项目、文化植入项

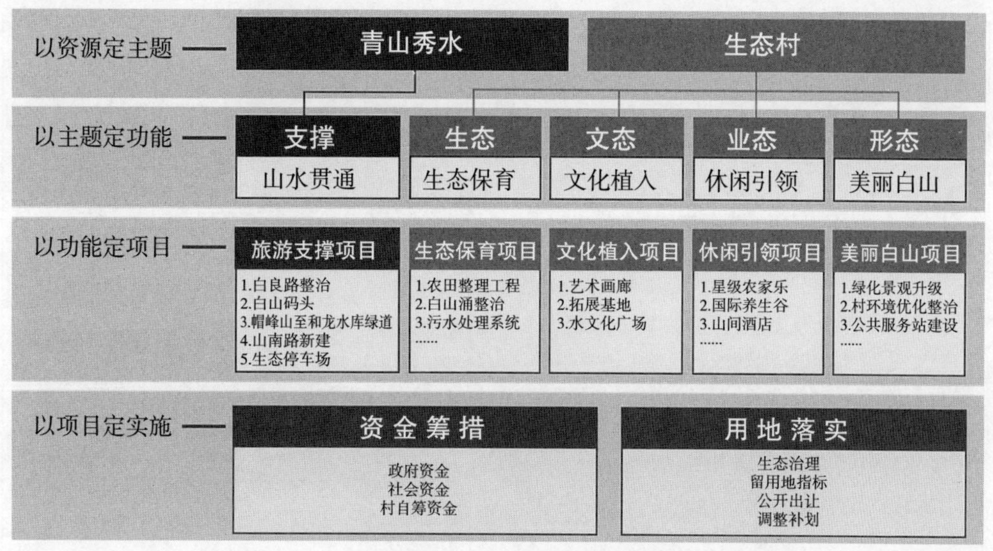

图3　白山村村庄发展策划模式

目、休闲引领项目、美丽白山项目。

（4）以项目定实施：资金筹措采用“多口筹钱，一口花钱”的策略，包括借助政府资金、引入社会资金，村自筹资金等途径。用地落实采用改造和生态治理、留用地指标、公开出让、调整补划等途径。

（五）村域规划——“五位一体”系统引导村庄空间发展

1. 功能片区划定——村域“一盘棋”式统筹考虑

将全村域作为一个整体，不仅考虑村建设用地的规划建设（主要为农民居住生活用地、村经济发展用地等），同时将非建设用地（主要为农村生态涵养地和农田水域等）也纳入规划进行通盘考虑。白山村划分为五大功能区，包括产业经济发展区、居住区、公共服务基础设施配套区、农业发展区和生态控制区（图4）。

居住区、公共服务基础设施配套区以及产业经济发展区主要为村民生活服务的村建设用地，规划严格限定其边界，防止其过度扩张而造成对基本农田等的侵占；农业发展区和生态控制区主要为农村非建设用地，主要功能为农业生产，同时兼有发展乡村旅游功能，此区域严格控制与农业生产或乡村旅游无关的建设项目。

2. 建设用地布局——协调“共性”和“个性”用地布局

村用地布局主要在村建设用地范畴内进行规划，重点考虑“共性用地”与“个性用地”之间的协调。“共性用地”主要包括村生活用地、村属公共服务设施用地、村属道路交通用地、村属市政设施用地和村公园绿地等，是保障村民基本生活所必需的用地；同时结合白山村自身的资源本底特色，增设“个性用地”（村经济发展用地、商业设施用地，主要为发展乡村旅游相关的服务设施用地），发展乡村旅游配套产业，建设星级农家乐、养生谷、山间酒店等旅游服务设施项目。两大用地之间通过农田和自然山体分割，既保障了旅游项目的高

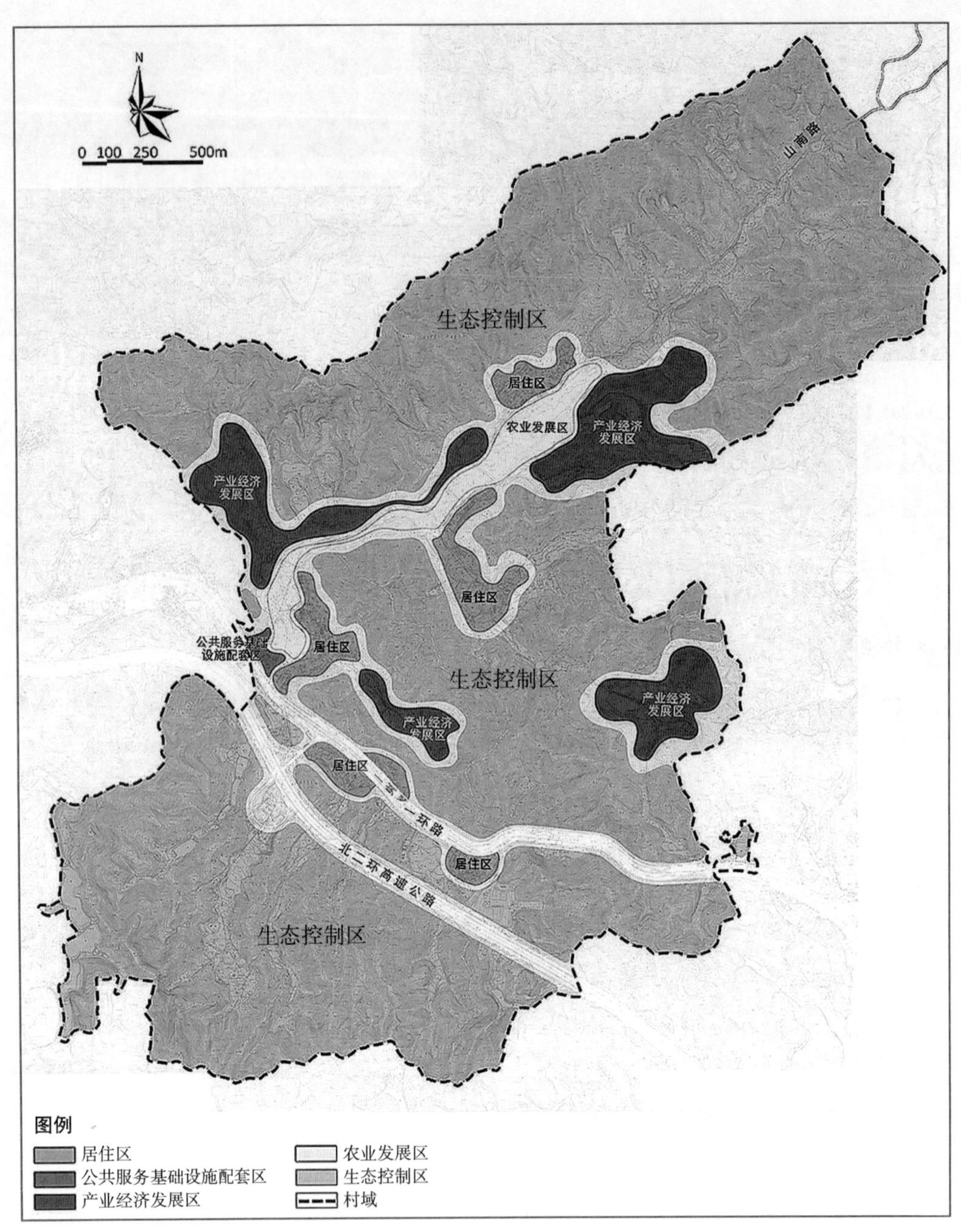

图4 白山村功能片区划分

质量，也避免了对本地村民的干扰（图5）。

3. 村民住房建设——“拆危、改造与新建”三管齐下

白山村现有泥砖房和危旧房196处，其中仍有村民居住的有96户。规划按照村民自愿的原则，对于部分不愿搬迁的村民，其泥砖房采用原地改造的方式，但需按照《广州市城乡规划技术规定（试行）》（2012）的要求，每户住宅建筑基底面积控制在80平方米以内，建筑面积控制在280平方米以内。对于现无人居住（户主迁出）的危旧房，在与户主取得沟通的前提下，进行拆除；或虽有人居住，但愿意搬迁的村民的危旧房和泥砖房，由镇

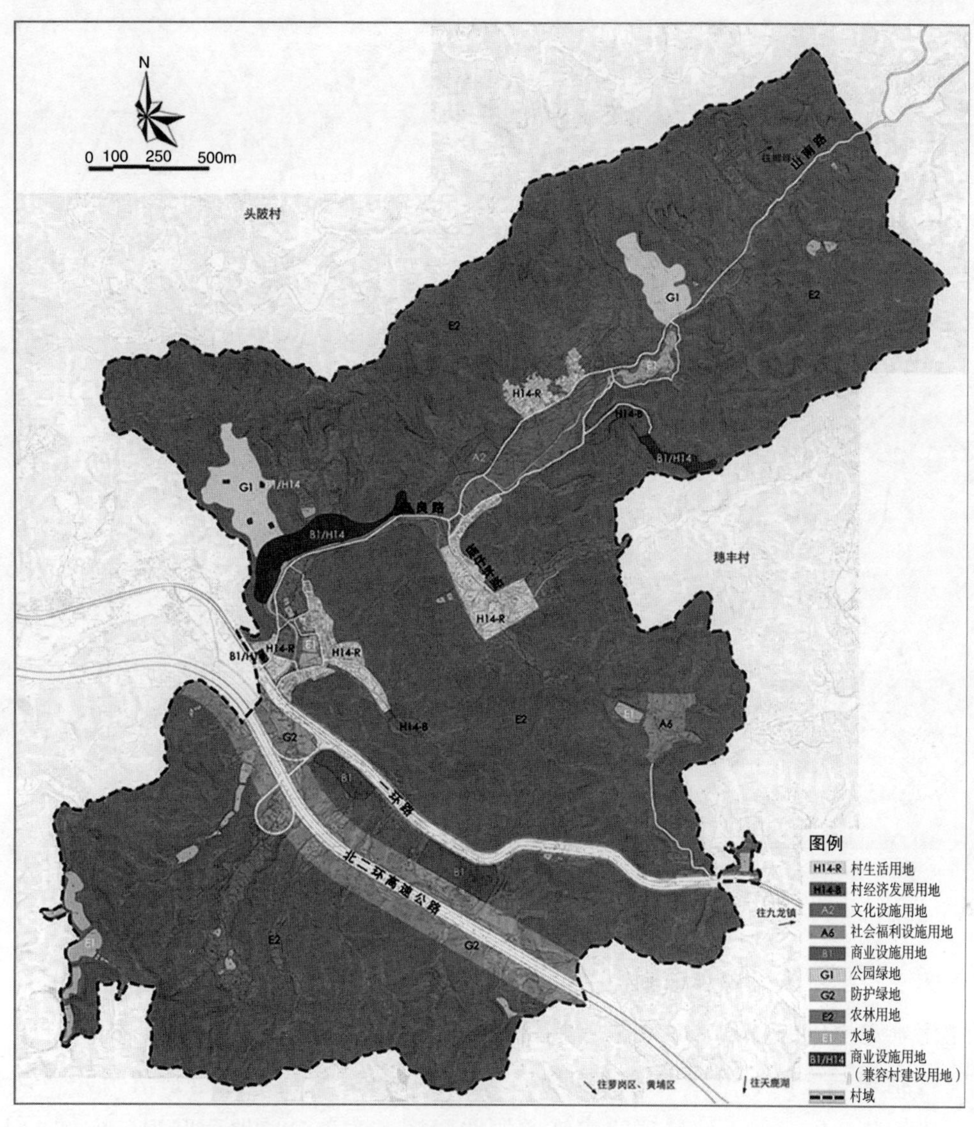

图5　白山村土地使用规划

(区）政府以新建农民公寓的方式进行集中安置，农民公寓建设以多层为主，小高层为辅，首层设置杂物间，用于放置农具（图6）。

4. 基础设施建设——协调考虑“生产型”与“生活型”设施

从村民日常活动的角度出发，将村设施分为“生产型”和“生活型”两大类。“生产型”设施主要分布在农田之间，如农田水利设施，主要方便村民的农业生产活动使用；“生活型”设施则相对集中布置，利于形成村的公共活动中心，以增强村的“凝聚力”和“认知感”。白山村围绕村委规划建设了卫生站、文化活动室、老人活动中心、幼儿园、篮球场等设施。

5. 景观风貌整治——“三次景观面”整治，突出岭南村落特色

岭南特色村落的基本要素主要是民居、道路（里巷）、祠堂、鱼塘以及其他自然环境等，重点对这几个方面的要素提出整治要求，以突出岭南村落特色。根据白山村现状特点，

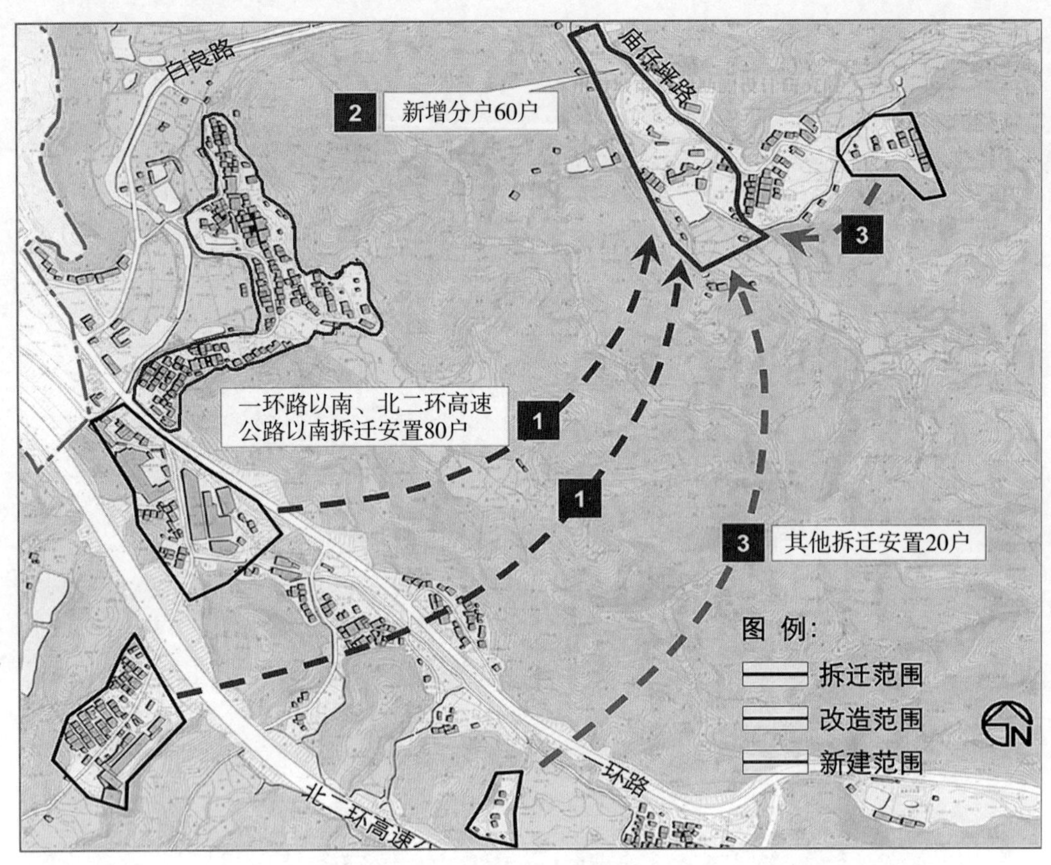

图6 白山村村民住房建设指引

结合视觉感受，将村落景观界面划分三个层次，即由人文建构筑物构成的“一次景观面”、由村庄绿化景观构成的“二次景观面”和由山体林相景观构成的“三次景观面”：①“一次景观面”包括建筑立面、道路、活动广场、基础设施等。整治重点包括清洁并整饰建筑立面、统一建筑色调以及对无坡屋顶的建筑增加坡屋檐；改善道路路面状况，实施沥青罩面，增加路灯、标识牌；增加户外活动广场，完善市政基础设施和公共服务设施等。②“二次景观面”包括宅前屋后绿化、滨水绿化、道路和节点绿化等。整治重点包括鼓励村民在宅前屋后空地种植瓜果蔬菜，减少裸露空地；提升滨水区、道路和节点绿化，并适当引入木棉等观赏树种。③“三次景观面”包括原生山体植被群落、风景林等。整治重点包括恢复裸露山体植被，保育现状原生的以荔枝和龙眼为主的常绿阔叶林，重要视觉节点引入木棉等观赏树（图7）。

（六）建设计划——设立“项目库”，实现村庄自我发展

制订完善的实施计划，将规划实施的资金、责任落实到政府部门，由政府主导规划实施，同时引入市场发展机制，尝试通过农地流转，引入社会资金，扩充资金流入渠道。将村庄规划最终落实到具体的建设项目上，制订细致的实施计划，包括项目名称、项目位置、用地规模、建设规模、完成时间、投资估算、资金来源、建设主体等内容，促进规划落地实施

图7 白山村“三次景观面”整治示意

(图8)。

在充分尊重村民意愿的前提下，按照“功能定项目”的思路，白山村从“支撑、生态、文态、业态和形态”5个方面设置了含37个项目的“项目库”，并分派到2013－2015年的三年实施计划当中。其中，2013年规划了23个项目，重点是以改善村民生产生活环境、打通旅游通道，为发展乡村生态旅游奠定基础；2014年规划了8个项目，重点是通过旅游公司引入文化和旅游项目，发展乡村生态旅游，提高村民收入，增加村民的就业机会；2015年规划了6个项目，重点是建设村民住房安置区以解决90户村民住房安置的问题，建设国家4A级生态旅游景区和广州市民的周末休闲地。同时，在规划中明确了哪些是政府投入的资金、哪些是需要引入的社会资金，并对社会资金的引资渠道都有通盘考虑。

（七）实施保障

1. 用地保障——以“三规合一”，确保规划落地

再好的规划，如果不能落地，最终将变为一纸空谈。白山村尝试将村庄规划与土地利用规划（简称“土规”）、城市规划的图斑进行叠加分析（图9），找出三个规划存在矛盾的地

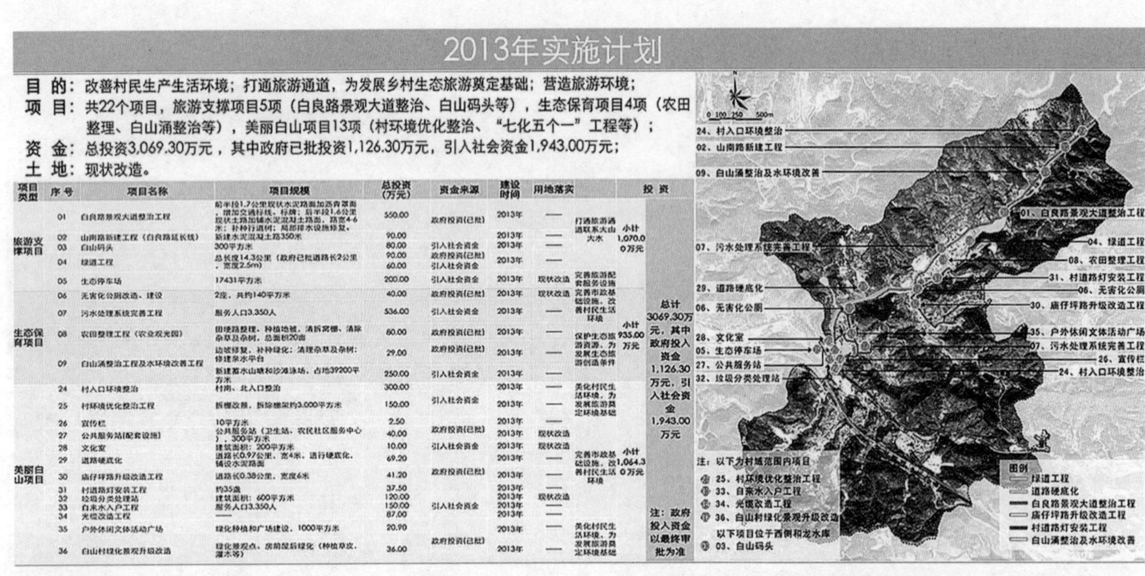

2013年实施计划

目　的： 改善村民生产生活环境；打通旅游通道，为发展乡村生态旅游奠定基础；营造旅游环境；

项　目： 共22个项目，旅游支撑项目5项（白良路景观大道整治、白山码头等），生态保育项目4项（农田整理、白山涌整治等），美丽白山项目13项（村环境优化整治、“七化五个一”工程等）；

资　金： 总投资3,069.30万元，其中政府已批投资1,126.30万元，引入社会资金1,943.00万元；

土　地： 现状改造。

项目类型	序号	项目名称	项目规模	总投资(万元)	资金来源	建设时间	用地落实	项目作用	投资（小计）	投资（总计）
旅游支撑项目	01	白良路景观大道整治工程	前半段1.7公里现状水泥路面加沥青罩面，增加交通标线、标牌；后半段1.6公里现状土路加铺水泥混凝土路面，路宽4-6米；补种行道树；局部排水设施修复。	550.00	政府投资(已批)	2013年	—	打通旅游通道联系大山大水	小计1,070.00万元	总计3069.30万元，其中政府投入资金1,126.30万元，引入社会资金1,943.00万元 注：政府投入资金以最终审批为准
	02	山南路新建工程（白良路延长线）	新建水泥混凝土路350米	90.00		2013年	—			
	03	白山码头	300平方米	80.00	引入社会资金	2013年	—			
	04	绿道工程	总长度14.3公里（政府已批道路长2公里，宽度2.5m）	90.00 60.00	政府投资(已批) 引入社会资金	2013年	—			
	05	生态停车场	17431平方米	200.00	引入社会资金	2013年	现状改造	完善旅游配套服务设施		
生态保育项目	06	无害化公厕改造、建设	2座，共约140平方米	40.00	政府投资(已批)	2013年	现状改造	完善市政基础设施，改善村民生活环境	小计935.00万元	
	07	污水处理系统完善工程	服务人口3,350人	536.00	引入社会资金	2013年	—			
	08	农田整理工程（农业观光园）	田埂路整理、种植绿被、清拆窝棚、清除杂草及杂树，总面积20亩	80.00	政府投资(已批)	2013年	—	保护生态旅游资源，为发展生态旅游创造条件		
	09	白山涌整治工程及水环境改善工程	边坡修复、补种绿化；清理杂草及杂树；修建亲水平台	29.00	政府投资(已批)	2013年	—			
			新建蓄水山塘和沙滩泳场，占地39200平方米	250.00	引入社会资金	2013年	—			
美丽白山项目	24	村入口环境整治	村南、北入口整治	300.00	引入社会资金	2013年	—	美化村民生活环境，为发展旅游奠定环境基础	小计1,064.30万元	
	25	村环境优化整治工程	拆棚改屋，拆除棚架约3,000平方米	150.00		2013年	—			
	26	宣传栏	10平方米	2.50	政府投资(已批)	2013年	—			
	27	公共服务站(配套设施)	公共服务站（卫生站、农民社区服务中心），300平方米	40.00		2013年	现状改造			
	28	文化室	建筑面积：200平方米	10.00	引入社会资金	2013年	现状改造	完善市政基础设施，改善村民生活环境		
	29	道路硬底化	道路长0.97公里，宽4米，进行硬底化，铺设水泥路面	69.20	政府投资(已批)	2013年	—			
	30	庙仔坪路升级改造工程	道路长0.38公里，宽度6米	41.20		2013年	—			
	31	村道路灯安装工程	约35盏	37.50	引入社会资金	2013年	—			
	32	垃圾分类处理站	建筑面积：600平方米	120.00		2013年	现状改造			
	33	自来水入户工程	服务人口3,350人	150.00		2013年	—			
	34	光缆改造工程	—	87.00		2013年	—			
	35	户外休闲文体活动广场	绿化种植和广场建设，1000平方米	20.90	政府投资(已批)	2013年	—	美化村民生活环境，为发展旅游奠定环境基础		
	36	白山村绿化景观升级改造	绿化景观点、房前屋后绿化（种植草皮、灌木等）	36.00		2013年	—			

2014年实施计划

目　的： 通过旅游公司引入文化和旅游项目，发展乡村生态旅游；解决200人就业；村经济收入达到100万；实现村民收入翻一番，增加村民的就业机会；

项　目： 共12个项目，文化植入项目3项（艺术画廊、青少年拓展基地、水文化广场）；休闲引领项目6项（青青农庄及其配套设施、农贸市场、山间酒店、体验式农家乐客家坞、农家亲子旅馆）；美丽白山项目3项（入口植物园、白良路两侧建筑立面整饰、森林运动公园配套设施）；

资　金： 总投资17,232.00万元，全部通过引入社会资金；

土　地： 土地出让用地1.97公顷（艺术画廊）；落实留用地指标0.8公顷（客家坞部分）；通过三规合一调整用地，预支指标7.3公顷（青青农庄及其配套设施部分、农贸市场、山间酒店、体验式农家乐、客家坞部分）；现状改造6.1公顷（农家亲子旅馆、水文化广场[乐百氏整治]）；生态治理15.9公顷（青少年拓展基地、青青农庄及其配套设施部分）；

项目类型	序号	项目名称	项目规模	总投资(万元)	资金来源	建设时间	用地落实	项目作用	投资（小计）	投资（总计）
文化植入项目	10	艺术画廊	用地：49,695平方米	3,000.00	引入社会资金	2014年	土地出让	传统文化融合现代理念，发展乡村旅游，增加村民收入	小计3,600.00万元	总计17,232.00万元，全部通过引入社会资金
	11	青少年拓展基地	用地：65,124平方米	500.00		2014年	生态治理			
	12	水文化广场(乐百氏整治)	用地：17,887平方米	100.00		2014年	现状改造			
休闲引领项目	13	青青农庄及其配套设施	用地：99,969平方米	800.00	引入社会资金	2014年	生态治理/预支指标	结合休闲、度假，发展生态旅游，提高村民收入，增加村民就业机会	小计12,000.00万元	
	14	农贸市场	用地：3,000平方米	500.00		2014年	预支指标			
	15	山间酒店	用地：24,000平方米	3,200.00		2014年	预支指标			
	16	体验式农家乐	用地：11,427平方米	1,500.00		2014年	预支指标			
	17	客家坞	用地：36,000平方米	3,000.00		2014年	留用地/预支指标			
	18	农家亲子旅馆	用地：42730平方米	3,000.00		2014年	现状改造			
美丽白山项目	37	入口植物园	用地：22,000平方米	200.00	引入社会资金	2014年	—	美化村民生活环境，为发展旅游奠定环境基础	小计1,632.00万元	
	38	白良路两侧建筑立面整饰	建筑面积：43,200平方米	432.00	引入社会资金	2014年	—			
	39	森林运动公园配套设施	用地：430,000平方米	1000.00	引入社会资金	2014年	—			

2015年实施计划

目　的： 建设村民住房安置区，解决80户村民住房安置的问题；建设国家4A级生态旅游景区和广州市民的周末休闲地；解决400人就业；村经济收入达到300万；村民人均年收入达到广州平均水平；

项　目： 共5个项目，休闲引领项目5项（国学公馆、乡村俱乐部、国际养生谷、康复疗养基地、住房安置项目）；

资　金： 总投资18,000.00万元，全部通过引入社会资金；

土　地： 土地出让用地5.9公顷（国学公馆、乡村俱乐部、康复疗养基地）；政府征收用地11.04公顷（国际养生谷）

项目类型	序号	项目名称	项目规模	总投资(万元)	资金来源	建设时间	用地落实	项目作用	投资（小计）	投资（总计）
休闲引领项目	19	国学公馆	用地：30,000平方米	3,500.00	引入社会资金	2015年	土地出让	结合休闲、度假，发展生态旅游，提高村民收入，增加村民就业机会	小计18,000.00万元	总计18,000.00万元，全部通过引入社会资金
	20	乡村俱乐部	用地：11,404平方米	1,500.00		2015年	土地出让			
	21	国际养生谷	用地：110,425平方米	6,000.00		2015年	政府征收			
	22	康复疗养基地	用地：18,000平方米	2,000.00		2015年	土地出让			
	23	住房安置项目	用地：46,772平方米	5,000.00		2015年	返迁留用地指标	满足村民住房安置需求		

图8　白山村村庄建设“项目库”

方，并通过生态治理置换用地、落实留用地指标、预支指标和征收出让等方式进行解决。

首先，对接《白云区土地利用总体规划（2010－2020）》。原则上在土地利用规划建设用地范围内开展村庄规划编制，从长远规划角度，在建设用地总量不变并不涉及基本公田保护区的前提下，通过移动土地利用规划的建设用地图斑，优化村庄建设用地布局，并提出了对土地利用规划的调整建议。对移动的建设用地图斑，在土地利用规划调整前用虚线表示，作为村庄长远规划的建议。

其次，对接《帽峰山控制性详细规划（2012）》。确保白山村规划与控制性详细规划（简称“控规”）确定的重点功能区规划、道路、重大市政基础设施、公共服务设施、公园绿地、历史文化保护区等相协调。对于部分规划符合“土规”但与“控规”有矛盾的地块，通过“控规”调整程序来实现；对于“控规”与村民矛盾特别突出的，近期仅做整治规划，控制发展规模，远期通过置换“空心村”等方式，实现村民利益与政府要求的平衡。

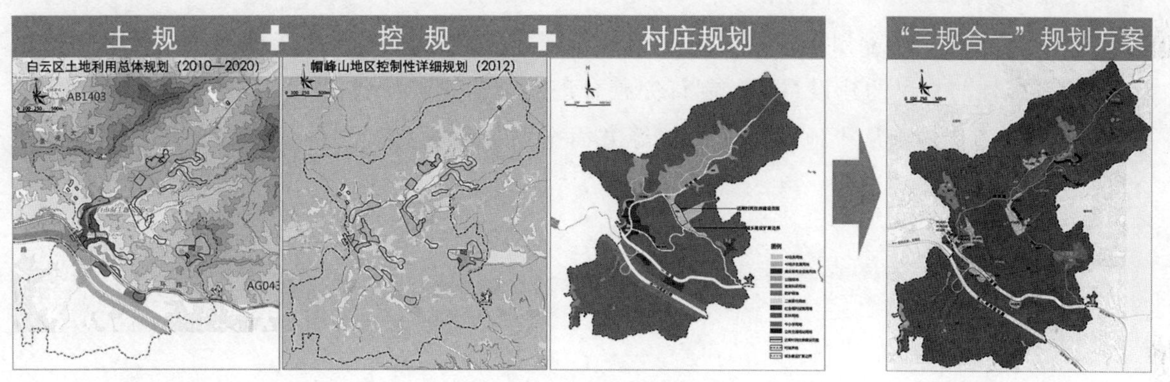

图9　白山村村庄规划“三规合一”

2. 参与保障——实施“规划工作坊”，引导村民参与

村庄归根结底是村民自己的村庄，规划建设村民自己的家园，村民期盼什么，需要什么，他们最有发言权（黄升旗，2010）。我国城乡发展进程短，“公众参与”机制建立的时间也不长，加上村民的知识水平和文化素养有限，直接影响了村民参与乡村建设的程度与深度（汤海孺，等，2013）。由于传统村民参与并没有有效调动“村民自己做规划”的积极性，绝大部分村民在成果公示后才知道，事后参与特点明显（徐明尧，等，2012）。白山村规划运用了“规划工作坊”的方法，即在方案编制的各个阶段，规划师与村民一起进行分组讨论规划方案，规划师向村民展示易看懂的图片，用粤语讲解规划方案，听取和记录村民的意见，并及时反馈到规划成果中，以达到与村民共同协商村庄规划建设问题。工作坊又细分为规划解读、规划讨论、规划答疑三个环节。规划解读环节主要由规划编制单位把规划设计初步成果，整理成通俗易懂的规划图和文字，以一名规划技术人员向全体村民代表进行介绍；规划讨论环节，村民代表分组进行讨论，每组发放一套规划图纸，并由规划师组织本组村民围绕主题有序地进行讨论，解释规划、记录村民意见；规划答疑环节由规划师汇总针对村民提出的问题，并进行集中解答。从效果来看，由于实现了村民自己做规划，“规划工作

坊”活动极大地推动了规划成果的实施。

三、结语

新型城市化发展大背景下，村庄规划在规划思想上有着较大的转变，应以促进实施为核心导向。村庄规划如果仅从单一的空间规划角度出发，往往不能从根本上解决村庄的发展问题。实施型村庄规划应该是包括发展策划、村域规划、建设计划和实施保障于一体的系统性规划：

（1）发展策划着重解决村庄特色发展问题，主要针对村庄的特色及资源进行合理的分配，进行系统的发展策划；

（2）村域规划解决空间发展问题，主要包括功能片区、建设用地、村民住房、基础设施以及景观整治等方面的内容；

（3）建设计划将策划与规划对应到具体的建设项目，解决可操作性问题，充分考虑项目的可实施性与村民的建设意见，制订完善合理的分期建设计划；

（4）实施保障则从土地、村民参与等方面全面推动村庄规划的实施，保障村庄建设工作的顺利开展。

（作者：宋瑞，广州市城市规划勘测设计研究院，高级工程师；王锋，广州市城市规划勘测设计研究院）

参考文献

[1] 黄升旗．我国新型城市化问题探讨［J］．中国集体经济，2010（6）：45-47.

[2] 汤海孺，柳上晓．面向操作的乡村规划管理研究——以杭州市为例［J］．城市规划，2013，37（3）：59-65.

[3] 王冠贤，朱倩琼．广州市村庄规划编制与实施的实践、问题及建议［J］．规划师，2012（5）：81-85.

[4] 徐明尧，陶德凯．新时期公众参与城市规划编制的探索与思考——以南京市城市总体规划修编为例［J］．城市规划，2012，36（2）：73-81.

[5] 有田博之．日本的村镇建设［J］．王宝刚，译．小城镇建设，2002（6）：86-89.

[6] 叶斌，王耀南，郑晓华，等．困惑与创新——新时期新农村规划工作的思考［J］．城市规划，2010，34（2）：30-35.

加强中外社团间合作，促进新型城镇化建设

——美国保尔森基金会与中国有关团体合作介绍

2012年，保尔森基金会（PI）与其合作伙伴中国国际经济交流中心（简称“国经中心”，CCIEE）携手发布倡议，在中国推动可持续城镇化。在此过程中，保尔森基金会与国经中心启动了一系列项目，旨在帮助决策者、研究人员和政府官员深入理解实施可持续城镇化实践方面的最新发展情况和政策。在该活动中，中国市长协会一直以来都是保尔森基金会与国经中心的重要合作伙伴。

保尔森基金会是一家设在芝加哥大学的独立的非党派机构。该基金会成立于2011年，创始人是美国第74任财长及高盛前首席执行官亨利·保尔森（Henry M. Paulson，Jr.），致力于推动全球环境保护及中美两国的可持续经济增长，并加深两国之间的相互了解。保尔森先生是一名自然保护主义者、商业领袖以及忠诚的公务人员，他所创建的基金会一直遵循上述价值理念。目前，该基金会从事的多个活动，都旨在推动相关培训、教育和合作，以便培育城镇可持续发展方面的最佳实践。中国国际经济交流中心是在民政部注册的一级社团，成立于2009年。其主管单位是国家发展和改革委员会。国经中心的主要业务范围和服务领域是研究经济问题、开展国内外经济交流、促进国内外经济合作和提供咨询服务。

一、愿为可持续城镇化有所为

中国国家主席习近平将城镇化列为其宏伟经济改革方案的核心内容之一。中国正经历历史上最大规模的人口迁移活动。据估算，到2020年，中国的城市人口将新增3亿人，约等于美国目前的总人口。在城市消费者激增，进一步发展中国经济的同时，人口问题、食品安全、清洁用水供应和交通堵塞等问题也将继续成为各界关注焦点。中国以及全世界都将很快感受到这一快速城镇化给资源、交通、能源、水和空气质量等需求带来的影响。因此，保尔森基金会相信，作为一个至关重要的领域，可持续城镇化是包括社团在内的中美各方可以携手合作，为城市、公民和环境做出积极影响和作为的良机。

在这一全球城市变革的过程中，市长们发挥着重要的作用。到2020年，全世界将会出现50个人口超过1 000万人的全球性大都市。中国一些城市的规模届时将远大于其他国家。市长们则肩负着实施城镇化这一极具挑战性的任务，不仅为经济增长、就业增长和投资机会

的增长而努力，同时也为在他们城市中实施可持续实践而努力。

中国的市长们与世界各国的市长们一样在工作中有着相似的轻重缓急，但他们也面临着独一无二的各种挑战。保尔森基金会旨在帮助市长们获得成功所需的技能和知识，并通过可持续发展规划项目奖，为应对可持续城镇化的种种挑战、创新可解决的方案而提供激励机制。

二、可持续城镇化主要项目：城市评估工具

（一）保尔森城市评估工具

作为可持续城镇化项目的一部分，保尔森基金会开发了一个独特的评估工具——保尔森城市评估工具（PCAT）。它可以帮助城市领导评估他们的城市所面临的可持续性挑战，并清楚地了解他们的城市在包括形态、交通、能源、气候、空气和水等在内的关键的可持续性和宜居性指标方面是否达标。掌握了这些信息后，市长及主要利益相关方可以更好地分配时间、资源和工作，以取得最大的成效。

该评估工具在中国尚属首创，是在麦肯锡公司为美洲开发银行开发用于整个拉丁美洲范围的快速评估工具基础上改进而成的。保尔森基金会、能源基金会中国可持续城市项目、能源创新政策和技术有限责任公司、中国城市发展研究院以及其他专家和实践者提出了修改意见。在此基础上，该评估工具针对中国的城市进行了调整。

PCAT 城市评估工具本着以“以人为本”的科学发展观为核心，从城市形态、交通、建筑、水、能源、气候、固体废弃物、空气 8 个方面评价城市的生态建设，着重强调人在城市中的生活宜居度，共 61 项指标。在指标评价上，采用“交通灯”反馈分级系统：用红、黄、绿三种颜色来评估每个获得的数据，绿色表示最佳，黄色次之，红色则需要提高。我们结合各项国家规范和各生态城市标准来确定“交通灯”系统的分级标准。PCAT 城市评估工具的应用范围，为城市建成区的全部或其中某一区域以及新城、新区的规划项目。

（二）关于保尔森城市评估工具的具体开发

在对保尔森城市评估工具进行设计和改进的过程中，我们的第一步是采访中国的有关政策制定者、市长、学者以及城市规划专家。对地方领导者来说，最大的挑战之一就是如何确定政策重点的轻重缓急。以长沙为例，时任市长是一名交通运输方面的专家。他很自然地将重点放在城市的交通发展上，但同样严重的问题是，交通系统发展的副产品出现了，那就是对城市绿地的侵占以及人行道同步建设的缺失。

虽然中国充斥着各种不同经济和环境标准下的排名，但根据国内和国际标准制定的快速评估工具却是凤毛麟角。因此，我们首先将目光投向了国际组织中可资利用的模型。该模型应该可以针对中国的情况进行调整并按照不同城市进行细化。于是，我们找到了美洲开发银行在拉丁美洲城市可持续化项目中使用的快速评估工具。

美洲开发银行的快速评估工具主要用于将收集到的数据根据交通、城镇规划、清洁用水、清洁空气等涉及城镇化多个范畴的国家和国际标准进行评级。我们对该工具进行了定制，花了两年时间开发出保尔森城市评估工具。除了创建一个具有直觉性的简单评估工具之外，我们还旨在开发出一个工具可以在6个月的时间里为政策制定者提供评估意见。每届市长的任期通常为四至五年，因此，该工具的快速时间框架可使他们有机会对报告和建议做出反应。我们在工具开发过程中采访的许多中国市长和专家指出，他们通常会收到关于进行3年期深入研究的申请，这实际上只给他们留下了两到三年的时间解决研究中发现的各种问题。虽然时间跨度更长的研究得出的结果可能会更详细，但我们采访的所有专家都认为，与之相比，6个月的分析所确定的趋势并无太大不同。

之后，我们开始与中西方专家合作，对美洲开发银行的工具进行修订，开发出了保尔森城市评估工具的初始版本。一些相关的内容得以保留，适用于拉丁美洲却不适合中国的其他措施，如安全、市长选举、教育措施和相关问题等，因为与课题内容不符而遭到舍弃。获得可资利用的初始版本后，在中国举办了几次研讨会，召集了中国和国际上领先的可持续发展和城镇化专家就工具达成一致意见，并尽可能广泛地从实践者那里寻求更多信息。

在此过程中，我们汇集了各领域的领导，包括美洲开发银行负责在拉丁美洲管理该工具的专家、协助开发和部署其评估工具的麦肯锡公司专家、中国可持续化问题专家以及交通、城市规划与设计、水质、污染相关问题和能效等具体部门的专家的意见。几个对中国城镇化或可持续性具体领域问题有着专门研究的美国智库、大学、公司和个人专家都对保尔森城市评估工具的内容提供了反馈。此外，我们的中方合作伙伴中国城市发展研究院，是在中国城市发展和城镇化研究方面的中国领先专业机构，保留着关于中国市政统计的最大数据库。他们将此数据使用在了保尔森城市评估工具的开发中。中国城市发展研究院在创建该工具的过程中，也在中国政府内部以及清华大学建筑学院等领先的学术机构中进行了广泛咨询。

（三）关于保尔森城市评估工具的具体运用

保尔森城市评估工具已经在两个处于快速城镇化进程中的中国城市进行了试点：一个是河北省保定市，一个是湖南省长沙市。保定位于中国人口最稠密的地区之一，也是中国多家大的可再生能源制造企业的所在地。虽然可持续能源已占当地 GDP 的 20%，但该城市仍然因为其制造业部门的能源使用而名列中国污染最严重城市第三名。受保定市市长于群的邀请，保尔森基金会在保定开展保尔森城市评估工具试点，以交通、城镇规划、用水和用电这四个城镇化领域为重点，旨在将保定市变成中国最领先的可持续发展城市之一。在于群市长将保定这个总人口 1 000 万人、城市人口 100 万人的城市变成中国领先的可持续发展城市的整体努力中，他将该工具用作该努力的组成部分。根据规划，“保定将成为承接北京疏散非首都核心功能中的工业、部分服务业以及部分行政性、事业性服务机构的重要平台。”在涉及城镇化规划时，该城市领导层一直都有向该目标积极靠拢的明晰意图。根据上述分析，我们发现：

就交通领域而言，保定市拥有足够的道路满足该市的交通需求，但随着国内发展趋势，乘用车保有量也在不断增加。道路规划和公交系统也需加大改善力度。尤其是，由于有意愿乘坐公交的人士远多于可提供公交车数量，人均公交车占有量进入黄色类别区域，因此需要更多公共交通。保定市在步行区和自行车道的建设实施上也落后于绿色类别。

在城镇规划领域，有两个趋势与推动保定市可持续发展背道而驰，那就是不断降低的人口密度和在建社区中综合社区的减少。事实上，我们已将不断降低的人口密度这一统计列入红色类别区域。为解决上述问题，实现保定市城市规模的最大化，我们建议逐步形成依靠公共交通的更大人口密度，发展综合社区，特别是在靠近高铁车站的区域。

在用水领域，保定市达到并超过了节水目标，并享受较低的工业和家庭用水费率。多项用水指标均在绿色类别之下，唯一的例外是漏水管道，我们将之加上小红旗标志，作为急需关注的领域。我们也无法确定漏水率从 2010 年的 4% 升至 2011 年的 12% 的相关原因。

保定的居民和商业用电量相对较高。在商业用电方面，我们建议引进更多具有绿色商业举措的企业，用以抵消目前主导该市工业构成的诸多能源密集型企业所带来的影响，从而对该市的产业结构进行合理化安排。在居民用电方面，我们相信可以通过引进公民教育活动来教会消费者采取哪些步骤节能，保定市也将从中获益。

保尔森城市评估工具也在长沙市进行了试点。长沙正处于从一个内陆欠发达城市向快速成长中的中心城市转变的进程中。该市不但是该省的经济增长引擎，同时也是中南地区的经济增长驱动器，在经济增长方面，在中南六省首府中也是遥遥领先。

长沙市 370 万人口主要集中在几个中心区，中心区的城镇化率约为 90%，其中芙蓉中央商务区宣称其人口密度已经达到 100%。但是，与日本等世界上人口最稠密城市的人口密度相比，长沙市区仍然有着继续发展城镇化的空间，特别是，如果长沙市的基础设施、各项系统和城镇规划也能与时俱进，长沙市将可容纳更多人口。由于农民工大量涌入城市中心区，长沙市的人口在下一个 10 年中预计增加至 800 万人左右，因此，亟待将可持续发展的最佳实践融入其城镇规划中。

长沙正面临着与世界各地快速城镇化过程中的其他城市面临的相同问题：交通堵塞、工业效率低和高耗能消费。因此，保尔森基金会和国经中心一直都专注于对城镇化、交通、公共绿地、能源消费和水资源消费 5 个重点部门的分析和建议。根据评估工具的结果，我们发现：

长沙市的城镇化率正在稳定提升，目前已经超过湖南省以及全国的平均水平。长沙市各区之间城镇化率差异较大，市中心和更靠近市区的城区水平较高，原因是有大量农民工离开农村地区前往这些地区寻找工作机会。因此，该测量结果属于应予以关注的黄色分类区域。我们建议长沙市继续寻找可以保护和支持农民工及其家人发展的方式，因为这一人口流入趋势将不可能放缓。此外，我们建议长沙市政府与邻近各区合作，启动一个“边缘开发”计划，因为这些地区正在面临人口外流到市区的情况，使得这些地区失去了充足的农村劳动力。

在交通领域，长沙市曾做出很大的努力，希望将公共交通系统变得更为环保，但该市的公交系统需要特别注意与城镇化的进展保持与时俱进。由于私人轿车保有量快速提高，人均道路面积不足，长沙市正在经历严重的交通堵塞。同时，长沙市在提供充足的人行道方面也有很多工作要做。

虽然长沙市的公共绿地面积总量在缓慢增加，但远低于国家平均水平。公共绿地总密度略有提升，但人均绿地面积出现剧降。绿地面积属于红色类别，需要立即加以关注。城市中心的绿地面积与经济和旅游的发展相辅相成，相互促进。为解决该问题，我们建议长沙市实施包括绿地在内的建筑相关举措，创建可容纳更多人口流动的交通系统，如自行车道和人行道等，且均要远离机动车道。

长沙市在整体节能方面取得了重大进步。2011 年，长沙市单位 GDP 能耗大幅下降，与上一年相比下降 22.52%。在地区级城市中，长沙市人均电耗最低，但人均居民电耗最高，显示长沙市需要强调降低居民电耗。在水资源领域，长沙市因附近的湖泊以及湘江、浏阳河和捞刀河三条大河而拥有丰富的水资源。长沙市将把建成一套高性能污水处理系统作为其工作重点，目前在污水处理方面已经超过全国平均水平。但是，该市人均水耗仍然居高不下。该市应探寻其他替代方式推动更佳的节水措施，例如对供水网络进行大修、引进节水装置，以及开展公民教育活动。

三、可持续城镇化的其他项目

（一）未来城市：现代中国的城市可持续性研讨会

保尔森基金会每年都与国经中心和中国市长协会合作，在北京举办一届“未来城市：现代中国的城市可持续性研讨会”。研讨会将国际和国内专家、实践者和思想家汇集一堂，通过对解决城市规划和环境挑战的专家级演示共同探讨推动可持续发展的创新方法。

研讨会旨在提供切实可行的方法，解决决策者和市长们在当前城市快速增长中所面临的一些主要挑战，包括以人为本建设城市、经济增长取之有道、城市建设中绿色公交先行等，由此解决私人轿车激增所带来的严重交通堵塞问题，提供清洁用水和改善空气质量的方法。

中国市长协会与美国市长协会的领导曾是前两届研讨会的主旨发言人。我们还曾有幸邀请到两任北京市市长分享他们如何在取得经济发展的同时，推动北京以可持续的方式不断发展的经验。此外，洛杉矶市前市长安东尼·维拉奥格萨在 2011 年研讨会上分享了洛杉矶如何从美国一个雾霾首府成长为领先的绿色城市的心路历程。在研讨会期间，费城市市长迈克尔·纳特在接受《财富》杂志编辑采访时谈到了洛杉矶市为了“变绿”而采取的措施，包括复兴滨水区域、与 NRG 公司合作，将该市的足球体育场改建成一处全绿色建筑，用以对该市 99.4% 的垃圾进行循环再利用或将其制作成堆肥。纳特市长之后主持了本基金会在费城举办的首次市长培训项目，并抽出大量时间与代表团介绍了他的决策情况和该城市可持续发展办公室的架构等。

2014 年，年度研讨会的重点转到了关注建筑节能标准所能带来的重大影响上，而这正是中国能有所作为的一个重要议题。研讨会的主题是“21 世纪建筑——优化建筑绩效，构建可持续未来”，在北京将全球领先的有关专家学者和实践者汇聚一堂，就推动节能建筑的最佳实践进行为期一天的探讨。根据联合国政府间气候变化专门委员会的报告，建筑物的能源消耗超过世界上任何其他部门，约占全球温室气体排放的40%。中国目前正是全球领先的建筑工地，正可借推动建筑节能的东风为温室气体减排做出重要贡献。

会议建议中国也可采取一些简单的措施推动各种改变。其一，根据最新科技和目前大力推行的实践案例制定高质量的建筑节能法规。其二，从单个建筑中收集供暖/制冷和能源利用数据，使政府部门、建筑业主、公共事业公司和建筑使用者可以价廉物美的方式调整其节能行为。推行改变其行为的激励措施，如激励项目的创新使用和提高节能意识的运动，能够鼓励人们更多采用节能电器和绿色三星建筑标准。

我们非常荣幸地邀请到了深圳市市长许勤到会，向大家介绍了深圳市在可持续发展以及推广绿色建筑方面的卓越举措。而且，我们也邀请芝加哥市前市长理查德·戴利到会进行了一次立意深刻的演讲。他谈到如何推动芝加哥市的绿色市政建筑，使得政府部门在绿色建筑发展方面以身作则，起到模范带头作用。下届研讨会可能把重点转向可再生能源方面。

（二）市长培训项目

保尔森基金会与国经中心和中国市长协会合作，推出了一个针对市长和可持续发展事务官员的可持续城镇化最佳实践年度培训项目。该项目于2013年启动，已形成系统性的逐省参加模式，确保所有参与者有着共同的挑战和目标。因此，我们每年都邀请不同省份的市长参加项目。代表团第一周在清华大学学习，之后前往美国。在美国的第一周将在芝加哥大学参加各可持续发展领域的领先实践者举办的讲座。芝加哥市以其颇具创新意识的前市长理查德·戴利领导和推行的可持续性项目而闻名。市长培训项目的首个代表团来自北京，重点学习的是可持续发展理念和实践。这是一个为期三周的项目，包括在芝加哥、费城和纽约的各种课程和实地考察。课程重点是交通、城市规划和再开发、地区一体化发展、保障房、水资源管理与气候变化应急规划。代表团直观地了解了哪些做法在美国是有效的，哪些是无效的。在诸多案例中，美国都是中国的前车之鉴，说明了“二战”之后推动城镇化、开发郊区的做法有多么不明智。虽然郊区有着良好的环境，但迫使人们大量使用轿车，偏离了更为传统的以较小城市街区承载混居社区的城市规划。

第二个代表团来自广东省，代表团在芝加哥学习一周之后，拜访了迈阿密市，探讨该城市如何在2008年全球金融危机之后将引进的可持续举措作为其城市复兴的计划之一。与许多城市一样，迈阿密市接纳了区域性可持续发展的理念，启动了一个范围覆盖四个县、无预算、自愿运作的委员会，在推行解决迈阿密市重大挑战的地区性解决方案方面取得了巨大成就。

在面临水灾和推动灵活海岸线政策方面，迈阿密市与广东省有着诸多的相似之处。迈阿密市还拥有一个重要港口，承担拉美各国与美国之间的诸多贸易。代表团受到了迈阿密市前市长曼尼·迪亚兹的热情接待，并会见了迈阿密比奇市市长。这位市长是水灾治理问题方面的前沿领域专家，而该问题会对海港城市所赖以生存的旅游业造成巨大影响。代表团还受到时任迈阿密大学校长、克林顿政府时期美国前卫生部长多娜·莎拉拉的热情接待。莎拉拉女士是城市政治和市长职务方面的专家，无论是在迈阿密大学时在可持续发展和海岸恢复力方面从事尖端研究，还是担任白宫内阁秘书长、卫生部长，她都能在相关事务上提供自己的真知灼见。项目结束时，各位市长还向我们提供了关于会议和讨论话题的珍贵反馈意见。此外，市长们还撰写了提交省级领导以及可供中国市长协会发表的报告。我们由此确定了2015年项目的新重点话题：可持续性领导力。毫无疑问，领导力的原则能够超越不同的政治制度而显示出其共性。

（三）可持续发展规划项目奖

保尔森基金会和国经中心的可持续发展规划项目奖于2013年启动，每年都颁发给一个针对严重城镇化挑战做出创新、可扩展和有效解决方案的中国可持续发展项目。该奖旨在为实施可持续发展方面的最先进实践创建一个积极的激励机制，将这些行动推向更广泛的受众，并通过一个由业界专家组成的评委会来对中国城市做出的卓越成就加以认可。

评委会由芝加哥市前市长理查德·戴利先生领导，成员包括自然保护、发展、经济学和金融学领域的多位中美重要领袖。评委会将确定并审查合格项目，分析项目并将之与规划项目奖的标准进行对比，最终挑选出胜出的项目。

2013年11月7日，保尔森基金会和国经中心在北京将第一届“可持续发展规划项目奖”授予嘉兴世合新农村项目。评委会之所以评选该项目作为最终获奖者，是因为它用一种创新的方式来应对中国目前日益增长的大规模城镇化挑战。该项目通过在节约用水、能源效率和交通技术方面采用开创性的实践，应对了城镇化进程中的三大挑战：空气、土地和水。这一创新项目还直接创造了新的就业机会，并将推动这一快速发展的区域实现可持续经济增长。该项目奖由保尔森基金会主席、美国前财政部长、高盛集团前主席和首席执行官亨利·保尔森（Henry Paulson）先生和国经中心理事长、中国前副总理曾培炎先生向获胜项目所在城市的市长颁发。

2014年11月10日，保尔森基金会和国经中心在北京将第二届“可持续发展规划项目奖”授予深圳国际低碳城项目。评委会选择该项目是因为“深圳项目反映了设计、规划、和实施大型低碳城项目的一种综合、前瞻的思维方式”。

低碳城项目坐落在深圳欠发达社区，在制订社区复兴计划时，策划者认真考虑了居住在该区的人们，这使得该项目有别于中国其他城市项目。没有为了建新楼而拆除现有建筑，让居民搬迁，该项目重点投资于提升改造现有建筑和旧厂房，同时改善环境（如清理当地河流）。这些提高鼓励了高端、低碳工业项目的有机发展以及专注于当地人民需求的经济发展。深圳市市长许勤代表项目组织方领取了该奖项。

保尔森基金会主席亨利·保尔森在谈到2014年的获奖项目时说道，“这个奖项为开发创新的、可持续发展和可扩展的解决方案提供了激励机制，并促进了中美之间的合作。该奖项旨在鼓励经济、政治以及其他领域的领导者竭力寻求真正挑战的实际解决方式。”

我们与国经中心和中国市长协会之间的合作伙伴关系已经产生了多个实际项目，也带来了正能量。得益于大学、研究单位和参加市长培训项目代表团的市长们的努力，新的合作伙伴关系已经形成，也有新的解决方案提出，以供中国的决策者们考虑。

四、加强高端智库建设，促进新型城镇化

2014 年，韩国科学技术政策研究院参与并完成《未来 10 年预测研究报告》。该报告在优先领域和必须发展的技术推导过程中，十分注重与国外比较，以及技术领先性与市场投资关注点之间的关系。他们为此聘请了 2 000 多个专家，从产学研、专利、论文、情报、影响力指数等方面综合评估，对 120 项关键技术与国际最高水平国家进行比对。

全国政协委员蓝闽波曾提交了一份《联合各类资源，推进高水平专业化智库建设》的提案。他认为，目前我国类似韩国的发展规划和战略报告大多出自科技专家和管理专家。专家们对自己的专业领域提出见解，相关部门再根据这些建议，制定相关规划，确实对我国科技发展起到一定的引领作用。“但产业所涉及的不仅是科学问题，它更是一个系统工程，仅由科学家判定产业发展是不全面的。”科技和产业的关系需要不同专业的人员多角度进行研究。他还认为，各类科技学会、协会是由专家组成的社会团体，他们来自于不同的科研单位和企业，应该将他们发展成为建设我国科技和产业智库的重要力量。

智库是“思想库”“脑库”“外脑”、咨询公司、智囊团或其他智囊组织的通称，是由多方面专家、研究人员组成的跨学科公共研究机构，为决策者提供政策建议和决策咨询，通过各种研究成果和公共媒体影响公共政策的制定和社会舆论。独立性和非营利性是国际上智库普遍恪守的准则。但蓝闽波对智库的独立性认为，独立性不意味着不接受社会和政府资金资助，非营利性也不是不能用研究成果换取运营经费。“斯坦福研究院对中国化学化工研究机构研究能力的评价报告就被中国有相关合作的大型跨国公司高价收购了。”蓝闽波认为，只要建立起科学的采购标准和程序，智库成果采购制度能激励智库产出更优质的报告。

2015 年年初，中共中央办公厅、国务院办公厅印发了《关于加强中国特色新型智库建设的意见》，从推进国家治理体系、治理能力现代化和增强国家软实力的战略高度，为今后一个时期中国智库建设和发展设定了目标和方向。

2015 年 3 月 25 日，主管全国学会、协会、研究会的中国科协下发了《中国科协关于贯彻落实中央群团工作部署，加强和改进科协工作的意见》，指出：“认真落实党中央关于中国特色新型智库建设的部署，发挥好科协组织在科技战略、规划、布局、政策等方面的决策咨询作用，加大科技创新智库建设力度，努力成为创新引领、国家倚重、社会信任、国际知名的高端科技创新智库。围绕科技发展重大问题以及国家重大产业发展和区域发展战略，深入调查研究，提出有价值的对策建议。着眼于推动健全完善国家科技决策咨询制度，积极开展第三方创新评估，提高科学性、权威性，服务科学决策。”

以上充分说明中国为智库的纵横发展正在开创前所未有的良好的舆论环境，多层设计的政策导向。保尔森基金会坚信，在中国不断加强高端智库建设，保护境外非政府组织在中国

境内依法开展活动等方针指引下，如果包括美国社会团体在内的中外社团精诚合作，那么，在实现中国新型城镇化中必将有所作为。

（作者：戴青丽（Deborah Lehr），保尔森基金会资深战略顾问；魏蕾（Leigh Wedell），保尔森基金会首席可持续发展官）

海口：国际旅游岛助推城市快速发展

一、城市资源环境与城市发展条件

（一）海口资源环境

海口，位于海南国际旅游岛的最北端，海南省会，行政辖区包括琼山、秀英、龙华、美兰四个区，土地面积2 304平方公里，海域面积830平方公里。

海口地处低纬度热带北缘，属于热带海洋性季风气候，是一座洋溢着热带海滨风光、海岛都市风情的生态旅游城市。海口地区构造运动复杂，现今还分布着我国目前规模居首位的火山群，是第四纪火山的天然博物馆，同时也是我国唯一的热带海岛城市火山。海口地区是海南岛移民最先涉足的区域，多种移民文化在这里集中体现，并与本土文化有机融合，形成了独具特色的海口地方文化与传统。海口市还荣获“国家环境保护模范城市”和“中国人居环境奖”称号，是世界卫生组织指定的全国第一个“健康城市”试点市。独特的地理位置，复杂的构造运动，悠久的历史，灿烂的文化，造就了海口美丽神奇、丰富多彩的旅游资源。

（二）海口城市发展条件

1. 国民经济持续平稳增长

海口市国民经济多年来保持平稳增长。2014年海口市实现国内生产总值（GDP）1 005.51亿元，比上年增长9.2%。人均地区生产总值46 000元，比上年增长7.7%，按年均汇率折算为7 418美元。

第三产业贡献率较高。第一、二、三产业比例由上年的6.2∶22.9∶70.9调整为5.5∶21.4∶73.1。第一、二、三产业对经济增长的贡献率分别为-1.6%、14.1%和87.5%。其中，第三产业对经济增长的贡献率比上年提高14.2个百分点，拉动全市经济增长8个百分点。

2. 旅游产业起步早、发展较快

1988年海南建省、设经济特区，海口的政务和商务活动日趋繁忙，带动了娱乐业的兴

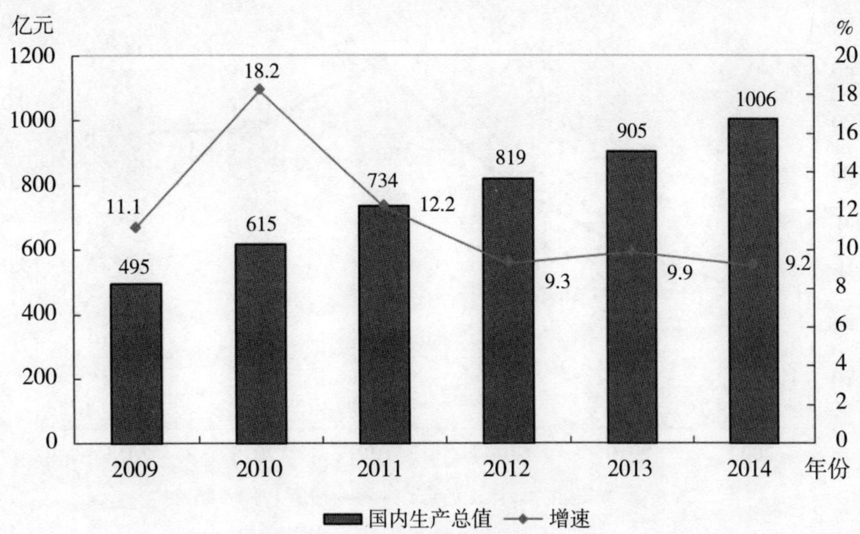

图1　海口市2009-2014年国内生产总值（亿元）及增速

资料来源：2014年海口市国民经济和社会发展统计公报。

起。1992年邓小平南巡讲话之后，海口旅游业迅速崛起，当年接待国内外游客人数突破100万人次；到20世纪90年代中期，寰岛泰德、金海岸罗顿、宝华海景等一批高档商务和度假酒店相继建成，1996年游客接待量突破200万人次；1999年美兰机场正式建成通航，次年海口的游客接待量即突破300万人次，2008年达到637.9万人次；2014年海口市接待国内外游客量达到1130.7万人，旅游总收入达142.02亿元。全市A级旅游景区9家，新评1家。星级宾馆酒店45家，其中五星级宾馆酒店7家、四星级宾馆酒店14家。

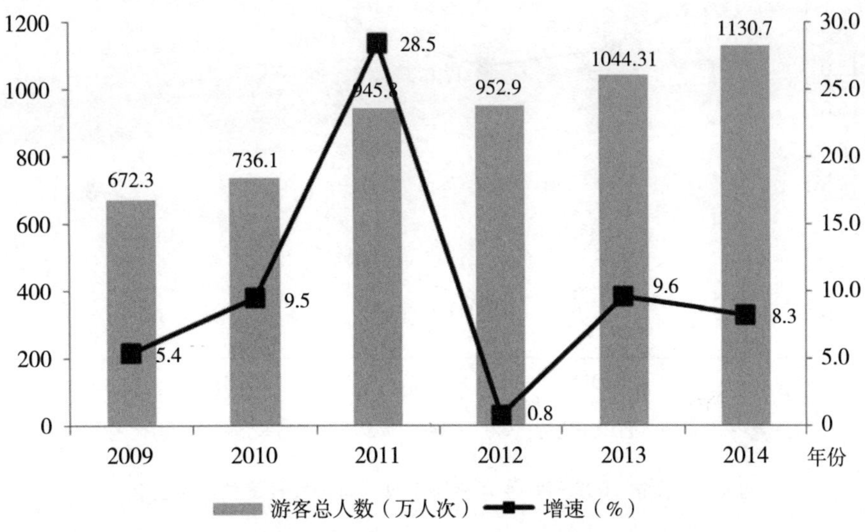

图2　海口市2009-2014年国内外游客总人数及增速

资料来源：2009-2014年海口市国民经济和社会发展统计公报。

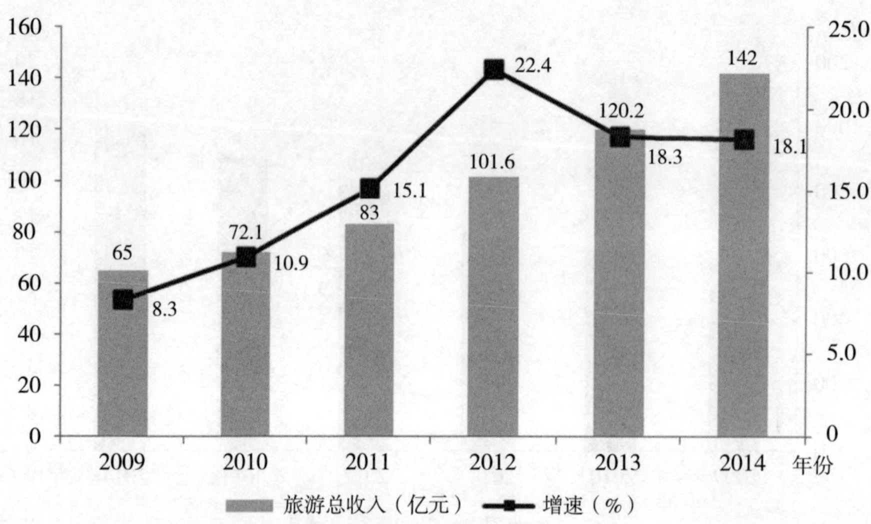

图3　海口市2009-2014年旅游总收入及增速

资料来源：2009-2014年海口市国民经济和社会发展统计公报。

3. 旅游业已成为海口国民经济支柱产业

海口旅游经过30多年的发展，已具一定规模。2014年旅游总收入达到142亿元，相当于全市GDP的14.1%，相当于第三产业增加值的19.3%。“十二五”期间，海口旅游业总收入年均增长18.5%，高于同期全市GDP年均增长率（13.1%）和第三产业增加值的年均增长率（15.6%）。海口旅游业已成为海口国民经济的支柱产业和第三产业的龙头产业。

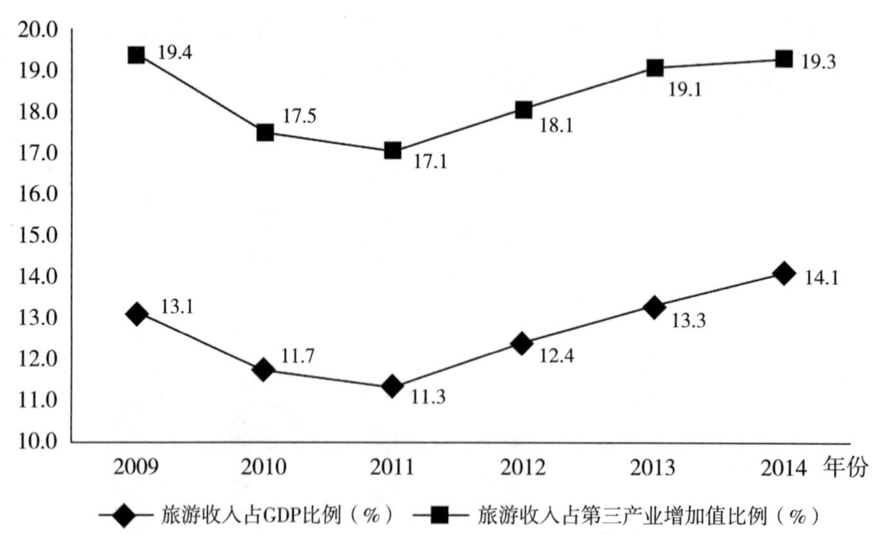

图4　海口市2009-2014年旅游总收入与国民经济关联性变化

资料来源：2009-2014年海口市国民经济和社会发展统计公报。

二、海口发展定位

（一）新版总规编制的背景

1994 年，由中国旅游协会咨询中心和海口市旅游局联合编制完成的海口市第一版旅游发展规划，为海口旅游的发展起了重要指导作用。《海口市旅游发展规划（1994－2010）》提出将海口市建成集观光、娱乐、购物、美食、会议、度假、康复为一体，经济繁荣、文化发达、环境优美、旅游管理和服务全面与国际标准接轨，具有热带海岛特色的综合性多功能的现代化国际旅游城市。该版规划在一定时期内较好地指导了海口市城市建设和旅游发展，但随着时间推移，海口市旅游业的发展环境也发生了变化，主要体现在：

1. 旅游业的发展上升到国家战略

党的十六届五中全会提出的“加快建设资源节约型、环境友好型社会”，并作为国民经济与社会发展中长期规划的一项战略任务，对我国产业结构调整与经济增长方式转变已经起到了重要作用，包括旅游业在内的第三产业和生态型经济得到大力发展，为旅游业与相关业态的融合发展增添了推动力。2009 年 12 月 1 日《国务院关于加快发展旅游业的意见》提出，要“把旅游业培育成国民经济的战略性支柱产业和人民群众更加满意的现代服务业”，将旅游业的发展上升到国家战略的高度。

此外，2008 年 1 月 1 日起执行的《全国年节及纪念日放假办法》和《职工带薪年休假条例》带来的公民休假制度改革也对海口旅游环境带来深远的影响。

2. 海南国际旅游岛建设

2007 年 4 月 26 日，海南省第五次党代会正式提出“扩大旅游开放，推动国际旅游岛建设”，并向国务院申报建立“海南国际旅游岛综合试验区”。2008 年，国务院函复海南省人民政府，同意海南进一步发挥经济特区优势，在旅游业对外开放和体制机制改革方面积极探索，先行试验。随着《国务院关于加快发展旅游业的意见》的颁布，2009 年 12 月 31 日，《国务院关于推进海南国际旅游岛建设发展的若干意见》出台（国发〔2009〕44 号），从政策上保证了海南建设国际旅游岛的顺利推进。

在国际旅游岛建设目标指引下，2008 年 12 月编制完成的《海南国际旅游岛规划纲要》明确了海南旅游业发展的战略目标：把海南建成旅游国际化程度高、生态环境优美、文化魅力独特、社会文明祥和的世界一流的海岛型国际旅游目的地。该规划对海口旅游总体定位为：海南国际旅游岛和南海区域旅游组织中心与服务基地，世界一流的热带滨海国际旅游目的地城市。作为海南省首府城市，海口旅游发展面临新的定位与目标要求。

（二）新版总规对海口城市发展的定位

《海口市旅游发展总体规划（2010－2020）》将海口定位为“世界一流滨海休闲旅游目的地城市、我国旅游业改革创新示范城市、海南国际旅游岛旅游综合服务中心、南海旅游组织与服务基地”。

世界一流滨海休闲旅游目的地城市——建设面向全球和全岛的旅游交通服务网络、高品质的接待设施，提供优质的服务、丰富的休闲娱乐与户外活动，营造国际化的都市氛围和安全、友好的旅游环境，具备组织大型节事活动的综合能力，拥有专业化的旅游服务团队，成为国内外旅游文化交流、旅游职业教育与培训的重要基地。

我国旅游业改革创新示范城市——创造性地贯彻国家赋予的政策，加快体制机制创新，成为各种旅游开发新理念、新模式、新项目的先行先试区。

海南国际旅游岛旅游综合服务中心——放大中心城市功能，推进旅游要素的转型升级，使海口成为世界一流海岛休闲度假旅游目的地的组织者、推动者、协调者和服务者。

南海旅游组织与服务基地——构筑南海乃至更大区域的旅游协作网络，建设现代化的基础设施，为南海旅游资源开发提供强有力的综合保障。

三、海口旅游发展思路与策略

（一）海口旅游发展思路

《海口市旅游发展总体规划（2010-2020）》提出以全面提高海口城乡地区的宜游性和宜居性为目标，以改革创新与服务平台建设、新业态领引的旅游产品与市场开发、海南国际旅游岛首府城市新形象塑造为根本任务，将海口建设成为海南“开放之岛、绿色之岛、文明之岛、和谐之岛”上满意度最高、最具吸引力的旅游大都市。包括五大发展战略：

1. 构建强大的区域性旅游服务平台

建设政府主导下的旅游公共服务体系，搭建旅游产业领引下的政策与管理机制平台，培育与筑造国际知名品牌旅游企业总部基地。

2. 打造国际影响力的旅游目的地

落实海口旅游国际化的实施内容和要求，开发主题化的特色旅游吸引物体系，构建和谐发展的旅游空间网络，强化海口城市旅游功能，塑造海口“海韵椰城，欢乐港湾”旅游形象，建设高效、市场化的旅游营销网络。

3. 创建特色旅游文化品牌

通过文化建设促进旅游，通过旅游带动文化建设。提升传统文化，营造休闲文化，突出养生文化，培育时尚文化，实现文化旅游与旅游文化并举发展。

4. 旅游与相关产业联动发展

重点强化旅游与会展、商业、金融、保险、文化、体育、教育、医疗卫生、房地产等服务业的互融与联动发展。

5. 强化多层级的区域旅游协作

打造以海口为中枢的琼北旅游圈、海南岛旅游圈和南海区域旅游圈，强化海口与大珠三角区域的旅游联动，深化海口与北部湾及东南亚地区旅游目的地城市的旅游合作。

（二）海口旅游发展策略

1. 打造八大重点产品和十大主题线路

以资源和环境为基础、市场需求为导向、发展战略为指引，以差异化与特色化为根本，海口市将观光旅游、休闲度假旅游与专项旅游相结合，满足需求与引导消费相结合，热带生态与海口地域文化相结合，提出重点开发包括健康旅游、时尚休闲旅游、商务会展旅游、文化旅游、乡村旅游、观光旅游、节庆赛事旅游和城市旅游在内的八大旅游产品。

同时，打造品牌化十大主题产品线路，包括：风景海口——海岛都市风光之旅；韵味海口——历史人文体验之旅；欢乐海口——都市娱乐休闲之旅；活力海口——户外时尚运动之旅；品质海口——高端定制度假之旅；健康海口——热带避寒养生之旅；节日海口——商务会展与节事之旅；逍遥海口——自助自驾自由之旅；经典夜海口——风情体验之旅；浪漫海口——婚庆蜜月爱情之旅。

2. 提出“二、三、四、五”的旅游市场开发定位

二大核心市场——入境旅游核心目标市场为港澳台和日韩俄等东北亚以及东南亚地区传统客源市场，北美、澳洲、北欧等地区高尔夫专项市场，西欧文化旅游专项市场；国内旅游核心目标市场为珠三角、长三角和京津冀三大都市群地区及海南本省；

三大基础市场——巩固提升都市休闲、商务会议和避寒养生旅游市场；

四大专项市场——品牌化打造高尔夫度假、游艇邮轮、自驾游市场；

五大潜力市场——积极开拓定制度假、医疗旅游、奖励旅游、修学旅游、毕业旅行市场。

3. 构筑“一轴、一带、五区”的全市旅游产业总体布局

结合“中强、西拓、东优、南控”的城市空间发展策略，以主城区为重点优化配套，集群发展，海口市提出构筑“一轴、一带、五区”的旅游发展空间格局。

一轴——北部滨海旅游发展轴；

一带——南渡江生态休闲旅游带；

五区——滨海中部都市旅游综合服务区、滨海西部商务会展休闲度假旅游发展区、滨海东部生态休闲度假旅游发展区、羊山时尚休闲度假旅游发展区、南部乡村休闲旅游发展区。

4. 以六大引擎性项目为引领，建设一批旅游项目库

围绕特色资源，对接市场需求，着力开发“海口国家地质公园、海口国家湿地公园、海口假日海滩旅游区、海口骑楼老街文化休闲旅游区、东海岸国家级旅游度假区以及希望之舟（东海岸人工旅游岛）”六大引擎性项目。并以此为引领，建设一批旅游项目库，包括：重点提升或鼓励类旅游项目，如各类主题公园、旅游度假区、历史文化景点、乡村旅游点、国际旅游主题小镇等；城市型项目，包括邮轮游艇码头、会展中心、购物餐饮设施、文博设施、各类公园等。

5. 对城市功能进行旅游化改造

如塑造红树林生态海岸、椰城风情海岸、温泉度假海岸三段主题海岸；培育东海岸和西

海岸人工旅游岛两大增长引擎；营造三类旅游功能空间；建设“椰风海韵”风情大道；构筑城市绿色慢行游憩系统；构建多处城市观景新平台；开发海口夜间游览、夜间娱乐、夜间休闲等夜间旅游项目。

6. 以项目为抓手，推进近期建设

包括加快推进海口国家地质公园、海口国家湿地公园在内的一批重大项目建设；积极申报 2 个国家 5A 级旅游景区、2 个国家级旅游度假区；打造一批品牌酒店，建设市内免税购物公园、奥特莱斯小镇等大型购物中心，三条特色餐饮街，以及国际旅游主题小镇、邮轮游艇码头、海南国际会展中心、海南文化体育中心、滨海滨河步行与自行车专用道、旅游交通集散体系等。

四、海口城市发展

（一）旅游业发展带动城市活力提升

旅游业是带动能力极强的产业。海口旅游业的高速发展带动了一、二、三产业的快速发展；如：精细开发热带农业观光和休闲渔业旅游项目，推动了特种农业的产业化发展，形成旅游与第一产业的互促和互动；围绕饮料加工、农产品加工、医药等海口特色产业开发工业观光项目，提升其知名度，形成旅游与第二产业的互动；立足海南国际旅游岛首府城市定位，重点强化旅游与会展、商业、金融、保险、文化、体育、教育、医疗卫生、房地产等服务业的互融与联动发展，培育了海口旅游新业态。

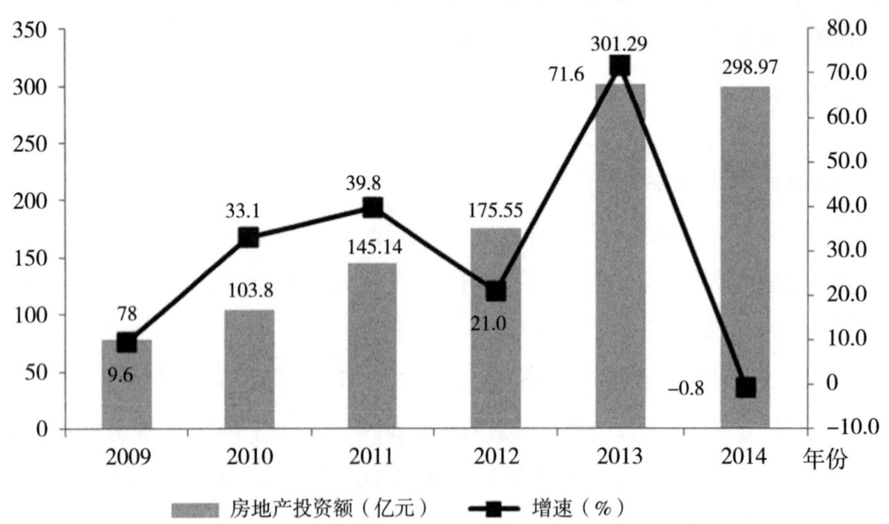

图 5 海口市 2009-2014 年房地产投资变化

资料来源：2009-2014 年海口市国民经济和社会发展统计公报。

（二）城市旅游功能的改造带动宜居城市的建设

海口市以旅游产业引领城市经济发展，以增强旅游竞争力为核心，以旅游者为本，在体现海口地方特色的同时，加强城市特色景观的营建和城市环境的美化，把城市视为开放的大景区来建设，实现城市即景区、景区即城市的融合效果，提升海口旅游的综合价值，塑造了“景”城形象。同时，以旅游发展为导向进行城市整治改造、开展基础设施配套规划建设，提高旅游景点之间与旅游服务设施之间的可达性。此外，创造了轻松、便捷的城市旅游氛围；构筑了城市休闲游憩系统，丰富和提升城市旅游活动的内容和品质。如此种种，都带动了海口市宜居城市的建设。

（三）旅游的发展促进了文化遗产的保护

海口是国家级历史文化名城，拥有众多的历史文化遗产，见证了从滨水到滨海、从内陆到海洋、从封闭到开放的城市发展过程；众多历史古迹、建筑、古村镇几经沉浮，古韵依旧。

海口旅游的发展还促进了文化遗产的保护。以海口骑楼老街为载体的南洋文化和以古城、古村为载体的历史名城文化，经各种旅游主题化、精品化的开发后，成了海口文化旅游的特色品牌，同时也保留了历史上的实景生活气息，堪称一座活着的海口近代历史博物馆。

五、结语

不同城市成长有不同的模式。海口借势海南国际旅游岛建设，利用自身的独特优势，通过旅游业带动其他产业，发展特色产业，增强城市活力；通过城市旅游功能培育提升城市品质，提高城市宜居性；通过旅游形象塑造，强化海口特色风貌，使海口成为旅游助推发展的样板城市。

（作者：周建明，中国城市规划设计研究院文化与旅游规划研究所，教授级高级城市规划师）

苏州申报“李光耀世界城市奖”对中国城市的启示

2014 年 6 月，苏州荣获第三届“李光耀世界城市奖”，成为获得该奖项的第一座亚洲城市。提名委员会主席马凯硕表示：“苏州的领导人在城市规划方面着眼全局，并在规划早期就注重对历史文化遗产的保护。苏州在经济发展和古城保护中成功获得了平衡，发展蜕变为一个宜居且充满活力的城市，具有令人自豪的城市特色。苏州对中国和世界其他国家的城市而言，都是一个值得学习的范本。”苏州的获奖是城市综合实力的体现，是城市软实力提升的国际认可，是对中国治理现代化探索的认可，对新型城镇化战略下的中国城市发展启示深远。

图 1　苏州金鸡湖

一、什么是“李光耀世界城市奖”

“李光耀世界城市奖”（Lee Kuan Yew World City Prize）由新加坡政府于 2009 年 6 月 22 日设立，是一项国际性奖项，每两年颁发一次，旨在奖励以远见和创新思维进行城市规划和管理工作，或者解决许多城市面临的环境挑战，并能以纵观全局的方式为不同社区带来社会、经济及环境效益的城市及其领导人和组织。截至目前已颁发三届，获奖城市分别为西班牙毕尔巴鄂、美国纽约和中国苏州。

“李光耀世界城市奖”着重于 4 个城市主旨：可持续性（Sustainability），宜居性

(Livability)，城市活力（Vibrancy)，城市生活质量（Quality of Life)。与其他城市规划奖项不同，“李光耀世界城市奖”更关注城市的宜居程度和永续性的活力。其评奖标准主要考察四个方面：第一，通过以城市转型为目标的战略愿景、行动规划、实施举措，展现城市政府的领导和治理能力。第二，在战略、规划和实施途径中，创新模式和标准。第三，在理念和实践层面，对其他城市具有良好的示范和推广作用。第四，在城市长期发展过程中，城市转型实施取得成功效果。

“李光耀世界城市奖”评选严格。该奖项不接受自我推荐，只能由城市规划等相关领域具有领导地位的学者、政府官员及国际组织领导人组成的第三方提名。所有符合资格的被提名方都将经过提名委员会及理事会的两轮严格遴选程序，包括申报材料评选、回访问卷和现场考察等。提名委员会和理事会的成员均由公私领域相关学科的著名业内人士、决策者、学者及专家担任，如在城市规划专业领域享有盛誉的彼得·霍尔、刘太格、仇保兴等。由于该奖项两年才评选一次，奖项争夺的激烈程度可想而知。2010 年共有 77 个城市参评，2012 年有 62 个城市参评，2014 年也有 36 个城市与苏州同台竞争。

二、苏州为什么能获奖

2014 年与苏州一同入围第二轮评选的城市还有日本的横滨市、哥伦比亚的麦德林市。这两个城市申报的内容也极富竞争力。麦德林是哥伦比亚第二大城市，总人口约 350 万人。她是南美地区过度城镇化的典型代表，贫民窟和犯罪问题非常突出。麦德林市政府采取了非常规的创新手段，用“点穴式”的小项目，取得了大效果。通过建设连接贫民窟与市中心的通勤缆车系统和方便山腰贫民窟居民出行的城市电动扶梯、为贫民窟提供必要的市政基础设施、增加公共空间等项目，增强了贫民窟地区与城市中心区的联系，改变了贫民窟与城市其他地区割裂的状态，让贫民窟居民更好地融入城市的就业和生活当中，贫民窟的高失业率、高犯罪率等问题得到了有效改善，全市谋杀犯罪率成功由 1991 年的每 10 万人 380.6 起降到了 2012 年的每 10 万人 52.3 起。横滨是日本第三大城市，常住人口约 370 万人，是东京都市圈边缘以环境宜居、生活成本适宜、家庭氛围浓郁为特色的卫星城。横滨建立了政府与土地业主、市民深入合作的创新模式，为土地私有制度下城市公共利益的实现提供了途径，如“横滨港未来 21”地区的成功更新就得益于这种操作模式。另外，横滨的成就还包括通过市民、企业的合作，实现垃圾减量，建设智慧城市，构建智能能源管理系统等。

相比这两座城市，苏州能够最终夺魁，从申报的角度来看，可以归结于以下三个方面：第一，拥有高水平的城市规划和良好的实施管理。第二，申报主题选择准确。第三，对“李光耀世界城市奖”传递的价值观理解深入。

（一）苏州高水平的城市规划和良好的实施管理

苏州的确享有很好的政府管理和全面的城市规划。苏州具有悠久的城市规划传统，在中国城市规划和人居环境建设史上地位突出。平江图上水陆双棋盘的独特城市肌理和精妙绝伦

图2　麦德林通勤缆车

图3　横滨港未来21片区

的苏州园林都是苏州人民留给全世界的宝贵遗产。

改革开放以来，苏州共编制过三版城市总体规划，也是各具特色，既有先进的理念和长远的眼光，又解决了当时的特殊矛盾，通过规划的有效实施，实现了城市快速成长阶段的健康、可持续发展。

20 世纪 80 年代末，随着经济发展带来的城镇化动力的增长，苏州古城已难以满足城市人口和产业集聚的需要。是拆古城、增加开发强度，还是跳出古城、拓展新区，这是当时苏州城市规划必须解决的难题。国内大部分城市选择了前一条道路。但苏州 1986 版总体规划充分认识到了古城的历史价值，也前瞻性地预见到苏州产业发展的巨大潜力，明确提出了跳出古城发展新区，疏解和保护古城，实现经济发展和遗产保护双赢的策略。历史证明，这版规划确立的全面保护古城、跳出古城发展新区的指导思想，有效地保护了古城风貌，为苏州的城市框架打下了良好的基础。

20 世纪 90 年代中期，随着沪宁高速公路全线贯通，以上海为龙头的沪宁发展带日趋成熟。1986 版总体规划确定的新区位于古城西侧，显然与上海为主导的经济流向不一致。因此，借苏州工业园区建设之机，1996 版总体规划适时对城市空间格局进行调整，提出了“东园西区，一体两翼”的城市空间发展骨架和“四角山水”、“真山真水园中城”的山水

图 4　苏州 1986 版城市总体规划

图 5　苏州 1996 版城市总体规划

格局，以工业园区为载体，重点向古城东部区域拓展，主动对接以上海为中心的区域经济流向。这版规划有效引导了苏州从 20 世纪 90 年代到 21 世纪初的快速发展，初步确立了苏州作为大城市的空间骨架，并且明确了大尺度下城市与山水环境的关系。

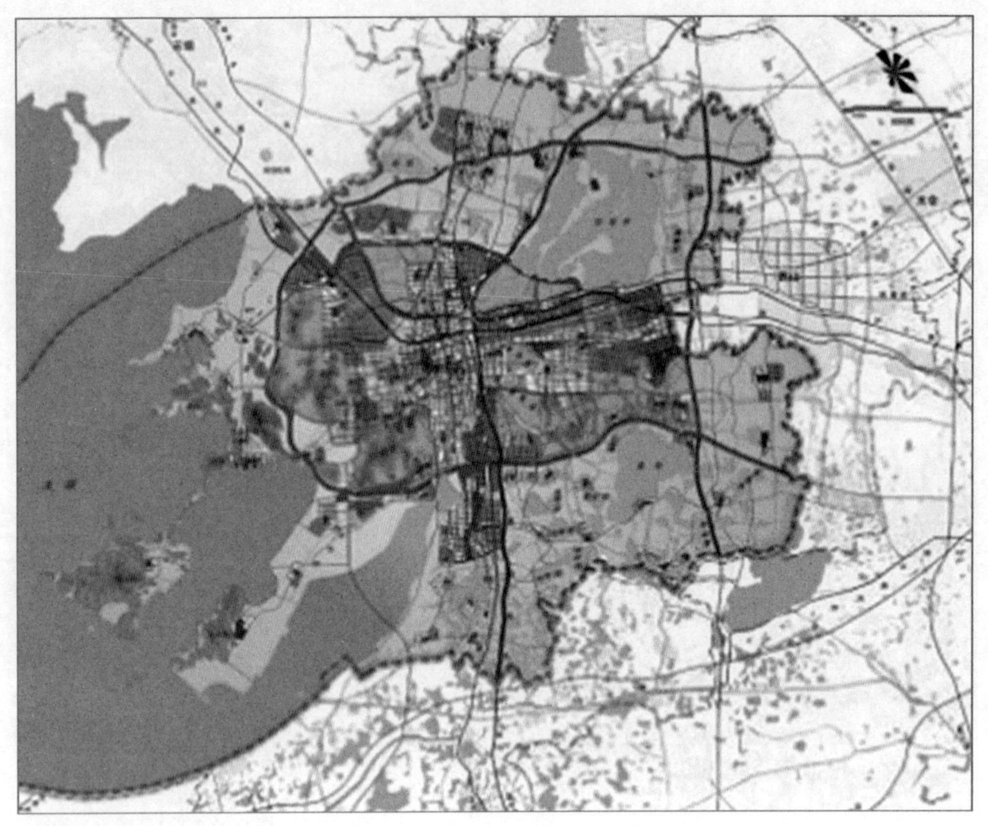

图6　苏州2007版城市总体规划

2000年以后，借中国加入WTO的东风，苏州外向型经济高速发展，城市快速扩张，土地资源迅速消耗，生态环境急剧恶化。在此背景下，苏州启动了新一轮的城市总体规划编制工作，提前谋划，确定了重现“青山清水新天堂”的发展目标，并提出转变模式、精明增长，由外延扩张走向内涵增长。通过这版规划的实施，有效遏制了城市的无序蔓延，城市发展逐渐回归到合理的轨道。

（二）苏州申报的主题与内容

结合对“李光耀世界城市奖”的理解，苏州最终将申报的主题确定在转型和让城市大多数人获益两个方面，既突出苏州的综合协调发展，彰显苏州转型发展的独特价值和综合竞争力，也突出苏州在文化、经济、环境等方面发展的创新经验，并展示苏州转型发展的巨大变化。

21世纪初是苏州发展最快，也是矛盾最集中的阶段，城市面临四大方面的挑战：一是如何提高产业附加值，并且在经济增长过程中惠及广大居民；二是如何转变依靠土地资源快速大量消耗的经济发展模式；三是如何保护好城市文化特色和历史遗产；四是如何避免生态环境质量下降。2007版城市总体规划在苏州“一体两翼”的空间结构基础上提出“东进沪西、北拓平相、南优松吴、西控太湖、中核主城”的空间战略，并从功能、产业、资源、文化、环境、民生等方面明确了转型发展的方向和措施，如提高科技创新能力，推动经济增长由资源消耗型向创新驱动型转变；培育服务型产业，增加就业，提高居民收入水平；确定城市增长边界，保障土地、水、能源、环境等资源底线，土地从“增量供给”逐渐向“存量盘活”转变；疏散古城，发展新城等。

在2007版城市总体规划的指导下，苏州在城市发展建设中采取了一系列有针对性的举措。

（1）经济发展和提升：政府积极支持开发区建立特色产业园区、创新型园区、知识产权示范区以及其他特殊功能区。推进高新技术产业和生产性服务业发展，并不断推进制造业的产业升级。同时，推动工业园区由单一功能片区向城市综合性功能新区转型。代表性的实施项目包括环金鸡湖中央商务区建设等。

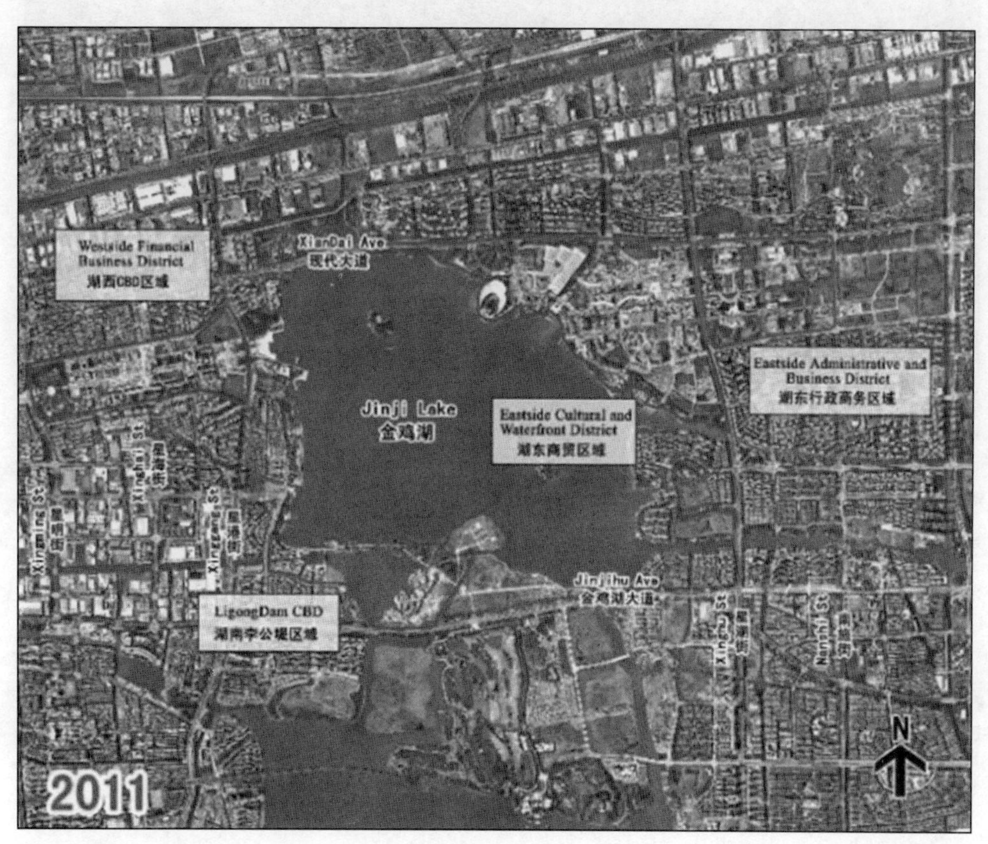

图7　环金鸡湖中央商务区

（2）文化保护与传承：编制《苏州历史文化名城保护规划》，制定《苏州市古建筑保护条例》、《苏州市非物质文化遗产保护条例》等地方法规。疏解古城功能和发展建设新城并重，降低古城保护压力，控制古城人口容量，疏解交通，优化环境。全面保护古城风貌，明确了古城的综合保护框架，将古城划分为54个街坊进行保护、更新和整治。代表性的实施项目包括平江路历史街区改造、山塘街改造等。

（3）生态保护与改善：从小山水格局走向兼有传统与现代的大山水的生态格局，在保持传统水乡特色和园林景观的基础上，强化对湖泊、山体等大山水的保护。制定了《苏州湿地保护条例》、《苏州市城市绿化条例》、《太湖、阳澄湖水源保护条例》等一系列地方法

图8　平江路历史街区

规。完善城市市政基础设施建设，提高废水、废物、废气等污染物的处理水平。加强河流水系的疏浚和污染水体治理。推进城市郊野公园和公共绿地建设，如城市西南部的石湖景区生态修复工程等。

图9　石湖生态修复效果

(4) 社会保障与和谐：推动社会保障向均衡协调发展，提高保障待遇、缩小城乡差距、加强外来人员保障。逐步将城市低收入困难家庭纳入住房保障体系。大力投资城市公共交通（如地铁）建设，推进城市公共服务设施建设（如教育、医疗、文体设施等），初步实现基本公共服务均等化。

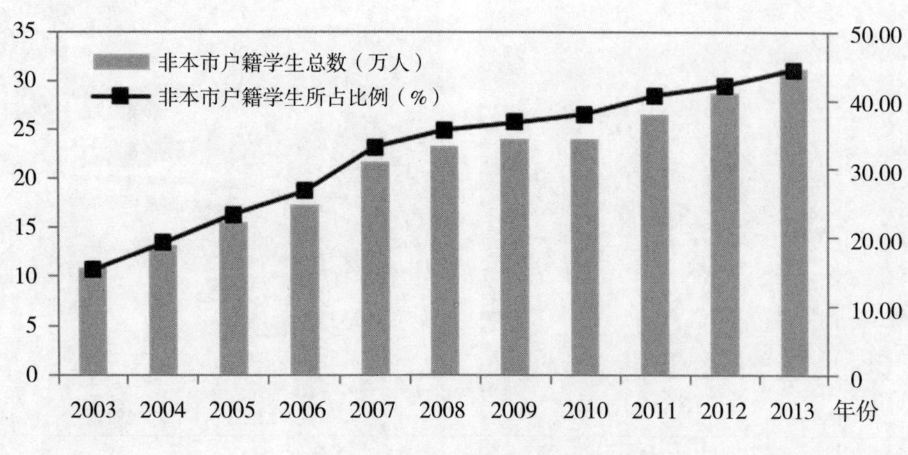

图10 外来人口享受义务教育的水平

通过规划指导下的一系列实施举措，苏州城市经济持续稳定增长，发展模式逐渐由“资源依赖”向“创新驱动”方式转变；历史文化保护与经济发展良好协调，城市吸引力持续增强；城市环境质量不断改善；城市生活品质、公共服务水平明显提高，外来人口等弱势群体保障加强，广大居民从城市发展中普遍获益。

（三）向获奖城市取经——“李光耀世界城市奖”的价值导向

前两届获奖城市毕尔巴鄂和纽约成功诠释了“李光耀世界城市奖”的价值导向。

1. 毕尔巴鄂：战略规划引领下的城市文化复兴

几十年前，毕尔巴鄂还是西班牙一个衰败的港口小城。18－19世纪一度因钢铁及造船业而兴旺发达，20世纪逐渐丧失工业竞争力，1983年更遭遇淹没城市的洪灾。20世纪80年代后期，毕尔巴鄂启动战略规划研究以指导城市复兴建设，出台了面向2030年的《毕尔巴鄂—2030》发展规划，强调地方自主复兴的动力，提出了包括建设创新科技园、启动旧城更新计划、开始河道治理和工业园改造、加强城市文化复兴建设四大发展策略。

在战略规划的指引下，25年来，市政府大力推动了25个项目的实施，包括历史街区改造、港口扩建、工业升级转移和产业园区建设、河道治理和复兴、基础设施建设、公共设施建设、邻里社区改造等，著名的毕尔巴鄂古根海姆博物馆正是这一时期建设的成果。伴随着这些项目的实施，毕尔巴鄂实现了城市经济和历史文化的复兴，就业岗位不断增多，失业率下降，城市人口恢复增长，公共空间增加且品质提高。如今，毕尔巴鄂已转型为欧洲生活、旅游、投资条件最好的城市之一，“宜居”是这座城市最大的特点。因其在规划指引下转型发展所取得的成就，2010年毕尔巴鄂获得首届“李光耀世界城市奖”。

图 11　毕尔巴鄂港口地区更新前后对比

图 12　毕尔巴鄂火车站地区更新前后对比

2. 纽约：更绿色更美好

纽约一直是世界城市的翘楚。但“9·11”事件之后，人们对这种经济高度集聚、建设密度极高的城市空间产生了怀疑。布伦伯格市长就职以来，致力于重塑纽约的吸引力。以《纽约规划（PLANYC）》为蓝图，以“更绿色、更美好”为目标，在社区住房保障、公共空间供给、棕地升级改造、水系综合整治、供水系统升级、交通可持续建设、能源建设、空气质量改善、固体垃圾减量、减少碳排放等方面提出了相应的规划策略，并开展了一系列卓有成效的工作。特别是过去10年内进行的三大城市改造工程，展现了城市规划和管理的远见和创新思维。布鲁克林大桥公园通过改造废弃码头、综合利用港口和城市设施，创建了城市新型空间的典范；由曼哈顿下中城西部一条长约2公里的高架铁路改造而成的曼哈顿高线公园，是纽约市政府汇集私人投资和公共资金建成的曼哈顿核心区域首个空中花园，为周边地区提供了宝贵的公共空间，还带动了区域房地产升值；2007年以来大力推行的“骑自行车出行”运动则是一项推广低碳生活、减少环境污染、减轻公共交通压力的举措，纽约不仅建设了环绕全市的自行车道，设立有关交通标识，还通过立法保障骑自行车出行的安全。

规划及实施对城市发展产生了持续影响。过去10年，纽约的犯罪率减少了35%；用于城市公园新建的资金增加了38亿美元；建成了450公里的自行车专用道；城市吸引力持续提升，旅游总人数增加到5020万人次/年。因其在战略规划指引下、政府强力主导的一系列公共项目的良好运作，2012年纽约获得第二届“李光耀世界城市奖”。

综合以上两个成功案例，可以看出“李光耀世界城市奖”所传递出的新加坡价值观：推崇强人政治和精英管治；看重长远的规划引导，并由政府持续推动；任何经验都必须可实施，可推广，可持续；最终要实现经济成功、社会和谐、文化多元。简而言之，就是要有良好的治理能力、创新的发展模式、可推广的示范意义和有成效的实施效果。对于该奖评选而

图13　纽约高线公园

图14 布鲁克林大桥公园

言，就是要在申报内容中体现强力高效的政府领导力、长效的战略规划和思路、操作性强的政策措施、有带动力的实施性项目，以及可操作、可复制、可推广的发展模式。正如“李光耀世界城市奖”提名委员会主席马凯硕总结的那样：“所有‘李光耀世界城市奖’得主的共同点是：都享有很好的政府管理和全面的城市规划。”

三、对中国城市有什么启示

“李光耀世界城市奖”始终强调，获奖城市的创新发展模式应当具有可操作、可复制、可推广的价值和意义。作为东部先发展地区的城市，苏州快速工业化和城镇化的过程是中国城市发展的集中缩影。苏州在不同发展阶段触及的各类问题，既是苏州的问题，也是中国绝大多数城市将要碰到的问题。因此，苏州转型发展的实践对中国其他城市甚至广大发展中国家城市都具有启发意义。

就苏州荣获“李光耀世界城市奖”而言，首先，它向中国传递了国际社会城市发展评价的主流价值导向——多元、人本、可持续，这与中央提出的走新型城镇化道路的要求是高度一致的。回顾世界城市理论和评价体系的演进过程也可以看出这种价值取向的变化。在20世纪80年代弗里德曼提出“世界城市假说”的时候，其关注的重点还是金融、商务、航运、国际组织等反映城市经济实力的指标。到2000年左右，英国拉夫堡大学全球化与世界城市研究中心（GaWC）首次对世界城市进行排名时，其选择的指标也仅限于金融、法律、会计等商务服务领域。但到了2010年左右，无论是GaWC还是社会学家萨森等，对世界城市的评价标准都已从金融、贸易扩展到创新、文化、宜居等领域，强调只有经济、社会、文化、环境多元协调、充满活力和可持续的城市才是真正有竞争力的世界城市。

其次，它显示了科学规划、有效实施和良好管理对城市发展的重要性。无论是历届"李光耀世界城市奖"得主，还是其他国际先进城市的发展经验，都表明，有远见卓识、可操作性强的城市规划是建设良好人居环境的基本前提。在良好规划的基础上，"一张蓝图干到底"，按照规划实施和建设则是实现良好人居环境的重要手段。当然，"三分建设、七分管理"，强力有效和不断创新的城市治理是维护良好人居环境的最终保障。

最后，它为中国城市树立自信注入了力量，说明只要坚持正确的发展方向，中国城市也可以成为领先全球的范例。只要按照新型城镇化建设的要求，以人为本，关注城市中大多数人的利益，让城市的发展成果惠及包括外来人口在内的广大民众；超越经济繁荣，追求更加平衡、可持续的发展，实现经济发展与环境改善、文化保护、社会和谐等的协调统一；坚持规划引领，不断提高城市建设和治理水平；中国特色的新型城镇化道路和丰富多彩的城镇、乡村必然可以谱就人类城乡发展史和人居环境建设史上的璀璨篇章。

（作者：缪杨兵，范嗣斌，均为中国城市规划设计研究院高级城市规划师）

以新型城镇化推进广东区域协调发展的调研报告

2013 年年底，中央召开全国新型城镇化工作会议，对全国城镇化建设作出了重要的战略部署，进一步明确了新型城镇化的发展路径、主要目标和战略任务。2014 年 6 月 15 日，广东省委、省政府召开城镇化工作会议，全面部署广东省新型城镇化工作。在此背景下，针对广东推进新型城镇化中面临的挑战与机遇，2014 年 8 月 25 日至 9 月 14 日，中组部、广东省委组织部与美国保尔森基金会共同举办了“可持续城镇化高级研究班”，学员来自珠三角和粤东、粤西、粤北地区 12 个地市分管规划建设工作的副市长和县（区）书记。

可持续城镇化高级研究班在实地调查、学习借鉴国内外城市群建设经验的基础上，思考和探索推动广东区域协调发展之路，集思广益，形成此调研报告。

改革开放以来，广东省城镇化步伐加快，成为推动广东经济社会发展和现代化建设的重要动力。2013 年年末，广东省城镇化率达 67.76%，基本达到中等发达国家水平，其中珠三角城市群成为我国三大城市群之一，城镇化率达 83.84%，已经达到了发达国家水平。但广东省城镇化建设任重道远，城镇化质量亟待提高，区域发展很不平衡，存在规划“碎片化”、产业“同质化”、发展“两极化”等问题。所以，在广东省加快转型升级的关键时期，必须遵循世界城市化发展的规律，认真借鉴国内外城市群和可持续发展的做法和经验，加快促进区域协调发展和推进新型城镇化，努力实现“三个定位、两个率先”的目标。

一、坚持分类指导，加快打造升级核心城市圈层

要坚持总体规划和分类指导相结合，以核心城市的大都市圈为集聚辐射、示范带动，通过重塑粤港澳、融合广深珠，凝聚欠发达地区。推动圈层扩散、点轴扩散，形成大中小城市协调发展的现代化新型城镇化体系。

（一）重塑粤港澳

改革开放以来，广东省珠江三角洲地区与香港特别行政区、澳门特别行政区同呼吸、共命运，形成了优势互补、互惠互利的经济共同体。当前，在广东加快新型城镇化进程的关键时期，深入研究珠港澳问题，以战略的眼光和思维审视珠港澳的关系，挖掘其内生发展动

力，增强区域核心竞争力，塑造全新的“粤港澳”城市群，是一个具有现实、长远意义的重大课题。要以 CEPA① 和粤港、粤澳合作框架为基础，以打造大珠三角优质生活圈为目标，以国际化、法制化为手段，以广州南沙、深圳前海、珠海横琴三大平台为重要抓手，率先在环保、食品安全、知识产权保护、个人所得税等经济、民生领域全面与香港、澳门以及国际接轨，打造一个适宜现代服务业发展的广大领域，与上海竞争，力保国际门户和中国龙头地位，进一步提升珠三角区域发展的整体竞争力，形成亚太地区最具活力和国际竞争力的世界级城镇群。要加强珠港澳交通、市政等基础设施对接，加快港珠澳大桥建设进度，开展大桥单 Y 型变双 Y 型的可行性研究，推动经济一体化发展。加快推进合作交流创新机制，探索广东区域内居民自由出入港澳通关政策，推动三地之间人员流动；同时，可在粤港澳区域内实行三种货币、三个监管当局、实行各自的金融货币政策的前提下，加强金融领域的交流与合作，在确保区域金融安全的基础上，探索货币自由流通的政策。重塑粤港澳不仅是一项重大课题，也是一项理论性、法制性、政策性很强的系统工程。为此，这一设想的实现，从思想上要深入探讨，几方协调，顶层设计，上下统筹，求同存异，听取民意，逐步达成共识；从实践上先易后难，分期实施。相信只要坚持勇于开拓，不断实践，这一战略性的变革终将展现。

（二）融合广深珠

近年来，以广州、深圳、珠海为核心的三大经济圈一体化建设已取得显著成效，但融合发展还有待深化，省级层面对全域一体化工作的统筹协调也有待加强。当前，继续发挥广州、深圳、珠海的辐射带动作用，推动珠三角“广佛肇”、“深莞惠”和“珠中江”三大都市区融合发展，促进环珠三角地区外围城市融入珠三角地区，一方面可以主动承接国内外产业扩张和转移，另一方面可以对接和延伸珠三角产业链，为珠三角的转型升级提供空间，形成“广佛肇 + 清远、云浮”、“深莞惠 + 汕尾、河源”、“珠中江 + 阳江”（“9 + 5”）的三大新型都市圈，推进区域协调发展，共建世界级城镇群。一是建立与城市群发展模式相适应的地方治理体系。当前，广东的经济和人口规模已经超过了许多国家和经济体，在市场经济体制仍不成熟的“行政区经济”运行时期，三大新型都市圈内部的行政分割和区际协调的矛盾突出。因此，建立与城市群发展模式相适应的地方治理体系至关重要。可以在三大新型都市圈各设立一个省委省政府的派出机构，并在其直接指导和领导下，着手组建三个基于经济权限的过渡性大都市区机构。其机构权力来自于省政府下放、中心城市政府适当上收两方面，并赋予规划、环保、统计和监督、指导等职能，同时，按区域设立金融、海关、电力等中央派驻机构，设立土地、工程、政府采购等交易中心，加快推进以要素为重点的市场体系建设，打破行政区划限制，消除行政壁垒和地方保护，推动资金、人才、技术等要素自由流

① CEPA：英文全称为 Mainland and Hong Kong Closer Economic Partnership Arrangement 及 Mainland and Macao Closer Economic Partnership Arrangement，中文全称分别是《内地与香港关于建立更紧密经贸关系的安排》及《内地与澳门关于建立更紧密经贸关系的安排》。是中华人民共和国中央政府与香港及澳门两个特别行政区政府签订的特别政策，先后于 2003 年 6 月 29 日及 10 月 18 日签订。

动，促进大都市区的政治经济一体化。二是推广“双语”制度。以广州、深圳、珠海等核心城市为试点，推行“双语”制度，10～20年内逐步将英语作为官方的第二语言，然后在其他城市全面铺开，在南中国形成一个5 000万人口的英语区，加快推动与国际的交流和合作。三是积极推动都市圈层城市在各个领域务实合作。主要是围绕基础设施建设、产业分工协作、要素市场体系构建、区域科技创新，推动三大都市圈开展深度合作、务实合作。要加快推进产业规划和转型升级，统筹规划圈内大中小城市功能定位和产业布局，强化城市间职能分工与协作，大力发展节能环保、新一代信息技术、生物、高端装备制造、新能源、新材料和新能源汽车等战略性新兴产业，提高服务业比重，增强城市在国际分工和产业发展中的竞争力。要打造珠三角核心城市间的“黄金走廊”。以广州、深圳、珠海为主要枢纽，大力发展多元化公共交通体系，加快三大新型都市圈内的高速公路、城市快速通道、地铁、城际铁路等“同城化”轨道交通网络，抓好深中通道等道路建设，推动珠三角公交一体化，与港澳轨道交通相衔接，建立珠三角主要城市1小时宜居生活圈。要探索建立城市群成本共担和利益共享机制。统筹推进能源基础设施一体化；加快都市圈内“一卡通”服务平台建设，统一信息交换标准和规范，进一步推进珠三角城市间互联互通，促进基础设施和公共服务设施共建共享。

（三）凝聚欠发达地区

地城镇化发展很不平衡，粤东、粤西、粤北地区城镇化率分别比珠三角地区低24.79、44.12和38.54个百分点，其中粤西和粤北地区甚至低于全国平均水平。加快新型城镇化，推进广东区域协调发展，要从全省大局出发，既要抓好特大城市功能提升和大城市有序发展，又要把粤东、粤西、粤北地区等欠发达地区凝聚起来，推动中小城市和小城镇协调发展。因此，在加快三大新型经济圈层组团发展的同时，要着力优化城镇化空间结构，在继续凝聚区域核心功能的基础上，积极培育粤东城镇群、粤西城镇群和韶关都市区，打造引领粤东、粤西、粤北地区加快发展的增长极，促进全省大中小城市协调发展。粤东地区应加快推进汕潮揭同城化，促进与梅州的区域协作，培育辐射带动粤东北、赣东南和闽西南地区的重要增长极。粤西地区应推动湛江、茂名等市中心城区扩容提质，建设面向北部湾和东盟的区域性重化工和机械产业基地，打造“双城”协同发展的粤西城镇群。粤北地区应以韶关国家生态文明先行示范区为重点，联合清远等市打造北江经济带，形成辐射带动粤北区域发展的增长极。当前，粤东、粤西、粤北地区的城镇化工作重点，应该按照省委、省政府的部署和要求，凝聚力量、整合资源，强化措施，狠抓“三大抓手”，全力推进城镇化建设，力促振兴发展。在交通基础设施方面，要积极争取国家的交通政策，加大投入，加快综合交通规划实施，加速推进高速路网、高（快）速铁路贯通粤东、粤西、粤北地区，进一步畅通连接珠三角、连接内陆的通道，使粤东、粤西、粤北地区成为珠三角的经济腹地。同时，研究全面取消省内高速公路收费政策，可借鉴海南省的经验和做法，把路费加到油费中，多用多收，加快市场要素的流通，更好地推动粤东、粤西、粤北产业的发展。在产业园区和新区建设方面，继续出台更加优惠的扶持政策和措施，在财政支付、产业发展、基础设施建设、民生事业发展、布局重点项目等方面多向粤东、粤西、粤北地区倾斜，加快推动工业化与城镇化互动发展。省级层面上，在东、西、北地区各片区选出一个市作为产业园区和新区建设试点，通过国家战略平台的搭建和政策创新，赋予特殊扶持政策，集中资源全力支持其产业园区和新区建设，力争通过3~5年的时间取得实效，为振兴发展起到示范和带动作用。同时，粤东、粤西、粤北地区各市要以建设新城新区为载体，抓好招商引资和承接产业转移，致力推动产业集聚化、高端化，以城聚产，以产兴市，积极培育壮大自己的主导产业，扩大城市就业容量，带动本地劳动力充分就业，避免有城无产、有城无人。一些小城镇侧重于发展“一镇一品”、“特色专业镇”，以小产业、特色产业集聚人口，促进城镇化可持续发展，形成全省大中小城市和小城镇协调发展、产业布局科学合理的城市体系。同时，要注重旧区改造与新区开发有机结合，加大投入，加快教育、卫生、文化等领域均等化，交通、通信等服务同城化，社会管理、生态环保一体化，推动城市扩容提质，使老城区焕发新活力，为城市群新型社会形态和可持续发展提供坚实基础。

二、强化城市群区域发展协调机制

据调查，区域系统内的“经济单元”处于自然状态下，各个城市若没有人为创造因素，协同效率最大值仅为40%。由此可见，跨区域协调尤为关键。相对美国地方政府的“零碎化”管理体制而言，我国“由上而下”管理体制在区域协调上有着明显的优势。美国城市发展非常重视区域协调，从20世纪60年代成立国家区域规划委员会开始，至今美国共有大大小小500多个区域协调委员会。这些机构不仅研究国家政策对城市发展的影响，而且推动政府之间开展有效合作。在广东省城镇化过程中，由于行政区域划分、考核指标失衡、法制不够健全等原因，一些区域发展不协调的现象逐步显现，如跨城市的河流污染治理、跨区域的空气污染整治等问题。建立完善跨区域城市发展协调机制迫在眉睫，围绕打造珠三角世界级城市群、粤东汕潮揭城市群、粤西茂湛阳临港经济城市群、粤北生态型经济城市群为目标，并以此为平台建立城市群管理协调模式，创新城市群要素市场管理机制，破除行政壁垒和垄断，促进生产要素自由流动和优化配置，推动跨区域城市间产业分工、基础设施、环境治理等协调联动。

一是加强省级对城市群区域发展的统筹协调。在珠三角地区城市群中有许多类型的行政管理体制并存，包括香港和澳门两个特别行政区（SAR）、深圳和珠海两个经济特区，以及省、市区、县等多种行政管理体制，行政管理体制的差异增加了区域协调的难度。行政分割直接导致各城市在产业布局、基础设施和交通网络建设中都自然以行政区为单位，城市之间的协调难度较大。这对城市群内基础设施的合理配置和有效运营形成障碍。建议成立省级城镇化区域发展协调机构，负责协调解决城市群政策规定、基础设施、产业互补、环境整治等方面问题，建立完善能发挥协调作用及各利益主体参与的多层次的全面协商机制，加强港澳与珠三角之间、珠江三角洲内部地区之间、城市群之间的协调，推动官方机构的协调、政府政策的协调，强化城市群区域规划立法保障和实施监督，统筹区域规划、产业布局和财政投入，加快生产要素的流动和项目联动，共建共享，探索区域公共资源一体化管理，推进政府间高效协同开展工作。

二是成立跨地区的城乡发展规划委员会和生态环境保护委员会。芝加哥市1909年制定的城市规划，指导了城市近百年建设。由此看出，城市规划的科学制定、依法执行非常重要。广东省及各地市在城市建设方面制订出台不少规划，但是规划之间协调较少、衔接不够，随意乱改现象比较严重。这说明规划的科学性不足，也反映了规划的权威性不够。建议在做实“广佛肇+清远、云浮”、“深莞惠+汕尾、河源”、“珠中江+阳江”经济圈联席会议的基础上，成立跨区域城乡发展规划委员会和生态环境保护委员会，由“三大”新型城市群党政主要领导、政府相关部门、专家以及社会人士组成，作为联席会议的实体化落实机构，进一步强化政府在推进城镇化进程中的宏观调控和指导协调作用。①城乡发展规划委员会，主要负责加强对跨区域基础设施的统一规划管理以及城市间规划建设问题的协调。在此基础上，要做实规划，从跨区域层面明确各城市群发展目标、空间结构和开发方向，确定各城市的功能定位和分工，统筹交通基础设施和信息网络布局，做到与省的规划相统一、相衔接，推进城乡规划一体化。同时，要通过出台条例等形式把规划固定下来，增强其权威性和严肃性，避免朝令夕改。②生态环境保护委员会，主要是负责创建低碳生态城市生态环境保护从总体规划编制到建设实施全过程的组织协调、督促检查等工作。借鉴美国城市的绿色低碳发展理念，充分发挥生态环境保护委员会的协调组织作用，通过打造一批跨区域绿色节能示范项目、制定出台一些绿色环保激励政策、实施公交优先发展战略以及加强水源涵养、污水治理、生态净化、大气治理和森林城市建设等工作，加快改善城市生态环境。

三是发挥跨区域社会组织联盟作用。在美国城市化建设中，非政府组织作为个人与政府之间不可或缺的中间环节而存在，它们承担了很大部分原属于政府所负责城镇化建设任务，减轻了地方政府的负担和成本。在核心城市内部，芝加哥率先建立起政府和市场、社会的多边协作机制，其最突出的标志就是在一系列重大决策事务上邀请民间组织有效参与。民间组织的高度专业化，使得他们提出的建议、制定的标准既切合实际，又能引领产业发展方向。因此，推进广东区域协调发展，要充分发挥社会组织的协调作用，建立跨区域民间社团等非政府组织关于城市化发展的协调对话机制，拓宽公众参与协调区域和社区事务的渠道，推动社会各界参与城市化建设，形成多元参与、多元投资的生动局面。

三、完善区域协调发展的保障机制

新型城镇化是一项系统工程，涉及城市和农村诸多方面，必须加强各方面的改革，为广东区域协调发展建立健全保障机制。

（一）完善资源配置机制

在新型城镇化及城乡一体化发展中，借鉴美国“经营城市”的经验，摒弃政府以往“大包大揽”的做法，坚持市场化改革方向，进一步健全市场机制，把市场对资源配置的基础性作用与政府统筹的调控性作用结合起来，打破行政垄断和市场分割，加快建立统一开放、公平竞争、生产要素自由流动的区域大市场，合理引导城镇化发展的规模、速度、节奏，优化结构和布局。在体制机制上，逐步减少按行政等级来配置公共资源和经济资源的做法，做到公共资源按照公平原则、经济资源按照效率原则来配置。公平原则，即保障欠发达地区城市群的协调发展，加大对欠发达地区的支持力度，通过建立农民与市民共享的保障机制和构建城乡平等的就业、培训及子女受教育机会等机制，大力推进基本公共服务覆盖工作，基本实现城乡、区域和不同社会群体间基本公共服务制度的统一、标准的一致和水平的均衡。效率原则，即要按照市场化手段来配置资源，摈弃输血式供给，采取竞争性配置方式，比如财政转移支付资金要在保障公平的基础上，增强对资金使用效率较高、投入产出效益较好的欠发达地区的支持力度，激发其活力，促进区间竞争，发挥各自能动性，自觉增强城镇化建设的资金调配使用效益；在土地利用年度计划指标分配上，优先向土地利用效率较高的欠发达地区倾斜，采用“以奖代拨”办法，按照“以增量撬动存量、以增量激活存量、以存量换取增量”和“多劳多得、多干多配”的方式加强调控；探索推行用地指标交易制度，有偿使用的方式，破解城镇土地利用粗放低效问题，进一步提高城镇节约集约用地水平。

（二）设立区域合作发展基金

在区域合作发展过程中，为了避免产业同构、市场雷同和恶性竞争，应该统筹配置好区域内产业布局、市场布局、资源配置，对于一些发展比较落后的地区和在区域合作中利益受损或获利较少的地区，通过设立投资贸易促进基金、研发创新基金、项目风险基金、产业发展协调基金、人才培养和就业指导基金、区域内地区发展平衡基金等区域合作发展基金对其进行补贴或发展扶持，保证区域合作的顺利推进和区域内的均衡发展，构建区域合作的利益分享机制。

（三）完善生态补偿机制

要加大财政扶持力度，建立生态补偿机制，对城市群里生态环境保护贡献较大的城市进行资源、生态、耕地、区域的补偿。一要建立市场补偿机制，通过价格、成本、税收等多种形式，激励各个地区在新型城镇化过程中主动改善生态环境，通过市场化手段，建立健全生态环境资源权益交易的市场机制。二要运用生态 GDP① 指标对各地区进行生态文明建设评

① 绿色 GDP 是有缺陷的。“一个明显的缺陷是，绿色 GDP 本身反映的是经济社会发展带来的环境资源损失，体现的是负能量，而没有反映出生态环境自身的正能量，即其产生的正面的生态效益。”所谓生态效益，即十八大报告提出的生态产品，包括涵养水源、净化大气环境、保育土壤、固碳释氧和生物多样性保育等方面，即生态系统服务功能。公开资料显示，一个完整的绿色 GDP 核算体系由两部分构成，包括五类自然资源耗减成本（耕地资源、矿物资源、森林资源、水资源、渔业资源）和两大项生态环境退化成本（环境污染和生态破坏）。绿色 GDP 难以推行的一个重要原因在于只做减法。实施绿色 GDP，扣除了生态环境损失成本，会使一些地区的经济增长数据大大下降，有可能影响地方官员的“政绩”，导致地方接受起来有难度。中国林科院森林生态环境与保护研究所首席专家王兵研究员率先提出了“生态 GDP”的概念。建议应在原有绿色 GDP 核算体系的基础上加入生态效益，形成生态 GDP，才能完整地反映经济与社会、环境与社会的相互影响关系，也更利于地方接受。

价，在原有绿色GDP核算体系的基础上加上生态效益，通过评价，合理测算各个地区的生态补偿标准。对于经济发展相对落后、地方财政薄弱的“生态涵养区”和“生态保护区”，其生态GDP与现有GDP的差值，即可作为需要补偿的缺口，由其他地区补偿。三要鼓励地区间横向援助，生态环境受益地区通过资金补助、定向援助、对口支援等多种形式，对重点生态功能区进行补偿，实现不同区域的经济和环境互补，推动不同区域城镇化的协调发展。至于生态补偿具体如何运行，将另文探讨。

（四）完善科学考核体系

改革现行的GDP考核方式，调整优化现有的考核体系，改革现有条块划分的统计模式，建立大都市区统计区统计指标体系，进一步增强对体现都市区（圈）整体竞争力、发展质量和区域协同的指标考核，强化对经济结构、科技创新、劳动就业、公共服务、公共安全、资源消耗、环境损害、生态效益以及外来人口公共服务覆盖面等方面的人均指标考核，同时，在指标体系中设置正向激励指标和负向约束指标，不断引导和激发各级政府全面正确履行职能。把大都市边缘新城和次中心节点的建设成效纳入城市政府考核体系中，引导城镇群、都市圈（区）健康发展。建立以地均产出为条件的中心城区扩容提质支持引导机制，分类指导，实行差别化，因地制宜制定科学反映城市不同发展阶段、发展特征的指标考核体系，对用地效益高的中心城区，突出发展规模、结构调整和功能开发等方面的考核；对用地效益较低或用地较为紧缺的中心城区，突出发展效益、功能开发等方面指标考核。建立健全动态评估和通报机制，委托第三方中介机构，每年对各地城镇化发展水平进行考核评估，以蓝皮书形式公开发布，全面接受社会监督。

完善干部交流机制。畅通城市都市区、城市群内人才流动的渠道，建立人才保障体系。要加强对领导干部、现有城镇建设各种专门人员的教育培训，采取委托培养、组织进修以及各种专题班等形式，造就一批擅长城市建设、运营、管理的人才队伍。要加强干部双向交流融合，选派省直单位、珠三角地区优秀干部或具有专业知识的人员到粤东、粤西、粤北地区任职、挂职；选派粤东、粤西、粤北地区优秀干部到省直单位和珠三角地区任职、挂职锻炼，学习先进地区的理念和发展经验。要创设有利于推动新型城镇化建设的“绿色人才通道”，通过多种形式聚集人才、培养人才、使用人才、保障人才，使人才工作更好地服务于新型城镇化建设。

（供稿：可持续城镇化高级研究班）

附录篇

附录 1

2014 年中国城市发展大事记

2014 年 1 月 1 日 安徽省住房和城乡建设厅组织编制的《安徽省县城规划编制标准》正式实施。该标准是全国第一个县城规划编制标准，有效弥补了目前县城规划编制标准的缺失。

2014 年 1 月 6 日 国务院办公厅公布《国务院关于同意设立陕西西咸新区的批复》(以下简称《西咸批复》)。《西咸批复》指出，建设西咸新区，对于创新城市发展方式、深入实施西部大开发战略、引领和带动西部地区发展、扩大向西开放具有重要意义。同日，国务院办公厅公布《国务院关于同意设立贵州贵安新区的批复》（以下简称《贵安批复》)。《贵安批复》指出，建设贵安新区，对于探索欠发达地区后发赶超途径、发展内陆开放型经济、建设生态文明社会具有重要意义。

2014 年 1 月 7 日 由三省一市和国家八部委组成的长三角区域大气污染防治协作机制启动，并在上海召开第一次工作会议。这次会议建立了“会议协商、分工协作、共享联动、科技协作、跟踪评估”五个工作机制，并明确了协作机制的五项具体职能。

2014 年 1 月 7 日 环境保护部与全国 31 个省（自治区、直辖市）签署了《大气污染防治目标责任书》，明确了各地空气质量改善目标和重点工作任务，进一步落实了地方政府环境保护责任，为实现全国环境空气质量改善目标提供了坚实保障。

2014 年 1 月 8 日 国家能源局公布了第一批创建新能源示范城市名单，全国共有 81 个城市和 8 个产业园区入围。新能源示范城市是指在城市区域能源发展中充分利用当地丰富的太阳能、风能、地热能、生物质能等可再生能源，使其在能源消费中达到较高比例或较大利用规模的城市。

2014 年 1 月 9 日 环境保护部召开全国环保工作会议，部署了 2014 年全国环保工作的重点任务。大气、水体、土壤污染治理，是国务院确定的本届政府环境保护的三项重点工作，也是 2014 年环境保护部在全面深化生态环境保护领域改革的同时，需要全力推进的三项重点工作。

2014 年 1 月 10 日 住房和城乡建设部印发《住房城乡建设部利用遥感监测辅助城乡规划督察工作管理办法（试行)》。这是住房和城乡建设部第一个关于遥感督察工作的规范性文件，明确了遥感督察工作的任务、工作原则、工作程序、工作保障措施以及各级规划主管部门和部派城乡规划督察员的职责分工，对深入推进遥感督察工作有着非常重要的现实意义。

2014年1月10日 我国首个国家生态保护综合试验区——三江源国家生态保护综合试验区建设暨三江源生态保护和建设二期工程在青海省西宁市、玉树藏族自治州同时启动。工程涉及玉树、果洛、黄南、海南4个藏族自治州的21个县和格尔木市唐古拉山镇。

2014年1月11日 全国国土资源工作会议第二次全体会议在北京召开。会议部署了2014年重点工作，主要包括以下10个方面：一是严防死守保护耕地；二是节约集约用好资源；三是加强和改善土地调控；四是积极稳妥推进重点领域改革；五是扎实开展不动产统一登记和土地调查监测；六是加强矿政管理推进地质找矿突破；七是切实维护群众合法权益；八是强化执法督察工作；九是推进生态国土建设；十是巩固教育实践活动成果。

2014年1月14日 住房和城乡建设部根据《国家园林城市申报与评审办法》和《国家园林县城城镇标准和申报评审办法》等相关文件要求，综合现场考查和评审结果，公布了2013年国家园林城市、县城和城镇命名名单。

2014年1月15日 以西咸新区信息产业园为主体，“西安—西咸新区云计算服务创新发展试点示范”正式获得国家发改委、国家工信部批复。这是迄今为止西部唯一国家级云计算示范城市，西咸新区也成为全国七个示范城市中唯一的城市新区。

2014年1月19日 新华社授权发布中共中央、国务院印发的《关于全面深化农村改革加快推进农业现代化的若干意见》（以下简称《意见》）。《意见》要求，要抓紧构建新形势下的国家粮食安全战略，严守耕地保护红线，划定永久基本农田，深化农村土地制度改革，不断提升农业综合生产能力，坚决破除体制机制弊端，坚持农业基础地位不动摇，加快推进农业现代化。《意见》首次提出，赋予农民对承包地承包经营权抵押、担保权能。同时提出允许农村集体经营性建设用地出让、租赁、入股，与国有土地同等入市、同权同价。

2014年1月21日 住房和城乡建设部印发《乡村建设规划许可实施意见》（以下简称《意见》）。《意见》分乡村建设规划许可的原则、乡村建设规划许可的适用范围、乡村建设规划许可的内容、乡村建设规划许可的主体、乡村建设规划许可的申请、乡村建设规划许可的审查和决定、乡村建设规划许可的变更、乡村建设规划许可的保障措施8部分。

2014年1月24日 住房和城乡建设部下发《住房城乡建设部关于开展县（市）城乡总体规划暨“三规合一”试点工作的通知》（以下简称《通知》）。《通知》指出，为贯彻落实党的十八大、十八届三中全会以及中央城镇化工作会议精神，全面推动城乡发展一体化，在县（市）探索经济社会发展、城乡、土地利用规划的“三规合一”或“多规合一”，住房和城乡建设部决定开展县（市）城乡总体规划暨“三规合一”试点工作。

2014年1月26日 财政部发布《关于城乡建设用地增减挂钩试点有关财税政策问题的通知》（以下简称《通知》）。《通知》明确，增减挂钩项目单位需要举借债务的，应当与开展增减挂钩项目所需自筹资金相适应，从严控制债务规模。《通知》还指出，在实施增减挂钩中，要做好农村居民的拆迁补偿安置工作，规范项目支出管理，加大财政支持力度。

2014年1月28日 为贯彻落实《国务院关于加快发展养老服务业的若干意见》（国发〔2013〕35号），住房城乡建设部、民政部等部门联合印发了《关于加强养老服务设施规划建设工作的通知》（建标〔2014〕23 号，以下简称《通知》）。《通知》要求，各地要结合老年人口规模、养老服务需求，明确养老服务设施建设规划，并将有关内容纳入城市、镇总体规划，加强区域养老服务设施统筹协调，推进城乡养老服务一体化。

2014 年 2 月 7 日 国务院总理李克强主持召开国务院常务会议，听取关于 2013 年全国人大代表建议和全国政协委员提案办理工作汇报，决定合并新型农村社会养老保险和城镇居民社会养老保险，建立全国统一的城乡居民基本养老保险制度。

2014 年 2 月 8 日 国家发展和改委委员会、中国气象局等 12 个部门联合印发了《全国生态保护与建设规划（2013-2020 年）》（以下简称《规划》）。《规划》提出了强化生态建设的气象保障、防治水土流失、推进重点地区综合治理、保护生物多样性、保护地下水资源以及森林、草原、荒漠、湿地与河湖、农田、城市、海洋七大生态系统 12 项建设任务。

2014 年 2 月 8 日 北京市发布首都城镇化发展分析报告，显示北京城镇化率达到 86.2%，与高收入国家城镇化水平接近，产业结构也与高收入国家基本一致。目前，北京城镇化水平仅比上海低 3.6 个百分点，居全国第二位。

2014 年 2 月 11 日 国土资源部发布 2013 年国土资源有关统计数据，2013 年全国国有建设用地供应同比增长 5.8%，全国 105 个主要监测城市地价总体水平持续上涨。2013 年全国土地出让收入总金额达 4.1 万亿元。

2014 年 2 月 11 日 上海市市政府常务会议原则通过《关于深化拓展城市网格化管理，积极探索和推进城市综合管理的若干意见》，上海城市网格化管理实施以来，相关体制机制、管理标准和信息平台已日趋成熟，初步形成了全市一张网的管理格局。

2014 年 2 月 11 日 据环境保护部消息称，根据生态系统的整体性而确定的“环保大部制”改革正在稳步推进。根据这一框架，环境保护部将实行独立而统一的环境监管，建立起陆海统筹的生态系统保护修复和污染防治区域联动机制。目前，在大气污染防治方面，京津冀、长三角、珠三角等重点区域已陆续建立联防联控协作机制。

2014 年 2 月 11 日 遭遇大火的独克宗古城恢复重建的总规划出台，计划投入 12 亿元，2014 年年底前完成民居基本恢复，三年内完成全部重建工作。据了解，独克宗古城重建过程中，将充分尊重历史、尊重民族文化、尊重民俗民风，修旧如旧，努力恢复古城原貌。为保护生态，重建将以板岩等新型材料替代木材。

2014 年 2 月 13 日 从湖北省发展和改委委员会获悉，《武汉城市圈区域发展规划（2013-2020 年）》已获批。在批复中，国家发展和改委委员会要求湖北省率先在优化结构、节能减排、自主创新等重要领域和关键环节的改革上实现新突破。按照规划，武汉城市圈将建设成为全国两型社会建设示范区、全国自主创新先行区、全国重要的先进制造业和高技术产业基地、全国重要的综合交通运输枢纽、中部地区现代服务业中心和促进中部地区崛起的重要增长极。

2014 年 2 月 13 日 四川省环境保护厅发布，按照国家要求，四川省 2014 年将首次开展生态环境地面试点监测，监测地点为唐家河自然保护区森林生态系统。2014 年岷江、沱江流域跨界断面水质超标资金扣缴监测，将增加总磷考核指标，推动各级政府综合治理水环境污染。

2014年2月19日 国土资源部下发《关于强化管控落实最严格耕地保护制度的通知》(以下简称《通知》)。《通知》要求，除生活用地及公共基础设施用地外，原则上不再安排城市人口500万以上特大城市中心城区新增建设用地，全国人均城市建设用地目标将严格控制在100平方米以内。各地要将保护耕地作为土地管理的首要任务，全面强化规划统筹、用途管制、用地节约和执法监管，加快建立共同责任、经济激励和社会监督机制，严守18亿亩耕地红线，确保耕地实有面积基本稳定、质量不下降。加大土地规划计划管控力度。

2014年2月19日 住房城乡建设部和国家文物局联合下发通知，公布了第六批中国历史文化名镇（村）名单。178个镇（村）榜上有名，其中河北省武安市伯延镇等71个镇为中国历史文化名镇、北京市房山区南窖乡水峪村等107个村为中国历史文化名村。

2014年2月19日 为贯彻落实中央城镇化工作会议精神，做好历史文化街区保护工作，住房和城乡建设部与国家文物局联合下发通知，决定开展中国历史文化街区的申报认定工作。

2014年2月19日 《贵州贵安新区总体方案》经国务院原则同意。贵安新区将着力推进体制机制创新，探索欠发达地区城市发展建设新模式，到2015年，贵安新区城市主体框架及相关服务体系基本建成，重点产业园区要素聚集能力显著提高，一批以战略性新兴产业、高端服务业为代表的企业集中布局，内陆开放型经济体系初步建立。

2014年2月22日 湖南省启动经济社会发展规划、城乡规划和土地利用总体规划的“三规合一”试点工作。试点工作将按照城乡一体、全域控制、部门协作的要求，以城乡规划为基础，以经济社会发展规划为目标，以土地利用规划提出的用地为边界，编制县（市）城乡总体规划，实现一个县（市）一张图，县（市）域全覆盖。

2014年2月25日 中共中央总书记、国家主席、中央军委主席习近平在北京市考察工作时强调，建设和管理好首都，是国家治理体系和治理能力现代化的重要内容。习近平指出，城市规划在城市发展中起着重要引领作用，考察一个城市首先看规划，规划科学是最大的效益，规划失误是最大的浪费，规划折腾是最大的忌讳。

2014年2月26日 中共中央总书记、国家主席、中央军委主席习近平在北京主持召开座谈会，就推进京津冀协同发展提出7点要求。一是要着力加强顶层设计，抓紧编制首都经济圈一体化发展的相关规划；二是要着力加大对协同发展的推动；三是要着力加快推进产业对接协作；四是要着力调整优化城市布局和空间结构；五是要着力扩大环境容量生态空间，加强生态环境保护合作；六是要着力构建现代化交通网络系统；七是要着力加快推进市场一体化进程。

2014年2月28日 宁夏首次编制空间发展战略规划，是宁夏回族自治区城乡规划工作的一个重要创新。事实上，这也是国内第一个以省域为单位编制的空间规划。规划正在提请自治区党委常委会审议，审议通过后报自治区人大常委会制定《实施〈宁夏空间发展战略规划〉条例》，确立空间规划的法律地位，将空间规划作为编制城乡规划、土地利用总体规划、经济社会发展规划等各项规划的法定依据。

2014年3月1日　《北京市地下文物保护管理办法》（以下简称《办法》）正式施行，它是全国第一部省级地下文物保护的专项规章。《办法》要求市文物部门建立全市地下文物埋藏情况数据库，标明地下文物埋藏区和重点监测区，并对实际考古调查、勘探、发掘的结果进行记录。监测区内的建设工程应向文物行政部门备案，文物部门则将加强对监测区的日常巡查监管。

2014年3月3日　《国务院办公厅关于推进城区老工业区搬迁改造的指导意见》（以下简称《意见》）发布。《意见》提出，力争到2022年基本完成城区老工业区搬迁改造任务，把城区老工业区建设成为经济繁荣、功能完善、生态宜居的现代化城区。

2014年3月5日　国务院总理李克强在十二届全国人大二次会议上作政府工作报告时指出，2014年要推进以人为核心的新型城镇化，坚持走以人为本、四化同步、优化布局、生态文明、传承文化的新型城镇化道路，遵循发展规律，积极稳妥推进，着力提升质量。

2014年3月5日　国务院总理李克强在政府工作报告中指出，要完善住房保障机制。以全体人民住有所居为目标，坚持分类指导、分步实施、分级负责，加大保障性安居工程建设力度，2014年新开工700万套以上，其中各类棚户区470万套以上，加强配套设施建设；年内基本建成保障房480万套，让翘首以盼的住房困难群众早日迁入新居。

2014年3月5日　国家发展和改委委员会主任徐绍史在国务院举行的一次记者会上指出，2013年我国经济发展有两个“首次”。一个是首次成为世界第一大货物贸易国，另一个是第三产业占GDP比重首次超过第二产业，达到46.1%。这标志着三大产业结构发生了历史性剧变。徐绍史说，中国只要保持7%左右的增长速度，就可以到2020年实现全面建成小康社会。

2014年3月6日　农业部部长韩长赋在两会的记者会上表示，关于农村土地问题，实际是三块地，第一块地是农户的承包地，第二块是农村集体建设用地，第三块是宅基地。在土地流转中不能搞“大跃进”，不能搞强迫命令，要有序流转。所谓有序流转就是依法、自愿、有偿。一是要保障农民的权益，二是流转要和当地农村劳动力和人口转出去多少相适应、要和当地的技术装备水平相适应，要和社会化服务的程度相适应。

2014年3月7日　甘肃省省域城镇体系规划编制工作座谈会在兰州召开。中国城市规划设计研究院就甘肃省省域城镇体系规划纲要框架情况进行了专题汇报。甘肃省副省长张广智指出，省域城镇体系规划是甘肃省实施城乡规划管理，合理配置省域空间资源，优化城乡空间布局，统筹基础设施和公共设施建设的基本依据。规划部门要按照国家要求和甘肃省城镇发展规律，坚持城乡统筹规划，因地制宜，分类指导，促进区域协调发展。

2014年3月11日　上海公布了《关于编制上海新一轮城市总体规划的指导意见》（以下简称《意见》）。根据《意见》，在2020年基本建成“四个中心”和社会主义现代化国际大都市的基础上，上海将努力建设成为具有全球资源配置能力、较强国际竞争力和影响力的全球城市，为打造中国经济升级版，实现中华民族伟大复兴的中国梦作出应有贡献。

2014年3月11日　国务院对发展改革委《关于报送赣闽粤原中央苏区振兴发展规划（送审稿）的请示》予以批复。

2014年3月14日 国家文物局明确要求各地的抗日战争历史遗迹，凡是条件具备的，都将在2014年9月前向公众开放。据介绍，目前我国涉及日本侵华及中国抗日战争的全国重点文物保护单位共有186处。

2014年3月16日 中共中央、国务院印发《国家新型城镇化规划（2014-2020年）》（以下简称《规划》）。《规划》是今后一个时期指导全国城镇化健康发展的宏观性、战略性、基础性规划。城镇化是现代化的必由之路，是解决农业农村农民问题的重要途径，是推动区域协调发展的有力支撑，是扩大内需和促进产业升级的重要抓手。制定实施《规划》，努力走出一条以人为本、四化同步、优化布局、生态文明、文化传承的中国特色新型城镇化道路，对全面建成小康社会、加快推进社会主义现代化具有重大现实意义和深远历史意义。

2014年3月18日 据国家文物局消息称，3年前国家文物局会同住房和城乡建设部提出的“名城濒危名单”建议2014年将正式付诸实施，将对国家历史文化名城保护状况进行评估，对于保护不力、破坏严重的名城，将列入濒危名单予以警告。

2014年3月19日 住房和城乡建设部副部长齐骥介绍全国住房信息联网工作进展时指出，目前全国40个房地产重点监测城市的住房信息已与住房和城乡建设部联网，信息系统自动记录设区城市增量房的交易信息。对没有信息系统前的存量房纸介合同，住房和城乡建设部要求各地抓紧录入到信息系统中，相当多城市已经完成这一工作。

2014年3月20日 财政部表示，为促进并轨顺利进行，地方政府原用于廉租住房建设的资金来源渠道，需整合用于公共租赁住房以及2014年以前的在建廉租住房。

2014年3月24日 北京市规划委主任黄艳对外表示，2014年北京将对执行10年的城市总体规划进行调整和修改，城乡接合部被纳入规划中。解决北京的“城市病”要放在京津冀区域内治理，要把非首都核心职能的产业发展，尽可能压缩疏解到周边。将周边城市建成具有竞争力的“城市群”，城市功能相互衔接、匹配、分担。目前，北京、河北、天津正在联合做规划，把一部分首都溢出的、不符合“政治、文化、国际交往、科技创新中心”的核心职能疏解到周边。把非建设地区和生态保护的地方划红线，拿出资源、工具和政策来保证地方提升生态环境质量。

2014年3月25日 国务院发展研究中心和世界银行联合发布《中国：推进高效、包容、可持续的城镇化》报告。该报告提出了构建新型城镇化模式的六大优先领域：第一，改革土地管理制度；第二，改革户籍制度，推进基本公共服务均等化，促进具备技能的劳动者自由流动；第三，将城市融资建立在更可持续的基础之上，同时建立有效约束地方政府的财政纪律；第四，改革城市规划和设计；第五，应对环境压力；第六，改善地方政府治理。

2014年3月26日 《河北省委、省政府关于推进新型城镇化的意见》（以下简称《意见》）出台。《意见》明确指出，将落实京津冀协同发展国家战略，以建设京津冀城市群为载体，充分发挥保定和廊坊首都功能疏解及首都核心区生态建设的服务作用，进一步强化石家庄、唐山在京津冀区域中的两翼辐射带动功能，增强区域中心城市及新兴中心城市多点支撑作用。

2014年3月26日 国土资源部部长姜大明在不动产登记工作第一次部际联席会议上指

出，从2014年开始，用3年左右时间全面建立不动产统一登记制度；用4年左右时间，运行统一的不动产登记信息管理基础平台，实现不动产审批、交易和登记信息实时互通共享以及依法查询，形成不动产统一登记体系。

2014年3月28日　国务院法制办就《城镇住房保障条例（征求意见稿）》（以下简称《意见稿》）公开征求意见。《意见稿》从规划与建设，保障性住房的申请、使用与退出，租赁补贴，社会力量参与，监督管理和法律责任等方面对城镇住房保障工作进行了规范。《意见稿》规定，对住房困难的最低生活保障家庭等住房救助对象优先给予保障。

2014年3月29-30日　长三角城市第十四次市长联席会议日前在盐城召开，“自贸区效应”成为与会30个城市市长热议的话题。与会市长认为，长三角已经走过了区域一体化的第一阶段，即经济要素一体化，实现了人流、物流、技术流、资金流和信息流的聚集和辐射。现在，长三角区域进入到了第二个发展阶段，即制度一体化，是经济、社会、人口、资源、环境“五位一体”的一体化。

2014年3月30日　国家发展和改革委员会正式批复将苏州市列为“国家发展改革委城乡发展一体化综合改革试点”。这意味着苏州城乡发展一体化试点晋升至国家层面。从“省级试点”晋升到“国家试点”，将为苏州城乡发展一体化创造“改革红利”，也赋予苏州更大的担当。按照国家发展和改委委员会批复的苏州市城乡发展一体化综合改革试点总体方案，苏州将积极破解难题，打造新型城镇化发展、共同富裕、“四化”同步发展、公共服务均等化、生态文明、和谐社会、土地资源节约集约利用、城乡金融制度改革8个示范区。

2014年3月31日　国务院批准《晋陕豫黄河金三角区域合作规划》，以探索省际交界地区合作发展新路径，推动晋陕豫黄河金三角地区合作发展。

2014年4月9日　公安部、住房和城乡建设部、国家文物局三部门联合出台一份旨在加强历史文化名城名镇名村及文物建筑消防安全工作的指导意见。这是我国首个由多家职能部门联合制订的强化文物古建筑消防安全工作的规范性文件。指导意见要求，各级政府应将历史文化名城名镇名村及文物建筑的消防安全工作纳入工作考评，建立多部门消防工作协调机制，对失职渎职或发生重特大火灾事故的依法依纪追究相关人员责任。

2014年4月10日　国务院总理李克强在博鳌亚洲论坛2014年年会上指出，落实以人为核心的新型城镇化规划，从破解城乡之间和城市内部二元结构问题入手，有序推进转移人口市民化，政府加大支持力度与运用市场手段相结合，将在2014年更大规模改造各类棚户区。在谈及中国经济发展寻找新的动力时，李克强指出，要向调结构要动力，围绕缩小城乡、区域差距和解决产业结构不合理等问题，以结构改革推动结构调整。加快弥补服务业这块“短板”，把“营改增”试点扩大到邮政电信等更多服务领域，用税收的杠杆来培育壮大生产性和生活性服务业，更多运用社会资本，增加养老、健康、旅游、文体等生活性服务供给。

2014年4月11日　住房和城乡建设部发出通知，决定在全国组织开展老楼危楼安全排查工作。

2014年4月13日　《云南省新型城镇化规划（2014-2020年）》出台。

2014年4月15日 重庆市启动主城区文物保护与城市规划的“一张图”管理，这是该市为实现文物保护与城市规划的有机结合和有效管理的最新举措。

2014年4月17日 国家发展和改革委员会召开全国“十三五”规划编制工作电视电话会议，主任徐绍史宣布启动编制国民经济和社会发展第十三个五年规划。徐绍史要求规划编制必须强化全球视野和战略思维，正确处理好政府与市场的关系，科学设定规划目标指标，积极推进市县规划体制改革，坚持开放民主编制规划，使“十三五”规划更加适应时代要求，更加符合发展规律，更加反映人民意愿。

2014年4月17日 交通运输部宣布，预计2016年年底前，全国大中型城市初步实现公交一卡通的跨市域、跨交通方式使用；到2020年，基本实现全国范围内的公共交通一卡通互联互通，全国联网。

2014年4月19日 国家发展改革委主任徐绍史在2014年中国城镇化高层国际论坛上表示，国家发展和改委委员会将从人口管理制度、土地管理制度、创新城镇化资金保障机制、健全城镇住房制度、强化生态环境保护制度5方面改革入手，推进中国特色新型城镇化道路建设。

2014年4月24日 《环境保护法》修订案通过。修订后的《环境保护法》，进一步明确了政府对环境保护的监督管理职责，完善了生态保护红线、污染物总量控制、环境监测和环境影响评价、跨行政区域联合防治等环境保护基本制度，强化了企业污染防治责任，加大了对环境违法行为的法律制裁，还就政府、企业公开环境信息与公众参与、监督环境保护作出了系统规定，增强了法律的可执行性和可操作性。

2014年4月25日 住房和城乡建设部公布《住房城乡建设部关于做好2014年住房保障工作的通知》（以下简称《通知》）。《通知》要求，为探索发展共有产权住房，确定北京、上海、深圳、成都、淮安、黄石为共有产权住房试点城市，试点城市要按照实施方案积极稳妥推进试点，在12月底前报送试点工作总结，相关省（直辖市）住房城乡建设部门要加强对试点工作的督促指导。

2014年4月25日 住房城乡建设部、文化部、国家文物局、财政部联合发布《关于切实加强中国传统村落保护的指导意见》，旨在加强传统村落保护，改善人居环境，实现传统村落的可持续发展。

2014年4月25日 住房城乡建设部、文化部、国家文物局、财政部四部门联合出台指导意见，要求切实加强中国传统村落保护。据专家估计，全国有较高保护价值的传统村落现存不到5000个。与此同时，传统村落遭到破坏的状况日益严峻。根据指导意见，四部门提出，用3年时间，使列入中国传统村落名录的村落文化遗产得到基本保护，具备基本的生产生活条件、基本的防灾安全保障、基本的保护管理机制，逐步增强传统村落保护发展的综合能力。截至目前，已有两批1561个村落列入中国传统村落名录。

2014年4月26日 中国十大古城镇联盟在山东省淄博市周村区成立。十大古城镇成立联盟在国内尚属首次，开创了中国古建文化遗产保护联盟新思路。参加本次联盟大会的古城镇有周庄、南浔、周村、阆中、呈坎、平遥、襄阳、同里、西塘、洪江十大古城镇。

2014年4月28日　中共中央政治局常委、国务院总理李克强在重庆主持召开座谈会，研究依托黄金水道建设长江经济带，为中国经济持续发展提供重要支撑。会上，国家发展和改委委员会负责人汇报了长江经济带建设总体考虑和相关规划。上海、江苏、浙江、安徽、江西、湖北、湖南、四川、重庆、云南、贵州等11个长江经济带覆盖省（直辖市）政府主要负责人汇报了对建设长江经济带的思考和建议。

2014年4月29日　京津冀交通一体化工作座谈会暨第二次交通运输工作联席会议在天津市召开。与会代表达成一致意见，协同推进京津冀交通运输规划对接，形成区域交通“一张图”。京津冀将共同加快京秦高速、京台高速、唐廊高速、滨石高速、津保铁路等建设；共同向国家争取促进津冀港口发展的优惠政策，推进天津自贸区建设、通关一体化；共同深化研究京津公共交通向河北省延伸事宜等。京津冀一体化航空、铁路大格局也已经形成。

2014年4月29日　住房和城乡建设部就切实做好2014年住房保障工作下发通知明确，2014年全国城镇保障性安居工程计划新开工700万套以上，其中各类棚户区470万套以上；计划基本建成480万套。同时，要求各地加大省级补助支持力度；建立省级巡查机制，加强对目标任务进展情况的督促检查；指导市县尽早开工建设，提高建成比例，尽快投入使用，确保完成年度开工和建成任务。

截至2014年4月底，据住房和城乡建设部消息，全国城镇保障性安居工程已开工286万套，基本建成125万套，分别占全年目标任务的40%和25%，与2013年同期基本持平。

2014年5月1日　为保障京津用水安全，张家口提出“京津冀水源涵养功能区”控制目标，对用水总量、用水效率、水土治理等指标进行控制，要求到“十二五”末，该市万元工业增加值用水量与“十一五”末相比降低32%。

2014年5月3日　湖北省武汉市启动《城市总体规划》、《土地利用总体规划》及《综合交通规划》修编工作，作为引导城市发展转型的顶层设计。同时，加快推进编制《武汉2049远景发展战略重大问题2014-2020年立法规划》、修编《武汉建设国家中心城市规划纲要》、研究制定并完善适合实情的人口发展政策等重要工作。“武汉2049”远景发展战略确定了完善立法计划和规划体系、城市规划建设、生态保护等九大方面共40个重点督办事项。

2014年5月4日　《甘肃省新型城镇化规划（2014-2020年）》（以下简称《规划》）出台。从空间布局上看，《规划》重点强调加快推进形成以丝绸之路经济带甘肃段为轴线、以区域性中心城市和城市组团发展为支撑的“一群两带多组团”城镇化布局。《规划》对甘肃省新型城镇化发展目标很明确，到2020年，甘肃省城镇常住人口将达到1350万人以上，城镇化率达到50%以上；按户籍统计，非农业人口达到1100万人以上，城镇化率达到38%以上，努力实现350万左右农业转移人口在城镇落户。

2014年5月6日　据《中国建设报》消息称，四川省在灾后恢复重建规划工作中，除指导各地全面推进灾后规划外，还筛选了3县、7镇（乡）和19村作为灾后城镇乡村规划的示范点，提高了灾后规划编制质量，为灾后规划起到示范带动作用。截至2013年7月底，组织完成了《城镇体系规划》、《城乡住房规划》和70余项城、镇、乡、村规划编制任务，为灾区恢复重建规划作出了贡献。

2014年5月9日 由中国社会科学院财经战略研究院、社会科学文献出版社、中国社科院城市与竞争力研究中心共同举办的《城市竞争力蓝皮书：中国城市竞争力报告No.12》在京发布。蓝皮书指出，2013年位列宜居城市十强的城市分别是：珠海、香港、海口、三亚、厦门、深圳、舟山、无锡、杭州和上海。

2014年5月12日 修改后的《宜宾市城市总体规划（2013-2020）》（以下简称《总体规划》）获四川省政府批准。按照规划，宜宾在《总体规划》确定的1887平方公里的规划区范围内，将实行城乡规划统一管理。按照因地制宜、城乡统筹发展要求，根据市域内不同地区条件，有重点地发展县城和基础条件好、发展潜力大的建制镇，优化城镇布局，促进农村经济快速发展。

2014年5月12日 武汉市启动《城市总体规划》、《土地利用总体规划》、《武汉市新型城镇化暨全域城乡统筹规划（2014-2030年）》及《综合交通规划》修编工作，作为引导城市发展转型顶层设计。同时，加快推进编制《武汉2049远景发展战略重大问题2014-2020年立法规划》、修编《武汉建设国家中心城市规划纲要》、研究制定并完善适合实情的人口发展政策等重要工作。

2014年5月13日 据在贵州召开的第二届中国水安全会议消息称，我国多地正试点开展以水生态文明城市建设为载体、探索保障水安全的新途径。据了解，确定的第一批水生态文明建设试点城市46个，第二批54个试点城市也已通过专家评审，这些城市将着重探索保障水安全的途径。

2014年5月14日 住房和城乡建设部下发通知要求，开展全国农村危房现状调查。同时，为全面把握和评估全国农村人居环境状况，住房和城乡建设部将开展农村人居环境调查，建立全国农村人居环境信息系统。

2014年5月15日 《住房城乡建设部关于建立全国农村人居环境信息系统的通知》发布。住房和城乡建设部正在加快建立全国农村人居环境信息系统，将在2015年年初基本查清全国58.8万个行政村的人居环境“家底”。全国农村人居环境信息系统涵盖全国所有行政村（含乡镇政府驻地行政村），按照一村一表采集信息，主要包括地址信息、基本情况、基础设施、公共环境、建设管理以及照片信息6类41项指标。目前，不少农村地区“脏乱差”的现象仍然较为突出。“家底”调查清楚之后，要制度化地推进全国农村人居环境改善，并将全面启动农村生活垃圾专项治理，5年内使全国90%的生活垃圾得到处理。

2014年5月16日 国务院办公厅印发《关于改善农村人居环境的指导意见》，明确了因地制宜、分类指导，量力而行、循序渐进等基本原则，强调要按照改善农村人居环境的总体要求，根据各地经济社会发展实际，科学确定不同地区的具体目标、重点、方法和标准，防止生搬硬套和“一刀切”，防止大拆大建，慎砍树、禁挖山、不填湖、少拆房。

2014年5月22日 青海省政府发布《青海省新型城镇化规划（2014-2020年）》（以下简称《规划》）。《规划》提出，到2020年，青海省城镇化格局明显优化，规模结构更加合理，以1个大城市、4个区域性中心城市、8个左右新兴城市和80个重点城镇为主体的新型城镇化格局基本形成。

2014年5月25日　《江苏省新型城镇化与城乡发展一体化规划（2014－2020年）》（以下简称《规划》）正式出台。根据《规划》，到2020年，江苏省常住人口城镇化率达到72%，新型城镇化与城乡发展一体化质量将显著提升。

2014年6月3日　据中国政府网发布的《国务院办公厅关于加强城市地下管线建设管理的指导意见》提出，我国计划用10年左右时间，建成较为完善的城市地下管线体系，使地下管线建设管理水平能够适应经济社会发展需要，应急防灾能力大幅提升。

2014年6月4日　深圳建设国家自主创新示范区获批，成为我国首个以城市为基本单元的国家自主创新示范区。深圳国家自主创新示范区是我国继北京中关村、武汉东湖高新区和上海张江之后的第四个自主创新示范区，也是我国首个以城市为基本单元的国家自主创新示范区。

2014年6月5日　住房和城乡建设部发布《住房和城乡建设部关于做好2014年村庄规划、镇规划和县域村镇体系规划试点工作的通知》（以下简称《通知》）。《通知》提出，在各地推荐申报的基础上，经遴选，确定辽宁省盘锦市大洼县等5个县开展县域村镇体系规划试点，天津市武清区河西务镇等17个镇开展镇规划试点，江西省赣州市瑞金市黄柏镇向阳村等10个行政村开展村庄规划试点。

2014年6月5日　据国家发展和改委委员会消息，国家发展和改委委员会有关方面已初步将京津冀区域划分为四大功能分区，即西、北部生态保护和生态产业发展区（覆盖承德、张家口），中部优化调整区（北京、天津、廊坊、唐山）、南部制造业与耕作业区（覆盖石家庄、保定、沧州）、东部滨海临港产业发展区（覆盖秦皇岛、唐山、天津、沧州）。在四大功能分区的基础上，京津冀的总体布局也已具雏形，即“两核三轴一带三重点”，“三轴”指京津塘主轴、京—保—石拓展轴、京—唐—秦拓展轴，“一带”指沿海经济带，三个重点开发地区包括中关村、天津滨海新区、曹妃甸工业区。

2014年6月6日　习近平总书记在主持召开中央全面深化改革领导小组第三次会议上强调，推进人的城镇化重要的环节在于户籍制度，加快户籍制度改革，是涉及亿万农业转移人口的一项重大举措。总的政策要求是全面放开建制镇和小城市落户限制，有序放开中等城市落户限制，合理确定大城市落户条件，严格控制特大城市人口规模，促进有能力在城镇稳定就业和生活的常住人口有序实现市民化，稳步推进城镇基本公共服务常住人口全覆盖。

2014年6月6日　住房和城乡建设部开展2014年国家级风景名胜区执法检查，检查涉及群众举报、媒体曝光及其他随机抽取的部分国家级风景名胜区。

2014年6月7日　住房城乡建设部、国家发展改革委、财政部联合发出通知，要求各地切实做好2014年农村危房改造工作。

2014年6月9日　湖北省住房和城乡建设厅编制印发了《湖北省绿色生态城区示范技术指标体系（试行）》。

2014年6月17日　《福建省新型城镇化规划（2014－2020年）》（以下简称《规划》）出炉。《规划》明确了“推进农业转移人口市民化，优化城镇化布局形态，强化城镇化发展产业支撑，提高城镇综合承载能力，推进城乡发展一体化，创新城镇化发展体制机制”六大任务，阐明了福建新型城镇化的发展方向、目标和战略任务。

2014 年 6 月 19 日 国土资源部正式发布《节约集约利用土地规定》（以下简称《规定》）。《规定》首先明确通过土地利用总体规划，确定建设用地的规模、布局、结构和时序安排，对建设用地实行总量控制。土地利用总体规划确定的约束性指标和分区管制规定不得突破。国土资源主管部门应当通过规划、计划、用地标准、市场引导等手段，有效控制特大城市新增建设用地规模，适度增加集约用地程度高、发展潜力大的地区和中小城市、县城建设用地供给，合理保障民生用地需求。在“完善市场配置，促进用地提效”方面，《规定》扩大了土地有偿使用范围。

2014 年 6 月 19－20 日 国务院副总理汪洋在重庆调研农村改革工作时表示，要紧紧围绕使市场在资源配置中起决定性作用和更好发挥政府作用，推进农村改革创新，加快建立健全有利于激发农村内部发展活力和营造良好外部环境的制度安排。要尊重基层和群众首创精神，鼓励探索实践，搞好试点试验，及时总结推广好的经验和做法，不断将农村改革引向深入。

2014 年 6 月 20 日 住房和城乡建设部村镇建设司司长赵晖在第八届环境技术产业论坛上说，截至 2012 年，我国城市污水处理率已达到 87%，但村庄的污水处理率只有 8%。此外，截至 2012 年，县城的污水处理率接近 80%，但建制镇的污水处理率不到 30%。

2014 年 6 月 21 日 上海组织专门研讨会，聚焦新一轮城市总体规划编制，讨论“迈向全球城市的产业升级与竞争力提升”。据悉，在上海新一轮城市总体规划中，上海的城市定位已经发生变化：在 2020 年基本建成“四个中心”和社会主义现代化国际大都市的基础上，2040 年要努力建设成为具有全球资源配置能力、较强国际竞争力和影响力的全球城市。

2014 年 6 月 21 日 “南海丝绸之路文化遗产保护研讨会”在海南海口召开，与会专家共同谋划如何借海南、广东、广西、福建、江苏、浙江、山东 7 省（自治区）9 市之力，正式申请将“海上丝绸之路”纳入世界文化遗产。来自国家文物局、国家海洋局、中国博物馆协会丝绸之路专业委员会、国家水下文化遗产保护中心及台湾、香港等有关领导、专家参与研讨并共同发起《南海丝绸之路文化遗产保护共同宣言》。

2014 年 6 月 22 日 在卡塔尔首都多哈召开的第 38 届世界遗产大会上宣布：由扬州牵头的中国大运河项目成功入选世界文化遗产名录，成为中国第 46 个世界遗产项目。同时，本届遗产大会批准通过“丝绸之路：起始段和天山廊道的路网”世界遗产名录申请报告，中国与吉尔吉斯斯坦、哈萨克斯坦联合提交的这一文化遗产项目正式列入世界遗产名录。

2014 年 6 月 30 日 中共中央政治局召开会议，审议通过了《关于进一步推进户籍制度改革的意见》。会议指出，加快户籍制度改革是涉及亿万农业转移人口的一项重大措施。要坚持以人为本，着力促进有能力在城镇稳定就业和生活的常住人口有序实现市民化，稳步推进城镇基本公共服务常住人口全覆盖。要坚持积极稳妥、规范有序，既要鼓励各地大胆实践、积极探索，又要指导地方尊重客观规律，尊重群众意愿，不搞指标分配，不搞层层加码。要优先解决好进城时间长、就业能力强、可以适应城镇和市场竞争环境的人，使他们及其家庭在城镇扎根落户，有序引导人口流向。要积极推进城镇基本公共服务由主要对本地户籍人口提供向对常住人口提供转变，逐步解决在城镇就业居住但未落户的农业转移人口享有城镇基本公共服务问题。

2014年6月30日　成渝经济区两大城市群规划——成都城市群和南部城市群发展规划正式发布。

2014年7月1日　作为国内首部省级生态文明建设地方性法规，《贵州省生态文明建设促进条例》正式施行。

2014年7月1日　《大理市大理古城保护管理办法》（以下简称《办法》）正式施行。《办法》明确规定，大理市古城保护管理局的主要职责之一为依法征收和管理古城维护费。

2014年7月2日　《关于对世界文化遗产丽江古城保护规划的意见》（以下简称《意见》）在国家文物局官网发布，《意见》原则上同意云南省文物局所报的丽江古城保护规划，但对规划提出了多条修改意见，包括应遏制丽江古城的商业化倾向，严格控制周边新建项目。《意见》还提出，鉴于近期丽江古城火灾频发，应进一步完善有针对性的消防安全专项规划。

2014年7月3日　河南省政府正式发布了《河南省新型城镇化规划（2014－2020年）》。

2014年7月13日　《京津冀区域发展报告（2014）》在北京大学发布。该报告由北京大学首都发展研究院牵头，联合京津冀三地研究部门，邀请32位权威专家共同编写。报告就稳妥疏解首都非核心功能、建立京津冀区域协调机制等六方面进行了探讨。

2014年7月21日　国务院办公厅印发《关于进一步加强棚户区改造工作的通知》，部署有效解决棚户区改造中的困难和问题，进一步加强棚户区改造工作，扎实推进改造约1亿人居住的城镇棚户区和城中村。

2014年7月24-25日　国务院总理李克强在山东济南、德州考察时表示，基础设施建设是以人为核心的新型城镇化要害所在，特别在县一级基础薄弱、需求巨大。政府要加大投入，更要通过改革，创新投融资方式，吸引社会资金进入，加快建设，造福当代，惠及子孙。

2014年7月28日　中国社科院财经战略研究院、中国社科院城市与竞争力研究中心发布2014年《中国住房发展（中期）报告》。报告指出，2014年上半年，全国楼市进入结构性过剩阶段，房价调整期恐持续两三年。

2014年7月30日　《国务院关于进一步推进户籍制度改革的意见》（以下简称《意见》）正式发布。《意见》要求，取消农业户口与非农业户口性质区分和由此衍生的蓝印户口等户口类型，统一登记为居民户口。建立与统一城乡户口登记制度相适应的教育、卫生计生、就业、社保、住房、土地及人口统计制度。《意见》称，全面放开建制镇和小城市落户限制，有序放开中等城市落户限制，合理确定大城市落户条件，严格控制特大城市人口规模。

2014年7月30日　《广西壮族自治区新型城镇化规划（2014－2020年）》（以下简称

《规划》）正式印发。《规划》提出要走“以人为本、集约高效、绿色发展、四化同步、城乡一体、多元特色”的新型城镇化道路。根据《规划》，到2020年，广西常住人口城镇化率为54%，户籍人口城镇化率为34.5%，新增城镇人口700万人，600万农业转移人口和其他常住人口落户城镇。

2014年7月31日 国务院同意建立推进新型城镇化工作部际联席会议制度，由国家发展和改委委员会牵头，统筹推进国家新型城镇化规划实施和政策制定落实，推进土地管理、财税金融等重点领域和关键环节改革。

2014年7月31日 国务院总理李克强主持召开振兴东北地区等老工业基地工作会议，强力吹响“二次振兴东北”的号角。从上半年GDP增速来看，东北地区显然压力较大，整体经济都在中下游水平，不仅GDP大大低于全国平均水平，而且吉林、黑龙江排名相对靠后。当前东北地区所面临的形势，既有普遍性的共性问题，其他省份或多或少也正在经历同样的阵痛和困惑，也有地区特色的个性问题，比如“历史旧账”较重，这需要有针对性解决方案。对此，李克强总理开出了“三味药”：一是进一步推进简政放权激发市场活力，为企业经营和创新创业提供公平市场环境；二是加强民生保障，增加公共产品有效供给；三是紧扣转方式、调结构，做强实体经济。

2014年8月1日 国土资源部、财政部、住房城乡建设部、农业部、国家林业局联合印发《关于进一步加快推进宅基地和集体建设用地使用权确权登记发证工作的通知》。

2014年8月3日 首都规划建设委员会召开第33次全体会议，研究《北京市城市总体规划》的修改工作。中共中央政治局委员、市委书记、首规委主任郭金龙在这次会议上对总规修改提出五点要求：一是突出“瘦身健体”，一方面下决心调整疏解非首都核心功能，另一方面在构建“高精尖”经济结构上积极作为；二是突出国际一流，努力打造城市建设精品力作，特别是把城市开发强度降下来，把“摊大饼”式的发展遏制住，把绿色空间长上去；三是要突出文化传承，处理好古都风貌保护和现代化建设的关系，延续城市历史文脉，造福人民群众；四是突出破解难题，把生态文明建设和城市环境治理作为重要内容，进一步优化城市空间布局；五是突出改革创新，使修改后的规划更好地反映首都特点、北京特色和时代特征。

2014年8月5日 环境保护部发布今年上半年全国环境质量状况，环境状况结果显示，实施空气质量新标准的161个城市按照《环境空气质量标准》（GB 3095－2012）的年均值进行评价，仅舟山、拉萨9个城市达标，其余152城市环境空气质量均未达标。

2014年8月6日 为贯彻落实京津冀协同发展重大国家战略，推进津冀两地市场深化合作，天津市与河北省签署了《交通一体化合作备忘录》。优化整合港口、铁路、公路、航空等各种交通方式，共同构建安全、便捷、高效、绿色、经济的现代综合交通运输体系。

2014年8月8日 江西省政府办公厅转发省住房城乡建设厅《关于严格执行城镇总体规划集约节约利用建设用地的意见》，重申坚决遏制城镇建设规模无序扩张。

2014年8月15日 《重庆市统筹城乡重点改革总体方案》（以下简称《方案》）正式出炉。《方案》不仅明确了改革的重点和目标，还指明了改革的方向，是未来重庆市统筹城乡改革的“风向标”。各地在推进改革的过程中，均可依据本地实际情况，积极推动五个方面的改革：一是建立健全新型农业经营体系；二是深化农民工户籍制度改革；三是完善农村金融服务体系；四是完善地票制度功能，重点完善地票使用及交易机制、完善复垦管理工作机制、建立完善“三农”权益保障机制、构建农村综合产权交易服务体系；五是健全农村现代流通体系。

2014年8月19日　《国务院关于近期支持东北振兴若干重大政策举措的意见》（以下简称《意见》）发布。《意见》提出11个方面35条政策措施，从基建项目、国企改革到产业支持等领域明确了扶持举措。

2014年8月19日　《安徽省城镇体系规划（2011-2030）》（以下简称《规划》）获批，预期到2020年安徽省城镇化水平将达58%，城镇人口3900万人；2030年全省城镇化水平将达70%左右，城镇人口5100万人左右。这是全国第三个经国务院同意批复的至2030年的省域城镇体系规划。根据《规划》，近期安徽省将发展形成“一圈一带一群”的城镇空间结构，其中“一圈”为合肥都市圈，“一带”为沿江（皖江）城市带，“一群”为皖北城市群。在此基础上，远期将加快发展芜马都市圈和淮蚌合芜宣发展（轴）带，形成“两圈两带一群”的城镇空间结构。

2014年8月29日　据国家发展和改委委员会消息，国家发展和改委委员会、工业和信息化部等8部门发布《促进智慧城市健康发展的指导意见》，提出到2020年建成一批特色鲜明的智慧城市。建成的智慧城市将实现“五化”：一是公共服务便捷化；二是城市管理精细化；三是生活环境宜居化；四是基础设施智能化；五是网络安全长效化。

2014年9月1日　由福建省城乡规划设计研究院和福建省城市规划学会共同编制的《福建省绿道规划建设标准》（以下简称《标准》），经省住房城乡建设厅批准为福建省工程建设地方标准。《标准》自10月30日起执行。

2014年9月4日　京津冀协同发展领导小组第三次会议在北京召开。国务院副总理、京津冀协同发展领导小组组长张高丽主持会议并讲话。会议讨论了京津冀区域功能定位，审议了京津冀交通一体化、生态环境保护、产业协同发展三个重点领域率先突破工作方案和支持京津冀协同发展重大改革政策措施，研究部署下一阶段工作。

2014年9月11日　据《中国建设报》消息，为贯彻落实全国工程质量治理两年行动电视电话会议精神，住房和城乡建设部派出督察工作组，对北京、天津等15个省（直辖市、自治区）开展工程质量治理两年行动督察工作。

2014年9月13-15日　2014中国城市规划年会在海口召开。这是我国城市规划行业规模最大、学术水平最高、参与性最强的行业性盛会，每年举办一次。本届年会主题为：城乡治理与规划改革。由中国城市规划学会主办，海口市人民政府、海南省住房和城乡建设厅协办，中国城市规划设计研究院、海口市会展局、海口市规划局共同承办。参会人数达6000余人。

2014年9月15日　据《中国建设报》消息，住房和城乡建设部发出通报，命名内蒙古自治区通辽市等8个城市为国家园林城市。根据《国家园林城市申报与评审办法》，2013

年，住房和城乡建设部对2012年申报城市组织了综合评审。通辽、鄂尔多斯、宁德、高密、泸州、咸阳、灵武、中卫8个城市按照评审意见，认真查找不足，积极整改落实，经所在省级城乡建设主管部门审核把关及专家现场核实，达到国家园林城市标准要求，被命名为国家园林城市。

2014年9月16日 中共中央政治局常委、国务院总理李克强主持召开推进新型城镇化建设试点工作座谈会并作重要讲话。他说，我国经济保持中高速增长、迈向中高端水平，必须用好新型城镇化这个强大引擎。新型城镇化是一个综合载体，不仅可以破解城乡二元结构、促进农业现代化、提高农民生产和收入水平，而且有助于扩大消费、拉动投资、催生新兴产业，释放更大的内需潜力，顶住下行压力，为中国经济平稳增长和持续发展增动能。必须认真贯彻中央城镇化工作会议精神，按照科学发展的要求，遵循规律，用改革的办法、创新的精神推进新型城镇化，促进“新四化”协同发展，取得新的突破。

2014年9月16日 住房和城乡建设部召开2014年中国城市无车日活动新闻发布会。部总规划师唐凯在会上强调，要以无车日活动为契机，制定发展绿色交通的永久性措施。围绕如何推进步行和自行车交通基础设施建设，唐凯从规划和设计层面提出三点要求：一是要重视步行和自行车交通系统与空间环境一体化规划；二是步行和自行车交通系统离不开以道路为主体的精细化、人性化设计；三是要加强步行和自行车交通与其他交通方式的衔接。

2014年9月16日 住房和城乡建设部公布的数据显示，截至8月份，我国2014年已开工保障性安居工程650万套，基本建成400万套，分别达到年度目标任务的92%和83%，完成投资9500亿元人民币。对于下一阶段的工作，住房和城乡建设部部长陈政高表示主要有四个方面：一是要确保完成全年保障房建设的目标任务，保开工、保建成，未开工的地方9月份必须全部开工。二是在棚户区改造中既要注重实物安置也要注重货币安置，在公租房保障上既要注重实物配租也要注重租金补助。三是继续加大巡查力度。四是2015年要继续加大保障性安居工程建设力度，合理确定建设任务；工矿、林区、垦区、棚户区改造要在摸清底数的基础上，打一场攻坚战；进一步研究完善已建成的保障性住房的使用和管理体制机制。

2014年9月16日 从国务院召开的推进新型城镇化建设试点工作座谈会上获悉，新型城镇化试点名单已确定，共有62个试点城市入选，首批“镇改市”试点名单只拟定了两个镇，分别是浙江温州龙港镇和吉林延边二道白河镇。

2014年9月18日 据《经济参考报》报道，为推进城镇化、缓解大城市病，现阶段国家发展和改委委员会已正式启动编制跨省区城市群规划。规划或于2015年年底前编制完成，并上报国务院批准实施。为发挥城市群的战略平台作用，此前，国家发展和改委委员会已经印发《关于开展跨省级行政区城市群规划编制工作的通知》。

2014年9月19日 据中国政府网消息，国务院正式批复同意《国家应对气候变化规划(2014－2020年)》。

2014年9月22日 中国举办城市无车日活动。本届活动的主题为“我们的街道，我们的选择”，重点关注交通对城市生活质量的影响，鼓励重新分配和设计街道及公共空间，促进多种交通方式在道路空间分配上的平衡。

2014年9月22日　据《中国建设报》消息，“珠三角全域规划”的编制工作正在稳步推进。全域规划期限暂定为2020年，以珠三角地区地理信息为基础，将近期重点项目、空间政策、区域现代社会治理体系等制订成为行动计划；借鉴国内外同类型城市群规划的工作经验，对相应空间作出安排和谋划，确定总目标和次一级目标；突出从城市到乡村全范围规划的特点，统筹产业、交通、生态等各项规划，并根据珠三角发展现状提出优化发展的策略，以全区域的尺度统筹生产、生活、生态空间元素，形成分工协作、功能互补的城市群格局。

2014年9月23日　第五届中国（天津滨海）国际生态城市论坛暨博览会、2014（第九届）中国城市发展与规划大会在天津滨海新区召开。本届大会延续“生态城市创造和谐未来”的永久主题，聚焦“生态城市与美好家园”的年度主题，紧扣十八届三中全会相关精神，结合滨海新区建设宜居生态型城区的生动实践，探寻发展生态城市的新思路和新举措。

2014年9月23日　《陕西省新型城镇化规划（2014-2020年）》发布，提出要坚持以人为本、生态环保、保护文化、创新体制的原则，科学施策，适度超前，改善城市基础设施条件，完善公共服务设施，增强城市综合承载能力。

2014年9月25日　《国务院关于依托黄金水道推动长江经济带发展的指导意见》明确，长江经济带覆盖上海、江苏、浙江、安徽、江西、湖北、湖南、重庆、四川、云南、贵州11省（直辖市），面积约205万平方公里，人口和生产总值均超过全国的40%。以沿江综合运输大通道为轴线，以长江三角洲、长江中游和成渝三大跨区域城市群为主体，以黔中和滇中两大区域性城市群为补充，以沿江大中小城市和小城镇为依托，促进城市群之间、城市群内部的分工协作。

2014年9月25日　国土资源部就近期下发的《关于推进土地节约集约利用的指导意见》举行通气会。国土资源部规划司司长董祚继在会上表示，目前城市新区扩张问题比较普遍，也比较严重，今后将严格管控城市新区用地。2013年国土资源部进行了全面的摸底调查，发现全国391个城市的新区规划人均城市建设用地197平方米，已建成区人均城市建设用地达到161平方米，这远超过人均100平方米的国家标准。今后确需设立城市新区的，必须以人口密度、用地产出强度和资源环境承载能力为基准，以符合土地利用总体规划为前提。国土资源部将在严格掌握标准的前提下予以规范和支持。但是第一必须符合国家标准，第二必须符合土地规划和城市规划。

2014年10月8日　推进新型城镇化工作部际联席会议第一次会议召开，该会议提出，要充分发挥好推进新型城镇化工作部际联席会议制度的平台作用，统筹推进国家新型城镇化规划实施和政策制定落实，协调解决重大问题。为此，要协调搞好配套政策的研究、制定和落实，推进人口管理等重点领域和关键环节改革。按照新标准，特大城市是指城区人口500万人以上的城市，按照2010年的数据就只有16个，包括北京、上海、天津、广州、武汉、西安等，以直辖市和省会城市以及计划单列市为多。

2014年10月9日 山东省委、省政府公布了《山东省新型城镇化规划（2014－2020年）》（以下简称《规划》）。《规划》共11篇42章，确定了今后一段时期山东城镇化发展的目标和工作任务，明确了未来全省新型城镇化的发展路径和主要措施。

2014年10月14日 国务院批复《中国—新加坡天津生态城建设国家绿色发展示范区实施方案》（以下简称《方案》），明确通过《方案》实施，着力优化城市空间布局，促进绿色低碳发展，推动资源节约高效循环利用，努力把中国—新加坡天津生态城建设成为生产发展、生活富裕、生态良好的宜居城区，为探索中国特色新型城镇化道路提供示范。

2014年10月18日 以"人居环境与科学规划"为主题的中国城市规划设计研究院60周年学术报告会在京举行。两院院士吴良镛到会。邹德慈院士以"明天的城市，走向何方"为题作了演讲；崔恺院士阐述了城市保护与发展的关系；王瑞珠院士与大家分享了莫干山会议的启示；崔功豪教授提出了规划变革的思路；原建设部部长汪光焘通过对法治与城乡规划编制进行思考，提出了当前的三项重要工作：要重视丰富科技知识和熟悉法律规定，要创新大数据、信息化时代的规划编制方法，要着手科研技术规范修订。

2014年10月18日 在全国城市基础设施建设经验交流会上，住房和城乡建设部部长陈政高提出7点要求：第一，要树立正确的政绩观，城市建设，既要重视城市的面子，也要重视里子；既要重视地上，更要重视地下。第二，水是宝贵的自然资源和环境要素。优先考虑把有限的雨水留下，建设自然积存、自然渗透、自然净化的海绵城市，既减轻了城市排水压力，又补充了地下水，一举多得。要用10年左右时间建成较完善的城市排水防洪工程体系。第三，城市新区要推进综合管廊建设，用3年左右时间，在全国36个大中城市全面启动地下综合管廊试点工程。第四，垃圾是资源，是城市矿产而不是包袱，必须大幅提高垃圾回收率。第五，不仅要把污水处理好，还要提高中水回用率。第六，在基础设施建设中，着力推动绿色节能。第七，建立完整的基础设施信息系统。

2014年10月22日 由住房和城乡建设部组织编制的《海绵城市建设技术指南——低影响开发雨水系统构建（试行）》发布实施，为各地深入开展海绵城市建设提供指导和依据。下一步，住房和城乡建设部将组织设市城市、区、县开展海绵城市建设试点示范工作，以点带面，扩大推广。

2014年10月29日 国务院印发《关于调整城市规模划分标准的通知》，对原有城市规模划分标准进行了调整，明确了新的城市规模划分标准。一是城市类型由四类变为五类，增设了超大城市。二是将小城市和大城市分别划分为两档，细分小城市主要为满足城市规划建设的需要，细分大城市主要是实施人口分类管理的需要。三是人口规模的上下限普遍提高。小城市人口上限由20万人提高到50万人，中等城市的上下限分别由20万人、50万人提高到50万人、100万人，大城市的上下限分别由50万人、100万人提高到100万人、500万人，特大城市下限由100万人提高到500万人。四是将统计口径界定为城区常住人口。城区是指在市辖区和不设区的市，区、市政府驻地的实际建设连接到的居民委员会所辖区域和其他区域。

2014年10月29日 《青海省生态文明先行示范区建设实施方案》获国家发展和改委

委员会等六部委批复。由此，青海正式列入国家首批生态文明建设先行示范区。

2014年10月30日 湖南省政府印发了《湖南省推进新型城镇化实施纲要（2014－2020年）》（以下简称《纲要》）。《纲要》提出要在2020年内全省城镇化率达到58%，还提出适时调整行政区划，优化城镇体系结构，从2014年起所有城镇全面放开落户限制。

2014年10月30日 厦门市召开“多规合一”专题研讨会，探讨在已运行的发改、国土和规划“三规合一”的基础上，进一步整合涉及环保、海洋、林业、文化、教育、体育、卫生、交通等部门的规划职能，力争整个城建规划都只看“一张图”。2014年9月，厦门在省内率先整合发改、国土和规划三部门的规划职能，形成“三规合一”，有效避免了建设用地与非建设用地“规划打架”。从近三个月来的运行情况来看，新编制大大缩短了建设项目的审批时限，大大简化了审批手续。实行“三规合一”后，从项目建议书至施工许可核发，总审批时限由原来的122个工作日缩短至49个工作日，前期工作总时限压缩了1/3以上。

2014年10月31日 全球首个“世界城市日”活动全球启动仪式在上海举行。首个“世界城市日”的主题为“城市转型与发展”。

2014年11月1日 《关于严禁在历史建筑、公园等公共资源中设立私人会所的暂行规定》正式施行。为贯彻落实《中共中央办公厅、国务院办公厅转发住房城乡建设部等部门〈关于严禁在历史建筑、公园等公共资源中设立私人会所的暂行规定〉的通知》，住房和城乡建设部下发通知，将对“会所中的歪风”整治情况进行跟踪督察，对检查中发现确实存在公园中设立私人会所等问题的，将予以通报批评，限期整改；整改仍不合格的，将公告撤销其国家园林城市、中国人居环境奖称号或取消其申报、考核资格。

2014年11月3日 由住房城乡建设部信息中心、国家测绘地理信息局国土测绘司、国家遥感中心等单位联合主办的第九届中国智慧城市建设技术研讨会暨设备博览会在北京国际会议中心举行，会议以“创新·融合·服务”与“大数据”为主题，集中展示智慧城市建设最新技术和方案，深度探讨大数据时代智慧城市建设的机制体制问题。

2014年11月5日 由中国建筑工业出版社、清华大学建筑学院主办的《中国人居史》首发式暨人居历史与文化学术研讨会在北京举办。《中国人居史》的作者吴良镛先生是中国科学院和中国工程院院士、中国人居环境科学的创建者。该书梳理了我国古代人居建设的历程，从人居文化复兴的角度对我国未来人居建设提出了基本看法。人居历史与文化学术研讨会随后召开。清华大学建筑与城市研究所副所长武廷海主持了研讨会，中国工程院院士、中国建筑设计研究院研究员傅熹年，故宫博物院院长单霁翔，中国建筑学会原秘书长、原城乡建设环境保护部设计局局长张钦楠等数十位专家作了精彩的发言报告。

2014年11月9日 《武汉城市圈“两型”社会建设综合配套改革试验行动方案（2014－2015年）》正式出台，成为圈内9个城市如何实现“一体化”的最新行动指南。

2014年11月11日 酝酿十多年的《广州市历史文化名城保护规划》已获省政府审议通过，并于该日起正式生效。

2014年11月17日 国务院副总理张高丽在全国进一步推进户籍制度改革工作电视电话会议上强调，推进户籍制度改革，要遵循规律、积极稳妥，坚持从实际出发，全面实施差别化落户政策；坚持存量优先，逐步满足符合条件的农业转移人口落户需求；坚持加快中小城市发展，增强集聚人口和提供公共服务的能力，确保与新型城镇化发展相适应。要以人为本、顺应民意，充分尊重城乡居民自主定居的意愿，切实保障农业转移人口合法权益，加快推进城镇基本公共服务常住人口全覆盖，在制度安排上为各类社会群体提供更多选择，最大限度释放改革红利。要统筹配套、协同推进，抓紧制定《居住证管理办法》，做好户籍制度改革与教育、就业、医疗、养老、住房保障、农村产权、财力保障等相关领域改革的衔接。

2014 年 11 月 18 日 住房和城乡建设部召开全国农村生活垃圾治理工作电视电话会议，推广四川、山东等地农村生活垃圾治理经验，部署全面推进农村生活垃圾治理工作，提出全面启动农村生活垃圾 5 年专项治理，使全国 90% 村庄的生活垃圾得到处理。

2014 年 11 月 18 日 国家卫生计生委发布《中国流动人口发展报告 2014》（以下简称《报告》）。《报告》指出，现在全国流动人口的总量是 2.45 亿人，超过总人口的 1/6，流动人口总的流向趋势没有改变，特别是特大城市人口聚集态势还在加强，如北京、上海吸纳跨省流动人口的趋势进一步增强。

2014 年 11 月 18 日 据国家发展和改革委员会网站消息，国家发展改革委在东北地区全面启动独立工矿区改造搬迁工程。目前，10 个独立工矿区的改造搬迁工程已全面开工。通过实施改造搬迁工程，将显著改善矿区发展条件和居民生产生活条件，有效解决制约独立工矿区转型发展的突出瓶颈问题，增强独立工矿区的内生发展动力，对于东北地区应对今年以来经济下行压力、稳增长惠民生也将发挥重要作用。

2014 年 11 月 23 日 住房和城乡建设部规划司明确将东莞作为住房和城乡建设部总规编制与审批改革试点城市，并要求该市积极围绕部的总规改革思路，大胆探索 2030 年总规编制新方法，加快总规编制工作进度，为部的工作决策和其他城市提供样板和经验借鉴。

2014 年 11 月 25 日 在各地初步评价的基础上，经传统保护村落发展专家委员会评审认定，住房和城乡建设部、文化部、国家文物局、财政部、国土资源部、国家旅游局等联合公布第三批中国传统村落名录，全国共有 994 个村落榜上有名。自 2012 年以来，我国已经公布两批 1561 个村落列入了中国传统村落名录，其中 327 个村落列入 2014 年第一批中央财政支持范围。加上此次入选村落，共计 2555 个传统村落将获得保护。

2014 年 11 月 25 日 宁夏回族自治区十一届人大常委会第十三次会议审议通过了《宁夏回族自治区空间发展战略规划的条例》，以地方立法的形式将空间规划的编制、修改、实施、监督纳入法制化轨道。这是宁夏首次编制空间发展战略规划，也是国内第一个以省域为单位编制的空间规划。

2014 年 11 月 27－29 日 第九届中国城镇水务发展国际研讨会与新技术设备博览会在南宁市召开。大会由中国城市科学研究会、中国城镇供水排水协会、广西壮族自治区住房和城乡建设厅及南宁市人民政府联合举办，得到国家住房城乡建设部、环境保护部、广西壮族自治区人民政府和国际水协（IWA）的鼎力支持。大会以“提高用水效率，治理水体污染，确保用水安全”为主题，设大会开幕式、综合论坛和 20 多个分论坛，吸引了国内外水业同行 2000 余人参会。开幕式由中国城镇供水排水协会副会长、秘书长邵益生主持。

2014年12月2日 北京市副市长陈刚在北京名城委专家工作会上提出，北京当前进行的总体规划修改中，将在空间布局上为旧城减负，旧城要疏解功能，减少建设量，人口疏解则本着自愿的原则。首先要从大的空间布局上，给旧城、给文保区减负。要减少建设量，减少人为活动，减少低端产业。旧城里经营低端商业活动，吸引大量外来人口，这样一些业态都要进行调整。高、中、低端业态都要根据规划进行有序的疏解。要留住乡愁，留住非物质文化遗产。同时，还要从精细化管理、依法行政的角度对旧城进行治理，包括停车环境等。

2014年12月3日 全国城市地下管线综合管理试点工作启动，山东德州成为首个试点城市。

2014年12月5日 中共中央政治局召开会议，分析研究2015年经济工作。本次会议总结了2014年经济发展成果，认为中国经济发展形势总体是好的，并作出中国进入经济发展新常态的判断。2015年将继续坚持稳中求进工作总基调，更加注重转方式、调结构。会议还强调了2015年经济工作七大重点，包括财政货币政策、产业结构、农业、区域发展、改善民生、经济体制改革、扩大内需。

2014年12月6日 据国务院扶贫办主任刘永富在全国贫困村旅游扶贫试点工作座谈会上指出，国家发展改革委、财政部、国家旅游局、国务院扶贫办等七部门联合印发了《关于实施乡村旅游富民工程推进旅游扶贫工作的通知》，明确了到2015年扶持约2000个贫困村开展乡村旅游，到2020年，支持6000多个贫困村开展乡村旅游。

2014年12月9日 中央经济工作会议在北京召开，首次明确了“经济发展新常态”的九大趋势性变化，提出“认识新常态，适应新常态，引领新常态，是当前和今后一个时期我国经济发展的大逻辑”。会议从“消费需求”、“投资需求”、“出口和国际收支”、“生产能力和产业组织方式”、“生产要素相对优势”、“市场竞争特点”、“资源环境约束”、“经济风险积累和化解”、“资源配置模式和宏观调控方式”九大方面，全面阐述了经济发展新常态下的九大趋势性变化。会上将“京津冀协同发展”列入明年经济工作的主要任务。会议提出，优化经济发展空间格局，要完善区域政策，促进各地区协调发展、协同发展、共同发展。西部开发、东北振兴、中部崛起、东部率先的区域发展总体战略，要继续实施。各地区要找准主体功能区定位和自身优势，确定工作着力点。要重点实施“一带一路”、京津冀协同发展、长江经济带三大战略。

2014年12月14日 针对我国地下管线现状不明、“家底”不清问题，住房和城乡建设部、工业和信息化部、新闻出版广电总局、安监总局和能源局联合发出通知，要求在全国范围内开展地下管线普查，2015年年底前完成普查并建立完善城市地下管线综合管理信息系统和专业管线信息系统。

2014年12月15日 北京新机场工程正式获得批复。国家发展和改革委员会发布了关于北京新机场工程可行性研究报告的批复：为满足北京地区航空运输需求，增强我国民航竞争力，促进北京南北城区均衡发展和京津冀协同发展，以及更好服务全国对外开放，同意建设北京新机场。

2014年12月16日 国务院副总理张高丽在杭州调研城市规划建设工作座谈会上表示，

做好城市规划建设工作，对于推动新型城镇化、有效治理“城市病”、促进经济社会持续健康发展、提高群众生活水平至关重要。我们一定要增强责任感和使命感，把思想和行动统一到党中央、国务院的决策部署上来。张高丽强调，要统筹兼顾、突出重点，采取有针对性的措施，大力提升城市规划建设水平。要提高城市规划的科学性、权威性、严肃性，更好地发挥对城市建设的调控、引领和约束作用；要加强城市设计、完善决策评估机制、规范建筑市场和鼓励创新，提高城市建筑整体水平；要加大投入，加快完善城市基础设施，增强城市综合承载能力；要强化监督管理和落实质量责任，扭住关键环节，着力提高建筑工程质量；要注重保护历史文化建筑，牢牢把握地域、民族和时代三个核心要素，为城市打造靓丽名片，留住城市的人文特色和历史记忆。同时，要加强农村建筑风貌管控，做好传统村落和传统民居的保护工作。

2014年12月17日 国土资源部公布《关于发布全国耕地质量等别调查与评定主要数据成果的公告》。这是自2009年国土资源部完成对全国耕地质量等级首次全面调查与评定后，第二次全面清查全国耕地质量等别及其分布状况。根据全国耕地质量等别及其分布状况的调查评定数据，中国耕地目前耕地平均质量等级总体偏低，中、低等耕地面积占耕地评定面积的70.6%。

2014年12月19日 住房和城乡建设部部长陈政高在全国住房城乡建设工作会议上作了题为《勇于担当，突破重点，努力开创住房城乡建设事业新局面》的讲话，全面总结2014年住房城乡建设工作，对2015年的工作任务作出部署。在部署2015年住房城乡建设工作时，陈政高要求，全系统要主动适应经济发展新常态，紧紧围绕提高人民群众居住水平、提升城市综合承载能力、改善城乡人居生态环境，统筹谋划，突出重点，扎实推进，务求实效，努力开创住房城乡建设事业新局面。一是要保持房地产市场平稳健康发展。二是要深入推进工程质量治理、城市基础设施建设和农村生活垃圾治理三项工作。三是要在“大力提高建筑业竞争力，实现转型发展；加强城市设计工作；下力气治理违法建设；狠抓建筑节能；推进城市洁净工程；全面启动村庄规划”六个方面努力实现新突破。

2014年12月22日 甘肃省住房和城乡建设厅公布了《甘肃省城镇体系规划（2013-2030年)》（以下简称《规划》）成果主要内容，广泛征求公众意见。《规划》提出构建“一廊四轴多中心”空间布局，建立起以都市圈、都市区等现代城镇簇群为主体形态，“核心突出、特色多元、城乡美丽、功能协调”的城乡统筹协调发展新格局。

2014年12月23日 国务院总理李克强签署第656号国务院令，公布《不动产登记暂行条例》，自2015年3月1日起施行。

2014年12月23日 据《中国建设报》消息，云南省住房和城乡建设厅制定出台了《云南省城镇特色规划编制暂行办法》，规定该省各州、市、县、镇编制总体规划时，应将城镇特色规划作为专项规划同步编制，以法定规划指导各城镇建设，使之更具民族特色、地域特点和历史文化特征，突出每个城镇的特色主题形象。

2014年12月24日 中德全方位战略伙伴关系中的重要组成部分——中德低碳生态城市试点示范工作在京启动。

2014年12月26日 由中国社会科学院财经院、中国社会科学院城市与竞争力研究中心及社会科学文献出版社共同编著的《中国住房发展报告（2014-2015）》发布。

2014年12月26日 京津冀协同发展工作推进会议在北京召开。中共中央政治局常委、国务院副总理、京津冀协同发展领导小组组长张高丽主持会议并讲话。张高丽强调，京津冀协同发展的顶层设计已经取得阶段性成果，下一步要把工作重点从总体谋划转向推进实施，对确定的各项任务要狠抓落实、务求实效。要抓紧修改完善规划纲要，加快编制相关领域专项规划，确保在一个目标下协同、一张蓝图下推进。要深入研究体制机制改革、强化创新驱动、开展试点示范等重大问题，优先启动一批有共识、看得准、能见效的非首都核心功能疏解项目，加快推动交通一体化、生态环保、产业转移三个重点领域率先突破，抓紧确定2015年的重点工作和重大项目清单。

2014年12月29日 国土资源部公布了全国土地利用数据分析报告，截至2013年12月31日，全国城镇土地总面积为858.1万公顷（12872万亩）。其中，城市面积占47%，建制镇面积占53%。

2014年12月29日 中国国家信息中心宏观经济形势课题组发布报告称，2015年中国经济将呈现稳中缓降态势，预计GDP（国内生产总值）增长7%左右，政策方面建议继续实施积极的财政政策，适当扩大财政赤字。

2014年12月29日 《历史文化名城名镇名村街区保护规划编制审批办法》正式施行。

2014年12月30日 上海交通大学城市科学研究院编著的《中国城市群发展报告2014》发布。报告显示，目前，中国六大城市群综合指数水平的排名依次为：长三角、珠三角、京津冀、山东半岛、中原经济区、成渝经济区。

（作者：金晓春，中国城市规划设计研究院学术信息中心副主任；郭磊，中国城市规划设计研究院学术信息中心规划师）

附录2

2014年度中国城市相关政策法规索引

名　称	批号(文号)	发布机构	发布日期
国务院关于同意设立陕西西咸新区的批复	国函〔2014〕2号	国务院	2014-01-06
国务院关于同意设立贵州贵安新区的批复	国函〔2014〕3号	国务院	2014-01-06
住房城乡建设部关于印发县(市)域城乡污水统筹治理导则(试行)的通知	建村〔2014〕6号	住房和城乡建设部	2014-01-09
住房城乡建设部关于命名2013年国家园林城市、县城和城镇的通报	建城〔2014〕4号	住房和城乡建设部	2014-01-14
住房城乡建设部关于印发《乡村建设规划许可实施意见》的通知	建村〔2014〕21号	住房和城乡建设部	2014-01-21
国务院办公厅关于促进地理信息产业发展的意见	国办发〔2014〕2号	国务院办公厅	2014-01-22
住房城乡建设部关于开展县(市)城乡总体规划暨"三规合一"试点工作的通知	建规〔2014〕18号	住房和城乡建设部	2014-01-24
关于城乡建设用地增减挂钩试点有关财税政策问题的通知	财综〔2014〕7号	财政部	2014-01-26
住房城乡建设部等部门关于加强养老服务设施规划建设工作的通知	建标〔2014〕23号	住房和城乡建设部等	2014-01-28
交通运输部、公安部、国家发展改革委、工业和信息化部、住房城乡建设部、商务部、国家邮政局关于加强和改进城市配送管理工作的意见	交运发〔2013〕138号	交通运输部、公安部、国家发展改革委等	2014-02-06
关于强化管控落实最严格耕地保护制度的通知	国土资发〔2014〕18号	国土资源部	2014-02-13
南水北调工程供用水管理条例	国务院令第647号	国务院	2014-02-16
住房城乡建设部、国家文物局关于公布第六批中国历史文化名镇(村)的通知	建规〔2014〕27号	住房和城乡建设部、国家文物局	2014-02-19
住房城乡建设部、国家文物局关于开展中国历史文化街区认定工作的通知	建规〔2014〕28号	住房和城乡建设部、国家文物局	2014-02-19
国务院关于建立统一的城乡居民基本养老保险制度的意见	国发〔2014〕8号	国务院	2014-02-21
国务院办公厅关于落实中共中央国务院关于全面深化农村改革加快推进农业现代化若干意见有关政策措施分工的通知	国办函〔2014〕31号	国务院办公厅	2014-02-23
国家发展改革委关于浙江嘉善县域科学发展示范点建设方案的批复	发改地区〔2013〕419号	国家发展改革委	2014-02-28
国务院办公厅关于推进城区老工业区搬迁改造的指导意见	国办发〔2014〕9号	国务院办公厅	2014-03-03

续表

名　称	批号(文号)	发布机构	发布日期
国务院关于支持福建省深入实施生态省战略加快生态文明先行示范区建设的若干意见	国发〔2014〕12号	国务院	2014-03-10
国务院关于赣闽粤原中央苏区振兴发展规划的批复	国函〔2014〕32号	国务院	2014-03-11
住房城乡建设部等部门关于开展生活垃圾分类示范城市(区)工作的通知	建城〔2014〕39号	住房和城乡建设部、国家发展改革委、财政部等	2014-03-14
住房城乡建设部、国家发展改革委关于开展《全国城镇供水设施改造与建设"十二五"规划及2020年远景目标》中期评估的通知	建办城函〔2014〕158号	住房和城乡建设部、国家发展改革委	2014-03-17
城镇住房保障条例(征求意见稿)		国务院法制办公室	2014-03-28
住房城乡建设部关于做好2014年村庄规划、镇规划和县域村镇体系规划试点工作的通知	建村〔2014〕44号	住房和城乡建设部	2014-03-28
国务院关于晋陕豫黄河金三角区域合作规划的批复	国函〔2014〕40号	国务院	2014-03-31
国务院关于长沙市城市总体规划的批复	国函〔2014〕45号	国务院	2014-04-04
国务院关于洞庭湖生态经济区规划的批复	国函〔2014〕46号	国务院	2014-04-14
住房城乡建设部关于2013年中国人居环境奖获奖名单的通报	建城〔2014〕17号	住房和城乡建设部	2014-04-16
住房城乡建设部关于做好2014年住房保障工作的通知	建保〔2014〕57号	住房和城乡建设部	2014-04-22
住房城乡建设部、文化部、国家文物局、财政部关于切实加强中国传统村落保护的指导意见	建村〔2014〕61号	住房和城乡建设部、文化部、国家文物局、财政部	2014-04-25
住房城乡建设部关于成立传统民居保护专家委员会的通知	建村函〔2014〕111号	住房和城乡建设部	2014-04-28
住房城乡建设部关于2014年建设宜居小镇、宜居村庄示范工作的通知	建村函〔2014〕105号	住房和城乡建设部	2014-04-28
住房城乡建设部、中国气象局关于做好暴雨强度公式修订有关工作的通知	建城〔2014〕66号	住房和城乡建设部、中国气象局	2014-05-04
住房城乡建设部关于全面开展农村危房现状调查的通知	建村函〔2014〕120号	住房和城乡建设部	2014-05-14
国务院办公厅关于印发2014-2015年节能减排低碳发展行动方案的通知	国办发〔2014〕23号	国务院办公厅	2014-05-15
住房城乡建设部关于建立全国农村人居环境信息系统的通知	建村函〔2014〕121号	住房和城乡建设部	2014-05-15
国务院办公厅关于改善农村人居环境的指导意见	国办发〔2014〕25号	国务院办公厅	2014-05-16
节约集约利用土地规定	国土资源部令第61号	国土资源部	2014-05-22
关于推进城镇养老服务设施建设工作的通知	民发〔2014〕116号	民政部、国土资源部、财政部等	2014-05-28
国务院办公厅关于加强城市地下管线建设管理的指导意见	国办发〔2014〕27号	国务院办公厅	2014-06-03
国务院关于同意设立青岛西海岸新区的批复	国函〔2014〕71号	国务院	2014-06-03
国务院关于同意设立内蒙古二连浩特重点开发开放试验区的批复	国函〔2014〕74号	国务院	2014-06-05

续表

名　称	批号(文号)	发布机构	发布日期
住房城乡建设部关于公布2014年村庄规划、镇规划和县域村镇体系规划试点名单的通知	建村〔2014〕82号	住房和城乡建设部	2014-06-05
住房城乡建设部、国家发展改革委、财政部关于做好2014年农村危房改造工作的通知	建村〔2014〕76号	住房和城乡建设部、国家发展改革委、财政部	2014-06-07
住房城乡建设部办公厅关于做好第三批城市步行和自行车交通系统示范项目工作的通知	建办城函〔2014〕343号	住房城乡建设部办公厅	2014-06-10
国务院办公厅关于调整河北衡水湖等4处国家级自然保护区的通知	国办函〔2014〕55号	国务院办公厅	2014-06-16
国务院关于同意设立大连金普新区的批复	国函〔2014〕76号	国务院	2014-06-23
住房城乡建设部关于加快城市道路桥梁建设改造的通知	建城〔2014〕90号	住房和城乡建设部	2014-06-23
国务院关于珠江—西江经济带发展规划的批复	国函〔2014〕87号	国务院	2014-07-08
住房城乡建设部办公厅关于开展加强和改进住房公积金服务专项督查工作的通知	建办金函〔2014〕394号	住房和城乡建设部办公厅	2014-07-11
住房城乡建设部关于印发《村庄规划用地分类指南》的通知	建村〔2014〕98号	住房和城乡建设部	2014-07-11
国务院关于同意将浙江省湖州市列为国家历史文化名城的批复	国函〔2014〕88号	国务院	2014-07-14
住房城乡建设部、中央农办、环境保护部、农业部关于落实《国务院办公厅关于改善农村人居环境的指导意见》有关工作的通知	建村〔2014〕102号	住房和城乡建设部等	2014-07-14
住房城乡建设部、文化部、国家文物局、财政部关于公布2014年第一批列入中央财政支持范围的中国传统村落名单的通知	建村〔2014〕106号	住房和城乡建设部、文化部等	2014-07-16
住房城乡建设部等部门关于公布全国重点镇名单的通知	建村〔2014〕107号	住房和城乡建设部、国家发展改革委等	2014-07-21
国务院关于进一步推进户籍制度改革的意见	国发〔2014〕25号	国务院	2014-07-24
国务院关于全国对口支援三峡库区合作规划(2014-2020年)的批复	国函〔2014〕96号	国务院	2014-07-30
国务院办公厅关于进一步加强棚户区改造工作的通知	国办发〔2014〕36号	国务院办公厅	2014-08-04
国务院关于同意将黑龙江省齐齐哈尔市列为国家历史文化名城的批复	国函〔2014〕98号	国务院	2014-08-06
国务院关于近期支持东北振兴若干重大政策举措的意见	国发〔2014〕28号	国务院	2014-08-08
住房城乡建设部、国家发展改革委关于进一步加强城市节水工作的通知	建城〔2014〕114号	住房和城乡建设部、国家发展和改革委员会	2014-08-08
国务院关于促进旅游业改革发展的若干意见	国发〔2014〕31号	国务院	2014-08-09
国务院办公厅关于支持铁路建设实施土地综合开发的意见	国办发〔2014〕37号	国务院办公厅	2014-08-11
国务院关于公布第一批国家级抗战纪念设施、遗址名录的通知	国发〔2014〕34号	国务院	2014-08-24
关于印发促进智慧城市健康发展的指导意见的通知	发改高技〔2014〕1770号	国家发展改革委	2014-08-27

续表

名　称	批号(文号)	发布机构	发布日期
住房城乡建设部、文化部、国家文物局关于做好中国传统村落保护项目实施工作的意见	建村〔2014〕135号	住房城乡建设部、文化部、国家文物局	2014-09-05
国务院关于依托黄金水道推动长江经济带发展的指导意见	国发〔2014〕39号	国务院	2014-09-12
国务院关于进一步做好为农民工服务工作的意见	国发〔2014〕40号	国务院	2014-09-12
国务院关于支持汕头经济特区建设华侨经济文化合作试验区有关政策的批复	国函〔2014〕123号	国务院	2014-09-15
国务院关于国家应对气候变化规划(2014-2020年)的批复	国函〔2014〕126号	国务院	2014-09-17
住房城乡建设部关于落实国家新型城镇化规划完善工程建设标准体系的意见	建标〔2014〕139号	住房和城乡建设部	2014-09-22
住房城乡建设部关于印发城市综合交通体系规划交通调查导则的通知	建城〔2014〕141号	住房和城乡建设部	2014-09-25
国务院关于同意设立四川天府新区的批复	国函〔2014〕133号	国务院	2014-10-02
国务院办公厅关于同意中国—新加坡天津生态城建设国家绿色发展示范区实施方案的复函	国办函〔2014〕81号	国务院办公厅	2014-10-03
历史文化名城名镇名村街区保护规划编制审批办法	住房和城乡建设部令第20号	住房和城乡建设部	2014-10-15
住房城乡建设部关于印发海绵城市建设技术指南——低影响开发雨水系统构建(试行)的通知	建城函〔2014〕275号	住房和城乡建设部	2014-10-22
国务院关于调整城市规模划分标准的通知	国发〔2014〕51号	国务院	2014-10-29
国务院办公厅关于促进国家级经济技术开发区转型升级创新发展的若干意见	国办发〔2014〕54号	国务院办公厅	2014-10-30
国务院办公厅关于实施公路安全生命防护工程的意见	国办发〔2014〕55号	国务院办公厅	2014-11-03
国务院关于支持鲁甸地震灾后恢复重建政策措施的意见	国发〔2014〕57号	国务院	2014-11-04
住房城乡建设部等部门关于公布第三批列入中国传统村落名录的村落名单的通知	建村〔2014〕168号	住房城乡建设部、文化部、国家文物局等	2014-11-17
国务院关于乌鲁木齐市城市总体规划的批复	国函〔2014〕149号	国务院	2014-11-18
住房城乡建设部关于加强城市轨道交通线网规划编制的通知	建城〔2014〕169号	住房和城乡建设部	2014-11-20
不动产登记暂行条例	国务院令第656号	国务院	2014-11-24
住房城乡建设部关于贯彻落实《关于严禁在历史建筑、公园等公共资源中设立私人会所的暂行规定》的通知	建城函〔2014〕298号	住房和城乡建设部	2014-11-24
住房城乡建设部等部门关于开展城市地下管线普查工作的通知	建城〔2014〕179号	住房和城乡建设部、工业和信息化部等	2014-12-01
国务院办公厅关于进一步动员社会各方面力量参与扶贫开发的意见	国办发〔2014〕58号	国务院办公厅	2014-12-04
国务院办公厅关于公布内蒙古毕拉河等21处新建国家级自然保护区名单的通知	国办发〔2014〕61号	国务院办公厅	2014-12-05
住房城乡建设部关于2014年国家级风景名胜区执法检查结果的通报	建城函〔2014〕308号	住房和城乡建设部	2014-12-10
住房城乡建设部等部门关于公布2014年第二批列入中央财政支持范围的中国传统村落名单的通知	建村〔2014〕180号	住房城乡建设部、文化部等	2014-12-17

续表

名　称	批号(文号)	发布机构	发布日期
住房城乡建设部办公厅关于做好国家级风景名胜区内重大建设工程项目选址方案核准工作的通知	建办城〔2014〕53 号	住房和城乡建设部办公厅	2014 - 12 - 17
住房城乡建设部关于坚决制止破坏行为加强保护性建筑保护工作的通知	建规〔2014〕183 号	住房和城乡建设部	2014 - 12 - 18
住房城乡建设部办公厅关于贯彻落实《历史文化名城名镇名村街区保护规划编制审批办法》的通知	建办规〔2014〕56 号	住房和城乡建设部	2014 - 12 - 26

（作者：金晓春，中国城市规划设计研究院学术信息中心副主任；郭磊，中国城市规划设计研究院学术信息中心规划师）

附录 3

中国城市基本数据(2012 年)

城市名称	Name of cities	行政级别 Admini-strative level	行政区域土地面积(平方公里) Total land area of administrative region(sq. km)	年末总人口(万人) Total population at year-end (10 000 persons)	六普常住人口(万人) Total residents of the Sixth National Population Census (10 000 persons)	建成区面积(平方公里) Area of built-up district (sq. km)	地区生产总值(万元) Gross regional product (10 000 yuan)	人均地区生产总值(元) Per capita gross regional product(yuan)	用水普及率(%) Water coverage rate(%)	污水处理率(%) Wastewater treatment rate(%)	人均公园绿地面积(平方米) Per capita public green space(sq. m)	生活垃圾处理率(%) Domestic garbage treatment rate(%)
北京市	Beijing	直辖市	16 411	1 297.5	1 961.24	1 261	178 794 000	87 475	100.00	83.16	11.87	99.12
天津市	Tianjin	直辖市	11 760	993.2	1 293.87	722	128 938 800	93 173	100.00	88.24	10.54	99.81
河北省	Hebei											
石家庄市	Shijiazhuang	地级市	15 848	1 005.3	1 016.38	216	45 002 098	43 552	100.00	95.86	14.17	100.00
唐山市	Tangshan	地级市	13 472	741.8	757.73	247	58 616 363	76 643	100.00	94.81	14.99	100.00
秦皇岛市	Qinhuangdao	地级市	7 802	291.2	298.76	95	11 393 664	37 804	100.00	92.54	20.22	100.00
邯郸市	Handan	地级市	12 065	993.1	917.47	117	30 242 864	32 650	100.00	97.51	21.00	100.00
邢台市	Xingtai	地级市	12 433	747.7	710.41	72	15 320 620	21 361	100.00	84.01	11.36	99.73
保定市	Baoding	地级市	22 185	1 172.1	1 119.44	141	27 209 000	24 053	100.00	92.00	9.15	100.00
张家口市	Zhangjiakou	地级市	36 873	468.4	434.55	86	12 335 529	28 139	100.00	91.31	11.18	89.29
承德市	Chengde	地级市	39 548	376.9	347.32	113	11 819 213	33 791	100.00	96.64	24.82	100.00
沧州市	Cangzhou	地级市	14 053	744.4	713.41	61	28 124 212	38 949	100.00	95.88	9.94	92.61
廊坊市	Langfang	地级市	6 429	433.2	435.88	64	17 943 291	40 598	100.00	87.31	13.24	95.70
衡水市	Hengshui	地级市	8 837	442.4	434.08	46	10 110 263	23 101	99.72	80.35	12.01	100.00
辛集市	Xinji	县级市	951	63	61.59	29	3 415 778	54 219	99.22	100.00	8.96	100.00
藁城市	Gaocheng	县级市	836	81	77.51	18	4 753 244	58 682	96.93	99.95	10.22	90.41
晋州市	Jinzhou	县级市	619	55	53.77	16	2 009 307	36 533	100.00	97.10	9.55	100.00

续表

城市名称 Name of cities		行政级别 Admini-strative level	行政区域土地面积(平方公里) Total land area of administrative region(sq. km)	年末总人口(万人) Total population at year - end (10 000 persons)	六普常住人口(万人) Total residents of the Sixth National Population Census (10 000 persons)	建成区面积(平方公里) Area of built - up district (sq. km)	地区生产总值(万元) Gross regional product (10 000 yuan)	人均地区生产总值(元) Per capita gross regional product(yuan)	用水普及率(%) Water coverage rate(%)	污水处理率(%) Wastewater treatment rate(%)	人均公园绿地面积(平方米) Per capita public green space(sq. m)	生活垃圾处理率(%) Domestic garbage treatment rate(%)
新乐市	Xinle	县级市	524	50	48. 77	13	1 560 814	31 216	100. 00	99. 09	9. 85	100. 00
鹿泉市	Luquan	县级市	603	40	43. 29	19	2 900 051	72 501	100. 00	97. 06	9. 97	100. 00
遵化市	Zunhua	县级市	1 509	74	73. 70	23	5 198 179	70 246	100. 00	89. 18	12. 27	100. 00
迁安市	Qian'an	县级市	1 208	74	72. 82	36	9 009 168	121 746	100. 00	97. 61	16. 86	100. 00
武安市	Wu'an	县级市	1 806	80	81. 90	30	5 804 439	72 555	100. 00	95. 68	15. 09	100. 00
南宫市	Nangong	县级市	861	48	46. 90	20	787 599	16 408	99. 75	80. 09	12. 45	98. 89
沙河市	Shahe	县级市	859	42	49. 84	15	2 047 245	48 744	100. 00	100. 00	13. 62	100. 00
涿州市	Zhuozhou	县级市	742	65	60. 35	34	2 075 326	31 928	100. 00	97. 26	10. 15	80. 89
定州市	Dingzhou	县级市	1 274	122	116. 52	28	2 397 006	19 648	100. 00	91. 54	8. 08	97. 24
安国市	Anguo	县级市	486	41	37. 03	13	926 853	22 606	100. 00	93. 39	11. 30	100. 00
高碑店市	Gaobeidian	县级市	618	57	64. 03	17	1 176 400	20 639	100. 00	94. 99	8. 24	94. 00
泊头市	Botou	县级市	1 007	61	58. 43	20	1 600 988	26 246	100. 00	100. 00	8. 07	100. 00
任丘市	Renqiu	县级市	1 012	85	82. 25	44	5 436 342	63 957	100. 00	98. 03	8. 01	100. 00
黄骅市	Huanghua	县级市	1 545	47	54. 85	28	2 340 150	49 790	100. 00	98. 12	11. 13	100. 00
河间市	Hejian	县级市	1 333	83	81. 03	19	2 301 312	27 727	100. 00	100. 00	12. 47	100. 00
霸州市	Bazhou	县级市	801	63	62. 30	18	3 204 402	50 864	100. 00	96. 99	12. 27	95. 49
三河市	Sanhe	县级市	634	58	65. 20	20	4 251 348	73 299	100. 00	92. 73	17. 79	100. 00
冀州市	Jizhou	县级市	877	35	36. 20	17	792 848	22 653	100. 00	100. 00	14. 89	100. 00
深州市	Shenzhou	县级市	1 245	57	56. 61	19	1 195 555	20 975	100. 00	90. 03	8. 06	100. 00
山西省	Shanxi											
太原市	Taiyuan	地级市	6 977	365. 8	420. 16	310	23 114 326	54 440	100. 00	84. 50	10. 35	100. 00
大同市	Datong	地级市	14 127	319. 4	331. 81	108	9 313 878	27 815	100. 00	82. 39	12. 93	86. 56
阳泉市	Yangquan	地级市	4 570	132. 1	136. 85	53	6 019 519	43 702	100. 00	94. 32	9. 51	100. 00

续表

城市名称 Name of cities		行政级别 Administrative level	行政区域土地面积(平方公里) Total land area of administrative region(sq. km)	年末总人口(万人) Total population at year-end (10 000 persons)	六普常住人口(万人) Total residents of the Sixth National Population Census (10 000 persons)	建成区面积(平方公里) Area of built-up district (sq. km)	地区生产总值(万元) Gross regional product (10 000 yuan)	人均地区生产总值(元) Per capita gross regional product(yuan)	用水普及率(%) Water coverage rate(%)	污水处理率(%) Wastewater treatment rate(%)	人均公园绿地面积(平方米) Per capita public green space(sq. m)	生活垃圾处理率(%) Domestic garbage treatment rate(%)
长治市	Changzhi	地级市	13 896	336. 1	333. 46	59	13 286 098	39 523	96. 30	92. 21	9. 87	100. 00
晋城市	Jincheng	地级市	9 425	218. 2	227. 91	42	10 128 134	44 257	96. 50	94. 99	13. 24	100. 00
朔州市	Shuozhou	地级市	10 674	173. 5	171. 49	42	10 071 198	58 205	98. 60	97. 25	10. 71	87. 93
晋中市	Jinzhong	地级市	16 392	325. 0	324. 94	50	9 865 596	30 093	97. 01	96. 23	12. 85	77. 47
运城市	Yuncheng	地级市	14 181	519. 5	513. 48	52	10 686 498	20 628	94. 00	91. 62	9. 98	95. 00
忻州市	Xinzhou	地级市	25 117	310. 0	306. 75	32	6 209 439	20 081	93. 04	95. 00	7. 10	
临汾市	Linfen	地级市	20 275	425. 2	431. 66	54	12 210 801	28 031	92. 89	90. 45	1 322. 00	100. 00
吕梁市	Lvliang	地级市	21 239	393. 7	372. 71	22	12 304 159	32 709	95. 02	88. 34	11. 90	100. 00
古交市	Gujiao	县级市	1 584	22	20. 51	16	323 984	14 727	97. 45	86. 70	7. 99	100. 00
潞城市	Lucheng	县级市	630	23	22. 69	8	970 590	42 200	97. 11	95. 20	8. 41	100. 00
高平市	Gaoping	县级市	946	48	48. 49	18	2 346 777	48 891	97. 97	85. 00	11. 93	100. 00
介休市	Jiexiu	县级市	744	41	40. 65	18	1 510 400	36 839	100. 00	97. 50	9. 46	80. 40
永济市	Yongji	县级市	1 221	44	44. 47	23	1 199 074	27 252	98. 83	85. 83	14. 80	65. 00
河津市	Hejin	县级市	593	40	39. 55	22	1 846 676	46 167	90. 91	86. 06	15. 00	
原平市	Yuanping	县级市	2 571	49	49. 12	11	1 051 970	21 469	99. 83	92. 57	3. 39	100. 00
侯马市	Houma	县级市	221	24	24. 00	19	909 918	37 913	100. 00	91. 60	11. 66	100. 00
霍州市	Huozhou	县级市	764	30	28. 29	15	865 912	28 864	97. 05	79. 95	9. 39	
孝义市	Xiaoyi	县级市	946	49	46. 88	22	3 905 013	79 694	85. 19	75. 28	7. 41	100. 00
汾阳市	Fenyang	县级市	1 175	42	41. 62	12	1 153 031	27 453	90. 00	50. 11	6. 50	
内蒙古自治区	Inner Mongolia											
呼和浩特市	Huhhot	地级市	17 453	230. 3	286. 66	210	24 755 700	84 534	98. 63	80. 03	15. 09	98. 17
包头市	Baotou	地级市	27 768	223. 5	265. 04	186	34 095 400	125 709	99. 43	85. 04	12. 62	97. 00
乌海市	Wuhai	地级市	1 754	54. 8	53. 29	63	5 625 710	103 242	97. 53	92. 58	14. 34	85. 45

续表

城市名称 Name of cities		行政级别 Admini-strative level	行政区域土地面积(平方公里) Total land area of administrative region(sq. km)	年末总人口(万人) Total population at year - end (10 000 persons)	六普常住人口(万人) Total residents of the Sixth National Population Census (10 000 persons)	建成区面积(平方公里) Area of built - up district (sq. km)	地区生产总值(万元) Gross regional product (10 000 yuan)	人均地区生产总值(元) Per capita gross regional product(yuan)	用水普及率(%) Water coverage rate(%)	污水处理率(%) Wastewater treatment rate(%)	人均公园绿地面积(平方米) Per capita public green space(sq. m)	生活垃圾处理率(%) Domestic garbage treatment rate(%)
赤峰市	Chifeng	地级市	90 021	461. 2	434. 12	89	15 693 540	36 360	91. 67	85. 77	14. 40	100. 00
通辽市	Tongliao	地级市	59 535	319. 8	313. 92	87	16 918 500	53 976	92. 67	100. 00	15. 52	100. 00
鄂尔多斯市	Ordos	地级市	86 752	152. 1	194. 07	134	36 568 000	182 680	99. 37	99. 52	26. 39	98. 00
呼伦贝尔市	Hulunbeier	地级市	253 356	266. 4	254. 93	28	13 358 200	52 649	91. 19	87. 52	22. 17	91. 48
巴彦淖尔市	Bayannur	地级市	64 413	186. 7	166. 99	38	8 133 300	48 812	93. 37	87. 50	8. 51	96. 95
乌兰察布市	Ulanqab	地级市	59 448	287. 0	214. 36	42	7 811 700	36 721	92. 01	98. 00	32. 78	98. 05
霍林郭勒市	Huolinguole	县级市	585	8	10. 22	22	2 950 038	368 755	74. 51	84. 83	2. 29	100. 00
满洲里市	Manzhouli	县级市	732	17	24. 95	27	1 759 226	103 484	98. 92	84. 02	12. 87	90. 91
牙克石市	Yakeshi	县级市	27 590	35	36. 63	94	1 901 512	54 329	91. 51	84. 47	12. 84	80. 33
扎兰屯市	Zhalantun	县级市	16 800	42	35. 22	20	1 486 485	35 393	91. 58	85. 08	12. 90	95. 13
额尔古纳市	Eerguna	县级市	28 958	8	11. 04	10	369 968	46 246	83. 96	82. 76	13. 10	85. 02
根河市	Genhe	县级市	20 012	16	7. 67	47	349 223	21 826	86. 09	85. 24	12. 93	96. 67
丰镇市	Fengzhen	县级市	2 704	34	24. 56	22	1 269 004	37 324	60. 94	80. 09	20. 85	100. 00
乌兰浩特市	Wulanhaote	县级市	2 728	32	32. 71	39	1 300 027	40 626	84. 69	60. 79	12. 66	100. 00
阿尔山市	Aershan	县级市	7 409	5	6. 83	10	127 315	25 463	18. 57		2. 00	
二连浩特市	Erlianhaote	县级市	4 013	3	7. 42	27	679 245	226 415	100. 00	100. 00	16. 85	100. 00
锡林浩特市	Xilinhaote	县级市	14 780	18	24. 59	41	1 945 374	108 076	93. 44	71. 85	10. 62	100. 00
辽宁省	Liaoning											
沈阳市	Shenyang	副省级市	12 980	724. 8	810. 62	455	66 025 865	80 480	100. 00	87. 11	12. 45	100. 00
大连市	Dalian	副省级市	12 574	590. 3	669. 04	395	70 028 306	102 922	100. 00	95. 10	12. 24	100. 00
鞍山市	Anshan	地级市	9 255	350. 4	364. 59	167	24 293 160	69 211	98. 56	80. 01	10. 98	100. 00
抚顺市	Fushun	地级市	11 272	219. 3	213. 81	131	12 363 686	58 512	96. 51	71. 65	9. 69	100. 00
本溪市	Benxi	地级市	8 411	153. 2	170. 95	108	11 123 567	64 459	91. 34	87. 40	9. 66	99. 06

续表

城市名称 Name of cities		行政级别 Admini-strative level	行政区域土地面积（平方公里）Total land area of administrative region (sq. km)	年末总人口（万人）Total population at year-end (10 000 persons)	六普常住人口（万人）Total residents of the Sixth National Population Census (10 000 persons)	建成区面积（平方公里）Area of built-up district (sq. km)	地区生产总值（万元）Gross regional product (10 000 yuan)	人均地区生产总值（元）Per capita gross regional product (yuan)	用水普及率（%）Water coverage rate (%)	污水处理率（%）Wastewater treatment rate (%)	人均公园绿地面积（平方米）Per capita public green space (sq. m)	生活垃圾处理率（%）Domestic garbage treatment rate (%)
丹东市	Dandong	地级市	15 290	240.5	244.47	77	10 153 733	42 171	97.50	84.99	10.84	100.00
锦州市	Jinzhou	地级市	9 891	307.9	312.65	72	12 427 098	40 002	100.00	82.56	9.23	100.00
营口市	Yingkou	地级市	5 242	235.1	242.85	110	13 811 809	56 583	98.98	89.33	10.34	
阜新市	Fuxin	地级市	10 355	191.6	181.93	77	5 599 635	31 049	99.68	55.49	11.79	90.91
辽阳市	Liaoyang	地级市	4 736	180.3	185.88	103	10 004 881	53 877	100.00	85.53	9.13	100.00
盘锦市	Panjin	地级市	4 065	128.8	139.25	67	12 449 563	87 153	100.00	100.00	10.59	100.00
铁岭市	Tieling	地级市	12 985	302.2	271.77	38	9 753 258	32 130	97.74	89.58	9.92	83.98
朝阳市	Chaoyang	地级市	19 731	340.6	304.46	58	9 206 331	30 765	98.82	64.32	8.12	100.00
葫芦岛市	Huludao	地级市	10 415	280.0	262.35	75	7 193 325	27 709	100.00	85.01	14.90	100.00
新民市	Xinmin	县级市	3 297	69	65.78	18	4 157 555	60 254	91.17	100.00	8.30	100.00
瓦房店市	Wafangdian	县级市	3 794	100	94.22	39	9 573 342	95 733	100.00	86.25	13.29	100.00
普兰店市	Pulandian	县级市	2 896	93	74.12	33	7 158 278	76 971	99.50	25.50	9.00	100.00
庄河市	Zhuanghe	县级市	4 086	91	84.13	40	7 549 765	82 964	99.80	100.00	13.80	100.00
海城市	Haicheng	县级市	2 570	109	129.39	33	8 035 803	73 723	97.09	100.00	5.79	100.00
东港市	Donggang	县级市	2 399	61	62.75	28	4 749 172	77 855	100.00	64.06	9.18	94.14
凤城市	Fengcheng	县级市	5 515	58	54.39	18	4 234 628	73 011	84.20	85.06	8.90	100.00
凌海市	Linghai	县级市	2 585	53	50.81	20	2 454 993	46 321	100.00	100.00	9.40	100.00
北镇市	Beizhen	县级市	1 694	52	51.49	53	1 359 351	26 141	77.91	100.00	3.08	100.00
盖州市	Gaizhou	县级市	2 946	72	69.16	155	2 192 651	30 453	89.47	58.24	6.14	100.00
大石桥市	Dashiqiao	县级市	1 598	72	70.49	33	4 999 379	69 436	100.00	25.42	8.50	100.00
灯塔市	Dengta	县级市	1 170	45	49.61	12	2 237 544	49 723	95.16	100.00	11.19	100.00
调兵山市	Diaobingshan	县级市	262	24	24.14	19	1 614 486	67 270	99.01	87.18	9.02	100.00
开原市	Kaiyuan	县级市	2 838	53	54.56	48	4 102 975	77 415	100.00	100.00	10.22	100.00

续表

城市名称 Name of cities		行政级别 Admini-strative level	行政区域土地面积（平方公里） Total land area of administrative region(sq. km)	年末总人口（万人） Total population at year-end (10 000 persons)	六普常住人口（万人） Total residents of the Sixth National Population Census (10 000 persons)	建成区面积（平方公里） Area of built-up district (sq. km)	地区生产总值（万元） Gross regional product (10 000 yuan)	人均地区生产总值（元） Per capita gross regional product(yuan)	用水普及率（%） Water coverage rate(%)	污水处理率（%） Wastewater treatment rate(%)	人均公园绿地面积（平方米） Per capita public green space(sq. m)	生活垃圾处理率（%） Domestic garbage treatment rate(%)
北票市	Beipiao	县级市	4 469	58	49.62	14	2 182 446	37 628	95.94	92.95	7.44	
凌源市	Lingyuan	县级市	3 278	66	57.07	25	1 821 108	27 593	94.74	100.00	8.49	88.89
兴城市	Xingcheng	县级市	2 116	55	54.62	30	1 267 045	23 037	100.00	57.97	11.14	100.00
吉林省	Jilin											
长春市	Changchun	副省级市	20 604	756.9	767.44	434	44 566 446	58 691	99.70	86.15	13.76	96.39
吉林市	Jilin	地级市	27 126	430.8	441.32	166	24 300 668	56 244	98.00	94.00	12.01	100.00
四平市	Siping	地级市	14 080	336.3	338.52	54	11 228 017	33 150	71.44	75.02	8.15	35.94
辽源市	Liaoyuan	地级市	5 140	122.0	117.62	46	6 051 273	49 479	98.22	84.86	7.52	100.00
通化市	Tonghua	地级市	15 608	224.6	232.44	49	8 811 232	39 111	87.37	89.84	11.81	96.54
白山市	Baishan	地级市	17 485	127.9	129.61	36	64 30 212	50 158	81.00	53.15	9.87	100.00
松原市	Songyuan	地级市	21 090	289.8	288.01	47	16 054 206	55 177	95.31	93.01	11.86	90.48
白城市	Baicheng	地级市	25 745	200.0	203.24	42	6 155 007	30 576	98.09	60.21	7.87	95.48
九台市	Jiutai	县级市	3 375	70	61.17	26	3 329 470	47 564	88.37	93.82	5.09	83.54
榆树市	Yushu	县级市	4 712	131	116.06	28	3 418 803	26 098	65.02	81.30	4.69	62.02
德惠市	Dehui	县级市	3 435	83	74.84	27	3 433 828	41 371	55.63	43.80	5.04	96.75
蛟河市	Jiaohe	县级市	6 364	45	44.72	13	1 963 987	43 644	69.47	72.61	13.89	100.00
桦甸市	Huadian	县级市	6 625	45	44.48	19	2 715 604	60 347	94.09	85.21	13.92	100.00
舒兰市	Shulan	县级市	4 557	66	64.57	26	1 855 429	28 113	92.92	65.01	6.86	100.00
磐石市	Panshi	县级市	3 867	54	50.58	30	2 851 106	52 798	74.36	85.67	5.71	94.83
公主岭市	Gongzhuling	县级市	4 028	108	109.29	36	3 444 236	31 891	98.07	94.32	5.76	100.00
双辽市	Shuangliao	县级市	3 121	41	42.07	30	1 807 945	44 096	87.59	89.08	6.73	100.00
梅河口市	Meihekou	县级市	2 174	62	61.52	24	2 477 829	39 965	92.59	69.47	9.07	92.93
集安市	Jiân	县级市	3 342	22	23.23	14	830 423	37 747	87.84	34.71	9.69	100.00

续表

城市名称 Name of cities		行政级别 Admini-strative level	行政区域土地面积（平方公里）Total land area of administrative region（sq. km）	年末总人口（万人）Total population at year－end（10 000 persons）	六普常住人口（万人）Total residents of the Sixth National Population Census（10 000 persons）	建成区面积（平方公里）Area of built－up district（sq. km）	地区生产总值（万元）Gross regional product（10 000 yuan）	人均地区生产总值（元）Per capita gross regional product（yuan）	用水普及率（%）Water coverage rate（%）	污水处理率（%）Wastewater treatment rate（%）	人均公园绿地面积（平方米）Per capita public green space（sq. m）	生活垃圾处理率（%）Domestic garbage treatment rate（%）
临江市	Linjiang	县级市	3 008	17	17. 50	8	835 418	49 142	94. 59	26. 90	11. 00	100. 00
洮南市	Taonan	县级市	5 031	43	43. 21	17	1 105 534	25 710	100. 00	87. 02	7. 88	100. 00
大安市	Daan	县级市	4 879	41	43. 10	14	1 214 146	29 613	90. 43	88. 04	9. 70	100. 00
延吉市	Yanji	县级市	1 748	52	56. 30	41	3 009 137	57 868	95. 08	90. 59	9. 50	98. 57
图们市	Tumen	县级市	1 142	12	13. 45	9	391 273	32 606	93. 37	30. 88	10. 58	99. 85
敦化市	Dunhua	县级市	11 957	46	48. 35	31	1 568 725	34 103	95. 96	87. 60	21. 75	100. 00
珲春市	Hunchun	县级市	5 161	22	24. 18	18	1 250 687	56 849	82. 25	50. 01	8. 47	79. 19
龙井市	Longjing	县级市	2 208	17	17. 72	10	376 288	22 135	97. 56	15. 05	12. 22	100. 00
和龙市	Helong	县级市	5 069	19	18. 95	11	545 926	28 733	97. 47	26. 32	5. 07	100. 00
黑龙江省	Heilongjiang											
哈尔滨市	Harbin	副省级市	53 068	993. 5	1063. 60	383	45 502 155	45 810	100. 00	91. 62	10. 06	85. 30
齐齐哈尔市	Qiqihar	地级市	42 469	559. 1	536. 70	140	11 760 768	22 139	98. 61	72. 87	10. 02	50. 14
鸡西市	Jixi	地级市	22 531	185. 9	186. 22	79	5 823 381	31 076	98. 88	33. 33	9. 61	67. 57
鹤岗市	Hegang	地级市	14 657	108. 5	105. 87	51	3 582 393	32 968	80. 99	41. 53	14. 98	
双鸭山市	Shuangyashan	地级市	23 209	150. 4	146. 26	51	5 654 312	37 490	99. 79	77. 48	14. 74	81. 93
大庆市	Daqing	地级市	21 522	281. 6	290. 45	233	40 010 695	142 067	91. 11	32. 51	14. 32	52. 32
伊春市	Yichun	地级市	32 759	125. 2	114. 81	165	2 600 327	20 686	73. 47	37. 33	20. 41	
佳木斯市	Jiamusi	地级市	32 704	239. 3	255. 21	98	6 682 943	27 774	93. 88	39. 88	13. 88	82. 95
七台河市	Qitaihe	地级市	6 221	92. 4	92. 05	68	2 989 081	32 308	93. 42	42. 13	11. 91	100. 00
牡丹江市	Mudanjiang	地级市	38 405	259. 6	279. 87	76	9 810 518	37 001	95. 65	42. 04	10. 55	100. 00
黑河市	Heihe	地级市	68 240	172. 8	167. 39	19	3 660 823	18 892	92. 05	99. 70	14. 64	72. 54
绥化市	Suihua	地级市	34 954	557. 0	541. 82	28	10 579 799	18 474	95. 31	99. 32	7. 66	70. 59
双城市	Shuangcheng	县级市	3 112	82	82. 56	24	3 703 335	45 163	99. 37	61. 31	12. 16	

续表

城市名称 Name of cities		行政级别 Administrative level	行政区域土地面积(平方公里) Total land area of administrative region(sq. km)	年末总人口(万人) Total population at year-end (10 000 persons)	六普常住人口(万人) Total residents of the Sixth National Population Census (10 000 persons)	建成区面积(平方公里) Area of built-up district (sq. km)	地区生产总值(万元) Gross regional product (10 000 yuan)	人均地区生产总值(元) Per capita gross regional product(yuan)	用水普及率(%) Water coverage rate(%)	污水处理率(%) Wastewater treatment rate(%)	人均公园绿地面积(平方米) Per capita public green space(sq. m)	生活垃圾处理率(%) Domestic garbage treatment rate(%)
尚志市	Shangzhi	县级市	8 891	62	58. 54	40	2 198 431	35 459	98. 80	82. 00	11. 65	87. 56
五常市	Wuchang	县级市	7 512	101	88. 12	22	2 784 264	27 567	95. 81		14. 05	
讷河市	Nehe	县级市	6 648	73	62. 59	14	1 081 379	14 813	89. 43	100. 00	12. 60	10. 00
虎林市	Hulin	县级市	9 334	16	31. 79	11	639 905	39 994	98. 48	80. 00	14. 96	100. 00
密山市	Mishan	县级市	7 731	34	40. 75	22	971 085	28 561	100. 00	100. 00	12. 30	100. 00
铁力市	Tieli	县级市	6 730	38	34. 94	44	669 706	17 624	81. 30	32. 00	14. 31	
同江市	Tongjiang	县级市	6 300	11	17. 98	10	408 780	37 162	48. 07	100. 00	11. 14	
富锦市	Fujin	县级市	8 227	39	43. 72	16	1 258 529	32 270	100. 00	100. 00	7. 59	100. 00
绥芬河市	Suifenhe	县级市	422	7	13. 23	24	1 113 204	159 029	61. 51	100. 00	6. 37	
海林市	Hailin	县级市	8 711	40	40. 09	14	1 519 142	37 979	99. 60	96. 00	13. 73	100. 00
宁安市	Ning'an	县级市	7 891	44	43. 75	11	1 535 489	34 897	100. 00	100. 00	11. 62	100. 00
穆棱市	Muling	县级市	6 212	29	29. 33	38	1 470 717	50 714	100. 00	100. 00	13. 45	
北安市	Bei'an	县级市	7 194	39	43. 64	20	644 426	16 524	76. 82	96. 09	9. 92	
五大连池市	Wudalianchi	县级市	9 874	36	32. 64	19	453 028	12 584	88. 30	99. 98	9. 93	
安达市	Anda	县级市	3 586	49	47. 28	26	3 350 706	68 382	83. 79	99. 88	3. 71	91. 68
肇东市	Zhaodong	县级市	3 905	94	90. 31	34	4 461 925	47 467	94. 55	100. 00	13. 11	
海伦市	Hailun	县级市	4 667	84	76. 94	20	977 340	11 635	96. 74		5. 61	
上海市	Shanghai	直辖市	6 340	1 426. 9	2 301. 92	886	201 817 200	85 373	100. 00	91. 29	7. 08	83. 59
江苏省	Jiangsu											
南京市	Nanjing	副省级市	6 587	638. 5	800. 37	653	72 015 700	88 525	100. 00	94. 60	13. 94	100. 00
无锡市	Wuxi	地级市	4 627	470. 1	637. 44	316	75 681 500	117 357	100. 00	95. 52	14. 61	100. 00
徐州市	Xuzhou	地级市	11 259	990. 5	857. 72	274	40 165 800	46 877	98. 08	87. 02	16. 09	99. 98
常州市	Changzhou	地级市	4 372	364. 8	459. 24	183	39 698 700	85 039	100. 00	93. 76	12. 49	100. 00

续表

城市名称 Name of cities		行政级别 Admini-strative level	行政区域土地面积(平方公里) Total land area of administrative region(sq. km)	年末总人口(万人) Total population at year-end (10 000 persons)	六普常住人口(万人) Total residents of the Sixth National Population Census (10 000 persons)	建成区面积(平方公里) Area of built-up district (sq. km)	地区生产总值(万元) Gross regional product (10 000 yuan)	人均地区生产总值(元) Per capita gross regional product(yuan)	用水普及率(%) Water coverage rate(%)	污水处理率(%) Wastewater treatment rate(%)	人均公园绿地面积(平方米) Per capita public green space(sq. m)	生活垃圾处理率(%) Domestic garbage treatment rate(%)
苏州市	Suzhou	地级市	8 488	647.8	1 045.99	437	120 116 500	114 029	100.00	91.85	15.34	100.00
南通市	Nantong	地级市	8 001	765.2	728.36	156	45 586 700	62 506	100.00	90.00	12.82	100.00
连云港市	Liangyungang	地级市	7 615	511.0	439.35	140	16 034 200	36 470	100.00	83.21	13.72	100.00
淮安市	Huaián	地级市	10 072	546.8	480.17	136	19 209 100	39 992	99.20	78.60	12.04	72.57
盐城市	Yancheng	地级市	16 972	822.4	726.22	95	31 200 000	43 172	100.00	85.40	11.98	100.00
扬州市	Yangzhou	地级市	6 591	458.4	446.01	128	29 332 000	65 692	99.02	92.95	17.32	100.00
镇江市	Zhenjiang	地级市	3 847	271.4	311.41	120	26 304 200	83 650	100.00	90.01	16.93	100.00
泰州市	Taizhou	地级市	5 787	506.4	461.89	70	27 016 700	58 378	100.00	85.15	9.53	100.00
宿迁市	Suqian	地级市	8 555	560.3	471.92	70	15 220 300	31 722	100.00	85.03	12.54	100.00
江阴市	Jiangyin	县级市	987	121	159.51	55	25 353 800	209 536	100.00	93.82	14.72	100.00
宜兴市	Yixing	县级市	1 997	108	123.55	70	10 859 800	100 554	100.00	88.14	16.00	100.00
新沂市	Xinyi	县级市	1 571	107	92.06	34	3 501 600	32 725	95.93	75.01	9.90	100.00
邳州市	Pizhou	县级市	2 088	180	145.80	42	5 134 900	28 527	96.69	62.76	10.51	100.00
溧阳市	Liyang	县级市	1 535	79	74.95	25	5 592 000	70 785	100.00	84.07	9.44	100.00
金坛市	Jintan	县级市	976	55	55.20	22	37 38 100	67 965	100.00	85.72	12.11	100.00
常熟市	Changshu	县级市	1 276	107	151.05	98	18 701 900	174 784	100.00	90.12	19.35	100.00
张家港市	Zhangjiagang	县级市	990	91	124.68	67	20 505 800	225 338	100.00	91.73	13.81	100.00
昆山市	Kunshan	县级市	932	74	164.49	72	27 253 200	368 286	100.00	93.50	15.12	100.00
太仓市	Taicang	县级市	823	47	71.19	46	9 551 190	203 217	100.00	90.82	13.10	100.00
启东市	Qidong	县级市	1 208	112	97.25	22	5 891 385	52 602	100.00	80.23	9.49	100.00
如皋市	Rugao	县级市	1 492	143	126.71	25	5 901 669	41 270	100.00	84.73	11.17	100.00
海门市	Haimen	县级市	939	100	90.76	22	6 630 971	66 310	100.00	84.96	9.55	100.00
东台市	Dongtai	县级市	3 221	114	99.03	34	5 066 899	44 446	100.00	80.57	12.02	100.00

续表

城市名称 Name of cities		行政级别 Administrative level	行政区域土地面积(平方公里) Total land area of administrative region(sq. km)	年末总人口(万人) Total population at year-end (10 000 persons)	六普常住人口(万人) Total residents of the Sixth National Population Census (10 000 persons)	建成区面积(平方公里) Area of built-up district (sq. km)	地区生产总值(万元) Gross regional product (10 000 yuan)	人均地区生产总值(元) Per capita gross regional product(yuan)	用水普及率(%) Water coverage rate(%)	污水处理率(%) Wastewater treatment rate(%)	人均公园绿地面积(平方米) Per capita public green space(sq. m)	生活垃圾处理率(%) Domestic garbage treatment rate(%)
大丰市	Dafeng	县级市	3 059	73	70. 67	26	3 933 600	53 885	100. 00	71. 55	8. 62	100. 00
仪征市	Yizheng	县级市	857	56	56. 40	39	3 702 700	66 120	99. 95	88. 70	9. 78	100. 00
高邮市	Gaoyou	县级市	1 922	82	74. 47	24	3 360 000	40 976	96. 18	83. 51	9. 78	100. 00
丹阳市	Danyang	县级市	1 047	81	96. 07	26	8 305 068	102 532	100. 00	85. 02	9. 66	100. 00
扬中市	Yangzhong	县级市	331	28	33. 50	12	3 602 000	128 643	100. 00	88. 15	9. 63	100. 00
句容市	Jurong	县级市	1 387	59	61. 77	23	3 368 600	57 095	100. 00	85. 93	11. 45	100. 00
兴化市	Xinghua	县级市	2 395	157	125. 35	35	5 123 600	32 634	100. 00	69. 78	13. 32	100. 00
靖江市	Jingjiang	县级市	656	67	68. 44	34	6 008 500	89 679	100. 00	82. 43	10. 23	100. 00
泰兴市	Taixing	县级市	1 170	120	107. 39	24	5 435 500	45 296	100. 00	81. 98	9. 02	100. 00
姜堰市	Jiangyan	县级市	928	79	72. 86	23	4 058 600	51 375	100. 00	88. 10	8. 47	100. 00
浙江省	Zhejiang											
杭州市	Hangzhou	副省级市	16 571	700. 5	870. 04	453	78 020 058	88 962	100. 00	95. 49	15. 45	100. 00
宁波市	Ningbo	副省级市	9 816	577. 7	760. 57	290	65 822 064	86 228	100. 00	88. 14	10. 56	100. 00
温州市	Wenzhou	地级市	11 874	800. 2	912. 21	204	36 691 842	40 103	100. 00	83. 38	12. 95	100. 00
嘉兴市	Jiaxing	地级市	3 915	344. 5	450. 17	90	28 905 730	63 704	100. 00	90. 12	13. 64	100. 00
湖州市	Huzhou	地级市	5 820	261. 4	289. 35	88	16 643 045	57 350	100. 00	90. 12	16. 36	100. 00
绍兴市	Shaoxing	地级市	8 256	440. 8	491. 22	115	36 540 321	82 966	100. 00	95. 02	15. 17	100. 00
金华市	Jinhua	地级市	10 942	470. 6	536. 16	74	27 107 675	50 269	100. 00	87. 96	11. 92	96. 01
衢州市	Quzhou	地级市	8 845	252. 8	212. 27	64	9 722 460	38 476	100. 00	85. 38	13. 51	100. 00
舟山市	Zhoushan	地级市	1 455	97. 2	112. 13	56	8 531 767	87 883	99. 86	82. 07	14. 58	100. 00
台州市	Taizhou	地级市	9 411	591. 0	596. 88	116	29 112 616	48 505	100. 00	86. 09	11. 51	100. 00
丽水市	Lishui	地级市	17 298	262. 6	211. 70	33	8 941 046	42 244	100. 00	86. 57	10. 99	100. 00
建德市	Jiande	县级市	2 364	51	43. 08	9	2 477 268	48 574	100. 00	86. 47	10. 78	100. 00

续表

城市名称 Name of cities		行政级别 Admini-strative level	行政区域土地面积（平方公里）Total land area of administrative region（sq. km）	年末总人口（万人）Total population at year – end（10 000 persons）	六普常住人口（万人）Total residents of the Sixth National Population Census（10 000 persons）	建成区面积（平方公里）Area of built – up district（sq. km）	地区生产总值（万元）Gross regional product（10 000 yuan）	人均地区生产总值（元）Per capita gross regional product（yuan）	用水普及率（%）Water coverage rate（%）	污水处理率（%）Wastewater treatment rate（%）	人均公园绿地面积（平方米）Per capita public green space（sq. m）	生活垃圾处理率（%）Domestic garbage treatment rate（%）
富阳市	Fuyang	县级市	1 808	66	71. 77	25	5 418 339	82 096	100. 00	86. 78	8. 69	100. 00
临安市	Lin′an	县级市	3 124	53	56. 67	15	3 813 458	71 952	100. 00	89. 01	8. 44	100. 00
余姚市	Yuyao	县级市	1 501	84	101. 07	46	7 090 713	84 413	100. 00	81. 65	10. 08	100. 00
慈溪市	Cixi	县级市	1 361	104	146. 24	42	9 582 077	92 135	100. 00	84. 10	12. 91	100. 00
奉化市	Fenghua	县级市	1 268	48	49. 17	19	2 742 507	57 136	100. 00	77. 52	9. 83	100. 00
瑞安市	Rui′an	县级市	1 271	122	142. 47	23	5 593 195	45 846	100. 00	81. 21	9. 98	100. 00
乐清市	Leqing	县级市	1 174	127	138. 93	19	5 994 291	47 199	99. 57	41. 28	4. 73	67. 56
海宁市	Haining	县级市	668	67	80. 70	34	5 812 532	86 754	100. 00	85. 51	13. 93	100. 00
平湖市	Pinghu	县级市	537	49	67. 18	18	4 228 412	86 294	100. 00	86. 21	12. 36	100. 00
桐乡市	Tongxiang	县级市	727	68	81. 58	38	5 268 713	77 481	100. 00	85. 72	13. 50	100. 00
诸暨市	Zhuji	县级市	2 311	107	115. 79	38	8 219 025	76 813	100. 00	85. 01	10. 83	100. 00
上虞市	Shangyu	县级市	1 403	78	77. 94	26	5 774 648	74 034	100. 00	82. 07	11. 26	100. 00
嵊州市	Shengzhou	县级市	1 790	74	67. 98	41	3 639 848	49 187	100. 00	75. 32	10. 67	100. 00
兰溪市	Lanxi	县级市	1 312	67	56. 05	33	2 311 298	34 497	95. 40	80. 04	9. 46	100. 00
义乌市	Yiwu	县级市	1 105	75	123. 40	100	8 060 304	107 471	100. 00	86. 84	10. 06	100. 00
东阳市	Dongyang	县级市	1 747	83	80. 44	37	3 735 844	45 010	100. 00	76. 92	9. 77	100. 00
永康市	Yongkang	县级市	1 048	58	72. 35	35	3 920 925	67 602	100. 00	76. 03	9. 47	100. 00
江山市	Jiangshan	县级市	2 019	60	46. 79	16	2 161 944	36 032	95. 40	84. 76	10. 97	100. 00
温岭市	Wenling	县级市	836	121	136. 68	32	6 838 377	56 516	100. 00	83. 80	11. 04	100. 00
临海市	Linhai	县级市	2 171	118	102. 88	40	3 877 696	32 862	100. 00	84. 49	12. 20	100. 00
龙泉市	Longquan	县级市	3 059	29	23. 46	13	859 459	29 637	100. 00	75. 00	16. 65	100. 00
安徽省	Anhui											
合肥市	Hefei	地级市	11 445	710. 5	570. 25	378	41 643 400	55 186	99. 76	98. 70	11. 50	100. 00

续表

城市名称 Name of cities		行政级别 Administrative level	行政区域土地面积(平方公里) Total land area of administrative region(sq. km)	年末总人口(万人) Total population at year-end (10 000 persons)	六普常住人口(万人) Total residents of the Sixth National Population Census (10 000 persons)	建成区面积(平方公里) Area of built-up district (sq. km)	地区生产总值(万元) Gross regional product (10 000 yuan)	人均地区生产总值(元) Per capita gross regional product(yuan)	用水普及率(%) Water coverage rate(%)	污水处理率(%) Wastewater treatment rate(%)	人均公园绿地面积(平方米) Per capita public green space(sq. m)	生活垃圾处理率(%) Domestic garbage treatment rate(%)
芜湖市	Wuhu	地级市	5 988	383.4	226.31	146	18 736 339	48 742	100.00	91.90	13.56	95.00
蚌埠市	Bengbu	地级市	5 952	367.8	316.45	115	8 902 164	27 999	100.00	98.45	8.87	100.00
淮南市	Huainan	地级市	2 584	243.8	233.39	102	7 817 510	33 489	98.70	97.86	11.75	99.40
马鞍山市	Maanshan	地级市	4 049	228.4	136.63	86	12 320 000	56 217	100.00	93.60	15.83	96.02
淮北市	Huaibei	地级市	2 741	218.3	211.43	80	6 205 393	29 278	99.00	97.36	14.50	100.00
铜陵市	Tongling	地级市	1 200	74.2	72.40	52	6 213 008	84 819	99.91	80.77	14.03	100.00
安庆市	Anqing	地级市	15 318	620.4	531.14	81	13 597 027	25 592	97.21	95.83	9.08	67.00
黄山市	Huangshan	地级市	9 807	147.3	135.90	54	4 249 452	28 773	98.10	89.76	14.66	100.00
滁州市	Chuzhou	地级市	13 523	452.1	393.79	77	9 707 413	24 651	99.81	92.40	13.86	100.00
阜阳市	Fuyang	地级市	9 776	1 039.8	759.99	90	9 624 981	12 616	92.57	88.28	9.60	93.28
宿州市	Suzhou	地级市	9 787	651.7	535.29	67	9 149 528	17 308	99.28	94.21	10.69	100.00
六安市	Liuan	地级市	17 976	710.3	561.17	68	9 182 000	16 248	100.00	88.96	14.41	99.95
亳州市	Bozhou	地级市	8 374	612.6	485.07	43	7 156 572	14 642	91.18	96.92	10.29	100.00
池州市	Chizhou	地级市	8 272	161.9	140.25	37	4 174 466	29 471	98.28	90.26	17.10	99.91
宣城市	Xuancheng	地级市	12 453	279.6	253.29	48	7 574 700	29 636	97.62	83.76	11.49	100.00
巢湖市	Chaohu	县级市	2 046	89	78.07	43	2 098 599	23 580	92.20	84.95	12.20	100.00
桐城市	Tongcheng	县级市	1 546	76	66.45	26	1 966 140	25 870	92.54	81.42	8.64	100.00
天长市	Tianchang	县级市	1 751	64	60.28	29	2 112 849	33 013	96.03	98.99	12.57	100.00
明光市	Mingguang	县级市	2 350	64	53.27	24	924 768	14 450	90.53	91.25	3.77	85.83
界首市	Jieshou	县级市	667	79	56.20	18	1 008 032	12 760	82.59	93.54	4.41	70.95
宁国市	Ningguo	县级市	2 487	39	37.69	26	1 829 619	46 913	88.10	92.13	11.09	100.00
福建省	Fujian											
福州市	Fuzhou	地级市	13 066	655.3	711.54	240	42 182 887	58 304	99.37	84.70	11.32	98.23

续表

城市名称 Name of cities		行政级别 Admini-strative level	行政区域土地面积（平方公里）Total land area of administrative region (sq. km)	年末总人口（万人）Total population at year – end (10 000 persons)	六普常住人口（万人）Total residents of the Sixth National Population Census (10 000 persons)	建成区面积（平方公里）Area of built – up district (sq. km)	地区生产总值（万元）Gross regional product (10 000 yuan)	人均地区生产总值（元）Per capita gross regional product (yuan)	用水普及率（%）Water coverage rate (%)	污水处理率（%）Wastewater treatment rate (%)	人均公园绿地面积（平方米）Per capita public green space (sq. m)	生活垃圾处理率（%）Domestic garbage treatment rate (%)
厦门市	Xiamen	副省级市	1 573	190. 9	353. 13	264	28 170 697	77 392	100. 00	90. 70	11. 38	99. 00
莆田市	Putian	地级市	4 131	329. 3	277. 85	55	12 027 880	42 957	99. 46	84. 40	12. 71	98. 53
三明市	Sanming	地级市	23 094	274. 2	250. 34	33	13 392 862	53 422	99. 87	84. 02	12. 59	97. 77
泉州市	Quanzhou	地级市	11 015	693. 2	812. 85	193	47 264 953	57 291	98. 75	87. 13	13. 70	99. 02
漳州市	Zhangzhou	地级市	13 334	482. 5	481. 00	56	20 177 971	41 433	99. 70	88. 89	12. 41	98. 96
南平市	Nanping	地级市	26 308	313. 9	264. 55	28	9 967 580	37 756	100. 00	84. 00	13. 53	98. 97
龙岩市	Longyan	地级市	19 028	297. 7	255. 95	42	13 746 498	53 590	99. 45	89. 90	11. 90	99. 02
宁德市	Ningde	地级市	13 452	342. 3	282. 20	23	10 777 262	38 015	99. 13	86. 88	13. 82	100. 00
福清市	Fuqing	县级市	1 518	129	123. 48	41	6 072 480	47 073	99. 94	81. 03	12. 01	99. 01
长乐市	Changle	县级市	672	69	68. 26	22	4 350 867	63 056	99. 49	79. 00	16. 64	90. 41
永安市	Yong'an	县级市	2 932	33	34. 70	22	2 464 195	74 673	98. 11	85. 53	11. 10	97. 74
石狮市	Shishi	县级市	160	32	63. 67	26	5 001 440	156 295	99. 34	80. 00	12. 20	98. 66
晋江市	Jinjiang	县级市	642	107	198. 64	36	12 138 880	113 447	99. 31	81. 19	11. 31	98. 70
南安市	Nan'an	县级市	1 985	152	141. 85	29	6 589 862	43 354	91. 51	78. 28	9. 77	98. 01
龙海市	Longhai	县级市	1 315	83	87. 78	35	4 818 704	58 057	97. 44	80. 16	14. 84	98. 67
邵武市	Shaowu	县级市	2 859	31	27. 51	17	1 466 798	47 316	100. 00	87. 03	15. 81	95. 35
武夷山市	Wuyishan	县级市	2 814	23	23. 36	9	981 325	42 666	96. 32	84. 89	13. 27	100. 00
建瓯市	Jian'ou	县级市	4 233	54	45. 22	13	1 409 943	26 110	96. 15	54. 89	10. 83	98. 23
建阳市	Jianyang	县级市	3 378	35	28. 94	11	1 115 571	31 873	99. 06	89. 90	13. 58	100. 00
漳平市	Zhangping	县级市	2 976	28	24. 02	10	1 417 032	50 608	96. 43	73. 20	14. 40	98. 04
福安市	Fu'an	县级市	1 880	65	56. 36	12	2 686 760	41 335	99. 07	80. 44	10. 78	100. 00
福鼎市	Fuding	县级市	1 526	58	52. 95	19	2 106 453	36 318	98. 92	82. 16	10. 69	100. 00
江西省	Jiangxi											
南昌市	Nanchang	地级市	7 402	507. 9	504. 26	208	30 005 236	58 715	98. 90	89. 66	12. 03	100. 00

续表

城市名称 Name of cities		行政级别 Admini-strative level	行政区域土地面积(平方公里) Total land area of administrative region(sq. km)	年末总人口(万人) Total population at year-end (10 000 persons)	六普常住人口(万人) Total residents of the Sixth National Population Census (10 000 persons)	建成区面积(平方公里) Area of built-up district (sq. km)	地区生产总值(万元) Gross regional product (10 000 yuan)	人均地区生产总值(元) Per capita gross regional product(yuan)	用水普及率(%) Water coverage rate(%)	污水处理率(%) Wastewater treatment rate(%)	人均公园绿地面积(平方米) Per capita public green space(sq. m)	生活垃圾处理率(%) Domestic garbage treatment rate(%)
景德镇市	Jingdezhen	地级市	5 261	166. 7	158. 75	75	6 282 524	39 151	99. 60	69. 56	15. 65	100. 00
萍乡市	Pingxiang	地级市	3 831	192. 4	185. 45	44	7 330 597	39 186	100. 00	89. 46	11. 53	100. 00
九江市	Jiujiang	地级市	18 823	508. 6	472. 88	100	14 201 046	29 785	100. 00	99. 23	17. 00	100. 00
新余市	Xinyu	地级市	3 178	120. 5	113. 89	70	8 303 232	72 266	100. 00	96. 78	18. 45	100. 00
鹰潭市	Yingtan	地级市	3 560	124. 0	112. 52	26	4 821 747	42 449	96. 33	94. 73	12. 39	100. 00
赣州市	Ganzhou	地级市	39 379	926. 7	836. 84	89	15 084 851	17 873	100. 00	63. 14	12. 02	100. 00
吉安市	Ji'an	地级市	25 372	505. 5	481. 03	46	10 062 610	18 660	94. 72	91. 24	16. 95	100. 00
宜春市	Yichun	地级市	18 669	573. 1	541. 96	60	12 476 000	22 855	95. 15	93. 10	14. 99	100. 00
抚州市	Fuzhou	地级市	18 820	417. 8	391. 23	55	8 250 400	20 922	98. 24	78. 03	16. 44	100. 00
上饶市	Shangrao	地级市	22 791	760. 3	657. 97	47	12 653 897	19 077	99. 76	90. 02	13. 76	100. 00
乐平市	Leping	县级市	1 974	91	81. 04	19	2 075 446	22 807	100. 00	81. 45	17. 48	100. 00
瑞昌市	Ruichang	县级市	1 423	46	41. 90	15	1 070 119	23 263	97. 16	95. 45	12. 18	100. 00
共青城市	Gongqingcheng	县级市	308	7		14	589 720	84 246	75. 00	50. 00	27. 17	100. 00
贵溪市	Guixi	县级市	2 493	62	55. 85	27	2 773 888	44 740	91. 73	45. 85	12. 09	100. 00
瑞金市	Ruijin	县级市	2 448	68	61. 89	24	889 236	13 077	92. 53	69. 39	14. 50	100. 00
南康市	Nankang	县级市	1 740	83	78. 76	30	1 228 860	14 806	99. 39	42. 92	13. 12	100. 00
井冈山市	Jinggangshan	县级市	1 276	16	15. 23	9	440 396	27 525	80. 48	89. 25	44. 10	100. 00
丰城市	Fengcheng	县级市	2 845	139	133. 64	42	3 146 623	22 638	90. 01	81. 50	12. 23	100. 00
樟树市	Zhangshu	县级市	1 290	60	55. 51	26	2 340 246	39 004	89. 10	85. 45	12. 03	100. 00
高安市	Gaoan	县级市	2 439	85	81. 16	54	1 512 388	17 793	100. 00	30. 97	12. 98	100. 00
德兴市	Dexing	县级市	2 082	33	29. 32	7	1 221 086	37 003	99. 38	68. 28	16. 46	100. 00
山东省	Shandong											
济南市	Jinan	副省级市	8 177	609. 2	681. 40	363	48 036 762	69 444	100. 00	97. 29	10. 31	91. 98

续表

城市名称 Name of cities		行政级别 Administrative level	行政区域土地面积(平方公里) Total land area of administrative region(sq. km)	年末总人口(万人) Total population at year-end (10 000 persons)	六普常住人口(万人) Total residents of the Sixth National Population Census (10 000 persons)	建成区面积(平方公里) Area of built-up district (sq. km)	地区生产总值(万元) Gross regional product (10 000 yuan)	人均地区生产总值(元) Per capita gross regional product(yuan)	用水普及率(%) Water coverage rate(%)	污水处理率(%) Wastewater treatment rate(%)	人均公园绿地面积(平方米) Per capita public green space(sq. m)	生活垃圾处理率(%) Domestic garbage treatment rate(%)
青岛市	Qingdao	副省级市	11 282	769. 6	871. 51	375	73 021 100	82 680	100. 00	91. 34	14. 58	100. 00
淄博市	Zibo	地级市	5 965	423. 7	453. 06	238	35 572 100	77 876	100. 00	96. 19	15. 40	100. 00
枣庄市	Zaozhuang	地级市	4 563	394. 8	372. 91	146	17 029 205	45 262	99. 24	92. 62	14. 63	98. 50
东营市	Dongying	地级市	7 950	185. 5	203. 53	111	30 006 600	145 395	100. 00	92. 17	18. 55	100. 00
烟台市	Yantai	地级市	13 746	650. 3	696. 82	273	52 813 800	75 672	99. 87	97. 00	21. 30	100. 00
潍坊市	Weifang	地级市	16 143	878. 9	908. 62	157	40 124 300	43 681	100. 00	96. 61	17. 67	100. 00
济宁市	Jining	地级市	11 423	847. 1	808. 19	125	31 893 700	39 165	100. 00	94. 39	11. 07	100. 00
泰安市	Tai'an	地级市	7 762	558. 9	549. 42	114	25 470 100	41 850	100. 00	94. 03	19. 85	100. 00
威海市	Weihai	地级市	5 797	253. 6	280. 48	138	23 378 600	92 148	100. 00	95. 70	25. 08	100. 00
日照市	Rizhao	地级市	5 348	288. 1	280. 10	96	13 525 700	47 851	100. 00	93. 54	21. 87	100. 00
莱芜市	Laiwu	地级市	2 246	126. 3	129. 85	81	6 314 100	48 212	100. 00	91. 23	18. 49	100. 00
临沂市	Linyi	地级市	17 191	1 083. 8	1 003. 94	186	30 128 100	29 808	100. 00	97. 00	20. 04	100. 00
德州市	Dezhou	地级市	10 356	577. 5	556. 82	124	22 305 600	39 710	100. 00	97. 00	25. 14	100. 00
聊城市	Liaocheng	地级市	8 703	594. 5	578. 99	70	21 467 500	36 573	98. 38	91. 02	11. 70	100. 00
滨州市	Binzhou	地级市	9 600	380. 9	374. 85	88	19 877 262	52 591	100. 00	95. 71	18. 26	100. 00
菏泽市	Heze	地级市	12 239	957. 3	828. 77	84	17 873 557	21 461	100. 00	75. 18	11. 69	100. 00
章丘市	Zhangqiu	县级市	1 855	102	106. 42	36	6 787 431	66 543	100. 00	89. 10	16. 43	100. 00
胶州市	Jiaozhou	县级市	1 324	81	84. 31	45	7 542 822	93 121	100. 00	92. 51	12. 13	100. 00
即墨市	Jimo	县级市	1 780	113	117. 72	53	7 879 704	69 732	100. 00	88. 24	12. 23	100. 00
平度市	Pingdu	县级市	3 167	138	135. 74	50	7 044 700	51 049	100. 00	88. 01	10. 73	100. 00
莱西市	Laixi	县级市	1 568	74	75. 02	82	5 298 800	71 605	100. 00	97. 11	15. 00	100. 00
滕州市	Tengzhou	县级市	1 496	169	160. 37	53	8 308 457	49 162	100. 00	92. 95	13. 39	100. 00
龙口市	Longkou	县级市	901	64	68. 83	41	8 450 429	132 038	99. 96	87. 20	12. 80	100. 00

续表

城市名称 Name of cities		行政级别 Administrative level	行政区域土地面积(平方公里) Total land area of administrative region(sq. km)	年末总人口(万人) Total population at year-end (10 000 persons)	六普常住人口(万人) Total residents of the Sixth National Population Census (10 000 persons)	建成区面积(平方公里) Area of built-up district (sq. km)	地区生产总值(万元) Gross regional product (10 000 yuan)	人均地区生产总值(元) Per capita gross regional product(yuan)	用水普及率(%) Water coverage rate(%)	污水处理率(%) Wastewater treatment rate(%)	人均公园绿地面积(平方米) Per capita public green space(sq. m)	生活垃圾处理率(%) Domestic garbage treatment rate(%)
莱阳市	Laiyang	县级市	1 732	87	87. 86	42	2 815 174	32 358	99. 72	97. 00	13. 30	100. 00
莱州市	Laizhou	县级市	1 878	86	88. 39	40	5 787 359	67 295	100. 00	96. 98	14. 31	100. 00
蓬莱市	Penglai	县级市	1 129	45	45. 11	35	4 254 477	94 544	94. 05	97. 02	13. 79	100. 00
招远市	Zhaoyuan	县级市	1 432	57	56. 62	30	5 511 196	96 688	100. 00	97. 02	18. 56	100. 00
栖霞市	Qixia	县级市	2 016	62	58. 96	16	2 012 926	32 467	97. 50	94. 66	11. 77	100. 00
海阳市	Haiyang	县级市	1 909	66	63. 87	54	2 774 175	42 033	99. 21	96. 98	14. 60	100. 00
青州市	Qingzhou	县级市	1 569	92	94. 04	49	4 491 222	48 818	100. 00	97. 03	25. 46	100. 00
诸城市	Zhucheng	县级市	2 151	109	108. 62	42	5 815 962	53 357	100. 00	97. 01	23. 53	100. 00
寿光市	Shouguang	县级市	1 990	105	113. 95	38	6 181 142	58 868	100. 00	97. 01	23. 61	100. 00
安丘市	Anqiu	县级市	1 712	95	92. 69	38	2 211 913	23 283	100. 00	95. 27	25. 05	100. 00
高密市	Gaomi	县级市	1 527	88	89. 56	45	4 458 220	50 662	100. 00	97. 01	23. 85	100. 00
昌邑市	Changyi	县级市	1 628	58	60. 35	25	2 979 500	51 371	100. 00	92. 84	20. 89	100. 00
曲阜市	Qufu	县级市	815	64	64. 05	27	2 984 368	46 631	100. 00	97. 01	15. 00	100. 00
兖州市	Yanzhou	县级市	664	64	61. 84	37	5 061 900	79 092	100. 00	90. 71	12. 61	100. 00
邹城市	Zoucheng	县级市	1 616	116	111. 67	42	6 713 200	57 872	99. 82	86. 24	15. 00	100. 00
新泰市	Xintai	县级市	1 933	140	131. 59	66	7 510 800	53 649	100. 00	94. 45	19. 44	100. 00
肥城市	Feicheng	县级市	1 277	98	94. 66	44	6 188 169	63 145	100. 00	91. 52	18. 93	100. 00
文登市	Wendeng	县级市	1 829	64	67. 36	44	7 046 410	110 100	100. 00	97. 01	22. 02	100. 00
荣成市	Rongcheng	县级市	1 526	67	71. 44	71	8 000 672	119 413	100. 00	96. 98	22. 37	100. 00
乳山市	Rushan	县级市	1 654	57	57. 25	31	3 692 916	64 788	100. 00	95. 17	18. 10	100. 00
乐陵市	Leling	县级市	1 172	70	65. 24	30	1 868 528	26 693	98. 57	80. 02	6. 25	100. 00
禹城市	Yucheng	县级市	990	53	49. 00	49	2 062 861	38 922	100. 00	97. 00	14. 10	100. 00
临清市	Linqing	县级市	950	76	71. 96	24	2 852 600	37 534	99. 63	93. 59	12. 10	100. 00

续表

城市名称 Name of cities		行政级别 Administrative level	行政区域土地面积（平方公里）Total land area of administrative region (sq. km)	年末总人口（万人）Total population at year-end (10 000 persons)	六普常住人口（万人）Total residents of the Sixth National Population Census (10 000 persons)	建成区面积（平方公里）Area of built-up district (sq. km)	地区生产总值（万元）Gross regional product (10 000 yuan)	人均地区生产总值（元）Per capita gross regional product (yuan)	用水普及率（%）Water coverage rate (%)	污水处理率（%）Wastewater treatment rate (%)	人均公园绿地面积（平方米）Per capita public green space (sq. m)	生活垃圾处理率（%）Domestic garbage treatment rate (%)
河南省	Henan											
郑州市	Zhengzhou	地级市	7 446	1 072.5	862.71	373	55 497 869	62 054	100.00	95.82	6.03	89.75
开封市	Kaifeng	地级市	6 444	544.4	467.65	94	12 070 542	25 922	97.12	88.25	7.84	98.40
洛阳市	Luoyang	地级市	15 236	709.7	654.99	187	29 811 236	45 316	92.78	99.85	6.94	85.07
平顶山市	Pingdingshan	地级市	7 904	545.6	490.47	72	14 957 963	30 380	96.68	97.00	10.24	92.06
安阳市	Anyang	地级市	7 352	593.0	517.32	108	15 668 969	30 624	100.00	97.70	9.44	100.00
鹤壁市	Hebi	地级市	2 182	163.1	156.92	61	5 457 806	34 456	93.72	82.79	14.40	88.73
新乡市	Xinxiang	地级市	8 249	617.0	570.82	110	16 197 714	28 598	98.94	87.80	10.12	100.00
焦作市	Jiaozuo	地级市	4 071	367.3	354.01	102	15 513 469	44 029	99.82	86.10	9.90	97.34
濮阳市	Puyang	地级市	4 266	421.3	359.87	118	9 896 987	27 654	89.15	84.99	12.36	91.28
许昌市	Xuchang	地级市	4 996	494.2	430.75	80	17 161 891	39 947	96.83	96.96	10.39	96.27
漯河市	Luohe	地级市	2 617	275.0	254.43	60	7 971 238	31 211	92.33	70.61	14.93	99.48
三门峡市	Sanmenxia	地级市	10 496	226.1	223.40	30	11 273 204	50 408	98.07	96.55	15.50	92.39
南阳市	Nanyang	地级市	26 509	1 206.3	1 026.37	147	23 407 260	23 086	70.96	48.74	17.76	82.17
商丘市	Shangqiu	地级市	10 704	934.1	736.30	62	13 972 750	19 029	61.46	72.69	5.81	67.17
信阳市	Xinyang	地级市	18 847	855.2	610.91	73	13 973 205	22 347	95.17	83.99	14.14	93.20
周口市	Zhoukou	地级市	11 961	1 229.2	895.38	60	15 747 181	17 734	92.78	80.48	10.23	78.83
驻马店市	Zhumadian	地级市	15 083	899.2	723.12	65	13 735 463	19 592	77.83	92.05	9.81	91.89
巩义市	Gongyi	县级市	1 043	81	80.79	26	5 278 013	65 161	95.56	54.89	14.78	100.00
荥阳市	Xingyang	县级市	943	66	61.38	30	4 580 493	69 401	92.03	90.11	11.24	98.65
新密市	Xinmi	县级市	1 001	80	79.73	30	5 129 160	64 115	86.67	85.06	13.33	100.00
新郑市	Xinzheng	县级市	887	65	75.81	29	5 313 974	81 753	68.80	84.99	8.28	100.00
登封市	Dengfeng	县级市	1 217	70	66.86	39	4 311 803	61 597	73.38	90.03	8.43	92.80

续表

城市名称 Name of cities		行政级别 Administrative level	行政区域土地面积(平方公里) Total land area of administrative region(sq. km)	年末总人口(万人) Total population at year-end (10 000 persons)	六普常住人口(万人) Total residents of the Sixth National Population Census (10 000 persons)	建成区面积(平方公里) Area of built-up district (sq. km)	地区生产总值(万元) Gross regional product (10 000 yuan)	人均地区生产总值(元) Per capita gross regional product(yuan)	用水普及率(%) Water coverage rate(%)	污水处理率(%) Wastewater treatment rate(%)	人均公园绿地面积(平方米) Per capita public green space(sq. m)	生活垃圾处理率(%) Domestic garbage treatment rate(%)
偃师市	Yanshi	县级市	949	88	66. 67	121	4 321 509	49 108	96. 60	95. 23	9. 43	100. 00
舞钢市	Wugang	县级市	641	34	31. 38	37	1 027 791	30 229	95. 82	84. 71	10. 73	99. 14
汝州市	Ruzhou	县级市	957	106	92. 79	17	3 204 341	30 230	50. 85	97. 35	8. 41	98. 82
林州市	Linzhou	县级市	2 062	108	78. 97	21	4 037 843	37 387	91. 98	81. 04	10. 20	100. 00
卫辉市	Weihui	县级市	859	52	49. 57	20	1 036 441	19 932	97. 39	100. 00	8. 04	100. 00
辉县市	Huixian	县级市	2 007	84	74. 04	26	2 765 802	32 926	95. 77	92. 04	7. 12	100. 00
沁阳市	Qinyang	县级市	624	49	44. 77	23	3 005 767	61 342	94. 90	83. 36	8. 52	93. 10
孟州市	Mengzhou	县级市	542	38	36. 71	15	2 281 915	60 050	97. 24	95. 77	10. 21	97. 73
禹州市	Yuzhou	县级市	1 461	127	113. 19	35	4 035 510	31 776	94. 69	96. 95	8. 46	76. 84
长葛市	Changge	县级市	650	67	68. 71	51	3 703 704	55 279	84. 61	99. 96	14. 97	100. 00
义马市	Yima	县级市	112	17	14. 48	15	1 617 646	95 156	88. 96	41. 04	11. 16	49. 12
灵宝市	Lingbao	县级市	3 011	74	72. 10	17	4 412 404	59 627	93. 62	70. 74	9. 73	96. 96
邓州市	Dengzhou	县级市	2 360	175	146. 82	40	2 834 572	16 198	81. 22	87. 18	6. 55	100. 00
永城市	Yongcheng	县级市	2 021	152	124. 04	47	3 644 380	23 976	80. 52	92. 75	8. 47	90. 22
项城市	Xiangcheng	县级市	1 083	138	100. 37	30	1 957 668	14 186	99. 00	85. 64	8. 84	94. 46
济源市	Jiyuan	县级市	1 894	69	67. 58	38	4 400 957	63 782	99. 89	93. 00	10. 86	100. 00
湖北省	Hubei											
武汉市	Wuhan	副省级市	8 494	821. 7	978. 54	520	80 038 200	79 482	100. 00	88. 78	9. 92	100. 00
黄石市	Huangshi	地级市	4 586	261. 5	242. 93	72	10 409 500	42 703	100. 00	88. 00	12. 44	100. 00
十堰市	Shiyan	地级市	23 680	346. 0	334. 08	66	9 556 800	28 471	94. 76	89. 81	11. 34	100. 00
宜昌市	Yichang	地级市	21 084	399. 0	405. 97	124	25 088 900	61 517	100. 00	90. 48	14. 10	89. 90
襄阳市	Xiangyang	地级市	19 728	594. 0	550. 03	144	25 019 600	45 167	97. 91	90. 05	11. 48	88. 97
鄂州市	Ezhou	地级市	1 594	109. 4	104. 87	60	5 603 900	53 192	100. 00	90. 13	15. 20	100. 00

续表

城市名称 Name of cities		行政级别 Admini-strative level	行政区域土地面积（平方公里）Total land area of administrative region（sq. km）	年末总人口（万人）Total population at year－end（10 000 persons）	六普常住人口（万人）Total residents of the Sixth National Population Census（10 000 persons）	建成区面积（平方公里）Area of built－up district（sq. km）	地区生产总值（万元）Gross regional product（10 000 yuan）	人均地区生产总值（元）Per capita gross regional product（yuan）	用水普及率（%）Water coverage rate（%）	污水处理率（%）Wastewater treatment rate（%）	人均公园绿地面积（平方米）Per capita public green space（sq. m）	生活垃圾处理率（%）Domestic garbage treatment rate（%）
荆门市	Jingmen	地级市	12 404	302. 3	287. 37	53	10 852 600	37 649	100. 00	91. 50	10. 11	100. 00
孝感市	Xiaogan	地级市	8 910	526. 9	481. 45	38	11 051 600	20 934	96. 62	92. 30	11. 43	100. 00
荆州市	Jingzhou	地级市	14 067	663. 3	569. 17	69	11 960 200	20 912	98. 43	83. 90	9. 69	100. 00
黄冈市	Huanggang	地级市	17 457	748. 2	616. 21	41	11 928 800	19 220	98. 01	96. 32	12. 86	95. 03
咸宁市	Xianning	地级市	10 049	297. 9	246. 26	64	7 609 900	30 791	92. 30	87. 55	14. 13	100. 00
随州市	Suizhou	地级市	9 636	256. 9	216. 22	45	5 905 200	27 163	91. 86	93. 48	10. 00	100. 00
大冶市	Daye	县级市	1 566	95	90. 97	27	4 102 390	43 183	97. 72	81. 42	5. 30	
丹江口市	Danjiangkou	县级市	3 121	46	44. 38	28	1 300 165	28 264	100. 00	96. 38	10. 79	100. 00
宜都市	Yidu	县级市	1 357	40	38. 46	20	3 447 354	86 184	100. 00	92. 61	13. 54	95. 42
当阳市	Dangyang	县级市	2 159	49	46. 83	19	3 022 343	61 680	97. 97	85. 00	9. 03	100. 00
枝江市	Zhijiang	县级市	1 310	49	49. 60	20	2 927 700	59 749	100. 00	90. 77	9. 37	98. 76
老河口市	Laohekou	县级市	1 032	53	47. 15	27	2 081 915	39 281	100. 00	90. 93	9. 38	94. 99
枣阳市	Zaoyang	县级市	3 277	112	100. 47	34	3 759 206	33 564	100. 00	92. 97	11. 47	100. 00
宜城市	Yicheng	县级市	2 115	57	51. 25	19	2 019 429	35 429	97. 30	84. 99	8. 59	100. 00
钟祥市	Zhongxiang	县级市	4 488	106	102. 25	23	2 974 900	28 065	100. 00	83. 84	11. 31	100. 00
应城市	Yingcheng	县级市	1 103	67	59. 38	46	1 748 685	26 100	92. 48	79. 28	8. 56	95. 24
安陆市	Anlu	县级市	1 355	63	56. 86	22	1 253 300	19 894	97. 21	45. 89	9. 01	100. 00
汉川市	Hanchuan	县级市	1 659	111	101. 55	26	2 888 118	26 019	94. 91	80. 65	6. 16	41. 67
石首市	Shishou	县级市	1 427	65	57. 70	23	1 089 020	16 754	99. 93	79. 68	11. 62	100. 00
洪湖市	Honghu	县级市	2 519	94	81. 94	40	1 441 852	15 339	93. 35	78. 57	12. 47	94. 74
松滋市	Songzi	县级市	2 177	85	76. 59	25	1 533 108	18 037	99. 02	85. 03	10. 76	100. 00
麻城市	Macheng	县级市	3 747	117	84. 91	27	1 855 783	15 861	98. 65	61. 65	9. 12	95. 14
武穴市	Wuxue	县级市	1 246	80	64. 42	24	1 810 435	22 630	94. 51	88. 89	10. 94	87. 74

续表

城市名称 Name of cities		行政级别 Admini-strative level	行政区域土地面积(平方公里) Total land area of administrative region(sq. km)	年末总人口(万人) Total population at year – end (10 000 persons)	六普常住人口(万人) Total residents of the Sixth National Population Census (10 000 persons)	建成区面积(平方公里) Area of built – up district (sq. km)	地区生产总值(万元) Gross regional product (10 000 yuan)	人均地区生产总值(元) Per capita gross regional product(yuan)	用水普及率(%) Water coverage rate(%)	污水处理率(%) Wastewater treatment rate(%)	人均公园绿地面积(平方米) Per capita public green space(sq. m)	生活垃圾处理率(%) Domestic garbage treatment rate(%)
赤壁市	Chibi	县级市	1 723	53	47.84	26	2 445 000	46 132	98.32	83.01	7.49	78.57
广水市	Guangshui	县级市	2 647	95	75.59	72	1 892 229	19 918	96.76	32.58	10.06	
恩施市	Enshi	县级市	3 972	81	74.96	20	1 230 958	15 197	90.77	90.87	9.87	100.00
利川市	Lichuan	县级市	4 607	92	65.41	14	733 502	7 973	78.51	44.04	4.36	92.54
仙桃市	Xiantao	县级市	2 538	155	117.51	67	4 441 958	28 658	100.00	85.59	9.23	100.00
潜江市	Qianjiang	县级市	2 004	103	94.63	50	4 417 600	42 889	100.00	81.07	10.06	100.00
天门市	Tianmen	县级市	2 622	164	141.89	80	3 212 167	19 586	97.64	84.43	12.18	100.00
湖南省	Hunan											
长沙市	Changsha	地级市	11 816	660.6	704.10	316	63 999 097	89 903	99.98	99.43	8.92	100.00
株洲市	Zhuzhou	地级市	11 247	395.8	385.71	125	17 613 222	45 235	100.00	89.10	10.27	100.00
湘潭市	Xiangtan	地级市	5 006	291.8	275.22	77	12 823 929	46 249	97.85	86.02	8.75	100.00
衡阳市	Hengyang	地级市	15 303	800.2	714.83	158	19 577 018	27 258	94.06	62.24	7.62	100.00
邵阳市	Shaoyang	地级市	20 830	801.3	707.17	54	10 284 120	14 406	82.64	86.33	7.99	96.47
岳阳市	Yueyang	地级市	15 087	573.0	547.61	84	21 999 170	39 968	99.95	88.78	9.00	100.00
常德市	Changde	地级市	18 910	629.0	571.46	82	20 385 039	35 475	99.44	77.83	14.21	100.00
张家界市	Zhangjiajie	地级市	9 516	170.1	147.81	32	3 389 855	22 658	96.75	78.27	16.83	100.00
益阳市	Yiyang	地级市	12 320	481.9	430.79	65	10 202 773	23 572	82.95	86.67	7.83	100.00
郴州市	Chenzhou	地级市	19 342	509.8	458.35	72	15 172 679	32 848	100.00	80.96	10.24	100.00
永州市	Yongzhou	地级市	22 897	620.3	519.43	58	10 595 951	20 239	98.92	70.67	7.20	100.00
怀化市	Huaihua	地级市	27 624	516.5	474.17	60	10 010 673	21 018	97.70	85.30	7.55	100.00
娄底市	Loudi	地级市	8 119	437.8	378.46	46	10 026 518	26 367	98.29	80.42	9.53	100.00
浏阳市	Liuyang	县级市	4 998	142	127.95	25	8 111 256	57 122	95.08	98.05	4.85	100.00
醴陵市	Liling	县级市	2 157	105	94.74	27	3 955 347	37 670	99.53	74.53	7.24	100.00

续表

城市名称 Name of cities		行政级别 Admini-strative level	行政区域土地面积(平方公里) Total land area of administrative region(sq. km)	年末总人口(万人) Total population at year-end (10 000 persons)	六普常住人口(万人) Total residents of the Sixth National Population Census (10 000 persons)	建成区面积(平方公里) Area of built-up district (sq. km)	地区生产总值(万元) Gross regional product (10 000 yuan)	人均地区生产总值(元) Per capita gross regional product(yuan)	用水普及率(%) Water coverage rate(%)	污水处理率(%) Wastewater treatment rate(%)	人均公园绿地面积(平方米) Per capita public green space(sq. m)	生活垃圾处理率(%) Domestic garbage treatment rate(%)
湘乡市	Xiangxiang	县级市	1 967	92	78. 82	86	2 317 473	25 190	93. 75	70. 24	8. 18	90. 36
韶山市	Shaoshan	县级市	247	12	8. 60	5	495 681	41 307	97. 14	70. 85	9. 82	100. 00
耒阳市	Leiyang	县级市	2 656	143	115. 16	39	3 021 344	21 128	95. 64	68. 96	6. 60	100. 00
常宁市	Changning	县级市	2 064	97	81. 04	25	1 988 618	20 501	97. 86	52. 78	6. 74	41. 65
武冈市	Wugang	县级市	1 549	83	73. 49	16	904 674	10 900	98. 85	69. 78	10. 69	100. 00
汨罗市	Miluo	县级市	1 562	77	69. 21	74	2 954 848	38 375	97. 47	77. 55	7. 47	70. 58
临湘市	Linxiang	县级市	1 754	53	49. 83	15	1 596 772	30 128	95. 81	72. 15	7. 19	100. 00
津市市	Jinshi	县级市	557	26	25. 09	21	870 687	33 488	99. 18	92. 16	9. 78	100. 00
沅江市	Yuanjiang	县级市	2 020	75	66. 63	14	1 760 340	23 471	91. 84	95. 69	4. 49	100. 00
资兴市	Zixing	县级市	2 747	38	33. 73	25	2 226 103	58 582	93. 24	68. 70	9. 59	100. 00
洪江市	Hongjiang	县级市	2 289	44	47. 80	6	735 553	16 717	90. 67	88. 07	15. 17	100. 00
冷水江市	Lengshuijiang	县级市	439	37	32. 71	19	2 124 334	57 414	97. 21	85. 35	12. 00	82. 47
涟源市	Lianyuan	县级市	1 912	118	99. 55	16	1 834 020	15 543	95. 17	94. 84	2. 48	100. 00
吉首市	Jishou	县级市	1 058	30	30. 21	20	963 150	32 105	84. 79	92. 33	7. 51	100. 00
广东省	Guangdong											
广州市	Guangzhou	副省级市	7 434	822. 3	1 270. 19	1 010	135 512 072	105 909	99. 70	82. 73	19. 64	80. 38
韶关市	Shaoguan	地级市	18 463	326. 5	282. 62	88	9 064 760	31 702	97. 39	81. 88	11. 78	100. 00
深圳市	Shenzhen	副省级市	1 997	287. 6	1 035. 84	863	129 500 601	123 247	100. 00	96. 10	16. 60	95. 13
珠海市	Zhuhai	地级市	1 724	106. 6	156. 25	124	15 037 642	95 471	99. 69	86. 55	19. 02	100. 00
汕头市	Shantou	地级市	2 064	532. 9	538. 93	214	14 250 138	26 231	96. 12	90. 23	13. 10	65. 70
佛山市	Foshan	地级市	3 798	377. 7	719. 74	155	66 130 223	91 259	100. 00	91. 63	10. 86	94. 21
江门市	Jiangmen	地级市	9 505	391. 8	445. 07	157	18 803 941	42 028	98. 41	88. 15	16. 92	100. 00
湛江市	Zhanjiang	地级市	13 325	785. 2	699. 48	106	18 602 206	24 531	99. 40	96. 64	12. 92	97. 72

续表

城市名称 Name of cities		行政级别 Admini-strative level	行政区域土地面积(平方公里) Total land area of administrative region(sq. km)	年末总人口(万人) Total population at year-end (10 000 persons)	六普常住人口(万人) Total residents of the Sixth National Population Census (10 000 persons)	建成区面积(平方公里) Area of built-up district (sq. km)	地区生产总值(万元) Gross regional product (10 000 yuan)	人均地区生产总值(元) Per capita gross regional product(yuan)	用水普及率(%) Water coverage rate(%)	污水处理率(%) Wastewater treatment rate(%)	人均公园绿地面积(平方米) Per capita public green space(sq. m)	生活垃圾处理率(%) Domestic garbage treatment rate(%)
茂名市	Maoming	地级市	11 425	748.9	581.75	102	19 361 785	32 678	99.81	85.81	12.12	100.00
肇庆市	Zhaoqing	地级市	14 891	427.6	391.65	94	14 623 503	36 864	99.96	85.39	22.67	98.51
惠州市	Huizhou	地级市	11 343	341.9	459.84	229	23 675 499	50 873	97.63	92.06	14.91	100.00
梅州市	Meizhou	地级市	15 864	521.4	423.85	48	7 459 800	17 425	77.69	53.34	11.85	100.00
汕尾市	Shanwei	地级市	5 271	347.2	293.55	39	6 104 079	20 608	93.74	85.57	12.89	79.96
河源市	Heyuan	地级市	15 642	355.1	295.02	31	6 152 596	20 536	100.00	89.39	12.11	100.00
阳江市	Yangjiang	地级市	7 956	282.5	242.17	48	8 870 330	36 096	100.00	83.50	11.12	100.00
清远市	Qingyuan	地级市	19 036	405.7	369.84	71	10 250 321	27 320	99.98	83.57	11.52	100.00
东莞市	Dongguan	地级市	2 460	187.0	822.02	107	50 101 727	58 804	97.32	95.11	16.53	100.00
中山市	Zhongshan	地级市	1 784	152.0	312.13	48	24 410 432	77 527	100.00	90.70	14.33	100.00
潮州市	Chaozhou	地级市	3 146	264.8	266.95	42	7 066 543	26 252	100.00	86.20	12.80	100.00
揭阳市	Jieyang	地级市	5 266	673.9	588.43	68	13 967 948	23 532	63.68	80.82	15.91	92.11
云浮市	Yunfu	地级市	7 779	287.0	236.72	71	5 404 494	22 539	99.07	98.56	12.82	100.00
增城市	Zengcheng	县级市	1 616	85	103.71	32	8 502 115	100 025	100.00	25.94	13.29	48.56
从化市	Conghua	县级市	1 975	60	59.34	25	2 450 686	40 845	88.94	83.43	14.05	100.00
乐昌市	Lechang	县级市	2 421	51	39.78	20	822 486	16 127	95.62	68.95	10.76	94.00
南雄市	Nanxiong	县级市	2 326	48	31.62	11	867 578	18 075	94.15	75.28	12.13	
台山市	Taishan	县级市	3 285	98	94.11	26	3 106 067	31 695	91.40	87.62	11.00	100.00
开平市	Kaiping	县级市	1 659	68	69.92	32	2 406 475	35 389	96.11	80.30	11.29	100.00
鹤山市	Heshan	县级市	1 083	36	49.49	21	1 985 032	55 140	100.00	81.70	13.31	100.00
恩平市	Enping	县级市	1 698	50	49.28	19	1 220 756	24 415	94.66	80.54	9.43	100.00
廉江市	Lianjiang	县级市	2 840	171	144.31	92	2 581 605	15 097	92.59	51.37	30.08	97.70
雷州市	Leizhou	县级市	3 662	169	142.77	51	1 865 773	11 040	73.72	96.15	8.19	100.00

续表

城市名称 Name of cities		行政级别 Admini-strative level	行政区域土地面积（平方公里）Total land area of administrative region(sq. km)	年末总人口（万人）Total population at year-end (10 000 persons)	六普常住人口（万人）Total residents of the Sixth National Population Census (10 000 persons)	建成区面积（平方公里）Area of built-up district (sq. km)	地区生产总值（万元）Gross regional product (10 000 yuan)	人均地区生产总值（元）Per capita gross regional product(yuan)	用水普及率（%）Water coverage rate(%)	污水处理率（%）Wastewater treatment rate(%)	人均公园绿地面积（平方米）Per capita public green space(sq. m)	生活垃圾处理率(%) Domestic garbage treatment rate(%)
吴川市	Wuchuan	县级市	876	111	92. 73	18	2 072 445	18 671	84. 16	81. 03	10. 41	93. 85
高州市	Gaozhou	县级市	3 276	169	128. 87	27	3 716 366	21 990	100. 00	92. 67	11. 39	100. 00
化州市	Huazhou	县级市	2 354	162	117. 88	25	3 249 113	20 056	76. 62	75. 31	4. 20	100. 00
信宜市	Xinyi	县级市	3 081	136	91. 37	24	2 985 024	21 949	100. 00	85. 11	8. 74	100. 00
高要市	Gaoyao	县级市	2 186	79	75. 31	21	3 019 706	38 224	91. 38	81. 86	18. 50	100. 00
四会市	Sihui	县级市	1 262	50	54. 29	50	3 903 063	78 061	93. 08	80. 70	8. 76	86. 78
兴宁市	Xingning	县级市	2 104	118	96. 29	17	1 234 683	10 463	91. 05	68. 51	11. 29	100. 00
陆丰市	Lufeng	县级市	1 541	181	135. 83	20	1 820 643	10 059	91. 95	89. 94	7. 86	
阳春市	Yangchun	县级市	4 054	115	84. 95	28	2 559 470	22 256	98. 56	79. 86	9. 62	100. 00
英德市	Yingde	县级市	5 634	109	94. 20	25	1 843 068	16 909	97. 60	91. 05	17. 13	
连州市	Lianzhou	县级市	2 668	51	36. 76	23	973 430	19 087	85. 05	51. 37	13. 75	100. 00
普宁市	Puning	县级市	1 635	238	205. 56	37	4 204 424	17 666	98. 93	74. 25	0. 81	88. 97
罗定市	Luoding	县级市	2 327	123	95. 90	21	1 195 845	9 722	97. 08	89. 77	11. 71	60. 00
广西壮族自治区	Guangxi											
南宁市	Nanning	地级市	22 244	713. 5	665. 87	242	25 031 812	35 133	95. 38	94. 79	13. 04	100. 00
柳州市	Liuzhou	地级市	18 597	372. 3	375. 87	172	18 206 066	47 795	97. 93	90. 90	13. 42	97. 48
桂林市	Guilin	地级市	27 809	522. 1	474. 80	66	14 850 212	30 849	88. 30	91. 01	10. 29	100. 00
梧州市	Wuzhou	地级市	12 588	329. 5	288. 22	39	8 325 790	28 523	95. 78	87. 48	8. 47	100. 00
北海市	Beihai	地级市	3 337	168. 1	153. 93	67	6 307 923	40 418	99. 72	82. 45	10. 28	100. 00
防城港市	Fangchenggang	地级市	6 222	91. 6	86. 69	34	4 439 937	50 302	100. 00	68. 53	7. 94	95. 24
钦州市	Qinzhou	地级市	10 843	391. 7	307. 97	86	6 913 216	22 147	99. 76	66. 98	7. 44	95. 69
贵港市	Guigang	地级市	10 602	529. 9	411. 88	67	6 791 828	16 281	99. 97	86. 88	13. 20	97. 00
玉林市	Yulin	地级市	12 835	691. 9	548. 74	67	11 020 800	19 822	100. 00	99. 08	11. 17	100. 00

续表

城市名称 Name of cities		行政级别 Admini-strative level	行政区域土地面积(平方公里) Total land area of administrative region(sq. km)	年末总人口(万人) Total population at year - end (10 000 persons)	六普常住人口(万人) Total residents of the Sixth National Population Census (10 000 persons)	建成区面积(平方公里) Area of built - up district (sq. km)	地区生产总值(万元) Gross regional product (10 000 yuan)	人均地区生产总值(元) Per capita gross regional product(yuan)	用水普及率(%) Water coverage rate(%)	污水处理率(%) Wastewater treatment rate(%)	人均公园绿地面积(平方米) Per capita public green space(sq. m)	生活垃圾处理率(%) Domestic garbage treatment rate(%)
百色市	Baise	地级市	36 202	408. 6	346. 68	35	7 552 415	21 539	100. 00	61. 92	9. 23	100. 00
贺州市	Hezhou	地级市	11 855	226. 4	195. 41	32	3 942 144	19 904	64. 46	68. 41	11. 70	100. 00
河池市	Hechi	地级市	32 907	411. 6	336. 93	19	4 927 088	14 472	95. 18	88. 87	6. 50	100. 00
来宾市	Laibin	地级市	13 409	260. 7	209. 97	35	5 142 945	24 183	96. 67	77. 34	10. 50	99. 80
崇左市	Chongzuo	地级市	17 386	245. 4	199. 43	22	5 305 064	26 288	92. 60	50. 87	8. 55	63. 97
岑溪市	Cenxi	县级市	2 770	92	77. 21	8	1 890 394	20 548	97. 90	80. 10	16. 89	100. 00
东兴市	Dongxing	县级市	589	14	14. 47	10	624 504	44 607	71. 43	71. 34	11. 09	85. 88
桂平市	Guiping	县级市	4 071	192	149. 69	29	2 172 459	11 315	95. 31	74. 16	5. 72	97. 81
北流市	Beiliu	县级市	2 452	143	113. 22	19	2 090 025	14 616	100. 00	98. 18	9. 83	100. 00
宜州市	Yizhou	县级市	3 857	66	55. 86	11	877 880	13 301	100. 00	70. 06	10. 57	100. 00
合山市	Heshan	县级市	366	14	11. 45	7	333 531	23 824	100. 00	80. 78	7. 48	86. 15
凭祥市	Pingxiang	县级市	645	11	11. 22	3	362 035	32 912	98. 92	70. 14	8. 76	88. 07
海南省	Hainan											
海口市	Haikou	地级市	2 305	161. 6	204. 62	124	8 187 550	38 634	99. 98	88. 10	11. 32	100. 00
三亚市	Sanya	地级市	1 919	57. 3	68. 54	47	3 309 625	46 366	98. 91	79. 73	18. 98	100. 00
三沙市	Sansha	地级市	200 013	0. 1								
五指山市	Wuzhishan	县级市	1 129	11	10. 41	6	165 802	15 073	89. 47	62. 25	9. 82	100. 00
琼海市	Qionghai	县级市	1 710	50	48. 32	25	1 450 245	29 005	89. 13	49. 43	14. 97	100. 00
儋州市	Danzhou	县级市	3 394	98	93. 24	25	1 762 908	17 989	99. 86	36. 25	9. 71	100. 00
文昌市	Wenchang	县级市	2 485	59	53. 74	15	1 585 489	26 873	92. 86	53. 49	4. 50	100. 00
万宁市	Wanning	县级市	1 884	62	54. 56	11	1 349 786	21 771	93. 02	98. 30	14. 49	98. 24
东方市	Dongfang	县级市	2 256	48	40. 83	16	1 140 219	23 755	94. 86	29. 41	9. 80	100. 00
重庆市	Chongqing	直辖市	82 374	3 343. 4	2 884. 62	1 052	114 096 000	38 914	93. 84	90. 07	18. 13	99. 28

续表

城市名称 Name of cities		行政级别 Administrative level	行政区域土地面积（平方公里） Total land area of administrative region (sq. km)	年末总人口（万人） Total population at year-end (10 000 persons)	六普常住人口（万人） Total residents of the Sixth National Population Census (10 000 persons)	建成区面积（平方公里） Area of built-up district (sq. km)	地区生产总值（万元） Gross regional product (10 000 yuan)	人均地区生产总值（元） Per capita gross regional product (yuan)	用水普及率（%） Water coverage rate (%)	污水处理率（%） Wastewater treatment rate (%)	人均公园绿地面积（平方米） Per capita public green space (sq. m)	生活垃圾处理率（%） Domestic garbage treatment rate (%)
四川省	Sichuan											
成都市	Chengdu	副省级市	12 121	1 173. 3	1 404. 76	516	81 389 438	57 624	98. 26	92. 15	13. 66	100. 00
自贡市	Zigong	地级市	4 381	328. 5	267. 89	100	8 847 971	32 787	75. 08	90. 20	8. 45	90. 48
攀枝花市	Panzhihua	地级市	7 401	111. 9	121. 41	66	7 400 348	60 391	93. 22	65. 44	8. 80	96. 75
泸州市	Luzhou	地级市	12 236	505. 2	421. 84	101	10 304 538	24 317	90. 82	83. 76	9. 16	100. 00
德阳市	Deyang	地级市	5 910	391. 5	361. 58	64	12 802 046	35 945	98. 57	89. 20	9. 67	100. 00
绵阳市	Mianyang	地级市	20 248	545. 4	461. 39	108	13 464 220	27 056	99. 02	91. 81	10. 03	100. 00
广元市	Guangyuan	地级市	16 311	311. 7	248. 41	45	4 686 575	18 627	94. 66	77. 81	12. 17	78. 47
遂宁市	Suining	地级市	5 323	376. 1	325. 26	69	6 824 097	20 908	79. 55	93. 94	8. 79	86. 35
内江市	Neijiang	地级市	5 385	426. 6	370. 28	45	9 781 812	26 341	97. 52	83. 00	8. 02	74. 41
乐山市	Leshan	地级市	12 723	355. 1	323. 58	64	10 377 500	30 386	93. 06	76. 38	8. 09	96. 96
南充市	Nanchong	地级市	12 477	759. 6	627. 86	101	11 803 603	18 757	96. 99	80. 24	9. 76	85. 06
眉山市	Meishan	地级市	7 140	350. 4	295. 05	45	7 752 152	26 168	96. 69	86. 81	11. 33	100. 00
宜宾市	Yibin	地级市	13 271	546. 6	447. 19	80	12 427 582	27 865	95. 96	75. 99	14. 19	94. 98
广安市	Guang'an	地级市	6 341	468. 5	320. 55	34	7 522 228	23 410	93. 57	99. 66	16. 28	99. 90
达州市	Dazhou	地级市	16 582	695. 6	546. 81	36	11 354 673	20 685	73. 18	61. 47	9. 82	81. 20
雅安市	Yaan	地级市	15 046	156. 5	150. 73	28	3 980 524	26 157	99. 14	61. 65	9. 54	93. 14
巴中市	Bazhong	地级市	12 293	390. 0	328. 31	18	3 904 003	11 823	93. 84	81. 57	7. 57	77. 72
资阳市	Ziyang	地级市	7 960	505. 9	366. 51	41	9 847 194	27 283	93. 93	86. 32	9. 10	95. 18
都江堰市	Dujiangyan	县级市	1 208	61	65. 80	35	2 081 845	34 129	88. 76	54. 59	9. 86	92. 75
彭州市	Pengzhou	县级市	1 421	80	76. 29	21	2 130 951	26 637	67. 08	85. 79	9. 04	83. 76
邛崃市	Qionglai	县级市	1 384	66	61. 28	20	1 504 282	22 792	82. 81	77. 02	10. 81	92. 63
崇州市	Chongzhou	县级市	1 090	67	66. 11	25	1 634 346	24 393	96. 27	50. 08	12. 14	95. 63

续表

城市名称 Name of cities		行政级别 Admini-strative level	行政区域土地面积(平方公里) Total land area of administrative region(sq. km)	年末总人口(万人) Total population at year-end (10 000 persons)	六普常住人口(万人) Total residents of the Sixth National Population Census (10 000 persons)	建成区面积(平方公里) Area of built-up district (sq. km)	地区生产总值(万元) Gross regional product (10 000 yuan)	人均地区生产总值(元) Per capita gross regional product(yuan)	用水普及率(%) Water coverage rate(%)	污水处理率(%) Wastewater treatment rate(%)	人均公园绿地面积(平方米) Per capita public green space(sq. m)	生活垃圾处理率(%) Domestic garbage treatment rate(%)
广汉市	Guanghan	县级市	548	61	59. 11	45	2 519 501	41 303	85. 31	49. 67	7. 36	98. 96
什邡市	Shifang	县级市	820	44	41. 28	13	1 886 051	42 865	78. 19	82. 50	10. 02	99. 83
绵竹市	Mianzhu	县级市	1 246	51	47. 79	14	1 635 946	32 077	95. 94	85. 76	11. 15	100. 00
江油市	Jiangyou	县级市	2 720	89	76. 21	30	2 421 431	27 207	89. 57	81. 05	9. 60	100. 00
峨眉山市	Emeishan	县级市	1 181	43	43. 71	18	1 636 277	38 053	84. 64	93. 77	12. 43	98. 77
阆中市	Langzhong	县级市	1 875	88	72. 89	24	1 381 853	15 703	96. 73	75. 51	9. 31	83. 39
华蓥市	Huaying	县级市	464	36	27. 84	11	1 003 486	27 875	100. 00	36. 14	8. 75	81. 16
万源市	Wanyuan	县级市	4 051	60	40. 76	9	1 008 511	16 809	64. 62	0. 01	25. 07	100. 00
简阳市	Jianyang	县级市	2 215	148	107. 12	24	3 108 037	21 000	96. 87	74. 62	6. 44	76. 47
西昌市	Xichang	县级市	2 657	64	71. 24	36	3 340 454	52 195	81. 73	80. 28	9. 41	100. 00
贵州省	Guizhou											
贵阳市	Guiyang	地级市	8 034	374. 5	432. 26	230	17 003 048	38 447	94. 49	95. 07	12. 81	95. 68
六盘水市	Liupanshui	地级市	9 914	322. 5	285. 13	39	7 386 526	25 877	91. 86	66. 11	2. 53	100. 00
遵义市	Zunyi	地级市	30 762	771. 4	612. 71	65	13 439 251	22 001	99. 07	79. 63	8. 08	95. 21
安顺市	Anshun	地级市	9 267	284. 4	229. 76	39	3 526 171	15 454	91. 24	85. 36	1. 75	64. 71
毕节市	Bijie	地级市	26 853	858. 0	653. 75	42	8 779 637	13 461	91. 73	100. 00	14. 99	100. 00
铜仁市	Tongren	地级市	18 003	426. 5	309. 32	45	4 439 100	14 379	78. 83	98. 20	2. 66	93. 81
清镇市	Qingzhen	县级市	1 492	50	46. 78	52	1 441 585	28 832	86. 44	99. 94	6. 11	100. 00
赤水市	Chishui	县级市	1 852	31	23. 71	10	494 452	15 950	79. 57	85. 57	5. 57	100. 00
仁怀市	Renhuai	县级市	1 788	68	54. 65	12	3 294 649	48 451	93. 58	85. 19	1. 58	91. 43
兴义市	Xingyi	县级市	2 908	83	78. 31	32	1 999 630	24 092	92. 48	83. 81	7. 59	100. 00
凯里市	Kaili	县级市	1 306	50	47. 90	54	1 198 477	23 970	72. 67	100. 00	14. 97	100. 00
都匀市	Duyun	县级市	2 274	48	44. 37	29	1 101 648	22 951	99. 13	100. 00	8. 22	98. 57

续表

城市名称	Name of cities	行政级别 Admini-strative level	行政区域土地面积(平方公里) Total land area of administrative region(sq. km)	年末总人口(万人) Total population at year - end (10 000 persons)	六普常住人口(万人) Total residents of the Sixth National Population Census (10 000 persons)	建成区面积(平方公里) Area of built - up district (sq. km)	地区生产总值(万元) Gross regional product (10 000 yuan)	人均地区生产总值(元) Per capita gross regional product(yuan)	用水普及率(%) Water coverage rate(%)	污水处理率(%) Wastewater treatment rate(%)	人均公园绿地面积(平方米) Per capita public green space(sq. m)	生活垃圾处理率(%) Domestic garbage treatment rate(%)
福泉市	Fuquan	县级市	1 688	33	28. 39	19	796 294	24 130	97. 73	71. 15	9. 89	100. 00
云南省	Yunnan											
昆明市	Kunming	地级市	21 012	543. 5	643. 22	298	30 111 433	46 256	93. 37	99. 06	9. 50	99. 90
曲靖市	Qujing	地级市	28 904	637. 4	585. 51	66	14 001 655	23 661	100. 00	90. 13	9. 34	100. 00
玉溪市	Yuxi	地级市	15 285	214. 1	230. 35	44	10 001 749	43 037	96. 06	81. 85	18. 75	100. 00
保山市	Baoshan	地级市	19 637	255. 6	250. 65	25	3 899 564	15 397	86. 92	80. 36	7. 54	98. 97
昭通市	Zhaotong	地级市	22 621	583. 3	521. 35	36	5 555 967	10 528	97. 36	91. 09	5. 57	100. 00
丽江市	Lijiang	地级市	21 219	119. 0	124. 48	25	2 122 389	16 870	100. 00	93. 80	31. 34	100. 00
普洱市	Pu'er	地级市	45 385	251. 7	254. 29	24	3 668 537	14 286	98. 10	80. 73	10. 95	94. 98
临沧市	Lincang	地级市	24 469	236. 4	242. 95	17	3 529 771	14 376	88. 83	78. 45	6. 49	98. 81
安宁市	Anning	县级市	1 302	27	34. 13	21	2 131 027	78 927	94. 74	88. 48	15. 66	100. 00
宣威市	Xuanwei	县级市	6 053	151	130. 29	33	2 059 647	13 640	99. 46	100. 00	9. 51	100. 00
楚雄市	Chuxiong	县级市	4 512	51	58. 86	39	2 208 943	43 313	99. 14	96. 96	14. 97	100. 00
个旧市	Gejiu	县级市	1 587	39	45. 98	13	1 675 311	42 957	91. 54	89. 98	10. 13	100. 00
开远市	Kaiyuan	县级市	1 950	28	32. 27	21	1 244 102	44 432	62. 87	97. 60	10. 89	100. 00
蒙自市	Mengzi	县级市	2 228	38	41. 72	30	1 028 512	27 066	99. 34	83. 97	8. 84	100. 00
文山市	Wenshan	县级市	2 977	49	48. 15	20	1 406 442	28 703	97. 84	70. 60	9. 22	100. 00
景洪市	Jinghong	县级市	6 959	41	51. 99	24	1 249 101	30 466	100. 00	75. 02	16. 00	100. 00
大理市	Dali	县级市	1 815	61	65. 20	45	2 551 705	41 831	94. 68	92. 30	7. 79	94. 83
瑞丽市	Ruili	县级市	1 020	13	18. 06	25	396 362	30 489	100. 00	97. 26	7. 30	100. 00
芒市	Mangshi	县级市	2 987	37	38. 99	17	637 998	17 243	99. 57	84. 72	14. 30	100. 00
西藏自治区	Tibet											
拉萨市	Lasa	地级市	29 518	50. 4	55. 94	66	2 601 358	45 019	75. 22	0. 07	4. 44	100. 00

续表

城市名称 Name of cities		行政级别 Administrative level	行政区域土地面积(平方公里) Total land area of administrative region(sq. km)	年末总人口(万人) Total population at year-end (10 000 persons)	六普常住人口(万人) Total residents of the Sixth National Population Census (10 000 persons)	建成区面积(平方公里) Area of built-up district (sq. km)	地区生产总值(万元) Gross regional product (10 000 yuan)	人均地区生产总值(元) Per capita gross regional product(yuan)	用水普及率(%) Water coverage rate(%)	污水处理率(%) Wastewater treatment rate(%)	人均公园绿地面积(平方米) Per capita public green space(sq. m)	生活垃圾处理率(%) Domestic garbage treatment rate(%)
日喀则市	Rikaze	县级市	3 654	11	12.04	26	418 513	38 047	76.17		31.45	78.49
陕西省	Shaanxi											
西安市	Xian	副省级市	10 108	796.0	846.78	375	43 661 000	51 166	100.00	90.10	10.81	99.84
铜川市	Tongchuan	地级市	3 882	85.3	83.44	44	2 733 060	32 556	94.58	85.23	10.60	88.23
宝鸡市	Baoji	地级市	18 117	383.9	371.67	98	13 743 280	36 826	100.00	94.59	13.30	100.00
咸阳市	Xianyang	地级市	10 189	527.9	509.60	83	15 736 770	31 982	96.38	88.85	14.74	93.23
渭南市	Weinan	地级市	13 134	565.1	528.61	63	11 537 980	21 717	99.76	84.17	12.17	86.83
延安市	Yan'an	地级市	37 037	235.4	218.70	36	12 710 200	57 876	86.85	88.02	9.58	88.02
汉中市	Hanzhong	地级市	27 246	384.3	341.62	34	7 545 720	22 084	80.54	90.06	14.96	86.78
榆林市	Yulin	地级市	43 578	374.6	335.14	52	26 698 800	79 587	88.42	70.29	10.26	98.57
安康市	Ankang	地级市	23 536	306.0	262.99	38	4 969 080	18 878	90.51	86.01	9.83	97.79
商洛市	Shangluo	地级市	19 292	248.8	234.17	22	4 233 100	18 097	67.95	98.25	9.86	100.00
兴平市	Xingping	县级市	508	61	54.16	20	1 451 959	23 803	98.33	72.29	12.94	75.34
韩城市	Hancheng	县级市	1 621	40	39.12	18	2 332 153	58 304	99.88	71.03	8.49	98.78
华阴市	Huayin	县级市	817	26	25.81	7	676 270	26 010	92.73	70.82	8.36	100.00
甘肃省	Gansu											
兰州市	Lanzhou	地级市	13 086	321.5	361.62	199	15 638 180	43 175	93.93	67.73	8.88	100.00
嘉峪关市	Jiayuguan	地级市	2 935	19.8	23.19	63	2 691 460	115 123	100.00	82.31	14.34	100.00
金昌市	Jinchang	地级市	8 896	46.7	46.41	39	2 433 884	52 157	99.48	99.85	14.29	100.00
白银市	Baiyin	地级市	21 158	175.7	170.88	58	4 337 651	25 274	100.00	65.30	8.45	83.96
天水市	Tianshui	地级市	14 313	375.7	326.25	46	4 128 747	12 593	79.13	83.50	6.34	100.00
武威市	Wuwei	地级市	33 238	190.0	181.51	31	3 415 423	18 759	90.38	93.85	14.92	98.98
张掖市	Zhangye	地级市	41 924	130.8	119.95	37	2 919 280	24 204	100.00	85.78	29.80	100.00

续表

城市名称 Name of cities		行政级别 Administrative level	行政区域土地面积（平方公里）Total land area of administrative region (sq. km)	年末总人口（万人）Total population at year-end (10 000 persons)	六普常住人口（万人）Total residents of the Sixth National Population Census (10 000 persons)	建成区面积（平方公里）Area of built-up district (sq. km)	地区生产总值（万元）Gross regional product (10 000 yuan)	人均地区生产总值（元）Per capita gross regional product (yuan)	用水普及率（%）Water coverage rate (%)	污水处理率（%）Wastewater treatment rate (%)	人均公园绿地面积（平方米）Per capita public green space (sq. m)	生活垃圾处理率（%）Domestic garbage treatment rate (%)
平凉市	Pingliang	地级市	11 170	234.0	206.80	36	3 245 086	15 607	99.34	90.16	8.14	99.23
酒泉市	Jiuquan	地级市	193 974	98.8	109.59	41	5 745 681	52 116	100.00	92.76	8.97	98.18
庆阳市	Qingyang	地级市	27 119	262.3	221.12	25	5 293 638	23 882	98.47	90.14	6.01	92.25
定西市	Dingxi	地级市	19 609	296.3	269.86	23	2 232 711	8 157	91.99	82.63	10.36	94.00
陇南市	Longnan	地级市	27 914	284.9	256.77	14	2 259 756	8 809	64.37	93.33	1.47	99.66
玉门市	Yumen	县级市	13 496	16	15.98	26	1 302 563	81 410	100.00	70.59	9.65	96.89
敦煌市	Dunhuang	县级市	31 200	19	18.60	12	782 635	41 191	100.00	97.93	11.37	98.25
临夏市	Linxia	县级市	89	24	27.45	20	380 313	15 846	85.58	80.02	3.21	98.01
合作市	Hezuo	县级市	2 291	9	9.03	9	235 053	26 117	81.37	60.87	5.79	85.19
青海省	Qinghai											
西宁市	Xining	地级市	7 665	198.5	220.87	75	8 510 857	38 034	99.99	71.18	10.61	92.52
格尔木市	Golmud	县级市	119 174	13	21.52	31	2 899 966	223 074	100.00	55.89	5.35	97.96
德令哈市	Delingha	县级市	27 765	8	7.82	47	473 385	59 173	98.32	26.65	6.19	96.61
宁夏回族自治区	Ningxia											
银川市	Yinchuan	地级市	9 025	167.2	199.31	135	11 509 344	56 528	92.08	100.00	13.83	92.71
石嘴山市	Shizuishan	地级市	5 310	74.2	72.55	103	4 099 688	55 566	99.98	90.01	22.58	86.79
吴忠市	Wuzhong	地级市	16 757	141.6	127.38	45	3 150 281	24 166	89.77	89.97	19.81	98.82
固原市	Guyuan	地级市	13 047	154.2	122.82	37	1 584 544	12 619	95.86	66.96	8.98	90.74
中卫市	Zhongwei	地级市	17 441	120.0	108.08	36	2 505 881	22 779	70.05	100.00	17.61	100.00
灵武市	Lingwu	县级市	4 539	24	26.17	11	2 510 887	104 620	93.10	86.03	14.93	95.53
青铜峡市	Qingtongxia	县级市	2 525	28	26.47	27	1 192 706	42 597	99.07	84.37	13.92	83.84
新疆维吾尔自治区	Xinjiang											
乌鲁木齐市	Urumqi	地级市	13 788	257.8	311.26	384	20 040 727	59 645	99.95	84.75	9.20	91.43

续表

城市名称 Name of cities		行政级别 Admini-strative level	行政区域土地面积(平方公里) Total land area of administrative region(sq. km)	年末总人口(万人) Total population at year - end (10 000 persons)	六普常住人口(万人) Total residents of the Sixth National Population Census (10 000 persons)	建成区面积(平方公里) Area of built - up district (sq. km)	地区生产总值(万元) Gross regional product (10 000 yuan)	人均地区生产总值(元) Per capita gross regional product(yuan)	用水普及率(%) Water coverage rate(%)	污水处理率(%) Wastewater treatment rate(%)	人均公园绿地面积(平方米) Per capita public green space(sq. m)	生活垃圾处理率(%) Domestic garbage treatment rate(%)
克拉玛依市	Karamay	地级市	7 735	37.6	39.10	57	8 107 054	135 018	100.00	92.47	9.58	100.00
吐鲁番市	Turpan	县级市	13 589	28	27.34	13	665 150	23 755	98.70	62.76	26.44	98.96
哈密市	Hami	县级市	85 587	47	47.22	34	2 094 376	44 561	100.00	86.35	9.08	98.90
昌吉市	Changji	县级市	8 215	37	42.63	49	2 602 612	70 341	100.00	97.43	9.78	98.63
阜康市	Fukang	县级市	8 529	17	16.50	10	1 209 469	71 145	96.11	96.31	10.60	95.56
博乐市	Bole	县级市	7 956	27	23.56	20	636 911	23 589	98.88	100.00	11.21	89.29
库尔勒市	Korla	县级市	7 267	55	54.93	68	5 921 146	107 657	100.00	95.74	10.46	95.65
阿克苏市	Akesu	县级市	13 564	50	53.57	38	1 239 856	24 797	100.00	100.00	14.64	100.00
阿图什市	Atus	县级市	16 151	25	24.04	8	279 690	11 188	95.50	76.74	1.77	96.67
喀什市	Kashi	县级市	555	55	50.66	53	1 321 538	24 028	100.00	98.01	11.11	89.47
和田市	Hetian	县级市	510	33	32.23	26	410 704	12 446	97.19	84.98	7.67	88.24
伊宁市	Yining	县级市	676	52	51.51	37	1 367 965	26 307	99.97	85.01	9.41	100.00
奎屯市	Kuitun	县级市	1 110	16	16.63	25	1 058 464	66 154	100.00	68.52	8.65	100.00
塔城市	Tacheng	县级市	4 353	17	16.10	14	587 605	34 565	93.58	86.47	12.47	95.45
乌苏市	Wusu	县级市	13 729	23	29.89	25	1 246 778	54 208	88.46	77.92	6.81	93.62
阿勒泰市	Aletai	县级市	11 481	20	19.01	11	453 683	22 684	96.23	13.80	18.69	95.00
石河子市	Shihezi	县级市	6 007	62	38.01	30	2 904 071	46 840	100.00	58.62	10.69	100.00
阿拉尔市	Alar	县级市	4 196	17	15.86	36	926 356	54 492	95.45	79.85	11.52	100.00
图木舒克市	Tumushuke	县级市	1 927	16	13.57	14	361 713	22 607	64.01	49.64	25.80	
五家渠市	Wujiaqu	县级市	710	12	9.64	14	943 306	78 609	100.00	82.62	11.32	82.19
北屯市	Beitun	县级市	911	6	7.63	21	163 210	27 202	80.14	99.99	0.71	85.56

一、数据来源（Data Resources）

1. 行政级别（Administrative level）

2. 行政区域土地面积（Total land area of city's administrative region）

3. 年末总人口（Total population at year-end）

4. 建成区面积（Area of built-up district）

5. 地区生产总值（Gross regional product）

6. 城市人均地区生产总值（Per capita gross regional product）

以上数据来源：国家统计局城市社会经济调查司．中国城市统计年鉴（2013）［M］．北京：中国统计出版社，2014.

（注：该年鉴未发表2012年全国368个县级市的人均地区生产总值，本数据根据地区生产总值除以年末总人口得到。2004年1月6日国家统计局发布《关于改进和规范地区GDP核算的通知》（国统字〔2004〕4号），要求各省、区、市统一使用常住人口计算人均GDP，本统计得到的县级市人均地区生产总值并不一定确切反映城市的实际情况。）

7. 污水处理率（Wastewater treatment rate）

8. 生活垃圾处理率（Domestic garbage treatment rate）

9. 用水普及率（Water coverage rate）

10. 人均公园绿地面积（Per capita public green space）

以上数据来源：中华人民共和国住房和城乡建设部．中国城市建设统计年鉴（2012年）［M］．北京：中国计划出版社，2013.

二、指标解释（Data Illumination）

1. 行政级别：按行政级别分组，全国657个城市分为：4个直辖市，15个副省级城市，270个地级市，368个县级市。

——《中国城市统计年鉴（2013）》第3页

2. 行政区域土地面积：是指在该行政区划内的全部土地面积（包括水面面积）。计算土地面积以行政区划为准。

——《中国城市统计年鉴（2013）》第485页

3. 年末总人口：是指本市本年12月31日24时的人口总数，为公安部门的户籍人口数。

——《中国城市统计年鉴（2013）》第485页

4. 六普常住人口：以2010年11月1日零时为标准时点进行的第六次全国人口普查中的常住人口，包括居住在本乡镇街道、户口在本乡镇街道或户口待定的人；居住在本乡镇街道、离开户口登记地所在的乡镇街道半年以上的人；户口在本乡镇街道、外出不满半年或在境外工作学习的人。不包括常住在省内的境外人员。

——《第六次全国人口普查数据公报》

5. 建成区面积：指市政区范围内经过征用土地和实际建设发展起来的非农业生产建设地段，包括市区集中连片的部分以及分散在近郊区与城市有着密切联系，具有基本完善的市政公用设施的城市建设用地（如机场、污水处理厂、通信电台）。

——《中国城市统计年鉴（2013）》第485页

6. 地区生产总值：指按市场价格计算的一个地区所有常住单位在一定时期内生产活动的最终成果。

——《中国城市统计年鉴（2013）》第485页

7. 用水普及率：指报告期末城区内用水人口与总人口的比率。计算公式为：

用水普及率 = 城区用水人口/（城区人口 + 城区暂住人口）×100%

——《中国城市建设统计年鉴（2012 年）》第 616 页

8. 污水处理率：指报告期内污水处理总量与污水排放总量的比率。计算公式：

污水处理率 = 污水处理总量/污水排放总量 ×100%

——《中国城市建设统计年鉴（2012 年）》第 616 页

9. 人均公园绿地面积：指报告期末城区内平均每人拥有的公园绿地面积。计算公式：

人均公园绿地面积 = 城区公园绿地面积/（城区人口 + 城区暂住人口）

——《中国城市建设统计年鉴（2012 年）》第 616 页

10. 生活垃圾处理率：指报告期内生活垃圾处理量与生活垃圾产出量的比率。计算公式：

生活垃圾处理率 = 生活垃圾处理量/生活垃圾产生量 ×100%

——《中国城市建设统计年鉴（2012 年）》第 617 页

注释：

1. 2012 年 6 月 21 日，民政部发布《民政部关于国务院批准设立地级三沙市的公告》，经国务院批准，撤销海南省西沙群岛、南沙群岛、中沙群岛办事处，设立地级三沙市。《中国城市统计年鉴（2013）》中，三沙市区行政区域土地面积为 200 013 平方公里；根据三沙市人民政府网，三沙市陆地面积约 10 平方公里，海域面积约 200 万平方公里；根据海南省人民政府网，三沙市涉及岛屿面积 13 平方公里，海域面积为 260 多万平方公里。本统计采用《中国城市统计年鉴（2013）》的数据，可能与其他渠道统计数据存在出入，仅供参考。

2. 2012 年 8 月 17 日，国务院发布《国务院关于同意江苏省调整苏州市部分行政区划的批复》（国函〔2012〕102 号），撤销县级吴江市，设立苏州市吴江区。根据《苏州市 2010 年第六次全国人口普查主要数据公报》，原县级吴江市的常住人口为苏州市统计的一部分，故在本次“2012 年中国城市基本数据”的统计工作中，不再重复计数苏州市的这一部分人口。

3. 2012 年 9 月 30 日，国务院发布《国务院关于同意山东省调整青岛市部分行政区划的批复》（国函〔2012〕153 号），撤销青岛市黄岛区、县级胶南市，设立新的青岛市黄岛区。根据《青岛市 2010 年第六次全国人口普查主要数据公报》，原县级胶南市的常住人口为青岛市统计的一部分，故在本次“2012 年中国城市基本数据”的统计工作中，不再重复计数青岛市的这一部分人口。

4. 2010 年 11 月 26 日，国务院发布《国务院关于同意湖北省襄樊市更名的批复》（国函〔2010〕129 号），同意襄樊市更名为襄阳市。《中国城市统计年鉴（2013）》中已更名为襄阳市，但《中国城市建设统计年鉴（2012 年）》和六普数据仍沿用襄樊市的称谓。在本次“2012 年中国城市基本数据”的统计工作中，统一采用“襄阳市”这一称谓。

5. 《中国城市统计年鉴（2013）》未统计以下城市的建成区面积：福建省福清市、长乐市、石狮市、晋江市、南安市、邵武市、武夷山市、建瓯市、建阳市、漳平市、福安市和福鼎市，山东省兖州市，湖南省洪江市，广东省陆丰市，广西壮族自治区合山市，西藏自治区日喀则市，青海省格尔木市。在本次“2012 年中国城市基本数据”的统计工作中，上述数据取自《中国城市建设统计年鉴（2012 年）》。

6. 目前，由于各城市户籍改革步伐进展不一，一些地区已经把暂住人口完全纳入当地人口管理范畴，而另一些地区则仍维持原来的户籍人口管理办法，把暂住人口排除在外，导致各城市总人口概念差异较大。因此，本统计中的总人口及在此基础上计算出的各项人均指标均采用所引资料中的定义，可能与其他渠道统计数据存在出入，仅供参考。

（数据收集整理：毛其智，清华大学教授，国际欧亚科学院院士；胡若函，清华大学建筑学院博士研究生）

附录 4

2013 年中国人居环境奖获奖名单

中国人居环境奖是由建设部于 2000 年设立的全国人居环境建设领域的最高荣誉奖项，目的是为了表彰在城乡建设和管理中坚持以人为本、全面协调可持续的科学发展观，树立正确的政绩观，不断加强城乡基础设施和生态环境建设，切实改善人居环境，努力构建资源节约、环境友好的社会主义和谐社会，为实现全面建设小康社会做出突出贡献的城市。住房和城乡建设部 2014 年 2 月 24 日公布了 2013 年度的中国人居环境奖获奖名单（建城〔2014〕17 号），授予江苏省镇江市、安徽省池州市、山东省东营市、江苏省宜兴市、浙江省长兴县 2013 年中国人居环境奖；授予北京市海淀区翠湖湿地公园生态保护项目等 36 个项目 2013 年中国人居环境范例奖。目前，全国共有 35 个城市获得中国人居环境奖。以下是 2013 年中国人居环境奖获奖名单及中国人居环境范例奖获奖名单：

中国人居环境奖：

1. 江苏省镇江市
2. 安徽省池州市
3. 山东省东营市
4. 江苏省宜兴市
5. 浙江省长兴县

中国人居环境范例奖：

1. 北京市海淀区翠湖湿地公园生态保护项目
2. 天津市文化中心环境建设工程
3. 天津市郭家沟生态村提升改造项目
4. 河北省涞源县地下综合管廊建设项目
5. 河北省邯郸市数字化城市管理项目
6. 河北省秦皇岛市在水一方住宅小区建筑能源节约与利用项目
7. 黑龙江省哈尔滨市何家沟综合整治工程
8. 上海市长宁区废弃物综合处置中心建设项目
9. 上海市杨浦区新江湾城人文生态社区建设项目

10. 上海市杨浦区五角场地区智能交通系统建设项目
11. 江苏省常熟市碧溪新区城乡统筹垃圾处理与资源化利用项目
12. 江苏省昆山市陆家镇小城镇人居环境建设项目
13. 江苏省江阴市新桥镇新型社区建设项目
14. 江苏省宿迁市幸福新城危旧片区改造示范工程
15. 江苏省淮安市古淮河环境治理工程
16. 浙江省杭州市中东河综合整治与保护开发工程
17. 浙江省杭州市区公共厕所提升改造工程
18. 浙江省嘉兴市南湖新区能源节约型示范区建设工程
19. 浙江省丽水市城区街头绿地建设项目
20. 浙江省临海市紫阳街历史街区保护开发建设项目
21. 山东省潍坊市数字化城市管理拓展提升项目
22. 山东省诸城市新型农村社区建设项目
23. 山东省沂源县节能改造温暖万家工程
24. 河南省漯河市沙澧河开发建设项目
25. 湖北省襄阳市污水处理厂污泥和餐厨垃圾处理项目
26. 湖南省长沙市洋湖湿地生态修复与保护暨洋湖湿地公园建设项目
27. 湖南省郴州市苏仙区西河沙滩公园建设项目
28. 湖南省株洲市城市管理与体制创新项目
29. 广东省深圳市深圳湾滨海休闲带建设项目
30. 重庆市璧山县低碳生态绿岛建设项目
31. 重庆市荣昌县濑溪河流域水环境综合治理工程
32. 宁夏回族自治区中卫市老城区宜居家园城中村及棚户区改造建设项目
33. 宁夏回族自治区吴忠市市区建筑节能项目
34. 新疆维吾尔自治区克拉玛依市克拉玛依区信息技术推动城市管理机制创新项目
35. 新疆维吾尔自治区库车县老城区历史文化街区保护工程
36. 新疆维吾尔自治区天池景区环境综合整治工程

（资料整理：廖远涛，雷轩，广州市城市规划勘测设计研究院）

附录 5

2013 年国家园林城市、县城和城镇命名名单

住房和城乡建设部对所有申报国家园林的城市、县城和城镇组织了评审，于 2014 年 1 月 14 日公布了 2013 年度国家园林城市、县城和城镇名单。河北省邢台市等 37 个城市为国家园林城市，河北省临漳县等 37 个县城为国家园林县城，山西省贾家庄镇等 14 个镇为国家园林城镇。目前，国家园林城市共进行了 16 批次的评选。以下为 2013 年国家园林城市、县城和城镇名单：

一、国家园林城市（共 45 个）

1. 河北省邢台市
2. 陕西省咸阳市
3. 山西省大同市
4. 山西省朔州市
5. 江苏省盐城市
6. 浙江省建德市
7. 浙江省金华市
8. 浙江省丽水市
9. 安徽省滁州市
10. 福建省晋江市
11. 福建省宁德市
12. 江西省鹰潭市
13. 江西省抚州市
14. 山东省莱州市
15. 山东省诸城市
16. 山东省德州市
17. 山东省滨州市
18. 山东省高密市
19. 山东省菏泽市
20. 湖北省当阳市
21. 湖北省随州市
22. 湖北省恩施市
23. 湖北省仙桃市
24. 湖南省郴州市
25. 广东省阳江市
26. 广东省清远市
27. 广西壮族自治区梧州市
28. 广西壮族自治区北流市
29. 四川省自贡市
30. 四川省德阳市
31. 四川省泸州市
32. 四川省眉山市
33. 云南省普洱市
34. 云南省开远市
35. 云南省芒市
36. 宁夏回族自治区灵武市
37. 宁夏回族自治区中卫市
38. 西藏自治区拉萨市
39. 甘肃省金昌市
40. 甘肃省敦煌市

41. 内蒙古自治区通辽市
42. 内蒙古自治区鄂尔多斯市
43. 新疆维吾尔自治区乌鲁木齐市
44. 新疆维吾尔自治区阿勒泰市
45. 新疆维吾尔自治区五家渠市

二、国家园林县城（共37个）

1. 河北省临漳县
2. 河北省邱县
3. 河北省张北县
4. 河北省怀来县
5. 河北省平泉县
6. 山西省黎城县
7. 山西省长子县
8. 山西省灵石县
9. 山西省古县
10. 浙江省常山县
11. 浙江省龙游县
12. 江西省新干县
13. 山东省临朐县
14. 山东省费县
15. 山东省莒南县
16. 山东省临沭县
17. 河南省栾川县
18. 河南省鲁山县
19. 河南省长垣县
20. 湖北省房县
21. 湖北省嘉鱼县
22. 广西壮族自治区鹿寨县
23. 重庆市奉节县
24. 重庆市巫山县
25. 重庆市酉阳土家族苗族自治县
26. 云南省晋宁县
27. 云南省嵩明县
28. 云南省禄劝彝族苗族自治县
29. 云南省罗平县
30. 云南省华宁县
31. 云南省易门县
32. 陕西省扶风县
33. 甘肃省两当县
34. 新疆维吾尔自治区尉犁县
35. 新疆维吾尔自治区泽普县
36. 新疆维吾尔自治区巩留县
37. 新疆维吾尔自治区尼勒克县

三、国家园林城镇（共14个）

1. 山西省贾家庄镇
2. 江苏省木渎镇
3. 江苏省淀山湖镇
4. 江苏省梅李镇
5. 江苏省洛阳镇
6. 浙江省新塍镇
7. 江西省八景镇
8. 河南省竹林镇
9. 河南省仓头镇
10. 河南省岸上乡
11. 重庆市三汇镇
12. 重庆市长寿湖镇
13. 重庆市双河镇
14. 四川省友爱镇

（资料整理：廖远涛，雷轩，广州市城市规划勘测设计研究院）

附录6

全国“美丽乡村”首批创建试点名单

为深入贯彻党的十八大精神，加快推进美丽乡村建设，农业部2013年启动了“美丽乡村”创建活动。按照《农业部办公厅关于开展“美丽乡村”创建活动的意见》（农办科〔2013〕10号）和《农业部办公厅关于组织开展“美丽乡村”创建试点申报工作的通知》（农办科〔2013〕30号）的要求，农业部按照规定程序对各省相关主管部门推荐的名单进行了研究，最终确定北京市韩村河村等1100个乡村为全国“美丽乡村”创建试点乡村，并于2013年11月18日公布了试点名单：

北京市

房山区韩村河镇韩村河村、门头沟区妙峰山镇樱桃沟村、通州区于家务乡仇庄村、顺义区马坡镇石家营村、昌平区十三陵镇康陵村、大兴区长子营镇留民营村、怀柔区渤海镇北沟村、平谷区大华山镇挂甲峪村、密云县溪翁庄镇黑山寺村、延庆县千家店镇

天津市

西青区辛口镇水高庄村、精武镇小南河村、北辰区双街镇双街村、武清区大碱厂镇南辛庄村、大孟庄镇蒙村店村、宝坻区八门城镇欢喜庄村、宁河县岳龙镇小闫村、静海县双塘镇西双塘村、大丰堆镇史家庄村、蓟县穿芳峪镇毛家峪村

河北省

石家庄市高新区东佐村、正定县正定镇塔元庄村、赞皇县土门乡秦家庄村、平山县北冶乡黄安村、晋州市周家庄乡第九生产队、唐山市滦南县姚王庄镇李营村、乐亭县胡家坨镇大黑坨村、迁西县汉儿庄乡太阳峪村、遵化市兴旺寨乡何家裕村、秦皇岛市山海关区石河镇望峪村、北戴河区戴河镇西古城村、昌黎县十里铺乡西山场村、邯郸市涉县河南店镇石岗村、磁县陶泉乡南王庄村、永年县姚寨乡西河东堡村、武安市淑村镇白沙村、邢台市巨鹿县西郭城镇河北庄村、威县洺州镇戚霍寨村、沙河市白塔镇栾卸村、保定市易县西山北乡于家庄、博野县南小王乡大北河村、高碑店市辛立庄镇平辛庄村、张家口市张北县油篓沟乡喜顺沟村、蔚县南留庄镇白后堡村、阳原县东城镇东城村、万全县洗马林镇沙地房村、承德市开发区冯营子乡冯营子村、承德县下板城镇朝梁子村、平泉县卧龙镇八家社区、滦平县张百湾镇

周台子村、围场满族蒙古族自治县御道口乡御道口村、河间市故仙乡小故仙村、廊坊市安次区落垡镇邢官营村、广阳区白家务乡兴隆场村、永清县刘街乡土楼胜利村、霸州市南孟镇西粉营村、衡水市枣强县大营镇芍药村、武强县周窝镇周窝村、故城县青罕镇南王庄村

山西省

太原市杏花岭区中涧河乡长沟村、清徐县王答乡北录树村、古交市马兰镇营立村、大同市南郊区口泉乡、阳泉市郊区荫营镇上千亩坪村、平定县锁簧镇前锁簧村、平定县岔口乡甘泉井村、长治市郊区西白兔乡南村、长治县振兴新区振兴村、长治县荫城镇荆圪道村、晋城市阳城县北留镇皇城村、沁水县郑村镇湘峪村、高平市米山镇侯家庄村、朔州市朔城区南榆林乡青钟村、怀仁县马辛庄乡鲁沟村、晋中市榆次区东阳镇庞志村、昔阳县大寨镇大寨村、介休市龙凤镇张壁村、运城市临猗县耽子镇高堆村、闻喜县东镇镇上镇村、绛县横水镇新庄村、夏县庙前镇西村、忻州市定襄县神山乡崔家庄村、岢岚县大涧乡吴家庄村、河曲县文笔镇蚰蜒茆村、临汾市曲沃县史村镇西海村、翼城县南唐乡符册村、吉县东城乡柏东村、吕梁市方山县圪洞镇庄上村、孝义市新义街道办事处贾家庄村

内蒙古自治区

呼和浩特市新城区保合少乡恼包村、赛罕区金河镇根堡村、和林格尔县舍必崖乡小甲赖村、包头市九原区哈业胡同镇、固阳县银号乡银号村、达尔罕茂明安联合旗乌克镇大汗海村、赤峰市元宝山区元宝山镇木头沟村、松山区王府镇敖包村、林西县五十家子镇五十家子村、克什克腾旗热水镇、翁牛特旗乌丹镇赛沁塔拉嘎查、喀喇沁旗王爷府镇、宁城县汐子镇汐子村、通辽市科尔沁区丰田镇建新村、科尔沁左翼中旗舍伯吐镇那仁嘎查、开鲁县东风镇、扎鲁特旗鲁北镇哈日朝鲁嘎查、鄂尔多斯市东胜区罕台镇撖家塔村、准格尔旗十二连城乡五家尧村、鄂托克旗阿尔巴斯苏木赛乌素嘎查、伊金霍洛旗阿勒腾席热镇乌兰木伦村、呼伦贝尔市海拉尔区哈克镇团结村、莫力达瓦达斡尔族自治旗塔温敖宝镇顺斯堤村、额尔古纳市恩和俄罗斯民族乡、阿荣旗音河达斡尔鄂温克民族乡富吉村、巴彦淖尔市临河区双河镇进步村、五原县新公中镇永联村、磴口县沙金套海苏木巴音毛道嘎查、乌拉特前旗西小召镇公田村、杭锦后旗陕坝镇春光村、乌兰察布市凉城县麦胡图镇、丰镇市巨宝庄镇巨宝庄村、兴安盟科尔沁右翼前旗巴拉格歹办事处兴安村、扎赉特旗好力保乡永兴村、突泉县六户镇巨兴村、突泉县东杜尔基镇杜祥村、锡林郭勒盟西乌珠穆沁旗浩勒图高勒镇脑干哈达嘎查、太仆寺旗千斤沟镇后店村、太仆寺旗贡宝拉格苏木道海嘎查、多伦县蔡木山乡一家河村

辽宁省

沈阳市苏家屯区八一街道办事处来胜堡村、东陵区祝家街道办事处田家洼村、棋盘山开发区望滨街道办事处闫家村、辽中县冷子堡镇社甲村、辽中县潘家堡镇蔡伯街村、鞍山市台安县高力房镇乔坨村、岫岩满族自治县新甸镇合顺村、海城市西柳镇、抚顺市抚顺县后安镇佟庄村、新宾满族自治县永陵镇赫图阿拉村、清原满族自治县南口前镇王家堡村、清原满族

自治县南山城镇大北岔村、本溪市本溪满族自治县东营坊乡、桓仁满族自治县五里甸镇老黑山村、丹东市振安区五龙背镇、宽甸满族自治县长甸镇河口村、东港市北井子镇獐岛村、凤城市凤山街道办事处大梨树村、锦州市黑山县段家乡蛇山子村、龙栖湾新区娘娘宫镇祥茂村、北镇市观音阁街道办事处河洼村、营口市盖州市九寨镇九寨村、阜新市阜新蒙古族自治县大固本镇梅力营子村、阜新蒙古族自治县卧凤沟乡公官营子村、彰武县哈尔套镇富有村、辽阳市弓长岭区汤河镇、辽阳县唐马寨镇康明村、盘锦市大洼县新兴镇腰岗子村、大洼县唐家镇北窑村、盘山县胡家镇红岩村、盘山县得胜镇得胜村、铁岭市昌图县三江口镇刘胡村、调兵山市晓南镇锁龙沟村、开原市庆云堡镇兴隆台村、朝阳市朝阳县南双庙乡双庙村、建平县万寿街道办事处小平房村、喀喇沁左翼蒙古族自治县官大海农场、凌源市东城街道办事处辛杖子村、葫芦岛市南票区虹螺岘镇板石沟、绥中县塔山屯镇、建昌县魏家岭乡宁杖子村、建昌县小德营子乡新立屯村

吉林省

长春市朝阳区乐山镇糖坊村、绿园区合心镇岳家村、双阳区齐家镇曙光村、农安县合隆镇陈家店村、九台市苇子沟镇拉拉屯村、九台市纪家镇二十家子村、榆树市大坡镇西山村、榆树市恩育乡红庙村、德惠市米沙子镇太平沟村、吉林市蛟河市新农街道办事处南荒地村、桦甸市桦郊乡友谊村、舒兰市金马镇金马村、舒兰市莲花乡东大村、磐石市松山镇爱耕村、四平市梨树县梨树镇高家村、伊通满族自治县河源镇保南村、公主岭市环岭街道办事处火炬村、双辽市辽东街道办事处勃山村、辽源市东辽县金州乡德志村、通化市东昌区金厂镇、通化县快大茂镇赶马河村、通化县英额布镇、柳河县安口镇烧锅村、集安市榆林镇榆林村、白山市江源区大阳岔镇小洋桥村、抚松县仙人桥镇黄家崴子村、临江市六道沟镇三道阳岔村、松原市宁江区大洼镇房身村、宁江区伯都乡杨家村、扶余市蔡家沟镇珠山村、扶余市弓棚子镇广发村、白城市洮北区平安镇中兴村、洮南市万宝镇新丰村、大安市四棵树乡建设村、延边朝鲜族自治州延吉市朝阳川镇仲坪村、图们市月晴镇水口村、敦化市雁鸣湖镇腰店村、珲春市板石镇孟岭村、和龙市西城镇金达莱村、汪清县汪清镇春和村

黑龙江省

哈尔滨市呼兰区双井街道办事处护路村、阿城区金龙山镇吉兴村、方正县伊汉通乡得莫利村、宾县宾州镇友联村、通河县富林乡德兴村、双城市农丰满族锡伯族镇双利锡伯族村、尚志市元宝镇元宝村、五常市二河乡新庄村、齐齐哈尔市龙江县鲁河乡鲁河村、甘南县兴十四镇兴十四村、克东县克东镇光明村、鸡西市滴道区滴道河乡金铁村、鸡东县鸡林朝鲜族乡鸡林村、密山市白鱼湾镇湖沿村、鹤岗市萝北县太平沟乡太平沟村、双鸭山市友谊县凤岗镇、宝清县宝清镇红新村、大庆市龙凤区龙凤镇向阳村、肇州县二井镇实现新村、肇源县义顺乡东义顺村、林甸县东兴乡旭日村、杜尔伯特蒙古族自治县烟筒屯镇当奈村、伊春市嘉荫县保兴乡互助村、铁力市年丰朝鲜族乡吉松村、佳木斯市东风区建国镇建国村、抚远县乌苏镇赫哲族村、牡丹江市东宁县东宁镇夹信子村、绥芬河市绥芬河镇、宁安市江南朝鲜族满族

乡明星村、穆棱市下城子镇保安新村、黑河市北安区赵光镇东丰村、五大连池市龙镇发展村、绥化市北林区东富乡、望奎县望奎镇红五村、兰西县红光乡红光村、青冈县祯祥镇、安达市卧里屯乡、肇东市肇东镇东跃村、海伦市向荣乡向荣村、大兴安岭地区呼玛县白银纳鄂伦春族民族乡白银纳村

上海市

闵行区浦江镇新风村、宝山区罗店镇天平村、嘉定区华亭镇毛桥村、浦东新区周浦镇棋杆村、书院镇塘北村、金山区廊下镇中华村、松江区泖港镇、青浦区朱家角镇张马村、奉贤区庄行镇新叶村、崇明县横沙乡

江苏省

南京市江宁区谷里街道周村、江宁区横溪街道石塘村、六合区竹镇镇大泉村、溧水区洪蓝镇傅家边村、高淳区桠溪镇蓝溪村、无锡市锡山区东港镇山联村、惠山区阳山镇、江阴市华士镇华西村、江阴市顾山镇红豆村、宜兴市湖㳇镇张阳村、徐州市贾汪区青山泉镇马庄村、丰县华山镇大程庄村、沛县张寨镇陈油坊村、新沂市邵店镇沂北村、常州市武进区雪堰镇雅浦村、金坛市薛埠镇上阮村、苏州市吴中区东山镇三山村、常熟市支塘镇蒋巷村、张家港市南丰镇永联村、昆山市张浦镇姜杭村、吴江区同里镇北联村、太仓市城厢镇东林村、南通市通州区东社镇香台村、海门市海永乡、连云港市赣榆县塔山镇土城村、淮安市淮阴区码头镇码头村、金湖县塔集镇陆河村、盐城市盐都区潘黄街道仰徐村、盐都区郭猛镇杨侍村、东台市梁垛镇临塔村、大丰市大中镇恒北村、扬州市广陵区泰安镇金湾村、仪征市铜山办事处长山村、高邮市菱塘回族乡、镇江市丹徒区世业镇、丹阳市后巷镇前巷村、扬中市新坝镇新治村、句容市后白镇、泰州市姜堰区沈高镇河横村、姜堰区溱潼镇湖南村、泰兴市黄桥镇祁巷村、宿迁市宿豫区顺河镇林苗圃居委会、泗阳县李口镇八堡村

浙江省

杭州市桐庐县江南镇、淳安县文昌镇王家源村、淳安县枫树岭镇下姜村、临安市板桥镇上田村、温州市永嘉县大若岩镇埭头村、永嘉县岩头镇下日川村、文成县西坑畲族镇西坑社区梧溪村、文成县黄坦镇培头村、嘉兴市嘉善县大云镇、嘉善县姚庄镇、海宁市盐官镇桃园村、桐乡市石门镇桂花村、湖州市南浔区和孚镇荻港村、安吉县溪龙乡黄杜村、安吉县山川乡高家堂村、绍兴市绍兴县王坛镇南岸村、绍兴县漓渚镇棠棣村、新昌县澄潭镇坑下村、诸暨市东白湖镇斯宅村、诸暨市东和乡十里坪村、金华市武义县桃溪镇陶村、磐安县尖山镇管头村、义乌市城西街道何斯路村、义乌市佛堂镇桥西村、永康市江南街道园周村、衢州市开化县桐村镇黄石村、开化县音坑乡下淤村、龙游县大街乡贺田村、龙游县沐尘畲族乡沐尘村、江山市贺村镇永兴坞、舟山市定海区干览镇新建村、普陀区展茅街道沙井村、台州市黄岩区头陀镇白湖塘村、黄岩区屿头乡布袋坑村、仙居县淡竹乡石盟垟村、丽水市莲都区大港头镇利山村、遂昌县大柘镇大田村、遂昌县三仁畲族乡坑口村、庆元县屏都街道洋背村、庆元县淤上乡局下村

安徽省

合肥市长丰县水湖镇费岗村、肥西县官亭镇回民社区、庐江县汤池镇果树村、芜湖市繁昌县孙村镇中分村、南陵县大浦村大浦新村、蚌埠市禹会区秦集镇宗洼村、怀远县鲍集镇薛场村、五河县头铺镇八岔村、淮南市潘集区祁集镇陈郢村、凤台县丁集乡张巷社区、马鞍山市当涂县护河镇桃花村、淮北市濉溪县濉溪镇蒙村、铜陵市铜陵县西联乡犁桥村、安庆市怀宁县洪铺镇五桥村、枞阳县会宫镇会官村、潜山县痘姆乡求职村、望江县高士镇童岭村、桐城市范岗镇樟枫村、黄山市屯溪区黎阳镇凤霞村、黄山区甘棠镇庄里村、黄山区新明乡猴坑村、徽州区福溪乡光明村、歙县雄村乡卖花渔村、休宁县海阳镇盐铺村、黟县宏村镇宏村村、黟县西递镇西递村、祁门县渚口镇渚口村、滁州市来安县汊河镇相官村小李庄、全椒县石沛镇黄栗树村、凤阳县小溪河镇小岗村、阜阳市颍东区正午镇田楼居委会、太和县旧县镇张槐村、界首市林场红石桥新村、宿州市埇桥区桃源镇光明村、灵璧县虞姬乡虞姬村、六安市金安区木厂镇新庄村、裕安区苏埠镇南楼村、寿县安丰镇梧桐村、舒城县桃溪镇红光村、金寨县双河镇河西村、亳州市谯城区十河镇大周村、利辛县王人镇曹店村、利辛县永兴镇诸王村、池州市贵池区乌沙镇乌沙社区、石台县矶滩乡沟汀村、宣城市郎溪县凌笪乡钱桥村、宁国市港口镇山门村

福建省

福州市晋安区寿山乡寿山村、闽侯县白沙镇孔元村、连江县潘渡乡贵安村、永泰县嵩口镇月洲村、永泰县塘前乡芋坑村、平潭综合实验区平潭县白青乡国彩村、莆田市城厢区华亭镇涧口村、涵江区白沙镇坪盘村、荔城区西天尾镇后黄村、仙游县园庄镇岭北村、三明市梅列区列西街道小蕉村、将乐县万安镇万安村、泰宁县梅口乡水际村、永安市小陶镇八一村、泉州市安溪县湖头镇山都村、永春县五里街镇高垅村、德化县国宝乡佛岭村、晋江市磁灶镇大埔村、南安市码头镇大庭村、南安市康美镇兰田村、漳州市漳浦县南浦乡后坑村、诏安县梅岭镇田厝村、长泰县马洋溪生态旅游区山重村、平和县文峰镇三坪村、华安县仙都镇大地村、龙海市东园镇东宝村、南平市顺昌县埔上镇张墩村、浦城县富岭镇双同村、建瓯市小松镇湖头村、建阳市潭城街道考亭村、建阳市将口镇芹口村、龙岩市新罗区龙门镇洋畲村、长汀县策武镇南坑村、上杭县古田镇五龙村、连城县宣和乡培田村、漳平市永福镇西山村、宁德市蕉城区金涵乡上金贝村、寿宁县犀溪镇西浦村、福安市赛岐镇狮子头村、福鼎市硖门畲族乡柏洋村

江西省

南昌市江西省蚕桑茶叶研究所凤凰村、南昌县蒋巷镇上村、新建县樵舍镇朱坊村、安义县长均乡观察村、进贤县前坊镇太平村、景德镇市乐平市礼林镇围渡村、萍乡市湘东区麻山镇幸福村、上栗县福田镇战山村、九江市庐山区海会镇、星子县温泉镇、湖口县大垅乡联丰村、彭泽县马当镇船形村、新余市孔目江经济生态区欧里镇昌坊村、仙女湖区九龙山乡、鹰潭市余江县黄庄乡藕塘村、贵溪市雷溪乡、赣州市章贡区沙石镇火燃村、经济技术开发区谭东镇龙井村、上犹县社溪镇沙村、崇义县上堡乡水南村、宁都县田埠乡东龙村、于都县靖石

乡黄沙村、兴国县方太乡宝石村、南康市横市镇增坑村、吉安市吉州区兴桥镇钓源村、青原区富滩镇张家渡村、吉安县横江镇濠云村、峡江县水边镇湖洲村、泰和县马市镇蜀口村、永新县高溪乡大塘村、井冈山市厦坪镇菖蒲村、宜春市袁州区竹亭镇南池村、奉新县甘坊镇横桥村、上高县塔下乡田北村、靖安县香田乡石马村、丰城市董家镇付家村、抚州市黎川县日峰镇永兴桥村、宜黄县棠阴镇民主村、金溪县秀谷缜先锋村、上饶市三清山风景名胜区三清乡上西坑村、玉山县怀玉乡玉峰村、铅山县武夷山镇、横峰县红桥垦殖场白沙岭分场、婺源县江湾镇、婺源县大鄣山乡通源村

山东省

济南市历城区西营镇藕池村、长清区双泉镇、商河县贾庄镇南庞村、章丘市宁家埠镇向高村、淄博市淄川区双杨镇藏梓村、博山区山头街道乐疃村、临淄区金山镇东崖村、高青县常家镇樊家村、枣庄市峄城区榴园镇北孙庄村、山亭区城头镇西城头村、滕州市洪绪镇龙庄村、东营市东营区龙居镇、垦利县垦利街道左一村、广饶县李鹊镇、烟台市莱阳市姜疃镇濯村、莱州市金仓街道、蓬莱市刘家沟镇马家沟村、栖霞市桃村镇国路夼村、潍坊市临朐县城关街道东朱封村、青州市何官镇南张楼村、寿光市孙家集镇岳寺高村、寿光市双王城生态经济园区、济宁市微山县西平乡西平村、泗水县泗张镇王家庄村、曲阜市小雪街道武家村、泰安市岱岳区天平街道大陡山村、岱岳区满庄镇滩清湾村、宁阳县鹤山乡、新泰市龙廷镇掌平洼村、威海市文登市界石镇、荣成市寻山街道青鱼滩村、荣成市成山镇西霞口村、乳山市冯家镇唐家店子村、日照市东港区西湖镇竖旗岭村、莱芜市莱城区大王庄镇竹园子村、临沂市沂水县泉庄镇、沂水县院东头镇、苍山县卞庄街道代村、莒南县洙边镇、蒙阴县野店镇毛坪村、临沭县曹庄镇朱村、德州市德城区黄河涯镇、齐河县刘桥乡洪州社区、乐陵市黄夹镇梁锥希森新村、聊城市东昌府区湖西办事处姜堤村、冠县兰沃乡韩路村、高唐县清平镇、临清市松林镇亢庙村、滨州市沾化县富国街道西刘村、博兴县湖滨镇柳桥村、邹平县韩店镇西王村、菏泽市牡丹区马岭岗镇穆李村、东明县武胜桥镇玉皇新村

河南省

郑州市二七区侯寨乡、巩义市小关镇水道口村、巩义市大峪沟镇民权村、荥阳市环翠峪管委会二郎庙村、新密市超化镇黄固寺村、开封市开封县朱仙镇、洛阳市孟津县平乐镇平乐村、孟津县送庄镇梁凹村、栾川县庙子镇庄子村、伊川县彭婆镇许营村、平顶山市汝州市庙下镇小寨村、宝丰县赵庄乡袁庄村、安阳市龙安区龙泉镇、安阳县永和乡西街村、滑县留固镇温庄村、鹤壁市淇县北阳镇卧羊湾村、新乡市新乡县七里营镇刘庄村、新乡县合河乡前村村、卫辉市顿坊店乡比干社区、辉县市上八里镇松树坪村、焦作市修武县岸上乡岸上村、博爱县金城乡西金城村、济源市承留镇卫佛安村、许昌市禹州市磨街乡玉泉村、濮阳市濮阳县五星乡安寨村、漯河市舞阳县莲花镇半李村、临颍县杜曲镇北徐庄村、三门峡市灵宝市大王镇后地村、灵宝市焦村镇杨家村、卢氏县文峪乡庙沟村、南阳市宛城区瓦店镇逵营村、西峡县丹水镇谭沟村、内乡县余关乡黄楝村、邓州市穰东镇穰西社区、商丘市民权县龙塘镇吴堂

村、虞城县张集镇林堂村、永城市芒山镇柿园村、信阳市平桥区五里店街道办事处郝堂村、新县香山湖管理区水塝村、商城县伏山乡里罗城村、固始县方集镇小畈村、周口市扶沟县韭园镇湾赵村、沈丘县冯营乡李寨村、淮阳县葛店乡朱庄村、驻马店市确山县竹沟镇鲍棚村、遂平县槐树乡李兴楼村

湖北省

武汉市东西湖区东山办事处内燃村、蔡甸区奓山街道星光村、江夏区法泗街大路村、黄石市阳新县兴国镇宝塔村、十堰市张湾区西沟乡相公村、郧县茶店镇樱桃沟村、竹山县麻家渡镇罗家坡村、丹江口市官山镇吕家河村、宜昌市兴山县峡口镇普安村、秭归县水田坝乡王家桥村、宜都市五眼泉乡鸡头山村、枝江市问安镇关庙山村、襄阳市南漳县巡检镇峡口村、谷城县五山镇堰河村、鄂州市鄂城区长港镇峒山村、荆门市京山县孙桥镇沙岭湾村、沙洋县高阳镇歇张村、钟祥市石牌镇彭墩村、孝感市云梦县城关镇西王村、安陆市棠棣镇李园村、汉川市庙头镇中心村、荆州市监利县朱河镇花园村、石首市桃花山镇李花山村、洪湖市瞿家湾镇、松滋市斯家场镇万年桥村、黄冈市团风县团风镇黄湖郧阳村、罗田县九资河镇圣仁堂村、英山县温泉镇百丈河村、浠水县兰溪镇盐客树村、蕲春县张榜镇下车门村咸宁市咸安区双溪桥镇九彬村、嘉鱼县官桥镇官桥村、崇阳县白义镇油市村、赤壁市沧湖开发区普安村、随州市曾都区南郊办事处椅子山村、广水市武胜关镇桃源村、恩施土家族苗族自治州恩施市芭蕉侗族乡戽口村、利川市毛坝乡夹壁村、宣恩县高罗镇板寮村、咸丰县黄金洞乡麻柳溪村、来凤县三胡乡黄柏园村、仙桃市三伏潭镇栗林嘴村、潜江市园林办事处工农村、天门市天门市岳口镇健康村、神农架林区松柏镇八角庙村委会

湖南省

长沙市望城区靖港镇、望城区格塘镇杨家山村、长沙县福临镇金坑桥村、长沙县开慧镇、宁乡县金洲镇关山社区、浏阳市北盛镇马战村、株洲市茶陵县下东乡黄堂村、炎陵县霞阳镇山垅村、醴陵市浦口镇贯古村、湘潭市雨湖区姜畲镇梅花村、湘乡市东山街道办事处张江村、韶山市韶山村、衡阳市南岳区拜殿乡拜殿村、衡阳县金兰镇金沙村、衡山县白果镇涓水村、邵阳市邵东县堡面前乡大羊村、新邵县寸石镇龙竹村、隆回县虎形山瑶族乡、岳阳市华容县护城乡五星村、平江县园艺场园艺村、汨罗市白水镇西长村、常德市汉寿县岩汪湖镇岩汪湖村、桃源县茶庵铺镇茶庵铺村、桃源县马鬃岭镇木槎桥村、石门县秀坪园艺场、津市市灵泉镇、贺家山原种场大洲分场、张家界市永定区王家坪镇石堰坪村、武陵源区天子山镇泗南峪居委会、桑植县洪家关白族乡实竹坪村、益阳市赫山区八字哨镇金家堤村、高新区谢林港镇清溪村、南县青树嘴镇四美村、南县浪拔湖镇南红村、沅江市三眼塘镇荷花村、郴州市北湖区华塘镇三合村、苏仙区望仙镇和平村、桂阳县黄沙坪街道办事处沙坪村、汝城县土桥镇黄家村、永州市冷水滩区伊塘镇、祁阳县下马渡镇栗山村、蓝山县新圩镇上清涵村、怀化市鹤城区黄岩管理处白马村、会同县青朗乡客寨村、芷江侗族自治县木叶溪乡小渔溪村、靖州苗族侗族自治县寨牙乡大林村、娄底市双峰县甘棠镇盐井村、新化县奉家镇下团村、涟

源市杨市镇、湘西土家族苗族自治州凤凰县管庄乡大湾村、花垣县麻栗场镇立新村、永顺县高坪乡西米村、龙山县苗儿滩镇捞车河村

广东省

广州市番禺区南村镇坑头村、花都区梯面镇红山村、南沙区横沥镇冯马三村、萝岗区九龙镇洋田村、增城市正果镇黄屋村、韶关市乳源瑶族自治县游溪镇八一瑶族新村、珠海市斗门区连洲镇连江村、斗门区斗门镇南门村、金湾区平沙镇平塘社区、万山区担杠镇外伶仃洋村、汕头市潮阳区和平镇合浦社区、潮南区陇田镇东华村、南澳县深澳镇后花园村、佛山市南海区九江镇烟南村、江门市鹤山市鹤城镇五星村、湛江市徐闻县曲界镇龙门村、吴川市黄陂镇水潭村、茂名市茂南区镇盛镇彭村、肇庆市德庆县官圩镇金林村、惠州市惠阳区平潭镇阳光村、梅州市梅县松口镇大黄村、梅县南口镇桥乡村、大埔县百侯镇侯南村、蕉岭县三圳镇、汕尾市陆河县螺溪镇螺溪村、河源市连平县坡头镇、阳江市阳春市合水镇平北村、中山市三乡镇古鹤村、揭阳市揭西县京溪园镇粗坑村、云浮市郁南县连滩镇兰寨村

广西壮族自治区

柳州市融水苗族自治县融水镇新国村古选屯、三江侗族自治县丹洲镇丹洲村、桂林市兴安县严关镇杉树村委马头山村、永福县百寿镇瓦瑶生态园、灌阳县黄关镇龙吟村毛栗坪屯、龙胜各族自治县和平乡龙脊村、恭城瑶族自治县莲花镇竹山村委红岩村、平乐县桥亭乡显堆村委大塘口自然村、荔浦县东昌镇东阳村扒齿屯、梧州市苍梧县梨埠镇沙地村、藤县和平镇座洞村、岑溪市归义镇荔枝村、北海市合浦县廉州镇马江村、防城港市东兴市东兴镇竹山村、钦州市钦南区康熙岭镇高沙村、玉林市福绵管理区沙田镇六龙村、陆川县沙坡镇高庆村、兴业县葵阳镇四新村、北流市民乐镇罗政村、百色市田阳县百育镇四那村那生屯、田东县祥周镇中平村、平果县果化镇龙色村龙东屯、靖西县新甲乡新荣村古风屯、西林县普合苗族乡新丰村、贺州市八步区贺街镇西南村新兴寨、昭平县文竹镇桂花村、钟山县钟山镇榕马村、富川瑶族自治县朝东镇秀水村、河池市宜州市屏南乡合寨村果地屯、来宾市兴宾区凤凰镇龙岩村委长福村、忻城县城关镇板河村内城屯、象州县象州镇石里村、武宣县东乡镇河马村委下莲塘村、金秀瑶族自治县三江乡古范村、崇左市扶绥县渠旧镇濑滤村、大新县雷平镇新立村、凭祥市新鸣村板小屯

海南省

海口市琼山区三门坡镇龙鳞村、三亚市市辖区凤凰镇槟榔村、三亚市市辖区吉阳镇南丁村、五指山市毛阳镇毛贵村、南圣镇红合村、琼海市潭门镇、博鳌镇朝烈村、儋州市那大镇石屋村、和庆镇美万新村、文昌市东路镇永丰村、万宁市长丰镇文通村、东方市大田镇报白村、定安县定城镇水冲坡村委会、龙湖镇桐树村、屯昌县屯城镇后久塘村、乌坡镇冯宅村、澄迈县金江镇龙坡村委会、老城镇罗驿村、福山镇敦茶村、临高县调楼镇洋林下村、白沙黎族自治县福门镇老周三村、元门乡罗帅村、乐东黎族自治县佛罗镇丹村、陵水黎族自治县光坡镇旺村

重庆市

万州区太安镇凤凰村、涪陵区南沱镇连丰村、沙坪坝区曾家镇虎峰山村、北碚区金刀峡镇胜天湖村、万盛经济开发区万东镇五和村、巴南区二圣镇集体村、渝北区统景镇印盒村、黔江区小南海镇新建村、长寿区石堰镇麒麟村、江津区吴滩镇郎家村、合川区涞滩镇、永川区南大街办事处黄瓜山村、南川区木凉乡汉场坝村、綦江区永城镇复兴村、潼南县崇龛镇临江村、铜梁县南城街道鱼溅村、大足区宝顶镇倒庙村、荣昌县古昌镇玉带村、璧山县正兴镇卫寺村、梁平县合兴镇龙滩村、城口县岚天乡岚溪村、河鱼乡、丰都县江池镇横梁村、垫江县太平镇牡丹村、武隆县仙女山镇、忠县拔山镇杨柳村、开县南门镇莲池村、云阳县清水土家族乡清水村、奉节县兴隆镇三桥村、巫山县官渡镇杨坝村、骡坪镇茶园村、巫溪县尖山镇大包村、石柱土家族自治县黄水镇万胜坝村、秀山土家族苗族自治县孝溪乡檬子村、酉阳土家族苗族自治县黑水镇大泉村、彭水苗族土家族自治县润溪乡白果村

四川省

成都市温江区和盛镇友庆社区、双流县彭镇羊坪社区、郫县友爱镇农科村、新津县文井乡李柏村、都江堰市虹口乡高原村、自贡市自流井区农团乡东升村、沿滩区黄市镇红旗村、攀枝花市米易县普威镇独树村、泸州市江阳区华阳街道西岸村、泸县福集镇龙桥文化生态园、德阳市旌阳区新中镇龙居村、罗江县慧觉镇黄荆村、广汉市连山镇锦花村、绵竹市遵道镇棚花村、绵阳市涪城区杨家镇团阳寺村、安县花荄镇联丰村、江油市新安镇黑滩村、广元市利州区龙潭乡建设村、昭化区紫云乡紫云村、苍溪县石门乡文家角村、遂宁市船山区唐家乡东山村、射洪县沱牌镇百战村、内江市市中区永安镇太平寺村、乐山市市中区土主镇铁牛村、井研县集益乡繁荣村、南充市南部县火峰乡化林村、营山县东升镇玉帝村、西充县凤鸣镇双龙桥村、眉山市东坡区白马镇龚村、丹棱县双桥镇梅湾村、青神县白果乡甘家沟村、宜宾市珙县巡场镇箐林村、广安市广安区大龙乡果坝村、华蓥市阳和镇祝家坝村、达州市开江县甘棠镇龙井坝村、大竹县庙坝镇长乐村、雅安市雨城区中里镇张沟村、汉源县双溪乡申沟村、巴中市巴州区清江镇巾字村、通江县沙溪镇王坪村、平昌县驷马镇元峰村、资阳市雁江区碑记镇半月村、简阳市贾家镇菠萝村、阿坝藏族羌族自治州汶川县三江镇河坝村、甘孜藏族自治州丹巴县格什扎乡布科村、凉山彝族自治州西昌市西乡凤凰村

贵州省

贵阳市花溪区青岩镇龙井村、乌当区新堡乡马头村、白云区牛场乡蓬莱村、观山湖区百花湖乡石操村、开阳县南江乡龙广村、开阳县禾丰乡马头村、清镇市红枫湖镇大冲村、六盘水市水城县米箩镇倮么村、盘县普古乡舍烹村、遵义市红花岗区深溪镇高坊村、绥阳县温泉镇双河村、道真仡佬族苗族自治县隆兴镇浣溪村、务川仡佬族苗族自治县大坪镇龙潭村、湄潭县湄江镇核桃坝村、余庆县白泥镇、习水县大坡乡笼灯村、安顺市西秀区大西桥镇鲍屯村、平坝县天龙镇天龙村、镇宁布依族苗族自治县大山镇大寨村、黄果树风景名胜区黄果树镇石头寨村、铜仁市江口县太平乡云舍村、印江土家族苗族自治县朗溪镇河西村、石阡县坪

山乡尧上村、松桃苗族自治县正大乡苗王城村、黔西南布依族苗族自治州兴义市万峰林街道办事处、兴义市郑屯镇民族村、兴仁县屯脚镇鲤鱼坝村、毕节市七星关区青场镇青坝村、大方县羊场镇桶井村、金沙县岩孔镇板桥村、织金县熊家场乡白马村、黔东南苗族侗族自治州施秉县牛大场镇牛大场村、三穗县台烈镇寨头村、剑河县岑松镇温泉村、黎平县茅贡乡地扪村、雷山县西江镇西江村、黔南布依族苗族自治州荔波县玉屏社区福利村、贵定县盘江镇音寨村、罗甸县董当乡大井村、龙里县羊场镇走马村、龙里县湾寨乡场坝村

云南省

昆明市西山区团结街道办事处和平社区、禄劝彝族苗族自治县翠华镇兴隆村、曲靖市麒麟区沿江乡庄家圩社区、会泽县金钟镇乌龙村、玉溪市通海县秀山街道办事处大树社区、保山市隆阳区板桥镇北汉庄村、腾冲县界头镇、昭通市昭阳区永丰镇三甲村、盐津县中和镇清河社区、丽江市古城区七河镇共和村、宁蒗彝族自治县永宁乡落水村、玉龙纳西族自治县拉市镇、普洱市澜沧县惠民镇景迈村、西盟县勐卡镇马散村、临沧市沧源佤族自治县勐角乡翁丁村、楚雄彝族自治州永仁县永定镇太平地村、武定县狮山镇狮山村委会、红河哈尼族彝族自治州建水县西庄镇团山村、石屏县宝秀镇郑营村、弥勒市西三镇可邑村、文山壮族苗族自治州砚山县干河彝族乡马鞍山村、马关县仁和镇阿峨新寨村、西双版纳傣族自治州景洪市勐罕镇曼听村、大理白族自治州大理市大理镇龙龛村龙下登村、漾濞彝族自治县苍山西镇光明村、德宏傣族景颇族自治州瑞丽市勐卯镇姐东村喊沙村、芒市风平镇法帕村、怒江傈僳族自治州泸水县鲁掌镇三河村、迪庆藏族自治州维西傈僳族自治县塔城镇

西藏自治区

拉萨市尼木县吞巴乡、曲水县南木乡、曲水县才纳乡才纳村、堆龙德庆县羊达乡通嘎村、达孜县邦堆乡林阿村、昌都地区类乌齐县桑多镇恩达村、边坝县草卡镇苏东行政村、山南地区乃东县泽当镇金鲁居委会、扎囊县扎塘镇羊噶居委会、贡嘎县吉雄镇扎庆社区、日喀则地区日喀则市聂日雄乡、南木林县艾玛乡恰热村、江孜县江孜镇东郊村、拉孜县曲下镇吉如村、那曲地区聂荣县色庆乡帕玉村、林芝地区林芝县鲁朗镇扎西岗村、工布江达县巴河镇东玛村、波密县倾多镇热西村、察隅县古玉乡罗马村

陕西省

西安市阎良区新兴街道办井家村、蓝田县焦岱镇鲍旗寨村、周至县楼观镇周一村、户县甘亭镇东韩村、铜川市耀州区锦阳路街道办事处水峪村、耀州区董家河镇王家砭村、宝鸡市凤翔县城关镇周家门前村、眉县金渠镇田家寨村、太白县黄柏塬镇、咸阳市杨凌区五泉镇斜上村、泾阳县三渠镇挡驾桥村、彬县太峪镇、淳化县石桥镇咀头村、渭南市临渭区官道镇武赵村、大荔县埝桥镇黄营村、澄城县王庄镇水洼村、富平县庄里镇王庄村、延安市子长县杨家园则镇、吴起县铁边城镇铁边城村、汉中市汉台区铺镇狮子村、城固县桔园镇刘家营村、勉县勉阳镇黄家沟村、留坝县武关驿镇河口村、榆林市靖边县红墩界镇尔德井村、佳县坑镇

赤牛村、安康市汉阴县城关镇五一村、平利县长安镇、旬阳县石门镇、商洛市丹凤县棣花镇万湾村、商南县城关镇任家沟村、山阳县漫川关镇

甘肃省

兰州市永登县武胜驿镇、皋兰县什川镇、榆中县来紫堡乡冯湾村、金昌市金川区宁远堡镇中牌村、金川区双湾镇、永昌县城关镇金川东村、白银市白银区水川镇桦皮川村、景泰县中泉乡龙湾村、天水市麦积区伯阳镇曹石村、武山县马力镇北顺村、武威市凉州区黄羊镇上庄村、民勤县三雷镇中陶村、天祝藏族自治县天堂镇天堂村、张掖市甘州区长安乡前进村、山丹县位奇镇芦堡村、平凉市灵台县西屯乡店子村、庄浪县南湖镇石阳村、酒泉市肃州区银达镇、玉门市赤金镇、庆阳市庆城县玄马镇孔桥村、华池县南梁镇、定西市安定区青岚山乡大坪村、陇西县首阳镇首阳村、临洮县八里铺镇王家大庄村、漳县四族乡牙里村、陇南市武都区马街镇姜家山村、两当县张家乡、临夏回族自治州永靖县太极镇大川村、广河县庄窠集镇大庄村、和政县三十里铺镇三十里铺村

青海省

西宁市大通县东峡镇元墩子村、大通县景阳镇小寨村、大通县景阳镇土关村、湟源县日月乡山根村、湟源县日月乡日月山村、湟源县和平乡小高陵村、湟中县共和镇苏吉尔村、湟中县拦隆口镇班仲营村、湟中县李家山镇新添堡村、海东地区民和回族土族自治县马场垣乡翠泉村、民和回族土族自治县马场垣乡下川口村、乐都县瞿昙镇官隆湾村、乐都县蒲台乡李家台村、互助土族自治县丹麻镇松德村、互助土族自治县塘川镇高羌村、互助土族自治县东沟乡大庄村、海北藏族自治州门源县泉口镇大庄村、门源县东川镇孔家庄村、门源县珠固乡东旭村、贵德县河西镇格尔家村、贵德县尕让乡松巴村

宁夏回族自治区

银川市金凤区良田镇和顺新村、灵武市郝家桥镇王家嘴村、石嘴山市惠农区燕子墩乡路家营村、平罗县陶乐镇王家庄村、吴忠市利通区扁担沟镇同利村、利通区金积镇秦坝关村、同心县丁塘镇新华村、同心县王团镇沟南村、青铜峡市叶盛镇、青铜峡市瞿靖镇瞿靖村、固原市隆德县城关镇杨店村、隆德县神林乡辛平村、隆德县沙塘镇清泉村、彭阳县古城镇皇甫村、彭阳县新集乡团结村、彭阳县城阳乡杨坪村、中卫市沙坡头区迎水桥镇夹道村、沙坡头区柔远镇冯庄村、中宁县石空镇太平村、中宁县大战场镇宁原村

新疆维吾尔自治区

乌鲁木齐市乌鲁木齐县水西沟镇、吐鲁番地区吐鲁番市亚尔乡、鄯善县连木沁镇巴扎村、鄯善县东巴扎乡、哈密地区伊吾县苇子峡乡沙依巴克恰村、昌吉回族自治州昌吉市佃坝乡二畦村、玛纳斯县乐土驿镇、玛纳斯县旱卡子滩乡加尔苏瓦提村、博尔塔拉蒙古自治州博乐市贝林哈日莫敦乡、精河县茫丁乡、巴音郭楞蒙古自治州且末县阿热勒乡、克孜勒苏柯尔

克孜自治州阿图什市阿扎克乡、阿克苏地区阿克苏市良种场托万克乔格达勒村、新和县依其艾日克乡加依村、喀什地区麦盖提县央塔克乡跃进村、和田地区和田县拉依喀乡库木艾日克村、墨玉县喀尔赛乡赛先巴扎村、于田县奥依托格拉克乡兰干吾斯塘村、伊犁哈萨克自治州伊宁县阿热吾斯塘乡古库热提曼村、霍城县芦草沟镇四宫村、特克斯县喀拉达拉镇琼库什台村、塔城地区沙湾县大泉乡三道沟村、阿勒泰地区布尔津县杜来提乡

大连市

旅顺口区铁山街道王家村、长海县獐子岛镇、瓦房店市许屯镇东马屯村、普兰店市石河街道石河村、庄河市光明山镇小营村

青岛市

崂山区王哥庄街道青山社区、城阳区城阳街道后田社区、开发区灵珠山街道办事处、平度市南村镇姜家埠村、即墨市龙山街道办事处石源村

宁波市

象山县石浦镇、奉化市萧王庙街道滕头村、镇海区庄市街道光明村、鄞州区下应街道湾底村、余姚市泗门镇

厦门市

同安区洪塘镇郭山村、同安区莲花镇军营村、翔安区新圩镇

新疆生产建设兵团

农一师十团、农三师四十八团、农六师一零五团、农六师共青团农场、农八师石河子总场北泉镇

黑龙江农垦总局

宝泉岭管理局普阳农场、红兴隆管理局红旗岭农场、建三江管理局七星农场、牡丹江管理局八五七农场、牡丹江管理局海林农场、北安管理局尾山农场、九三管理局鹤山农场、齐齐哈尔管理局富裕牧场第二管理区

广东农垦总局

茂名农垦局建设农场9队、阳江农垦局平岗农场、湛江农垦局华海糖业发展有限公司勇士12队

（资料整理：廖远涛，雷轩，广州市城市规划勘测设计研究院）

附录 7

中国城市幸福感调查推选活动资料（2007－2014）

一、中国城市幸福感调查推选活动概况

中国城市幸福感调查推选活动是由新华社《瞭望东方周刊》、中国市长协会《中国城市发展报告》联合主办，自 2007 年至今已连续成功举办八年。活动采用《瞭望东方周刊》在多年调查研究分析的基础上研发的我国首个城市幸福感评价体系，通过公众调查及城市材料申报的方式对居住在城市的人们幸福感进行调查。活动旨在全面检测中国城市幸福感以及城市科学发展与和谐社会建设成果，展现民众的幸福生活。活动推选幸福城市典范，推介幸福案例。活动凭借其公正性、权威性、广泛性已成为中国最具影响力的活动之一，当选城市的形象得到了进一步的提升。这项活动成为新华社品牌活动之一。

二、历年中国城市幸福感调查推选活动介绍及特色

（一）2007－2008 年

当一个国家中的大部分人尚未解决温饱问题的时候，发展经济无疑会提高人的生存率和幸福感；而当经济发展到一定程度之后，经济与幸福的关联度就会减弱。

100 年前，世界上最大的城市是伦敦，那时的伦敦有 650 万人口。但 100 年后的 2007 年，这个数字仅仅相当于东京的 1/4。联合国有统计数字表明，截至 2006 年年底，生活在城市和乡村的居民一样多……每座城市都以自己独特的美丽紧紧吸引了城外的人。城里的人，城外的人，他们对于城市有什么样的感受，城市的哪些方面拨动了人们心底最深处的幸福神经呢？带着这些疑问与思考，新华社《瞭望东方周刊》与中国市长协会《中国城市发展报告》开展了旨在了解我国各主要城市居民的幸福感状况的调查活动——“中国最具幸福感城市调查推选活动”。

活动采用美国芝加哥大学商学院教授奚恺元的幸福学评价体系，采用入户调查、网络调

查、报纸调查等方式，2007年和2008年候选城市分别为35座和50座，调查内容涉及自然环境、交通状况、发展速度、文明程度、赚钱机会、医疗卫生水平、教育水平、房价、人情味、治安状况、就业环境、生活便利12个具体指标。

（二）2009-2012年

2009年是新中国成立60周年，为了更全面细致地了解人们对于幸福城市的理解和感受，本次调查活动所涉及的城市范围更广泛，将县级市也纳入进来。同时考虑到副省级/地级市和县级市在经济、人口等因素上的差别，对它们进行分析研究比较。活动组委会最终确定候选城市为50座副省级城市/地级市和50座县级市，通过60多万人的独立入户调查，全国报纸、手机短信、网络问卷等累计近3000万人的参与，最终20座城市（10座地级以上城市和10座县级城市）脱颖而出，获得“2009年中国最具幸福感城市”称号，另设了“建国六十年特别大奖”。本次调查，也是多年幸福城市调查活动中，首次加入了对县级市的调查，让县级市的经济发展与幸福程度首次进入大众的视线范围。

在首次加入县级市调查之后，2010年，活动组委会进一步加大了对县级城市的调查力度，并且扩大了调查范围，将候选城市锁定在120座城市当中，其中60座地级以上城市，60座县级城市，紧接着2011年候选城市继续增加为地级以上城市66座，县级城市52座。自2009年到2012年的幸福感城市，调查的城市范围始终锁定地级以上城市以及县级城市，并将更多的关注点放在了县级城市的发展与幸福程度上，不仅丰富了活动，也给民众一个不一样的视角，让读者感受到了更多丰富多彩、更加生动鲜活的幸福城市。

（三）2013-2014年

2013年，这一年幸福城市活动已连续成功举办了七届，进入第八个年度。城镇化过程是人民共享发展和改革成果的过程，城镇化的核心是人，让城市居民来评价城市，也是最具幸福感城市一贯秉承的宗旨。城市形象既是城市软实力的重要体现，也是国家形象、国家软实力的重要组成部分。新的时代主旋律昭示了城市的重要性。这一年我们将眼光投向了城市的软实力，突出了“中国形象”这一主题。本次调查候选城市为50座地级以上城市，调查内容为“中国城市形象+幸福感调查活动”，调查依据复旦大学国际公共关系研究中心研制的中国城市形象评价体系，首次对中国城市形象进行评价。

2014年幸福城市推选活动与中国城市文化软实力评价活动同时进行，最终产生了2014“中国最具幸福感城市”“中国最具文化软实力城市”。为了突出“中国文化·影响世界”这一主题，组委会广泛吸取国内外专家学者意见，特别制定了“中国城市幸福感、文化软实力评价体系”，涵盖城市文化魅力、城市文化活力、城市文化实力、城市文化传播力、城市形象、城市幸福感六大体系70个指标。

表1 2014中国城市系列调查评价指标体系（文化软实力、幸福感）

一级指标		二级指标	三级指标
一	城市文化魅力 释义:文化吸引力 设置奖项:最具文化魅力城市	传统文化	国家级重点文物保护单位数
			国家级非文物文化遗产数
		特色文化	你觉得你们城市文化有特色吗
		文化休闲娱乐生活	你觉得你们城市文化生活丰富吗
		文化吸引力	全年接待入境游客总人数
		文化凝聚力	你对所在城市的归属感强吗
二	城市文化活力 释义:文化创新力 设置奖项:最具文化活力城市	文化产业规模	人均文化产业增加值(元/人)
			文化产业增加值占GDP的比重
			文化创意产业增长率
		文化品牌	国家级文化(创意)产业基地(园区)数量
			文化(创意)产业上市公司数量
			国家级文化艺术大师数量
		文化创新	你认为所在城市的文化创新能力强吗
			文化(事业)产业投入占财政支出比例
		文化现象	是否有影响甚至引领全国乃至世界的文化现象
三	城市文化实力 释义:文化基础 奖项:最具文化实力城市	文化设施	公共图书馆数量
			公共博物馆数量
		文化教育	人均教育经费
			义务教育师生比
		市民文化素质	每万人口大学生人数
			市民文化素质
			你觉得所在城市的文化实力强吗
四	城市文化传播力 奖项:最具文化传播力城市	传播能力	百万人口拥有电视频道数量
			百万人口拥有广播频道数量
		传播投入	外宣经费占财政支出比
		传播渠道和平台	常设性的对外文化交流活动数量
五	城市形象 奖项:城市形象最佳城市	国际形象	你认为你的城市国际化程度高吗
			友好城市数量
		国内形象	城市形象知名度
			城市形象美誉度
			获得国家级城市称号数
六	城市幸福感 奖项:最具幸福感城市	城市幸福程度	(沿用原来的评价指标)

(四) 小结

从活动开办至今，每年活动都以不同的主题，给读者和城市管理者一个了解自己城市的切入点，同时也让城市通过不同的活动主题，展示出城市不一样的闪光点。

2007 年：“幸福更青睐哪些城市?”

2008 年：“改革开放三十年，哪些城市的居民更觉得幸福?”

2009 年：“60 年辉煌 · 60 年幸福”

2010 年：“创造幸福 · 享受尊严”

2011 年：“幸福民生 · 和谐中国”

2012 年：“民生幸福 · 成就中国”

2013 年：“美丽中国 · 幸福民生”

2014 年：“中国文化 · 影响世界”

一系列主题的背后，是城市各个角度幸福感的表现，也是活动组委会多年来对于城市幸福感研究中的多种解读与关注点。每一个方面都是建设幸福城市不可或缺的元素，又是值得我们特别关注的。

三、城市幸福感体系与释义

此次调查活动使用《瞭望东方周刊》城市幸福感测评中心的中国城市幸福感评价体系。该体系共 22 个指标，是《瞭望东方周刊》邀请国内外专家经过 8 年的理论与实践，研发而成的，是目前我国最具影响力和权威性的城市幸福感评价体系。

表 2　中国城市幸福感评价体系

序号	指　标	指标释义
1	住房现状	受访者对当地住房现状感到的幸福程度
2	物价(含房价)	受访者对当地含房价的物价感到的幸福程度
3	交通状况	受访者对当地整体交通状况感到的幸福程度
4	气候	受访者对当地的气温及天气舒适度感到的幸福程度
5	医疗便利程度和质量	受访者对当地医疗的便利程度和质量感到的幸福程度
6	环境和污染程度	受访者对当地的空气、水质及道路干净程度等感到的幸福程度,对当地的绿化、山水等感到的幸福程度
7	治安	受访者对当地整体的治安状况感到的幸福程度
8	养老	受访者对当地养老状况感到的幸福程度
9	人情味	受访者对当地人情味浓厚感到的幸福程度
10	餐饮娱乐和文化、体育设施	受访者对当地文化体育设施等感到的幸福程度,对当地的餐饮设计以及娱乐设施的便利感到的幸福程度
11	生活节奏	受访者对当地的生活节奏感到的幸福程度
12	文明程度	受访者对当地居民整体文明程度感到的幸福程度

续表 2

序号	指　标	指标释义
13	执法规范程度	受访者对当地执法文明程度感到的幸福程度
14	公共服务水平	受访者对当地公共服务质量感到的幸福程度
15	文化底蕴	受访者对当地的历史、传统等感到的幸福程度
16	购物便利性	受访者对当地购买各种生活相关产品的便利程度感到的幸福程度
17	赚钱机会	受访者对当地就业机会与赚钱机会感到的幸福程度
18	市民个人发展空间	受访者对个人发展感到的幸福程度
19	城市发展质量与速度	受访者对当地的发展和速度等感到的幸福程度
20	教育	受访者对当地学校质量、教学质量等感到的幸福程度
21	对外来人的包容度	受访者对外来人口感到的幸福程度
22	旅游度假	受访者旅游度假感到的幸福程度

四、调查方式

入户调查、电话调查、网络调查、材料申报。

各环节占总分比重分别为：

入户调查、电话调查占 60%；

网络调查占 10%；

材料申报占 30%。

五、回顾与总结

（一）2007－2014 年获奖城市（地级及以上城市）

表 3　历届获奖地级及以上城市（2007-2014）

序号	城市名	获奖年份	奖项	总获奖年数
1	杭州	2007	中国最具幸福感城市	8
		2008	中国最具幸福感城市	
		2009	建国六十年特别大奖	
		2010	最高荣誉奖——民生贡献大奖	
		2011	五周年特别荣誉大奖	
		2012	中国最美幸福城市最高荣誉大奖	
		2013	中国最具幸福感城市	
			中国形象最佳城市	
		2014	中国最具幸福感城市	
			中国最具文化软实力城市	

续表 3

序号	城市名	获奖年份	奖项	总获奖年数
2	成都	2007	中国最具幸福感城市	8
		2008	无	
		2009	建国六十年特别大奖	
		2010	最高荣誉奖——民生贡献大奖	
		2011	五周年特别荣誉大奖	
		2012	中国最美幸福城市最高荣誉大奖	
		2013	中国最具幸福感城市	
			中国形象最佳城市	
		2014	中国最具幸福感城市	
			中国最具文化软实力城市	
3	长沙	2007	无	7
		2008	中国最具幸福感城市	
		2009	中国最具幸福感城市	
		2010	金奖	
		2011	五周年特别荣誉大奖	
		2012	中国最具幸福感城市最高荣誉大奖	
		2013	中国最具幸福感城市	
			中国形象最佳城市	
		2014	中国最具幸福感城市	
			中国最具文化软实力城市	
4	南京	2007	无	6
		2008	无	
		2009	中国最具幸福感城市	
		2010	中国最具幸福感城市	
		2011	金奖	
		2012	中国幸福宜居城市大奖	
		2013	中国最具幸福感城市	
			中国形象最佳城市	
		2014	中国最具幸福感城市	
			中国最具文化软实力城市	
5	长春	2007	无	6
		2008	中国最具幸福感城市	
		2009	中国最具幸福感城市	
		2010	金奖	
		2011	无	
		2012	中国城市公共服务市民满意大奖	

续表3

序号	城市名	获奖年份	奖项	总获奖年数
5	长春	2013	中国最具幸福感城市	6
			中国形象最佳城市	
		2014	中国最具幸福感城市	
			中国最具文化软实力城市	
6	宁波	2007	中国最具幸福感城市	6
		2008	中国最具幸福感城市	
		2009	金奖	
		2010	无	
		2011	五周年特别荣誉大奖	
		2012	民生幸福城市大奖	
		2013	中国最具幸福感城市	
			中国形象最佳城市	
7	天津	2007	无	5
		2008	中国最具幸福感城市	
		2009	无	
		2010	无	
		2011	中国最具幸福感城市	
		2012	金奖	
		2013	中国最具幸福感城市	
			中国形象最佳城市	
		2014	中国最具幸福感城市	
			中国最具文化软实力城市	
8	西安	2007	无	4
		2008	无	
		2009	中国最具幸福感城市	
		2010	无	
		2011	无	
		2012	中国幸福城市特别荣誉大奖	
		2013	中国最具幸福感城市	
			中国形象最佳城市	
		2014	中国最具幸福感城市	
			中国最具文化软实力城市	
9	昆明	2007	无	4
		2008	中国最具幸福感城市	
		2009	中国最具幸福感城市	
		2010	金奖	
		2011	五周年特别荣誉大奖	
		2012	无	

续表 3

序号	城市名	获奖年份	奖项	总获奖年数
10	无锡	2007	无	4
		2008	中国最具幸福感城市	
		2009	无	
		2010	中国最具幸福感城市	
		2011	金奖	
		2012	中国幸福城市特别荣誉大奖	
11	珠海	2007	中国最具幸福感城市	3
		2011	中国最具幸福感城市	
		2014	中国最具幸福感城市	
12	重庆	2010	中国最具幸福感城市	3
		2011	中国最具幸福感城市	
		2014	中国最具文化软实力城市	
13	北京	2007	中国最具幸福感城市	3
		2013	中国形象最佳城市	
		2014	中国最具文化软实力城市	
14	上海	2007	中国最具幸福感城市	2
		2013	中国形象最佳城市	
15	岳阳	2014	中国最具幸福感城市	2
			中国最具文化软实力城市	
16	沈阳	2007	中国最具幸福感城市	1
17	中山	2007	中国最具幸福感城市	1
18	青岛	2007	中国最具幸福感城市	1
19	台州	2007	中国最具幸福感城市	1
20	唐山	2008	中国最具幸福感城市	1
21	佛山	2008	中国最具幸福感城市	1
22	绍兴	2008	中国最具幸福感城市	1
23	银川	2009	中国最具幸福感城市	1
24	南昌	2009	中国最具幸福感城市	1
25	广州	2010	中国最具幸福感城市	1
26	通化	2010	中国最具幸福感城市	1
27	南通	2012	中国最具幸福感城市	1
28	厦门	2013	中国最具幸福感城市	1
29	海口	2013	中国最具幸福感城市	1
30	大连	2014	中国最具幸福感城市	1

（二）2007－2014年获奖城市（县级市）及幸福乡镇

表4 历届获奖县级城市及幸福乡镇（2009-2014）

<table>
<tr><th>序号</th><th>城市名</th><th>获奖年份</th><th>奖项</th><th>总获奖年数</th></tr>
<tr><td rowspan="5">1</td><td rowspan="5">浙江余姚市</td><td>2009</td><td>中国最具幸福感城市</td><td rowspan="5">4</td></tr>
<tr><td>2010</td><td>民生贡献大奖</td></tr>
<tr><td>2011</td><td>金奖</td></tr>
<tr><td rowspan="2">2012</td><td>中国幸福城市最高荣誉大奖</td></tr>
<tr><td>中国城市民生成就大奖</td></tr>
<tr><td rowspan="4">2</td><td rowspan="4">辽宁海城市</td><td>2009</td><td>中国最具幸福感城市</td><td rowspan="4">4</td></tr>
<tr><td>2010</td><td>中国最具幸福感城市</td></tr>
<tr><td>2011</td><td>金奖</td></tr>
<tr><td>2012</td><td>中国幸福城市特别荣誉大奖</td></tr>
<tr><td rowspan="4">3</td><td rowspan="4">湖南长沙县</td><td>2009</td><td>中国最具幸福感城市</td><td rowspan="4">4</td></tr>
<tr><td>2010</td><td>中国最具幸福感城市</td></tr>
<tr><td>2011</td><td>金奖</td></tr>
<tr><td>2012</td><td>中国最具幸福感城市</td></tr>
<tr><td rowspan="5">4</td><td rowspan="5">江苏太仓市</td><td>2009</td><td>无</td><td rowspan="5">3</td></tr>
<tr><td>2010</td><td>中国最具幸福感城市</td></tr>
<tr><td>2011</td><td>中国最具幸福感城市</td></tr>
<tr><td rowspan="2">2012</td><td>金奖</td></tr>
<tr><td>中国幸福城市最高荣誉大奖</td></tr>
<tr><td rowspan="4">5</td><td rowspan="4">江苏宜兴市</td><td>2009</td><td>中国最具幸福感城市</td><td rowspan="4">3</td></tr>
<tr><td>2010</td><td>县级市民生贡献大奖</td></tr>
<tr><td>2011</td><td>金奖</td></tr>
<tr><td>2012</td><td>无</td></tr>
<tr><td rowspan="4">6</td><td rowspan="4">江苏江阴市</td><td>2009</td><td>无</td><td rowspan="4">2</td></tr>
<tr><td>2010</td><td>中国最具幸福感城市</td></tr>
<tr><td>2011</td><td>中国最具幸福感城市</td></tr>
<tr><td>2012</td><td>无</td></tr>
<tr><td rowspan="4">7</td><td rowspan="4">江苏吴江市</td><td>2009</td><td>中国最具幸福感城市</td><td rowspan="4">2</td></tr>
<tr><td>2010</td><td>无</td></tr>
<tr><td>2011</td><td>中国最具幸福感城市</td></tr>
<tr><td>2012</td><td>无</td></tr>
<tr><td rowspan="4">8</td><td rowspan="4">重庆永川区</td><td>2009</td><td>无</td><td rowspan="4">2</td></tr>
<tr><td>2010</td><td>无</td></tr>
<tr><td>2011</td><td>中国城市民生贡献奖</td></tr>
<tr><td>2012</td><td>中国最具幸福感城市</td></tr>
</table>

续表 4

序号	城市名	获奖年份	奖项	总获奖年数
9	重庆市云阳县	2011	中国最具幸福感城市 中国城市民生贡献奖	1
10	广东增城市	2009	中国最具幸福感城市	1
11	江苏江都市	2009	中国最具幸福感城市	1
12	山东邹平县	2009	中国最具幸福感城市	1
13	四川都江堰市	2009	中国最具幸福感城市	1
14	云南安宁市	2009	中国最具幸福感城市	1
15	山东胶州市	2010	中国最具幸福感城市	1
16	山东莱州市	2010	中国最具幸福感城市	1
17	山东滕州市	2010	中国最具幸福感城市	1
18	江苏昆山市	2011	中国最具幸福感城市	1
19	江苏(常州市)武进区	2011	中国最具幸福感城市	1
20	重庆铜梁县	2010	中国最具幸福感城市	1
21	河南巩义市	2012	中国最具幸福感城市	1
22	江苏张家港市	2012	中国最具幸福感城市	1
23	四川双流县	2012	中国最具幸福感城市	1
24	浙江慈溪市	2012	中国最具幸福感城市	1
25	浙江富阳市	2012	中国最具幸福感城市	1
26	重庆璧山县	2011	中国城市民生贡献奖	1
27	重庆江津区	2011	中国城市民生贡献奖	1
28	重庆渝北区	2011	中国城市民生贡献奖	1
29	重庆(云阳县)迎龙镇	2011	幸福乡镇	1
30	江苏(吴江市)震泽镇	2011	幸福乡镇	1
31	江苏(江阴市)新桥镇	2011	幸福乡镇	1
32	江苏(太仓市)城厢镇	2011	幸福乡镇	1
33	湖南(长沙县)榔梨镇	2011	幸福乡镇	1
34	辽宁(海城市)腾鳌镇	2011	幸福乡镇	1
35	重庆铜梁区	2014	中国最具文化魅力城区	1
36	重庆安居镇	2014	中国最具文化魅力古城	1

（三）2014 年中国最具文化软实力品牌

表 5　2014 年中国最具文化软实力品牌

序号	单位名	获奖年份	奖项	总获奖年数
1	今晚报	2014	中国最具文化软实力品牌	1
2	中广天择传媒	2014	中国最具文化软实力品牌	1
3	重庆火锅天下宴博物馆	2014	中国最具文化软实力品牌	1
4	西安城墙景区	2014	中国最具文化软实力品牌	1
5	西安印刷包装产业基地	2014	中国最具文化软实力品牌	1

六、活动影响

“中国最具幸福感城市调查推选活动”举办8年来，规模逐年增大，参与人数多，影响力强，累计7.5亿人次参与。超过300家网络媒体、200家地方平面媒体对该活动及相关事件进行了报道，新闻传播覆盖范围广，基本上覆盖了全国与地方的重要媒体。

七、历届获奖城市名单

2007年获奖城市：

杭州、沈阳、中山、宁波、青岛、台州、珠海、上海、北京、成都。

2008年获奖城市：

杭州、宁波、昆明、天津、唐山、佛山、绍兴、长春、无锡、长沙。

2009年获奖城市：

地级及以上城市：西安、南京、昆明、宁波、杭州、成都、银川、长沙、南昌、长春。

县级市：山东邹平县、江苏宜兴市、江苏吴江市、湖南长沙县、江苏江都市、浙江余姚市、云南安宁市、四川都江堰市、辽宁海城市、广东增城市。

（杭州、成都分别获得建国六十年特别大奖；宁波获得金奖）

2010中国最具幸福感城市：

地级及以上城市：杭州、成都、长沙、昆明、南京、长春、重庆、广州、通化、无锡。

县级市：江阴、宜兴、长沙县、余姚、滕州、铜梁、海城、太仓、莱州、胶州。

（杭州、成都分别获得最高荣誉奖——民生贡献特别大奖；昆明、长沙、长春分别获得金奖；宜兴、余姚分别获得民生贡献大奖；长沙获得民生满意大奖。）

2011中国最具幸福感城市：

地级及以上城市：天津市、重庆市、珠海市。

金奖：南京市、无锡市。

中国最具幸福感城市五周年特别荣誉大奖：

杭州市、成都市、宁波市、昆明市、长沙市。

县级市：

江阴市、吴江市、昆山市、江苏武进区、太仓市、重庆云阳县。

金奖：宜兴市、余姚市、长沙县、海城市。

幸福乡镇：

重庆（云阳县）迎龙镇、江苏（吴江市）震泽镇、江苏（江阴市）新桥镇、江苏（太仓市）城厢镇、湖南（长沙县）榔梨镇、辽宁（海城市）腾鳌镇。

中国城市民生贡献奖：

重庆江津区、重庆渝北区、重庆永川区、重庆云阳县、重庆璧山县。

2012 中国最具幸福感城市：

地级及以上城市：杭州、成都、宁波、南京、天津、长春、无锡、长沙、西安、南通。

其中：

杭州、成都分别获得中国最美幸福城市最高荣誉大奖；

宁波获得中国民生幸福城市大奖；

南京获得中国幸福宜居城市大奖。

长春获得中国城市公共服务市民满意大奖；

天津获得中国幸福城市金奖；

长沙获得中国最具幸福感城市最高荣誉大奖；

无锡、西安分别获得中国幸福城市特别荣誉大奖；

县级市：江苏张家港、江苏太仓、浙江余姚、重庆永川、浙江慈溪、浙江富阳、辽宁海城、湖南长沙县、四川双流县、河南巩义。

其中：

江苏太仓获得中国幸福城市最高荣誉大奖，同时获得中国最具幸福感城市金奖；

浙江余姚获得中国幸福城市最高荣誉大奖，同时获得中国城市民生成就大奖；

辽宁海城获得中国幸福城市特别荣誉大奖。

2013 年获奖名单：

中国最具幸福感城市：

杭州、成都、南京、西安、天津、长沙、宁波、长春、厦门、海口。

中国形象最佳城市：

成都、南京、杭州、西安、天津、长沙、宁波、长春、上海、北京。

2014 年获奖名单：

中国最具幸福感城市：

成都、杭州、南京、西安、天津、长春、长沙、岳阳、珠海、大连。

中国最具文化软实力城市：

南京、成都、西安、杭州、天津、长春、长沙、岳阳、北京、重庆。

中国最具文化魅力城区：重庆铜梁区

中国最具文化魅力古城：重庆安居镇

中国最具文化软实力品牌：

2014年幸福城市推选活动与“中国城市文化软实力”评价活动同步进行，以下单位获得了“2014中国最具文化软实力”的称号：

今晚报、中广天择传媒 、重庆火锅天下宴博物馆、西安城墙景区、西安印刷包装产业基地。

八、2014年中国城市未来发展国际论坛内容

（一）新华通讯社副社长于绍良先生在中国城市未来发展国际论坛上的致辞

（2014年10月31日 人民大会堂·北京厅）

各位嘉宾，女士们、先生们：

大家上午好！

联合国决定自2014年起将每年的10月31日设为“世界城市日”。今天是全球第一个“世界城市日”。我们有幸聚会一堂，在中国——一个正在推进大规模新型城镇化的国度，交流探讨“城市问题”，可以说，是对“世界城市日”极富价值的纪念。在此，我代表主办方之一的新华社，对各位莅临今天的论坛表示诚挚的欢迎和衷心的感谢。

刚才，我们一起收看了联合国秘书长潘基文先生精彩的致辞，我与大家一样，很有感触，很受启发。

中国经过长期不懈努力，各方面有了长足发展，但作为最大的发展中国家的基本国情没有变，其标志之一就是城镇化整体水平不高。中国有13亿人口，截至2013年年底，城镇化率还只是53.73%，远低于发达国家。

城镇化是国家现代化的必经之路。中国的决策者不仅意识到现实发展的短板，而且不失时机地做出了“顶层设计”和系统部署。2013年12月中央城镇化工作会议召开，今年3月《国家新型城镇化规划》正式公布，这在中国发展史上都是第一次。

按照我国的新型城镇化规划，到2020年，常住人口城镇化率要达到60%左右，户籍人口城镇化率达到45%左右，特别是将解决“三个1亿人”问题——也就是促进约1亿农业转移人口落户城镇、改造约1亿人居住的城镇棚户区和城中村、引导约1亿人在中西部地区就近城镇化。这是一个令人鼓舞的规划，同时也是充满前所未有的压力和挑战的规划，因为在一个既定的时空内完成如此人口规模的城镇化，在人类发展史上还没有先例。

完成这样的创举，只有走中国特色、科学发展的新型城镇化道路，但这不等于关起门来搞城镇化。城市是人类文明的重要成果，世界城市文明的精髓和要旨，对于各国城市化和城市治理都具有普遍意义，我们需要学习借鉴世界上优秀的城市文明成果。同时，学习借鉴不等于简单的拿来主义，需要坚持从我国实际出发合理吸收，不能搞“全面移植”，不能原路原样照搬照抄，尤其是必须规避那些先行者们留下的遗憾、败笔、痛苦和教训。潘基文秘书长推崇城市的可持续发展的理念，也正与中国决策者倡导的主张相契合。

城镇化、城市发展、城市治理是一个系统工程，涉及的问题非常多，而影响其进程与品质的力量更是错综复杂，其中就包括主流媒体舆论的影响和力量。联合国开发署的负责人特

别希望我讲讲主流媒体在城镇化进程的责任问题。这让我联想到，今年5月20日，潘基文秘书长专门访问新华社总部，与李从军社长会见，就曾谈到新华社这样的主流媒体在促进全人类和平与发展所起到的积极作用。这说明联合国高度重视主流媒体的影响。也正是那次访问，确定了由联合国开发计划署与新华社《瞭望东方周刊》共同主办“千年目标·百年梦想”系列城市主题活动和今天的论坛活动。

我想，一个良好有序的城镇化进程、一个良好健康的城市发展，应当是所有参与者的共同追求和共同责任。在波澜壮阔的城镇化历史进程中，主流媒体作为整个社会的信息中枢，不仅要当变革的观察者、时代的见证者、历史的记录者，更应成为“城市，让生活更美好”的积极建设者、正确引导者。

城镇化的核心是人。能不能有一个良好有序的城镇化进程，能不能有一个良好健康的城市发展，关键在人的认识和行为。媒体是影响人思维和行为的。让所有的参与者有正确的思维和行动，正是主流媒体的责任所在。在涉及利益关系复杂调整的过程中，媒体尤其是主流媒体至少要履行好如下责任——

引导正确舆论和促进共识的责任：城镇化的进程，媒体肯定要面对思想活动独立性、选择性、多变性、差异性明显增强的受众，走中国特色新型城镇化道路，既要借鉴世界各国城市化的成功经验，也要规避一些国家的深刻教训，更要从中国人口多、资源相对短缺、生态环境比较脆弱、城乡区域发展不平衡的国情出发，不仅要正确地看问题，而且要积极推动正确地解决问题，科学地处理各种利益关系，包括现实与长远、局部与整体、个人权益与共同利益等关系；包括树立过程论观念，让人们在解决问题中看到美好、看到希望、看到梦想就在前方；包括发挥建设性监督作用，促进政府提高科学管理能力和管理创新，使越来越多的受众思想理念认识，向正确的方向聚集，形成正能量。

提供公共服务的责任：为公众提供信息服务、生活服务、精神服务等，属于媒体的基本功能。新型城镇化是中国社会和中国人民的一场宏大实践，新问题、新经验、新趋势层出不穷，主流媒体需要贴近实际、贴近生活、贴近群众，发布准确信息，提供权威正确的解读，满足大众信息需求。

倡导和传承城市文明的责任：中国整体社会从农业文明向城市文明的转变，是一次短期内的剧烈大变动，城市文明的培育任重道远。媒体有责任弘扬社会主义核心价值观，传承中华优秀传统文化，结合新的时代条件，倡导科学文明生活方式，通过一点一滴的报道，影响和改变人们的思想和生活，发挥出思想导向、价值导向、行为导向、法治导向、人文导向、审美导向等方面的作用，促进人的现代化。

履行人文关怀的责任：农民进城市民化不仅是身份变更，更是每个进入城镇者的生活方式、日常习惯、社会关系、价值取向、精神需求等方面的全新变换。作为媒体，应更加注重深入人的精神世界、关心人的情感、启迪人的思想、激励人的全面发展，不仅贴近人，更要能贴心。

各位朋友：

作为中国最大的新闻信息传播机构和媒体集群，新华社综合运用立体多样的现代传播体系，立足国内、面向世界，及时传播中国政府为推动新型城镇化所做的努力。以本次论坛主办方《瞭望东方周刊》为例，就始终把传播中国城市绿色健康发展、城市科学治理、城市人性化发展等理念作为使命，并组织了“中国最具幸福感城市推选活动”等一系列活动，与专业研究者一起，独创了全面立体、较为科学完善的城市评估指标体系。面向未来，我们将进一步担负起时代赋予我们作为社会瞭望者的职责，尽我们的力量向世界讲述好中国城市的新故事，阐释好中国特色的新型城镇化道路。

各位来宾：

我相信，只要我们的城市领导者、管理者、企业、媒体，共同履行应尽的责任，就能无愧于我们的人民，无愧于我们推进中国特色新型城镇化的时代，中国的城市就必将开辟出可持续发展的美好未来。

谢谢大家！

（二）首个“世界城市日”中国发布幸福城市榜单

（新华社通稿内容）

新华社北京 10 月 31 日电，你的城市幸福吗？哪座城市最具文化影响力？31 日，在“中国城市未来发展国际论坛”上，“2014 中国最具幸福感城市”系列榜单发布。

“中国最具幸福感城市”调查推选活动由新华社《瞭望东方周刊》联合中国市长协会《中国城市发展报告》共同主办，迄今已连续举办 8 年，是目前中国最具影响力和公信力的城市调查推选活动。

本届推选活动从 8 月份启动后，累计 2300 多万人次参加了公众调查和抽样调查。经过活动组委会评审，成都、杭州、南京、西安、天津、长春、长沙、岳阳、珠海、大连十座城市荣获“2014 中国最具幸福感城市”荣誉称号。

与往届不同，本届推选活动推出系列奖与“中国城市文化软实力”评价活动同时进行。最终，南京、成都、西安、杭州、天津、长春、长沙、岳阳、北京、重庆十座城市获得“2014 中国最具文化软实力城市”称号。今晚报、中广天择传媒 、重庆火锅天下宴博物馆、西安城墙景区、西安印刷包装产业基地荣获了“2014 中国最具文化软实力品牌”称号。重庆铜梁区荣获“2014 中国最具文化魅力城区”，重庆安居镇获得“2014 中国最具文化魅力古城”称号。

据介绍，为了突出“中国文化 · 影响世界”这一主题，组委会广泛吸取国内外专家学者意见，特别制定了“中国城市幸福感、文化软实力评价体系”，涵盖城市文化魅力、城市文化活力、城市文化实力、城市文化传播力、城市形象、城市幸福感六大体系 70 个指标。

主办方表示，在首个“世界城市日”发布“中国最具幸福感城市”系列榜单，对于提升中国城市形象，推动中国城市走向世界，具有示范作用。

（供稿：新华社《瞭望东方周刊》）

编后语

2014 年是中国经济发展步入新常态的一年，也是城市发展步入新常态的一年。这一年，很多朋友都感受到了城市发展的寒意，认为冬天来了。然而，也是在这一年，思想领域却是异常活跃的。“大数据”、“多规合一”、“区域一体化”等新的规划理念与技术方法成为热门话题，百家争鸣，好不热闹。

新常态之“新”在于传统的城镇化发展难以适应经济社会发展的要求，需要转型升级，将传统的重发展轻传承、重经济轻人文、重空间轻社会的思维定式打破，采取新心态、新思路、新方法去解决问题；新常态之“常”则在于问题还是老问题，依旧是创造一个和美的人类栖居环境。

本年度的《中国城市发展报告》便是在新常态的背景下编写的，在结构上基本延续了往年的框架，即为新常态之“常”。蒋正华先生撰写序言一，陈政高部长撰写序言二。全书共分为六篇：综论篇、论坛篇、观察篇、专题篇、案例篇以及附录篇。

综论篇对 2014 年中国城市的发展做了中英文综述，对中国城市发展的十大事件做了回顾。此外，还对中国城市交通发展以及中国城市信息化进展做了系统性的论述。

论坛篇邀请了邹德慈、林树森、仇保兴等多位院士、专家和部分省部级领导对南沙、京津冀等热点区域的发展进行了高屋建瓴的谋划；就气候变化对沿海城市安全的影响、城市噪声问题等一些关注热度不高但却意义非凡的城市问题提出了独特的见解。

观察篇除讨论“两会”关注的热点问题外，还特别增加食品质量安全问题，并从管理者角度对我国舆情发展问题进行了专业论述，大大丰富了本年度《中国城市发展报告》的内容。

专题篇则紧扣时代热点，集中关注了地方债务、公共安全评价、公立医院管理效率、大数据、绿色建筑等问题。

案例篇对海口的国际旅游、中外社团合作、广州新农村建设等经验进行了介绍，还对苏州申报“李光耀世界城市奖”进行了经验推广。

同时，我们继续整理了有关城市规划、建设、管理方面的各类重要数据和信息作为附录资料，收辑于全书末尾，方便读者查阅。

《中国城市发展报告（2014）》之“新”体现在我们的主题不再局限于就城市论城市，我们邀请了多领域的专家一起来为我们的城市发展献言献策，如食品质量健康、公立医院管理效率、地方债务等话题，都很值得我们思考与讨论。

自2005年国际欧亚科学院中国科学中心承办《中国城市发展报告》以来，已整整10周年。这10年，我们不断地探索与创新，认真做好每一年的年度报告；这10年，我们作为城市的记录者，见证着中国城市的发展。这10年的梦想与笃行，换来的是《中国城市发展报告》的光荣与美誉。在此，衷心地感谢为《中国城市发展报告》做出贡献的同仁。相信下一个10年，我们的《中国城市发展报告》必将更加出彩。

最后，由于《中国城市发展报告》涉及专业面广，疏漏之处在所难免，恳请关心《中国城市发展报告》的城市领导、专家学者、研究人员和社会各界读者不吝批评指正！同时，对数十位参加《中国城市发展报告》编写的院士、专家及相关人员的辛勤工作表示感谢。

戴　逢

2015年6月18日

（作者：戴逢，国际欧亚科学院中国科学中心城市科学部副主任，国际欧亚科学院院士）